RISING STARS Mathematics

Year 3

Concept developed by

Caroline Clissold and Cherri Moseley

Year 3 Author Team

Caroline Clissold, Belle Cottingham, Steph King

Homework Sheets written by

Jo Chambers

Practice Book written by

Paul Broadbent

Teacher's Guide

ISBN: 978-1-78339-530-9

First published in 2016 by
Rising Stars UK Ltd, part of Hodder Education,

An Hachette UK Company

Carmelite House
50 Victoria Embankment
London EC4Y 0DZ

www.risingstars-uk.com

Authors: Caroline Clissold, Belle Cottingham, Steph King

Programme consultants: Caroline Clissold, Cherri Moseley, Paul Broadbent

Publishers: Fiona Lazenby and Alexandra Riley

Editorial: Kate Baxter, Jane Carr, Sarah Chappelow, Jan Fisher, Lucy Hyde, Jackie Mace, Jane Morgan, Denise Moulton, Christine Vaughan

Answer checking: Deborah Dobson

Project manager: Sue Walton

Text design: Steve Evans and Mark Walker

Illustrations by Steve Evans

Cover design: Steve Evans and Words & Pictures

Printed by Ashford Colour Press Ltd, Gosport, Hants

A CIP record for this book is available from the British Library.

Contents

Introduction

What is *Rising Stars Mathematics*?

Rising Stars Mathematics is a primary mathematics programme developed specifically for the 2014 National Curriculum Programmes of Study. The programme offers a complete solution to primary mathematics, adapting the best teaching and learning approaches from high-performing jurisdictions such as Shanghai and Singapore, but written bespoke to develop mathematics mastery in the context of UK classrooms.

Rising Stars Mathematics has been designed, developed and written by UK mathematics experts and educators to meet the Mathematics Textbook Guidance produced by the National Centre for Excellence in the Teaching of Mathematics (NCETM).

> 'A high-quality mathematics textbook is an educational resource that can be used by pupils in lessons and independently, and that also provides both subject knowledge and pedagogy support to teachers of mathematics. It is a comprehensive learning tool, providing support for the development of both procedural fluency and conceptual understanding in mathematics.'
>
> NCETM, January 2015
> (https://www.ncetm.org.uk/files/21383193NCETM+Textbook+Guidance.pdf)

Following these guidelines, *Rising Stars Mathematics*:

- provides the rigour teachers expect from quality schemes, without the prescription of scripted day-by-day lesson plans
- contains all the resources and CPD support teachers need to design outstanding mathematics lessons
- offers a wealth of opportunities for children to explore, practise, embed and extend learning
- follows the Concrete-Pictorial-Abstract approach to deepen children's understanding of mathematical concepts
- covers all the curriculum content with a wide variety of teaching ideas whilst respecting teachers' professionalism, to enable them to decide how best to teach their classes.

The pedagogy, approach and rationale

Rising Stars Mathematics is designed to develop fluency, build conceptual understanding and embed reasoning through an enquiry-based approach. It provides a 'light touch' comprehensive structure that allows teachers to retain the control, freedom and flexibility to adapt the timing and teaching activities to meet the needs of their own class. This means that they can focus their time and skills on teaching outstanding lessons in their own way. Carefully organised to provide a clear route through the yearly programmes of study, the curriculum concepts are revisited in a spiral way to reinforce and extend understanding and make links between content areas.

The programme has been developed based on the following key pedagogical beliefs:

1. Mathematical understanding is developed through using **concrete, pictorial** and **abstract** representations.
2. High-quality **textbooks used effectively as teaching tools** support teachers in explaining mathematical concepts clearly, encourage investigative thinking, questioning, discussion and application, all while encouraging children to engage with the wonder of mathematics (see page 6).
3. Children will only fully understand topics and **master concepts** through **step-by-step teaching** and **intelligent practice**. This means teaching concepts at a slower pace and dealing with each aspect of that concept in very small steps, in order to give children time to embed understanding. To achieve mastery, therefore, it is important to spend more time on teaching fewer topics in greater depth rather than moving on to a new topic or concept every few days (see page 6).
4. Mathematics is an interconnected subject in which children need to be able to **make connections** across mathematical ideas. This enables them to develop fluency, mathematical reasoning and problem-solving skills (see page 7).
5. Using **precise mathematical vocabulary** from the beginning is vital in ensuring children's understanding. **Rich talk and discussion** between teachers and children, and amongst peers, using mathematical terminology and constant probing questioning is an essential tool in the ongoing assessment of conceptual understanding for all children (see page 7).

Each of these key points of pedagogy is expanded on and explained in the following sections.

1. Concrete-Pictorial-Abstract (CPA) approach

Rising Stars Mathematics is based on the belief that mathematical understanding is developed through using **concrete, pictorial** and **abstract** (or symbolic) representations. Children will travel along this continuum again and again, often revisiting previous stages when a concept is extended.

Children use **concrete** objects to help them make sense of the concept or problem. This could be anything from real or plastic fruit, to straws, counters, cubes or something else meaningful. Whatever the objects are, they can be moved, grouped and rearranged to illustrate the problem. As the child's experience and confidence grows, they may no longer need physical objects to actually move around. Instead, they draw them. These simple **pictures** to represent the problem could be pictures of real objects they have used in the past, objects mentioned in the problem or something else meaningful. As understanding develops, children move on to use some form of **abstract** representation. This could be giving values to rectangular bars (bar model) to identify what is known and what is unknown, using a symbol to stand for a number, or something else.

It is important to realise that these are not stages gone through once, but a continuum. There will be occasions when a particular child will use concrete, pictorial and abstract representations all in one session. A child who uses abstract representations in one area may need concrete representations in another. On a different occasion, a child may need to revisit a concrete representation before moving on to a pictorial or abstract one.

Using the CPA approach encourages children to start by modelling a problem with concrete objects, before moving on to pictorial and abstract representations. It is important to ensure that a variety of manipulatives are available in all classrooms, not just for Key Stage 1 children. This will help children to develop their understanding more quickly and securely.

A variety of representations are used throughout *Rising Stars Mathematics*. These are both the teacher's and children's toolkit for illustrating and understanding a concept or a particular problem. Children will need to explore the various representations for themselves and be allowed the opportunity to choose which representations they use for a particular activity. (See pages 12–14 for examples and explanations of the main concrete resources and pictorial representations used throughout the *Rising Stars Mathematics* programme.)

2. Textbooks as teaching tools

Rising Stars Mathematics follows the Singapore and Shanghai approach to the use of textbooks. In these high-performing jurisdictions the textbook is a starting point for high-quality teaching. Teachers lead the usage of the textbook with the whole class as a starting point for high-quality teaching, rather than giving a textbook to children to work through on their own. This latter misuse of published resources unfortunately became common in England over a number of years and led to textbooks being seen as synonymous with poor-quality lessons. However, when used effectively as a teaching tool, evidence shows that this is not the case. Instead textbooks provide a framework for teachers to both introduce and develop new content, as well as providing a resource for children to refer back to as required.

The *Rising Stars Mathematics* Textbooks are designed specifically to be used as a teaching tool in conjunction with the teaching guidance and ideas provided in the corresponding Teacher's Guide pages. It is not intended that the Textbooks are given to children to work through in isolation. The Teacher's Notes tabs at the bottom of each Textbook page reference the relevant Teacher's Guide pages, so that the resources can be used in tandem.

The 'Let's learn' pages in the Textbooks should be used by the teacher as a starting point to introduce, teach, model and demonstrate new concepts. To support them in doing this, they can use the ideas in the Teacher's Guide or their own activities if preferred.

The 'Let's practise' pages in the Textbooks provide initial practice opportunities. They lead from basic practice and practice in context, to investigative, open-ended practice. These guided practice activities should be introduced by the teacher. The Teacher's Guide provides suggestions on questioning and how to give targeted support to children who may need additional help in order to move on with the group. The 'Let's practise' sections can be used to provide opportunities for independent working as appropriate for different children or as assessment opportunities to identify whether children have mastered the concept. This will then enable teachers to judge how much additional practice each child requires using the *Rising Stars Mathematics* Practice Books (or other practice materials that they choose to use).

3. The mastery approach

A mastery approach underpins the 2014 National Curriculum. This approach advocates spending longer on topics in order to embed understanding and developing rich connections across topics.

NCETM has identified further principles and features that characterise a mastery approach:

- Teachers reinforce an expectation that all pupils are capable of achieving high standards in mathematics.
- The large majority of pupils progress through the curriculum content at the same pace. Differentiation is achieved by emphasising deep knowledge and through individual support and intervention.
- Teaching is underpinned by methodical curriculum design and supported by carefully crafted lessons and resources to foster deep conceptual and procedural knowledge.
- Practice and consolidation play a central role. Carefully designed variation within this builds fluency and understanding of underlying mathematical concepts in tandem.
- Teachers use precise questioning in class to test conceptual and procedural knowledge, and assess pupils regularly to identify those requiring intervention so that all pupils keep up.

NCETM, October 2014
(https://www.ncetm.org.uk/public/files/19990433/Developing_mastery_in mathematics_october_2014.pdf)

In December 2012, The Advisory Committee on Mathematics Education (ACME) published a report called 'Raising the bar: developing able young mathematicians'. The report identified that England needs to increase the number of young mathematicians with a robust grasp of the range of mathematical ways of thinking and working, through experiencing a deep, rich, rigorous and challenging mathematics education. Children should not be accelerated through the school curriculum: 'acceleration encourages only a shallow mastery of the subject, and so promotes procedural learning at the expense of deep understanding'. Not allowing children enough time to secure deep understanding can lead to feelings of insecurity and dislike of the subject.

Consequently, there is an expectation in the 2014 National Curriculum that most children should 'move through the programmes of study at broadly the same pace'. Children should not be accelerated into a future year group's work. Instead, it is expected that children who grasp concepts rapidly should be challenged through being offered rich and sophisticated problems before any acceleration through new content. There is also the expectation that those who are not sufficiently fluent with earlier material should consolidate their understanding, including through additional practice, before moving on. The aim is for mastery, which is the approach used by many of the high-performing jurisdictions in the international league tables.

With this in mind, there are some important questions for schools to consider when teaching for mastery, which should be discussed and agreed with the whole staff:

- To support the expectation that all children are capable of achieving high standards, what are the implications for whole-class teaching, class groupings or setting within the school?
- How will differentiation be managed to enable all children to access what is being taught? How and when will intervention be given to ensure misconceptions are dealt with immediately and shared with the whole class, so that no children fall behind?
- How will questioning and scaffolding be varied to provide support as needed? What different problems will be provided so that children who grasp the concept quickly are given complex problems which deepen their knowledge of the same content?
- Is there enough focus on the important ability to recall facts and manipulate them to work out other facts, so that children develop the fluency which comes from deep knowledge and practice?
- How will enough time be allowed for different types of intelligent practice (basic practice, variations such as practice within different contexts, extended practice which goes deeper and deeper), so that longer can be spent on key concepts? Will more than one mathematics session per day be required?
- How will practice and consolidation be provided within different contexts, e.g. time, money or length, to ensure connections are made across different areas of mathematics?
- How will teaching focus on the development of deep structural knowledge and the ability to make connections?
- Is the use of precise mathematical vocabulary consistent across the school? Is correct vocabulary introduced from the beginning of teaching? Are all teaching staff comfortable with mathematical terminology?

Practice and variation

Intelligent practice underpins the mastery approach. 'Intelligent practice' is a term used to describe practice that develops procedural fluency while at the same time exposing mathematical structures, patterns and relationships in order to deepen conceptual understanding.

Intelligent practice is clearly structured and incorporates carefully-designed variations. These variations may be conceptual or procedural:

- Procedural variation can be introduced by extending a problem (e.g. varying the number, the unknown or the context), varying the processes of solving a problem or varying the application of a method (e.g. applying the same method to a group of similar problems).
- Conceptual variation can be introduced by varying the representation of a problem.

The practice in *Rising Stars Mathematics* is based on the principles of intelligent practice.

- The 'Let's practise' pages in the Textbook are clearly structured. Steps 1 and 2 comprise bare (or, decontextualised) practice and include procedural variations. Step 3 provides practice within a variety of contexts (including time, money and statistics) and Step 4 offers open-ended, investigative practice. By working their way through the practice, children will build procedural fluency across a range of question types and in a range of contexts, while also developing their understanding of the concepts covered in the 'Let's learn' pages.
- The corresponding 'Let's practise' pages in the Teacher's Guide extend the opportunities for conceptual variation by suggesting a range of physical and pictorial representations that teachers may want to use to support children's practice.
- The Practice Book offers further carefully-crafted practice exercises. These exercises have been planned to include structured variation of a number or unknown (procedural variation), a range of representations (e.g. a question on length may use a variety of visuals such as ribbons, snakes and pencils) and open questions (e.g. 'What do you notice?') that encourage children to reason and spot patterns.

Teachers can use the carefully-designed questions and exercises as a starting point to introduce intelligent practice into their teaching. However, they retain the freedom to develop their own questions and activities, incorporating variation that best suits the needs of their children.

4. Making connections

The 2014 National Curriculum states that:

> 'Mathematics is an interconnected subject in which pupils need to be able to move fluently between representations of mathematical ideas. The programmes of study are, by necessity, organised into apparently distinct domains, but pupils should make rich connections across mathematical ideas to develop fluency, mathematical reasoning and competence in solving increasingly sophisticated problems. They should also apply their mathematical knowledge to science and other subjects.'
>
> *National Curriculum in England*, Department for Education, 2013

In *Rising Stars Mathematics* there are a wide variety of opportunities to develop mathematics in other areas of the curriculum and in real life, e.g. the opening pages of each unit in the Textbook contain interesting photos and visuals to encourage children to identify instances of mathematics in the world around them, in order to make connections between what they are learning and how it might apply in real life. The programme is designed to provide opportunities to link together different areas of mathematics together, e.g. when children practise a concept, such as addition, they will have the opportunity to do this through an area of measure, e.g. length, mass, temperature or time. This has the benefit of allowing more time to be spent on the big ideas of mathematics within its everyday applications.

The units in *Rising Stars Mathematics* are structured to focus on one of four key mathematical themes: Number Sense, Additive Reasoning, Multiplicative Reasoning or Geometric Reasoning (see page 9). These cover concepts from the related Programmes of Study areas, incorporating Measurement and Statistics where appropriate. This ensures that the end-of-year statements for these areas are covered through a multitude of practice opportunities across the units.

5. Mathematical vocabulary

The 2014 National Curriculum states that:

> 'The National Curriculum for mathematics reflects the importance of spoken language in pupils' development across the whole curriculum – cognitively, socially and linguistically. The quality and variety of language that pupils hear and speak are key factors in developing their mathematical vocabulary and presenting a mathematical justification, argument or proof. They must be assisted in making their thinking clear to themselves as well as others, and teachers should ensure that pupils build secure foundations by using discussion to probe and remedy their misconceptions.'
>
> *National Curriculum in England*, Department for Education, 2013

Using correct mathematical language is crucial for thinking, learning and communicating mathematically. Children may build knowledge through remembering information that they hear, but it is only when they put these ideas into their own words that it becomes clear whether concepts have been learnt effectively. It is in listening to children talking about mathematics that teachers can best assess what they are actually learning and understanding, which in turn enables them to identify and address any misconceptions that might be developing.

Children should be encouraged to explain what they are doing and why they are doing it, through probing questioning from the teacher if necessary. Offering opportunities to use mathematical language frequently, e.g. by participating in paired activities, group discussions and games, will ensure that rich talk develops in the classroom. Spoken language in mathematics can be thought of as a rehearsal for recording, as well as an outcome in its own right. It allows children to extend and develop their reasoning skills as they explain and justify their thinking. It provides the opportunity to review existing knowledge, to explore new ideas and to extend their understanding.

The productive use of spoken language in mathematics allows children to evaluate their learning, support others' suggestions, challenge ideas, reason or justify and ask questions. Therefore, it is important to encourage children not just to learn and remember the correct vocabulary, but also to use these words regularly to communicate mathematically. Using mathematical vocabulary can help all children to make links across areas of mathematics, across the curriculum as a whole and also within real life situations. It can enable them to build confidence, communicate and problem-solve, so should be an integral part of every mathematics lesson.

Teachers need to plan the introduction of new words into lessons and provide opportunities for children to rehearse and use them on a regular basis. It is also essential that other adults working with children use mathematical vocabulary accurately and consistently. The 'Mathematical vocabulary' sections in the *Rising Stars Mathematics* Teacher's Guide identify key words that should be covered when teaching each concept. The glossary in the Textbook provides explanations for children and the glossary at the back of this Teacher's Guide offers detailed definitions on a wide variety of key mathematical terms.

Getting started with *Rising Stars Mathematics*

The components

Rising Stars Mathematics includes a wealth of resources for children and teachers. The pupil materials include full-colour Textbooks, single-colour write-in Practice Books and Homework Sheets (found at the back of the Teacher's Guides). The teacher materials comprise the Teacher's Guide and a variety of additional CPD, teaching resources, and digital teaching and learning resources be found on the My Rising Stars website. The contents for each of these components is summarised below.

Textbook

- Opportunities for children to develop problem-solving and reasoning skills.
- 14 units covering all the concepts to be learnt in Year 3.
- Glossary.

Practice Books

- 14 units providing further independent practice of all the concepts to be learnt in Year 3.
- Answers can be found on the My Rising Stars website.

Homework Sheets

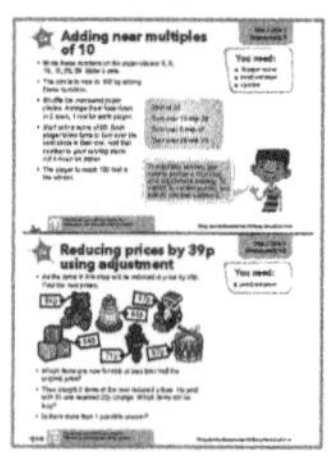

- 70 expansion activities to enable children to explore mathematics further outside the classroom.
- Ideal for engaging parents/carers in children's learning.

Teacher's Guide

- CPD guidance on the pedagogy, approach and how to use the *Rising Stars Mathematics* resources.
- Scope and sequence chart and curriculum mapping grids to aid planning.
- Non-prescriptive teaching guidance for all 14 units in the Textbook.
- Photocopiable Homework Sheets and answers.
- Glossary.
- Bibliography for further reading.

Website and digital resources

- **CPD resources** including:
  1. Short, sharp **CPD videos** providing bite-sized insights into key areas of importance when teaching mathematics, as well as background subject knowledge videos for every theme.
  2. Ready-made **INSET Training PowerPoint presentation** to offer a time-saving way to introduce the principles and resources of *Rising Stars Mathematics* to staff.
- **Planning resources** including:
  1. **Scope and sequence charts** and **curriculum mapping grids** for each year group.
  2. The Rising Stars ***Primary Maths Planning Framework*** and **posters** for long-term planning support.
  3. Editable **medium-term planning grids** including references to other useful resources.
  4. Mathematical vocabulary **glossaries**.
  5. **Bibliography** of research papers and recommended further reading, including guidance documents from NCETM.
- **Teaching resources** including:
  1. **Teacher Toolkit** containing useful digital tools, which can be used to model concepts on the interactive whiteboard. Tools include:

     - Counters
     - Numerals & Symbols
     - 100 Squares
     - Place Value & Abacus
     - Number Line
     - Clock & Timer
     - Calendar & Timezone
     - Money
     - Calculator
     - Dice, Coin & Number
     - 2D Shapes
     - Tangrams
     - 3D Shapes
     - Fraction Wall
     - Graphs & Charts
     - Geometry Instruments
  2. **eTextbook** – a digital version of the Textbook that can be displayed in the classroom on the interactive whiteboard or shared with parents/carers, so that children can access it from home. The eTextbook is enhanced with fun animations to help explain concepts.
  3. **Animations** from the eTextbook (available separately) are organised by unit, so they can be accessed quickly to play on the interactive whiteboard when required.

  4. PDFs of the **Teacher's Guide notes**, organised unit by unit, can be viewed anytime without needing the book to hand.
  5. Editable versions of the **Homework Sheets**.
  6. Printable versions of the colour **gameboards** from the Textbooks.
  7. Editable versions of the **game instructions** from the Teacher's Guide.
  8. **Answers** to the Practice Books and Homework Sheets.
- **Pupil resources** including:
  1. **eTextbook** – see Teaching resources above.
  2. **Animations** – see Teaching resources above.
  3. **Printable gameboards** and **instruction sheets** organised unit by unit.
  5. Editable versions of the **Homework Sheets** organised unit by unit.
  6. **Answers** to the Practice Books and Homework Sheets.

Themes

Rising Stars Mathematics is built around four themes: Number Sense, Additive Reasoning, Multiplicative Reasoning and Geometric Reasoning. Each covers the concepts from the related Programme of Study areas. This approach ensures that clear connections are made between areas of mathematics.

1. **Number Sense** is about understanding our number system, with a focus on how our numbers work and fit together, and applying this understanding in different contexts. Units on Additive Reasoning and Multiplicative Reasoning are usually preceded by a unit on Number Sense, which explores the understanding needed for the subsequent unit.
2. **Additive Reasoning** is about understanding addition and subtraction together and the relationship between them, and using this understanding to solve problems.
3. **Multiplicative Reasoning** is about understanding multiplication and division together and the relationship between them, and using this understanding to solve problems.
4. **Geometric Reasoning** is about understanding the properties of shapes and the relationships between them, using this understanding to solve problems related to measure and movement within space.

Measures and statistics are included throughout as contexts for all four themes. These contexts are examples and teachers may wish to select different contexts to support each concept. **Algebra** (a new domain in Year 6) appears in all themes as part of generalisation of mathematical understanding.

The unit structure

Each year level of *Rising Stars Mathematics* contains 14 units. These units all follow the same structure as explained below. The Textbook and Teacher's Guide work alongside each other. Each double-page spread in the Teacher's Guide contains a reproduction of the corresponding Textbook page for ease of reference. The Textbook has teaching notes tabs at the bottom of each page to enable teachers to quickly find the corresponding Teacher's Guide page.

Textbook and Teacher's Guide: unit opener pages

In the Textbook, each unit begins with engaging photos of mathematics in real life. These unit opener pages give children the opportunity to discuss what they see and explore what could be going on, looking for mathematics in the world around them. 'I wonder…' questions encourage thinking around the topic. This sets the scene for exploring the underlying concepts in more depth throughout the unit. Such discussions give the teacher the opportunity to check current understanding before moving on to the concept explanation, modelling, exemplification, practice and application.

The corresponding Teacher's Guide pages highlight the main mathematical focus of the unit, expected prior learning and key new learning to be covered throughout the unit. It also provides: support for making connections across areas of mathematics or between concepts; a 'Talk about' section that focuses on the use of precise mathematical vocabulary; a variety of activities and questions about the visuals in the Textbook to engage and explore with children; a list of questions for teachers to think about regarding organisation and planning. Finally, there is brief guidance to support teachers in checking understanding as the unit progresses.

Textbook and Teacher's Guide: concept pages

Each has two pages: 'Let's learn' and 'Let's practise'. The 'Let's learn' page begins with a discussion between the year group character guides, illustrating a possible misconception. The key information about the new concept to be learnt is explained, supported by relevant pictorial representations.

The 'Let's practise' section develops children's reasoning incrementally through guided practice. In *Rising Stars Mathematics*, the first steps provide bare, decontextualised practice. The third step gives practice in a context (e.g. an area of measurement or statistics), while the fourth step is a more open-ended, investigative practice of the concept.

The corresponding Teachers' Guide pages for these sections provide: a list of key mathematical vocabulary, representations and resources; useful background knowledge; activities for warming up, modelling and teaching, digging deeper through practice and follow-up activity ideas. There is also a section on ensuring progress, with ideas for supporting and broadening understanding. These are ideas which can be adapted to the needs of the class – there is no specific script. There are also notes on how to identify when the key concepts have been mastered and answers to the 'Let's practise' activities in the Textbook.

Textbook and Teacher's Guide: gameboard pages

Each unit contains fun activities to encourage children to apply their knowledge and skills, whilst consolidating conceptual understanding. The attractive colour gameboards for these are contained in the Textbooks. Two versions of games that can be played using each gameboard are provided and children are also encouraged to invent their own game using the gameboard. The invented games are often a useful means of assessing understanding.

The corresponding Teachers' Guide pages provide further detail about playing each of the games, including the mathematics focus, resources needed, instructions for how to play and support for making the game activities easier or harder. A photocopiable sheet of 'How to play' instructions is also provided, should teachers wish to send the games home as an out-of-class activity. Printable versions of the gameboards are available to download from the website.

Textbook and Teacher's Guide: 'And finally …' review pages

The final part of each unit is a review section, which provides a variety of assessment tasks. The Textbook pages include three assessment tasks, followed by a colourful 'Did you know?' fun facts section to complete the unit. (For further information about assessment see page 11.)

The corresponding Teachers' Guide review pages provide further detail of any resources needed, instructions for how to run the tasks and guidance on what to look for in children's responses, in order to evidence mastery. There is also some background knowledge about the 'Did you know?' facts and a summary list of all the concepts children are expected to have mastered by the end of the unit.

Introduction

Practice Books

The Practice Books provide further opportunities for children to consolidate understanding and explore, explain and reason through different types of practice activities. These activities include conceptual and procedural variations, in order to develop fluency and conceptual understanding. There is practice for every concept in the Textbook. The write-in format ensures that children always have a record of their work that they can refer back to,so that they can learn from their mistakes and see the progress they are making.

The relevant Practice Book pages for each concept in the Textbook are referenced at the top of the corresponding Teacher's Guide page for each new concept.

Homework Sheets

The photocopiable Homework Sheets can be found at the back of the Teacher's Guide. Editable versions are also available on the My Rising Stars website. They provide expansion activities for children to continue to explore mathematics outside the classroom. Two activities are provided for each of the concept pages in a unit.

The relevant Homework Sheets for each concept in the Textbook are referenced at the top of the corresponding Teacher's Guide page for each new concept.

Teaching a unit

Teachers are advised to begin by looking at the Teacher's Guide to familiarise themselves with the content to be covered within a particular unit and reviewing the related CPD videos on the website if necessary.

1. Develop subject knowledge

- Watch the short online CPD videos to develop background subject knowledge before planning lessons.
- Refresh knowledge by reviewing the INSET training presentations as necessary.

2. Design lessons

- Plan and design lessons using the suggested activities in the Teacher's Guide.
- Choose how much time to spend on each activity to fit the needs of each class.
- Gather all the concrete resources and visual representations needed.
- Review the recommended Teacher Toolkit tools and any relevant concept animations on the My Rising Stars website.

3. Explore new concepts

- Introduce the unit using the Textbooks as a teaching tool. Remember to check the teaching notes tab at the bottom of each page and the corresponding Teacher's Guide pages before the lesson.
- Play any relevant animations (from the eTextbook or direct from the website) to the class and discuss them together.
- Explore, model and teach new concepts to children using a variety of representations and practical resources, following the 'Let's learn' page.
- Use tools from the Teacher Toolkit to model concepts on the interactive whiteboard where appropriate.
- Embed conceptual understanding and dig deeper into concepts through intelligent practice, using the 'Let's practise' page.

4. Embed and expand understanding

- Consolidate understanding using the fun games to provide extra practice and aid mastery. Print extra copies of the game boards and instructions from the website as necessary.
- Set expansion or out-of-class activities using the Homework Sheets or Practice Books. Answers can be found on the website.
- Encourage parents/carers to engage with children's learning by sharing the eTextbook to view the pages and animations at home.
- Provide further independent practice using the Practice Books to deepen understanding of the concepts taught using the Textbooks.

5. Assess progress and mastery

- Review the content covered throughout the unit using the assessment tasks to ensure children have mastered the concepts.
- Finish the unit by finding out some fun mathematical facts in the 'Did you know?' section.
- Use *Rising Stars Assessment Half-Termly Progress Tests* to measure progress independently, if desired.

Timing

As a guide, the expectation is that each unit will take two to three weeks to teach. The length of time spent on each unit will vary depending on the topic, the number of new concepts covered within it and how quickly children master the concepts. If teachers are confident that children have mastered a concept, then it is perfectly acceptable to move on more quickly, just as it is important to allow children to spend longer on a topic if necessary to ensure that they have fully mastered it before moving on. It is better to spend more time on fewer topics to ensure that they are fully understood and children have embedded what they have learnt, so that they can remember and apply it later on.

Mixed-age classes

For schools with mixed-age classes, the *Rising Stars Mathematics* resources can be used to teach the same topic to the whole class, as long as this is done age-appropriately. The pitch should be year-group based, regardless of the perceived ability of children within those year groups. It is important that however the classroom is managed, each year group sticks to what is expected for that year in order to meet the National Curriculum Programme of Study requirements. Children should therefore all be using the Textbooks and Practice Books appropriate for their year group. As teachers in this kind of setting will know all too well, this is like teaching two or more classes. This brings huge challenges in planning and organisation, especially in small schools where there are three to four year groups per class.

However, because the units in *Rising Stars Mathematics* all have a main focus on one of four themes (Number Sense, Additive Reasoning, Multiplicative Reasoning or Geometric Reasoning), similar topics are generally covered in the same unit in each year group. Therefore corresponding units from Year 1 and Year 2, Year 3 and Year 4, Year 5 and Year 6 will work together neatly as they focus on the same themes, e.g. Unit 1 in all year groups across the *Rising Stars Mathematics* resources is focused on Number Sense, so teachers are able to focus on similar topics at a different level within mixed-age classes.

On the website, there are Medium-term Planning Grid templates which break down the units into half-termly plans. These may be useful for teachers of mixed-age classes to compare the different year groups.

Assessment

Assessment opportunities

Each unit in *Rising Stars Mathematics* provides the opportunity for teachers to check existing understanding through the opener pages. Discussions around what children can see, how they interpret what they see and their response to the 'I wonder…' questions will reveal children's current level of understanding.

Likewise, the cartoon at the beginning of each concept, provides an opportunity to check understanding through class discussion of the misconception or error. Throughout each unit, there are continual opportunities for assessment. Teachers will probe conceptual and procedural understanding through questioning and observation as they model and teach. The way children respond to the modelling and teaching provides the teacher with valuable information on what to spend a little more time and what to move through quickly, as well as information on individual needs.

The Textbook activities provide further assessment opportunities, particularly the non-routine, open-ended types of activities offered in Step 4.

The final review activities are particularly useful assessment tasks, since they are designed to give children the opportunity to demonstrate what they know and the concepts they have mastered. In this way assessment is ongoing throughout the unit, with a summative assessment at the end of each unit.

End points to be tested in Key Stage 2 national tests

Some elements of the National Curriculum cannot be assessed in statutory tests although they will need to be assessed by teachers as part of their statutory assessment of the whole National Curriculum. Over time, all the end point requirements that can be tested in the 2014 National Curriculum will be tested at the end of Key Stage 2. It is therefore important to make a note of these, particularly for teachers in Years 5 and 6, and to make sure children are up to speed with these requirements, e.g. Roman numerals need to be taught from Years 3 to 5. There is no mention of them in Year 6. However, they could be tested in the end of Year 6 tests. *Rising Stars Mathematics* suggests times when these can be rehearsed and reinforced during the warm-up activities, practice or follow-up tasks.

Measuring progress

In a new world of assessment free from levels, it is now up to teachers to decide how best to assess the progress their children are making against the new Programmes of Study. For schools who wish to do this using regular half-termly or end-of-term tests using an independent resource outside of the *Rising Stars Mathematics* teaching materials, the *Rising Stars Assessment Half-termly Progress Tests* are an ideal resource to measure progress and inform future learning. They are organised to assess the content in the same order that it is covered in the scope and sequence of the Rising Stars Mathematics units, so that teachers can be sure that children are not being tested on content that they have yet to be taught. For more information, please visit www.risingstars-uk.com.

Ensuring progress for all children

If we consider any particular concept area as a pool, some children will paddle, others will swim with armbands and others will swim freely. They are all in the same pool, but accessing it at different levels and in different ways. This is a good metaphor for how differentiation should be managed when following a mastery approach. It will ensure that the broad majority of children all move on together into a new pool, as required by the National Curriculum.

Rising Stars Mathematics assumes that all children within the class will be taught the same content and given the same opportunities to understand the concepts. The 'Let's learn: Modelling and teaching' and 'Let's practise: Digging deeper' sections both include suggestions for a variety of representations, models and images that can be used to explain the concepts. The expectation is not that all children should be able to use all representations or methods, but rather that different representations will trigger understanding for different children. By using a wide variety of representations like this and multiple ways to explain concepts, teachers give each individual child the best possible chance of finding something that works for them. Some children may fully grasp the concept being introduced using the first or second representation, however that does not mean the rest of the lesson is irrelevant for them. Seeing the concept represented in different ways will give them the opportunity to deepen their understanding and make connections between the different methods.

Rising Stars Mathematics recognises that in every class it is likely that there will be some children who will need more support than others to achieve understanding of concepts. The Teacher's Guide includes a section on 'Supporting understanding' for children who need a little more reinforcement. The same section also offers ideas for 'Broadening understanding', for those children who have a good understanding of the concept.

In order to give all children the best possible chance to make progress in mathematics, the *Rising Stars Mathematics* approach to differentiation is that it should be managed through support and intervention, not through changing the content. Difficulties and misconceptions should be addressed as they occur and children should be challenged through more demanding problems, rather than being accelerated to future curriculum content.

Some schools are organising mathematics so that there are two shorter sessions each day. The first session is used for teaching the concept, the second is for practice. Using *Rising Stars Mathematics* for this approach, teachers would focus on the 'Let's learn' part of the unit in the first session and on the 'Let's practise' section in the second session. During the second session, the teacher could work with children who have struggled to understand as a guided group, whilst others work through the three or four steps in the Textbook more independently. A further 15-minute intervention session may be offered later the same day. Intervention must be carried out immediately to ensure that the majority of children move through the materials at the same pace. Some schools may wish to pre-teach a small group of children. This 10-minute session could be used to revise what children already know about today's concept and its vocabulary, before the concept is extended in the main session.

Children with significant special needs may require an individual programme of work. Although these children are unlikely to master concepts as deeply as others, they should still aim for mastery at a level appropriate for the individual.

Fast finishers can be challenged to deepen their understanding by generalising. Depending on the concept, they might be asked if what they have just explored will always, sometimes or never be true. They might be asked to give an example of the concept in money or measures. Alternatively, some of the other strategies to embed problem solving could be used. *Rising Stars Mathematics* provides some suggestions for broadening understanding in every unit.

Resources and representations

Representations are hugely important in helping children to develop a conceptual understanding of what they are learning. *Rising Stars Mathematics* aims to encourage all teachers to make use of these with all children from Year 1 through to Year 6. In the past, manipulatives and visual representations have often only been used in Key Stage 2 for children struggling to grasp certain concepts, but they are necessary for all. There are two main types of representations: visual (pictorial) and manipulative (concrete apparatus).

The key manipulatives included in this programme are:

- Straws (Years 1-3)
- Base 10 apparatus
- Place-value counters
- Place-value cards
- Number rods
- Double-sided counters
- Bead strings
- Plates
- Digit cards
- Coins
- Counting sticks
- Interlocking cubes
- Coloured counters
- 2-D shapes
- 3-D shapes
- Clock faces
- 1–6 dice
- 1–10 dice
- Percentage cards
- Modelling clay
- Number cards
- Tangrams

See below for further details.

The key visual representations included in this programme are:

- Number tracks
- Ten frames
- 100 squares
- Number lines
- The bar model
- Place-value grids
- Gattegno charts

See below for further details.

Concrete manipulatives

Straws

Straws are a great resource to enable children to see the cardinality of numbers. They could make bundles of ten and compare tens and ones. They could put ten bundles together to make 100 and compare these. Straws are particularly useful for younger children, when they still need to see and touch quantities.

Base 10 apparatus

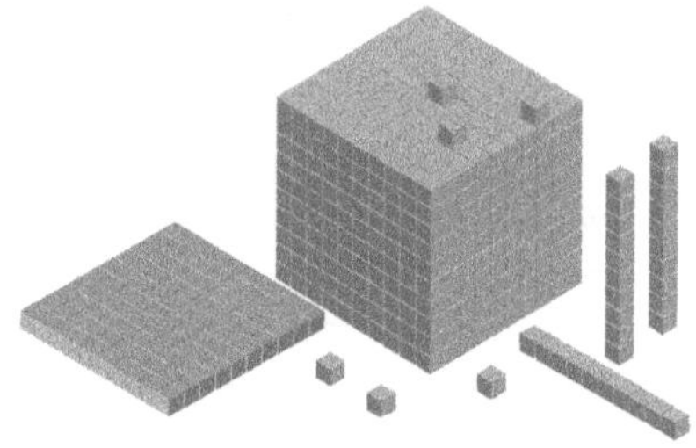

These are representations of numbers. In the first instance, the small cubes represent ones, the rods tens, the flats hundreds and the large cubes thousands. Children find these helpful because the size of the individual pieces helps to denote their value. Later, when children encounter decimals, the flats represent ones, the rods tenths and the small cubes hundredths. If children are familiar with using different manipulatives to represent numbers, it will be easy for them to make this transfer.

Place-value counters

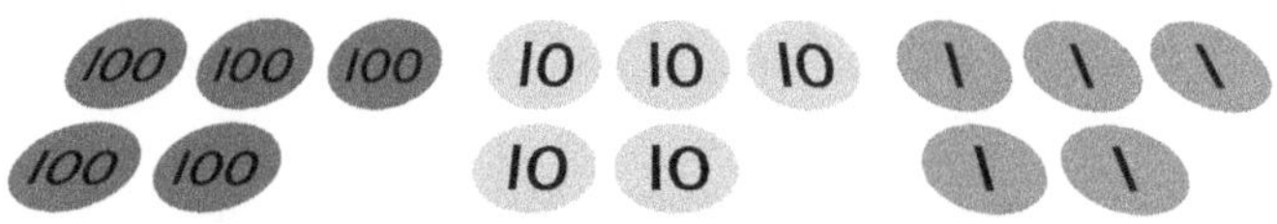

These also represent numbers. You can see clearly what each colour represents through the values written on each (often greens are hundreds, yellows are tens, and reds are ones). They are more abstract than Base 10 apparatus because the counters are all the same size and are therefore not proportional to their value. It is recommended that these are used in late Key Stage 1 and in Key Stage 2, when children are working with larger numbers. When children have used these, you may find that they can use any coloured counters and assign their own values to them.

Number rods

Coloured number rods are excellent for helping children to become flexible in their thinking about numbers. The rods represent any number that you would want them to represent. Assign a value to one and children can work out the values of the other rods. The rods are fractions of other rods, e.g. some are halves, quarters and eighths of others. This is a great resource to use when dealing with multiplication, division and fractions.

Coloured rods can also be used as bars to support thinking when using the bar model. Using a rod to represent a bar allows bars to be changed or manipulated to illustrate the problem under consideration. See the section on the bar model for further information on this.

Double-sided counters

These are great for helping children to develop reasoning and fluency. You could give children three counters each and ask them to show you 2, then 3, then 12. Children need to consider how they could represent 12 using three counters. The only rule is that one colour needs to represent the same number. So, two yellow sides could be 5 each and a red side could be 2. Or one yellow side could be 8 and one red side 4. There are numerous ways to represent 12 or other numbers using these counters.

Bead strings

Bead strings are helpful for early calculation. When children are familiar with them and know that each string of colour is 10, they can add, subtract, multiply and divide using them and develop the ability to do this without counting one at a time, e.g. for 10 + 6, they add 6 onto 10, without the need to count ten beads, six beads and then count them all. These can be used to represent other numbers, e.g. the whole string could represent 1, each coloured section would then be one tenth and one bead would be one hundredth. This flexibility makes the bead string a very useful manipulative for fractions, decimals and percentages.

Plates

Plates like these are another manipulative which help children to move on from counting everything, e.g. if they add 5 and 9, they put the plates together. They match the result with 10 and 4 to give the answer 14. Paper 10 frames can be cut and used to represent a number in exactly the same way.

Visual representations

The bar model

The bar model is a very effective visual representation. It helps children to make sense of problems. Take missing number statements such as 35 – □ = 16. We know that 35 is the larger number, so it will be the larger bar. A smaller bar of 16 can be drawn below it. Drawing a bar from the end of the 16 bar to fill the space to the end of the 35 bar represents the missing number. We can then work out the missing number by counting back from 35 to 16 or counting on from 16 to 35.

35	
16	?

This can support children as they work out families of addition and subtraction facts.

$a = b + c$

$a = c + b$

$a - b = c$

$a - c = b$

a	
b	c

Addition and subtraction calculations can be represented using this model, e.g.

1) Samir scored 145 points on a computer game, Alex scored 76 more points. How many points did Alex score?

145	76
?	

(Alex scored 221 points.)

2) Jenny had a collection of shells. She gave her friend 123 of them. She was left with 146. How many shells did she have before giving some to her friend?

123	146
?	

(Jenny had 269 shells.)

3) Ben went for a run. He ran 12.5 km to the shop and 6.75 km back. Then he stopped to talk to a friend. How much further did he need to run to get home?

12.5 km	
?	6.75 km

(Ben has to run another 5.75 km.)

4) Ella has some cherries. She eats two. Then she eats half of what is left. She now has six. How many did she have to begin with?

?		
6	6	2

(Ella started off with 14 cherries.)

This model can be used very effectively for representing multiplication, division and fractions, as well as ratio and proportion problems. It is often helpful to use double-sided counters or coloured rods to set out the problems first and then move on to drawing them as bars, e.g.

1) There are 27 red flowers in the garden. There are three times as many red flowers as there are white flowers. How many white flowers are there?

Red flowers			
White flowers			

If there are 27 red flowers, each part is worth 9. So there are 9 white flowers.

2) Sam had five times as many marbles as Tom. If Sam gives 26 marbles to Tom, the two friends will have exactly the same amount. How many marbles do they have altogether?

Tom's marbles	T				
Sam's marbles	S	S	S	S	S

Sam gives 26 marbles to Tom.

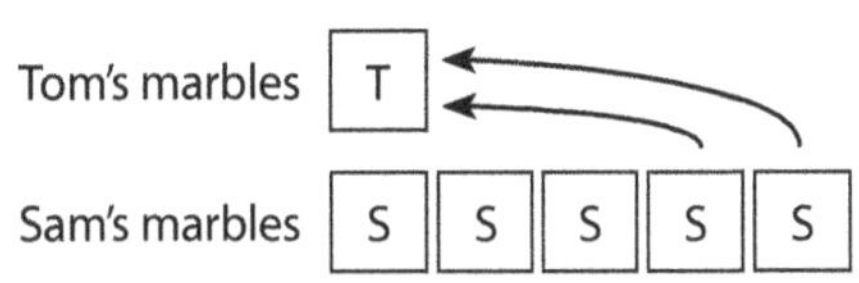

So, the model will look like this:

T	S	S
S	S	S

We now know that each part is worth 13. So they have 78 marbles altogether.

3) David spent $\frac{2}{5}$ of his money on a book. The book cost £10. How much money did he start off with?

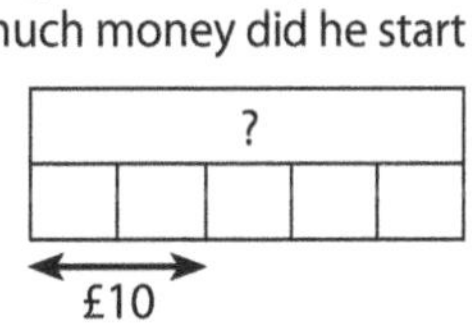

We know $\frac{2}{5}$ is equal to £10. Each part must be £5. So he started off with £25.

4) In Class 4, 80% of children like crisps. 75% of children who like crisps also like chocolate. What percentage of Class 4 like both crisps and chocolate?

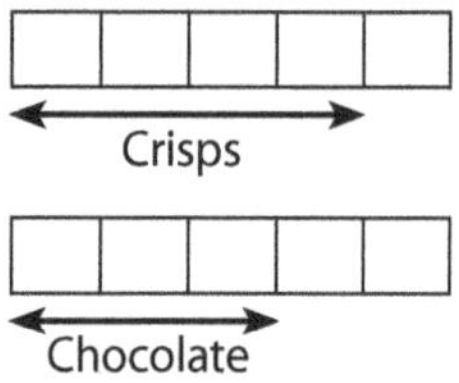

Each part in the model is worth 20%. So 60% of Class 4 like both crisps and chocolate.

5) A computer game was reduced in a sale by 20% and it now costs £48. What was the original price?

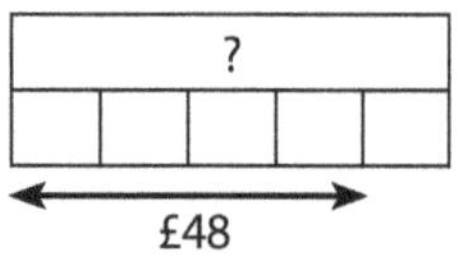

We know from this model that each part is worth £12. So, £12 is equivalent to the discount. Therefore the original cost was £60.

6) A gardener plants tulip bulbs in a flower bed. She plants 3 red bulbs for every 4 white bulbs. She plants 60 red bulbs. How many white bulbs does she plant?

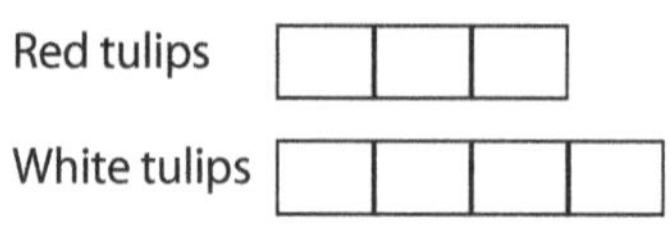

If she plants 60 red tulips, each part is worth 20. Therefore she must have planted 80 white bulbs.

Ten frames

There are different types of ten frames. This is one example.

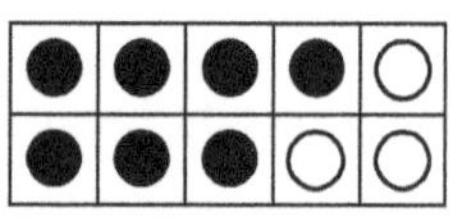

It draws out the odd and even properties of number. They are helpful for finding number bonds to 10, as well as for addition and subtraction.

These can also be used to represent fractions and decimals, e.g. if the whole frame is worth 1, what are the black counters worth? (0.7, $\frac{7}{10}$.)

Place-value grids

1000	100	10	1	.	10th	100th	1000th
				.			

Place-value grids are very useful for helping children to gain an understanding of the four main aspects of place value.

Gattegno charts

0.001	0.002	0.003	0.004	0.005	0.006	0.007	0.008	0.009
0.01	0.02	0.03	0.04	0.05	0.06	0.07	0.08	0.09
0.1	0.2	0.3	0.4	0.5	0.6	0.7	0.8	0.9
1	2	3	4	5	6	7	8	9
10	20	30	40	50	60	70	80	90
100	200	300	400	500	600	700	800	900
1000	2000	3000	4000	5000	6000	7000	8000	9000
10000	20000	30000	40000	50000	60000	70000	80000	90000

Gattegno charts are another useful resource that will help to secure children's conceptual understanding of place value.

Delivering the aims of the National Curriculum

Developing fluency

The first aim of the 2014 National Curriculum states that teachers must ensure that children: 'become fluent in the fundamentals of mathematics, including through varied and frequent practice with increasingly complex problems over time, so that pupils develop conceptual understanding and the ability to recall and apply knowledge rapidly and accurately'. Fluency includes:

- knowing number bonds for all numbers to 10, then 20 and 100.
- knowing multiplication facts up to 12 × 12.
- using these facts flexibly to create other facts, e.g. if you know that 6 × 7 = 42, you can work out that 6 × 70 = 420, 6 × 35 = 210 and so on.
- knowing efficient mental calculation strategies and written procedures for the four operations and using them efficiently.
- knowing when to use these methods appropriately. Children need to develop conceptual understanding, so that they know the facts and the procedures and how and why they work.

Developing reasoning skills

The second aim of the 2014 National Curriculum states that we should ensure that children: 'reason mathematically by following a line of enquiry, conjecturing relationships and generalisations, and developing an argument, justification or proof using mathematical language'.

Reasoning is about:

- making and testing predictions, conjectures or hypotheses
- searching for patterns and relationships
- making and investigating general statements by finding examples that satisfy them
- explaining and justifying solutions, results, conjectures, conclusions, generalisations and so on:
  - by testing
  - by reasoned argument
- disproving by finding counter-examples.

Many of the activities in *Rising Stars Mathematics* encourage reasoning. You can also provide extra activities to encourage reasoning. Only children can actually do the reasoning, but teachers can help them acquire and refine the necessary skills to do this. Teachers can also model reasoning by 'thinking out loud'.

The problem-solving strategies outlined in this introduction are useful ones to look at for developing reasoning. See also the introduction to the Textbooks, where there are some useful reminder prompts to help children think critically about reasoning and solving problems.

Strategies to embed problem solving

There are many strategies that will embed problem solving, which is the third aim of the 2014 National Curriculum. We need to ensure that children: 'can solve problems by applying their mathematics to a variety of routine and non-routine problems with increasing sophistication, including breaking down problems into a series of simpler steps and persevering in seeking solutions'.

Here are a few strategies that you might like to use, particularly when you work on activities that seek to deepen children's understanding of what you are teaching. Further guidance, detailed examples and activities using these strategies can be found in the Rising Stars *Problem Solving and Reasoning* programme developed by Tim Handley.

Always, sometimes, never

'Always, sometimes, never' is when you give children a statement and then ask whether it is always, sometimes or never true. This encourages the development of the skills of proof, generalisation and algebraic thinking. These are part of reasoning, which is the second aim of the National Curriculum. This strategy also encourages children to make connections between different areas of mathematics.

Another, another, another

'Another, another, another' is a strategy which involves giving children a statement and asking them to give you an example that matches it, and then another and another, e.g. say that $\frac{1}{2}$ and $\frac{2}{4}$ are equivalent fractions, then ask for another pair of equivalent fractions…and another…and another.

This strategy encourages children to give specific examples which meet a given general statement. It provides a good opportunity to assess children's conceptual understanding of an area of mathematics.

Convince me

'Convince me' activities are a useful way to encourage children to explore the structure of a mathematical concept. The teacher makes a statement to children and asks them to decide whether it is accurate or not, and then explain why. Their explanations to convince you allow them to develop their skills of reasoning in the context of mathematical proof, generalisation and algebraic thinking, which is the second aim of the National Curriculum.

Hard and easy

'Hard and easy' is an example of a strategy that encourages children to think closely about the structure of mathematics. It enables you to assess children's conceptual understanding of their mathematics. Ask them to give you an example of a 'hard' and 'easy' answer to a question and explain why one is 'hard' and the other is 'easy'. The choices children make when responding to this often provide valuable information about what they find difficult.

If this is the answer, what's the question?

'If this is the answer, what's the question?' activities encourage children to think creatively and explore the structure of mathematics. The strategy also allows children to develop their skills of generalisation. Give children an answer such as 25% and ask them to come up with as many questions as possible that could have that answer, e.g. 'What is $\frac{1}{4}$ of 100%?' or 'A jumper costs £15 in a sale and the original price was £20. What is the percentage discount?'

Mathematics stories

Giving children a number, geometric concept or measure and asking them to write its 'story', is a strategy that encourages children to explore everything they know about a mathematical concept. It is therefore particularly effective at developing children's subject knowledge, whilst also encouraging them to reason. Through telling a 'story', children are also likely to form and use their own generalisations and patterns, which can be a great starting point for further discussion.

Odd one out

'Odd one out' is a strategy which encourages conjecturing, making generalisations and reasoning about items in a set. All you need to do is give children a set of three or more numbers, shapes or statements and ask them to identify which is the odd one out and why. There will often be several potential responses involving each of the numbers, shapes or statements.

Peculiar, obvious, general

'Peculiar, obvious, general' is a strategy that encourages children to think about the structure of mathematics and to reason about it. Through focusing on what makes a peculiar, obvious or general example of a given statement, children have to think carefully about the statement given, the criteria needed to meet the statement, and what examples they could give.

Silly answers

'Silly answers' encourages children to make generalisations. In giving you a 'silly' answer to a question and explaining why it is such, they will have to reason about possible 'correct' answers. This will require them to consider the properties relating to the topic in the question, therefore deepening their conceptual understanding.

What do you notice?

The 'what do you notice?' strategy encourages children to look deeply at the structure of mathematics. By asking them 'What do you notice?' about a number, set of numbers, shape or mathematical statement, they will need to make their own generalisations and test them against specific examples.

What else do we know?

'What else do we know?' is a strategy that encourages children to see the links that exist in all areas of mathematics. It encourages them to reason and combine other known facts with a given statement, e.g. give children a statement such as 'If we know $8 \times 9 = 72$, what else do we know?' They could then create new statements by doubling, halving and multiplying or dividing by 10, such as $8 \times 90 = 720$, $8 \times 45 = 360$ and $4 \times 45 = 180$.

What's the same? What's different?

'What's the same? What's different?' is a strategy that encourages children to compare and contrast. Children will need to spot patterns and similarities, as well as making generalisations and connections between different aspects of mathematics.

Zooming in

'Zooming in' is a strategy that encourages children to reason about mathematical properties, e.g. give a criterion such as an odd number. Ask children to give an example that fits the criteria. Then 'zoom in' to give another criterion, e.g. an odd number which is also a multiple of 7. This strategy also encourages children to re-evaluate their decisions and helps them to try to make more reasoned choices for their initial 'answers'.

Effective questioning

Questioning is an important strategy which can help embed problem solving and reasoning into day-to-day mathematics teaching. It also allows you to assess children's conceptual understanding. Here are some examples of question structures and routines:

Can you give me an example of ...?

- a prime number which is not odd
- an irregular quadrilateral
- a percentage fraction and decimal equivalence

What is the quickest or easiest way to ...?

- find out if a number is prime
- find the area of a rectangle
- find out how many chairs will fit into our school hall

What are 7, 11 and 13 examples of ...?

What about 36?

What about 72 cm^2?

How can we be sure that ...?

- all multiples of 6 are multiples of 3
- the area of a triangle = $\frac{1}{2}$ base × height
- $\frac{6}{8}$ is equal to $\frac{12}{16}$

What's the link between ...?

- 12, 24 and 36
- $\frac{6}{8}$, 0.75 and 75%
- a rectangle and a square

Developing mental and written calculation skills

Mental calculation strategies

Throughout the 2014 National Curriculum Programme of Study for Mathematics, children are expected to use mental calculation strategies as appropriate. Very often, after written methods have been introduced, children tend to use these as their default methods for answering calculations, whether they are appropriate or not. It is therefore important to provide opportunities where children are given calculations and have to decide which methods would be the most efficient to solve them. This encourages them to continue using mental arithmetic as much as possible.

If schools still have copies of the 1999 National Numeracy Strategy Framework, teachers may find the section on mental calculation strategies for addition, subtraction, multiplication and division a useful reference tool for identifying key mental calculation strategies to teach and practise regularly. The 1999 QCA booklet, Teaching mental calculation strategies: guidance for teachers at key stages 1 and 2, is another useful resource.

Key mental calculation strategies include:

- Partition and recombine: $36 + 24 = 30 + 20 + 6 + 4 = 50 + 10 = 60$
- Sequencing: $135 + 78 = 135 + 70 + 8 = 205 + 8 = 213$
- Doubles and near doubles: $154 + 153 = \text{double } 154 - 1 = 307$
- Using number pairs to 10 and 100: $462 + 138 = 460 + 130 + 10 = 400 + 100 + 100 = 600$
- Adding near multiples of 10 and adjusting: $1458 + 2998 = 1458 + 3000 - 2 = 4456$
- Using known number facts: if we know that $12 \times 7 = 84$ then $12 \times 14 = 168$, $1.2 \times 7 = 8.4$, $2.4 \times 7 = 16.8$
- Bridging though tens, hundreds, tenths: $36 + 8 = 36 + 4 + 4 = 40 + 4 = 44$
- Using relationships between operations: if $256 + 135 = 391$, then $135 + 256$ must also be 391, $391 - 256$ must be 135 and $391 - 135$ must be 256
- Counting on: $365 - 178$, $178 + 22 = 200$, $200 + 165 = 365$, so $365 - 178 = 22 + 165 = 187$
- $\times 4$ by doubling and doubling again: 280×4, double $280 = 560$, double $560 = 1120$
- $\times 8$ by doubling, doubling and doubling again: 56×8, double $56 = 112$, double $112 = 224$, double $224 = 448$
- $\times 5$ by $\times 10$ and halving: $364 \times 10 = 3640$, half $3640 = 1820 = 364 \times 5$
- $\times 9$ by $\times 10$ then subtracting: $\times 1$ $17 \times 9 = (17 \times 10) - (17 \times 1) = 170 - 17 = 153$
- $\times 20$ by $\times 10$ and doubling: $470 \times 20 = 470 \times 10 \times 2 = 4700 \times 2 = 9400$
- $\times 25$ by $\times 100$ then halving and halving again: 37×25, $37 \times 100 = 3700$, half $3700 = 1850$, half $1850 = 925 = 37 \times 25$.

Rising Stars Mathematics encourages teachers to rehearse mental calculation strategies regularly with children during the 'Warming up' sections.

Mental strategies are often used in conjunction with written strategies, so the two do, in fact, go hand in hand. Children will use mental strategies to estimate the solution to a number statement. They will also use, e.g. their mental calculation skills in each column of a written calculation and when using an algorithm.

Approach to written algorithms

In the 2014 National Curriculum Programme of Study for Mathematics, formal written algorithms are introduced during Key Stage 2. It is not necessary to introduce any algorithms into Key Stage 1, these children should be focusing on mental calculation strategies. However, recording addition and subtraction in columns can be introduced if teachers wish to support understanding of place value and prepare for formal written methods later on.

When written algorithms are introduced, children need to develop a conceptual understanding of these and not just learn a method using a rote learning process. It is therefore very important that they use manipulatives, such as those outlined in the Resources and Representations section (see pages 12–14), when they learn a new method or use a method that they have previously learnt but are beginning to apply to larger numbers or decimals.

In Key Stage 2, Base 10 apparatus and place-value counters are very important for developing this conceptual understanding. It is useful for the teacher to model the procedure using this apparatus (which could be on the interactive whiteboard) and children follow their lead. The teacher should then model the written method and ask children to identify what is the same and what is different about the two methods. Some suggestions for how to model this for each operation are given below.

It is often a good idea, when beginning a series of lessons on one of the four operations, to write a selection of calculations on the whiteboard. Children can then discuss with a partner which methods would be the best to use. This highlights the fact that mental calculation strategies are often the most efficient methods to use.

Mental calculation uses the multiplicative property of place value and written methods use the positional property, e.g. if using the strategy of sequencing, one number needs to be partitioned, $246 + 132 = 246 + 100 + 30 + 2$. If subtracting 4567 and 1281, children will refer to the digits positioned in their columns. This is one reason that children need to have a deep conceptual knowledge of place value.

Addition

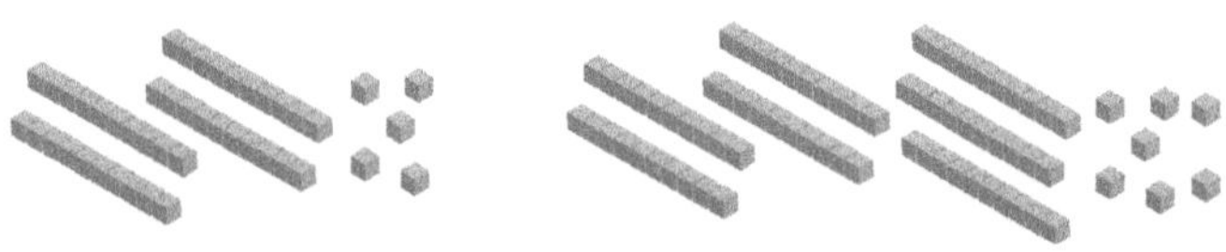

45 + 77

Encourage children to group the ones. They will have 12, 10 of which need to be changed to one ten. They then add the tens to give 12. 10 of these need changing to one hundred. Model the written method as children progress through each stage with the Base 10 apparatus.

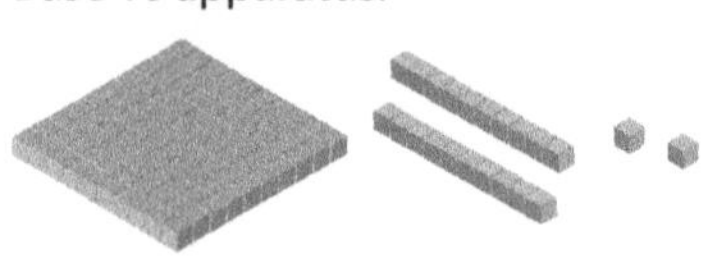

$$\begin{array}{r} 45 \\ +\ 77 \\ \hline 122 \\ {\scriptstyle 1\ 1} \end{array}$$

How are these models different?
How are they the same?

Using the correct vocabulary is also important. With addition, the vocabulary is:

augend + addend = sum

Subtraction

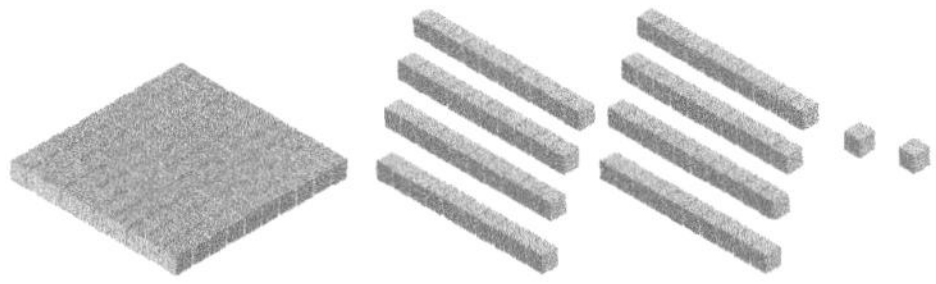

182 – 147

In this example, children set out 182. When they need to subtract 7 from 2, they can see that there are not enough ones. They therefore need to exchange a ten for 10 ones. They can then take away the other numbers. Again, teachers should model the written method as children progress through the stages of the calculation using the Base 10 apparatus.

Using the correct vocabulary is also important. With subtraction, the correct vocabulary is:

minuend – subtrahend = difference

Multiplication

Arrays are a key visual representation for multiplication. They highlight the links with repeated addition and division. In this example, 38 × 3, 38 is made three times using manipulatives and then grouped. The model below shows how the physical array links to the grid method and then to the written method:

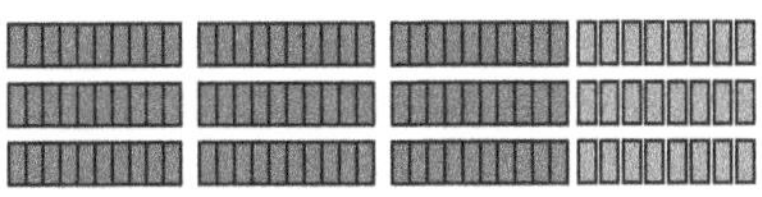

	30	8
3	90	24

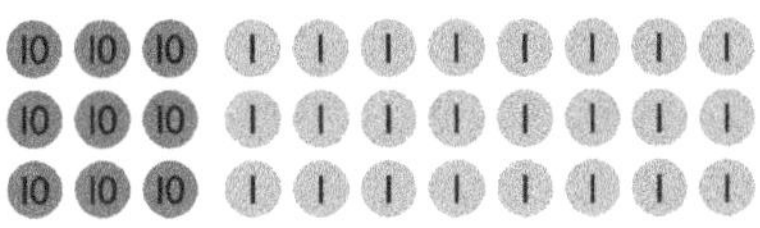

$$\begin{array}{r} 38 \\ \times\ \ 3 \\ \hline 114 \\ {\scriptstyle 2} \end{array}$$

What's different about all these models?
What's the same?

The correct vocabulary for multiplication is:

multiplicand × multiplier = product

Division

Division is basically grouping, i.e. how many groups of the divisor can be made out of the dividend? When children set out the number (the dividend) using manipulatives, they can clearly see how many groups of the divisor (the number they are dividing by) they can make out of the numbers of each particular value.

Step 1

135 ÷ 3

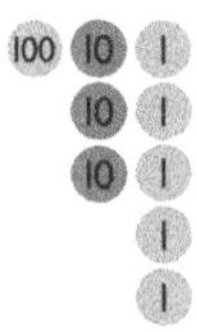

We can't make any groups of 3 hundred with the 1 hundred we have. Exchange the 1 hundred for 10 tens.

$3\overline{)135}$

What is different about these models?
What is the same

Step 2

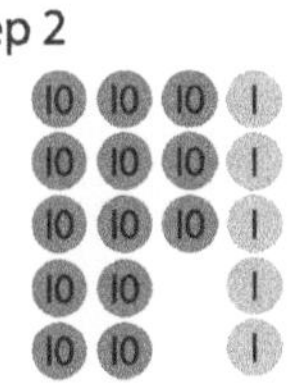

We now have 13 tens.

$3\overline{)\not{1}^{1}35}$

What is different about these models?
What is the same?

Step 3

We can make 4 groups of three 10s, leaving one 10

$$\begin{array}{r} 4\ \\ 3\overline{)\not{1}^{1}35} \end{array}$$

What is different about these models?
What is the same?

Step 4

We need to exchange the one 10 for ten 1s

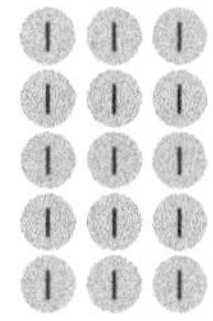

$$\begin{array}{r} 4\ \\ 3\overline{)\not{1}^{1}\not{3}^{1}5} \end{array}$$

What is different about these models?
What is the same

Step 5

We can make 5 groups of three 1s, giving an answer of 45

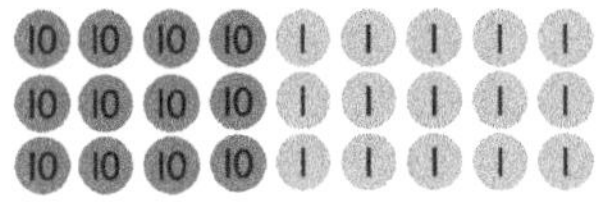

$$\begin{array}{r} 45 \\ 3\overline{)\not{1}^{1}\not{3}^{1}5} \end{array}$$

What is different about these models?
What is the same

The correct vocabulary for division is:

dividend ÷ divisor = quotient

Use of calculators

The 2014 National Curriculum states that: 'Calculators should not be used as a substitute for good written and mental arithmetic. They should therefore only be introduced near the end of Key Stage 2 to support pupils' conceptual understanding and exploration of more complex number problems, if written and mental arithmetic are secure. In both primary and secondary schools, teachers should use their judgement about when ICT tools should be used'.

It is extremely important that children do not learn to rely on calculators instead of being able to use mental and written calculation methods securely. The calculations given to children as practice should be carefully chosen, so that they are able to perform them using appropriate mental or written methods. However, when working on a real life problem with a large amount of data, teachers may wish to allow children to perform calculations on a calculator, so that they focus more deeply on the problem-solving task at hand.

Calculators are also a very effective way to rehearse recognising numbers for Key Stage 1 and understanding place value in both Key Stage 1 and Key Stage 2, e.g. to rehearse place value, give children the following instructions. They must work out what operation to use at each stage:

- key in 3
- put 5 in front of the 3 (they must add 50)
- put a 2 in front of the 5 (they must add 200)
- change the 5 to a 2 (they must subtract 30)

and so on.

Mathematics outside the classroom

Homework

Rising Stars Mathematics provides a range of homework options:

1. The Textbook can be sent home for children to complete a particular step in the 'Let's practise' section. Within the Textbook, children will have access to the concept explanation, modelling, exemplification, practice and application that they have already explored in the 'Let's learn' section. This enables them to pick up where they left off in class. For schools that do not wish to send Textbooks home, eTextbook versions on the website can be shared with parents/carers, so that the content can be accessed online from home.
2. All the gameboards and game instructions can be downloaded and printed from the website and sent home for children to play with parents/carers/siblings/friends. Children can also be asked to design their own game using the game boards in the Textbook.

3. There is a bank of Homework activities at the back of this Teacher's Guide, which can be used as expansion activities outside the classroom. There are two activities for each concept spread in the Textbook. These are also available as editable files on the website, enabling teachers to choose both the homework and its frequency.
4. The Practice Books provide a wide range of additional questions to consolidate and reinforce understanding of concepts taught using the Textbook in class. These extra practice activities can be set as homework or used as further practice within the classroom. Either way, they provide a good record for the child of their understanding and progress and will help teachers identify any misconceptions or gaps in understanding.

Engaging parents/carers

In order to engage parents/carers in their children's learning, it is important to share and explain the way in which mathematics is being taught in school and the key features and benefits of the *Rising Stars Mathematics* approach. An example of a letter to parents/carers is set out below:

Dear Parent/Carer,

As you know, mathematics is an integral part of your child's learning. We are using the innovative *Rising Stars Mathematics* programme to ensure mathematics is accessible for all children and that they achieve personal success in the subject.

Throughout the programme, there is a focus on the development of deep subject knowledge and the ability to make connections. The approach places importance on different types of practice, as well as the ability to recall facts and manipulate them to work out other facts.

The questioning in *Rising Stars Mathematics* is tailored to your child's needs, with a variety of different problems to solve. Any misconceptions are dealt with immediately. Children who grasp mathematical concepts quickly will be given complex problems which deepen their knowledge of the same content, rather than being accelerated into content from the next year level.

There is a focus on practice and spending longer on key concepts to embed understanding. This includes different types of practice, each of which requires a deeper level of understanding:

1. Basic practice, i.e. without any contexts
2. Variations or intelligent practice, this shows children patterns or helps them to make connections
3. Practice and consolidation within different contexts, e.g. time, money or length
4. Open-ended, investigative practice. This goes deeper and deeper, requiring greater reasoning.

Precise mathematical vocabulary will be taught from the start and used consistently throughout the school, including these terms:

Augend + addend = sum/total

Minuend − subtrahend = difference

Multiplicand × multiplier = product

Dividend ÷ divisor = quotient.

We are very excited to be using this unique programme and appreciate your continued support.

Yours faithfully,

The style of the *Rising Stars Mathematics* resources is clear and engaging, which will help to capture the interest of parents/carers. In the Textbook, explanations are supported by clear pictorial representations and followed by guided, step-by-step practice. This will enable parents/carers to quickly familiarise themselves with both what is being taught and how it is being approached. This is especially important if children are asked to complete activities from the Textbook as homework. Since the concepts are set out clearly in the 'Let's learn' section, children will be able to show and explain what they have been learning. Parents/carers will feel able to help without confusing their child by introducing a different method, particularly if they were taught mathematics in a different way themselves.

For schools that do not wish to send Textbooks home, online versions can be shared as eTextbooks and accessed online by parents/carers or children at home. These provide an enhanced version of the print Textbooks, with a number of pop-up animations throughout that help to explain key concepts. Parents/carers may wish to watch these with their child, to enable them to participate in their learning.

It may also be useful to share the school's Calculation Policy or the pages from this Teacher's Guide introduction on the *Rising Stars Mathematics* approach to mental arithmetic and written algorithms (see pages 16–17). This could help parents/carers understand how their child will be tackling calculations during practice or homework activities and explain how best they can support this

Planning grids

Year 3 scope and sequence

The following grid shows the concepts and objectives that are covered within each *Rising Stars Mathematics* Year 3 unit and provides page references to each of the various components.

Unit	Concept	Objectives	Textbook	Teacher's Guide	Practice Book	Homework Sheets
1	1a Tens and hundreds	• Count from zero in multiples of 100. • Find ten or 100 more or less than a given number.	12–13	26–7	4–6	178
	1b Hundreds, tens and ones	• Recognise the place value of each digit in a 3-digit number. • Read and write numbers up to 500 in numerals and words.	14–15	28–9	7–9	179
	1c Comparing and ordering numbers	• Recognise the place value of each digit in a 3-digit number. • Compare and order numbers up to 500.	16–17	30–1	10–12	180
	1d Representing numbers	• Identify, represent and estimate numbers to 500 using different representations.	18–19	32–3	13–17	181
2	2a Mental calculation strategies	• Add and subtract numbers mentally. • Add and subtract numbers with up to three digits. • Solve problems, including missing number problems, using number facts, place value and more complex addition and subtraction.	26–7	40–1	18–21	182
	2b Developing written methods	• Add and subtract numbers with up to three digits, using formal written methods of columnar addition and subtraction. • Estimate the answer to a calculation and use inverse operations to check answers.	28–9	42–3	22–4	183
3	3a 2s, 4s and 8s	• Recall and use multiplication and division facts for the three, four and eight multiplication tables. • Write and calculate mathematical statements for multiplication and division using the multiplication tables that they know, including for 2-digit numbers multiplied by single-digit numbers, mentally and progressing to formal methods.	36–7	50–1	25–8	184
	3b Commutativity	• Recall and use multiplication and division facts for the two, four and eight multiplication tables. • Write and calculate mathematical statements for multiplication and division using the multiplication tables that they know, including for 2-digit numbers multiplied by single-digit numbers, mentally and progressing to formal methods.	38–9	52–3	29–32	185
	3c Sharing and possibilities	• Write and calculate mathematical statements for multiplication and division using the multiplication tables that they know. • Solve problems involving multiplication and division, including correspondence problems in which n objects are connected to m objects.	40–1	54–5	33–5	186
4	4a Making and describing 3-D shapes	• Draw 2-D shapes and make 3-D shapes using modelling materials. • Recognise 3-D shapes in different orientations and describe them. • Solve one-step and two-step questions using information in scaled bar charts, pictograms and tables.	48–9	62–3	36–9	187
	4b Angles	• Recognise angles as a property of shapes or a description of a turn. • Identify right angles. • Identify whether angles are greater than or less than a right angle.	50–1	64–5	40–1	188
5	5a Counting in steps of different sizes	• Count from zero in multiples of four, eight, 50 and 100. • Find ten or 100 more or less than a given number. • Interpret and present data using bar charts, pictograms and tables.	58–9	72–3	42–5	189
	5b More about place value	• Recognise the place value of each digit in a 3-digit number. • Compare and order numbers to 1000. • Identify and represent numbers to 750 using different representations. • Read and write numbers to 750 in numerals and words. • Measure and compare mass (kg/g).	60–1	74–5	46–9	190
	5c Tenths	• Count up and down in tenths; recognise that tenths arise from dividing an object into ten equal parts and dividing single-digit numbers or quantities by ten. • Solve number and practical problems.	62–3	76–7	50–2	191

Unit	Concept	Objectives	Textbook	Teacher's Guide	Practice Book	Homework Sheets
6	6a Adding 3-digit numbers	• Add numbers mentally using number facts, place value. • Add numbers with up to three digits using the formal written methods of columnar addition where appropriate. • Estimate and use inverse operations to check answers to a calculation. • Solve addition and subtraction problems in contexts, deciding which operations and methods to use and why.	70–1	84–5	53–5	192
	6b Subtracting 3-digit numbers	• Subtract numbers mentally using number facts, place value. • Subtract numbers with up to three digits using the formal written methods of columnar subtraction where appropriate. • Estimate and use inverse operations to check answers to a calculation. • Solve addition and subtraction problems in contexts, deciding which operations and methods to use and why.	72–3	86–7	56–8	193
7	7a Showing numbers in different ways	• Identify, represent and compare numbers to 1000 using different representations. • Count up and down in tenths, recognise that tenths arise from dividing an object into ten equal parts and dividing single digits or quantities by ten.	80–1	94–5	59–61	194
	7b Unit and non-unit fractions	• Recognise and use fractions as numbers; unit and non-unit fractions with small denominators. • Compare and order unit fractions and fractions with the same denominator. • Solve number and practical problems.	82–3	96–7	62–4	195
	7c Adding and subtracting fractions	• Add and subtract fractions with the same denominator within one whole.	84–5	98–9	65–7	196
8	8a Multiplication tables	• Recall and use multiplication and division facts for the three, four and eight multiplication tables. • Write and calculate mathematical statements for multiplication and division using the multiplication tables that they know, including for 2-digit numbers multiplied by single-digit numbers, using mental and progressing to formal written methods.	92–3	106–7	68–71	197
	8b Multiplying and dividing by 5 and 20	• Write and calculate mathematical statements for multiplication and division using the multiplication tables that they know, including for 2-digit numbers multiplied by single-digit numbers, using mental and progressing to formal written methods.	94–5	108–9	72–4	198
	8c Missing number problems and scaling	• Solve problems, including missing number problems, involving multiplication and division, including positive integer scaling problems in which n objects are connected to m objects..	96–7	110–11	75–7	199
9	9a Lines	• Identify horizontal and vertical lines and pairs of perpendicular and parallel lines. • Draw 2-D shapes and make 3-D shapes using modeling materials. • Present data using tables.	104–5	118–19	78–80	200
	9b Turning	• Recognise angles as a property of shape or a description of a turn. • Identify right angles. • Recognise that two right angles make a half-turn, three make three quarters of a turn and four a complete turn. • Recognise 3-D shapes in different orientations and describe them.	106–7	120–1	81–3	201
10	10a Reading and writing numbers	• Read and write numbers up to 1000 in numerals and words. • Tell and read the time from an analogue clock, including using Roman numerals, and 12-hour clocks. • Estimate and read time with increasing accuracy to the nearest minute; record and compare time in terms of seconds, minutes and hours; use vocabulary such as o'clock, a.m./p.m., morning, afternoon, noon and midnight.	114–15	128–9	84–7	202
	10b Using place value	• Identify, represent and compare numbers to 1000 using different representations. • Count up and down in tenths, recognise that tenths arise from dividing an object into ten equal parts and dividing single-digit numbers or quantities by ten. • Interpret data using bar charts. • Know the number of seconds in a minute and the number of days in each month, year and leap year. • Compare durations of events.	116–17	130–1	88–90	203

Unit	Concept	Objectives	Textbook	Teacher's Guide	Practice Book	Homework Sheets
11	11a Adding 3-digit numbers	• Add numbers mentally including a 3-digit number and ones, tens and hundreds. • Add numbers with up to three digits using the formal written methods of columnar addition. • Estimate the answer to a calculation and use inverse operations to check answers. • Solve problems, including missing number problems, using number facts, place value and more complex addition.	124–5	138–9	91–3	204
	11b Subtracting 3-digit numbers	• Subtract numbers mentally including a 3-digit number and ones, tens and hundreds. • Subtract numbers with up to three digits using formal written methods of columnar subtraction. • Estimate the answer to a calculation and use inverse operations to check answers. • Solve problems, including missing number problems, using number facts, place value and more complex subtraction.	126–7	140–1	94–6	205
12	12a Representing whole numbers and tenths	• Identify, represent and compare numbers to 1000 using different representations. • Count up and down in tenths, recognise that tenths arise from dividing an object into ten equal parts and dividing single-digit numbers or quantities by ten. • Solve number and practical problems involving measure and compare lengths (m/cm/mm).	134–5	148–9	97–100	206
	12b Finding and using unit and non-unit fractions	• Recognise and use fractions as numbers; unit and non-unit fractions with small denominators. • Compare and order unit fractions and fractions with the same denominator. • Add and subtract amounts of money to give change, using both £ and p in practical contexts.	136–7	150–1	101–4	207
	12c Equivalent fractions	• Recognise and show, using diagrams, equivalent fractions with small denominators. • Add and subtract fractions with the same denominator within one whole. • Solve number and practical problems involving measure; compare, add and subtract: mass (kg/g).	138–9	152–3	105–7	208
13	13a Towards the written method for multiplication	• Write and calculate mathematical statements for multiplication and division using known multiplication tables, including for 2-digit numbers multiplied by single-digit numbers, using mental and progressing to formal methods.	146–7	160–1	108–13	209
	13b Towards the written method for division	• Write and calculate mathematical statements for multiplication and division using known multiplication tables, including for 2-digit numbers multiplied by single-digit numbers, using mental and progressing to formal methods.	148–9	162–3	114–16	210
14	14a All about 2-D shapes	• Draw 2-D shapes and describe them. • Interpret and present data using bar charts, pictograms and tables.	156–7	170–1	117–19	211
	14b Measuring perimeter	• Measure, compare, add and subtract: lengths (m/cm/mm). • Measure the perimeter of simple 2-D shapes. • Interpret and present data using bar charts, pictograms and tables.	158–9	172–3	120–3	212

Curriculum mapping grid

The following grid shows what children should be taught during Year 3, as laid out in the 2014 National Curriculum Programme of Study for Mathematics and how these are covered within the *Rising Stars Mathematics* Year 3 units.

Domain	Sub-domain	Statement	Unit 1	Unit 2	Unit 3	Unit 4	Unit 5	Unit 6	Unit 7	Unit 8	Unit 9	Unit 10	Unit 11	Unit 12	Unit 13	Unit 14
NUMBER	Number and place value	count from zero in multiples of four, eight, 50 and 100; find ten or 100 more or less than a given number	a				a									
		recognise the place value of each digit in a 3-digit number (hundreds, tens, ones)	b, c				b									
		compare and order numbers up to 1000	c				b									
		identify, represent and estimate numbers using different representations	d				b		a			b		a		
		read and write numbers up to 1000 in numerals and in words	b				b					a				
		solve number problems and practical problems involving these ideas					c									
	Addition and subtraction	add and subtract numbers mentally, including:														
		a 3-digit number and ones		a									a, b			
		a 3-digit number and tens											a, b			
		a 3-digit number and hundreds											a, b			
		add and subtract numbers with up to three digits, using formal written methods of columnar addition and subtraction		a, b				a, b					a, b			
		estimate the answer to a calculation and use inverse operations to check answers		b				a, b					a, b			
		solve problems, including missing number problems, using number facts, place value, and more complex addition and subtraction		a				a, b					a, b			
	Multiplication and division	recall and use multiplication and division facts for the three, four and eight multiplication tables			a, b					a						
		write and calculate mathematical statements for multiplication and division using the multiplication tables that they know, including for two-digit numbers multiplied by one-digit numbers, using mental and progressing to formal written methods			a, b, c					a, b					a, b	
		solve problems, including missing number problems, involving multiplication and division, including positive integer scaling problems and correspondence problems in which *n* objects are connected to *m* objects			c					c						
	Fractions	count up and down in tenths; recognise that tenths arise from dividing an object into ten equal parts and in dividing single-digit numbers or quantities by ten					c		a			b		a		
		recognise, find and write fractions of a discrete set of objects: unit fractions and non-unit fractions with small denominators												b		
		recognise and use fractions as numbers: unit fractions and non-unit fractions with small denominators							b					b		
		recognise and show, using diagrams, equivalent fractions with small denominators												c		
		add and subtract fractions with the same denominator within one whole [e.g. $\frac{5}{7} + \frac{1}{7} = \frac{7}{7}$]							b					c		
		compare and order unit fractions, and fractions with the same denominators							b					b		
		solve problems that involve all of the above							b					a, b, c		

Domain	Sub-domain	Statement	Unit 1	Unit 2	Unit 3	Unit 4	Unit 5	Unit 6	Unit 7	Unit 8	Unit 9	Unit 10	Unit 11	Unit 12	Unit 13	Unit 14
MEASUREMENT	Measurement	measure, compare, add and subtract: lengths (m/cm/mm); mass (kg/g); volume/capacity (l/ml)					b							a, c		b
		measure the perimeter of simple 2-D shapes														b
		add and subtract amounts of money to give change, using both £ and p in practical contexts												b		
		tell and write the time from an analogue clock, including using Roman numerals from I to XII, and 12-hour and 24-hour clocks										a				
		estimate and read time with increasing accuracy to the nearest minute; record and compare time in terms of seconds, minutes and hours; use vocabulary such as o'clock, a.m./p.m., morning, afternoon, noon and midnight										a				
		know the number of seconds in a minute and the number of days in each month, year and leap year										b				
		compare durations of events [e.g. to calculate the time taken by particular events or tasks]										b				
GEOMETRY	Properties of shapes	draw 2-D shapes and make 3-D shapes using modelling materials; recognise 3-D shapes in different orientations and describe them				a					a, b					a
		recognise angles as a property of shape or a description of a turn				b					b					
		identify right angles, recognise that two right angles make a half-turn, three make three quarters of a turn and four a complete turn; identify whether angles are greater than or less than a right angle				b					b					
		identify horizontal and vertical lines and pairs of perpendicular and parallel lines									a					
STATISTICS	Statistics	interpret and present data using bar charts, pictograms and tables					a				a	b				a, b
		solve one-step and two-step questions [e.g. 'How many more?' and 'How many fewer?'] using information presented in scaled bar charts and pictograms and tables				a										

Unit 1 All about numbers

Mathematical focus

★ Number: Number and place value

★ Measurement: length, money, volume/capacity

Prior learning

Children should already be able to:

- count in steps of two, three and five from zero, and in tens from any number, forward or backward
- recognise the place value of each digit in a 2-digit number (tens, ones)
- identify, represent and estimate numbers using different representations, including a number line
- compare and order numbers from zero up to 100; use <, > and = signs
- read and write numbers to at least 100 in numerals and in words
- use place value and number facts to solve problems.

Key new learning

- Count from zero in multiples of 100.
- Find ten or 100 more or less than a given number.
- Recognise the place value of each digit in a 3-digit number.
- Read and write numbers up to 500 in numerals and words.
- Compare and order numbers up to 500.
- Identify, represent and estimate numbers to 500 using different representations.

Making connections

- Counting in tens and hundreds, and finding ten and 100 more or less than a given number, can be practised in a wide range of contexts, including of money, length, mass, volume and capacity, and time.
- An understanding of place value underpins many topics that children will meet later, including decimals, percentages and powers of ten. It is important component of number sense, which is essential if children are to answer more complex questions and solve problems with ease.
- Children need to see plenty of examples that show that numbers do not only represent countable numbers of items, but are all around them in many forms, including money, time and other measures. This understanding will help them read scales and interpret data, and an appreciation of the use of numbers in everyday life will make maths seem more relevant to them.

Talk about

Introduce children to the properties of place value using the terms positional, multiplicative and additive. The positional property shows where the digit in a number is positioned. The multiplicative property shows what the number must be multiplied by to give its true value. The additive property is when all the values are added together to give the whole number, e.g. in the number 258, the two is placed in the hundreds position and must be multiplied by 100 to give a value of 200. The five is placed in the tens position and needs multiplying by ten to give its true value of 50. The eight is placed in the ones position and is multiplied by one to give its value of eight. These are then added to give the whole number: 200 + 50 + 8 = 258.

Engaging and exploring

Ask children to show you the costs of the sweets in the different jars with coins. Ask questions relating to the cost of two, three, four, etc. of one type of sweet. Children find the fewest coins to make these amounts. Discuss different methods to find this out. Link to counting in steps and multiplication facts: rehearse counting in steps of two, five and ten forwards and backwards from zero to the 12th multiple, then ask them to tell you a variety of related multiplication facts. Encourage children to tell you the commutative fact as well in each case, giving both in a complete sentence, e.g. '6 multiplied by 5 equals 30 and 5 multiplied by 6 equals 30' because multiplication is commutative. Also encourage them to tell you the related division facts.

Look at the picture of the boy against the height chart. Do children know how tall they are? Write some of their heights on the board, in metres and centimetres. Alternatively, invite volunteers to measure the heights of some of the class using a metre stick and ruler. Find out if they know how many centimetres are equivalent to a metre, two metres, half a metre, etc. Order the heights from shortest to tallest. Turning to the question in the Textbook, discuss how to find 10 cm more than 120 cm. Agree that you need to add a ten onto the ten that is already there. Rehearse finding ten more and ten less than other 2- and 3-digit numbers. Ask children to find ten more and less than the heights recorded on the board.

Ask children what they notice about the numbers on the three sheets of raffle tickets. What are their similarities and differences? e.g. they are all 3-digit numbers; the hundreds numbers on each sheet are the same but across all three they are different. They could make these using Base 10 apparatus. Ask them to look at the pattern of numbers on the pink sheet. Can they tell you what the hidden numbers on the blue and yellow sheets must be? Look at the first number on each sheet (186, 271, 461). Establish that these are also in ascending order. Ask children how they know, encouraging them to talk about the value of the hundreds digit. Discuss whether the numbers are odd or even and how they know. Which are multiples of five? Are there any other familiar multiples?

Ask children to describe the three money boxes using fractions. Establish that the smallest is about half the size of the medium sized one which is about half the size of the largest one. What fraction of the large one must the smallest one be? Agree a quarter. Ask children to imagine that the smallest one holds 100 pennies. How much would the other two hold? If the large one held 400 pennies how much would the other two hold? For each answer ask children to compare the two numbers, telling you which is the greatest and smallest. They could compare these using the 'is greater than' and 'is less than' symbols. Ask them what they would need to do to the amounts to make them equal.

Give children some time to look at and talk about the sandwich menu. Then ask them to choose two different items, read their prices and then find their sum, writing it in numerals and words. Write 'pounds' and 'pence' on the board so that they can spell these correctly. Discuss the coins in our monetary system. Give pairs coins and them to find those that they would need to make the amounts on the menu. Encourage them to use the fewest coins. Ask questions such as: *I have £5 and buy a prawn and mayonnaise sandwich. How much change will I receive?*

Things to think about

- Which problem-solving strategies are most appropriate? e.g.:
  - Another, another, another
  - What's the same? What's different?
  - Convince me …
- What equipment and concrete resources will you provide to allow children to explore different representations of number?
- Will you provide children with opportunities to measure items in order to compare their length/mass/volume?
- Is the classroom and school a number-rich environment, with plenty of examples of 2- and 3-digit numbers, and numbers written in numerals and words?

Checking understanding

You will know children have mastered these concepts when they can count from zero in multiples of 100 and find ten or 100 more or less than a given number. They will recognise the place value of each digit in a 3-digit number and be able to compare and order numbers up to 500 and read and write them in numerals and words. They will be able to identify, represent and estimate numbers to 500 using different representations.

1a Tens and hundreds

- **Count from zero in multiples of 100.**
- **Find ten or 100 more or less than a given number.**

Mathematical vocabulary

Ones, tens, hundreds, ten more, ten less, 100 more, 100 less, equivalent, count on, count back, multiples

Warming up

Rehearse number bonds for all numbers to ten. Once children are confident finding pairs, encourage them to think of creative ways of making a given number, e.g. for 8: $2\frac{1}{2} + 5\frac{1}{2}$, $1 + 2 + 3 + 2$, $9 - 1$. Repeat this for the other numbers, finishing with numbers that have a total of ten.

Background knowledge

Counting in steps of different sizes follows on from counting in ones, and understanding that there is an order in which we count and that the final number is the amount we have. Be aware that there are many connections to other areas of mathematics. Counting in steps of one through to 12 up to the 12th multiple helps children develop an understanding of multiplication facts. Counting in hundreds will help them count in hundredths in subsequent years. This also helps in developing mental calculation strategies such as rounding to the nearest hundred and adjusting (e.g. 245 + 99 would be 245 + 100 − 1). It also helps them to find one hundred more or less than a given number. Children should be proficient in counting in steps of ten by now and so be able to identify the tens digit in a number and increase or decrease this by ten.

Let's learn: Modelling and teaching

Counting in 10s and 100s

- Discuss what is meant by a multiple. You could rehearse counting in steps of different sizes to find multiples of, e.g. two or five.
- Look at the 10–1000 square in the Textbook and talk about what happens to the numbers as you move from left to right in each row, and as you move from top to bottom. Use the first row and final column to count together in tens and hundreds.
- All the numbers in the square are multiples of ten. What do children notice about them? Agree that they all end with zero. Provide a copy of a 10-1000 grid and ask children to colour the multiples of 100 and 50. Ask: *What do you notice?* Can children tell you why 50 is a multiple of ten? Choose some numbers from the square and ask questions such as: *Is this a multiple of 100? 50? How do you know?*
- Choose a multiple of ten and ask children to count on in tens from it. Repeat with hundreds.

Homework 1 and 2

Practice Book pp 4–6

100 Squares

Representations and resources

Base 10 apparatus, rulers, 10–1000 squares (optional), 100 squares (optional), 0–100 number lines (optional), number rods (optional).

1a Tens and hundreds

Let's learn

You need
- Base 10 apparatus
- ruler

9 tens are ninety so 10 tens must be tenty.

Sort of, but we don't say tenty. When we get to 10 tens the number moves into the hundreds so 10 tens is 100.

Counting in 10s and 100s

When you count in 10s and 100s, you are counting in multiples.

A multiple of a number is the product when that number and another number are multiplied together, e.g. 20 is a multiple of 10 because 10 × 2 = 20.

10	20	30	40	50	60	70	80	90	100
110	120	130	140	150	160	170	180	190	200
210	220	230	240	250	260	270	280	290	300
310	320	330	340	350	360	370	380	390	400
410	420	430	440	450	460	470	480	490	500
510	520	530	540	550	560	570	580	590	600
610	620	630	640	650	660	670	680	690	700
710	720	730	740	750	760	770	780	790	800
810	820	830	840	850	860	870	880	890	900
910	920	930	940	950	960	970	980	990	1000

10 or 100 more or less

To find 10 more than a number, count on 10. 10 more than 20 is 30. 10 more than 28 is 38.

To find 10 less than a number, count back 10. 10 less than 90 is 80. 10 less than 96 is 86.

To find 100 more than a number, count on 100. 100 more than 340 is 440. 100 more than 342 is 442.

To find 100 less than a number, count back 100. 100 less than 860 is 760. 100 less than 864 is 764.

12

Teacher's Guide

Before working through the *Textbook*, study page 26 of the *Teacher's Guide* to see how the concepts should be introduced. Read and discuss the page with the children. Provide concrete resources to support exploration.

10 or 100 more or less

- Give children Base 10 apparatus and ask them to make a number and then add ten to find ten more. You could start with multiples of ten and relate the numbers to the 10–1000 square in the Textbook. Then move on to numbers which are not multiples of ten, and examples which involve crossing a hundreds boundary. Encourage children to notice that the tens increase and the ones stay the same.
- Repeat for ten less, again paying close attention to what happens to the digits. Then move on to 100 more and 100 less. Discuss the vocabulary that comes up, e.g. more, less, add, take away, count on, count back. As children become confident, they can be encouraged to count on or back without using equipment.

Let's practise: Digging deeper

Step 1

In this task children need to count on in tens and then hundreds from the given numbers. For counting on in tens, they could make the numbers using Base 10 apparatus and then add ten sticks. For counting on in hundreds, add hundred flats.

Step 2

Make sure children understand how to use Base 10 apparatus to add 100. They should notice that the hundreds digit increases by one and the tens and ones digits stay the same. You could discuss why part a does not form part of the pattern seen in the answers to parts b–e. Agree that in b–e the tens digit is 8, but in part a it is zero. The second part of the task is similar, but this time children take away 100 and then ten. Encourage them to write down both stages in their answer. They should notice that when taking away 100, only the hundreds digit changes; when taking away ten, only the tens digit changes. If appropriate, you could discuss the pattern seen in parts g-l, where same number (110) has been subtracted from each.

Step 3

Show children a ruler marked in millimetres and centimetres. Establish that there are 10 mm in 1 cm. Demonstrate counting along the ruler in tens to illustrate that there are, e.g. 30 mm in 3 cm. If necessary, discuss how to measure with a ruler to ensure children measure from zero and not the end of the ruler. Ensure they record their answers using the correct units and understand that ascending order means from the smallest to the longest length.

Step 4

Discus Mia's statement. Do children know how many pennies there are in £1? What about in 50p and 10p? Do they agree with Mia? You could ask children to discuss, in pairs or as a class, how to tackle the problem. Agree that they could change the £1, 50p and 10p coins into pennies and then count them all, including the 20 pennies. Encourage children to use resources to help them count the number of pennies quickly and efficiently (e.g. a 100 square, 0–100 number line, number rods or Base 10 apparatus). They might find a series of bar models helpful.

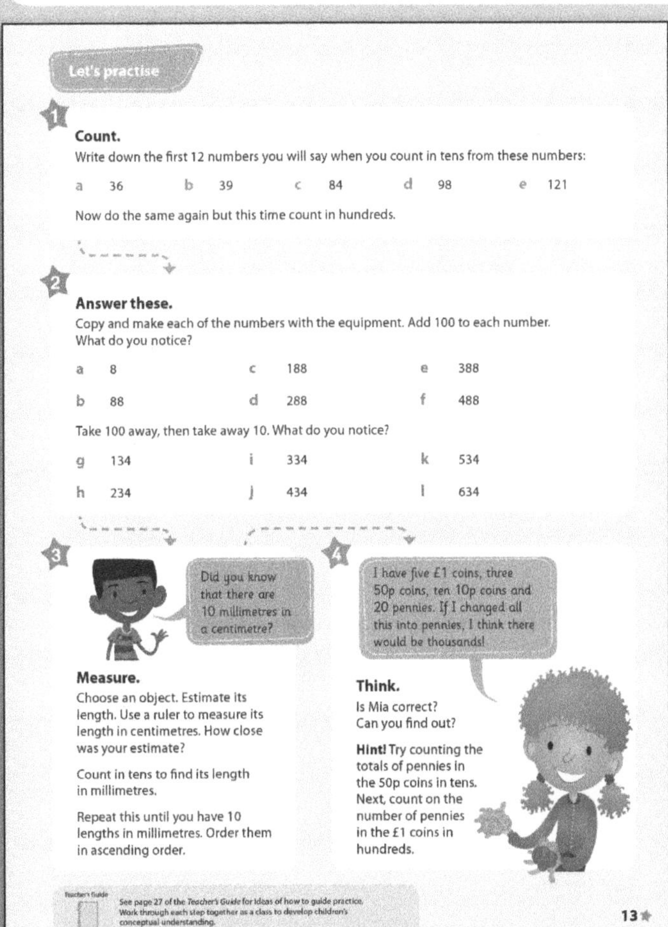
Let's practise

1 **Count.**
Write down the first 12 numbers you will say when you count in tens from these numbers:

a 36 b 39 c 84 d 98 e 121

Now do the same again but this time count in hundreds.

2 **Answer these.**
Copy and make each of the numbers with the equipment. Add 100 to each number. What do you notice?

a 8 c 188 e 388
b 88 d 288 f 488

Take 100 away, then take away 10. What do you notice?

g 134 i 334 k 534
h 234 j 434 l 634

3 Did you know that there are 10 millimetres in a centimetre?

Measure.
Choose an object. Estimate its length. Use a ruler to measure its length in centimetres. How close was your estimate?

Count in tens to find its length in millimetres.

Repeat this until you have 10 lengths in millimetres. Order them in ascending order.

4 I have five £1 coins, three 50p coins, ten 10p coins and 20 pennies. If I changed all this into pennies, I think there would be thousands!

Think.
Is Mia correct?
Can you find out?

Hint! Try counting the totals of pennies in the 50p coins in tens. Next, count on the number of pennies in the £1 coins in hundreds.

Teacher's Guide
See page 27 of the *Teacher's Guide* for ideas of how to guide practice. Work through each step together as a class to develop children's conceptual understanding.

13

Follow-up ideas

- Children could weigh 100 g of sand, rice or pasta into a plastic bag and then use it to help them weigh out estimates of multiples of 100 g.
- Children could set up their own café, pricing items to the nearest 10p or pound, make up menus, take orders, find total costs, take money and give change.
- You could ask children to make up a card game. They make two sets of cards. One in tens from ten to 100 and the other in hundreds from 100 to 1000. They shuffle the cards together and place them face down on the table and take it in turns to pick one. The aim is to get a run of multiples of tens or hundreds. The player that makes the longest run is the winner.

Ensuring progress

Supporting understanding

Some children may need to focus on adding and subtracting ten. Work with these in a focus group. You could show them how to count in tens using different models, e.g. a 0–100 number line.

Broadening understanding

You could link counting in hundreds to finding equivalent centimetres and metres. Give children a selection of metre measurements (e.g. 4 m, 7 m, 9 m) and ask them to count in hundreds to convert these to centimetres.

Concept mastered

Children can count from zero in multiples of 100 and find ten or 100 more or less than a given number.

Answers

Step 1

In tens

a 46, 56, 66, 76, 86, 96, 106, 116, 126, 136, 146, 156
b 49, 59, 69, 79, 89, 99, 109, 119, 129, 139, 149, 159
c 84, 94, 104, 114, 124, 134, 144, 154, 164, 174, 184, 194
d 98, 108, 118 ,128, 138, 148, 158, 168, 178, 188, 198, 208
e 121, 131, 141, 151, 161, 171, 181, 191, 201, 211, 221, 231

In hundreds

a 136, 236, 336, 436, 536, 636, 736, 836, 936, 1036, 1136, 1236
b 139, 239, 339, 439, 539, 639, 739, 839, 939, 1039, 1139, 1239
c 184, 284, 384, 484, 584, 684, 784, 884, 984, 1084,1184, 1284
d 198, 298, 398, 498, 598, 698, 798, 898, 998, 1098, 1198, 1298
e 221, 321, 421, 521, 621, 721, 821, 921, 1021, 1121, 1221, 1321

Step 2

a	108	**g**	34, 24
b	188	**h**	134, 124
c	288	**i**	234, 224
d	388	**j**	334, 324
e	488	**k**	434, 424
f	588	**l**	534, 524

Step 3

Answers will vary.

Step 4

Mia is incorrect. She would have 770 pennies.

1b Hundreds, tens and ones

- **Recognise the place value of each digit in a 3-digit number.**
- **Read and write numbers up to 500 in numerals and words.**

Homework 3 and 4

Practice Book pp 7–9

Place Value & Abacus

Mathematical vocabulary

Ten, twenty, thirty, forty, fifty, tens, ones, hundreds, equal to, more than, less than (fewer), most, least

Representations and resources

Base 10 apparatus, 1–6 dice, place-value grids, digit cards, plastic bags, sand, weighing scales.

Warming up

Rehearse calculation strategies, in particular addition pairs to ten (24 + 16, 57 + 23), rounding and adjusting (254 + 198 = 254 + 200 – 2), sequencing (243 + 125 = 243 + 100 + 20 + 5) and doubling (300 + 310 = 600 + 10). Write some calculations on the board that can be solved using one of these strategies, for children to answer on their whiteboards or on paper.

Background knowledge

A conceptual understanding of place value is vital for children if they are to succeed in mathematics. There are four important aspects of place value: positional, multiplicative, additive and Base 10. The positional aspect is when a digit is placed in the hundreds, tens or ones position. The multiplicative aspect is when you multiply the digit by the position it is in, e.g. in the number 755, 7 is in the hundred position so it must be multiplied by 100 to give its true value of 700. The additive aspect is when you add all the numbers together to make the whole number, e.g. 400 + 50 + 6 = 456. Base 10 involves the understanding that our number system increases and decreases in powers of ten. In this unit the first three aspects of place value are the focus. Children need to grasp the idea that we record 3-digit numbers in chunks of hundreds, tens and ones, so that they can correctly read the value of each digit.

1b Hundreds, tens and ones

You need
- Base 10 apparatus
- 1–6 dice
- place-value grids
- digit cards
- plastic bags
- sand
- weighing scales

Let's learn

Place value

3-digit numbers are made up of hundreds, tens and ones.

You can make a 3-digit number using Base 10 apparatus.

This is the number 755.

Place-value grids

A place-value grid tells you how many hundreds, tens and ones there are.

This grid shows the number 755.

Multiply each digit by its position to find its true value.

100	10	1
7	5	5

7 is in the hundreds position: 7 × 100 = 700
5 is in the tens position: 5 × 10 = 50
5 is in the ones position: 5 × 1 = 5

Now add all the numbers together:
700 + 50 + 5 = 755 or seven hundred and fifty-five

Teacher's Guide: Before working through the *Textbook*, study page 28 of the *Teacher's Guide* to see how the concepts should be introduced. Read and discuss the page with the children. Provide concrete resources to support exploration.

14

Let's learn: Modelling and teaching

Place value

- You could begin by asking what children can tell you about the number 755. Make the number using Base 10 apparatus, as in the Textbook, and ask: *How many hundreds? tens? ones?* Ask children to suggest some other 3-digit numbers and repeat using those.

Place-value grids

- You could give each child a place-value grid and a set of digit cards. Ask them to make 37 and place it in the correct position in their grid; then ask them to hold up the 3 and tell you what that number is. If they say 30, point out that it actually says 3. Ask: *What do you need to do to it to make 30?* Some children may say add a zero. It is important to help them understand that they multiply it by ten. Repeat this with different 2-digit numbers.
- Then move on to 3-digit numbers, starting with 755, as in the Textbook. You could relate this to the cartoon. Ask: *What mistake did Oli make?* Explore other 3-digit numbers. Encourage children to identify the positional, multiplicative and additive aspects of each number you look at. Encourage them to say and write each number in both numerals and words.
- Ask children to choose and write down some 3-digit numbers below 500. Encourage them to talk to a partner about what each digit represents and how it gets its real value. They could then pick one of their numbers and compare it with their partner's. Which is the highest number? Ask them to explain how they know.
- You could also discuss the idea of zero as a place holder. Ask children to make 201 with their Base 10 apparatus. Talk about how the zero holds the place of the tens, otherwise the number would read 21. Repeat this for other numbers where the zero is in the tens or ones position.

Let's practise: Digging deeper

Step 1

In this activity children use Base 10 apparatus to make each number. This will help them to visualise the hundreds, tens and ones. They then write the matching number statements, and write each number in words. Before children begin this activity, discuss the example given in the Textbook. Before they tackle parts e and f, you could review the use of zero as a place holder.

Step 2

In this activity, children generate six 3-digit numbers by rolling a dice three times for each number. They should record their numbers in a place-value grid. Encourage them to write down the value of each digit as they roll it. They work out the true value of each digit and then add them to make the whole number. Ask questions throughout to establish their confidence in talking about the positional, additive and multiplicative aspects of place value. Some children may still need to use Base 10 apparatus to help them visualise the number.

Step 3

Provide pairs of children with sand, three plastic bags (sealable sandwich type will be perfect) and weighing scales. They weigh the sand and pour or scoop it into the plastic bags. They should end up with bags weighing 200 g, 300 g and 400 g. They then take two bags, predict the sum of their masses and then weigh them to check. When they have found the sum, they write this in numerals and then words. Ask them to demonstrate how they found the sum using the hundred flats from the Base 10 apparatus and to write the sum in a place- value grid. They repeat this so that they have all possible combinations.

Step 4

Before children begin the task, write on the board some pairs of 3-digit numbers and ask children to tell you which is the larger number in each pair. Include some numbers where the hundreds digit is the same, e.g. 364 and 386. Prompt them with questions such as: *How many hundreds are there in this number? and this one? How many tens?* During the task, children throw a dice three times, make a note of the numbers thrown and then create two different 3-digit numbers using the same three digits. They identify the larger number and explain how they know. If appropriate, challenge children to find the largest possible number they can make with their three digits. What about the smallest?

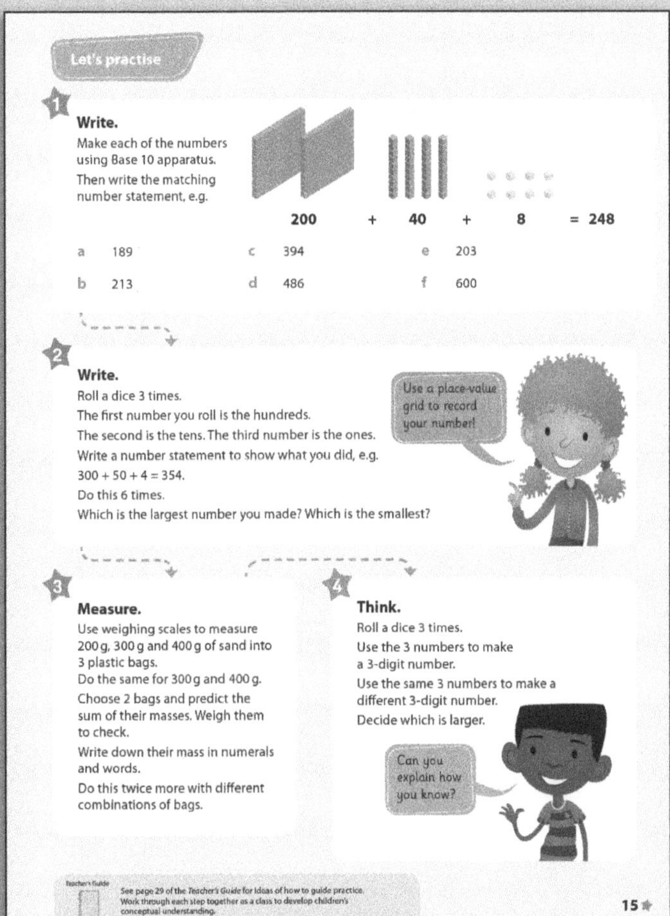
Let's practise

1 **Write.**
Make each of the numbers using Base 10 apparatus.
Then write the matching number statement, e.g.

200 + 40 + 8 = 248

a 189 c 394 e 203
b 213 d 486 f 600

2 **Write.**
Roll a dice 3 times.
The first number you roll is the hundreds.
The second is the tens. The third number is the ones.
Write a number statement to show what you did, e.g.
300 + 50 + 4 = 354.
Do this 6 times.
Which is the largest number you made? Which is the smallest?

3 **Measure.**
Use weighing scales to measure 200 g, 300 g and 400 g of sand into 3 plastic bags.
Do the same for 300 g and 400 g.
Choose 2 bags and predict the sum of their masses. Weigh them to check.
Write down their mass in numerals and words.
Do this twice more with different combinations of bags.

4 **Think.**
Roll a dice 3 times.
Use the 3 numbers to make a 3-digit number.
Use the same 3 numbers to make a different 3-digit number.
Decide which is larger.

Teacher's Guide
See page 29 of the *Teacher's Guide* for ideas of how to guide practice. Work through each step together as a class to develop children's conceptual understanding.

15

Ensuring progress

Supporting understanding

Some children may need help to create the numbers using Base 10 apparatus. You could work with them in a guided group. Begin by making 2-digit numbers and then progress to 3-digit numbers.

Broadening understanding

Encourage children to explain to a partner what each digit in a 3-digit number is and how to make the whole number. You could also ask them to make up some contextual problems involving adding, e.g. 300, 50 and 4, for the class to answer.

✓ Concept mastered

Children can recognise the place value of each digit in a 3-digit number and read and write numbers up to 500 in numerals and words.

Follow-up ideas

- You could give children the opportunity to estimate and weigh different items around the classroom and record their results in simple tables. Encourage them to weigh items in grams and write the mass in numerals and words. They could then record what the mass would be if it was 10 g/100 g more or less.
- Children could make a 3-digit number using digit cards on a place-value grid. They could then explore using other digit cards to make the number 100/ten/one larger or smaller, and explain what is happening.
- In pairs, one child writes a 3-digit number on paper. The other child then writes down the number that is ten more, ten less, 100 more and 100 less.

Answers

Step 1

a 100 + 80 + 9 = 189, one hundred and eighty-nine

b 200 + 10 + 3 = 213, two hundred and thirteen

c 300 + 90 + 4 = 394, three hundred and ninety-four

d 400 + 80 + 6 = 486, four hundred and eighty-six

e 200 + 3 = 203, two hundred and three

f 600 = 600, six hundred

Step 2

Answers will vary.

Step 3

500 g, five hundred grams

600 g, six hundred grams

700 g, seven hundred grams

Step 4

Answers will vary.

1c Comparing and ordering numbers

- **Recognise the place value of each digit in a 3-digit number.**
- **Compare and order numbers up to 500.**

Homework 5 and 6 | Practice Book pp 10–12 | Place Value & Abacus

Mathematical vocabulary

Capacity, volume, litres, millilitres, more than, less than, equivalent, equal to

Representations and resources

Pendulum, place-value cards, bottles, drinking glasses, water, Base 10 apparatus, three different containers per child, measuring cylinders.

Warming up

Focus on ways of making five. Use a pendulum, swinging it from side to side. As the pendulum swings one way, call out a number to five. As it swings the other way, children call out the number that goes with it to make five. You could repeat this for other numbers to ten, then multiples of ten to 100.

1c Comparing and ordering numbers

You need
- place-value cards
- glasses
- water
- Base 10 apparatus
- 3 different containers
- measuring cylinder

Let's learn

Comparisons

Capacity is the amount of liquid a container can hold.

Volume is the amount of liquid that is inside a container.

You can measure both capacity and volume in litres and millilitres.

Look at the glasses.

They each have a capacity of 500 ml.

You can see that the volumes are different.

Comparing and ordering numbers

Look at the numbers 225, 475 and 350.

The largest number in the hundreds column is 4. So 475 is the largest number.

The smallest number in hundreds column is 2. So 225 is the smallest number.

You can compare the numbers using symbols.

225 < 350 < 475 or 475 > 350 > 225

If the hundreds digits of 2 numbers are the same, look at the tens.

If the tens digits are also the same then look at the ones.

100	10	1
2	2	5
4	7	5
3	5	0

< means 'is less than'

> means 'is greater than'

16

Teacher's Guide: Before working through the *Textbook*, study page 30 of the *Teacher's Guide* to see how the concepts should be introduced. Read and discuss the page with the children. Provide concrete resources to support exploration.

Background knowledge

In order to compare numbers, it is important to have a sound grasp of place value. As in Unit 1b – Hundreds, tens and ones, focus on the positional, multiplicative and additive aspects of place value. When comparing two numbers we use the symbols < ('is less than') and > ('is greater than'). It is also worth considering the equals sign, =, alongside these symbols for values that are equivalent.

Children often confuse capacity and volume so it is important to make it clear to them that capacity is the amount a container can hold and that the volume is how much is in it at a given time.

Let's learn: Modelling and teaching

Comparisons

- You could begin by discussing the difference between capacity and volume. Show children two bottles, one full, one half full, and explain that capacity is how much can fit into the bottles. Measure the water in the full bottle to show its capacity. Explain that the volume is the amount inside the bottle. Measure the water in the bottle that is half full to show the volume.
- Children should easily be able to order the drinks shown in the Textbook. You could give children, in groups, the opportunity to measure out the three amounts, then order them from smallest to greatest volume. Record the volumes using the correct units, millilitres.

Comparing and ordering numbers

- Review the positional, multiplicative and additive aspects of place value by asking children to make 3-digit numbers up to 500 using place-value cards, e.g. 468. They look at each card and describe what it is and how to make it: $400 = 4 \times 100$, $60 = 6 \times 10$ and $8 = 8 \times 1$; $400 + 60 + 8 = 468$.
- Then look at the place-value grid in the Textbook. This shows the three capacities of the glasses. Discuss how you know that 475 is the largest number and 225 the smallest.
- Write the 'is less than' and 'is greater than' symbols on the board. Ask children what they mean. Write a number on one side and invite a child to write a number on the other side so that they make a correct number statement. Then use the symbols to order the volumes in the three glasses, as in the Textbook. Introduce other volumes with the same hundreds digit, or hundreds and tens digits, as one of the three numbers, e.g. for 450 ml, ask: *Is this more or less than 475 ml? How do you know?* You could also ask children to make up their own greater than and less than number statements, using numbers up to 500 of their choice.

Let's practise: Digging deeper

Step 1

In this activity, children need to decide which number in each pair is the larger or smaller and use the < and > symbols correctly. For a hands-on approach, allow children to make the numbers using Base 10 apparatus; they could use pencils to make the > or < symbol and place them between the numbers. Expect children to explain how they decided which number is the larger or smaller.

Step 2

Observe how children approach part a. Some might order the first two, then decide where the third goes, and so on; others might look for any mass with a hundreds digit of one, then those with a hundreds digit of two, and so on. In either case, encourage them to explain how their understanding of place value helps them (e.g. 267 g is greater than 150 g because there are two hundreds which is more than one hundred). They then make comparison number statements using pairs of numbers. As they have ordered the masses from greatest to smallest, they could start with statements using >, but ensure they write some using <.

Step 3

Each child or pair needs three different-sized containers, a bottle of water and a measuring cylinder. The task asks children to pour different amounts of water from the bottle into each of the three containers, then order them from smallest to greatest volume. This can be tricky if the containers are different shapes so will take some reasoning. Prompt them with questions such as: *How is this container different from that one?* You could ask children to estimate how many millimetres there are in each container. When they measure the volumes using the measuring cylinder, ask them to round to the nearest 100 ml. They should explain how they know their comparison statements are correct with reference to the value of the hundreds digits in each case. For the final part, children work out what to do to their volumes to make them equal. Encourage them to consider what needs adding to the smallest volume and what needs subtracting from the greatest.

Step 4

Children use the numbers on the digit cards to create as many different 3-digit numbers as they can. Encourage them to work systematically, e.g. making the numbers with 3 in the hundreds first, and so on. Six numbers are possible; ensure they understand they can use the numbers more than once when making their pairs. When working on the final part of the task, they should notice that what you add to one number to make it equal to the higher one you subtract from the other number to make the lower one.

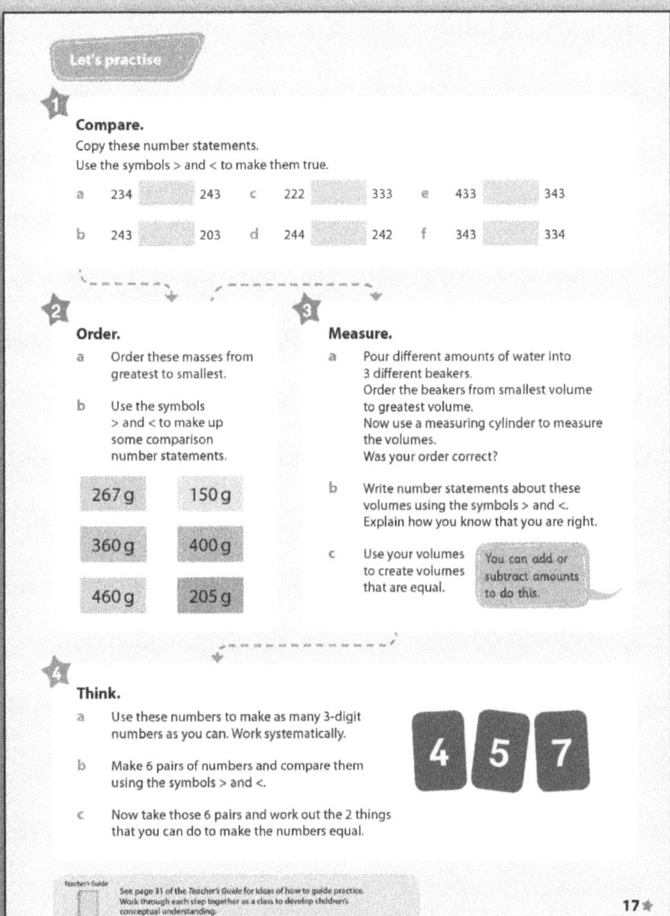
Let's practise

1 Compare.
Copy these number statements.
Use the symbols > and < to make them true.

a 234 ☐ 243   c 222 ☐ 333   e 433 ☐ 343
b 243 ☐ 203   d 244 ☐ 242   f 343 ☐ 334

2 Order.
a Order these masses from greatest to smallest.
b Use the symbols > and < to make up some comparison number statements.

267 g, 150 g, 360 g, 400 g, 460 g, 205 g

3 Measure.
a Pour different amounts of water into 3 different beakers. Order the beakers from smallest volume to greatest volume. Now use a measuring cylinder to measure the volumes. Was your order correct?
b Write number statements about these volumes using the symbols > and <. Explain how you know that you are right.
c Use your volumes to create volumes that are equal.
You can add or subtract amounts to do this.

4 Think.
a Use these numbers to make as many 3-digit numbers as you can. Work systematically.
b Make 6 pairs of numbers and compare them using the symbols > and <.
c Now take those 6 pairs and work out the 2 things that you can do to make the numbers equal.

4 5 7

Teacher's Guide
See page 31 of the *Teacher's Guide* for ideas of how to guide practice. Work through each step together as a class to develop children's conceptual understanding.

17

Follow-up ideas

- You could adapt Step 3 to give children practice estimating, measuring and ordering different masses in grams. Encourage them to measure to the nearest 100 g.
- Give children digit cards and ask them to generate four 3-digit numbers and order them from lowest to highest. They could then compare pairs of numbers, writing number statements using the symbols < and >.
- Ask children to write 20 3-digit numbers on pieces of card. They place these in a pile face down on the table. They take it in turns to pick a card each. They look at the two cards. The child with the highest number takes the two cards. Play continues until all the cards are used. For variation, they could play using the rule that the lowest number wins.

Ensuring progress

Supporting understanding

Place value is an important concept and must be mastered. It might be that some children will need more practice using Base 10 apparatus, partitioning cards and place-value grids to explore this further.

Broadening understanding

You could ask children to make up problems that involve ordering capacities or volumes to assess their depth of understanding in this concept.

Concept mastered

Children can recognise the place value of each digit in a 3-digit number and compare and order numbers up to 500.

Answers

Step 1

a 234 < 243 **d** 244 > 242

b 243 > 203 **e** 433 > 343

c 222 < 333 **f** 343 > 334

Step 2

a 460 ml, 400 ml, 360 ml, 267 ml, 205 ml, 150 ml,

b Answers will vary.

Step 3

Answers will vary.

Step 4

457, 475, 547, 574, 745, 754

Other answers will vary.

1d Representing numbers

- **Identify, represent and estimate numbers to 500 using different representations.**

Homework 7 and 8

Practice Book pp 13–17

Mathematical vocabulary

Represent, representations, equivalent, the same as

Warming up

Rehearse calculation strategies for subtraction, in particular counting on, rounding and adjusting, and sequencing. Write some calculations on the board that can be solved using one of these strategies for children to answer on their whiteboards or on paper, e.g. 23 – 19 (counting on: 19 + 1 + 3, answer = 4, rounding and adjusting: 23 – 20 = 3, 3 + 1 = 4), 26 – 9 (26 – 10 + 1), 36 –25 (36 – 20 – 5).

Background knowledge

In order to be flexible thinkers in mathematics, children need to see numbers represented in different ways, e.g. if they only see 25 as individual items this narrows their capacity to reason about numbers. Give children plenty of experience of using other representations such as cubes or counters (where one colour represents, e.g. tens and another colour represents ones) place-value counters, Base 10 apparatus and money. It is important to reinforce what each part of the representation represents. Also encourage them to draw representations of numbers. They could use lines and crosses to show tens and ones.

Representations and resources

Rulers, measuring cylinders, coloured counters, Base 10 apparatus, number rods, coins, other equipment for representing numbers (e.g. weighing scales, clocks with movable hands, interlocking cubes).

1d Representing numbers

You need
- ruler
- measuring cylinder
- coloured counters
- Base 10 apparatus
- number rods
- coins

Let's learn

10 is ten of something you can count, like 10 counters or 10 cubes.

Not always. We can show 10 in lots of different ways.

Representing numbers
There are lots of ways to represent numbers.
These pictures both show 125.

Numbers as measures
We also use numbers with measures.
These pictures show £1.25p and 1.25 kg.

18

Teacher's Guide

Before working through the *Textbook*, study page 32 of the *Teacher's Guide* to see how the concepts should be introduced. Read and discuss the page with the children. Provide concrete resources to support exploration.

Let's learn: Modelling and teaching

Representing numbers

- You could begin by asking children to show you ten using their fingers. Encourage them to be creative, e.g. five fingers, each representing two, four fingers on one hand representing two each and two fingers on the other each representing one. You could then repeat this using coloured counters. Give children a handful each. How can they show ten? e.g. they could have a red one to represent five, a yellow one to represent four and a green one to represent one or they could use one counter to represent ten. The only rule is that the same colour represents the same number.
- Next, look at the representations of 125 in the Textbook. Discuss each one, focusing on how the one hundred, two tens and five ones are represented. Can children think of any more ways of showing 125? How could they represent other numbers up to 500, e.g. for 450, four red counters each representing 100 and one blue representing 50, two yellow counters each representing 225. They could also use money in pounds and pence and length in metres and centimetres.
- You could show different items and ask children to estimate their masses. After they have done so invite children to weigh them and read the masses that they are. They compare their estimates and the actual masses. They then write these in two different ways, in grams and kilograms and grams.

Numbers as measures

- Remind children that we do not just use numbers to represent a number of things – often a number, with a unit, represents a measurement. Again, discuss the representations shown in the Textbook. What other measurements involving 125 can children think of? (e.g. 125 g, £125, £1.25). Give them the opportunity to show these measures, and others up to 500, e.g. 450, 275, using weighing scales, clocks, coins, etc.

Let's practise: Digging deeper

Step 1

Encourage children to adapt the representations shown in the Textbook (e.g. counters, cubes, money) and those you have discussed as a class, as well as any others they can think of. Encourage them to be creative, and perhaps think of more than one way of representing 150 using the same equipment, e.g. they could show 150p using a £1 coin and a 50p coin, or a £1 and five 10p coins. For equipment such as coloured counters, make sure they can explain what each colour represents.

Step 2

The second task asks children to take a random number of hundreds, tens and ones Base 10 apparatus and place them on the table. They estimate the value of their equipment and then find out the actual value. They then find the difference between their estimate and the actual number represented and repeat this five times. Model the activity before they begin to ensure that they all know what to do.

Step 3

Give children a ruler, measuring cylinder and a selection of coins. For the first part of this task children need to represent 250 on a classroom ruler. If necessary, remind children that there are 10 mm in 1 cm. Encourage them to look at their ruler. They should be able to 'see' that 25 cm represents 250 mm. For part b, ask children to look at the measuring cylinder so that they can 'see' what 500 ml would look like. Depending on the size of the container, they could describe 500 ml as a fraction of the whole cylinder. For part c, ask children to use a selection of coins to make 300 using them in different ways, e.g. three pound coins, two pound coins and two 50p coins. Each time, they need to describe to a partner what they have done.

Step 4

This task asks children to think about and write down where they have seen numbers in real life outside the classroom. This could include just numbers, e.g. bus numbers, car number plates, house numbers, as well as the different kinds of measures listed in the Textbook, e.g. in shops, on food packaging, on road signs, on clocks and timetables. You could ask children to write down numbers and measures as they think of them and then sort them into groups. In pairs, they discuss similarities and differences between their examples.

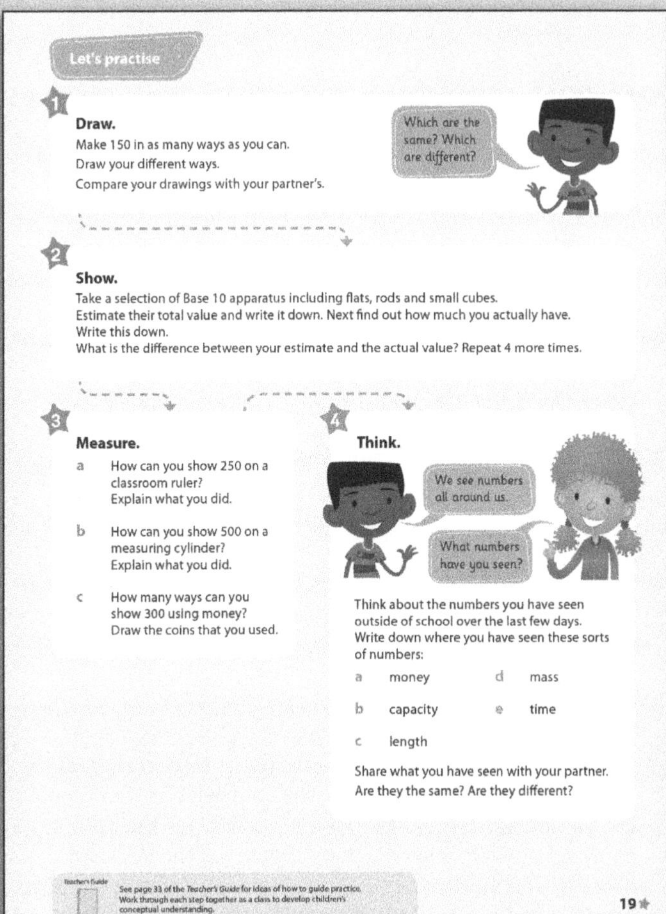

Let's practise

1 **Draw.**
Make 150 in as many ways as you can.
Draw your different ways.
Compare your drawings with your partner's.

2 **Show.**
Take a selection of Base 10 apparatus including flats, rods and small cubes.
Estimate their total value and write it down. Next find out how much you actually have.
Write this down.
What is the difference between your estimate and the actual value? Repeat 4 more times.

3 **Measure.**
a How can you show 250 on a classroom ruler? Explain what you did.
b How can you show 500 on a measuring cylinder? Explain what you did.
c How many ways can you show 300 using money? Draw the coins that you used.

4 **Think.**

Think about the numbers you have seen outside of school over the last few days.
Write down where you have seen these sorts of numbers:
a money
b capacity
c length
d mass
e time

Share what you have seen with your partner.
Are they the same? Are they different?

Teacher's Guide: See page 33 of the Teacher's Guide for ideas of how to guide practice. Work through each step together as a class to develop children's conceptual understanding.

19

Ensuring progress

Supporting understanding

Some children may find it difficult to show numbers in different ways. Using double-sided counters would be helpful. Work with them in a guided group and ask them to make different numbers using these. They should describe to the other members of the group what their counters represent.

Broadening understanding

Give children number rods to use. Ask them to set one of each piece out in order of size. Give them a starting number for the smallest piece. From this, they work out what all the other pieces represent.

Concept mastered

Children can recognise identify, represent and estimate numbers to 500 using different representations.

Follow-up ideas

- Children could use different things (e.g. Base 10 apparatus, counters, cubes and money) to represent a 3-digit number in different ways, then challenge a partner to work out what number is being represented and explain what each part of the representations shows.
- Pairs or small groups of children could use their ideas from Step 4 to make a poster showing where numbers are seen in everyday life. Encourage them to be creative, e.g. they could arrange their examples in categories, or draw a scene or series of scenes showing as many examples as possible.
- Ask children to make a poster for a classroom display, showing how they could represent 100 in as many ways as possible.

Answers

Step 1
Answers will vary.

Step 2
Answers will vary.

Step 3
Answers will vary.

Step 4
Answers will vary.

Unit 1 Pick!

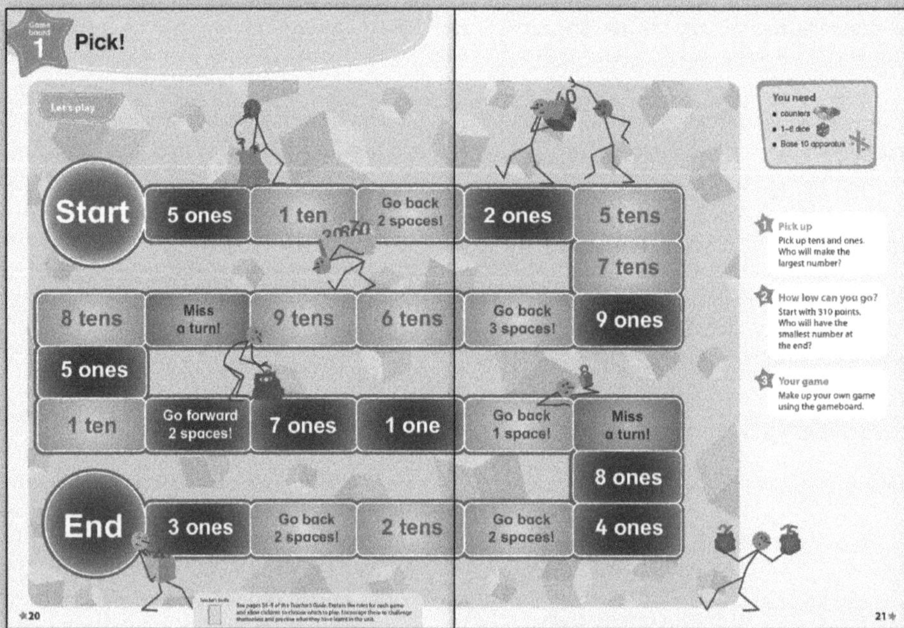

Game 1: Pick up

This game enables children to rehearse and reinforce the concept of place value. It focuses on tens and ones.

Maths focus

- Recognise the place value of each digit in a 3-digit number

Resources

1 counter per player (1 colour per player), 1–6 dice (1), Base 10 apparatus or similar.

How to play

This is a game for two or more players. Children place their counters on Start and take it in turns to roll the dice and move their counter that number of spaces. If they land on a 'pick' space, they collect this number of ones or tens in Base 10 apparatus (or similar). For all other spaces (e.g. miss a turn) they simply follow the instructions. To land on End they have to throw the exact number. If they do not, they move to End and then back the appropriate number of spaces. Once all players have landed on End, each player counts up the number of tens and ones they have collected to find their total score. They exchange ones for tens and tens for hundreds as appropriate. The winner is the player with the highest score.

Making it easier

You may need to play the game with some children first, then ask them to play independently.

Making it harder

You could ask children to keep a running total of their score after each turn.

Game 3: Your game

Children should invent their own game designing rules that use the concepts covered in the unit. Challenge children to make their game easier or harder.

Game 2: How low can you go?

This game enables children to rehearse and reinforce place value of 3-digit numbers. They start with a 3-digit number, taking away tens and ones as they play.

Maths focus

- Recognise the place value of each digit in a 3-digit number
- Read and write numbers up to 500 in numerals and words

Resources

1 counter per player (1 colour per player), 1–6 dice (1), Base 10 apparatus or similar.

How to play

This is a game for two or more players. Give each player 2 hundreds, 10 tens and 10 ones in Base 10 apparatus (or similar), and tell them that that they are each beginning the game with 310 points. Children then place their counters on Start and take it in turns to roll the dice and move their counter that number of spaces. If they land on a 'pick' space, they discard this number of ones or tens from their collection, exchanging tens for ones when necessary. For all other spaces (e.g. miss a turn) they simply follow the instructions. To land on End they have to throw the exact number. If they do not, they move to End and then back the appropriate number of spaces. Once all players have landed on End, each player counts up the number of tens and ones they have left to find their final score. They write this as an additive statement (e.g. 100 + 30 + 2 = 132) and in words (one hundred and thirty-two). The winner is the player with the lowest score.

Making it easier

Give children their 310 starting points as 30 tens and 10 ones.

Making it harder

Children could record the numbers they make, noting what they have done each time.

Choose a game to play.

Game 1: Pick up

You need:

- 1 counter per player (1 colour per player)
- 1–6 dice
- Base 10 apparatus

How to play

- Each place your counter on Start.
- Take turns to roll the dice. Move your counter that number of spaces.
- If you land on a Pick space, pick up the number of ones or tens.
- If you land on another space, do what it says.
- When you land on End, count up the number of tens and ones you have to find your total score.
- The winner is the player with the highest score.

HINT: You may need to exchange ones for tens or tens for hundreds.

Game 2: How low can you go?

You need:

- 1 counter per player (1 colour per player)
- 1–6 dice
- Base 10 apparatus

How to play

- Each player starts the game with 310 points: 2 hundreds, 10 tens and 10 ones.
- Each place your counter on Start.
- Take turns to roll the dice. Move your counter that number of spaces.
- If you land on a Pick space, take that number of ones or tens away from your collection.
- If you land on another space, do what it says.
- When you land on End, count up the number of tens and ones you have left to find your final score. Write the number as an additive statement and in words.
- The winner is the player with the lowest score.

HINT: If you need to take away a number of ones and do not have enough, exchange a ten for ones and continue.

Game 3: Your game

- Make up your own game using the gameboard.
- What are the rules for your game? Explain them to someone.

Please help your child by reading the instructions and playing the game together.

Unit 1 And finally ...

Assessment task 1

Resources

Place-value cards or Base 10 apparatus.

Running the task

You could prepare for this task by writing several 3-digit numbers on the board and asking questions such as: *How do you say this number? How many hundreds/tens/ones are there in this number?* Read out some more 3-digit numbers and ask children to write them on their whiteboards. If any children make the same mistake as Oli in the task, help them to see where they have gone wrong, by drawing a place-value grid on the board and asking, e.g. *If we put a three in this column, what does that mean?* If necessary, you could write numbers similar to the one that Oli has written and ask children what is wrong, e.g. write 200603 on the board and say *This is two hundred and sixty-three.* Can they tell you how it should be written?

During the task, listen to children you particularly wish to assess as they explain what Oli has done wrong. They should notice that Oli has written the number as he would speak it. They should be able to tell you that the four hundred is positioned in the hundreds position, the two tens in the tens position and the three ones in the ones position. Some children may benefit from being given Base 10 apparatus or place-value cards to use during their explanation.

Evidencing mastery

If children can explain and demonstrate the positional, multiplicative and additive properties of place value they are evidencing mastery.

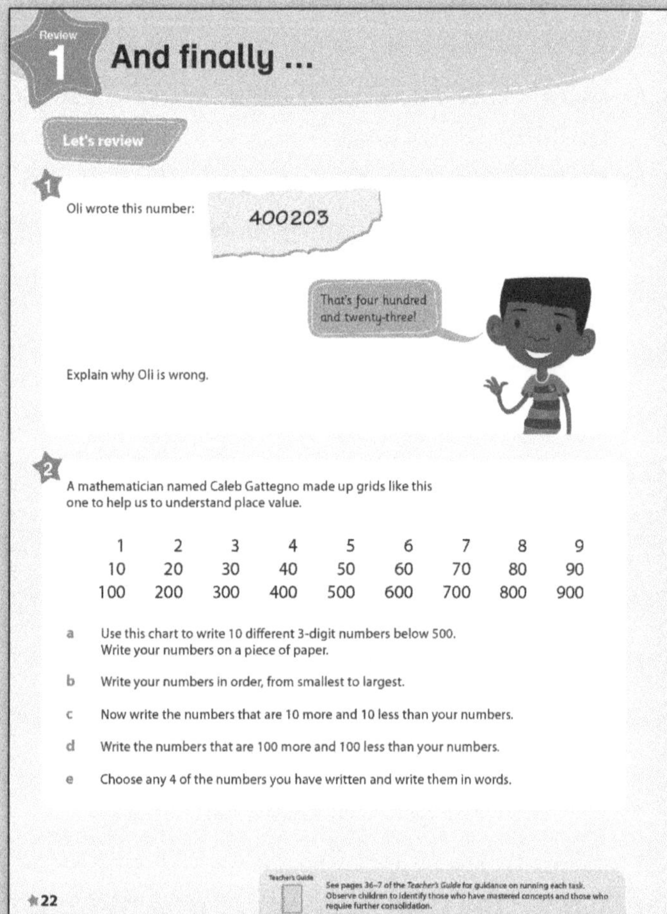

Review 1 And finally ...

Let's review

1 Oli wrote this number: 400203

Explain why Oli is wrong.

2 A mathematician named Caleb Gattegno made up grids like this one to help us to understand place value.

1	2	3	4	5	6	7	8	9
10	20	30	40	50	60	70	80	90
100	200	300	400	500	600	700	800	900

a Use this chart to write 10 different 3-digit numbers below 500. Write your numbers on a piece of paper.

b Write your numbers in order, from smallest to largest.

c Now write the numbers that are 10 more and 10 less than your numbers.

d Write the numbers that are 100 more and 100 less than your numbers.

e Choose any 4 of the numbers you have written and write them in words.

22

Teacher's Guide

See pages 36–7 of the *Teacher's Guide* for guidance on running each task. Observe children to identify those who have mastered concepts and those who require further consolidation.

Assessment task 2

Resources

Base 10 apparatus.

Running the task

Before children begin the task, discuss the Gattegno chart to ensure that they understand what it is. *What is happening along the top row?* Expect children to be able to tell you that the numbers increase by one. Repeat this for the other two rows. Ask them what they need to do to get from one to ten and then 100. Expect them to say that one is multiplied by ten to make ten and 100 to make 100. If children are unsure how to use the chart to make 3-digit numbers, make a number such as 247 using Base 10 apparatus and remind them of the additive aspect of place value: 200 + 40 + 7. They should then see that they can make 3-digit numbers from the chart by picking a number from each row of the table and combining them. Observe children to see if they are combining the numbers from the chart correctly. You could challenge them to make some 3-digit numbers using zero as a placeholder. How many numbers do they need to choose from the chart to do this? (Two – one from the hundreds row and one from either the tens or the ones row; or one – from the hundreds row.) Encourage children to read some of their numbers aloud.

When children order their numbers, assess their understanding by asking *How do you know?* Expect them to talk about place value, e.g. 'This number has five hundreds so it is bigger than that one, which only has two'. 'The hundreds digits are the same but this number has four tens and that one only has one ten'. They then write down the numbers that are ten more and ten less, and 100 more and 100 less, than their original numbers. Again, ask them to explain what they are doing. Finally, they choose four of their numbers and write them in words; the ability to do this indicates an understanding of place value; it is also important that children learn to spell number words correctly.

Evidencing mastery

Children who can write 3-digit numbers in numerals and words, order numbers correctly and find ten/100 more or less than 3-digit numbers are demonstrating mastery of place value.

3

a Count in hundreds from 125 to 925. Write down all the numbers that you count.

b Think of 5 different ways to represent 125. Draw them on a piece of plain paper.

Did you know?

1	2	3	4	5	6	7	8	9
−	=	≡	+	h	φ	?	ᔕ	ʔ

23

Assessment task 3

Resources

Base 10 apparatus, coins, cubes, counters, plain paper.

Running the task

Before children begin the task, practise counting in hundreds from a given starting number, e.g. 109, 110 and 111, for ten counts, and then back to the starting number. The task asks children to write down the numbers they count when counting in hundreds from 125 to 925. It then asks them to represent 125 in different ways. Provide them with equipment such as Base 10 apparatus, money, counters and cubes. As well as manipulatives, encourage them to draw visual representations such as a number line.

Evidencing mastery

If children can fluently count in hundreds from any given 2- or 3-digit number and explain the effect they are evidencing mastery. They should be able to represent numbers in different ways and explain how their representations work, with reference to hundreds, tens and ones.

Concepts mastered

- ☑ Children can count from zero in multiples of 100 and find ten or 100 more or less than a given number.
- ☑ Children can recognise the place value of each digit in a 3-digit number and read and write numbers up to 500 in numerals and words.
- ☑ Children can recognise the place value of each digit in a 3-digit number and compare and order numbers up to 500.
- ☑ Children can recognise identify, represent and estimate numbers to 500 using different representations.

Did you know?

The digits 1, 2, 3, … that we use today are based on the Hindu-Arabic numeral system which was developed over 1000 years ago. However, they were not used in Europe until the 1200s when the famous Italian mathematician, Fibonacci (1170–1245), brought them over. As a young boy, Fibonacci travelled with his father, a merchant, and first came across Hindu–Arabic numerals in Bugia (now Béjaïa, Algeria). He increased his understanding of this number system and its advantages during his later travels around the Mediterranean, and wrote about them in Liber Abaci (Book of Calculation), which he completed in 1202.

Up until then, Europeans used Brahmi numerals, as shown in the Textbook. These were first used in India in the 3rd century BCE. This was not a positional number system with a zero – instead there were separate symbols for each of the tens, and for 100 and 1000. In later years they introduced zero as a place holder.

You could remind children that when the Romans invaded England we used Roman numerals. Write on the board one to ten using Roman numerals and discuss any similarities and differences children can see between the three systems, e.g. in both Brahmi and Roman numerals the symbols for one, two and three are tally marks, although in Brahmi numerals the marks are horizontal and in Roman numerals they are vertical. Children may also see the similarity between the Brahmi and Hindu–Arabic numbers seven, eight and nine.

Unit 2 Mental and written calculation

Mathematical focus

- ★ Number: addition and subtraction
- ★ Statistics: interpret and present data
- ★ Measurement: length, money

Prior learning

Children should already be able to:

- recall and use addition and subtraction facts to 20 fluently and derive and use related facts up to 100
- add and subtract numbers using concrete objects, pictorial representations, and mentally
- show that addition of two numbers can be done in any order (commutative) and subtraction of one number from another cannot
- recognise the inverse relationship between addition and subtraction, and use this to check calculations and solve missing number problems
- use place value and number facts to solve problems.

Key new learning

- Add and subtract numbers mentally, including a 3-digit number and ones.
- Add and subtract numbers with up to three digits.
- Solve problems, including missing number problems, using number facts, place value and more complex addition and subtraction.
- Add and subtract numbers with up to three digits, using formal written methods of columnar addition and subtraction.
- Estimate the answer to a calculation and use inverse operations to check answers.

Making connections

- Mental addition and subtraction strategies rely on children's prior knowledge of place value and number sense, including number bonds, and the ability to count on and back.
- Children will develop the ability to decide which strategy is most efficient when answering addition and subtraction calculations and will apply this to problems involving measures.
- When children are asked to solve problems that involve collecting, representing and analysing data, they will invariably need to add and subtract, particularly for questions that begin with 'How many…' and 'How many more…'.

Talk about

Remind children that mental calculation strategies for addition and subtraction are very important because these can be quicker and more efficient than written methods. Discuss key strategies, such as using number facts, sequencing, bridging ten and adding near multiples of ten and adjusting. Inform children of the words for the numbers that are added and subtracted. Say *augend add addend equals sum* and *minuend subtract subtrahend equals difference*. Write number statements on the board to model this and expect children to repeat the mathematical vocabulary after you.

Engaging and exploring

Look at the pictogram and ask children if they know what this way of representing data is called. Establish that it is a pictogram and that each symbol represents two. *What does half a symbol represent?* Discuss what information the pictogram might show. Agree that it is likely to be the number of different coloured sweets in a packet. Ask children to work out and write down how many of each colour there are. Then ask questions that involve finding totals and differences. Observe children as they answer. Are they using their fingers or are they using number facts and other mental calculation strategies? e.g. the sum of blue and brown can be found by doubling seven and adding one, the sum of red and purple can be found by bridging ten (8 + 2 = 10, 10 + 4 = 14), the difference between brown and orange can be found by counting on. Use this as an opportunity to rehearse well-known mental calculation strategies for addition and subtraction. You could also give children a packet of sweets each and ask them to sort them into colours, then make their own pictogram.

Ask children to tell you how many cats there are in the picture. Observe children as they count. Do any children count the cats one at a time? Discuss how they could count more efficiently, e.g. they could count in twos, threes or fives or multiply groups of twos, threes or fives. Work through each of these methods together.

Look at the picture of the curry deal. Ask children what the opening deal is. Agree that it is an offer for £4 off. Ascertain that the curry and rice now costs £6.95. Ask children how they could work out the original cost. Establish that they could count on £4 from the £6 or simply use their number facts for ten. Give other prices for the curry and rice and ask children to find the original prices. Collect number statements to show the calculations that children have carried out, and use this opportunity to reinforce the vocabulary used in the Talk about section. Next give children original prices and ask them to work out the price under the offer. Give other amounts off, e.g. £2.50, £3.75, and repeat similar questions.

Ask children to describe what the page from the toy brochure shows. Establish that it is a list of the original prices of several toys and what they now cost in a sale. Ask questions such as: *By how much has the table football been reduced?* Expect children to be able to use a counting on or sequencing strategy to answer this. If they struggle to do so, demonstrate how they could count on using a number line or sequence by taking away £10 first and then £4. Rehearse these strategies for other amounts of money, initially in whole pounds. Repeat for the other toys.

Look at the picture of the pencils. Ask children to show how long 5 cm is on their ruler by moving their finger from zero to 5 cm. Ask them to draw a line of this length. Invite them to look carefully at the second pencil and to estimate the extra length from the tip of the shortest one. Ask them to draw a line to show their estimate for the length of the second pencil underneath their 5 cm line. Repeat for the longest pencil. Make up different lengths for the three pencils and ask children to work out totals and differences.

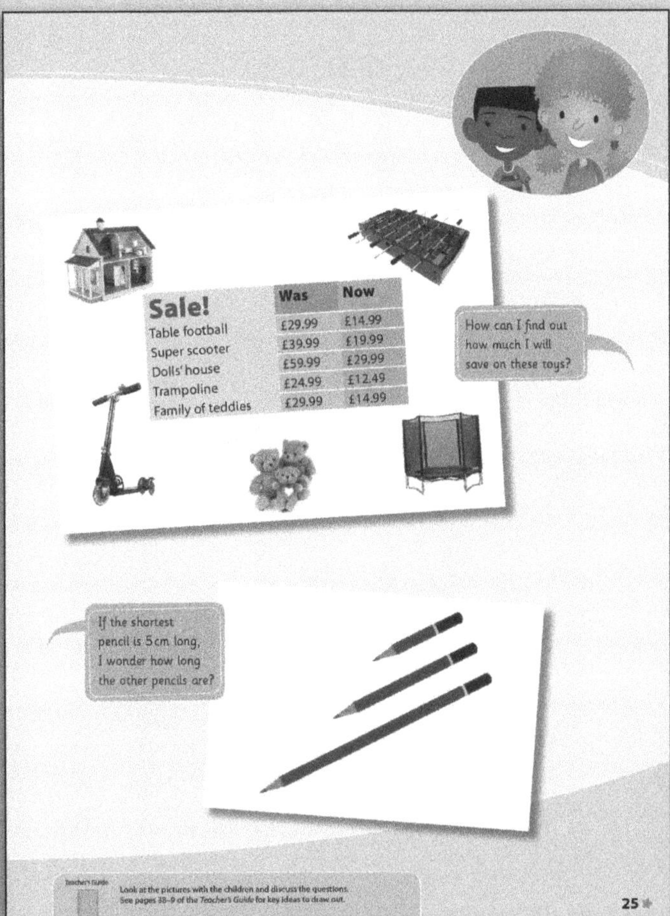

Checking understanding

You will know children have mastered these concepts when they can add and subtract numbers with up to three digits mentally. They will be able to add numbers with up to three digits using formal written methods. They will be able to solve problems using these skills, make estimates and use inverse operations to check their answers.

Things to think about

- How will you incorporate other key mental calculation strategies, e.g. sequencing?
- How will you use small step variation to progress from the vertical partitioning method for addition that children encountered in Year 2 to doing the same for 3-digit numbers before progressing to the formal written method?
- How will you use manipulatives and visual representations to help conceptual understanding of addition and subtraction with all children?
- How will you make links between addition and subtraction using the bar model?
- How will you ensure children experience practical opportunities to add and subtract numbers within the context of length, money and time?
- How will you develop children's understanding of pictograms and bar charts in order for them to be able to solve addition and subtraction problems?

2a Mental calculation strategies

- **Add and subtract numbers mentally.**
- **Add and subtract numbers with up to three digits.**
- **Solve problems, including missing number problems, using number facts, place value and more complex addition and subtraction.**

Mathematical vocabulary

Addition, subtraction, augend, addend, sum, minuend, subtrahend, difference

Warming up

Rehearse number bonds for all numbers to ten and 20. Write a number on the board, e.g. eight. Swing the pendulum from side to side. As it swings one way, call out a number below eight. As it swings the other way, children call out the number that goes with it to make eight. Repeat this for other numbers to ten and 20.

Background knowledge

Children need to develop a range of mental calculation strategies. Once children are taught written methods these often become their default method for answering all addition and subtraction calculations, even when a mental calculation strategy is more efficient.

This spread focuses on two important strategies: rounding and adjusting, and bridging ten. When rounding and adjusting, children decide which multiple of ten to add on to the augend and how much needs taking off (67 + 38 = 67 + 40 − 2). When bridging ten, children break a second number in order to make the augend a multiple of ten and hence the two numbers simpler to add (54 + 38 = 60 + 32 = 92).

Let's learn: Modelling and teaching

Rounding to the nearest 10 and adjusting

- Give each child a 100 square. *What is one less than ten?* Establish that to add nine to a number, they can add ten and subtract one. Similarly, to take away nine, they can subtract ten and add one. Practise this by asking children to take their finger for a walk on their 100 square, e.g. *Begin on square three, add ten, add nine, add 20, subtract nine.* Do all children end on square 33?
- Look at the first model in the Textbook and discuss what it shows. Agree that 30 is two more than 28, so you need to adjust the answer by subtracting two.
- Allow children to practise adding numbers ending in eight and nine using Base 10 apparatus. Next ask them to add 18 and 28 to different numbers using their 100 square and then, if appropriate, without visual support. Repeat for subtraction, using the second example in the Textbook.

Homework 9 and 10

Practice Book pp 18–21

100 Squares

Representations and resources

Pendulum, 100 squares, Base 10 apparatus, interlocking cubes, coins.

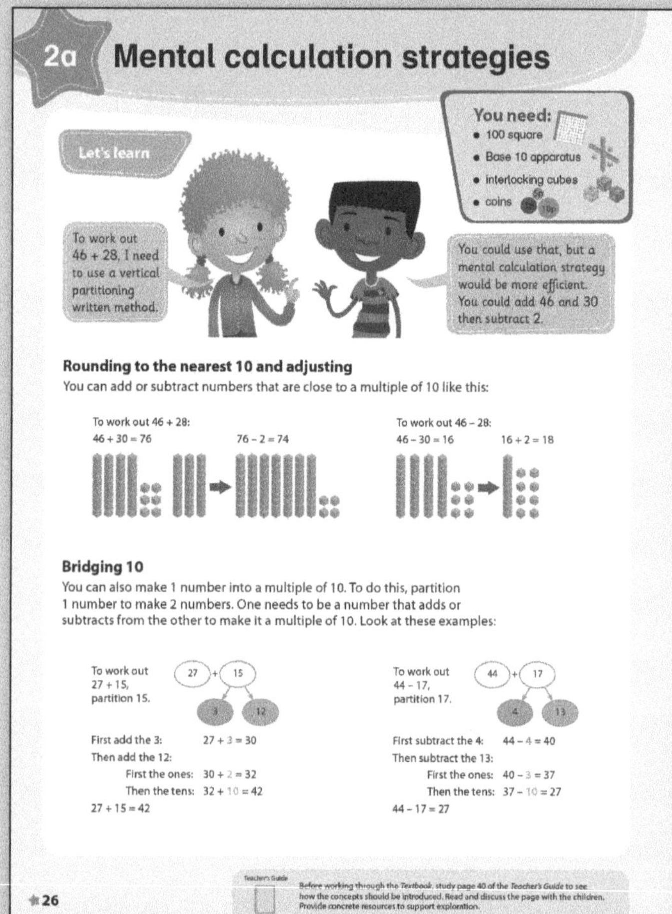

2a Mental calculation strategies

You need:
- 100 square
- Base 10 apparatus
- interlocking cubes
- coins

Let's learn

Rounding to the nearest 10 and adjusting

You can add or subtract numbers that are close to a multiple of 10 like this:

To work out 46 + 28:
46 + 30 = 76 76 − 2 = 74

To work out 46 − 28:
46 − 30 = 16 16 + 2 = 18

Bridging 10

You can also make 1 number into a multiple of 10. To do this, partition 1 number to make 2 numbers. One needs to be a number that adds or subtracts from the other to make it a multiple of 10. Look at these examples:

To work out 27 + 15, partition 15.

First add the 3: 27 + 3 = 30
Then add the 12:
First the ones: 30 + 2 = 32
Then the tens: 32 + 10 = 42
27 + 15 = 42

To work out 44 − 17, partition 17.

First subtract the 4: 44 − 4 = 40
Then subtract the 13:
First the ones: 40 − 3 = 37
Then the tens: 37 − 10 = 27
44 − 17 = 27

26

Teacher's Guide

Before working through the *Textbook*, study page 40 of the *Teacher's Guide* to see how the concepts should be introduced. Read and discuss the page with the children. Provide concrete resources to support exploration.

Bridging 10

- Discuss the Textbook example for addition using bridging ten. Give children interlocking cubes. Ask them to make the two numbers and then demonstrate the addition. Give them some more additions (e.g. 38 + 14) to practise in this way Choose some of the additions and ask children to show you the matching partitioning diagram.
- Look at the subtraction example. Again, ask children to model the calculation using interlocking cubes and then give them further practice using other numbers, e.g. 56 − 17. Ask children to work in pairs to draw the matching partitioning diagram.
- Work through some examples of sequencing for subtraction and compare this method with bridging ten. Which do they prefer? Stress that knowing number bonds for all numbers to ten is important for this strategy.

Let's practise: Digging deeper

Step 1

This task asks children to add and then subtract pairs of numbers using the rounding and adjusting strategy. Before they begin, check they remember that this means rounding a number to the next ten, adding (or subtracting) it and then subtracting (or adding) the extra ones. Give several examples where children need to add 8, 9, 18, 19, 28 and 29. Expect most children to be able to visualise the 100 square in their minds (particularly for the addition questions), but allow children who need support to use their 100 square or Base 10 apparatus.

Step 2

Before beginning the task, work through some examples of addition bridging ten, e.g. 25 + 26. Remind children that they could bridge by partitioning either number (26 = 21 + 5, so 25 + 5 = 30 and 30 + 21 = 51; 25 = 21 + 4, so 26 + 4 = 30 and 30 + 21 = 51). For subtraction, work through examples such as 34 – 19 and 74 – 52. For each question in the Textbook children should draw the model and clearly record what they are doing. For parts e-h, encourage them to justify why they used bridging ten or sequencing. Have all children used the same strategy for each part? If not, ask: *Convince me that your strategy is the most efficient.* Some children may benefit from using interlocking cubes as they work.

Step 3

For each calculation, children begin by making the first amount of money given. Encourage them to use the fewest possible coins. They then need to add or subtract the amounts given mentally, either using the strategy of rounding and adjusting or bridging ten. They then complete the calculation using coins (exchanging coins from the original amount for coins of a lower value if necessary). Do they get the same answer as when they worked it out mentally? Finally, they exchange coins to make the answer using the fewest possible coins.

Step 4

Children explore the possible new amounts when 19p is added to a selection of three coins. Encourage them to be systematic in their approach; e.g. they could find all the possible amounts that can be made with the 50p first, then all the amounts that can be made with the 20p. Once they have done this, only one further amount is possible (10p + 5p + 1p). Make sure they remember to add 19p to each and write down the new amounts.

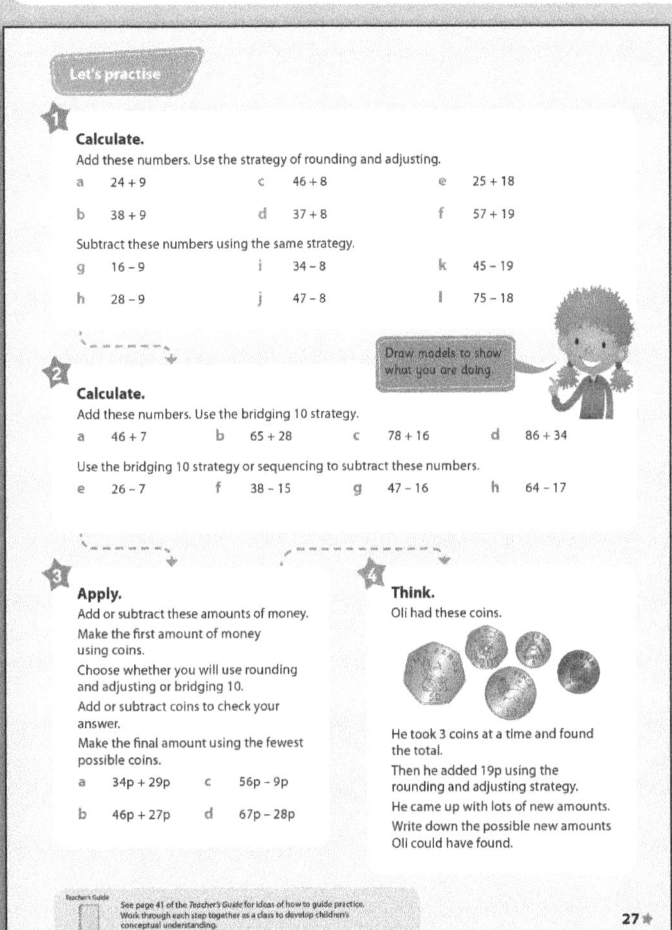

Let's practise

1 **Calculate.**

Add these numbers. Use the strategy of rounding and adjusting.

a 24 + 9 c 46 + 8 e 25 + 18

b 38 + 9 d 37 + 8 f 57 + 19

Subtract these numbers using the same strategy.

g 16 – 9 i 34 – 8 k 45 – 19

h 28 – 9 j 47 – 8 l 75 – 18

Draw models to show what you are doing.

2 **Calculate.**

Add these numbers. Use the bridging 10 strategy.

a 46 + 7 b 65 + 28 c 78 + 16 d 86 + 34

Use the bridging 10 strategy or sequencing to subtract these numbers.

e 26 – 7 f 38 – 15 g 47 – 16 h 64 – 17

3 **Apply.**

Add or subtract these amounts of money.

Make the first amount of money using coins.

Choose whether you will use rounding and adjusting or bridging 10.

Add or subtract coins to check your answer.

Make the final amount using the fewest possible coins.

a 34p + 29p c 56p – 9p

b 46p + 27p d 67p – 28p

4 **Think.**

Oli had these coins.

He took 3 coins at a time and found the total.

Then he added 19p using the rounding and adjusting strategy.

He came up with lots of new amounts.

Write down the possible new amounts Oli could have found.

Teacher's Guide See page 41 of the *Teacher's Guide* for ideas of how to guide practice. Work through each step together as a class to develop children's conceptual understanding.

27

Ensuring progress

Supporting understanding

Work with children in a focus group. Ask them to use Base 10 apparatus or interlocking cubes to show what is happening as they round and adjust. Ask them to explain what they are doing so that you can assess their understanding. If children are not confident in making given amounts of money, focus on this in Step 3 rather than rehearse the strategies from this spread.

Broadening understanding

You could explore, with children who are confident with the mental calculation strategies covered in the spread, how to add and subtract 3-digit numbers up to 500.

Concept mastered

Children can demonstrate, explain and use the mental calculation strategies of rounding and adjusting and bridging ten to add and subtract.

Follow-up ideas

- Children could make a card game, where they write a selection of 2-digit numbers onto 20 cards and then + 9, – 9, + 19, – 19, + 8, – 8, + 18, – 18 on eight others. They put them in two separate piles, take it in turns to pick one from each and then find sums and differences according to what the cards say.
- You could explore the rounding and adjusting strategy further by adding and subtracting 11, 12, 21, 22 and so on.
- Give children shopping catalogues and ask them to find items that interest them. Ask them to work out new prices if they should increase or decrease by £9, £19, £8, £18, etc.

Answers

Step 1

a 33 **g** 7
b 47 **h** 19
c 54 **i** 26
d 45 **j** 39
e 43 **k** 26
f 76 **l** 57

Step 2

a 53 **c** 94 **e** 19 **g** 31
b 93 **d** 120 **f** 23 **h** 47

Step 3

a 63p **c** 47p
b 73p **d** 39p

Step 4

There are ten possible amounts: 99p, 94p, 90p, 84p, 80p, 75p, 54p, 50p, 45p, 35p

2b Developing written methods

- **Add and subtract numbers with up to three digits, using formal written methods of columnar addition and subtraction.**
- **Estimate the answer to a calculation and use inverse operations to check answers.**

Homework 11 and 12

Practice Book pp 22–4

Representations and resources

Base 10 apparatus, cubes, metre sticks.

Mathematical vocabulary

Addition, subtraction, augend, addend, sum, minuend, subtrahend, difference

Warming up

Rehearse rounding to the nearest ten and adjusting. Do this for both addition and subtraction, e.g. 57 + 19 (57 + 20 – 1), 135 + 99 (135 + 100 – 1), 67 – 18 (67 – 20 + 2), 126 – 98 (126 – 100 + 2). You could include other important strategies, such as bridging ten, sequencing and near doubling (for addition).

Background knowledge

It is important that you continue to consider mental calculation strategies for the addition and subtraction of numbers, even though this concept focuses on written methods. However, when teaching written calculation methods ensure that you include some examples that cannot be answered efficiently using a mental strategy.

Introduce one step change at a time. In Year 2, children encountered addition using a partitioning vertical method (which deals with the most significant digit first) in Year 3, you begin with this method to introduce the addition of 3-digit numbers. It is important to reinforce that the short method is more efficient and it involves working from the least significant digit. For subtraction, the one step change is applying the method learned in Year 2 to 3-digit numbers.

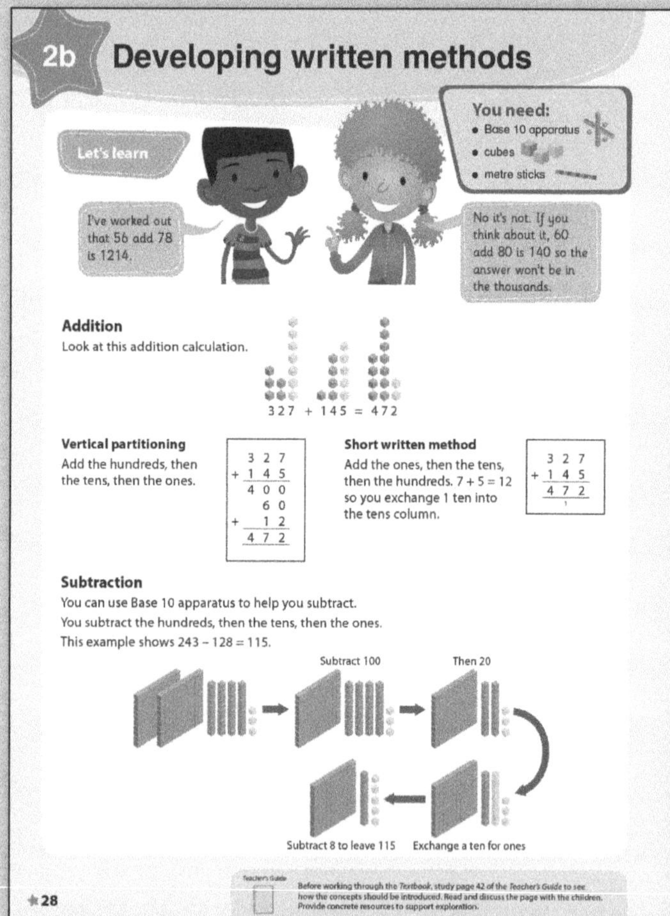

2b Developing written methods

Let's learn

You need:
- Base 10 apparatus
- cubes
- metre sticks

I've worked out that 56 add 78 is 1214.

No it's not. If you think about it, 60 add 80 is 140 so the answer won't be in the thousands.

Addition

Look at this addition calculation.

327 + 145 = 472

Vertical partitioning

Add the hundreds, then the tens, then the ones.

```
  3 2 7
+ 1 4 5
  4 0 0
    6 0
+   1 2
  4 7 2
```

Short written method

Add the ones, then the tens, then the hundreds. 7 + 5 = 12 so you exchange 1 ten into the tens column.

```
  3 2 7
+ 1 4 5
  4 7 2
    1
```

Subtraction

You can use Base 10 apparatus to help you subtract.
You subtract the hundreds, then the tens, then the ones.
This example shows 243 – 128 = 115.

Subtract 100 — Then 20 — Exchange a ten for ones — Subtract 8 to leave 115

Teacher's Guide: Before working through the *Textbook*, study page 42 of the *Teacher's Guide* to see how the concepts should be introduced. Read and discuss the page with the children. Provide concrete resources to support exploration.

28

Let's learn: Modelling and teaching

Addition

- Begin by writing Oli's calculation as a column calculation on the board. *What has he done wrong?* Establish that he has not exchanged the 1 ten from 14 ones. Review vertical partitioning with 2-digit numbers, e.g. 56 + 78. Remind children that you add the tens, then the ones, then add the results together. If necessary, use Base 10 apparatus or cubes to model the calculation.
- Focus on the Textbook example that models 327 + 145 using cubes. Ask children to make the two 3-digit numbers using coloured cubes, then add the numbers, working from the most to the least significant digit. For each step, write the corresponding part of the vertical partitioning calculation on the board.
- Discuss how this can be checked. Repeat for other 3-digit additions.
- Finally, look at the short written method for the calculation shown in the Textbook. Establish that for this method you work from the least to the most significant digit. Ensure children understand that, because 7 + 5 = 12, 10 ones need to be exchanged for one 10. Model the written method as they carry out the calculation. Give them more 3-digit additions to answer using the short method, e.g. 254 + 216, and Base 10 apparatus. You model the written addition.

Subtraction

- Use Base 10 apparatus to recap subtracting 2-digit numbers, again working from the most to the least significant digit. Then move on to 3-digit numbers, beginning with the example in the Textbook. Work through several examples in this way, with you recording. Make sure children can write the subtraction statement horizontally, e.g. 243 – 128 = 115.

Let's practise: Digging deeper

Step 1

For parts a–d, observe children to check they are able to combine and exchange the equipment appropriately and accurately. Similarly, do they remember that they need to work from the most significant digit for parts e–h but from the least significant digit for parts i–l?

Step 2

You may wish to decide which equipment it would be best for children to use for this task. All the calculations involve exchanging at least a ten; some involve exchanging tens and hundreds. Ask children to read their number statements to you, using the language of minuend, subtrahend and difference.

Step 3

Give pairs two metre sticks. Model putting them together and choosing a length between 1 m 50 cm and 2 m (e.g. 1 m 64 cm). Tell children that you are going to subtract 1 m 12 cm from the chosen length. Discuss different ways of doing this; e.g. count back 1 m 12 cm from 1 m 64 cm, count on from 1 m 12 cm or write a subtraction calculation (1 m 64 cm – 1 m 12 cm). During the task, pairs need to do this for themselves six times. They could use different methods for different lengths. Challenge children to justify their method: *Convince me that you have chosen the best method for your lengths.*

Step 4

You could either ask children to attempt this task independently, then hold a mini plenary to see how they are getting on, giving hints if necessary, or guide them with a series of questions. *What types of numbers will give an odd difference?* Ask children to take small numbers away from each other to find out, e.g. 9 and 4, 9 and 7, 8 and 4, 8 and 5. Establish that to give an odd difference one of the numbers must be odd and the other even. *One of Mia's numbers is an odd multiple of five. What can you say about the other number?* Agree that it must be even. *What are the odd multiples of five between 250 and 300?* From this children should be able to work out Mia's possible numbers.

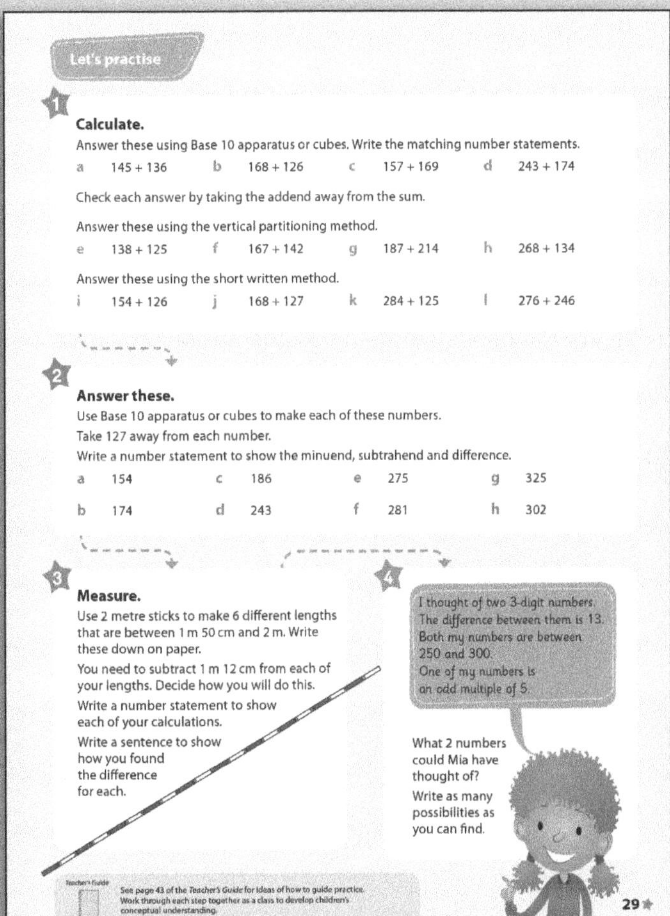
Let's practise

1 Calculate.

Answer these using Base 10 apparatus or cubes. Write the matching number statements.

a 145 + 136 b 168 + 126 c 157 + 169 d 243 + 174

Check each answer by taking the addend away from the sum.

Answer these using the vertical partitioning method.

e 138 + 125 f 167 + 142 g 187 + 214 h 268 + 134

Answer these using the short written method.

i 154 + 126 j 168 + 127 k 284 + 125 l 276 + 246

2 Answer these.

Use Base 10 apparatus or cubes to make each of these numbers.
Take 127 away from each number.
Write a number statement to show the minuend, subtrahend and difference.

a 154 c 186 e 275 g 325

b 174 d 243 f 281 h 302

3 Measure.

Use 2 metre sticks to make 6 different lengths that are between 1 m 50 cm and 2 m. Write these down on paper.

You need to subtract 1 m 12 cm from each of your lengths. Decide how you will do this.

Write a number statement to show each of your calculations.

Write a sentence to show how you found the difference for each.

4

What 2 numbers could Mia have thought of?

Write as many possibilities as you can find.

Teacher's Guide

See page 43 of the *Teacher's Guide* for ideas of how to guide practice. Work through each step together as a class to develop children's conceptual understanding.

29

Ensuring progress

Supporting understanding

Some children will need to have more practice adding and subtracting numbers with Base 10 apparatus. Work with them as a focus group until they have mastered this, initially without exchange and then including exchange. When they have mastered this, work with them on how to record their sums and differences.

Broadening understanding

Ask children to make up word problems that involve the addition and subtraction of 3-digit numbers. They could use digit cards to generate numbers. In this way they will also need to consider which way round to subtract the numbers

Concept mastered

Children can demonstrate and explain how to add and subtract numbers using manipulatives. They can use and explain the vertical partitioning and short written methods for addition.

Follow-up ideas

- Children could use digit cards to make pairs of 3-digit numbers. They find sums and differences using the written methods considered during this spread.
- You could ask children to add amounts of money that involve pounds and pence. Encourage them to choose the amounts they wish to add and to make these using coins. They could answer the calculations using a written method and then check by combining the coins.
- Give children shopping catalogues and ask them to find the difference between different amounts. They could do this practically or, if appropriate, using a written method. Encourage them to show what they are doing using the bar model.

Answers

Step 1

a	281	**g**	401
b	294	**h**	402
c	326	**i**	280
d	417	**j**	295
e	263	**k**	409
f	309	**l**	522

Step 2

a	27	**c**	59
b	47	**d**	116
e	148	**g**	198
f	154	**h**	175

Step 3

Answers will vary

Step 4

255 and 268

265 and 278, 252 and 265

275 and 288, 262 and 275

285 and 298, 272 and 285

282 and 295

Unit 2

Fish for sums and differences

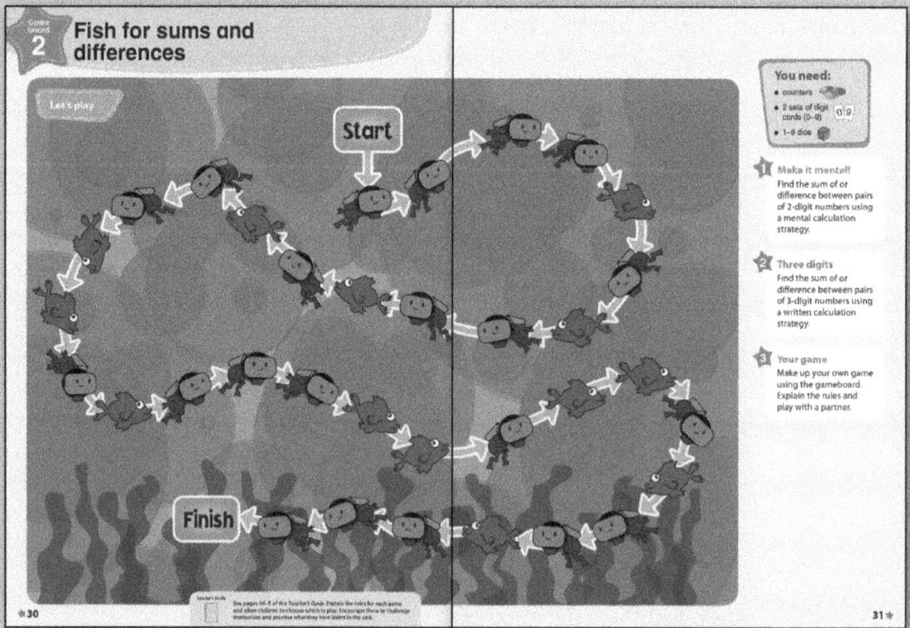

Game 1: Make it mental!

This game gives children practice in adding and subtracting using mental calculation strategies.

Maths focus

- Add and subtract numbers mentally

Resources

1 counter per player (1 colour per player), 0–9 digit cards (2 sets), 1–6 dice (1).

How to play

This game should be played in pairs. Players shuffle the two sets of digit cards together and place them in a pile, face down on the table. They each place their counter on Start. They then take turns to roll the dice and move their counter that number of spaces. If they land on a diver they do nothing. If they land on a fish they pick four digit cards and use them to make two 2-digit numbers. If they threw an odd number they find the difference between the two numbers. If they threw an even number they find the total. They choose the mental strategy they wish to use for their calculation and explain this to their partner. For each calculation that they get correct they score two points. The winner is the player with the higher total when both players reach Finish.

Making it easier

Encourage children to focus on one mental calculation strategy, e.g. bridging ten.

Making it harder

Encourage children to use one mental calculation strategy to add or subtract and then to check their answers using a second mental calculation strategy. You could ask them to use extra cards to make a 3-digit number and add and subtract a 2-digit number.

Game 2: Three digits

This game gives children practice in adding and subtracting using written calculation methods.

Maths focus

- Add numbers with up to three digits, using formal written methods of columnar addition

Resources

1 counter per player (1 colour per player), 0–9 digit cards (2 sets), 1–6 dice (1).

How to play

This game is for pairs. The basic rules are the same as for Game 1, including scoring. This time, when children land on a fish, they pick six digit cards and use them to make two 3-digit numbers less than 500. If they throw an odd number they subtract the two numbers. If they throw an even number they add them. For addition, they should use one of the written methods looked at during concept spread 2b–Developing written methods.. Encourage children to record their subtractions horizontally.

Making it easier

Give children manipulatives to use for support. You could also allow them to write the appropriate horizontal number statement, rather than using the formal written methods, for addition as well as subtraction.

Making it harder

Challenge children to find the highest possible total when they add and the smallest possible difference when they subtract.

Game 3: Your game

Children should invent their own game, designing rules that use the concepts covered in the unit. Challenge children to make their game easier or harder.

Fish for sums and differences

Choose a game to play.

Game 1: Make it mental!

You need:

- 1 counter per player (1 colour per player)
- 0–9 digit cards (2 sets)
- 1–6 dice

How to play

- Shuffle the digit cards and place them in a pile, face down. Each place your counter on Start.
- Take turns to roll the dice. Move your counter that number of spaces.
- If you land on a diver, do nothing.
- If you land on a fish, pick 4 digit cards and use them to make two 2-digit numbers.
  - If you rolled an odd number, find the difference between your 2 numbers.
  - If you rolled an even number, find the sum of your 2 numbers.
  - Choose what mental strategy to use and explain it to your partner.
  - For each calculation you get right, you score 2 points.
- Continue to play until you both reach Finish. The winner is the player with the most points.

Game 2: Three digits

You need:

- 1 counter per player (1 colour per player)
- 0–9 digit cards (2 sets)
- 1–6 dice

How to play

- Follow the basic instructions for Game 1.
- This time, if you land on a diver, do nothing.
- If you land on a fish, pick 6 digit cards and use them to make two 3-digit numbers.
  - If you rolled an odd number, find the difference between your 2 numbers.
  - If you rolled an even number, find the sum of your 2 numbers.
  - Answer using 1 of the written methods you have learnt.
  - For each calculation you get right, you score 2 points.
- Continue to play until you both reach Finish. The winner is the player with the most points.

Game 3: Your game

- Make up your own game using the gameboard.
- What are the rules for your game? Explain them to someone.

Please help your child by reading the instructions and playing the game together.

Unit 2 And finally ...

Assessment task 1

Running the task

This task requires children to use two mental strategies – rounding and adjusting, and bridging ten – to complete addition and subtraction calculations. Before they begin, recap both strategies using examples. Write a calculation, such as 57 + 19, on the board. *What strategy would you use to answer this?* Agree that 19 is close to 20, so you can round and adjust. Work through the steps in the calculation, first working out 57 + 20 = 77. Highlight the fact that you have added one to 19 to make 20. This is one 'too many', so you need to adjust by subtracting one: 77 – 1 = 76. Feed in the idea that you could also take one from 57 and add it to 19, to give the calculation 56 + 20. Then rehearse how to check the answer using sequencing. Repeat for several further calculations before moving on to some rounding and adjusting examples for subtraction, checking the answers by adding the difference and the subtrahend.

Next write 64 + 18 and discuss how to use the bridging ten strategy. *What do we need to add to 64 to get to the next ten?* Agree six, and that the 18 can be partitioned into six and 12. Model adding the six to 64 to make 70 and then the 12 to make a sum of 82. Then ask: *What do we need to add to 18 to get to the next ten?* Agree two, and that the 64 can be partitioned into two and 62. Model adding the two to 18 to make 20 and then the 62 to 82. Agree that both ways of bridging ten lead to the same answers. Repeat for several further calculations before moving on to subtraction. Children can then work on the questions in the Textbook independently.

Evidencing mastery

Children are evidencing mastery if they can explain and demonstrate how to add and subtract using the mental calculation strategies of rounding and adjusting and bridging ten.

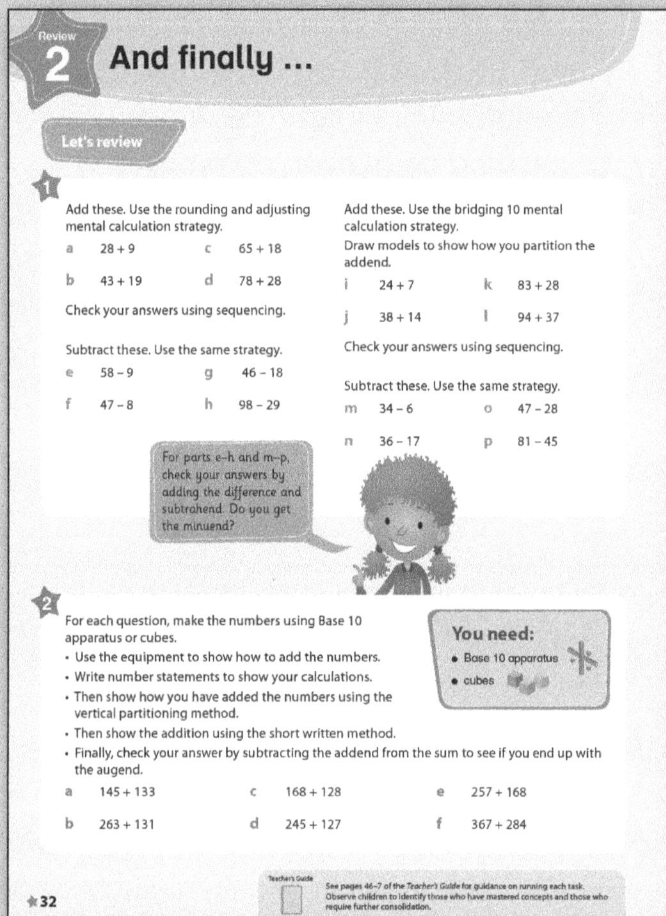
Review 2 And finally ...

Let's review

1

Add these. Use the rounding and adjusting mental calculation strategy.

a 28 + 9 c 65 + 18

b 43 + 19 d 78 + 28

Check your answers using sequencing.

Subtract these. Use the same strategy.

e 58 – 9 g 46 – 18

f 47 – 8 h 98 – 29

Add these. Use the bridging 10 mental calculation strategy.

Draw models to show how you partition the addend.

i 24 + 7 k 83 + 28

j 38 + 14 l 94 + 37

Check your answers using sequencing.

Subtract these. Use the same strategy.

m 34 – 6 o 47 – 28

n 36 – 17 p 81 – 45

For parts e–h and m–p, check your answers by adding the difference and subtrahend. Do you get the minuend?

2

For each question, make the numbers using Base 10 apparatus or cubes.

- Use the equipment to show how to add the numbers.
- Write number statements to show your calculations.
- Then show how you have added the numbers using the vertical partitioning method.
- Then show the addition using the short written method.
- Finally, check your answer by subtracting the addend from the sum to see if you end up with the augend.

a 145 + 133 c 168 + 128 e 257 + 168

b 263 + 131 d 245 + 127 f 367 + 284

You need:
- Base 10 apparatus
- cubes

32

Teacher's Guide
See pages 46–7 of the *Teacher's Guide* for guidance on running each task. Observe children to identify those who have mastered concepts and those who require further consolidation.

Assessment task 2

Resources

Base 10 apparatus, cubes.

Running the task

Stress to children that whenever possible mental calculation strategies should be used to answer addition and subtraction calculations. However, when these are not efficient because the numbers are too large or do not lend themselves to such methods, then written calculation methods should be used. Children made the first step towards the short written method by moving from 2-digit numbers (in Year 2) to 3-digit numbers. They did this practically using manipulatives and then set the calculations out in the same way as they did in Year 2 and answered them using a vertical partitioning method. They then explored how and why to move from this to adding the least significant digits first and missing out partitioning. This task asks them to work through all three aspects.

Work through an example with children before they tackle the task independently. Write a calculation, such as 234 + 148, on the board. Ask them to make these numbers using Base 10 apparatus or cubes and combine them, exchanging as necessary. They should then show this as a vertical partitioning calculation and then as the short written method. Discuss with children how they can check their answer. Establish that, because addition and subtraction are inverse operations, they can subtract the addend from the sum. If they have answered correctly, they should end up with the augend.

Some children may need to spend longer on vertical partitioning at this early stage in Year 3, which is fine..

Evidencing mastery

Children who can demonstrate how to move from combining manipulatives to the vertical partitioning method to the short written method for addition, and can explain what is happening in each stage, are demonstrating mastery.

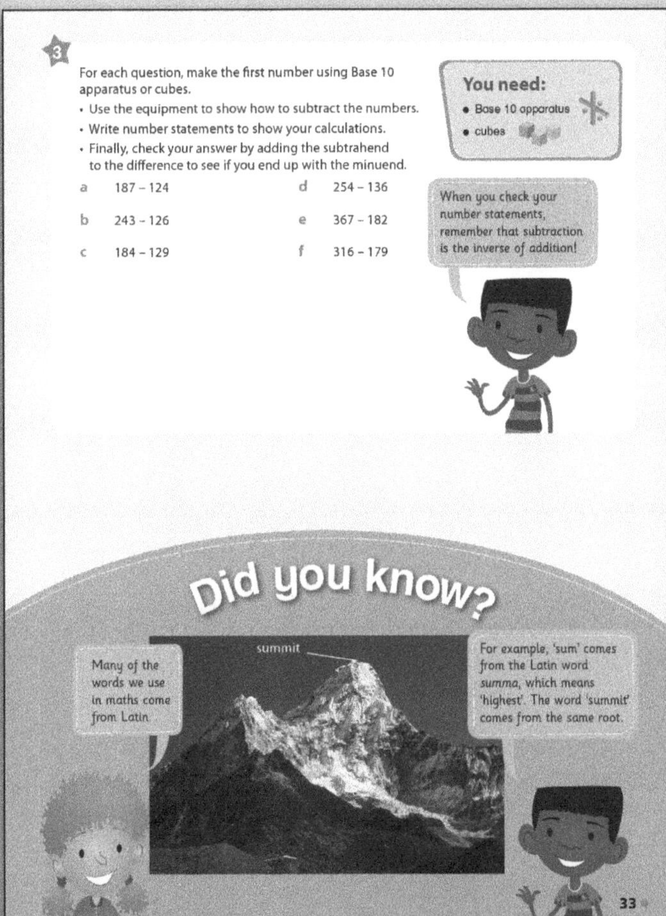

For each question, make the first number using Base 10 apparatus or cubes.

- Use the equipment to show how to subtract the numbers.
- Write number statements to show your calculations.
- Finally, check your answer by adding the subtrahend to the difference to see if you end up with the minuend.

a 187 – 124 d 254 – 136

b 243 – 126 e 367 – 182

c 184 – 129 f 316 – 179

You need:
- Base 10 apparatus
- cubes

When you check your number statements, remember that subtraction is the inverse of addition!

Did you know?

Many of the words we use in maths come from Latin.

summit

For example, 'sum' comes from the Latin word summa, which means 'highest'. The word 'summit' comes from the same root.

33

Assessment task 3

Resources

Base 10 apparatus, cubes.

Running the task

This task is similar to Task 2 but focuses on subtraction. Children need to make minuends using manipulatives and then practically take subtrahends away. Again, work through several examples before they begin the task, inviting children to instruct you on what to do. Identify any children who need to spend longer using manipulatives at this stage. Discuss with them how they can check their answer. Establish that, because addition and subtraction are inverse operations, they can add the subtrahend to the difference. If they have answered correctly, they should end up with the minuend.

Ensure that children make only the minuend using the equipment. They are taking away the subtrahend from this and so it does not exist as a separate amount. Whilst working with the manipulatives, children may begin with the most significant digit first. Encourage those who are ready to do so to begin with the least significant digit, as this will help them with the transition to the short written method for subtraction.

Evidencing mastery

Children who can demonstrate how to subtract 3-digit numbers using manipulatives, and can explain what is happening, are evidencing mastery at this stage in Year 3.

Concepts mastered

- ☑ Children can use, demonstrate and explain how to use the mental calculation strategies of rounding and adjusting and bridging ten to add and subtract.
- ☑ Children can demonstrate and explain how to add and subtract numbers using manipulatives. They can use and explain the vertical partitioning and short written methods for addition.

Did you know?

Many of the words we use in mathematics come from Latin. Latin originated in Ancient Roman times, having been developed in an old region of Italy, and was widely used across Europe in the days of the Roman Empire. Over the years the language has been lost from common parlance but is the root of many words we use today. It is still taught today and is particularly important in areas of medicine and science.

As noted in the Textbook, 'sum' comes from the Latin word *summa*, which means 'highest'. The word 'summit' comes from the same root. 'Augend' comes from the Latin *augendum*, 'a thing to be increased', as does the word 'augment' ('to increase'). 'Addend' comes from *addendum*, meaning 'an addition made to something'; we use 'addendum' in English in the context of additions to documents.

The word 'difference' comes from the Latin word *differentia*, meaning 'carrying away'. 'Minuend' stems from *minuendus*, which means 'to be diminished or make smaller'; children may be familiar with the related Italian term *diminuendo*, used in music to mean 'a gradual decrease in loudness'. 'Subtrahend' comes from *subtrahendum*, which means 'to delete from a list or take away'.

Unit 3

Ways to multiply and divide

Mathematical focus

- ★ **Number: multiplication and division, fractions**
- ★ **Measurement: money, length, time**
- ★ **Statistics: interpret and present data, solve problems**

Prior learning

Children should already be able to:

- recall and use multiplication and division facts for the two, five and ten multiplication tables
- count in threes
- calculate mathematical statements for multiplication and division, within the multiplication tables, and write them using the multiplication (×), division (÷) and equals (=) signs.

Key new learning

- Recall and use multiplication and division facts for the three, four and eight multiplication tables.
- Write and calculate mathematical statements for multiplication and division using the multiplication tables that they know, including for 2-digit numbers multiplied by single-digit numbers, mentally and progressing to formal written methods.
- Interpret and present data using pictograms and tables.
- Solve problems, including correspondence problems in which *n* objects are connected to *m* objects.

Making connections

- Multiplication and division facts have many real-life practical applications, including calculating with money and other measures. Fluency relies on solid number sense, including the ability to count in steps, e.g. twos, threes, fives and tens, ready recall of number facts and the strategies and confidence needed to work out other facts from known facts.
- Mastery of multiplication and division facts will help children read scales and interpret information presented in scaled bar charts, pictograms and tables, which they will meet in science, geography and other subjects.

Talk about

Remind children that multiplication is the same as repeated addition and adding groups of the same number. Division is repeated subtraction and taking away groups of the same number. Discuss the vocabulary of multiplicand, multiplier, product, dividend, divisor and quotient. Establish that multiplication is about finding the total of a number of groups of the multiplicand. Encourage children to read out calculations using formal vocabulary, e.g. multiplicand multiplied by multiplier equals product.

Remind children that multiplication and division calculations should be carried out using a mental calculation strategy wherever possible.

Engaging and exploring

Using the picture of the jars, begin by revising what is meant by multiplication, including the vocabulary of multiplicand, multiplier and product. Ask children for their ideas on how to find the total number of jars. Point out that the jars have been arranged in an array and agree that the total could be found by counting in ones, repeatedly adding 6 four times or using multiplication facts. Establish that there are 24 jars altogether and ask children to write the multiplication statement to show this: $6 \times 4 = 24$. Then give children counters and ask them to make different arrays and write the appropriate number statements.

Looking at the elephant, tell children that the average height of a male elephant is approximately four metres. Use a metre stick to demonstrate this horizontally and ask them to imagine it as a height. Ask children to work out how much smaller than the elephant a child who is 1 m tall is. Agree 3 m shorter. Encourage them to think of this in terms of fractions; agree $\frac{1}{4}$ of the size and link this to the concept of scaling down and division ($4\text{ m} \div 4 = 1\text{ m}$).

Draw two rectangles, so they are both the same length and the first is twice the width of the second. Agree that the smaller one has been scaled down to half the width. Give different widths for the larger rectangle, e.g. 12, 48, 120, 300, and ask children to tell you the width of the smaller rectangle. Give children two pairs of strips of paper that are the same size. They measure their lengths and widths. They then keep one of each as it is and scale the width and then the length of the other two by half.

Moving on to the giraffes, ask children to estimate how much taller the adult is than the baby. Agree that it is about three times as tall. Draw rectangles as for the elephant but, this time, so that they are both the same width and the second is three times the height of the shorter one. You could tell children that the taller one has been scaled up by three. Give different heights for the smaller rectangle, e.g. five. seven, nine, and ask children to tell you the height of the taller one. Make the link to multiplying by three. Children have counted in threes in Year 2, so encourage them to do this to find five, seven and nine multiplied by three.

Ask children to describe the sizes of the milk cartons in relation to each other, e.g. the smallest carton is one quarter the size of the biggest one; the middle carton is half the size of the biggest one; the smallest carton is half the size of the middle one.

Give the biggest carton a capacity, e.g. 2 litres, and ask children to tell you the capacities of the other two. Link this to scaling down, halving and dividing by two. Provide measuring equipment and bottles. Children could practically measure out, e.g. one litre and then measure half of that and then half of the last one. Repeat for other amounts.

For the hats and scarves, ask children how many combinations of one of each could be made. You could have three hats and four scarves, so that children can find out practically. You could then ask them to draw a model to show their thinking.

Make up similar problems for children to solve, e.g. using strawberry, vanilla and chocolate lollies. *Mia wanted two, how many possible combinations are there?*

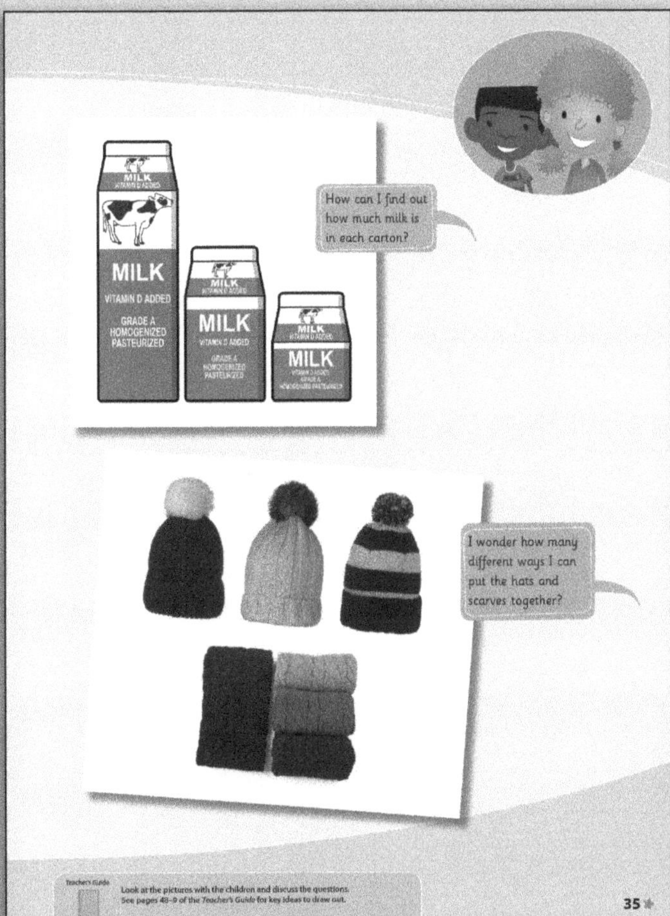

Things to think about

- How will you organise groupings?
- How will you use manipulatives and visual representations to help conceptual understanding with all children?
- How will you decide which strategies to use to encourage fluency, reasoning and problem solving?
- How will you ensure children experience practical opportunities to measure length, mass and capacity?

Checking understanding

You will know children have mastered these concepts when they can explain the links between multiplication and repeated addition, and between division and repeated subtraction. They can represent multiplication and division facts using arrays. They can explain and represent both operations as scaling up or down.

3a 2s, 4s and 8s

- **Recall and use multiplication and division facts for the two, four and eight multiplication tables.**
- **Write and calculate mathematical statements for multiplication and division using the multiplication tables that they know, including for 2-digit numbers multiplied by single-digit numbers, mentally and progressing to formal methods.**
- **Interpret and present data using pictograms and tables.**

Homework 13 and 14 | Practice Book pp 25–8 | Exploring multiplication

Representations and resources

Coins, strips of paper (up to 35 cm), rulers, scissors.

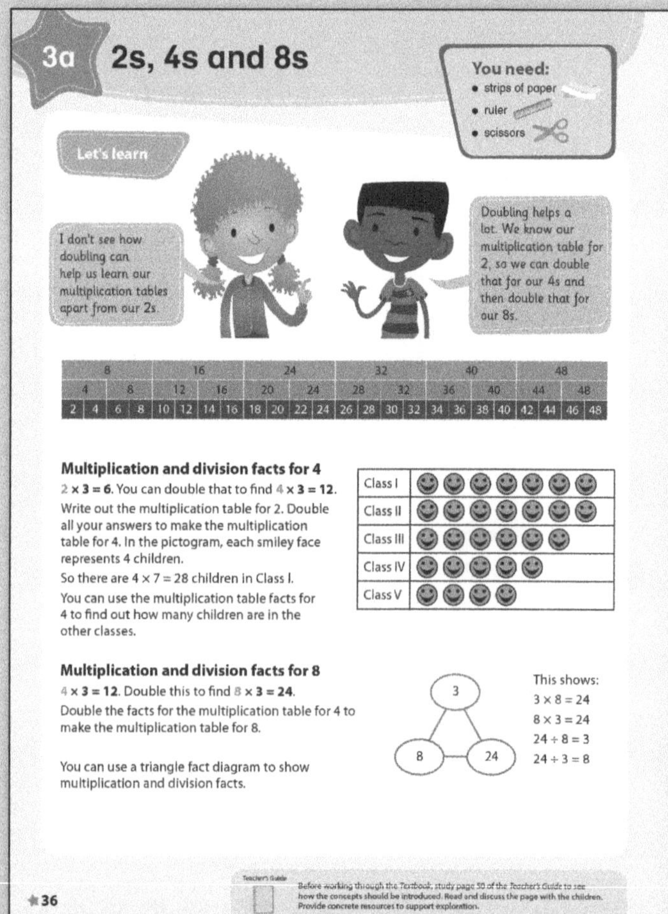
3a 2s, 4s and 8s

You need:
- strips of paper
- ruler
- scissors

Let's learn

I don't see how doubling can help us learn our multiplication tables apart from our 2s.

Doubling helps a lot. We know our multiplication table for 2, so we can double that for our 4s and then double that for our 8s.

8 16 24 32 40 48
4 8 12 16 20 24 28 32 36 40 44 48
2 4 6 8 10 12 14 16 18 20 22 24 26 28 30 32 34 36 38 40 42 44 46 48

Multiplication and division facts for 4
2 × 3 = 6. You can double that to find **4 × 3 = 12**.
Write out the multiplication table for 2. Double all your answers to make the multiplication table for 4. In the pictogram, each smiley face represents 4 children.
So there are 4 × 7 = 28 children in Class I.
You can use the multiplication table facts for 4 to find out how many children are in the other classes.

Class I
Class II
Class III
Class IV
Class V

Multiplication and division facts for 8
4 × 3 = 12. Double this to find **8 × 3 = 24**.
Double the facts for the multiplication table for 4 to make the multiplication table for 8.

You can use a triangle fact diagram to show multiplication and division facts.

3
8
24

This shows:
3 × 8 = 24
8 × 3 = 24
24 ÷ 8 = 3
24 ÷ 3 = 8

36

Teacher's Guide
Before working through the *Textbook*, study page 50 of the *Teacher's Guide* to see how the concepts should be introduced. Read and discuss the page with the children. Provide concrete resources to support exploration.

Mathematical vocabulary

Multiplication, division, multiplicand, multiplier, product, dividend, divisor, quotient, multiplication tables

Warming up

Ask children to count in threes, holding the appropriate number of fingers up as they do so. When they get to 11 × 3 and 12 × 3, they say 33 and 36. Next ask them to recite the multiplication tables and finally call out facts for them to answer. Repeat this for fours and eights.

Background knowledge

It is important that children learn their multiplication tables. Without instant recall of these facts, they will find it difficult to solve problems. Multiplication is commutative. It does not matter which way you multiply numbers, the answer is always the same. Therefore, children only need to learn half their multiplication facts, e.g. if they know that 3 × 6 = 18, they also know that 6 × 3 = 18. Division is not commutative. Multiplication and division are connected. Multiplication facts have corresponding division facts, e.g. 18 ÷ 6 = 3 and 18 ÷ 3 = 6. Arrays make this link obvious.

Let's learn: Modelling and teaching

Multiplication and division facts for 4

- Explain that if you know that 2 × 3 = 6, you can double this to find 4 × 3 = 12. Ask children to explain to a partner how doubling the multiplication table for two can help them find the one for four. Then give children the opportunity to explore the bar model and to tell you what they notice.
- Ask children to write out the multiplication table for four. They could make their own bar models, as in the Textbook, using strips of paper, e.g. for 8 × 4 they make four strips and label each strip '8'. They then write the appropriate multiplication and division facts.
- Look at the pictogram and discuss that each symbol represents four children. This is a good way to rehearse multiplication facts within the context of statistics. How many children are in Class 2? Class 3? Ask what the symbol would look like for one, two and three children.

Multiplication and division facts for 8

- Ask children to tell you what they would need to double to find the facts for the eight multiplication table. Then display a triangle fact diagram like those in the Textbook.
- Ask children to tell you what they notice. Can they write the four facts the model shows (3 × 8 = 24, 8 × 3 = 24, 24 ÷ 8 = 3, 24 ÷ 3 = 8)? Ask them to make up models for other facts and then write the associated facts. Emphasise that multiplication is commutative, but division is not. Ask them to say this in a sentence: *Multiplication is commutative – different calculation, same answer.* Remind them that division is the inverse of multiplication.
- Explore multiplying by eight using the bar model as shown in the Textbook. Can children see the links between the 2s, 4s and 8s? Ask them to find the common multiples, e.g. 8, 16 and 24. Can they tell you any others?

Let's practise: Digging deeper

Step 1

This task asks children to write down the multiplication facts for four up to 12 × 4. They then use their answers to write down the facts for eight up to 12 × 8. They need to explain to a partner how doubling can help them learn new facts. Encourage them to test each other on these facts. Ask them to think of other multiplication tables that can be learnt in this way, e.g. threes and sixes, sixes and twelves.

Step 2

Review the triangle fact diagram in Let's learn. The task asks children to find the missing number in each diagram: encourage them to use division facts to find the missing number. Children who do not have instant recall of the required facts can count on in multiples of the given number to see how many make the product. Children then make up some examples of their own for a partner to complete.

Step 3

Recap multiplication and division facts for two, four and eight. Observe children to see who can recall them quickly. You will need to give children long strips of paper. They need to find the products of the multiplications and then measure strips of paper to their lengths. Again, observe children to see if they can recall the facts quickly.

Step 4

Recap how to construct a pictogram. You could use the one in the Textbook or any that children might have drawn in class. Discuss the symbols and what they represent. Ask children to tell you the new values on the pictogram if the symbols represented two or eight. Children need to create a pictogram from the table, where each symbol represents four. Children need to work out what the last symbol will look like if the number of votes is not a multiple of four.

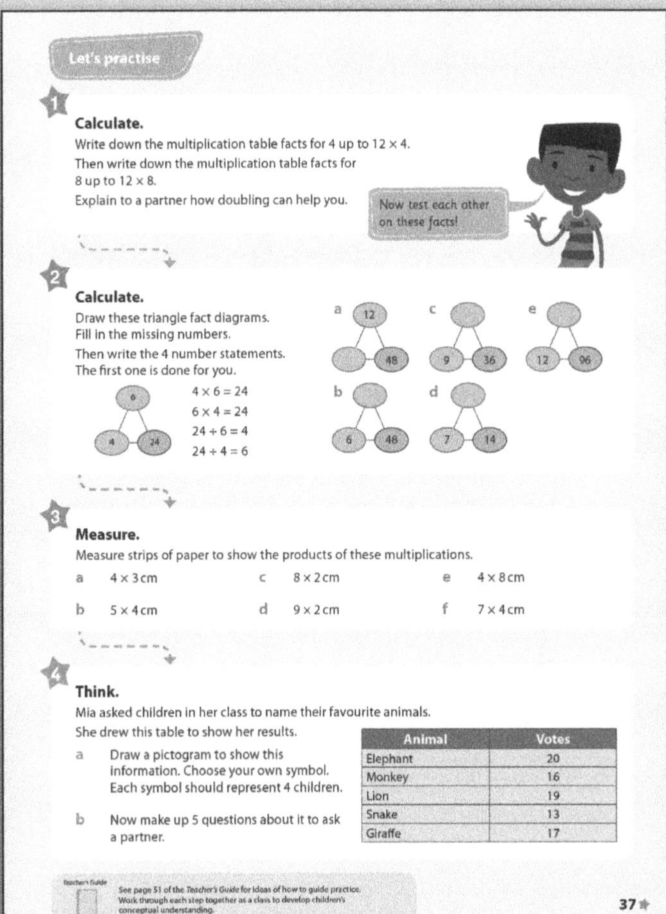

Let's practise

1 **Calculate.**
Write down the multiplication table facts for 4 up to 12 × 4.
Then write down the multiplication table facts for 8 up to 12 × 8.
Explain to a partner how doubling can help you.

2 **Calculate.**
Draw these triangle fact diagrams.
Fill in the missing numbers.
Then write the 4 number statements.
The first one is done for you.

4 × 6 = 24
6 × 4 = 24
24 ÷ 6 = 4
24 ÷ 4 = 6

3 **Measure.**
Measure strips of paper to show the products of these multiplications.

a 4 × 3 cm   c 8 × 2 cm   e 4 × 8 cm
b 5 × 4 cm   d 9 × 2 cm   f 7 × 4 cm

4 **Think.**
Mia asked children in her class to name their favourite animals.
She drew this table to show her results.

a Draw a pictogram to show this information. Choose your own symbol. Each symbol should represent 4 children.

b Now make up 5 questions about it to ask a partner.

Animal	Votes
Elephant	20
Monkey	16
Lion	19
Snake	13
Giraffe	17

Teacher's Guide
See page 51 of the *Teacher's Guide* for ideas of how to guide practice. Work through each step together as a class to develop children's conceptual understanding.

37

Ensuring progress

Supporting understanding

Encourage children who need support to refer to the multiplication facts they have written down when they test each other in Step 1, and again in Step 2. When they make up their own triangle fact diagrams, they should focus on the multiplication facts for two and four.

Broadening understanding

In Step 1, encourage children to try to recall the multiplication facts for eight, rather than working them out by doubling. In Step 2, let them choose which multiplication tables to use when making up their triangle fact diagrams. In Step 4, you could ask children to make a bar chart to show the information after they have completed the pictogram. The divisions need to go up in steps of four.

Concept mastered

Children can quickly recall facts for the two, four and eight multiplication tables and corresponding division facts.

Follow-up ideas

- Children could write the products for the two, four and eight multiplication tables on cards. They put them in a pile face down on the table. They take it in turns to pick one and write down as many different multiplication and division facts for the product as they can.
- Children write multiplication and division statements up to 12 × 8. They then use these to play a game of snap or pairs.
- Ask children to pick, e.g. food or pets, and then choose five or six and ask their classmates which is their favourite. They then create a pictogram with one symbol to represent four to show this information, or a bar chart with divisions on the vertical axis going up in twos or fours.

Answers

Step 1

Multiplication table facts for four.

Multiplication table facts for eight.

Step 2

a 4 **d** 2
b 8 **e** 8
c 4

Step 3

a 12 cm **d** 18 cm
b 20 cm **e** 32 cm
c 16 cm **f** 28 cm

Step 4

a Pictogram showing the following:

Elephant: $5\frac{1}{2}$ symbols

Monkey: $4\frac{1}{2}$ symbols

Lion: $3\frac{3}{4}$ symbols

Snake: $3\frac{1}{4}$ of a symbol

Giraffe: $4\frac{1}{4}$ symbols

b Answers will vary.

3b Commutativity

- **Recall and use multiplication and division facts for the three, four and eight multiplication tables.**
- **Write and calculate mathematical statements for multiplication and division using the multiplication tables that they know, including for 2-digit numbers multiplied by single-digit numbers, mentally and progressing to formal methods.**

Homework 15 and 16 | Practice Book pp 29–32 | Multiplication: Arrays

Representations and resources

Base 10 apparatus, counters, coins.

Mathematical vocabulary

Multiplication, division, multiplicand, multiplier, product, dividend, divisor, quotient, groups of, repeated addition, repeated subtraction

Warming up

Write an addition fact on the board, e.g. $6 + 3 = 9$. Ask children to generate as many other facts as they can from this, e.g. $3 + 6 = 9$, $9 - 3 = 6$, $60 + 30 = 90$, $90 - 60 = 30$, $120 + 60 = 180$, $45 - 30 = 15$. Encourage them to double, halve and multiply and divide the addends and the total by ten.

Background knowledge

Commutativity is a key principal in both addition and multiplication. Commutativity means that it does not matter in which order we add and multiply numbers, the answer will be the same. If we know that $7 \times 8 = 56$, we also know that $8 \times 7 = 56$. It is helpful to ask children to say, e.g. '$7 \times 8 = 56$ and $8 \times 7 = 56$ because multiplication is commutative'.

Arrays are an excellent visual representation or manipulative (if children are using counters) to demonstrate commutativity and the inverse relationship multiplication has with division. You could ask them to write the appropriate numbers by the rows and columns and the product in the middle. They will then be able to connect the two operations and tell you the four facts that they can derive from their array.

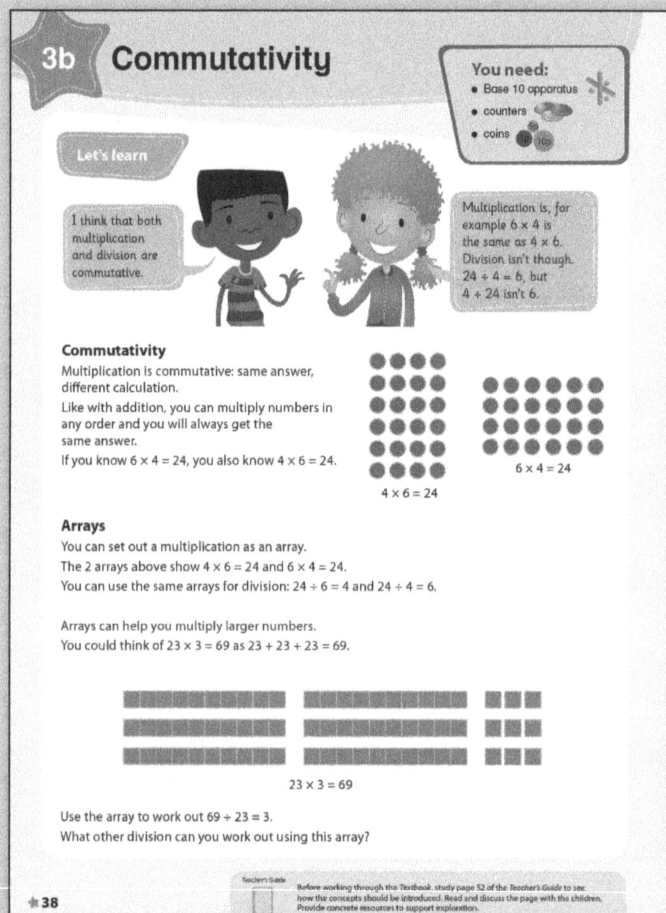
3b Commutativity

You need:
- Base 10 apparatus
- counters
- coins

Let's learn

I think that both multiplication and division are commutative.

Multiplication is, for example 6×4 is the same as 4×6. Division isn't though. $24 \div 4 = 6$, but $4 \div 24$ isn't 6.

Commutativity

Multiplication is commutative: same answer, different calculation.

Like with addition, you can multiply numbers in any order and you will always get the same answer.

If you know $6 \times 4 = 24$, you also know $4 \times 6 = 24$.

$4 \times 6 = 24$

$6 \times 4 = 24$

Arrays

You can set out a multiplication as an array.

The 2 arrays above show $4 \times 6 = 24$ and $6 \times 4 = 24$.

You can use the same arrays for division: $24 \div 6 = 4$ and $24 \div 4 = 6$.

Arrays can help you multiply larger numbers.

You could think of $23 \times 3 = 69$ as $23 + 23 + 23 = 69$.

$23 \times 3 = 69$

Use the array to work out $69 \div 23 = 3$.

What other division can you work out using this array?

Teacher's Guide

Before working through the *Textbook*, study page 52 of the *Teacher's Guide* to see how the concepts should be introduced. Read and discuss the page with the children. Provide concrete resources to support exploration.

38

Let's learn: Modelling and teaching

Commutativity

- Ask children to look at the arrays in the Textbook and to set them out using counters. Ask what is the same and what is different about their two arrays. Agree that the number of counters is the same and that the numbers of rows and columns are different. Ask them what they could to make them exactly the same. Agree they could turn one around. Discuss that multiplication is commutative and division is not.
- Refer to the cartoon and highlight that if children understand commutativity, they will only need to learn half of their multiplication facts. Next give children a multiplication statement using two, three, five or ten, such as $6 \times 5 = 30$. Ask them to write the other multiplication fact and the two division facts from this
- Practise multiplication facts for three and six. Emphasise that they can double the answers for three to give six, e.g. $8 \times 3 = 24$ so $8 \times 6 = 48$. Display the facts and ask them to write down the commutative facts.

Arrays

- Give children 24 counters and ask them to make as many different arrays as they can, recording the appropriate multiplication and division statements.
- Next give them Base 10 apparatus and ask them to make the array for 23×3, as shown in the Textbook, pointing out the repeated addition. Ask them what multiplication facts they can use to find the product; e.g. $2 \times 3 = 6$, so $20 \times 3 = 60$, and $3 \times 3 = 9$, therefore $23 \times 3 = 69$. They can group the Base 10 tens and ones to check. Encourage them to write down all their calculations using number statements. Repeat for other multiplication calculations, such as 42×3 and 23×4.

Let's practise: Digging deeper

Step 1

This task asks children to use a known fact to make other facts. Children need to use sets of three numbers to make up two multiplication and two division statements. Work through a few examples together, e.g. 2, 4, 8: $2 \times 4 = 8$, $4 \times 2 = 8$, $8 \div 2 = 4$ and $8 \div 4 = 2$. You could add variation to this activity, e.g. in part a, focus on three as the multiplicand and vary the multipliers so that they are 5, 6, 7, 8 with the appropriate products. Discuss the patterns that are building through this. Ask: *Why is the product is getting higher by three each time?* Expect children to tell you that each time an extra three is being added.

Step 2

Before children begin the task, work through an example such as 3×15. Ask children to make the array using Base 10 apparatus and write this as a repeated addition statement. They then find the product using known multiplication facts, e.g. 3×10 and 3×5, and check by counting the tens and then the ones. Children then write the multiplication statement for the array ($3 \times 15 = 45$). Next ask children what division statement they can see (45 take away groups of 15 gives three groups of 15: $45 \div 15 = 3$). Children can then work independently on the task.

Step 3

Give children a selection of coins. The task asks them to find a 5p coin and then to work out what four and then eight of these would be. Once they have an answer, they make the new amount and count in fives to check that they are correct. They then make the amount again using the fewest possible coins. They repeat this for 6p, using 5p and 1p coins, and then an amount that they choose. Encourage children to challenge themselves and make up a more difficult amount to work with.

Step 4

This task asks children to make up new multiplication and division facts from two given facts. Practise this before beginning the task. Encourage them to be creative and use doubling, halving and multiplying by powers of ten. Write $5 \times 4 = 20$ on the board and demonstrate other facts, e.g. $50 \times 4 = 200$, $200 \div 50 = 4$, $50 \times 40 = 2000$, $25 \times 40 = 1000$, $12.5 \times 40 = 500$, $500 \div 40 = 12.5$.

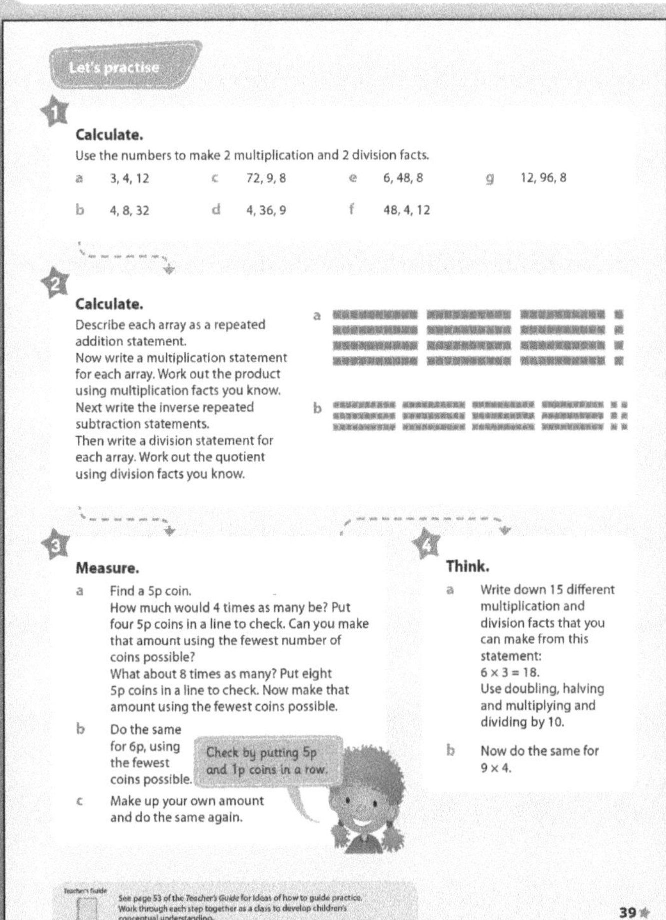

Let's practise

1 **Calculate.**

Use the numbers to make 2 multiplication and 2 division facts.

a	3, 4, 12	c	72, 9, 8	e	6, 48, 8	g	12, 96, 8
b	4, 8, 32	d	4, 36, 9	f	48, 4, 12		

2 **Calculate.**

Describe each array as a repeated addition statement.
Now write a multiplication statement for each array. Work out the product using multiplication facts you know.
Next write the inverse repeated subtraction statements.
Then write a division statement for each array. Work out the quotient using division facts you know.

a

b

3 **Measure.**

a Find a 5p coin.
How much would 4 times as many be? Put four 5p coins in a line to check. Can you make that amount using the fewest number of coins possible?
What about 8 times as many? Put eight 5p coins in a line to check. Now make that amount using the fewest coins possible.

b Do the same for 6p, using the fewest coins possible.

c Make up your own amount and do the same again.

4 **Think.**

a Write down 15 different multiplication and division facts that you can make from this statement: $6 \times 3 = 18$.
Use doubling, halving and multiplying and dividing by 10.

b Now do the same for 9×4.

Teacher's Guide

See page 53 of the *Teacher's Guide* for ideas of how to guide practice. Work through each step together as a class to develop children's conceptual understanding.

39

Ensuring progress

Supporting understanding

It is very important that you focus on arrays for making the link between multiplication and division. Give children pre-drawn arrays showing, e.g. five rows of four dots. They label the column and row and write 20 in the middle. Explore how, if taking away rows of four, there will be five and columns of five will be four

Broadening understanding

You could explore what happens if the divisor is doubled, halved or multiplied by ten in Step 1, e.g. $36 \div 4 = 9$ and $36 \div 2 = 18$. Here the divisor has been halved and the quotient has been doubled because there are more groups. Related division statements such as $72 \div 4$ can be manipulated in similar ways.

Concept mastered

Children can use known facts to generate others and explain their reasoning. They can use and explain arrays for single- and 2-digit numbers.

Follow-up ideas

- Children could collect data from the class, e.g. favourite animals or food, and create a pictogram where each symbol represents four children. They then make up questions for the other children to answer.
- Give children small plastic bags, sand and weighing scales. Ask them to weigh multiples of 100 g of sand and place them in the bags. They then work out the mass of three, four and eight bags. They do this by using and adapting known facts. They fill more bags of the masses and weigh the appropriate number to see if they are correct.

Answers

Step 1

Answers will vary.

Step 2

a $31 + 31 + 31 + 31 = 124$, $4 \times 31 = 124$ (I know that $3 \times 4 = 12$, so $30 \times 4 = 120$).

$124 - 31 - 31 - 31 - 31 = 0$, $124 \div 31 = 4$ (I know that $12 \div 4 = 3$, so $120 \div 4 = 30$).

b $42 + 42 + 42 = 126$, $42 \times 3 = 126$ (I know that $4 \times 3 = 12$, so $40 \times 3 = 120$).

$126 - 42 - 42 - 42 = 0$, $126 \div 42 = 3$ (I know that $12 \div 3 = 4$, so $120 \div 3 = 40$).

Step 3

a $5p \times 4 = 20p$ (20p), $5p \times 8 = 40p$ (20p, 20p).

b $6p \times 4 = 24p$ (20p, 2p, 2p), $6p \times 8 = 48p$ (20p, 20p, 5p, 2, 1p).

c Answers will vary.

Step 4

Answers will vary.

3c Sharing and possibilities

- **Write and calculate mathematical statements for multiplication and division using the multiplication tables that they know.**
- **Solve problems, including correspondence problems in which *n* objects are connected to *m* objects.**

Homework 17 and 18   Practice Book pp 33–5

Representations and resources

Interlocking cubes, paper circles, strips of paper, rulers, scissors, clocks with movable hands, t-shirts and shorts of different colours.

Mathematical vocabulary

Multiplication, division, multiplicand, multiplier, product, dividend, divisor, quotient, multiplication tables

Warming up

Practise clock time. Focus on minutes past. Ask children to use a clock to show you times such as ten minutes past six, 40 minutes past eight. For each they write the digital time, e.g. 6:10 and 8:40. Ask them to work out how many minutes it will be until the next o'clock time. Remind them that finding five minute intervals is straightforward because they can use their multiplication and division facts for five.

Background knowledge

Sharing is a form of division closely related to fractions, e.g. if 12 apples are shared between three children they will each receive a third of the total number of apples. It is not the inverse operation of multiplication. Repeated subtraction or groups is the inverse, not sharing. When working with fractions use the correct vocabulary of vinculum, denominator and numerator. Correspondence problems are those in which a set of objects are connected to another set of objects, e.g. *I have 3 hats and 4 coats, how many different outfits can I make?* When children tackle problems that involve finding all possibilities, they need to work systematically.

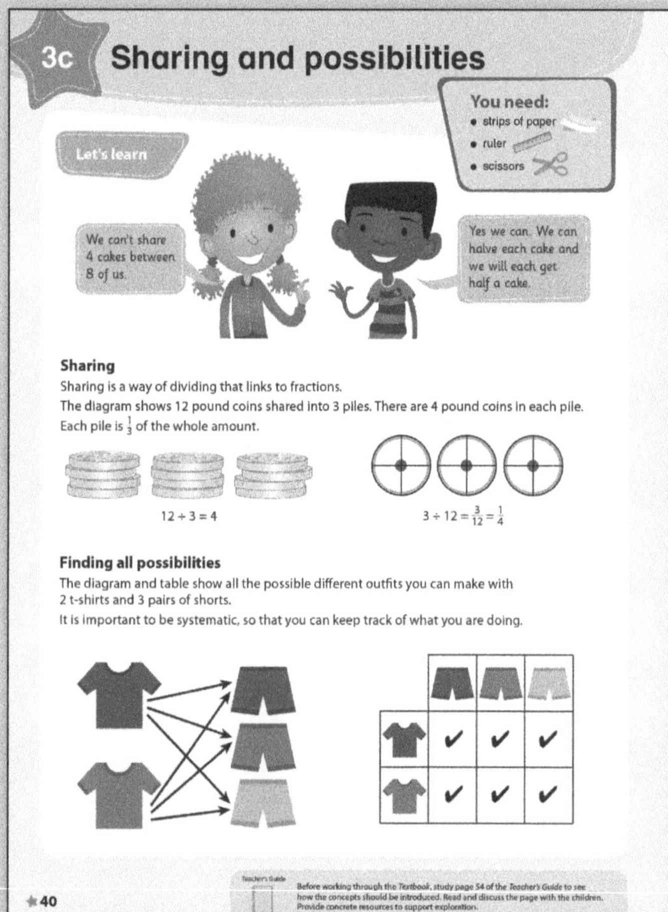
3c Sharing and possibilities

You need:
- strips of paper
- ruler
- scissors

Let's learn

Sharing

Sharing is a way of dividing that links to fractions.
The diagram shows 12 pound coins shared into 3 piles. There are 4 pound coins in each pile.
Each pile is $\frac{1}{3}$ of the whole amount.

$12 \div 3 = 4$ $3 \div 12 = \frac{3}{12} = \frac{1}{4}$

Finding all possibilities

The diagram and table show all the possible different outfits you can make with 2 t-shirts and 3 pairs of shorts.
It is important to be systematic, so that you can keep track of what you are doing.

40

Teacher's Guide: Before working through the *Textbook*, study page 54 of the *Teacher's Guide* to see how the concepts should be introduced. Read and discuss the page with the children. Provide concrete resources to support exploration.

Let's learn: Modelling and teaching

Sharing

- Look at the misconception cartoon in the Textbook. Model sharing the cakes using interlocking cubes or similar equipment. Establish that division is not commutative because 8 ÷ 4 is 2.
- Next look at the models in the Textbook for 12 ÷ 3 and 3 ÷ 12. Ask children to share 12 coins into three groups. Agree that each group has four in it. Provide each child with three paper circles and ask them what they would have to do to divide them by 12. Would there be groups of four? Agree that there would not but that each circle would need to be divided into four equal parts to give 12 parts in total. Children do this and cut out the parts. 3 ÷ 12 will be three of those parts which is equivalent to $\frac{1}{4}$.
- Discuss how a fraction is similar to a division symbol: instead of dots below and above the line there is a denominator and a numerator either side of a vinculum.
- Give children further examples, e.g. 6 ÷ 3 and 3 ÷ 6, 8 ÷ 2 and 2 ÷ 8. Let them use strips of paper that they can fold to help them work these out.

Finding all possibilities

- Look at the diagrams of the t-shirts and shorts in the Textbook. Agree that they show all the possible combinations of these that can be worn. The diagram and table show two effective ways of finding all the possibilities in a systematic manner. Use real shirts and shorts and invite children to prove that the table is correct.
- Ask them how they think this links to multiplication. Agree that, in the example in the Textbook, one t-shirt can be worn three times with the different pairs of shorts. As there are two t-shirts, they can multiply three by two. Give other examples for them to practically solve using the models shown and see if these link to multiplication, e.g. three hats and four coats.

Let's practise: Digging deeper

Step 1

This task asks children to share different numbers of cakes between different numbers of people. Before they begin, practise a few examples of cakes that can be shared as whole cakes and cakes that can be shared as fractions of the whole. During the task, children to draw pictures of circles to represent the cakes and show how they shared them.

Step 2

Recap the vocabulary for multiplication and division and ensure children know the meaning of multiplicand, multiplier, product, dividend, divisor and quotient. The task asks children to find two quotients when dividing pairs of numbers, so practise these, e.g. $10 \div 2$ and $2 \div 10$. Discuss reducing the fraction to its simplest term. Some children may be able to do this, but it is not essential for mastery at this level.

Step 3

Give children coins so that they can make the amounts of money in the problems. They should do this with the fewest coins. They then share each amount between Oli and his two friends. As they do this they exchange greater values of coins to smaller value, e.g. in the first amount they can share three pound coins. They exchange the last for ten pence coins and share those. There will be one left. They exchange the 50p and 20p to ten pence coins and then share them all.

Step 4

Children need to consider why Oli thought he could make ten different outfits. Agree he probably just added six and four. They then need to decide whether he is correct and explain their thinking. As they do this, they need to work out all the possibilities. They may simply multiply six and four. If so, ask them to prove this using a diagram or table, similar to those shown in the Textbook. Encourage them to be systematic and use one of the models in the Textbook.

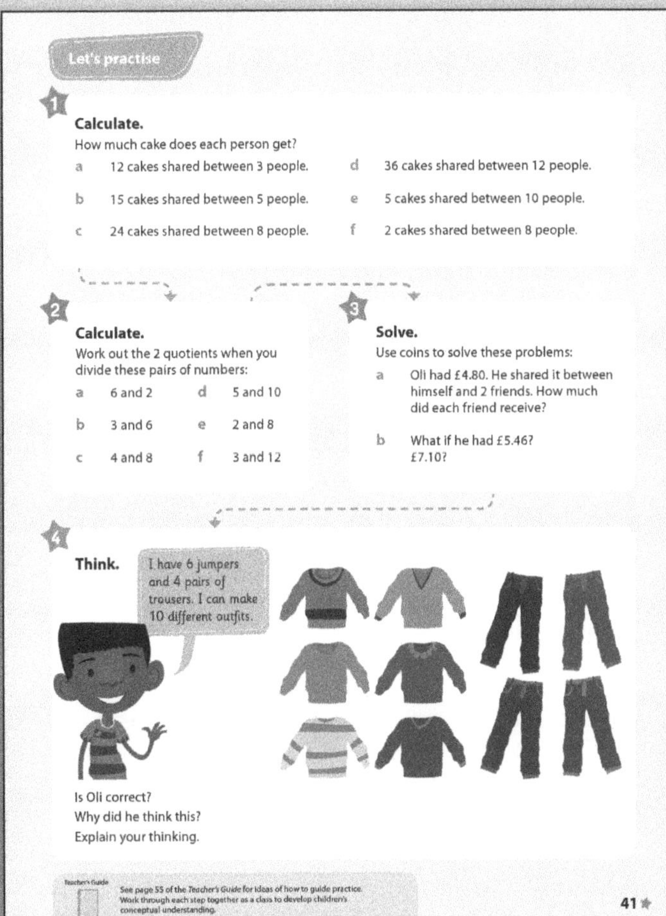
Let's practise

1 **Calculate.**

How much cake does each person get?

a 12 cakes shared between 3 people.
b 15 cakes shared between 5 people.
c 24 cakes shared between 8 people.
d 36 cakes shared between 12 people.
e 5 cakes shared between 10 people.
f 2 cakes shared between 8 people.

2 **Calculate.**

Work out the 2 quotients when you divide these pairs of numbers:

a 6 and 2
b 3 and 6
c 4 and 8
d 5 and 10
e 2 and 8
f 3 and 12

3 **Solve.**

Use coins to solve these problems:

a Oli had £4.80. He shared it between himself and 2 friends. How much did each friend receive?
b What if he had £5.46? £7.10?

4 **Think.**

Is Oli correct?
Why did he think this?
Explain your thinking.

Teacher's Guide
See page 55 of the *Teacher's Guide* for ideas of how to guide practice. Work through each step together as a class to develop children's conceptual understanding.

41

Follow-up ideas

- Children could work out an ice cream problem, which asks how many two-scoop cones can be made from the choices of vanilla, chocolate and strawberry scoops. They could price up the different flavours, e.g. vanilla 20p, chocolate 25p and strawberry 30p, and work out the cost of each possibility.
- Children could weigh out different amounts of sand and work out what quarters, eighths, thirds and/or fifths would be.
- Ask children to draw four different animals on paper and cut them out. They then work out how many different options a zoo could pick, if they only wanted to take three.

Ensuring progress

Supporting understanding

Observe children as they carry out each task. If any need support, use variation for each part, e.g. in Step 1 part a ask them to share three cakes between three, then six, nine, 12 and 15 people. Ask them to tell you what they notice about the pattern they make. They should be able to tell you that the answers are quotients of dividing by three. This will be particularly important for the questions with the fraction quotients, e.g. two cakes shared between two people, four people, six people and eight people.

Broadening understanding

For Steps 1 to 3, ask children to make up similar examples and to explain these to a partner. For Step 4, ask them to draw two models to show their systematic thinking. They could then make up similar problems to solve.

Concept mastered

Children can link sharing with fractions and solve associated problems correctly. They can find all possibilities in a developing systematic way.

Answers

Step 1

a 4
b 3
c 3
d 3
e $\frac{5}{10}$ or $\frac{1}{2}$
f $\frac{2}{8}$ or $\frac{1}{4}$

Step 2

a 3 and $\frac{2}{6}$ or $\frac{1}{3}$
b 2 and $\frac{3}{6}$ or $\frac{1}{2}$
c 2 and $\frac{4}{8}$ or $\frac{1}{2}$
d 2 and $\frac{5}{10}$ or $\frac{1}{2}$
e 4 and $\frac{2}{8}$ or $\frac{1}{4}$
f 4 and $\frac{3}{12}$ or $\frac{1}{4}$

Step 3

a Answers will vary but must be three amounts that add to £4.80, e.g. £2 + £2 + 80p.
b Answers will vary.

Step 4

Oli is incorrect. He can make 24 different outfits. Each jumper can be combined with four different trousers.

Unit 3

Double trouble!

Game 1: Lots of facts

In this game, children use known multiplication and division facts to generate other facts. It is designed to help them reinforce, practise and consolidate the facts and skills involved.

Maths focus

- Recall and use multiplication and division facts for the two, three, four, five, eight and ten multiplication tables

Resources

1 counter per player (1 colour per player), 1–6 dice (1), digit cards, stopwatch or minute timer.

How to play

This game should be played in pairs. Players shuffle the digit cards and place them face down in a pile. They place their counters on Start. They take it in turns to roll the dice and move that number of spaces. They take a digit card and use this and the number they landed on to generate as many related multiplication and division facts as they can in one minute; their partner times them. After the minute is up, their partner checks the facts to make sure they are correct. Each correct fact scores one point. The winner is the player with the highest total, once both players reach Finish.

Making it easier

Support children by encouraging them to use doubling and multiplying by ten to generate new facts. You could allow them to write out some of the multiplication tables before beginning.

Making it harder

Encourage children to use an extended range of strategies, e.g. halving (as well as doubling) and dividing by ten (as well as multiplying by ten). Challenge them to make up facts that involve fractions or decimals; they could score an extra point for these facts.

Game 2: Doubling and doubling

This game gives children an opportunity to practise doubling and doubling again, in order to score points.

Maths focus

- Use mental methods (doubling) to multiply by eight

Resources

1 counter per player (1 colour per player), 1–6 dice (1).

How to play

This game should be played in pairs. Players place their counters on Start. They take it in turns to roll the dice and move that number of spaces. They multiply the number they land on by two and then double and double again, so that they have multiplied by eight. The final answer is the number of points they score. The winner is the player with the highest total, once both players reach Finish.

Making it easier

You could ask children to double the number they land on twice to multiply by four.

Making it harder

Use the game to test children's recall of the multiplication table for eight.. Alternatively, they could multiply the number they land on by three, double for six and double again for 12.

Game 3: Your game

Children should invent their own game designing rules that use the concepts covered in the unit. Challenge children to make their game easier or harder.

Double trouble!

Choose a game to play.

Game 1: Lots of facts

You need:
- 1 counter per player (1 colour per player)
- 1–6 dice
- digit cards
- stopwatch or minute timer

How to play
- Shuffle the digit cards. Place them face down in a pile.
- Each place your counter on Start.
- Take turns to roll the dice. Move your counter that number of spaces.
- Take a digit card. Use the digit card and the number you landed on to make up as many multiplication and division facts as you can in one minute (your partner will time you).
- When your minute is up, ask your partner to check your facts. You score 1 point for every correct fact.
- The winner is the player with the highest total, once both players reach Finish.

Game 2: Doubling and doubling

You need:
- 1 counter per player (1 colour per player)
- 1–6 dice

How to play
- Each place your counter on Start.
- Take turns to roll the dice. Move your counter that number of spaces.
- Multiply the number you land on by 2, then double and double again (so that you have multiplied by 8).
- The final answer is the number of points you score.
- The winner is the player with the highest total, once both players reach Finish.

Game 3: Your game

- Make up your own game using the gameboard.
- Will your game use multiplying, doubling or something else?
- How will you make your game easier or harder?
- What are the rules for your game? Explain them to someone.

Please help your child by reading the instructions and playing the game together.

Unit 3 And finally ...

Assessment task 1

Resources

Base 10 apparatus.

Running the task

Before children begin, remind them that arrays are helpful in showing that it does not matter which way you multiply numbers together, the answer is always the same. They also help us understand that division is the inverse of multiplication. Ask children to set out a calculation such as 8×3 using Base 10 apparatus. Recap the different ways of looking at the array: repeated addition ($8 + 8 + 8$), multiplication (if necessary, stress that 8×3 gives the same answer as 3×8), repeated subtraction ($24 - 8 - 8 - 8 = 0$) and division (which is not commutative, $24 \div 3 = 8$ and $24 \div 8 = 3$).

Then work through an example similar to the one in the task, such as 47×3. Ask children to set out Base 10 apparatus to show the calculation and then discuss in pairs how they can use this to find the answer. Establish that they can add up the tens and then the ones. They then exchange 20 ones for 2 tens and 10 tens for one hundred to give an answer of 141. Finally, ask them if they could answer the question using known multiplication facts. Agree that they could use the fact that $4 \times 3 = 12$, to give $40 \times 3 = 120$ and add that to $7 \times 3 = 21$.

Some children may find answering 46×3 using known facts difficult. If so, model how to break down 46 to 40 + 6 and then find 40×3 by multiplying 4 by 3 and then 10; then work out 6×3 and add the two results together.

Children need to work through this process for a given calculation and then make up and answer their own calculations.

Evidencing mastery

If children can explain and demonstrate how to multiply using arrays and known facts, they are evidencing mastery.

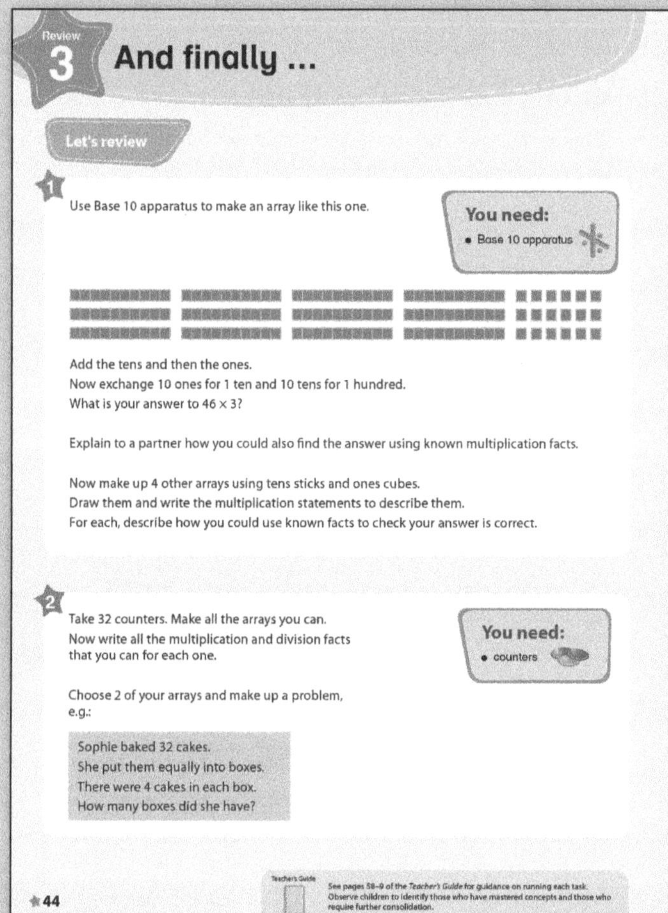
Review 3 And finally ...

Let's review

1 Use Base 10 apparatus to make an array like this one.

You need:
- Base 10 apparatus

Add the tens and then the ones.
Now exchange 10 ones for 1 ten and 10 tens for 1 hundred.
What is your answer to 46 × 3?

Explain to a partner how you could also find the answer using known multiplication facts.

Now make up 4 other arrays using tens sticks and ones cubes.
Draw them and write the multiplication statements to describe them.
For each, describe how you could use known facts to check your answer is correct.

2 Take 32 counters. Make all the arrays you can.
Now write all the multiplication and division facts that you can for each one.

You need:
- counters

Choose 2 of your arrays and make up a problem, e.g.:

Sophie baked 32 cakes.
She put them equally into boxes.
There were 4 cakes in each box.
How many boxes did she have?

44

Teacher's Guide
See pages 58–9 of the *Teacher's Guide* for guidance on running each task. Observe children to identify those who have mastered concepts and those who require further consolidation.

Assessment task 2

Resources

Counters.

Running the task

This task asks children to make as many arrays as they can with 32 counters. Before they begin, practise with 12 counters. Encourage them to work systematically and to explain how they know they have found all the possibilities. Discuss whether, e.g. the 2×6 and 6×2 arrays are the same and what this shows (the numbers and the answers are the same, but the calculation is different; this is a demonstration of commutativity). Next ask them to write down all the multiplication and division facts that they can for each of their different arrays for 12, including commutative facts. If necessary, remind them that multiplication and division are inverse operations and that, whilst multiplication is commutative, division is not. Children should be able to give an example to show this (e.g. $12 \div 6 = 2$ but $6 \div 12 = \frac{1}{2}$. Children should then be able to independently complete the same task using 32 counters.

The second part of the task asks children to make up a problem for two of their arrays. Again, you could explore this before they begin, using their arrays for 12. An example problem for 32 is given in the Textbook; a different example for 12 might be: *There are 6 skirts and 2 jumpers. How many different outfits can you make?* Ask children to work out the answer systematically and then compare it with the multiplication statement $6 \times 2 = 12$.

Evidencing mastery

If children can explain how to make arrays and how to make corresponding multiplication and division statements, and give examples, they are evidencing mastery.

3

Share 24 counters into groups of equal sizes.
Find all the possibilities.
Write a division statement for each one to show what you have done. Write the fraction of the whole that each group is.

Do this again for 36.

Choose you own number to explore.

You need:
• counters

How can you be sure you have found all the ways?

Did you know?

The French word *commuter* means 'to switch or substitute'.

The suffix *-ative* means 'tending to'. So 'commutative' means tending to switch or substitute. That is just what you can do when you multiply or add – switch the numbers around and you will get the same answer.

Lo-res placement

45

Assessment task 3

Resources

Counters.

Running the task

Before you begin, remind children that when we share we are dividing. We share things out equally into groups. The groups are parts of the whole amount and can be written as a fraction. Model an example using counters or by drawing on the board, e.g. show children ten counters randomly arranged, and then ten counters arranged in five groups of two. *Ten things have been shared into five groups. There are two in each group. Each group is $\frac{1}{5}$ of the whole.*

Discuss other structures for division. As well as sharing, they should be able to tell you about grouping (repeated subtraction) and scaling down. Ask them what is the same about the three methods and what is different. Expect clear explanations, e.g. that grouping means taking groups of the divisor away; scaling down is making something a certain amount smaller (and usually involves fractions, such as 'a quarter of the size'); and sharing means putting things into equal groups, so that each group is a fraction of the whole.

The task asks children to find as many ways as they can to share 24 counters into equal groups. As they do this, they write the appropriate division statement and what fraction one part is of the whole. Encourage them to work systematically if they do not do so independently. *How can you be sure you have found all the ways?*

Evidencing mastery

Children who can explain and demonstrate sharing objects into equal groups and fluently describe each group as a fraction are evidencing mastery. They understand the difference between sharing and grouping and understand that one group is a fraction of the whole.

Concepts mastered

- ☑ Children can quickly recall facts for the two, four and eight multiplication tables and corresponding division facts.
- ☑ Children can use known facts to generate others and explain their reasoning. They can use and explain arrays for single- and 2-digit numbers.
- ☑ Children can link sharing with fractions and solve associated problems correctly. They can find all possibilities in a developing systematic way.

Did you know?

The word 'commutative' comes from the French word *commuter* (to switch or substitute) and the suffix *-ative* (tending to). So commutative means 'tending to switch or substitute', which is what we can do when we multiply or add – switch the numbers around and we will get the same answer.

The term was first used in an 1814 memoir by François Servois, a French mathematician, priest and military officer. However, there are records of the use of the commutative property in multiplication and addition from much further back than this, e.g. the Egyptians used it for multiplication. The mathematician Euclid, who was alive sometime in the 3rd and 4th centuries BC, is known to have assumed the commutative property of multiplication in his book *Elements*. It came into more formal use in the late 18th and early 19th centuries. Today the commutative property is a well-known and basic property used in most branches of mathematics.

Unit 4 Angles and shapes

Mathematical focus

★ **Geometry: properties of shape**

★ **Statistics: interpret and present data**

Prior learning

Children should already be able to:

- identify and describe properties of 2-D and 3-D shapes including the number of sides and symmetry in a vertical line
- identify and describe properties of 3-D shapes including the number of edges, vertices and faces
- introduce right angles and compare with quarter turns
- find right angles in shapes
- sort shapes according to shapes with/without right angles.

Key new learning

- Draw 2-D shapes and make 3-D shapes using modelling materials.
- Recognise 3-D shapes in different orientations and describe them.
- Solve one-step and two-step questions using information in scaled bar charts, pictograms and tables.
- Recognise angles as a property of shapes or a description of a turn.
- Identify right angles.
- Identify whether angles are greater than or less than a right angle.

Making connections

- This unit offers opportunities to connect with the art curriculum, e.g. in the requirements that children should be taught to improve their mastery of art and design techniques, including making sculptures with a range of materials. You could ask children to make a selection of 3-D shapes, such as spheres and cuboids out of clay, then put the shapes together to make a sculpture of their choice. You could show children the works of famous artists such as Barbara Hepworth (*The Family of Man* and *Nine Figures on a Hill*) and ask them to look for shapes that they can see. Ask children to collect a range of 3-D shapes and create their own sculpture as Barbara Hepworth did. Connect shapes and fractions. Children should continue to recognise fractions in the context of shapes; it is important to give children the opportunity to explore this during shape and fraction lessons in order to consolidate their learning in both areas.

Talk about

It is important to use precise mathematical vocabulary from the beginning. This unit involves a good deal of vocabulary related to geometry, including the names of shapes (e.g. polygon, polyhedron, prism, pyramid) and properties (e.g. angle, edge, face, vertex). Ensure that children use this vocabulary correctly when identifying shapes and describing properties. You might like to create flashcards or posters to help children learn the vocabulary as they move through the unit.

Engaging and exploring

Give children some time to look at the photos in the Textbook and discuss with a partner what they notice before sharing ideas with the class. Provide children with modelling clay and ask them to make a ball. *What is the same and what is different between the snowball and the ball made from clay? What shape are they?* Encourage discussion and revisit the properties of the sphere including the number of edges and vertices.

Ask children: *What shapes is the castle made of?* Give children a mix of 3-D shapes and ask them to match their 3-D shapes to the shapes in the picture. Encourage children to name the shapes correctly and describe their properties. Visualising is an important skill for their future learning and it can be developed further by using physical prompts to describe the shapes they see. Encourage them to use logical and deductive language such as 'because', 'therefore', 'so' and 'must be', when naming and describing each shape.

Children work in small groups to make a cube made from magnetic spheres, interlocking cubes, building blocks and modeling clay. Ask each group to describe the hand movements to one-another when using different material to make the cube and encourage them to describe the properties of each shape. Children work in groups to make cubes from interlocking cubes, building blocks and modeling clay. Ask each group to describe the hand movements to one-another when using different materials to make the cube and encourage them to describe the properties of each shape. *How can you change a cube to a cuboid? Describe what is the same and different. What other materials can we use to make shapes?* Ask children to think of the materials used in real life to make a house. What shape are the bricks? Encourage discussion about the use of different shaped bricks used in building in real life.

Recap what is meant by right angle and quarter turns. Discuss with children how to use a rectangular ruler or a folded piece of paper to check whether or not a shape has a right angle. Show children an empty box and give them time to explore the angles that the faces of the box has. Then turn back to the picture. Encourage children to describe what they see. *How many right angles are there? Are they all the same size?*

Look at the picture of the road signs. Ask: *What is the same and what is different about the signs?* Allow children to talk about all aspects of the signs, including the shape, size and colour, before focusing their attention on the angles in the signs. Ask: *How many angles are there in each shape? Do all shapes have right angles?* Provide children with a sheet of paper and scissors and ask them to make a road sign they may have seen. Discuss the angles the signs may have.

Checking understanding

You will know children have mastered these concepts when they can make 3-D shapes using modelling materials. Children will be able to recognise 3-D shapes in different orientations and describe their properties. Children identify angles as a property of a shape. They can identify whether angles are right angles, greater than or less than a right angle. They are able to sort shapes according to their angles.

Things to think about

- What everyday objects will children use to explore 3-D shapes in different positions?
- What practical opportunities will children have to explore different size angles?
- What types of statistical tables can they use to record their findings?
- What material will children use to build 3-D shapes?
- How will you organise groupings for discussion and activities?
- What opportunities will you give children to explain their reasoning?
- What opportunities will you provide to build fluency?
- Which problem-solving strategies are most appropriate in this unit, e.g.:
    - ▶ What do you notice?
    - ▶ What is the same? What is different?
    - ▶ Another, another, another.
    - ▶ Convince me.

4a Making and describing 3-D shapes

- Draw 2-D shapes and make 3-D shapes using modelling materials.
- Recognise 3-D shapes in different orientations and describe them.
- Solve one-step and two-step questions using information in scaled bar charts, pictograms and tables.

Homework 19 and 20 | Practice Book pp 36–9 | 3D Shapes | 3-D shapes

Representations and resources

3-D shapes: cube, cuboid, cone, cylinder, sphere, triangular, pentagonal and hexagonal pyramid and prism, sphere, hemisphere, modelling clay, 24 long straws and 24 short straws, interlocking triangles, squares and cubes, building blocks, two large hoops, squared paper.

Mathematical vocabulary

Edge, end face, base, square based, pentagonal, hexagonal, pyramid, prism, tetrahedron, vertex, vertices, polyhedron, polygon

Warming up

Play a quick multiplying game to revise the multiplication tables for 4 and 8. Separate the class into two groups 'the 4s' and 'the 8s'. Say a number. The first group multiplies it by 4, the second group multiplies it by 8. Children write their answers on their whiteboards and show them. Share tips for multiplying by 4 and 8, e.g. when multiplying by 4, the number is doubled, then doubled again. When multiplying by 8, the number could be multiplied by 4 first, then double the answer. Demonstrate if necessary with sets of objects of 4 and 8. Adapt accordingly.

Background knowledge

A prism is a 3-D shape solid with two congruent polygons as bases and edges joining the corresponding vertices of the polygons. Prisms are named according to the base, i.e. triangular prism. A prism has the same cross-section along its length and its two end faces are identical. Cubes and cuboids are prisms. A cylinder is not a prism as its end faces are circles, not polygons. A face is a flat surface of a 3-D shape.

Model the correct use of terminology when describing properties of 3-D objects (faces, surfaces, vertex, vertices and edges).

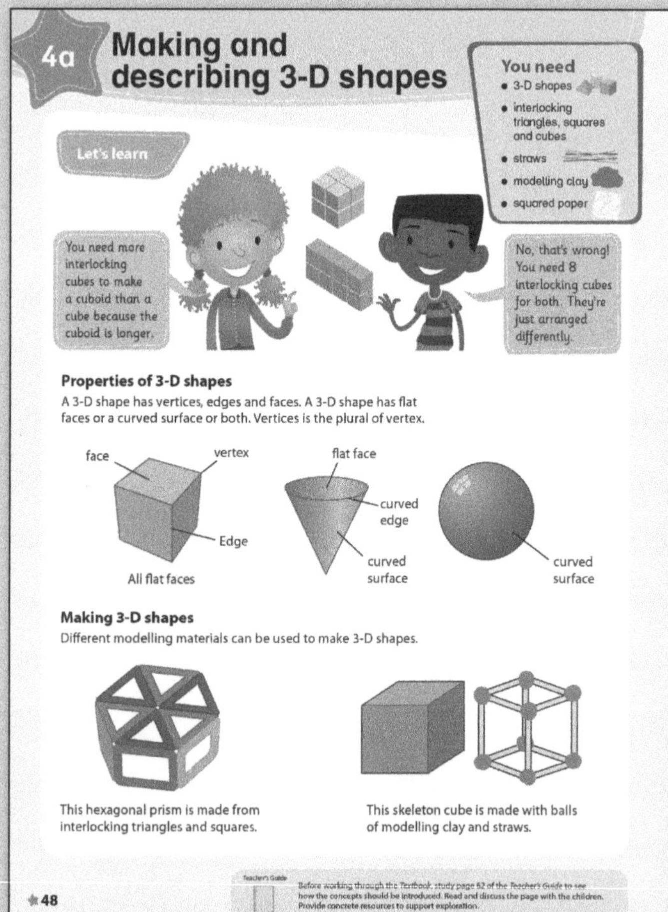

Let's learn: Modelling and teaching

Properties of 3-D shapes

- Using a set of 3-D shapes, encourage children to discuss edges, vertices (vertex), and faces using the correct mathematical language. Write on the board any words children are unsure of and a short explanation or drawing.
- Encourage children to describe the faces of a cone. *What other shapes have curved surfaces?* (sphere, cylinder) *Flat faces?* (pyramids, cuboids, prisms). Challenge them to find examples from their set of 3-D shapes or Textbook. Show children a polyhedron and explain that it is a solid shape with flat faces and no curved surfaces. Remind children of 'polygon': any closed 2-D shape with straight sides.
- Ask children to find a prism. Explain that a prism is the same size and shape all the way through the length. Compare a prism to a sliced loaf of bread. Each slice is the face of a prism and it can be different shapes, e.g. a square (cube or cuboid), triangle (triangle prism).
- Ask children to look for shapes with triangle faces and rectangle face sand to sort them into a Venn diagram made by overlapping two hoops on the floor.

Making 3-D shapes

- Explain that the skeleton of a shape is its frame. Using modelling clay and straws, invite children to make a cube. *Are the straws the same length? What does each straw and clay ball represent?*
- Using interlocking triangles and squares, ask children to make the hexagonal prism. Provide other material, e.g. interlocking cubes and triangles, and ask children to make and explore other 3-D shapes.

Let's practise: Digging deeper

Step 1

Children look at the shapes in different positions, identify and describe their properties. Children should record this information in a table. If they are unsure, show them physical 3-D shapes in different positions. Children should notice that all the sides and faces are the same.

Step 2

Begin by discussing clues to look for in a prism and pyramid, e.g. vertex on the top and triangle faces (pyramid), end faces the same shape (prism). Explain that the shape of the end faces determines the name of the shape, e.g. triangular prism. Children then group the shapes. Ensure they understand how to draw a bar chart and discuss what what 'other' means. Ensure children understand that cuboids and cubes are also prisms. Encourage discussion about the similarities and differences in the prisms in the Textbook.

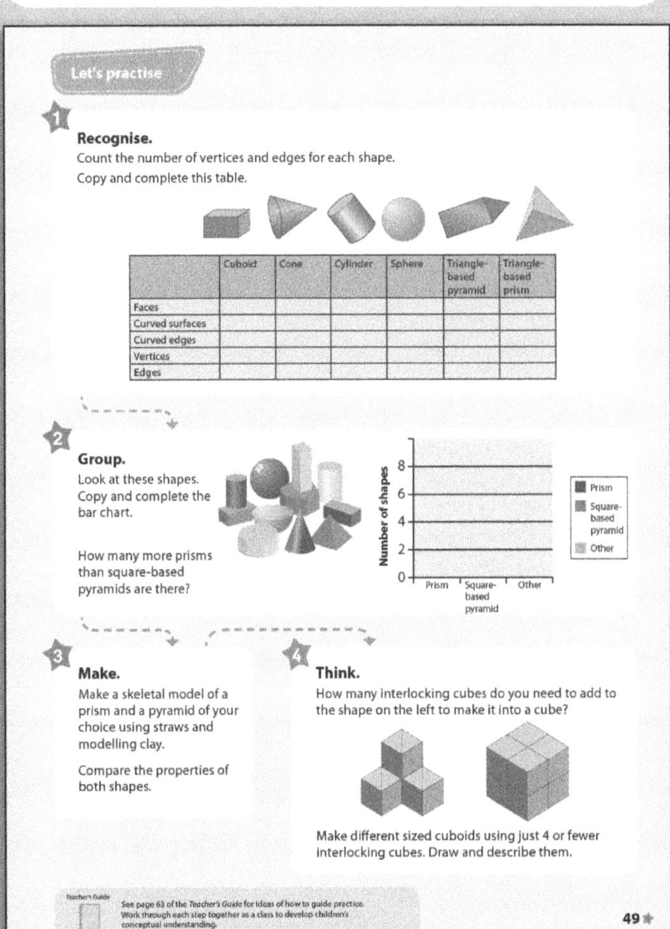

Let's practise

1 **Recognise.**

Count the number of vertices and edges for each shape.

Copy and complete this table.

	Cuboid	Cone	Cylinder	Sphere	Triangle-based pyramid	Triangle-based prism
Faces						
Curved surfaces						
Curved edges						
Vertices						
Edges						

2 **Group.**

Look at these shapes. Copy and complete the bar chart.

How many more prisms than square-based pyramids are there?

Number of shapes: 0, 2, 4, 6, 8

Prism, Square-based pyramid, Other

3 **Make.**

Make a skeletal model of a prism and a pyramid of your choice using straws and modelling clay.

Compare the properties of both shapes.

4 **Think.**

How many interlocking cubes do you need to add to the shape on the left to make it into a cube?

Make different sized cuboids using just 4 or fewer interlocking cubes. Draw and describe them.

Teacher's Guide

See page 63 of the *Teacher's Guide* for ideas of how to guide practice. Work through each step together as a class to develop children's conceptual understanding.

49

Follow-up ideas

- Children work in four mixed-ability groups: the 'triangle', 'square', 'rectangle' and 'circle group'. Each group uses different materials, e.g. magnets, building blocks, modelling clay, sticks, wooden blocks, interlocking shapes. They make models of 3-D shapes that have at least one face in the same shape as their group's name. Display the best shapes in the classroom.
- Children play 'Who am I?' in two groups. One group chooses a 3-D shape and says three clues about it. If the other group finds the shape after one clue, they get three points, after two clues, two points and after three clues, one point, e.g. *I have five faces, one is square, four are triangles. Who am I?* The groups swap round; the group with the most points wins.

Step 3

Encourage children to discuss the different prisms and pyramids they know. Discuss whether the straws need to be the same length. If children are unsure allow them to use different length straws and see whether the shape is what they expected.

Step 4

Children compare both shapes. Look out for those who only count the interlocking cubes they see. Ask children about the properties of a cube and encourage them to visualise the shape.

Give each child four small cubes and ask them to create different cuboids and compare their properties. Question children about the smallest/largest sized cuboid they can make.

Ensuring progress

Supporting understanding

Provide examples of 3-D shapes in different positions in the classroom, e.g. ball at the end of the room, cylinder pencils unsharpened in different positions. Ask children to describe the shapes they see and the ones they do not see.

Draw the shapes on the board, then write their key properties for children to refer to if they are stuck.

Broadening understanding

Challenge children to investigate whether there is a link between the number of vertices and the number of edges a 3-D shape has. Children could make a table and list different 3-D shapes, comparing the number of edges and vertices for each shape.

Concept mastered

Children can make 3-D shapes using modelling materials. They can recognise 3-D shapes in different orientations and describe their properties.

Answers

Step 1

	Cuboid	Cone	Cylinder	Sphere	Triangle based pyramid/ tetrahedron	Triangle based prism
Faces	6	1	2	0	4	5
Curved surfaces	0	1	1	1	0	0
Curved edges	0	1	2	0	0	0
Vertices	8	1	0	0	4	6
Edges	12	0	0	0	6	9

Step 2

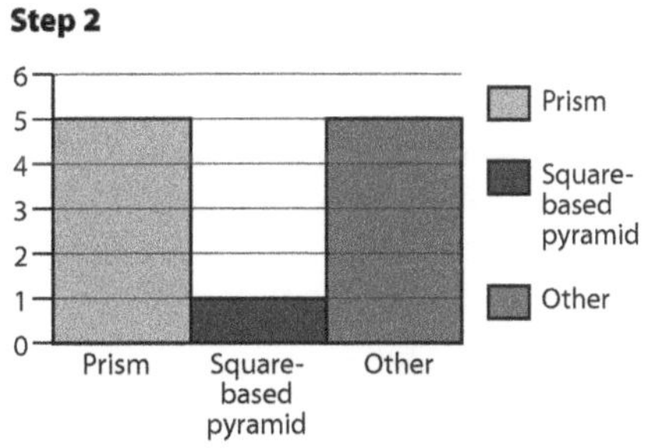

There are 4 more prisms than square-based pyramids.

Step 3

Individual answer.

Step 4

Four more cubes.

4b Angles

- **Recognise angles as a property of shapes or a description of a turn.**
- **Identify right angles.**
- **Identify whether angles are greater than or less than a right angle.**

Homework 21 and 22 | Practice Book pp 40–1 | Right angles

Mathematical vocabulary

Right angle, greater/ less than a right angle, measure, estimate

Warming up

Play a quick addition game to revise adding 2- and 3-digit numbers and ones. Separate the class into two groups: one focusing on 2-digit numbers and the other, 3-digit numbers.

Write two numbers on the board, e.g. 75 and 175. Ask children to add different single-digit numbers to them, one at a time, e.g. 3, 5, 8, 9. Children write their answers on their whiteboards and show them. Share tips for mentally adding numbers, e.g. looking for numbers that make 10 or, when adding 9, they add 10 first, then subtract 1. Repeat for different 3-digit and single-digit numbers.

Background knowledge

An angle is not the shape formed by two lines that meet, nor the point where the lines meet. It is a measure of turn – the size of rotation when you move from one line to the other. When turning from one direction to the other, there are always two angles involved: clockwise and anticlockwise. Children should know that a quarter turn is called a right angle and be able to identify right angles in shapes and objects around them.

Often, children associate the size of an angle with the size of the arms denoting that angle. They prefer the angle with long arms to be the larger angle. Direct children to the amount of turn, rather than to the space between the arms.

Representations and resources

3-D shapes: cube, cuboid, cone, cylinder, sphere, triangular pyramid and prism, sphere, regular and irregular 2-D shape models: triangles, squares, rectangles, quadrilaterals, pentagons, paper circle, straws, paper strips or geo-strips, rulers, coloured pencils, cuboid box.

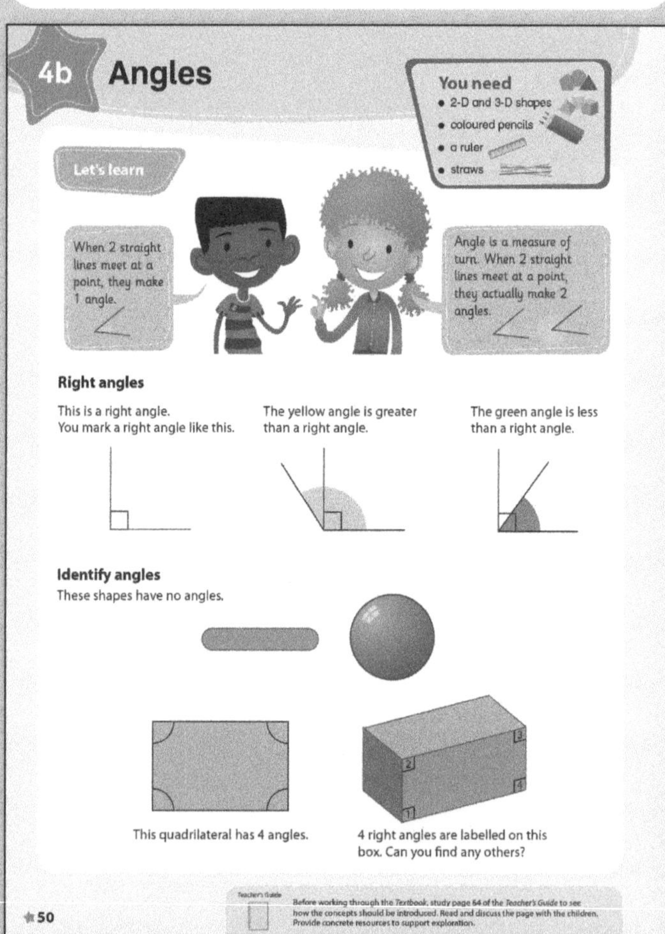
4b Angles

You need
- 2-D and 3-D shapes
- coloured pencils
- a ruler
- straws

Let's learn

When 2 straight lines meet at a point, they make 1 angle.

Angle is a measure of turn. When 2 straight lines meet at a point, they actually make 2 angles.

Right angles

This is a right angle. You mark a right angle like this.

The yellow angle is greater than a right angle.

The green angle is less than a right angle.

Identify angles

These shapes have no angles.

This quadrilateral has 4 angles.

4 right angles are labelled on this box. Can you find any others?

Teacher's Guide

Before working through the *Textbook*, study page 64 of the *Teacher's Guide* to see how the concepts should be introduced. Read and discuss the page with the children. Provide concrete resources to support exploration.

50

Let's learn: Modelling and teaching

Right angles

- Look at the misconception cartoon. Ask: *Is Oli correct? What is an angle?* Listen for their explanations. Draw on the board one straight and one curved line that meet. Highlight the fact that an angle is where two straight lines meet. Draw two *straight* lines and show the clockwise and anticlockwise angles created.
- Provide children with paper strips or geo-strips and encourage them to make different sized angles. Emphasise that the size of the angle does not depend on how long the strips are but how far the strip turns.
- Demonstrate how to make a right angle model by folding a circle of paper and use it to check the size of different angles.

Identify angles

- Discuss with children that not all shapes have angles, e.g. objects with round corners such as a ball. Help children to identify a range of angles in the environment, e.g. angles in the roof or windows. Group the angles into right angles, greater than or less than a right angle.
- Provide children with different models of 2-D shapes, e.g. different sized triangles. Remind children to look for the angles inside the shape rather than outside it. Show children a cuboid box similar to that in the Textbook. *What type of angles do rectangles and squares have?* Encourage generalising where possible.

Let's practise: Digging deeper

Step 1

Before starting, discuss with children the angles they know and how they can tell whether they are right angle, less or more than a right angle. Share their different methods with the rest of the class. Visualising the right angle will help them notice whether the other angles are greater or less than it.

Step 2

Children identify the angles in the shapes. They copy and complete the table. If children are unsure, provide them with different sized triangles, quadrilaterals, pentagon and cylinders. If they feel confident, ask them to draw the shapes, then investigate their angles. To extend, encourage generalising; e.g. children should notice that all cylinders, regardless of size, have no angles at all as they have curved edges.

Step 3

Most children should be able to make one right angle. However, they find it difficult making two or four right angles. Give children time to explore the task and allow them to work in pairs or small groups so they can share ideas. Encourage them to use precise mathematical language, including a quarter turn, clockwise and anticlockwise.

Step 4

Encourage children to draw irregular shapes. Ask them to name and describe the properties of each one. If children are unable to generalise, help them draw more shapes.

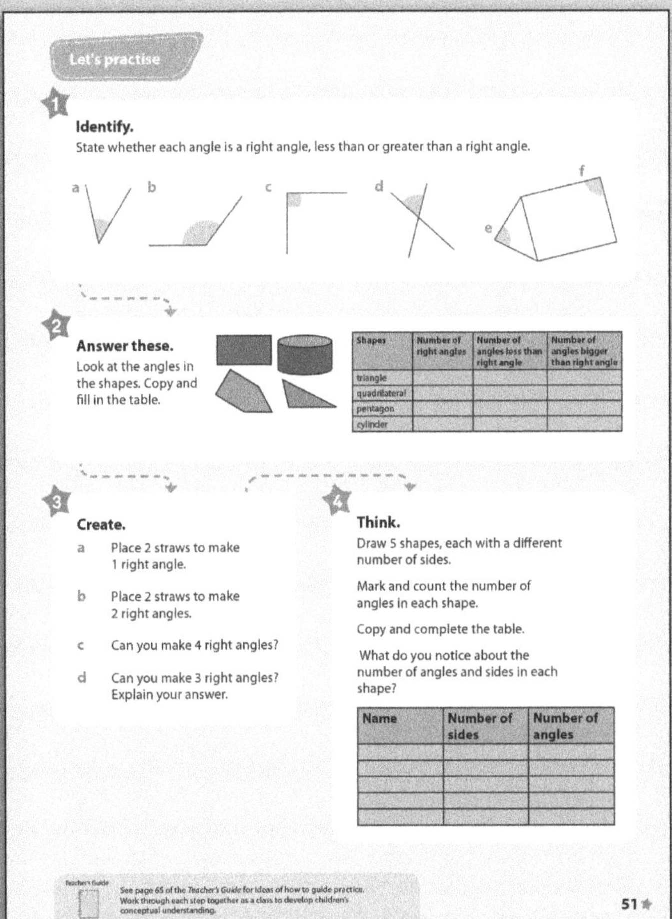

Let's practise

1 **Identify.**
State whether each angle is a right angle, less than or greater than a right angle.

2 **Answer these.**
Look at the angles in the shapes. Copy and fill in the table.

Shapes	Number of right angles	Number of angles less than right angle	Number of angles bigger than right angle
triangle			
quadrilateral			
pentagon			
cylinder			

3 **Create.**

a Place 2 straws to make 1 right angle.

b Place 2 straws to make 2 right angles.

c Can you make 4 right angles?

d Can you make 3 right angles? Explain your answer.

4 **Think.**
Draw 5 shapes, each with a different number of sides.

Mark and count the number of angles in each shape.

Copy and complete the table.

What do you notice about the number of angles and sides in each shape?

Name	Number of sides	Number of angles

Teacher's Guide
See page 65 of the *Teacher's Guide* for ideas of how to guide practice. Work through each step together as a class to develop children's conceptual understanding.

51

Ensuring progress

Supporting understanding

Provide children with lots of examples of right angles in different positions. Encourage them to use geostrips and a clip/fastener to make a right angle, moving the geostrip until they think that they have made a right angle. Visualising and estimating the size of a right angle makes it easier to identify right angles in different shapes. Allow children to use familiar shapes such as squares, rectangles and hexagons. Once they are confident with them, encourage use of irregular shapes.

Broadening understanding

Challenge children to look at the faces of different 3-D shapes such as prisms and pyramids and identify whether the angles they see are greater than, less than or equal to a right angle. Children could make a table of the angles of the faces of different prisms, e.g. a cuboid has six faces. Each face has four angles, hence all the faces of a cuboid have 24 angles. Repeat for the angles of a triangular prism, cuboid, pentagonal prism. *Is there a link between the number of the faces and the number of the angles each 3-D shape has?*

Concept mastered

Children can identify angles as a property of shapes. They can identify right angles and can identify whether angles are greater than or less than a right angle.

Follow-up ideas

- In pairs, children make three right-angled triangles (small, medium and large) on a geoboard. They compare the angles of each triangle. *Can you have a big angle in a small triangle?* Are all right angles the same? Repeat for different sized quadrilaterals.
- Give each pair of children three circular paper pizzas, each with 12 sections drawn on it. Children cut the first pizza so that each slice is a right angle size; the second pizza so that each slice is an angle less than a right angle; the third pizza into three slices each a different angle.

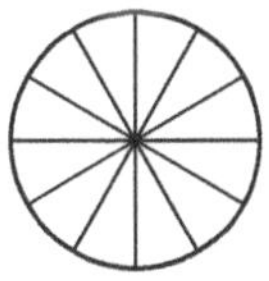

Answers

Step 1

a less than a right angle

b greater than a right angle

c right angle

d less than a right angle

e less than a right angle

f right angle.

Step 2

Shapes	Number of right angles	Number of angles less than right angle	Number of angles greater than right angle
triangle	0	2	1
quadrilateral	4	0	0
pentagon	2	1	2
cylinder	0	0	0

Step 3

Individual answer

Step 4

Individual answer

Unit 4 Angles win points!

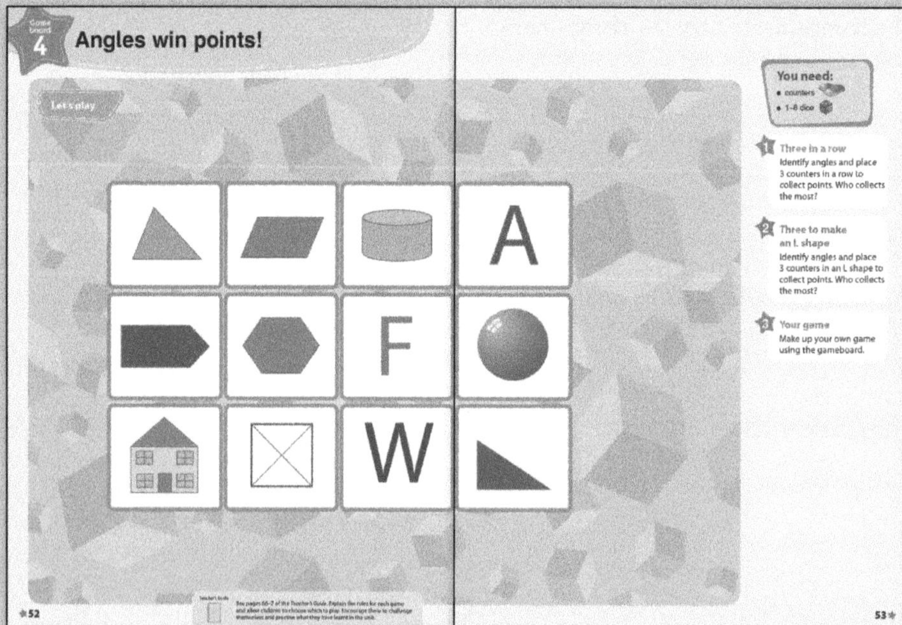

Game 1: Three in a row

This is a simple race game played in pairs. Children land on different shapes throughout the journey and try to identify the shape and angles they see.

Maths focus

- Identify right angles and angles as property of shape

Resources

6 counters per player (1 colour per player), 1-6 dice (1).

How to play

Children take turns to roll the dice. The child with the higher number chooses their counter colour and a square on the board. They roll the dice again and move along the board in any direction (up, down, left, right). They identify whether the angles in the shape or letter they land on are right angles or not. If correct, they place a counter in the square. If wrong, the other child places a counter if they answer correctly instead. If a child places three counters in a straight line they get 10 points. Other counters that are not in row of three are worth a total of 2 points. The winner is the player with the most points once all the counters are placed.

Making it easier

If stuck and unsure, children could 'call a friend' twice and ask for advice twice during the game.

Making it harder

Children could be asked to identify the number of vertices and whether the shape has a vertical line of symmetry.

Game 3: Your game

Children should invent their own game, designing rules that use the concepts covered in the unit.

Challenge children to make their game easier or harder.

Game 2: Three to make an L shape

This is a slightly more complex race game where the player who places three counters in an L shape collects points. Children land on different shapes and are required to identify whether the angles are right angles, greater than or less than a right angle.

Maths focus

- Identify right angles
- Identify whether angles are greater than or less than a right angle

Resources

6 counters per player (1 colour per player), 1-6 dice (1).

How to play

Children take turns to roll the dice. The child with the higher number chooses their counter colour and a square on the board. The child then looks at the shape or letter in the square they chose and says whether each of the angles in it are right angles, less than or greater than a right angle. If correct, they place a counter in the square. If wrong, the other child places a counter instead if they can correctly identify the shape and whether each of the angles are right angles, less than or greater than a right angle. The other child then has their turn. If a child places three counters to make a right angle or an L shape, they score 15 points. All other counters score a total of 4 points.

The winner is the player with the most points once all the counters are placed.

Making it easier

If stuck and unsure, children could 'call a friend' and ask for advice twice during the game.

Making it harder

Children could be asked to sketch the shapes on their whiteboard for an extra 2 bonus points.

Angles win points!

Choose a game to play.

Game 1: Three in a row

You need:

- 6 counters per player (1 colour per player)
- 1–6 dice

How to play

- Each roll the dice. The player with the higher number chooses a square to start from.
- Take turns to roll the dice and identify all the angles in the shape or letter you land on, including the right angles.
- If you do this correctly, put 1 of your counters on the square.
- Complete a line (row, column or diagonal) of 3 counters of the same colour to win 10 points (all counters not in a row are worth 2 points).
- The winner is the player who collects the most points.

Game 2: Three to make an L shape

You need:

- 6 counters per player (1 colour per player)
- 1–6 dice

How to play

- Each roll the dice. The player with the higher number chooses a square on the board.
- Take turns to identify whether the angles on the shape or letter you choose are right angles, greater than or less than a right angle.
- If you do this correctly, put 1 of your counters on the square.
- Complete an L shape of 3 counters of the same colour to win 15 points (counters not in an L shape are worth 4 points).
- The winner is the player who collects the most points.

Game 3: Your game

- Make up your own game using the gameboard.
- Can you think of a way to collect angles as you move along?
- The winner could be the player that collects the most right angles.
- What are the rules for your game? Explain them to someone.

Please help your child by reading the instructions and playing the game together.

Unit 4

And finally ...

Assessment task 1

Resources

3-D shapes, 2 hoops.

Running the task

Ensure children understand the task. They work in small groups and each group has a set of similar shapes. Encourage discussion and ask children to justify their answers. Establish that in group 1, the cube is the only shape that has all the faces in the shape of a square. The other shapes have all got at least one face in the shape of a triangle. In group 2, all the shapes apart from the sphere have a flat face and a curved surface, hence the sphere does not belong in the group.

For the second part of the task, provide children with two overlapping hoops. Ask them to group some or all the shapes in a different way, e.g. shapes that are prisms with at least five vertices and shapes that are not prisms. Is there any shape that will be in the middle of the hoops? Why? Establish that a square-based pyramid has five vertices but is not a prism.

To extend, ask children to work to separate the shapes in different groups and record the information in a bar chart. Ensure that they label the bar chart clearly, e.g. prisms, pyramids, shapes with one or more curved surfaces. Share answers and encourage children to describe the similar properties the shapes in each group have.

Evidencing mastery

Being able to describe and compare the properties of 3-D shapes, including the shape of their faces, the number of faces, edges and vertices shows a deeper understanding of the properties of 3-D shapes.

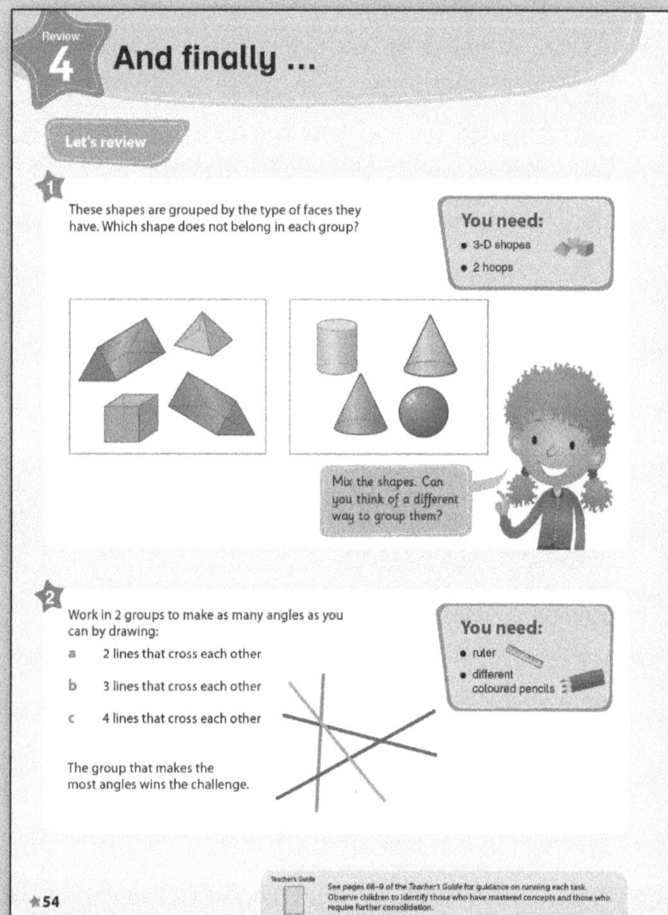
Review 4 And finally ...

Let's review

1 These shapes are grouped by the type of faces they have. Which shape does not belong in each group?

You need:
- 3-D shapes
- 2 hoops

Mix the shapes. Can you think of a different way to group them?

2 Work in 2 groups to make as many angles as you can by drawing:

a 2 lines that cross each other

b 3 lines that cross each other

c 4 lines that cross each other

The group that makes the most angles wins the challenge.

You need:
- ruler
- different coloured pencils

54

Teacher's Guide

See pages 68–9 of the *Teacher's Guide* for guidance on running each task. Observe children to identify those who have mastered concepts and those who require further consolidation.

Assessment task 2

Resources

Ruler, different coloured pencils.

Running the task

Explain to children that this question has many different answers depending on the positions of lines. Lines need to be long enough to pass the crossing point so that the angles are clear to see. Encourage children to look for shapes that are formed when lines cross (triangle, quadrilateral, pentagon, hexagon).

Ask children to 'think, pair, share.' How many possible angles are there when two lines cross? Discuss their answers and invite children to find all the angles. Remind them they are looking for the maximum number of angles to win the task. Children will notice that two lines cross at one point, and there are four angles at that point. Extend the task by asking children to think whether all angles can be right angles, or all angles could be less than a right angle or greater than a right angle.

Allow children to have time to explore the different angles that are formed.

Repeat for three and four lines. Is there a link between the points where the lines meet and the angles formed?

Extend this task by asking children to draw three and four lines that meet at right angles only and to describe the properties of the 2-D shapes formed. Alternatively, you could ask children to record the angles formed in a table and draw a bar chart to represent their work.

Evidencing mastery

Challenging children to make different sized angles is a good way to promote their mathematical reasoning and their decision making. It also shows a deep understanding of describing angles as properties of the 2-D shapes. Some children may attempt to generalise very quickly, saying that three lines make three angles, four lines make four angles and so on. They need more experience in noticing angles as properties of shapes.

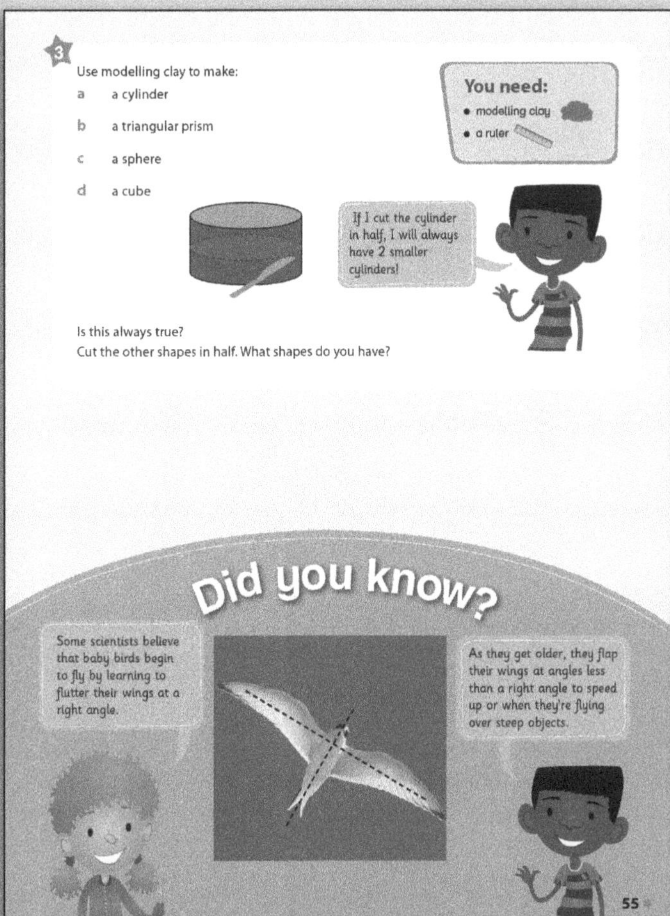

3

Use modelling clay to make:

a a cylinder

b a triangular prism

c a sphere

d a cube

You need:

- modelling clay
- a ruler

If I cut the cylinder in half, I will always have 2 smaller cylinders!

Is this always true?

Cut the other shapes in half. What shapes do you have?

Did you know?

Some scientists believe that baby birds begin to fly by learning to flutter their wings at a right angle.

As they get older, they flap their wings at angles less than a right angle to speed up or when they're flying over steep objects.

55

Concepts mastered

- ☑ Children can make 3-D shapes using modelling materials. They can recognise 3-D shapes in different orientations and describe their properties.
- ☑ Children can identify angles as a property of shapes. They can identify right angles and can identify whether angles are greater than or less than a right angle.

Assessment task 3

Resources

Modelling clay, ruler.

Running the task

Prior to starting the task, ask children to visualise each shape and describe its properties, including the number of vertices and edges. You could place 3-D shapes in different positions and help children to recognise and describe them, e.g. a cylindrical can could be tilted or placed horizontally against the wall, a tennis ball is half covered with one hand.

Discuss with children how they will make a curved surface and a flat face using modelling clay. If they are unsure ask them to think of what they need to do when making a snowball or building a sandcastle.

Ask children to predict what they think the shape will look like when halved. *Is it going to be a different shape? How many faces will it have? In how many ways can the shape be halved?* This is an opportunity to link finding half of a shape with the shape properties. Encourage children to explore all the shapes that can be created when shapes are halved and encourage their curiosity. *Will all cubes make two cuboids when halved? Will all cylinders make two smaller cylinders?* Give children time to question, investigate and generalise.

To extend, explore what would happen if prisms and pyramids are split into three or four parts.

Evidencing mastery

Children who make the shapes by themselves show that they are confident with the properties of each shape. Noticing what is the same and different between the shapes, questioning, exploring and generalising show a deep understanding of properties of shapes and fractions.

Children who are unsure how to halve a shape need more practice in finding fractions of 3-D shapes.

Children who are unsure whether the new shapes are prisms or not, need more practice in recognising different types of prism. Show them different types of prism in different positions, and explore their properties.

Did you know?

Angles are all around us. We use angles in sport when trying to score a goal in football or netball. Even animals and reptiles use angles in their lives. Frogs bend their legs at different angles to jump to escape predators.

Encourage children to think about the use of angles in real life to ignite the interest of learning maths, e.g. children could be asked to investigate questions such as 'Can you imagine a world without right angles?'. 'Are some angles more important than others?' could be the subject of a debate linking mathematics and literacy.

Unit
5
Number and place value

Mathematical focus

★ **Number: number and place value, fractions**

★ **Measurement: length, mass, money**

★ **Statistics: interpret and present data**

Prior learning

Children should already be able to:

- count from zero in multiples of 100
- recognise the place value of each digit in a 2-digit number
- compare and order numbers to 500
- identify, represent and estimate numbers to 500 using different representations
- read and write numbers to 500 in numerals and words.

Key new learning

- Count from zero in multiples of four, eight, 50 and 100.
- Find ten or 100 more or less than a given number.
- Interpret and present data using bar charts, pictograms and tables.
- Recognise the place value of each digit in a 3-digit number.
- Compare and order numbers to 1000.
- Identify and represent numbers to 750 using different representations.
- Read and write numbers to 750 in numerals and words.
- Measure and compare mass (kg/g).
- Count up and down in tenths; recognise that tenths arise from dividing an object into ten equal parts and dividing single-digit numbers or quantities by ten.
- Solve number and practical problems.

Making connections

- This unit presents opportunities for children to solve number and practical problems in a variety of measures contexts. Encourage children to measure, compare, add and subtract lengths (m/cm/mm), mass (kg/g) and volume/capacity (l/ml).
- Adding and subtracting amounts of money is an essential everyday skill that can be practised away from the classroom. Children should use both £ and p notation, recording them separately.

Talk about

It is important to use precise mathematical vocabulary from the beginning. When talking about place value, encourage children to describe the positional and multiplicative aspects of a number, e.g. in the number 325, the digit three is positioned in the hundreds position. To get its true value we multiply three by 100.

Engaging and exploring

Allow children to focus on each picture in turn and to discuss the accompanying question with a partner. Then bring the class together to share ideas.

Discuss the labels that are on the weighing scales and the value of the unlabelled marks. Revise counting in multiples of 100 from zero, noting the halfway points each time. Look at the place value of the number 325 and use partitioning to confirm the value of each digit. Encourage children to check the values using Base 10 apparatus. Discuss which hundreds boundaries 325 sits between and whether it is closer to 300 or 400. *How can we use the markings on the weighing scales to help us decide where 325 g sits?* Link to 350 g being halfway between 300 g and 400 g, and 25 g being half of 50 g.

Look at the snakes and ladders board. Ask children to find multiples of ten more or less than any given number.

Encourage them to investigate different combinations of the numbers from one to six that can be rolled with a conventional dice to equal 30 where not all rolls are the same, e.g. 5, 5, 5, 5, 6 and 4. Next challenge children to find out if it is possible to land on 30 by rolling the same number each time. Establish that this count will need to start from zero, marking the beginning of the snakes and ladders game. Children should recognise that, with conventional dice, all numbers except for four can be rolled continuously to reach 30.

For the picture of the tape measure and rope, discuss the length of the rope in centimetres and also in metres and centimetres. Revise the fact that 1 m = 100 cm using a metre stick. Ask children to tell you how many more centimetres are needed to make the rope two metres long, using mathematical language and number bonds to prove their thinking. Consider the question and discuss how place value can help to solve it. Suggest that the new length should be 196 cm or 187 cm, asking children to explain why a mistake has been made.

Model the picture of the clock using a geared clock. Ask children to give the time that is a number of hours or half an hour earlier or later than the time shown. Show the new time on your geared clock. Now ask children to use card clocks to model counting in steps of five or ten minutes from 12:35, looking carefully at the position of each hand. Challenge them to determine whether the count of ten minutes will ever cause the hour hand to land on an o'clock time. *How would the count need to change for this to be possible?* Discuss the question in the Textbook, looking carefully at some of the counting that children have already done. They should notice that every other time in the five-minute count is also in the ten-minute count because two lots of five minutes is equal to ten minutes.

Look at the coins. Invite children to count in one pounds up to ten pounds using coins. Think about different equivalences, e.g. two £1 coins are equal to a £2 coin, five £1 coins are equal to a £5 note. Show the equivalences using plastic coins and notes. Discuss how many pence there are in one pound. Ask children to recount the £1 coins but now as lots of 100 pennies. Again, look at some of the different equivalences as children count, e.g. a £2 coin is equal to 200 pennies and a £10 note is equal to 1000 pennies.

Checking understanding

You will know children have mastered these concepts when their counting assists them with adding and subtracting and they can make appropriate decisions about when to use their understanding of place value for solving addition and subtraction problems.

Things to think about

- How will you model and encourage the use of precise mathematical vocabulary when explaining thinking and reasoning?
- How will you share the language requirements with other adults before the start of a lesson or sequence of lessons?
- How will you use manipulatives and visual representations to help all children with their conceptual understanding? What have children used before? How can these be developed?
- How will you make effective use of additional adults? Could they support children to rehearse explanations and to model their own thinking?
- How will you incorporate problem solving so that children apply what they have learnt, including in a range of contexts?

5a Counting in steps of different sizes

- **Count from zero in multiples of four, eight, 50 and 100.**
- **Find ten or 100 more or less than a given number.**
- **Interpret and present data using bar charts, pictograms and tables.**

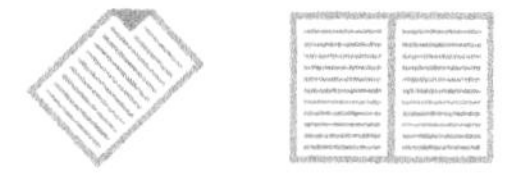

Homework 23 and 24 Practice Book pp 42–5

Representations and resources

Number rods for the numbers two, four and eight, 50p and £1 coins, Base 10 apparatus or place-value counters.

Mathematical vocabulary

Place value, multiples, more than, less than, digit

Warming up

Practise counting on and back in multiples of five and ten. Look carefully at the relationship between the counts and the patterns that emerge in relation to the ones digit. For the tens count, all the ones digits end in zero. For the fives count, the ones digits alternate between zero and five. Ask questions that draw on the relationship, e.g. having reached 80 when counting in tens, ask: *How many tens is that? How many fives?*

Background knowledge

It is important to relate the counting in this concept to the counting that children have done in Year 2. Look at the relationship and patterns between counting in twos and fours, i.e. every other count of two starting from zero is in the count of four. The patterns for fours and eights should be explored in the same way. These counts should be related to multiplication.

Children should also recognise and explain the relationship between counts of 5 and 50 and 10 and 100, including that every two steps of 50 are equal to a step of 100.

5a Counting in steps of different sizes

You need:
- 4 and 8 number rods
- 50p and £1 coins
- Base 10 apparatus
- place-value counters

Let's learn

Counting in steps of 4 and 8

You can use number rods to help you count.

Look at the start of a 4 count and an 8 count.

8		16	
4	8	12	16

The numbers in both counts are all even because you are counting in steps of an even number from zero.

All the numbers in the 8 count are also in the 4 count because every step of 8 is made up of 2 steps of 4.

Counting in steps of 50 and 100

Continue this count of 50p coins.
What amounts do you say?
What patterns do you notice?

50 100

10 or 100 more or less

When you count in steps of 10 from zero the ones digit remains the same: 0, 10, 20, 30, …

When you count in steps of 100 from zero both the tens digit and the ones digit remain the same: 0, 100, 200, 300, …

The same rule is also true for counting in steps of 10 or 100 from any number:

104, 114, 124, 134, 144 23, 123, 223, 323, 423

You can use these patterns to help you find 10 or 100 more or less than any number.

58

Teacher's Guide Before working through the *Textbook*, study page 72 of the *Teacher's Guide* to see how the concepts should be introduced. Read and discuss the page with the children. Provide concrete resources to support exploration.

Let's learn: Modelling and teaching

Counting in steps of 4 and 8

- Ask children to recreate the representation of the four and eight number rods shown in the Textbook, counting as they go and extending to 24.
- Establish that all the numbers in the count so far are even. Challenge children to explain why an odd number will never be in a count of four or eight from zero.
- Agree that all the numbers in the eight count are also in the four count, but not every number in the four count is in the eight count.

Counting in steps of 50 and 100

- Use 50 pence coins to recreate the count of 50. Encourage children to discuss any patterns that they see. Establish that, as 50 is a multiple of ten, the ones digit will always be zero. Prove this using a number line.
- Make links between 100 and 50 by counting out five £1 coins. Give the running total in pounds and pence, i.e. £1, £2, £3, £4, £5 and 100 pence, 200 pence, 300 pence, 400 pence, 500 pence.

10 or 100 more or less

- Explore counting in steps of ten and 100 from zero, looking carefully at the digits that remain the same and those that change. Use Base 10 apparatus to confirm thinking.
- Invite children to make 104 using Base 10 apparatus. They then add multiples of ten to replicate the count in the Textbook. Focus on the digits that remain the same and note how others change. Link back to the rule for counting in tens from zero. Counting in steps of 100 from 23 can be explored in the same way.

Let's practise: Digging deeper

Step 1

Children use number rods to continue counting forwards and backwards in multiples of four or eight. Encourage them to say the number of fours they have used rather than just the count number as this will help with further work on multiplication and division. Children go on to identify which numbers appear in both counts.

Step 2

Children should begin by making the numbers using Base 10 apparatus or place-value counters. They then find ten and 100 more and less of each number. Encourage them to explain how the digits change as they find the new numbers. Children can record their results in their own way.

Step 3

Children pick a number from the grid in the Textbook and use 50 pence or £1 coins to record a count in steps of 50 or 100 from zero to the chosen number. They should explain why some of the numbers can be reached by counting in steps of 50 or 100, whereas others can only be reached by counting in steps of 50. Relate this to steps of ten and five, where 20 and 30 can be reached in both counts, but 25 and 35 cannot.

Step 4

Children apply their knowledge of counting in steps of four and eight to help determine the scale used in a pictogram. They then use the scale to find the number of stickers collected by each child, drawing on knowledge of the counts they have been doing. The strategy of part-part-whole will support here as one whole (or a sticker on the pictogram) is worth eight, so each half part is worth four. Draw this out by asking questions such as: *Can you find the scale that Oli has used for his pictogram? What is the whole sticker worth? And the parts?*

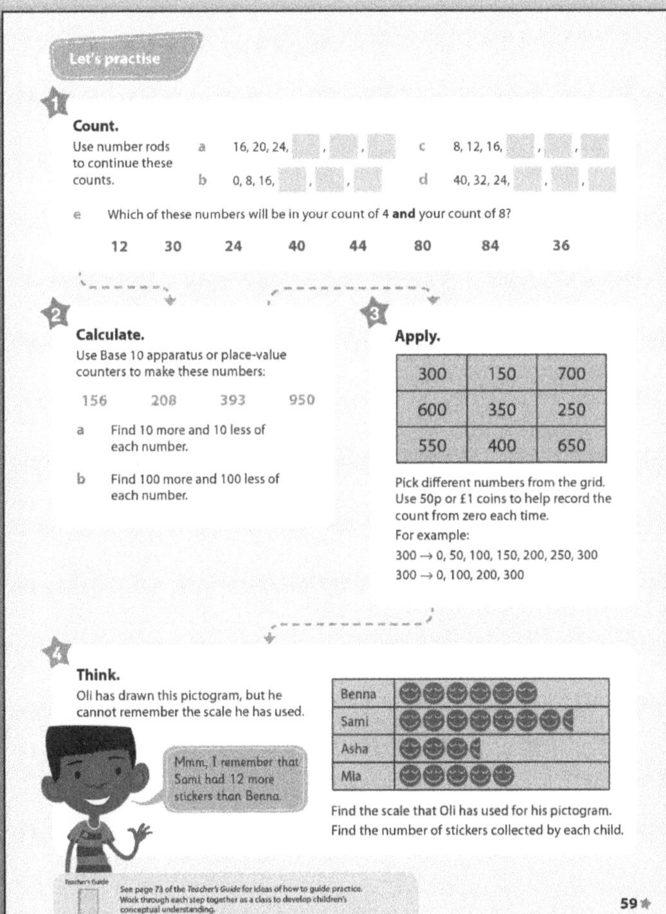
Let's practise

1 **Count.**

Use number rods to continue these counts.

a 16, 20, 24, ▢, ▢, ▢

b 0, 8, 16, ▢, ▢, ▢

c 8, 12, 16, ▢, ▢, ▢

d 40, 32, 24, ▢, ▢, ▢

e Which of these numbers will be in your count of 4 **and** your count of 8?

12 30 24 40 44 80 84 36

2 **Calculate.**

Use Base 10 apparatus or place-value counters to make these numbers:

156 208 393 950

a Find 10 more and 10 less of each number.

b Find 100 more and 100 less of each number.

3 **Apply.**

300	150	700
600	350	250
550	400	650

Pick different numbers from the grid. Use 50p or £1 coins to help record the count from zero each time.

For example:

300 → 0, 50, 100, 150, 200, 250, 300

300 → 0, 100, 200, 300

4 **Think.**

Oli has drawn this pictogram, but he cannot remember the scale he has used.

Find the scale that Oli has used for his pictogram.
Find the number of stickers collected by each child.

Teacher's Guide
See page 73 of the *Teacher's Guide* for ideas of how to guide practice. Work through each step together as a class to develop children's conceptual understanding.

59

Ensuring progress

Supporting understanding

Children could use number rods to make a count of two and then compare it with a count of four. Focus on the fact that it takes two steps of two to equal one step of four.

Broadening understanding

Further develop understanding of the relationship between the four and eight count or the 50 and 100 count by confirming that an even number of steps of four (or 50) are also steps of eight (or 100), whereas an odd number of steps of four (or 50), e.g. three steps of four (or 50), are not.

Concept mastered

Children can count in steps of four and eight and explain why some numbers appear in both counts. They can use the relationship between five and ten to count in steps of 50 and 100. They can find ten or 100 more or less than a given number.

Follow-up ideas

- Link the counts of four and eight to multiplication tables. Focus on the fact that multiples of eight are found by doubling multiples of four.
- Children solve problems involving money or length, e.g. *Oli has £12.50 in his pocket. He only has £1 coins and 50 pence coins. How many of each coin could he have? Mia has $12\frac{1}{2}$ m of ribbon. How many lengths of 100 cm can she cut? How many lengths of 50 cm?*

Answers

Step 1

a 28, 32, 36 **d** 16, 8, 0

b 24, 32, 40 **e** 24, 40, 80

c 20, 24, 28

Step 2

a 146 (156) 166
198 (208) 218
383 (393) 403
940 (950) 960

b 56 (156) 256
108 (208) 308
293 (393) 493
850 (950) 1050

Step 3

e.g.

400 → 100, 200, 300, 400

400 → 50, 100, 150, 200, 250, 300, 350, 400

Step 4

One sticker has a value of eight.

Benna: 48; Sami: 60; Asha: 28; Mia: 40

5b Writing and comparing numbers

- **Recognise the place value of each digit in a 3-digit number.**
- **Compare and order numbers to 1000.**
- **Identify and represent numbers to 750 using different representations.**
- **Read and write numbers to 750 in numerals and words.**
- **Measure and compare mass (kg/g).**

Homework 25 and 26 | Practice Book pp 46–9 | Place Value & Abacus

Representations and resources

Place-value counters, Base 10 apparatus, weighing scales, number lines, place-value grids.

Mathematical vocabulary

Place value, digit, position, multiplicative, additive reasoning, equal, more than, less than, greater than

Warming up

Use the 'Zooming in' strategy to reason about capacity. Give children a criterion, such as a capacity that is greater than 200 ml, and then 'zoom in' using the following criteria: a capacity that is less than half a litre; a capacity that is a multiple of 50 ml; a capacity that is not a multiple of 100 ml; a capacity that is 150 ml less than half a litre. This will zoom in to 350 ml. Repeat using other measures.

Background knowledge

When ordering numbers, it is important to focus on the most significant digit first, i.e. the one that has the greatest value. Children should be confident to explain when these digits have the same value or when they are different. It is useful to include 2- and 3-digit numbers that both start with the same digit, e.g. 346 and 39 or where the 2-digit number is say, 87 and the 3-digit number is 345 to focus on the importance of the position of the digit rather than just the digit itself. Look out for children who compare the digit 8 and 3 and identify 8 as being larger.

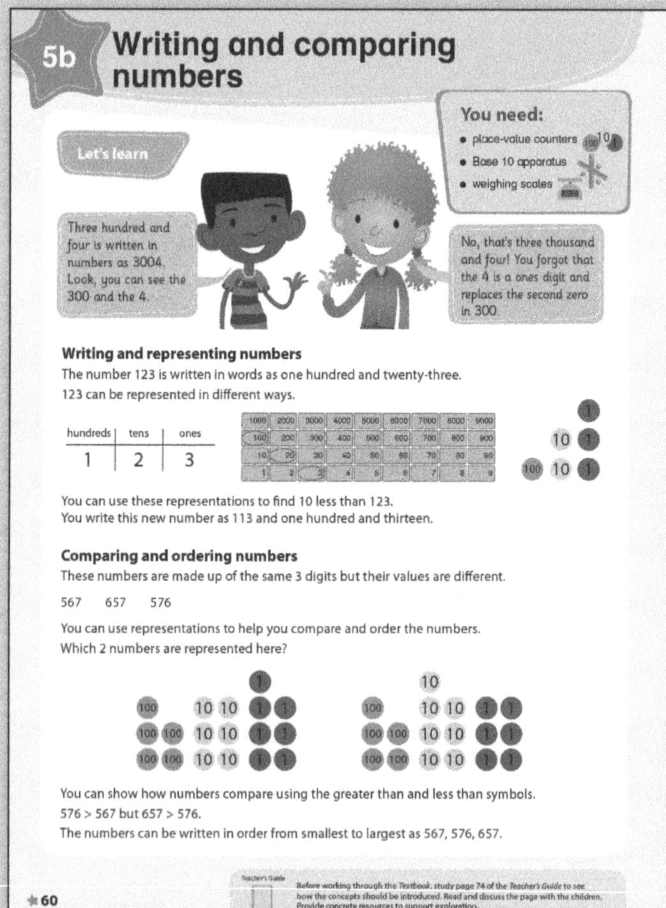
5b Writing and comparing numbers

You need:
- place-value counters
- Base 10 apparatus
- weighing scales

Let's learn

Three hundred and four is written in numbers as 3004. Look, you can see the 300 and the 4.

No, that's three thousand and four! You forgot that the 4 is a ones digit and replaces the second zero in 300.

Writing and representing numbers

The number 123 is written in words as one hundred and twenty-three.
123 can be represented in different ways.

hundreds	tens	ones
1	2	3

1000	2000	3000	4000	5000	6000	7000	8000	9000
100	200	300	400	500	600	700	800	900
10	20	30	40	50	60	70	80	90
1	2	3	4	5	6	7	8	9

You can use these representations to find 10 less than 123.
You write this new number as 113 and one hundred and thirteen.

Comparing and ordering numbers

These numbers are made up of the same 3 digits but their values are different.

567 657 576

You can use representations to help you compare and order the numbers.
Which 2 numbers are represented here?

You can show how numbers compare using the greater than and less than symbols.
576 > 567 but 657 > 576.
The numbers can be written in order from smallest to largest as 567, 576, 657.

60

Teacher's Guide: Before working through the *Textbook*, study page 74 of the *Teacher's Guide* to see how the concepts should be introduced. Read and discuss the page with the children. Provide concrete resources to support exploration.

Let's learn: Modelling and teaching

Writing and representing numbers

- Discuss how the words 'one hundred and twenty-three' relate to the digits in the number 123. Model the way that the positional and multiplicative aspects of each digit can be described, e.g. *In the number 123, the digit one is positioned in the hundreds position. To get its true value we multiply one by 100.*
- Refer to the misconception cartoon. Look carefully at the mistake that Oli has made and how the words 'three hundred and four' may have influenced it.
- Explore different representations of 123 (e.g. using place-value counters or the place-value chart), including partitioning in different ways, e.g. 123 = 120 + 3 or 100 + 10 + 13. Ask children to write in words and represent in different ways the result of adding ten and adding 100 to 123.

Comparing and ordering numbers

- Ask children to read out the three numbers in the Textbook and to think about the way these should be written in words. They will notice that the numbers all contain the same digits but the values are different because of the different positions of the digit each time.
- Look at the representations of two of the numbers in the Textbook. Invite children to match them with 567, 657 or 576. Discuss the positional and multiplicative aspects of each digit in the numbers 567 and 576.
- Model how other representations can be used to help make decisions when comparing numbers, e.g. the number line or a place-value grid.
- Focus on the use of the symbols < and > when comparing.

Let's practise: Digging deeper

Step 1

Children take turns to read the numbers written in words, use manipulatives to represent them and write the numbers using digits. Encourage children to describe the positional and multiplicative aspects of each digit as they write them. Some of the examples will require children to think carefully about the position of a zero as a place holder, e.g. in two hundred and ninety. Support this by asking: *What does the zero tell you?* (There are no ones in this number.)

Step 2

Children explore making different numbers with ten place-value counters. Two examples are given to show how the numbers and counters can vary. Children should record the different numbers they make each time. They could use a place-value grid to support their recording. Encourage them to check their workings by ensuring that the digits in each number sum to ten as there are ten counters, e.g. 433 as 4 + 3 + 3 = 10. Finally, children should pick three of their numbers and order them from smallest to largest, using their representations as an aid.

Step 3

This practical activity is set in the context of mass. Children use digital or balancing scales to weigh pairs of objects in the classroom. They are then required to use their knowledge of place value to make comparisons and record their findings using the symbols < or >, e.g. *If I know that a pencil case is heavier than a rubber, then a book which is heavier than the pencil case must be heavier than the rubber.*

Step 4

This task uses the strategy of 'Maths stories'. The example gathers together some of the representations and other aspects covered in the spread so far and relates them to the number 123.

When writing their own maths stories, encourage children to use or represent manipulatives and to draw on their knowledge of additive reasoning. Also encourage them to feature ways that are not included in the Textbook to represent their chosen numbers. Support discussion by asking questions, e.g. *How do you know that your partitioning is correct? If you know about 100 more than your number, what do you know about 200 more than your number?*

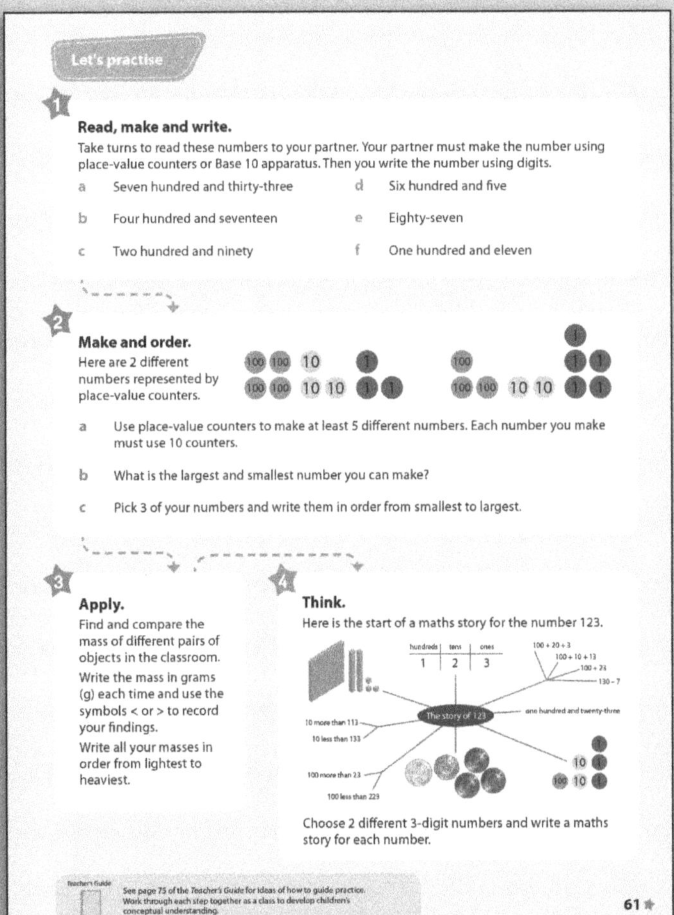
Let's practise

1 **Read, make and write.**
Take turns to read these numbers to your partner. Your partner must make the number using place-value counters or Base 10 apparatus. Then you write the number using digits.

a Seven hundred and thirty-three
b Four hundred and seventeen
c Two hundred and ninety
d Six hundred and five
e Eighty-seven
f One hundred and eleven

2 **Make and order.**
Here are 2 different numbers represented by place-value counters.

a Use place-value counters to make at least 5 different numbers. Each number you make must use 10 counters.
b What is the largest and smallest number you can make?
c Pick 3 of your numbers and write them in order from smallest to largest.

3 **Apply.**
Find and compare the mass of different pairs of objects in the classroom.
Write the mass in grams (g) each time and use the symbols < or > to record your findings.
Write all your masses in order from lightest to heaviest.

4 **Think.**
Here is the start of a maths story for the number 123.

Choose 2 different 3-digit numbers and write a maths story for each number.

Teacher's Guide
See page 75 of the *Teacher's Guide* for ideas of how to guide practice. Work through each step together as a class to develop children's conceptual understanding.

61

Follow-up ideas

- Children could measure and compare pairs of lengths or capacities, using the < and > symbols to record their findings. Challenge children to order the measurements or group them in different ways, e.g. more or less than 250 ml.
- Use catalogues or the Internet to compare prices of different items in pounds up to £750. Children record their findings using the < and > symbols and place a set in order from cheapest to most expensive.
- Investigate how Roman numerals are used to make the numbers one to 12 on a clock face. Focus on the use of V and X to make numbers that sit on either side of five and 10.

Ensuring progress

Supporting understanding

Groups of children could create a 'Maths story' for a 3-digit number less than 750. They could follow the example ideas in the Textbook but adapt them to suit their own number.

Broadening understanding

Use a range of logic-style problems based on the idea of using a given number of place-value counters to make different numbers, e.g. *Mia uses ten place-value counters to make two numbers. Her numbers have a difference of 150. Which numbers can she make?*

Concept mastered

Children can read and write numbers to 750 in words and numerals. They can represent numbers in many ways and use these to help them compare and order pairs or sets of numbers.

Answers

Step 1

a 733 **d** 605

b 417 **e** 87

c 290 **f** 111

Step 2

a Answers will vary

b 910 is the largest, 19 is the smallest

c Answers will vary

Step 3

Answers will vary

Step 4

Children's own 'Maths story' for a 3-digit number of their choice

5c Tenths

- **Count up and down in tenths; recognise that tenths arise from dividing an object into ten equal parts and dividing single-digit numbers or quantities by ten.**
- **Solve number and practical problems.**

Homework 27 and 28 | Practice Book pp 50–2 | Place Value & Abacus; Fraction Wall

Mathematical vocabulary

Fraction, tenth, half, quarter, divide, equal, whole, denominator

Representations and resources

Paper shapes, number line, clock, place-value chart, fraction bars, place-value grid, set of digit cards (1–9), Base 10 apparatus, paper strips.

Warming up

Draw this diagram on the board. Challenge children to complete it in as many ways as they can to show part-part-whole relationships. This will allow children to draw on their multiplication facts and place-value knowledge. Reinforce the inverse relationship between multiplication and division.

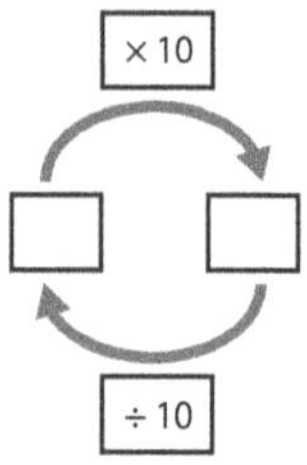

Background knowledge

Any division statement can be written as a fraction and every fraction can be written as a division statement. The divisor becomes the denominator and the dividend becomes the numerator. In this concept you will look at the effect of dividing single numbers by 10, e.g. 2 ÷ 10. It is important that children do not think that the largest number always goes first in a division! Ensure that you relate tenths to place value, in preparation for meeting decimal numbers in Year 4.

Let's learn: Modelling and teaching

Dividing by 10 to make tenths

- Revisit familiar fractions. Use different representations, including paper shapes, number lines and clocks, to focus on the concept of 'equal parts'. Also show representations that are not divided into equal parts.
- Refer to the misconception cartoon in the Textbook. Look carefully at the denominators and the size of the equal parts they represent. Extend the bar diagram in the Textbook to show the whole divided into halves as well as tenths. Encourage children to discuss the images in the Textbook. *How do you know each one shows tenths?*
- Use a place-value chart to explore the movement of the digits as you divide by ten. Start with the numbers 20 and 30. Model how the single digit, one, can also be divided by ten to show that $1 \div 10 = \frac{1}{10}$. Label the new column 'tenths' and further explore dividing two by ten. Look at the way in which division statements can be written as fractions and vice versa.

Counting in tenths

- Remind children that fractions are numbers in their own right and have a place on the number line. Just like whole numbers, the size of fractions will determine their position.

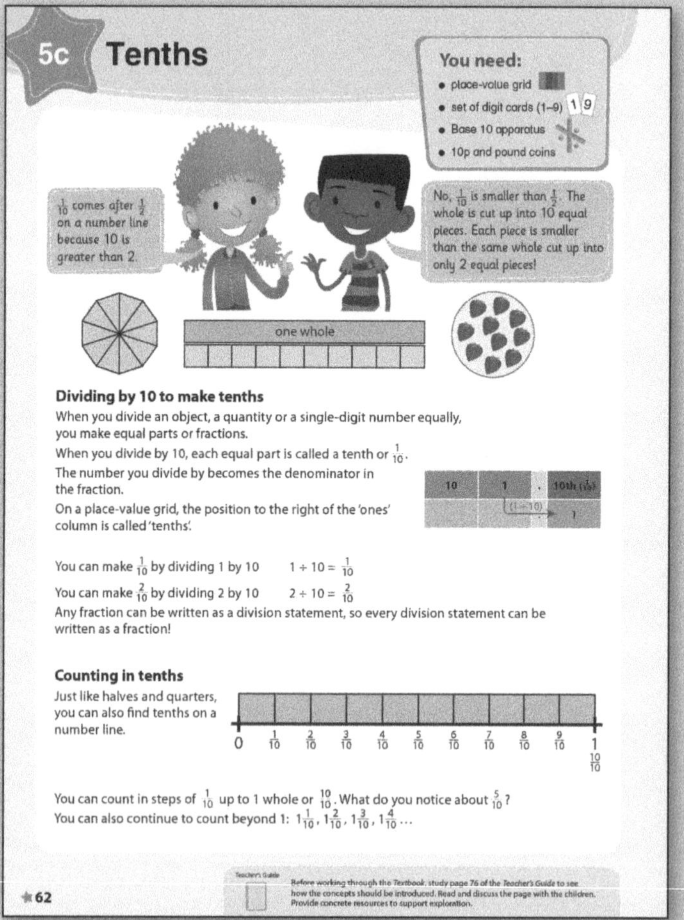

5c Tenths

You need:
- place-value grid
- set of digit cards (1–9)
- Base 10 apparatus
- 10p and pound coins

Dividing by 10 to make tenths

When you divide an object, a quantity or a single-digit number equally, you make equal parts or fractions.

When you divide by 10, each equal part is called a tenth or $\frac{1}{10}$.

The number you divide by becomes the denominator in the fraction.

On a place-value grid, the position to the right of the 'ones' column is called 'tenths'.

10	1	.	10th ($\frac{1}{10}$)
	(1 ÷ 10)	.	1

You can make $\frac{1}{10}$ by dividing 1 by 10 $1 \div 10 = \frac{1}{10}$

You can make $\frac{2}{10}$ by dividing 2 by 10 $2 \div 10 = \frac{2}{10}$

Any fraction can be written as a division statement, so every division statement can be written as a fraction!

Counting in tenths

Just like halves and quarters, you can also find tenths on a number line.

You can count in steps of $\frac{1}{10}$ up to 1 whole or $\frac{10}{10}$. What do you notice about $\frac{5}{10}$?

You can also continue to count beyond 1: $1\frac{1}{10}$, $1\frac{2}{10}$, $1\frac{3}{10}$, $1\frac{4}{10}$ …

62

Teacher's Guide

Before working through the Textbook, study page 76 of the Teacher's Guide to see how the concepts should be introduced. Read and discuss the page with the children. Provide concrete resources to support exploration.

- Encourage children to think about fractions that go beyond one, relating this to counting they have done previously in steps of a half or a quarter.
- Invite children to decide where they would place halves and quarters on a number line. *What could you do to help you check?* Using fraction bars to create a number line is a useful way to represent this concept.
- Count in tenths around the polygon in the Textbook. Agree that ten tenths are equal to one whole. Now focus on the fraction strip and number line. Look at the position of each of the tenths from zero to one and the equivalence of five tenths and one half.
- Count beyond one whole to reinforce the concept that fractions can be greater than one.

Let's practise: Digging deeper

Step 1

Remind children that they can use a place-value grid when working with tenths because our number system is based on tens, i.e. 10 ones equal 1 ten, 10 tens equal 100, 10 hundreds equal 1000 and so on. Children should move the digit cards one place to the right each time to represent dividing by ten. They should record the division statement they use and the fraction that results, e.g. $4 \div 10 = \frac{4}{10}$.

Step 2

Children are asked to reason about four different representations. Encourage children to explain, using fractional language, why some show tenths and some do not. Reinforce the concept of equal parts.

Step 3

Coins are used to show the relationship between tenths and a whole. Establish that the 10p coins are tenths because it takes ten of them to equal one whole pound. As children count in tenths, they exchange $\frac{10}{10}$ for one whole and continue the count in mixed numbers. They should record the total for the group counted, e.g. $1\frac{3}{10}$ and be able to explain how many lots of tenths this is, i.e. 13, or £1.30.

Step 4

Children continue to explore counting in tenths, on and back across one whole. They can use a number line, fraction bars, Base 10 apparatus, 10p coins and so on to support their counting if required. Children's solutions must match the criteria about Mia and Oli's counting each time. Challenge them to reason about Mia and Oli taking an equal number of steps and whether this results in a possible solution. Encourage children to think about how many steps are needed to reach one each time. Encourage children to represent their findings in a table.

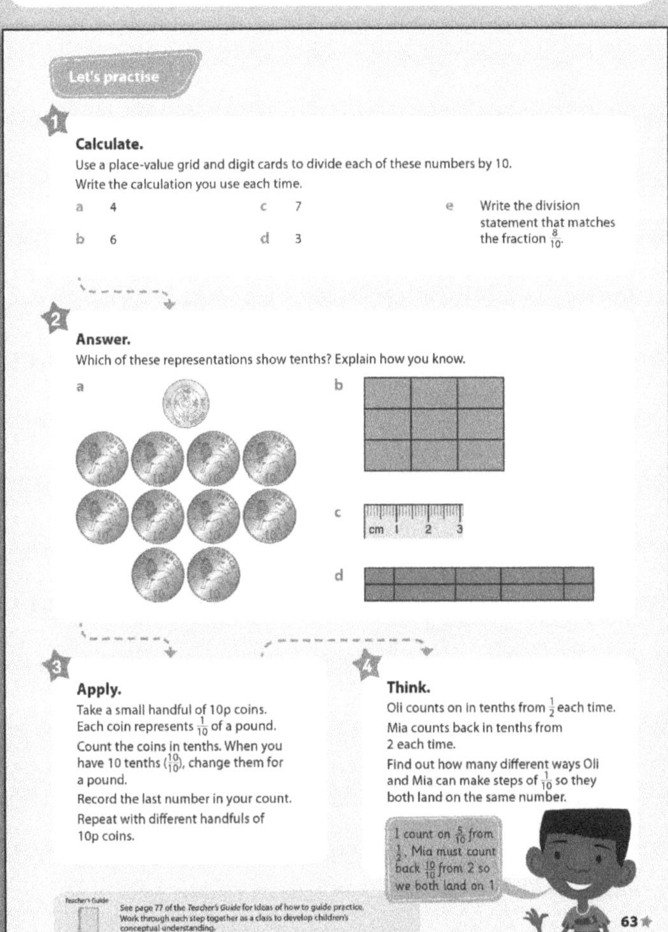

Let's practise

1 Calculate.

Use a place-value grid and digit cards to divide each of these numbers by 10.

Write the calculation you use each time.

a 4 c 7 e Write the division statement that matches the fraction $\frac{8}{10}$.

b 6 d 3

2 Answer.

Which of these representations show tenths? Explain how you know.

a b c d

3 Apply.

Take a small handful of 10p coins.
Each coin represents $\frac{1}{10}$ of a pound.

Count the coins in tenths. When you have 10 tenths ($\frac{10}{10}$), change them for a pound.

Record the last number in your count.

Repeat with different handfuls of 10p coins.

4 Think.

Oli counts on in tenths from $\frac{1}{2}$ each time.

Mia counts back in tenths from 2 each time.

Find out how many different ways Oli and Mia can make steps of $\frac{1}{10}$ so they both land on the same number.

Teacher's Guide

See page 77 of the *Teacher's Guide* for ideas of how to guide practice. Work through each step together as a class to develop children's conceptual understanding.

63

Follow-up ideas

- Continue to use the context of money to explore tenths of a pound. Children can describe amounts such as 90p as nine tenths of a pound.
- Begin to look at finding a tenth of an amount, linking this to multiplication facts and the place-value grid. Pose problems such as, *Oli has £20 and he gives Mia one tenth of his money. How much does he give Mia?*
- Explore patterns, shapes and other images that show tenths or use tenths in some way. This could include ten sections on the counting stick, on a metre ruler, on a weighing scale where 100 g is shown as $\frac{1}{10}$ of each kilogram, ten petals on a flower and so on.

Ensuring progress

Supporting understanding

Folding shapes or strips of paper helps to reinforce the concept of equal parts and enables children to compare the sizes of fractions of the same whole. Divide a strip of paper into ten equal parts. Count each part in tenths, to agree that a whole is made up of ten tenths.

Broadening understanding

Begin to introduce the equivalence of two tenths and one fifth. Encourage children to count in steps of two tenths, so establishing that it takes five steps of two tenths to complete a whole or that five groups of two tenths can be made from one whole.

Concept mastered

Children can identify or represent tenths in a variety of ways, including on a number line. They can count on and back in tenths, exchanging ten tenths and use a place-value grid to model dividing single digits by ten to create tenths, relating this to a division statement, e.g. $1 \div 10 = \frac{1}{10}$.

Answers

Step 1

a $4 \div 10 = \frac{4}{10}$ **c** $7 \div 10 = \frac{7}{10}$ **e** $8 \div 10$

b $6 \div 10 = \frac{6}{10}$ **d** $3 \div 10 = \frac{3}{10}$

Step 2

a and c show tenths

Step 3

Children's own examples, e.g. pick 15 cubes and show this as $1\frac{5}{10}$

Step 4

A table showing examples of counts, e.g.

Land on	Oli	Mia
$\frac{6}{10}$	1 step of $\frac{1}{10}$	14 steps of $\frac{1}{10}$
$\frac{5}{10}$	2 steps of $\frac{1}{10}$	13 steps of $\frac{1}{10}$
1 whole	5 steps of $\frac{1}{10}$	10 steps of $\frac{1}{10}$

Unit 5 Digit decisions!

Game 1: Make it large!

Children must choose the position of their digit cards wisely to get a higher 3-digit number than their opponent.

Maths focus

- Place value and order

Resources

2 sets of digit cards (0–9), sharp pencil, paperclip.

How to play

Each player uses their set of digit cards to make two 3-digit numbers. Children place one end of the paperclip over the centre of the spinner and position the pencil on the dot. They take turns to spin the spinner and decide in which column of the place-value grid to position the digit card that matches the number generated. Players should position each digit card so they have the best chance of making the highest number. Once a digit card has been placed, it cannot be moved. When all four numbers have been made, children order them from smallest to largest.

Making it easier

Children could play in pairs to make the largest possible number between them.

Making it harder

Children could play using the 0–9 digit cards only. They take turns to pick a card from their shuffled face-down pack and place it on the grid to make the highest number.

Game 2: Small numbers

To win this game, children must aim to make the lowest 3-digit number. Encourage them to think carefully about where they should position each digit card.

Maths focus

- Place value and order

Resources

2 sets of digit cards (0–9), sharp pencil, paperclip.

How to play

Each player uses their set of digit cards to make two 3-digit numbers. Children place one end of the paperclip over the centre of the spinner and position their pencil on the dot. They take turns to spin the spinner and decide in which column of the place-value grid to position the digit card that matches the number generated. Players should position each digit card so they have the best chance of making the lowest number. Once a digit card has been placed, it cannot be moved. When all four numbers have been made, children order them from largest to smallest.

Making it easier

Children could play in pairs to make the smallest possible number between them.

Making it harder

Children could play using the 0–9 digit cards only. They take turns to pick a card from their shuffled face-down pack and place it on the grid to make the smallest number.

Game 3: Your game

Children should invent their own game, designing rules that use the concepts covered in the unit. Challenge children to make their game easier or harder.

Digit decisions!

Choose a game to play.

Game 1: Make it large!

You need:

- 2 sets of digit cards (0–9)
- sharp pencil
- paperclip

How to play

- The aim is to make a larger 3-digit number than your opponent.
- Place one end of the paperclip over the dot in the centre of the spinner. Put the sharp end of the pencil on the dot. Take turns to flick the paper clip – where it lands is your number.
- Decide in which column of the place-value grid to place the digit card that matches the number you have generated. Think carefully because you cannot move it later!
- Make 2 numbers each. The player who has made the largest number wins the game.
- Order the 4 numbers from smallest to largest.

Game 2: Small numbers

You need:

- 2 sets of digit cards (0–9)
- sharp pencil
- paper clip

How to play

- The aim is to make a smaller 3-digit number than your opponent.
- Place one end of the paperclip over the dot in the centre of the spinner. Put the sharp end of the pencil on the dot. Take turns to flick the paperclip – where it lands is your number.
- Decide in which column of the place-value grid to place the digit card that matches the number you have generated. Think carefully because you cannot move it later!
- Make 2 numbers each. The player who has made the smallest number wins the game.
- Order the 4 numbers from largest to smallest.

Game 3: Your game

- Make up your own game using the gameboard.
- You could use a dice instead of a spinner so there are fewer digits to place.
- In one game, you could try to make your 2 numbers the largest number and the smallest number possible.
- Play your game with a partner.

Please help your child by reading the instructions and playing the game together.

Unit 5

And finally ...

Assessment task 1

Resources

Number rods, £1 and 50p coins (optional).

Running the task

Before children begin the task, remind them about some of the counting they have been doing in this unit. Tell children that you want to perform a count of eight from zero. *What numbers will be in my count?* Call out a range of numbers, some that could be included in a count of eight and others that could not. Ask children to tell you which numbers will be in your count of eight if you start from zero. Children explain the reasons for their choices.

The task itself can be run using just pencil and paper but, if appropriate, children could have access to number rods and £1 and 50p coins to support their thinking. For all sets of numbers that children are required to write, encourage them to explain their thinking and to give other examples that they know will be included in the count and others that will not.

Evidencing mastery

Mastery is evidenced if children can recognise and explain that multiples of 100 are also multiples of 50 because there are two lots of 50 in every 100. They should be able to apply the same reasoning to multiples of eight, recognising that these are also multiples of four. Children will be able to prove, using mathematical language or representations, why a number such as 12 is a multiple of four but not a multiple of eight.

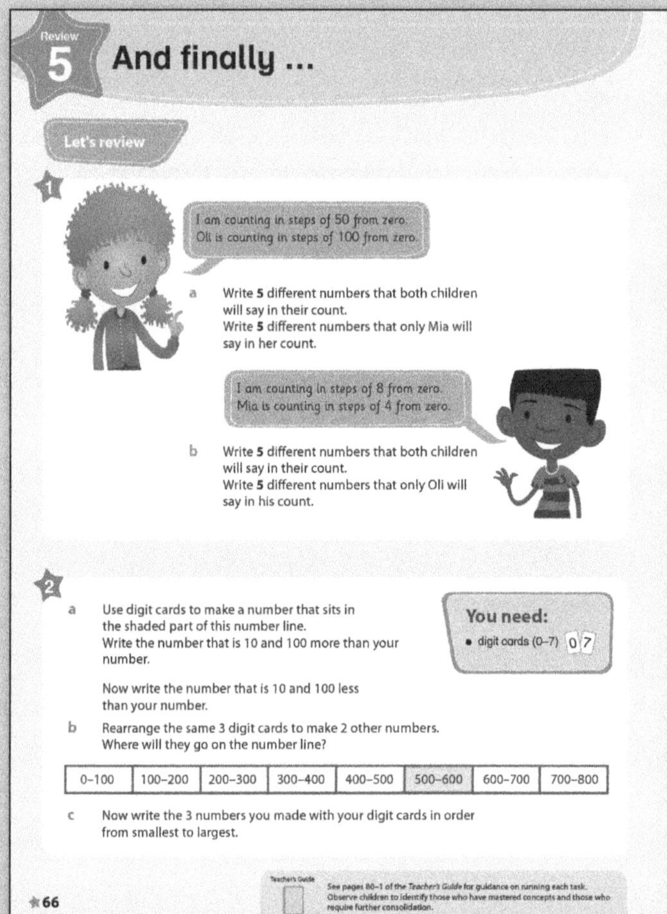
Review 5

And finally ...

Let's review

1

I am counting in steps of 50 from zero.
Oli is counting in steps of 100 from zero.

a Write **5** different numbers that both children will say in their count.
Write **5** different numbers that only Mia will say in her count.

I am counting in steps of 8 from zero.
Mia is counting in steps of 4 from zero.

b Write **5** different numbers that both children will say in their count.
Write **5** different numbers that only Oli will say in his count.

2

a Use digit cards to make a number that sits in the shaded part of this number line.
Write the number that is 10 and 100 more than your number.

Now write the number that is 10 and 100 less than your number.

b Rearrange the same 3 digit cards to make 2 other numbers.
Where will they go on the number line?

0–100	100–200	200–300	300–400	400–500	500–600	600–700	700–800

c Now write the 3 numbers you made with your digit cards in order from smallest to largest.

You need:
- digit cards (0–7) 0 7

66

Teacher's Guide
See pages 80–1 of the *Teacher's Guide* for guidance on running each task.
Observe children to identify those who have mastered concepts and those who require further consolidation.

Assessment task 2

Resources

Digit cards (0–7).

Running the task

Children can work in pairs for this task or on their own. They should be encouraged to look at the labels on the number line and identify the size of each interval as 100. The shaded part of the number line provides the focus for children to make a 3-digit number that could be positioned between 500 and 600. Encourage them to explain whether their number is closer to 500 or 600 and to describe the positional and multiplicative aspects of each digit.

Children apply their knowledge of place value to find the number that is ten and 100 more and less than the number they made with digit cards. They should be able to explain where these sit on the number line, i.e. when the number is 100 more or less, the tens and ones digits remain the same, but the number is positioned between 400 and 500 or between 600 and 700. The task continues as children rearrange the three digit cards to make two other 3-digit numbers and describe the position of these numbers on the number line. Children then order their digit cards from smallest to largest.

Evidencing mastery

Children have evidenced mastery if they can explain the value of each digit in a 3-digit number and can describe or show its position on the number line. They can find ten and 100 more or less than a number, recognising when the tens and ones digits will remain the same. They can also order their digits from smallest to largest, and use place-value to explain why their order is correct.

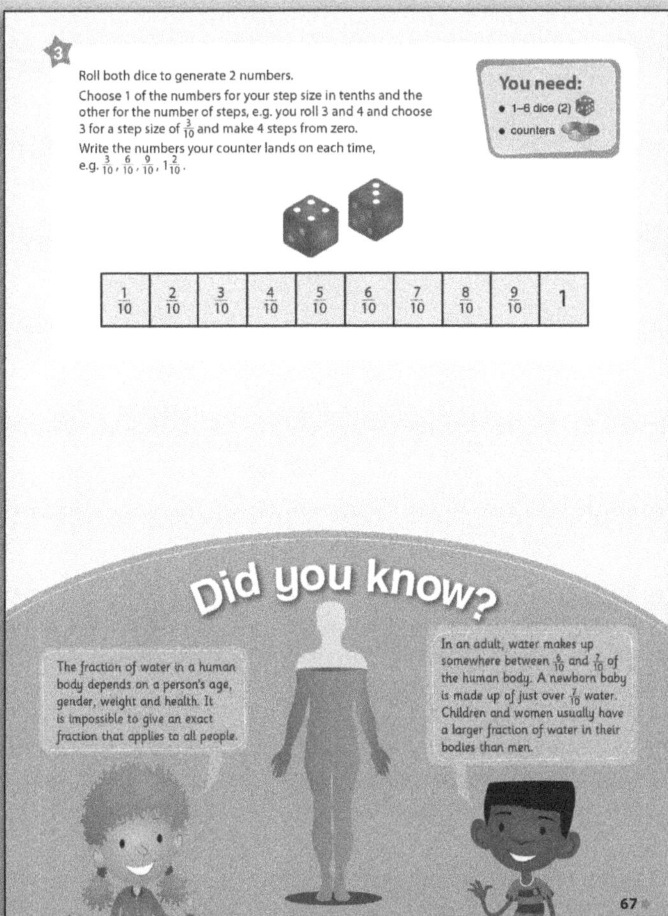
3

Roll both dice to generate 2 numbers.

Choose 1 of the numbers for your step size in tenths and the other for the number of steps, e.g. you roll 3 and 4 and choose 3 for a step size of $\frac{3}{10}$ and make 4 steps from zero.

Write the numbers your counter lands on each time, e.g. $\frac{3}{10}$, $\frac{6}{10}$, $\frac{9}{10}$, $1\frac{2}{10}$.

You need:
- 1–6 dice (2)
- counters

$\frac{1}{10}$	$\frac{2}{10}$	$\frac{3}{10}$	$\frac{4}{10}$	$\frac{5}{10}$	$\frac{6}{10}$	$\frac{7}{10}$	$\frac{8}{10}$	$\frac{9}{10}$	1

Did you know?

The fraction of water in a human body depends on a person's age, gender, weight and health. It is impossible to give an exact fraction that applies to all people.

In an adult, water makes up somewhere between $\frac{6}{10}$ and $\frac{7}{10}$ of the human body. A newborn baby is made up of just over $\frac{7}{10}$ water. Children and women usually have a larger fraction of water in their bodies than men.

67

Concepts mastered

- ☑ Children can count in steps of four and eight and explain why some numbers appear in both counts. They can use the relationship between five and ten to count in steps of 50 and 100. They can find ten or 100 more or less than a given number.
- ☑ Children can read and write numbers to 750 in words and numerals. They can represent numbers in many ways and use these to help them compare and order pairs or sets of numbers.
- ☑ Children can identify or represent tenths in a variety of ways, including on a number line. They can count on and back in tenths and use a place-value grid to model dividing single digits by ten to create tenths, relating this to a division statement, e.g. $1 \div 10 = \frac{1}{10}$.

Assessment task 3

Resources

Two 1–6 dice, counters.

Running the task

Remind children of some of the counting they have been doing in fraction steps. Challenge them to explain some of the ways that we can show tenths and how they arise, e.g. cutting a shape into ten equal parts, dividing a single digit by ten, so $3 \div 10 = \frac{3}{10}$. They should also explain that there are ten tenths in one whole.

Explain the rules of the task and model the example given in the Textbook. If necessary, explain that when children reach the end of the line, i.e. 1, they return to the beginning of the line to continue their count, adding the extra tenths to one whole. Also look at three steps of four tenths, agreeing that both counts finish on the same number but land on different numbers in between. This work begins to introduce the commutativity of fractions and multiplication. Look for children who recognise that five tenths are equivalent to one half.

Evidencing mastery

Children show mastery by counting fluently in tenths and exchanging ten tenths for a whole as they cross a boundary. They write fractions greater than one as a mixed number and begin to recognise that five tenths or $1\frac{5}{10}$ can be written as one half and $1\frac{1}{2}$.

Did you know?

This section looks at the fraction of water in a human body and relates it to tenths. Children could find out the fraction of water that makes up parts of the body, e.g. blood is nine tenths water, bones three tenths water.

The proportions of the human body also provide links with art, e.g. artists tend to use the rules that the eyes are half-way down the face and the nose half-way between the eyes and the chin. Children may find it interesting to use a tape measure to see if these rules are true.

Unit 6
Addition and subtraction

Mathematical focus

- ★ **Number: addition and subtraction, number and place value**
- ★ **Measurement: money, time, distance**
- ★ **Statistics: interpret and present data, solve problems**

Prior learning

Children should already be able to:

- add and subtract numbers mentally, including: a 3-digit number and ones
- add and subtract numbers with up to two digits
- recognise the place value of each digit in a 3-digit number (hundreds, tens, and ones)
- find 10 and 100 more or less than a given number.

Key new learning

- Add and subtract numbers mentally using number facts and place value.
- Add and subtract numbers with up to three digits using the formal written methods of columnar addition and subtraction where appropriate.
- Estimate and use inverse operations to check answers to a calculation.
- Solve addition and subtraction problems in contexts, deciding which operations and methods to use and why.

Making connections

- Children need to know how to apply methods of addition and subtraction in other areas of their mathematical learning, in other subjects at school and in real life, e.g. estimating, comparing and calculating different measures, including money in pounds and pence, is used both in the mathematics curriculum and everyday life. Familiarity with numbers could help children in their PE lessons to understand how much more or less they need to jump or run.
- The unit opener provides an opportunity to convert time between an analogue clock, using Roman numerals, and a normal analogue clock to solve a problem.
- You could link this unit with a 'cooking at school' project. Familiarity with 3-digit numbers could help children to understand better how much they have of an ingredient and how much they need.
- Children will also need to solve comparison, sum and difference problems using information presented in pictograms, tables and other graphs in the later years of Key Stage 2.

Talk about

It is important to use precise mathematical vocabulary from the beginning. To be able to understand whether to add or subtract, children need to understand and use sum, difference, more, less, how much more, how much less, compare, increase, decrease, plus, minus, take away, subtract, total, difference and altogether. They should be able to confidently use the words in context. Plan in how you will introduce these terms.

Engaging and exploring

Look together at the first photo. Discuss why children need to know how much money they have before deciding whether to buy an item. *How much money could there be in the photo? Is £20 a sensible estimate or a silly one? What about £1?* Ask children to give you other sensible and silly answers, explaining why. Encourage discussion about the value of each coin. Challenge children to think about different ways to calculate the total amount of money. Discuss the strategy of starting with the highest value and then adding the other values in order of decreasing size. Listen for children who prefer to group the coins, then add their values, e.g. 2p + 2p + 5p = 9p. Remind children to add two numbers at a time, then add the third number to the sum they found.

Agree that there is 99p in total. Discuss that the skipping rope is £1.99 which can also be written as 199p because there are 100 pennies in each pound. Challenge children to think of how much more money they need (£1 or 100p). Divide the class into groups and provide each table with different sums of coins, e.g. £3.50, £2.97, £4.20. Place items on each table with the price on, e.g. pencil case £2.99. Ask: *Do you have enough money to buy it? How much more money do you need? Will you receive any change?*

For the second photo, talk about the distances we need to travel to visit places. *Why is it important to know how far a place is?* Explain that one kilometre is 1000 metres and relate it to a distance from school so that children can visualise what each distance represents. Separate the class into three groups: Brighton, Cardiff and Paris. Ask children to estimate the difference between 500 km and each value. 243 km and 340 km can be rounded to 200 and 300 km which can be subtracted mentally from 500. 500 – 200 = 300 km and 500 – 300 = 200 km. Then ask children to suggest a strategy for calculating the exact difference. Challenge them to convince the class that they have found the most efficient strategy.

The picture of clocks encourages children to think about the ways that the times are displayed, including the use of Roman numerals. *What is the same? What is different?* Which clock do children find the easiest to use and understand? Revisit what each Roman numeral represents and explain some of the language used to describe time shown on an analogue clock, e.g. past, to, fractions of hours, etc. Discuss how many minutes there are in an hour, half an hour, a quarter of an hour, two hours and so on.

Show the times on two analogue clocks. Ask children to look at the time shown on the clock and compare it to the time the school starts. Write the time shown on the clock as a digital time to compare. Use the clocks to establish that the difference between the 8:35 a.m. and 8:50 a.m. is 15 minutes, hence the school starts in 15 minutes. If children are unsure, provide more examples of showing the time using analogue clocks, digital clocks and clocks that use Roman numerals.

Look at the diagram showing the number of dogs and cats at the Battersea home and talk about what it shows. Discuss why recording this data is important, e.g. to check there is housing available for all the animals, ordering food, cleaning products, employing staff and so on. Discuss the different ways that children have seen data presented, e.g. bar charts, pictograms, tally charts. If possible, show examples of each. Which ones do they find the easiest and the hardest to read? Encourage them to think of examples where each table can be used.

Discuss the scale used on the pictogram. If the whole circle represents 100 animals, what would half a circle represent? What about three-quarters of a circle? Link number, division and fractions. Challenge children to count the full circles they can see (five) and count in hundreds. Challenge them to estimate that there are more than 500 and less than 600 dogs and cats at the Battersea home and encourage them to explain the reasons for their answer.

Things to think about

- What type of manipulatives and visual representations will you use to help all children with their conceptual understanding of adding and subtracting 3-digit numbers?
- How will you create opportunities for children to practise addition and subtraction in real-life situations, including opportunities for meaningful role play?
- How will you provide time and opportunities for children to explain their reasoning?
- How will you organise your groupings?
- What opportunities will you provide to build fluency?
- Which problem-solving strategies are most appropriate?

Checking understanding

You will know children have mastered these concepts when they can solve addition and subtraction problems in different contexts, appropriately choosing and using number facts, showing understanding of place value, counting and mental and written methods. They will be able to find missing calculations and use estimating and inverse operations to check their answers. They can explain their decision making and justify their solutions.

6a Adding 3-digit numbers

- **Add numbers mentally using number facts and place value.**
- **Add numbers with up to three digits using the formal written methods of columnar addition where appropriate.**
- **Estimate and use inverse operations to check answers to a calculation.**
- **Solve addition and subtraction problems in contexts, deciding which operations and methods to use and why.**

Homework 29 and 30 | Practice Book pp 53–5 | Place Value & Abacus

Representations and resources

Place-value counters, interlocking cubes, Base 10 apparatus, cards or sticky notes, calculators, coins.

Mathematical vocabulary

Addition, total, sum, altogether, equal, estimate, more than, less than

Warming up

Play a quick multiplying game to revise the multiplying and division facts for three, four and eight. Give a mixture of multiplication and division questions, e.g. *What is 3 multiplied by 7? What is 21 divided by 3?* Listen for children who notice that multiplying and dividing are the opposite operations. Challenge children by asking them to write number statements for each calculation and derive the multiplying and division facts they know.

Background knowledge

It is important to raise children's awareness that there is a range of strategies they can use. Using real contexts is likely to start discussions about the methods that can be used to find a solution. Partitioning is a method of separating numbers into smaller units so that they are easier to work with. Numbers can be partitioned in other ways rather than tens and units. In the column method of addition, numbers are placed one above each other according to their place value. It is the method where numbers are 'carried' and borrowed'. Children will find this method challenging if they do not have a secure understanding of place value.

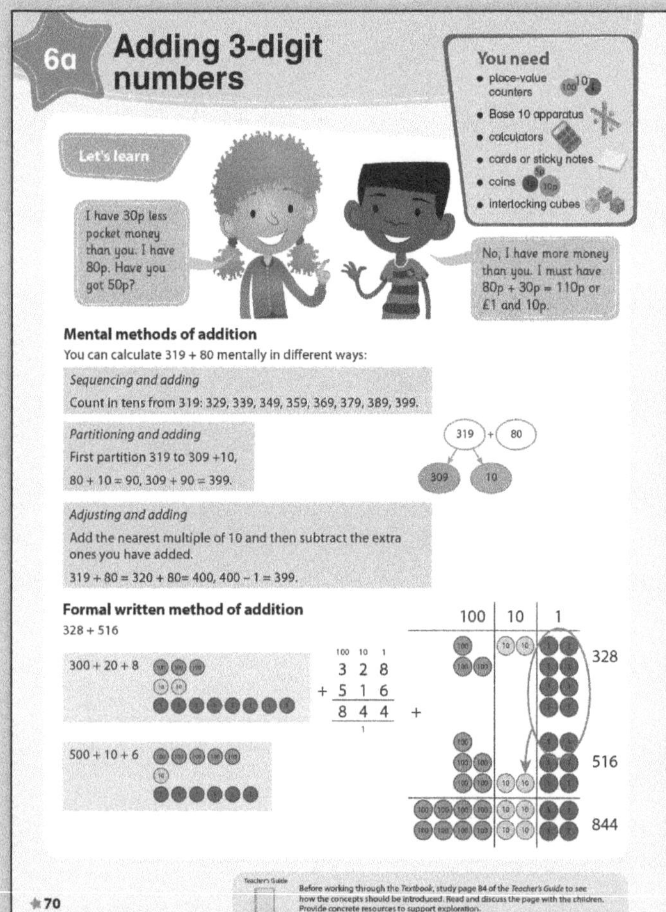
6a Adding 3-digit numbers

You need
- place-value counters
- Base 10 apparatus
- calculators
- cards or sticky notes
- coins
- interlocking cubes

Let's learn

I have 30p less pocket money than you. I have 80p. Have you got 50p?

No, I have more money than you. I must have 80p + 30p = 110p or £1 and 10p.

Mental methods of addition

You can calculate 319 + 80 mentally in different ways:

Sequencing and adding

Count in tens from 319: 329, 339, 349, 359, 369, 379, 389, 399.

Partitioning and adding

First partition 319 to 309 +10,

80 + 10 = 90, 309 + 90 = 399.

Adjusting and adding

Add the nearest multiple of 10 and then subtract the extra ones you have added.

319 + 80 = 320 + 80= 400, 400 − 1 = 399.

Formal written method of addition

328 + 516

300 + 20 + 8

500 + 10 + 6

328 + 516 = 844

★70

Let's learn: Modelling and teaching

Mental methods of addition

- Discuss the Textbook misconception cartoon. Use real money to show the amount that Oli has. Explain that it is very important to understand what the question is asking rather than assuming that 'more' means 'add' and 'less' means take away.
- Look at 319 + 80 and discuss what it shows. Give children interlocking cubes. Ask them to make the two numbers by using towers of hundreds, tens and ones and then demonstrate the methods used for addition in the Textbook. *Which method do they prefer? Why?* Give them more additions (e.g. 237 + 40, 524 + 80). *Who did it in another way? Is there another way to do it?*

Written methods

- Focus on the Textbook example 328 +516. Discuss the importance of estimating to check whether the answer is correct. Ask children to make the two 3-digit numbers using coloured counters or cubes, then add the numbers, working from the most to the least significant digit.
- Write the vertical partitioning calculation on the board. Discuss how this can be checked (by subtracting one number from the sum). Repeat for other 3-digit additions.
- Ensure that children understand that, because 8 + 6 = 14, you carry 1 ten into the tens column. Give children more examples to practise, encouraging them to discuss the benefits of different strategies.

Let's practise: Digging deeper

Step 1

Children are required to add pairs of 3-digit numbers and 2-digit numbers and 3-digit numbers and multiples of 100 using mental methods of their choice. They should be encouraged to explain their choice of method. Some children find mental calculations very difficult. Revisit the number bonds to 100 prior to the task and allow children time to talk through each calculation and work out the answer. To extend, ask children to use subtraction as the inverse of addition to check their answers.

Step 2

Children add pairs of numbers that require a written method of calculation. They should explain why this is the case. They make an estimate first and then use manipulatives to model each of the calculations. Encourage them to use the place value of digits when adding, e.g. 5 hundreds + 3 hundreds or 500 + 300 equals 8 hundreds or 800, rather than referring only to single digits (5 + 3).

Step 3

Remind children that £1 = 100p and ask them to change the prices into pennies when adding. Once they find the total amount, they can change back to pounds and pennies, e.g. £1.28p + 68p is the same as 128 + 68. Using a written method, children find the total to be 196p or £1 and 96p. Ask: *Explain how you added the numbers. Did anyone add the numbers in a different way? What do you have to do first when adding a price given in £ and one given in pence?* To challenge children, allow them to spend £10 and have a variety of items with prices up to and including £7.50.

Step 4

In the first part of the question, the numbers that need adding are given, while in the last three parts, children create their own calculations. They use estimation to find the numbers that need to be added so that the sum is within a certain range. Explain that the question has many answers. Can they find another one? Ask: *Can you make an easy and a difficult calculation? What makes it easy? What makes it difficult?* Use concrete materials if necessary or revise the strategies used when adding. Can they use subtraction to check their answers?

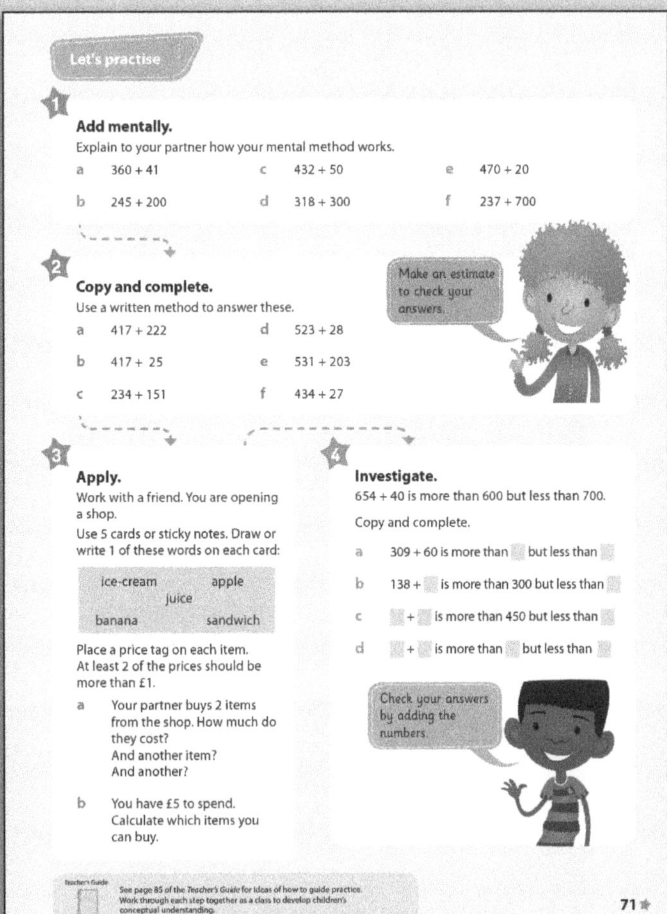
Let's practise

1 **Add mentally.**
Explain to your partner how your mental method works.

a 360 + 41 c 432 + 50 e 470 + 20
b 245 + 200 d 318 + 300 f 237 + 700

2 **Copy and complete.**
Use a written method to answer these.

a 417 + 222 d 523 + 28
b 417 + 25 e 531 + 203
c 234 + 151 f 434 + 27

3 **Apply.**
Work with a friend. You are opening a shop.
Use 5 cards or sticky notes. Draw or write 1 of these words on each card:

ice-cream apple juice banana sandwich

Place a price tag on each item.
At least 2 of the prices should be more than £1.

a Your partner buys 2 items from the shop. How much do they cost? And another item? And another?
b You have £5 to spend. Calculate which items you can buy.

4 **Investigate.**
654 + 40 is more than 600 but less than 700.
Copy and complete.

a 309 + 60 is more than ☐ but less than ☐
b 138 + ☐ is more than 300 but less than ☐
c ☐ + ☐ is more than 450 but less than ☐
d ☐ + ☐ is more than ☐ but less than ☐

See page 85 of the Teacher's Guide for ideas of how to guide practice. Work through each step together as a class to develop children's conceptual understanding.

71

Follow-up ideas

- Work in two groups. Each group throws a 1–6 dice five times. Use the numbers from the dice to make a 3-digit and 2-digit number. Add them up. Now rearrange the numbers so that the sum is as low as possible. *Could you have done it differently?* Repeat to find the highest possible sum. *Which group won?*
- Investigate whether the sum of two odd numbers is always odd, even, or sometimes even and sometimes odd. Would it make a difference if the odd numbers are single-digit, 2-digit or 3-digit numbers? Repeat for even numbers. Generalise where possible.
- Make up word problems where the answer is given, e.g. *This is the answer to a word problem: 231 + 109 = 340. What was the question?*

Ensuring progress

Supporting understanding

You may wish to focus on adding pairs of numbers that do not require any exchanging initially. It is important that children can talk about the place value of each digit in a 3-digit number and refer to this when adding before they are involved with more complex calculations. Continue to use manipulatives alongside a mental or written method.

Broadening understanding

Challenge children to create an easy and difficult question in each of the activities. By creating their own questions, children think about the numbers that can be used when adding the numbers mentally and with a written method. Challenge children to further explore more complex additions by giving them a target sum, e.g *Think of two numbers that add to make 320 or 500.*

Concept mastered

Children can fluently apply knowledge of number facts and place value to support mental work. They can explain the additive property of numbers and refer to it when using a formal written method.

Answers

Step 1

a	401	**d**	618
b	445	**e**	490
c	482	**f**	937

Step 2

a	639	**d**	551
b	442	**e**	734
c	385	**f**	461

Step 4

a 309 + 60 is more than 300 but less than 400

6b Subtracting 3-digit numbers

- Subtract numbers mentally using number facts and place value.
- Subtract numbers with up to three digits using the formal written methods of columnar subtraction where appropriate.
- Estimate and use inverse operations to check answers to a calculation.
- Solve addition and subtraction problems in contexts, deciding which operations and methods to use and why.

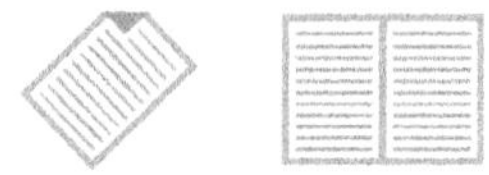

Homework 31 and 32 Practice Book pp 56–8

Representations and resources

Whiteboards and pens, Base 10 apparatus, number lines, tape measures, measuring jugs, water.

Mathematical vocabulary

Subtract, difference, take away, less than, more than, equal, partition, estimate, inverse, addition

Warming up

Separate the class into two groups. Say a 3-digit number, e.g. 521. One group finds ten or 100 more than the number, the other group finds ten or 100 less. Children write their answers on their whiteboards and show them clearly. Swap the groups so that each child has a go at counting on and back.

Background knowledge

It is very important to use manipulatives when teaching the concept of addition or subtraction. Many items can be used as manipulatives, e.g. Base 10 apparatus, number lines, beads, cubes, marbles, stationery items and money. Decomposition is used when subtracting numbers. It refers to breaking down tens into ones or hundreds into tens so that the required subtraction takes place. Working out change is a way to model decomposition. Writing the numbers on paper may help children visualise the numbers and decide what strategy they will use.

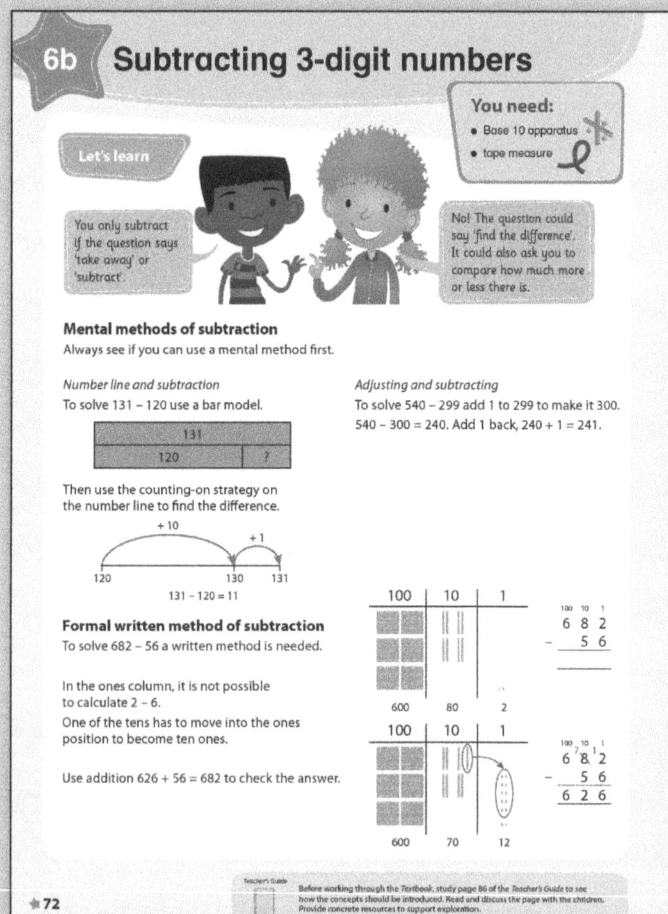

6b Subtracting 3-digit numbers

You need:
- Base 10 apparatus
- tape measure

Let's learn

Mental methods of subtraction

Always see if you can use a mental method first.

Number line and subtraction

To solve 131 – 120 use a bar model.

Then use the counting-on strategy on the number line to find the difference.

131 – 120 = 11

Adjusting and subtracting

To solve 540 – 299 add 1 to 299 to make it 300. 540 – 300 = 240. Add 1 back, 240 + 1 = 241.

Formal written method of subtraction

To solve 682 – 56 a written method is needed.

In the ones column, it is not possible to calculate 2 – 6.

One of the tens has to move into the ones position to become ten ones.

Use addition 626 + 56 = 682 to check the answer.

100	10	1
6	8	2
–	5	6

100	10	1
6	^{7}8	^{1}2
–	5	6
6	2	6

72

Before working through the *Textbook*, study page 86 of the *Teacher's Guide* to see how the concepts should be introduced. Read and discuss the page with the children. Provide concrete resources to support exploration.

Let's learn: Modelling and teaching

Mental methods of subtraction

- Use the misconception cartoon to discuss ways that questions can ask children to subtract. Give examples, using different terminology and ask children to explain what they understand by it. Challenge children to make up their own examples.
- Focus on subtraction calculations that can be solved using the mental method of subtracting multiples of ten or 100, e.g. discuss 850 – 200. Relate this to place value, e.g. 85 – 20 = 65, so 85 tens – 20 tens = 65 tens = 650.
- Use Base 10 apparatus or a number line to work through the examples in the Textbook. Explain that if the numbers in the number line are close to each other, it is easy to subtract mentally by partitioning the numbers and adding in steps from the smallest number to the biggest, e.g. 131 – 120 can be solved by adding 10 to 120, then adding 1, hence the answer is 11. Make sure children can write the subtraction statement horizontally, e.g. 131 – 120 = 11.

Formal written method of subtraction

- Compare the calculation 682 – 56 with other subtractions children have made. The numbers used are not multiples of ten nor close together on the number line. Establish that a formal written method would be appropriate.
- Agree that it is useful to first make an estimate by rounding. Then start with a simple example of columnar subtraction that does not involve exchanging e.g. 531 – 120.
- Model the example in the Textbook using Base 10 apparatus. Ask: *What is the same/different about the apparatus and the written method?*
- Allow children time to ask questions. Explain that the numbers have been partitioned in different ways. Provide different examples and work through them together.

Let's practise: Digging deeper

Step 1

All questions should be solved mentally, and children should relate methods to the numbers involved, e.g. finding the difference because the numbers are close together; using related number facts for two 2-digit numbers, partitioning and adjusting numbers and counting back in tens and hundreds.

Step 2

Children need to use written methods to answer the questions. Only one exchange is needed each time. Children should partition the number in different ways as required by the subtrahend. They should use the bar model to support the formal written method, matching the values each time. Ask: *Which method did you use? What other method could you have used? Which of these methods is quicker? Easier?* Listen to children's replies and revisit any strategies that they find tricky.

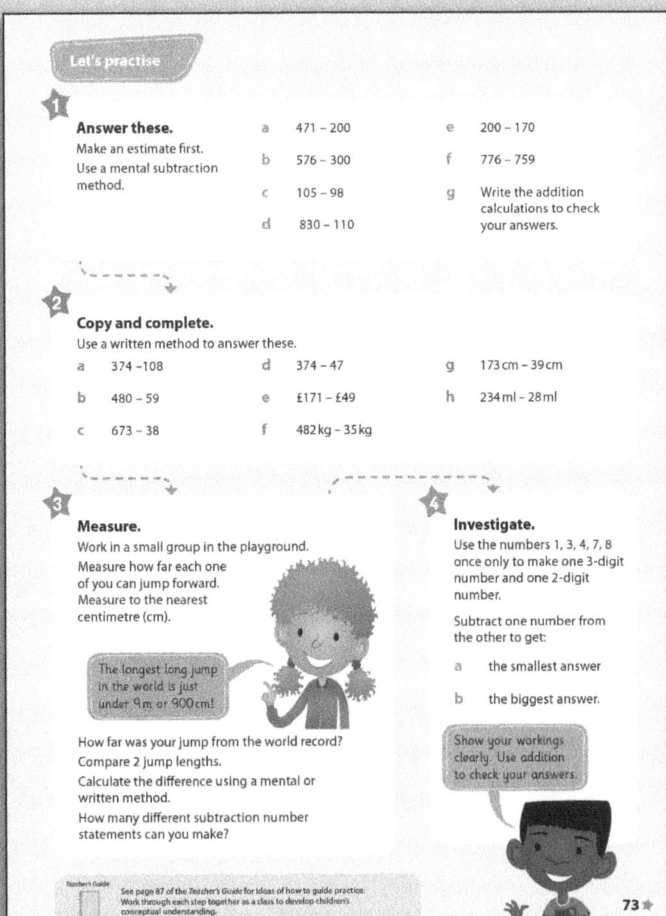
Let's practise

1 **Answer these.**
Make an estimate first.
Use a mental subtraction method.

a 471 – 200
b 576 – 300
c 105 – 98
d 830 – 110
e 200 – 170
f 776 – 759
g Write the addition calculations to check your answers.

2 **Copy and complete.**
Use a written method to answer these.

a 374 –108
b 480 – 59
c 673 – 38
d 374 – 47
e £171 – £49
f 482 kg – 35 kg
g 173 cm – 39 cm
h 234 ml – 28 ml

3 **Measure.**
Work in a small group in the playground.
Measure how far each one of you can jump forward.
Measure to the nearest centimetre (cm).

How far was your jump from the world record?
Compare 2 jump lengths.
Calculate the difference using a mental or written method.
How many different subtraction number statements can you make?

4 **Investigate.**
Use the numbers 1, 3, 4, 7, 8 once only to make one 3-digit number and one 2-digit number.

Subtract one number from the other to get:

a the smallest answer
b the biggest answer.

Teacher's Guide
See page 87 of the *Teacher's Guide* for ideas of how to guide practice. Work through each step together as a class to develop children's conceptual understanding.

73

Step 3

In this task, children record all measurements to the nearest centimetre so they are working with 3-digit numbers. Remind them that 1 m = 100 cm. Children should choose to use mental or written methods as appropriate and be encouraged to explain their choices. If the subtractions involve two exchanges, e.g. 214 – 127, encourage children to use estimates instead and find the difference between them, e.g. 214 can be rounded to 210 and 127 can be rounded to 130. 210 – 130 = 80 (because 21 tens – 13 tens = 8 tens.).

Step 4

In this task most children will create the two biggest numbers and subtract them to give the biggest results. They may create the two smallest numbers and subtract them to give the smallest result. Rather than telling children they are wrong, give them time to explore the task by asking them to subtract a different set of numbers, then another and another. Encourage children to record the results in an increasing order starting with the smallest difference they found. Allow children to use interlocking cubes or counters to help them visualise the question better. Encourage them to discuss their findings and help them generalise.

Ensuring progress

Supporting understanding

Start by revising the number bonds to 20 and 100 initially, then move to subtracting numbers that do not require any exchanging. Allow time for children to practise and ask questions. It is important that they can talk about the place value of each digit in a 3-digit number and refer to this when subtracting before they are involved with more complex calculations. Using manipulatives, e.g. pouring different quantities of water out of a measuring jug, may help children visualise the difference between subtracting a big and a small number from a given 3-digit number.

Broadening understanding

Challenge children to create similar tasks to the ones provided. *Can you make the questions easier/harder?* Encourage them to generalise where possible, e.g. when subtracting two numbers from the same number, the smaller the number you are subtracting, the bigger the result, e.g. 750 – 10 = 740 and 750 – 100 = 650. 740 > 650.

Concept mastered

Children can fluently apply knowledge of number facts and place value to support mental work. They use the written method and their knowledge of partitioning to subtract 3-digit numbers.

Follow-up ideas

- Ask children to solve addition and subtraction word problems involving money and time, that require mental and written methods of addition and subtraction. Remind children that one hour has 60 minutes (rather than 100!). Include one-step and two-step questions.
- Encourage children to make addition and subtraction questions when the answer is given, e.g. *My answer is 111. What is the question?*
- Split the class into two groups. Play the game 'I am thinking of a number' e.g. *I am thinking of a number. I add 85 to my number. My answer is 101. What was my number?* Children work in their group to make questions that require addition and subtraction for the other group. The group with the most correct answers wins.

Answers

Step 1				**Step 2**			
a	271	**f**	17	**a**	266	**f**	447 kg
b	276	**g**	200 + 271; 276 + 300; 98 + 7; 720 + 110; 170 + 30; 759 + 17	**b**	421	**g**	134 cm
c	7			**c**	635	**h**	206 ml
d	720			**d**	327		
e	30			**e**	£122		

Unit 6 Golden treasure!

Game 1: 999 coins

In this game children decide when to use a mental or a written method when adding and subtracting. They must also use their reasoning skills to make the correct decisions.

Maths focus

- Add and subtract 3-digit numbers mentally and using written methods

Resources

1–6 dice (1), 1 counter per player (1 colour per player).

How to play

Play in pairs. Players throw the dice and the player with the highest number chooses 419 or 318 gold coins to have in his treasure chest. Players take turns to roll the dice and move that number of spaces along the gameboard. They collect gold coins if they land on an orange box and subtract gold coins if they land on a purple box. If they have a choice of numbers, they choose the number of gold coins they wish. If they land on a green box, they follow the instructions. The first player to reach 999 gold coins wins the game. If no player does this, the winner is the player with the most coins at the end of the game. Players should check each other's calculations. If an answer is wrong, the coins are added to the other player.

Making it easier

Players could 'call a friend' and ask for advice twice during the game. If the numbers are difficult to add, children can use estimation rather than exact values.

Making it harder

Children get an extra ten coins for correctly explaining the reasons for using a mental or a written method.

Game 2: Bury the treasure!

This game provides children with the opportunity to add and subtract values using mental arithmetic or written methods. They must also use their reasoning skills.

Maths focus

- Add and subtract numbers mentally
- Subtract numbers including 2- and 3-digit numbers, using formal written methods of column subtraction

Resources

1–6 dice (1), 1 counter per player (1 colour per player), place-value counters, Base 10 apparatus.

How to play

Play as for Game 1, but this time players must finish the race with the least amount of gold coins in their treasure chest. If a player lands on a box with a choice of numbers, they choose one of them.

They must choose the smallest number to add on and the biggest number to subtract so that they finish with the least number of coins. Children should check each other's calculations. If a player makes a mistake, the other player removes the gold coins from their treasure chest instead.

Making it easier

Children can use estimation rather than exact values. They can use place-value counters or Base 10 apparatus to help them with the calculations.

Making it harder

Children can subtract an extra ten coins for correctly explaining the reasons for using a mental or a written method.

Game 3: Your game

Children should invent their own game, designing rules that use the concepts covered in the unit. Challenge children to make their game easier or harder.

Golden treasure!

Choose a game to play.

Game 1: 999 coins

You need:

- 1–6 dice
- 1 counter per player (1 colour per player)
- pencil and paper

How to play

- Each player rolls the dice. The player with the higher number decides whether to start with 419 or 318 gold coins.
- Take it in turns to roll the dice and move that number of spaces.
- If you land on 2 numbers, choose 1 of them. Collect coins on an orange box. Subtract coins on a purple box. Follow the instruction on a green box.
- Check each other's calculations using a mental or written method.
- The winner is the player who collects 999 gold coins first or finishes the game with the greater number of coins.

Game 2: Bury the treasure!

You need:

- 1–6 dice
- 1 counter per player (1 colour per player)
- pencil and paper

How to play

- Play as for Game 1. This time, you are trying to collect the least coins!
- Take it in turns to roll the dice and move on that number of spaces.
- If you land on 2 numbers, choose the smallest number to add on (orange box) and the biggest number to subtract (purple box). Follow the instructions on a green box.
- Check each other's calculations using a mental or written method.
- The winner is the player who runs out of coins first or who has the least amount of coins at the end!

Game 3: Your game

- Make up your own game using the gameboard.
- Can you think of a way to collect gold coins as you move along?
- How could you make your game easier or harder?

Please help your child by reading the instructions and playing the game together.

Unit 6 And finally ...

Assessment task 1

Running the task

Prior to starting the task, discuss use of diagrams in questions. Talk about the different ways that children have seen data presented, e.g. bar charts, pictograms, tally charts. Ask children why we present data in this way. Listen for their answers and share the best ones with the whole class, e.g. it is easy to compare, understand and construct. Challenge children to think of disadvantages of using the diagram in the question, e.g. how to show number 41 or 15? Encourage discussion about the importance of the scale so that we know exactly what the data represents. Children calculate the number of shells each class collected and then compare them. Encourage them to write number statements to show their calculations.

Remind children to make estimations first. Listen for children who fluently add and subtract multiples of tens and hundreds. Discuss a checking calculation each time. Children then calculate the total time for the school trip. This is a two-step problem that requires them to subtract first to find the time back, then add to find the total time. Remind children that there are 60 minutes in an hour, not 100! A formal written method should be used and children should explain their working on both steps.

Evidencing mastery

Children who know how to use the information represented in diagrams to answer questions show a clear mastery of the data. Those who recognise that a problem involves two steps of subtraction and addition and clearly show the number statements needed in each step demonstrate a deeper fluency and mastery.

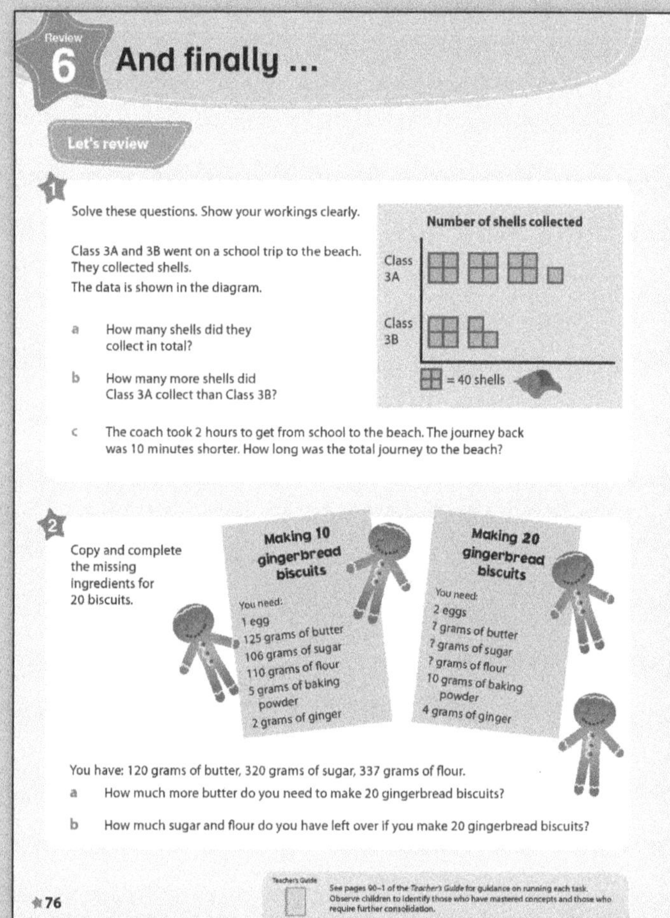

Assessment task 2

Running the task

Prior to starting the task, encourage children to discuss some of the mental and written calculations they have been doing recently, giving examples of calculations that would best suit a mental method and those that would not, e.g. they should recognise when doubling a big number they are adding the same number twice and could use an addition written or mental method. Also they should recognise that a subtraction with numbers that are close together on the number line can be more easily calculated using the mental method of counting on.

Children can work in pairs or in a group. Encourage them to talk to each other and explain the methods they are using and the reasons for their choice. Remind them to make an estimate first and always check whether their answer makes sense. Look for children who challenge themselves to add and subtract tens and hundreds mentally. Listen for children who use their number bonds to ten and 20 and manipulate them to work out number bonds to 100 or 200. Challenge children by giving them 500 grams of each of the ingredients. Can they make 40 biscuits? Adapt the number of biscuits made or the quantity of ingredients according to children's particular needs.

Evidencing mastery

You will know that children have mastered these concepts when they are able to decide quickly whether they are using a mental or written method and are able to explain their decisions. They will be able to use their knowledge of number facts and place value and use a range of strategies, including partitioning to work out the answers.

Concepts mastered

- ☑ Children can fluently apply knowledge of number facts and place value to support mental work. They can explain the additive property of numbers and refer to it when using a formal written method.
- ☑ Children use the written method and their knowledge of partitioning to subtract 3-digit numbers. Children use rounding to estimate and recognise that addition can be used to check a subtraction calculation.

Assessment task 3

Running the task

Word problems are the type of questions that most children find challenging. It is through practice that they will get better at them. Give children time to think about the question. Discuss why the phrases 'more than' and 'less than' can be tricky. 'More than' does not always mean you have to add and 'less than' does not always mean you have to subtract. Give some examples and children need to decide whether addition or subtraction is required, e.g. *Oli has two more brothers than Mia. Oli has three brothers. How many brothers does Mia have?*

Listen for children who give wrong answers and ask them to put the answer back in the question, e.g. Mia cannot have five brothers as Oli has the most brothers. Challenge children to make similar questions themselves. Use simple numbers to start with, so they do not worry about the arithmetic and instead concentrate on the method used. Once children feel more confident ask them to explain how they would solve the question in the Textbook.

Evidencing mastery

Obtaining the correct answer through correct use of mental strategies or written method shows that children are confident in adding and subtracting.

Did you know?

Discuss what happens at London Zoo. Have children been there? How many animals do they think live there altogether? Use the mathematical language children have learnt in the unit when asking questions about the zoo. Use interesting facts to practise addition and subtraction questions, e.g. in January 2015 there were 67 species of mammals, 108 species of birds and 270 species of fish. Write these numbers in the board and discuss with children the methods that they would use to add two of them.

Share with children a summary of stock taken in London Zoo. Ask children to work in two groups to create easy and difficult questions for each other using the facts below. Discuss why they thought some questions were more difficult than others. What methods did they use to answer them?

London Zoo	Species
Mammals	67
Birds	108
Reptiles	58
Amphibians	25
Fishes	270
Invertebrates	228
Total:	**Species: 756**

Unit 7

Writing and using fractions

Mathematical focus

★ **Number: number and place value, fractions**

★ **Measurement: time, length, money**

Prior learning

Children should already be able to:

- recognise the place value of each digit in a 3-digit number
- compare and order numbers up to 1000
- identify and represent numbers to 750 using different representations
- count from zero in multiples of four, eight, 50 and 100
- find ten or 100 more or less than a given number
- count on and back in fraction steps of $\frac{1}{2}$, $\frac{1}{3}$ and $\frac{1}{10}$.

Key new learning

- Identify, represent and compare numbers to 1000 using different representations.
- Count up and down in tenths, recognise that tenths arise from dividing an object into ten equal parts and dividing single digits or quantities by ten.
- Recognise and use fractions as numbers; unit and non-unit fractions with small denominators.
- Solve number and practical problems.
- Add and subtract fractions with the same denominator within one whole.
- Compare and order unit fractions and fractions with the same denominator.

Making connections

- In this unit children have opportunities to solve number and practical problems in a variety of contexts. They should measure, compare, add and subtract lengths (m/cm/mm) mass (kg/g) and volume/capacity (l/ml), recognising how they can use knowledge of place value and calculation strategies to help them.
- Understanding how to add and subtract amounts of money to give change provides a real-life context and can easily be practised away from the school setting.
- Children become more fluent in telling and writing the time and use related vocabulary to describe times in the day. They can sequence events in the day using the related vocabulary and use knowledge of the number of days in each month, year and leap year.
- They should time events in a variety of contexts, e.g. science, and recognise the number of seconds in a minute as they record and compare events.

Talk about

It is important to use precise mathematical vocabulary from the beginning using full sentences to model concepts and having high expectations that children will do the same, e.g. *Each part is worth a tenth because it takes ten of these parts to equal one whole.* This can be especially helpful when talking about the size of unit fractions and the effect the denominator has on the size, e.g. *As the denominator increases, the size of the number decreases.* It is a common misconception that $\frac{1}{10}$ is larger than $\frac{1}{2}$ because ten is larger than two.

Engaging and exploring

Ask children to make a sensible estimate about the total number of rowers they can see in the first picture. Be careful to distinguish between actual rowers and the coxes and, if necessary, explain the role of the coxes. Ask children to suggest a 'silly' estimate, explaining their choice.

Look at the number of rowers in each boat and challenge children to think about the best way to find the total number of rowers. Children should make links to counts of eight they have done previously. Manipulatives such as number shapes or cubes can be used to represent the number of rowers in each boat and to confirm the count.

Suggest there is a relationship between the boats in the first picture and the boat in the second.

Pose questions such as, *How many rowers will there be in five boats of four? How many boats of four are needed to have the same number of rowers as picture one?* Reinforce the relationship between four and eight and that each eight is made up of two groups of four.

Encourage children to think about where they see numbers around them, e.g. house numbers, telephone numbers, times, prices, lengths, car models, and so on. Ask if they know any telephone numbers that are only 3-digit numbers? (999, 101, 111, 911, 123.) Children should describe or show ways to represent the numbers, e.g. with Base 10 apparatus.

Focus on the number on the bus, perhaps writing down numbers of local bus services and looking for any patterns in the numbers, e.g. 103 and 203. Ask children to think about a way to show the number of the school bus. Look at adding a 100 flat to the number 109 shown in Base 10 apparatus or show moving on 100 on a place-value chart.

Challenge children to find the bus number that is 100 less than the bus in the picture. How about 200 more, ten or 20 more and less? Invite children to think creatively about how they could represent those numbers.

Ask children to tell you what they know about ten-pin bowling and the rules of the game. Ensure that they understand that a 'strike' is given for knocking all ten pins down in one go, and a 'spare' is given when all ten are knocked down in two goes. Children should draw on number bonds for ten to find all combinations of getting a 'spare'.

Refer to the comment about seeing tenths. What do children think is the 'whole' and what is a tenth? Agree that the whole is the whole group of ten pins and $\frac{1}{10}$ is one of the pins as it takes ten of them to equal the whole group. Count the pins in tenths up to one whole and back in tenths to zero.

Children could return to the combinations they found to score a 'spare' and begin to relate this to tenths, e.g. *I can knock down $\frac{3}{10}$ of the pins and then knock down another $\frac{7}{10}$ of the pins.*

Checking understanding

You will know children have mastered these concepts when they can represent fractions as numbers and explain how they know that, for unit fractions, as the denominator increases the size of the number decreases.

Things to think about

- How will you provide opportunities to build fluency in counting in steps of a constant size, including whole numbers and fraction steps?
- How will you organise groupings so that children who find the language of mathematics more difficult have the opportunity to sit with others who use language confidently?
- How will you check conceptual understanding by challenging children to show multiple representations of numbers and fractions?
- How will you draw out reasoning through carefully planned questions that require children to think, prove and explain?

7a Showing numbers in different ways

- **Identify, represent and compare numbers to 1000 using different representations.**
- **Count up and down in tenths, recognise that tenths arise from dividing an object into ten equal parts and dividing single digits or quantities by ten.**

Homework 33 and 34

Practice Book pp 59–61

Place value & Abacus

Representations and resources

Base 10 apparatus, place-value counters, coins.

Mathematical vocabulary

Place value, thousand, hundred, ten, one, exchange, place holder, tenth, numerator, denominator, unit fraction

Warming up

Rehearse number bonds for ten and 20, focusing on the relationship between the two sets of bonds, i.e. bonds for 20 are ten more than the bonds for ten. Give children random numbers from zero to ten. Encourage children to respond with the bond for 10 and also the bond for 20, explaining their decisions as they go, e.g. for three, children respond with *'Seven because three add seven equals ten and 17 because ten more than seven is 17.'* Children could use representations to prove their decisions each time. Also link each number bond to subtraction so that children are fluent with $3 + 7 = 10$ and $10 - 7 = 3$ so $3 + 17 = 20$ and $20 - 17 = 3$.

Background knowledge

Representing whole numbers and fractions using a variety of apparatus will help to secure children's conceptual understanding of place value. Base 10 apparatus and place-value counters are particularly effective in making place value explicit. Concrete resources such as these also help to develop confidence in counting across boundaries, e.g. from 999 to 1000. Encourage children to think carefully about how the new number is represented as each step of regrouping takes place starting with the ones.

When exploring fractions, draw attention to how the numerator and denominator relate to the divided and divisor in a division calculation, e.g. $3 \div 10 = \frac{3}{10}$ where three is the divided and ten the divisor.

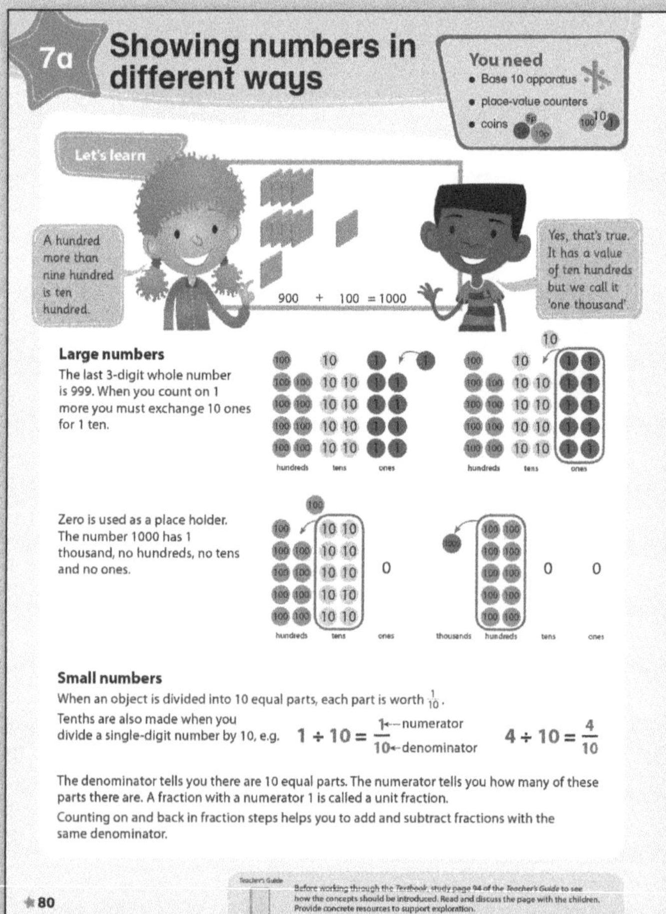

7a Showing numbers in different ways

You need
- Base 10 apparatus
- place-value counters
- coins

Let's learn

Large numbers

The last 3-digit whole number is 999. When you count on 1 more you must exchange 10 ones for 1 ten.

Zero is used as a place holder. The number 1000 has 1 thousand, no hundreds, no tens and no ones.

Small numbers

When an object is divided into 10 equal parts, each part is worth $\frac{1}{10}$.

Tenths are also made when you divide a single-digit number by 10, e.g. $1 \div 10 = \frac{1}{10}$ (1 ← numerator, 10 ← denominator) $4 \div 10 = \frac{4}{10}$

The denominator tells you there are 10 equal parts. The numerator tells you how many of these parts there are. A fraction with a numerator 1 is called a unit fraction.

Counting on and back in fraction steps helps you to add and subtract fractions with the same denominator.

80

Teacher's Guide: Before working through the *Textbook*, study page 94 of the *Teacher's Guide* to see how the concepts should be introduced. Read and discuss the page with the children. Provide concrete resources to support exploration.

Let's learn: Modelling and teaching

Large numbers

- Discuss the comments made by Mia and Oli in the misconception cartoon, looking carefully at the language used by both children and also at the equality of ten hundreds and one thousand. It may be useful to refer back to the effect of adding one more to 99.
- Using place-value counters, together, follow each step that is required on the place-value grid when one is added to 999. Reinforce that the largest digit in each place is nine and that when ten is reached, you exchange it.
- Focus on the use of zero as a place holder as each step in the exchange takes place and the need to create another position on the place-value grid for the thousands.

Small numbers

- Refer back to Unit 5c – Tenths where children used the place-value grid to divide single digits by ten to give tenths.
- The diagram in the Textbook clearly shows what happens to each of the numbers following the division and how the divisor becomes the denominator in the fraction.
- Introduce the term 'unit fraction' to represent any fraction that has a numerator of one and revisit how many tenths are equal to one whole in preparation for more counting beyond one. Children should recognise that the number of steps that complete a whole is the same as the value of the denominator.

Let's practise: Digging deeper

Step 1

Children use manipulatives to represent the number 879 and describe what they know about the value of each digit.

The task requires them to use the manipulatives to find a multiple of a hundred or ten more or less than 879, describing carefully the place value as they do so.

Step 2

The learning in this task is concerned with representing numbers rather than just calculating. For parts d and e children will need to think carefully and apply previous knowledge of ways they can represent counting in tenths.

Step 3

Children relate large numbers to money and use knowledge of place value to give change. Discuss what they know about the number of pennies in a pound and, therefore, the number of pennies in ten pounds. It would be useful for children to make each of the prices using Base 10 apparatus or place-value counters and use the finding the difference model to count on to 1000, exchanging as necessary. Encourage children to make the connection with number bonds for 1000.

Step 4

This is a more open task, again related to money. Children have already considered 10p as $\frac{1}{10}$ of a pound because it takes ten lots of ten pence to equal one pound. They should use coins to help reason about and find all possibilities. Challenge children to give some of their answers as fractions of a pound, e.g. 40p as $\frac{4}{10}$.

The problem develops as children are required to find amounts that sum to £1 or $\frac{10}{10}$ of a pound.

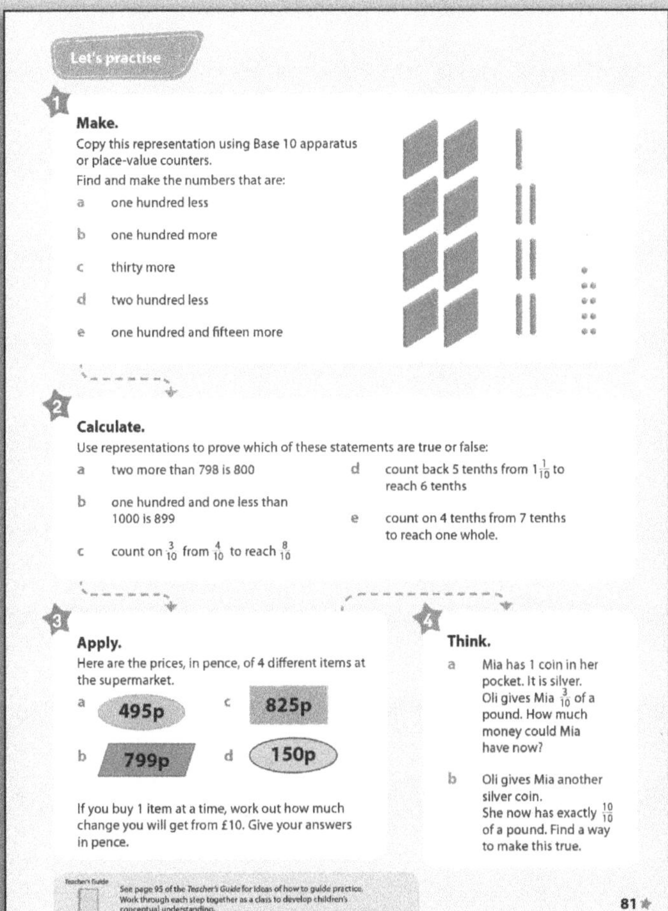
Let's practise

1 Make.
Copy this representation using Base 10 apparatus or place-value counters.
Find and make the numbers that are:

a one hundred less

b one hundred more

c thirty more

d two hundred less

e one hundred and fifteen more

2 Calculate.
Use representations to prove which of these statements are true or false:

a two more than 798 is 800

b one hundred and one less than 1000 is 899

c count on $\frac{3}{10}$ from $\frac{4}{10}$ to reach $\frac{8}{10}$

d count back 5 tenths from $1\frac{1}{10}$ to reach 6 tenths

e count on 4 tenths from 7 tenths to reach one whole.

3 Apply.
Here are the prices, in pence, of 4 different items at the supermarket.

a 495p

b 799p

c 825p

d 150p

If you buy 1 item at a time, work out how much change you will get from £10. Give your answers in pence.

4 Think.

a Mia has 1 coin in her pocket. It is silver. Oli gives Mia $\frac{3}{10}$ of a pound. How much money could Mia have now?

b Oli gives Mia another silver coin. She now has exactly $\frac{10}{10}$ of a pound. Find a way to make this true.

Teacher's Guide

See page 95 of the *Teacher's Guide* for ideas of how to guide practice. Work through each step together as a class to develop children's conceptual understanding.

81

Ensuring progress

Supporting understanding

Working in a focus group, ask children to match representations with their corresponding numbers. These representations can be photographs, drawings or physical examples using Base 10 apparatus or place-value counters. Include some numbers that are more tricky to distinguish between, e.g. 817 and 871, and those that have no matching representation. Children can then make or draw representations to go with these odd ones out.

Broadening understanding

Further develop counting on and back using place value with other larger multiples of tens and hundreds or combinations. Include examples that cross the thousands boundary.

Concept mastered

Children can represent numbers in different ways, applying knowledge of place value to describe the position and value of each digit in numbers up to 1000.

Follow-up ideas

- Find out about the heights of mountains around the world or the lengths of some of the rivers in different parts of, e.g. Europe. Encourage children to look carefully at place value when comparing and ordering, giving reasons for their choices, e.g. River Severn 354 km, Rhône 813 km, Meuse 925 km. Begin to look at the lengths of rivers that are just over 1000 km (Loire 1013 km) or mountains that are just over 1000 m (Mount Snowdon 1085 m) to further develop place value of one thousand.
- Use the Internet to find prices of items up to £1000, and calculate the amount of money left over in a budget of £1000.

Answers

Step 1

Representations to show each of the following numbers:

a 779 **d** 679

b 979 **e** 994

c 909

Step 2

Representations to prove that the following are true or false

a true **d** true

b true **e** false

c false

Step 3

a 505p **c** 175p

b 201p **d** 850p

Step 4

a Mia can start with 5p, 10p, 20p or 50p.

$\frac{3}{10}$ of a pound is equal to 30p so Mia could have 35p, 40p, 50p or 80p.

b Children's own examples to show that Mia could have had 20p to begin with and then added $\frac{3}{10}$ more to equal 50p and then Oli gave her a 50p coin to equal £1 which is equal to $\frac{10}{10}$ of a pound OR she started with 50p, then had 80p and Oli gave her a 20p coin.

7b Unit and non-unit fractions

- **Recognise and use fractions as numbers; unit and non-unit fractions with small denominators.**
- **Compare and order unit fractions and fractions with the same denominator.**
- **Solve number and practical problems.**

Homework 35 and 36 | Practice Book pp 62–4 | Fraction Wall

Representations and resources

Digit cards 0–100, coins, fraction bars, paper, ruler, scissors.

Mathematical vocabulary

Numerator, denominator, unit fraction, non-unit fraction, equal, division, compare, order, greater than, less than

Warming up

Rehearse number bonds for 100 in the context of money. Children find the change needed each time from £1 for a range of different prices. Using digit cards from 0–100 to represent the price each time, children write down the change and then describe or show the coins that can be used to make the change. Include extra reasoning by asking children to suggest some mystery prices and to match the clue about the change, e.g. *There is only one copper coin in the change or there are only three silver coins in the change.*

Background knowledge

It is a common misconception that a fraction such as $\frac{1}{10}$ is larger than $\frac{1}{4}$ because ten is larger than four. When numerators are the same (one in this case), the whole divided into ten equal parts results in smaller parts than the same whole divided into four equal parts. Explore this using real-life contexts such as, e.g.: *Would you rather have $\frac{1}{4}$ or $\frac{1}{10}$ of your favourite pizza?*

However, this is only always true when the numerators are both one (and later on, when the numerators are the same, e.g. both three) and the whole has the same value.

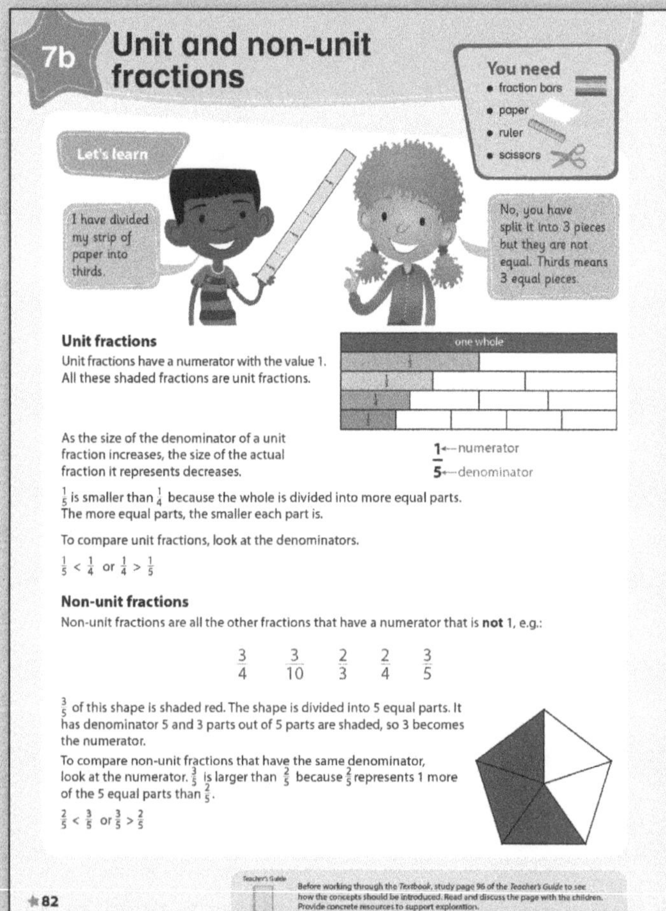

7b Unit and non-unit fractions

Unit fractions

Unit fractions have a numerator with the value 1. All these shaded fractions are unit fractions.

As the size of the denominator of a unit fraction increases, the size of the actual fraction it represents decreases.

$\frac{1}{5}$ is smaller than $\frac{1}{4}$ because the whole is divided into more equal parts. The more equal parts, the smaller each part is.

To compare unit fractions, look at the denominators.

$\frac{1}{5} < \frac{1}{4}$ or $\frac{1}{4} > \frac{1}{5}$

Non-unit fractions

Non-unit fractions are all the other fractions that have a numerator that is **not** 1, e.g.:

$\frac{3}{4}$ $\frac{3}{10}$ $\frac{2}{3}$ $\frac{2}{4}$ $\frac{3}{5}$

$\frac{3}{5}$ of this shape is shaded red. The shape is divided into 5 equal parts. It has denominator 5 and 3 parts out of 5 parts are shaded, so 3 becomes the numerator.

To compare non-unit fractions that have the same denominator, look at the numerator. $\frac{3}{5}$ is larger than $\frac{2}{5}$ because $\frac{2}{5}$ represents 1 more of the 5 equal parts than $\frac{2}{5}$.

$\frac{2}{5} < \frac{3}{5}$ or $\frac{3}{5} > \frac{2}{5}$

82

Teacher's Guide: Before working through the *Textbook*, study page 96 of the *Teacher's Guide* to see how the concepts should be introduced. Read and discuss the page with the children. Provide concrete resources to support exploration.

Let's learn: Modelling and teaching

Unit fractions

- Discuss Oli's misconception and revisit other fractions using a variety of representations such as fraction bars, e.g. quarters and tenths, describing them as arising from one whole divided into four or ten equal parts and each part is one quarter or one tenth.
- Use the fraction bars in the Textbook (or make your own from paper) to explore the unit fractions shown. Encourage children to count in fraction steps along the bars, reinforcing that $\frac{4}{4}$ are equal to one whole. Challenge them to describe the fraction of each bar not shaded. This will support addition in the next concept.
- Encourage children to refer to the numerator and denominator each time when describing or comparing fractions and, in this case, recognising that for unit fractions all numerators have the value one. Focus on the comparison of $\frac{1}{5}$ and $\frac{1}{4}$ in the Textbook and the language used to compare the parts. Remind children how they can use the symbols < and > to show comparisons.

Non-unit fractions

- Ask children to describe or show other fractions that they know with a numerator that does not have the value one (non-unit fractions). Look at the other examples in the Textbook. *How can we show or describe these?*
- The fraction $\frac{3}{5}$ is represented and described using language that makes links to division, i.e. dividing by five, and the denominator. The language also clearly describes the fraction of the shape shaded as three parts out of five parts. The three parts are shown by the value of the numerator. Challenge children to describe some of the other fractions ($\frac{3}{4}$, $\frac{3}{10}$, $\frac{2}{3}$ or $\frac{2}{4}$) in the same way.
- Focus on the comparison of $\frac{3}{5}$ and $\frac{2}{5}$ in the Textbook and the language used to compare the parts. Use the symbols < and > to compare the fractions.

Let's practise: Digging deeper

Step 1

Children should think first about the size of each fraction, looking at the denominator and describing how many equal parts there are in the whole. Fraction bars or the representation in the Textbook can be used to confirm decisions. Encourage children to refer back to some of the comparisons they have made to help them order a set of unit fractions.

Step 2

Children should identify the shaded part each time by using the language practised earlier, i.e. they should describe the first image as, e.g. $\frac{3}{4}$ *of this shape is shaded. I know it is* $\frac{3}{4}$ *because the shape is divided into 4 equal parts so it has denominator 4 and 3 parts out of 4 parts are shaded.* This task also introduces a fraction showing eighths so that children can employ the language as a way of identifying the fraction rather than, perhaps, drawing on a more familiar image.

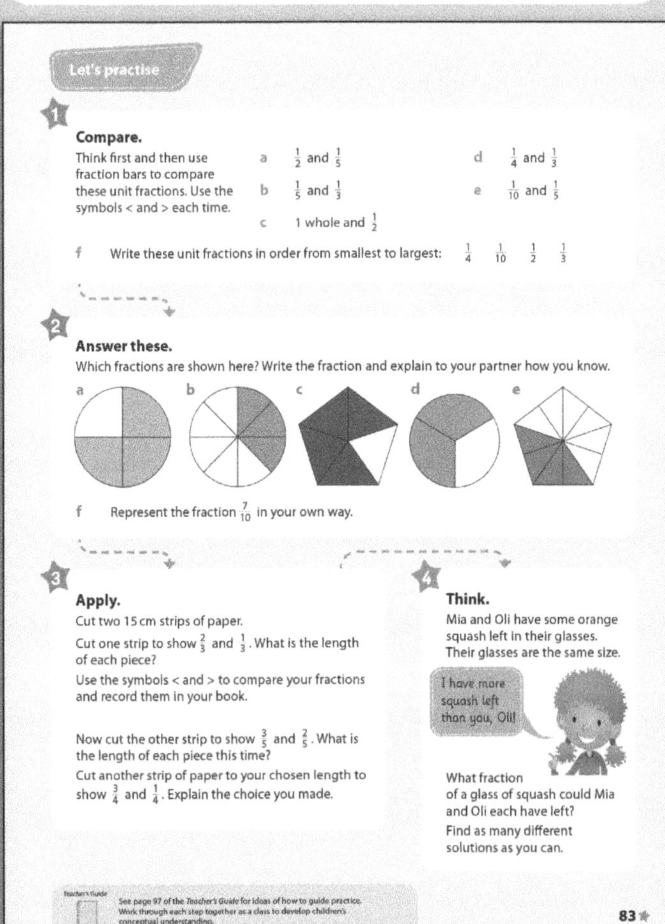

Let's practise

1 Compare.

Think first and then use fraction bars to compare these unit fractions. Use the symbols < and > each time.

a $\frac{1}{2}$ and $\frac{1}{5}$

b $\frac{1}{5}$ and $\frac{1}{3}$

c 1 whole and $\frac{1}{2}$

d $\frac{1}{4}$ and $\frac{1}{3}$

e $\frac{1}{10}$ and $\frac{1}{5}$

f Write these unit fractions in order from smallest to largest: $\frac{1}{4}$ $\frac{1}{10}$ $\frac{1}{2}$ $\frac{1}{3}$

2 Answer these.

Which fractions are shown here? Write the fraction and explain to your partner how you know.

a b c d e

f Represent the fraction $\frac{7}{10}$ in your own way.

3 Apply.

Cut two 15 cm strips of paper.

Cut one strip to show $\frac{2}{3}$ and $\frac{1}{3}$. What is the length of each piece?

Use the symbols < and > to compare your fractions and record them in your book.

Now cut the other strip to show $\frac{3}{5}$ and $\frac{2}{5}$. What is the length of each piece this time?

Cut another strip of paper to your chosen length to show $\frac{3}{4}$ and $\frac{1}{4}$. Explain the choice you made.

4 Think.

Mia and Oli have some orange squash left in their glasses. Their glasses are the same size.

I have more squash left than you, Oli!

What fraction of a glass of squash could Mia and Oli each have left?

Find as many different solutions as you can.

Teacher's Guide

See page 97 of the *Teacher's Guide* for ideas of how to guide practice. Work through each step together as a class to develop children's conceptual understanding.

83

Step 3

Children should apply multiplication and division facts to help split the 15 cm strip of paper accurately.

For the strip needed to show quarters, children should reason about the length of the strip to use. They could also use another 15 cm strip, folding it in half and half again, but they will need to be very careful when measuring each length.

Step 4

Encourage children to use a table or a list to record their ideas and to justify their solutions each time using the fractional language practised earlier.

Ensuring progress

Supporting understanding

Use fraction bars made from card for halves, thirds and quarters and spend time counting in fraction steps. Children should be able to explain that they have to take more steps to complete a whole using quarters than they do using halves or thirds. Discuss the size of each jump or step on the fraction bar or on a number line, reinforcing that quarters have smaller steps whereas thirds have fewer but larger steps so a step of $\frac{1}{3}$ is greater than a step of $\frac{1}{4}$.

Broadening understanding

For Step 4, encourage children to be systematic in finding solutions, e.g. when Mia has $\frac{1}{2}$ a glass left, Oli can have $\frac{1}{3}$, $\frac{1}{4}$, $\frac{1}{5}$, $\frac{1}{6}$ and so on of a glass left or when Mia has $\frac{9}{10}$ of a glass left, Oli can have $\frac{8}{10}$, $\frac{7}{10}$, $\frac{6}{10}$ and so on rather than randomly comparing fractions.

Concept mastered

Children can recognise and describe unit and non-unit fractions, referring to the value of the numerator to explain the difference between them.

Answers

Step 1

a $\frac{1}{2} > \frac{1}{5}$ and $\frac{1}{5} < \frac{1}{2}$

b $\frac{1}{3} > \frac{1}{5}$ and $\frac{1}{5} < \frac{1}{3}$

c $1 > \frac{1}{2}$ and $\frac{1}{2} < 1$

d $\frac{1}{3} > \frac{1}{4}$ and $\frac{1}{4} < \frac{1}{3}$

e $\frac{1}{5} > \frac{1}{10}$ and $\frac{1}{10} < \frac{1}{5}$

f $\frac{1}{10}, \frac{1}{4}, \frac{1}{3}, \frac{1}{2}$

Step 2

a $\frac{3}{4}$

b $\frac{3}{8}$

c $\frac{4}{5}$

d $\frac{2}{3}$

e $\frac{4}{10}$

f A representation showing $\frac{7}{10}$, e.g.

Step 3

15 cm strip cut into a 10 cm piece ($\frac{2}{3}$) and a 5 cm piece ($\frac{1}{3}$).

15 cm strip cut into a 9 cm piece ($\frac{3}{5}$) and a 6 cm piece ($\frac{2}{5}$).

For quarters, e.g. 12 cm strip cut into a 9 cm piece ($\frac{3}{4}$) and a 3 cm piece ($\frac{1}{4}$).

Step 4

A table, or list, of possible solutions for Mia and Oli, with Mia's fraction being greater each time.

e.g.

Mia	Oli
$\frac{9}{10}$	$\frac{8}{10}$
$\frac{1}{2}$	$\frac{1}{3}$
$\frac{1}{4}$	$\frac{1}{5}$
$\frac{2}{3}$	$\frac{1}{3}$

Follow-up ideas

- Explore other length strips of paper that children can use to find unit and non-unit fractions parts but set the criteria that each length cut must be in whole centimetres.
- Look at other examples, including sayings, where fractions are used to show or describe the size of a part or make comparisons, e.g. someone who thinks in a positive way is often described as 'having the glass half full'; 'possession is nine tenths of the law'; a quarter is a quarter of a dollar in the USA (i.e. 25 cents); $\frac{1}{2}$ a litre of milk and so on. Fractions even feature in this nursery rhyme, 'Half a pound of tuppenny rice, Half a pound of treacle. That's the way the money goes, Pop goes the weasel'.

7c Adding and subtracting fractions

- **Add and subtract fractions with the same denominator within one whole.**

Homework 37 and 38 | Practice Book pp 65–7 | Fraction Wall

Mathematical vocabulary

Numerator, denominator, unit fraction, non-unit fraction, whole, add, subtract, inverse, fraction bond

Representations and resources

Clocks, fraction bars, number shapes or interlocking cubes, number line, counters, paper circles.

Warming up

Use images of analogue clocks to display a set of times in a grid. Ensure that times include o'clock, quarter to and quarter past, half past, other multiples of ten and five minutes to and past the hour, e.g. 9:20 and 8:55 and others that are to the nearest minute, e.g. 1:09 or 7:36. Label some of the times as a.m. and p.m., others as morning, afternoon or evening and a clock showing 12 o'clock as noon or midnight.

Children work in pairs to practise reading the times or finding a given time that has been verbalised. Challenge them to order the times from earliest to latest, drawing on their knowledge of the vocabulary of time.

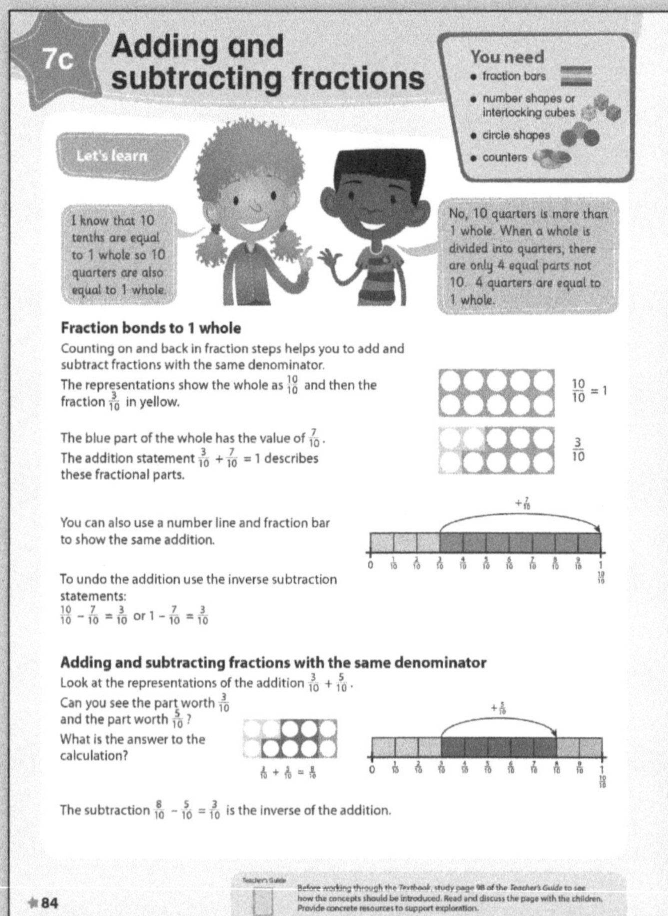
7c Adding and subtracting fractions

You need
- fraction bars
- number shapes or interlocking cubes
- circle shapes
- counters

Let's learn

I know that 10 tenths are equal to 1 whole so 10 quarters are also equal to 1 whole.

No, 10 quarters is more than 1 whole. When a whole is divided into quarters, there are only 4 equal parts not 10. 4 quarters are equal to 1 whole.

Fraction bonds to 1 whole

Counting on and back in fraction steps helps you to add and subtract fractions with the same denominator.

The representations show the whole as $\frac{10}{10}$ and then the fraction $\frac{3}{10}$ in yellow.

$\frac{10}{10} = 1$

$\frac{3}{10}$

The blue part of the whole has the value of $\frac{7}{10}$.
The addition statement $\frac{3}{10} + \frac{7}{10} = 1$ describes these fractional parts.

You can also use a number line and fraction bar to show the same addition.

$+\frac{7}{10}$

0 $\frac{1}{10}$ $\frac{2}{10}$ $\frac{3}{10}$ $\frac{4}{10}$ $\frac{5}{10}$ $\frac{6}{10}$ $\frac{7}{10}$ $\frac{8}{10}$ $\frac{9}{10}$ 1 $\frac{10}{10}$

To undo the addition use the inverse subtraction statements:
$\frac{10}{10} - \frac{7}{10} = \frac{3}{10}$ or $1 - \frac{7}{10} = \frac{3}{10}$

Adding and subtracting fractions with the same denominator

Look at the representations of the addition $\frac{3}{10} + \frac{5}{10}$.
Can you see the part worth $\frac{3}{10}$ and the part worth $\frac{5}{10}$?
What is the answer to the calculation?

$\frac{3}{10} + \frac{5}{10} = \frac{8}{10}$

$+\frac{5}{10}$

0 $\frac{1}{10}$ $\frac{2}{10}$ $\frac{3}{10}$ $\frac{4}{10}$ $\frac{5}{10}$ $\frac{6}{10}$ $\frac{7}{10}$ $\frac{8}{10}$ $\frac{9}{10}$ 1 $\frac{10}{10}$

The subtraction $\frac{8}{10} - \frac{5}{10} = \frac{3}{10}$ is the inverse of the addition.

84

Teacher's Guide
Before working through the *Textbook*, study page 98 of the *Teacher's Guide* to see how the concepts should be introduced. Read and discuss the page with the children. Provide concrete resources to support exploration.

Background knowledge

Children should have had plenty of opportunity to practise counting on and back in fraction steps up to and beyond one whole. Counting in this way builds the foundation for adding and subtracting fractions with the same denominators, e.g. the calculations, such as $\frac{4}{10} + \frac{3}{10}$, should be related to counting on $\frac{3}{10}$ from $\frac{4}{10}$, and the calculation $\frac{7}{10} - \frac{3}{10}$ related to counting back $\frac{3}{10}$ from $\frac{7}{10}$. As the fractions are made up of parts of equal size, we can complete them using knowledge of counting.

Let's learn: Modelling and teaching

Fraction bonds to 1 whole

- Remind children of some of the counting they have been doing in fraction steps. Ask them, in pairs, to choose fraction steps, e.g. halves, quarters or tenths, and practise counting on and back across one. Encourage them to also include counts in steps of $\frac{2}{10}$ or $\frac{3}{10}$.
- Reinforce that the denominators are the same so that they can count on or back in equal steps.
- Model the representation of $\frac{3}{10}$ and the remaining number of tenths left in the whole, as shown in the Textbook, using number shapes and fraction bars. Encourage children to count the three tenths and the remaining seven tenths. Use the seven number shape to confirm the addition. Make links to number bonds for ten as you model that $\frac{3}{10} + \frac{7}{10} = 1$.
- Discuss the number line and fraction bar representation of the same calculation shown in the Textbook. Ask children to identify each part of the calculation, i.e. *Where can you see $\frac{3}{10}$? Where can you see $\frac{7}{10}$?* Model how the calculation can be undone using the inverse and record the subtraction statements.

Adding and subtracting fractions with the same denominator

- Model on the calculation $\frac{3}{10} + \frac{5}{10}$, as shown in the Textbook, using number shapes and fraction bars. Invite children to explain to a partner where they can see the part worth $\frac{3}{10}$ and the part worth $\frac{5}{10}$ in each representation.
- Look at the number shapes and number line in the Textbook. Ask what is the same and what is different about the representations used previously for $\frac{3}{10} + \frac{7}{10}$ and the ones shown here for $\frac{3}{10} + \frac{5}{10}$. Children should notice that $\frac{3}{10}$ and $\frac{5}{10}$ are less than 1 whole.
- They should identify the addition calculation $\frac{3}{10} + \frac{5}{10} = \frac{8}{10}$. Again, look at how the addition can be undone using the inverse subtraction, recording the statement as $\frac{8}{10} - \frac{5}{10} = \frac{3}{10}$.

Let's practise: Digging deeper

Step 1

Refer to the conversation between Mia and Oli, focusing on the number of equal parts in a whole divided into tenths and a whole divided into quarters. To help with this task, children will need to know that the following are equal to one whole: $\frac{3}{3}$, $\frac{4}{4}$, $\frac{5}{5}$, $\frac{8}{8}$ and $\frac{10}{10}$. They should use number shapes or interlocking cubes.

Step 2

Children should draw on counting back in fraction steps to support subtraction. They could use counters on the number line to cover up the fractions they subtract, e.g. $\frac{7}{8} - \frac{3}{8} = \frac{4}{8}$. Encourage children to look out for equivalent fractions of $\frac{1}{2}$.

Step 3

Children use a circle shape or a fraction bar to represent one minute in time. Encourage them to think about the way in which they can represent the fractions given in the questions, i.e. $\frac{1}{4}$, $\frac{2}{4}$, $\frac{1}{2}$, $\frac{1}{3}$, $\frac{2}{3}$ and $\frac{3}{4}$, and what fraction of the whole is left each time. In this example, the whole is one minute, so children will need to draw on seconds as the unit of time that would represent fractions of a minute. Children should also draw on the knowledge that there are 60 seconds in one minute and use division and multiplication facts to help calculate.

Step 4

This task uses the strategy, 'If this is the answer, what is the question?'. Ensure that children can explain that the answer to each calculation will have the numerator three, but a denominator of their choice. Suggest that they can use manipulatives to support their thinking and help them reason about a range of solutions using addition and subtraction. Support children by asking: *How can you make the fraction equal to one whole? What does that tell you about the denominator? How about a fraction that is less than one whole?*

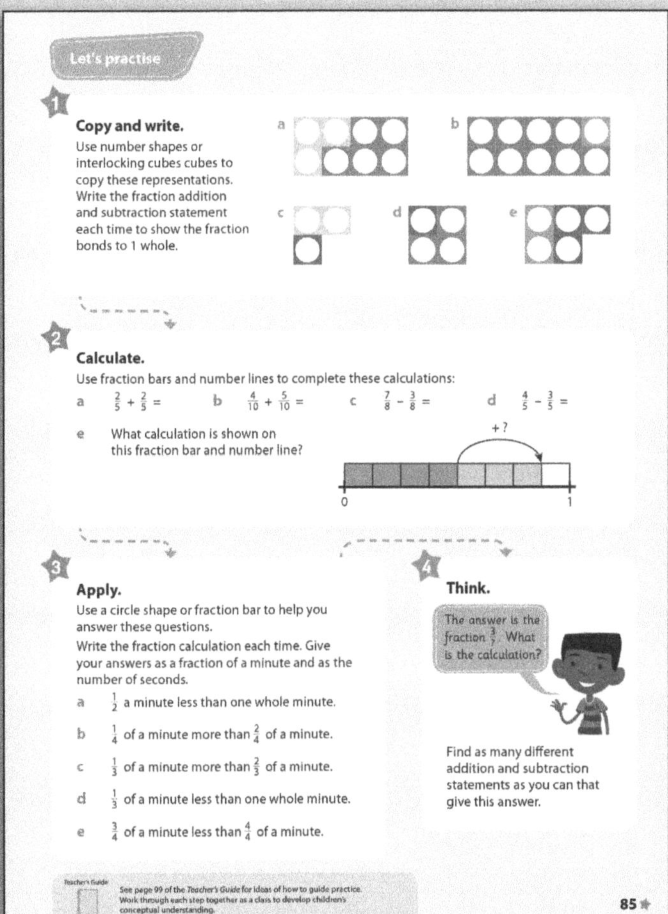
Let's practise

1 **Copy and write.**
Use number shapes or interlocking cubes cubes to copy these representations. Write the fraction addition and subtraction statement each time to show the fraction bonds to 1 whole.

a b c d e

2 **Calculate.**
Use fraction bars and number lines to complete these calculations:

a $\frac{2}{5} + \frac{2}{5} =$ b $\frac{4}{10} + \frac{5}{10} =$ c $\frac{7}{8} - \frac{3}{8} =$ d $\frac{4}{5} - \frac{3}{5} =$

e What calculation is shown on this fraction bar and number line?

3 **Apply.**
Use a circle shape or fraction bar to help you answer these questions.
Write the fraction calculation each time. Give your answers as a fraction of a minute and as the number of seconds.

a $\frac{1}{2}$ a minute less than one whole minute.

b $\frac{1}{4}$ of a minute more than $\frac{2}{4}$ of a minute.

c $\frac{1}{3}$ of a minute more than $\frac{2}{3}$ of a minute.

d $\frac{1}{3}$ of a minute less than one whole minute.

e $\frac{3}{4}$ of a minute less than $\frac{4}{4}$ of a minute.

4 **Think.**

Find as many different addition and subtraction statements as you can that give this answer.

Teacher's Guide

See page 99 of the *Teacher's Guide* for ideas of how to guide practice. Work through each step together as a class to develop children's conceptual understanding.

85

Ensuring progress

Supporting understanding

In Step 3, it would be useful for children to label the fractions of time on different circles or on different fraction bars. As a group, children could work and label the number of seconds in each fraction part before they begin to work through the questions.

Broadening understanding

Develop Step 4 by giving children a further criteria, e.g. If the answer is the fraction $\frac{6}{7}$, what is the calculation this time? This will encourage them to further explore addition of tenths and eighths or begin to think about other fractions with denominators less than ten, i.e. sixths, sevenths and ninths.

Concept mastered

Children can draw on understanding of counting in fraction steps of a constant size to help make sense of adding and subtracting fractions with the same denominator and find pairs of fractions that total one.

Follow-up ideas

- Pose a range of word problems where children need to apply knowledge of adding and subtracting fractions, also putting the problems in the context of measurement where appropriate, e.g. *Sam buys $\frac{4}{5}$ kg of potatoes and he uses $\frac{3}{5}$ kg in a recipe. What fraction of a kilogram of potatoes does Sam have left? Oli and Mia collect 10p coins. They have $\frac{9}{10}$ of a pound between them. What fraction of a pound can they each have?*

Answers

Step 1

a $\frac{3}{8} + \frac{5}{8} = \frac{8}{8}$ or 1 and 1 or $\frac{8}{8} - \frac{5}{8} = \frac{3}{8}$

b $\frac{9}{10} + \frac{1}{10} = \frac{10}{10}$ or 1 and 1 or $\frac{10}{10} - \frac{1}{10} = \frac{9}{10}$

c $\frac{1}{3} + \frac{2}{3} = \frac{3}{3}$ or 1 and 1 or $\frac{3}{3} - \frac{2}{3} = \frac{1}{3}$

d $\frac{1}{4} + \frac{3}{4} = \frac{4}{4}$ or 1 and 1 or $\frac{4}{4} - \frac{3}{4} = \frac{1}{4}$

e $\frac{2}{5} + \frac{3}{5} = \frac{5}{5}$ or 1 and 1 or $\frac{5}{5} - \frac{3}{5} = \frac{2}{5}$

Step 2

a $\frac{4}{5}$

b $\frac{9}{10}$

c $\frac{4}{8}$

d $\frac{1}{5}$

e $\frac{4}{8} + \frac{3}{8} = \frac{7}{8}$

Step 3

a $\frac{1}{2}$ minute, 30 seconds

b $\frac{3}{4}$ minute, 45 seconds

c 1 minute, 60 seconds

d $\frac{2}{3}$ minute, 40 seconds

e $\frac{1}{4}$ minute, 15 seconds

Step 4

Children's own set of solutions, e.g.

$\frac{10}{10} - \frac{7}{10} = \frac{3}{10}$ or $1 - \frac{7}{10} = \frac{3}{10}$

$\frac{7}{8} - \frac{4}{8} = \frac{3}{8}$

$\frac{2}{4} + \frac{1}{4} = \frac{3}{4}$

$\frac{2}{5} + \frac{1}{5} = \frac{3}{5}$

Unit 7 In a spin!

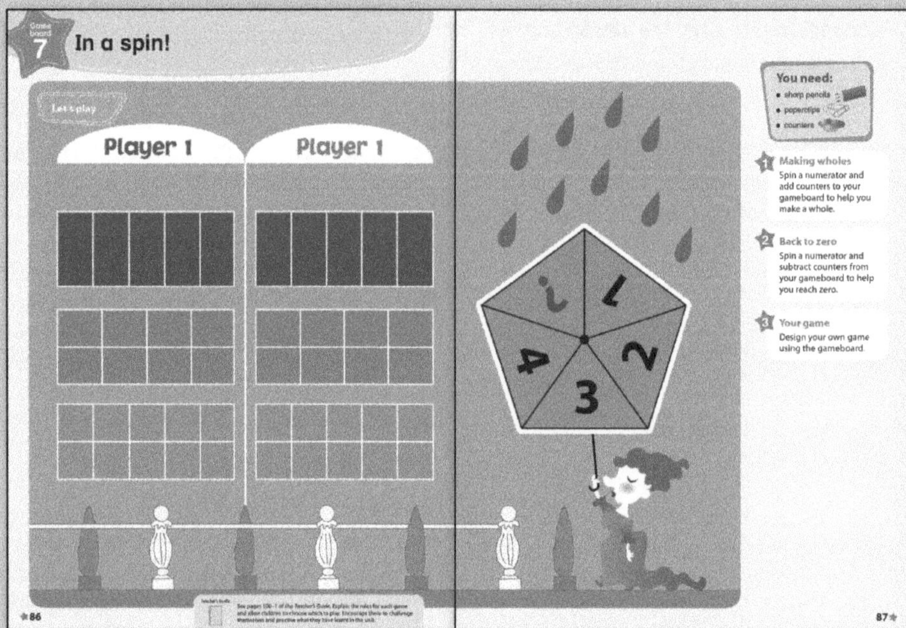

Game 1: Making wholes

This game gives children practice in adding non-unit fractions with the same denominator.

Maths focus

- Adding fractions with the same denominator

Resources

Sharp pencils, paperclips, counters.

How to play

Players take turns to put one end of a paperclip over the dot in the centre of the spinner and place the sharp end of a pencil on the dot. They flick the paperclip; where it lands is their numerator. The question mark is a numerator of their choice from one, two, three or four. They choose a gameboard to be the denominator, e.g. they spin a two and to add it to the gameboard divided into fifths so the fraction becomes $\frac{2}{5}$. They cover $\frac{2}{5}$ of the gameboard with two counters. Next time, if they spin a three, they can make it $\frac{3}{5}$ and write $\frac{2}{5} + \frac{3}{5} = 1$ for the same gameboard or start another. When a gameboard is completed, the player scores a point and removes the counters. Players miss a turn if an addition will take them beyond one on all three gameboards. The first player to reach five points is the winner.

Making it easier

Children use only one gameboard, e.g. the tenths, so when they spin a numerator the fraction is always tenths.

Making it harder

When an addition will take children beyond one on all three gameboards, they partition the fraction to complete the whole and use the rest of the fraction to start a new gameboard.

Game 3: Your game

Children should invent their own game, designing rules that use the concepts covered in the unit.

Game 2: Back to zero

This more complex game gives children practice in subtracting non-unit fractions with the same denominator.

Maths focus

- Subtracting fractions with the same denominator

Resources

Sharp pencils, paperclips, counters.

How to play

Before the game starts, children cover every space on each number gameboard with counters. Players take turns to spin for their numerator, as in Game 1. The question mark can be used as a numerator of their choice from one, two, three or four. They choose a gameboard from which to subtract their fraction and this becomes the denominator as in Game 1. They uncover the fraction of the gameboard by removing counters. They write the calculation, e.g. $1 - \frac{3}{8} = \frac{5}{8}$. On their next turn, if the child spins a four, they can decide to make it $\frac{4}{8}$ and write the calculation $\frac{5}{8} - \frac{4}{8} = \frac{1}{8}$ or start another gameboard, e.g. tenths, removing $\frac{4}{10}$. Each time zero is reached and a gameboard is fully uncovered, the player scores a point and covers the gameboard with counters so it can be used again. Players miss a turn if there is not a large enough fraction left to subtract on all three gameboards. The first player to reach five points is the winner.

Making it easier

Children use only one gameboard, e.g. the tenths, so when they spin a numerator the fraction is always tenths.

Making it harder

When there is not a large enough fraction left to subtract on all three gameboards, the player must add to the fraction instead, e.g. a player has $\frac{1}{10}$, $\frac{2}{8}$ and $\frac{2}{5}$ left on their gameboards and spins a four. They must then choose to add $\frac{4}{10}$ or $\frac{4}{8}$ or $\frac{4}{5}$ instead.

In a spin!

Choose a game to play.

Game 1: Making wholes

You need:
- sharp pencils
- paperclips
- counters

How to play
- Each player has 3 gameboards to fill with fifths, eighths or tenths.
- Take turns to spin the spinner to find a numerator 1, 2, 3 or 4. If you spin the question mark, choose any of these numerators.
- Cover this number of parts with counters on one of your gameboards and write the addition, e.g. $0 + \frac{2}{5} = \frac{2}{5}$.
- Score a point when a whole gameboard is complete. Uncover it so it can be used again.
- Miss a turn if an addition will make more than 1 whole on all 3 gameboards.
- The winner is the first player to score 5 points.

Game 2: Back to zero

You need:
- sharp pencils
- paperclips
- counters

How to play
- Each player has 3 gameboards covered with counters showing 1 whole in fifths, eighths or tenths.
- Take turns to spin the spinner to find a numerator 1, 2, 3 or 4. If you spin the question mark, choose any of these numerators.
- Uncover this number of parts on one of your gameboards and write the subtraction to show what is left, e.g. roll 2, uncover 2 fifths and write $1 - \frac{2}{5} = \frac{3}{5}$.
- Score a point when a gameboard is worth zero as no more can be subtracted. Then cover the gameboard with counters so it can be used again.
- Miss a turn if there is not a large enough fraction left to subtract on all 3 gameboards.
- The winner is the first player to score 5 points

Game 3: Your game

- You could use other fraction gameboards, e.g. quarters or sixths.
- You could score 2 points when a gameboard is covered by 3 fractions, e.g. $\frac{2}{5}$, $\frac{2}{5}$ and $\frac{1}{5}$.
- What are your rules? Explain them to someone.

Please help your child by reading the instructions and playing the game together.

Unit 7 And finally ...

Assessment task 1

Resources

Base 10 apparatus, place-value counters, place-value grid, digit cards.

Running the task

Before the task it may be useful to remind children about some of the different ways that they have been representing 3-digit numbers in this unit. You may wish to give them an example of a representation that they have covered and ask them to explain which number it is.

Check that children understand that the task is to check some comparisons that Mia and Oli have been doing. Children must interpret the number statements, making sense of the symbols < and >. If needed, prompt them to think about a manipulative they would like to use to help them. Ask them to explain the positional and multiplicative aspects of each digit, drawing on their knowledge of place value. Ask them to think about the advice they would give to someone who is comparing two numbers that start with the same digit.

Children are also required to order the set of numbers from smallest to largest.

Evidencing mastery

Children draw on various representations to show numbers in different ways, deciding and explaining which number is larger when comparing a pair or group of numbers. They recognise when zero is used as a place holder and read the number accurately. They apply knowledge of place value to describe the position and value of each digit in numbers up to 1000.

Look for children who use what they already know about comparing the pairs of numbers when ordering the whole set rather than starting again.

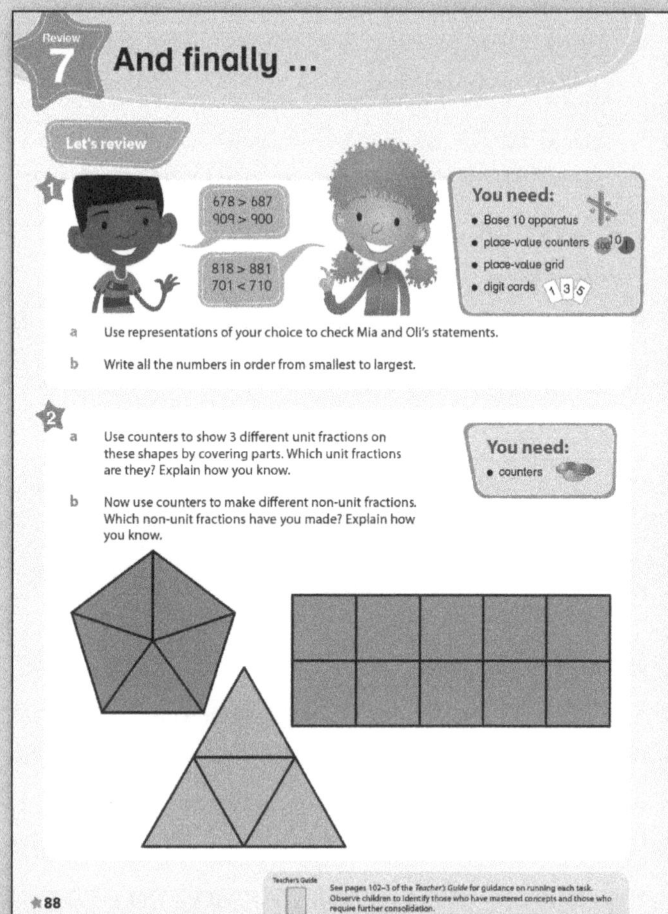
Review 7 And finally ...

Let's review

1

You need:
- Base 10 apparatus
- place-value counters
- place-value grid
- digit cards

a Use representations of your choice to check Mia and Oli's statements.

b Write all the numbers in order from smallest to largest.

2

a Use counters to show 3 different unit fractions on these shapes by covering parts. Which unit fractions are they? Explain how you know.

b Now use counters to make different non-unit fractions. Which non-unit fractions have you made? Explain how you know.

You need:
- counters

88

Teacher's Guide

See pages 102–3 of the *Teacher's Guide* for guidance on running each task. Observe children to identify those who have mastered concepts and those who require further consolidation.

Assessment task 2

Resources

Counters.

Running the task

Children must use three shapes that show a whole divided into a different number of equal pieces.

Encourage them to discuss each shape and explain which fractions they represent. You could ask them to count in fraction steps up to the whole.

Children must first use counters to represent unit fractions by covering parts and explain how they know each is correct, e.g. they could cover one part of the pentagon and explain this as one part out of the five parts are covered so this shows $\frac{1}{5}$. You could ask questions such as: *In a unit fraction, does the numerator always, sometimes or never have the value one? In a unit fraction, does the numerator always, sometimes or never have the value three?*

The task develops to include representations of non-unit fractions. Encourage children to work together with counters to show as many non-unit fractions as they can. Again, you could ask questions such as: *In a non-unit fraction, does the numerator always, sometimes or never have the value three?*

Evidencing mastery

Children explain the differences between a unit and non-unit fractions, giving examples of both.

They use representation to show a range of fractions and can explain that a unit fraction always has a numerator with a value of one.

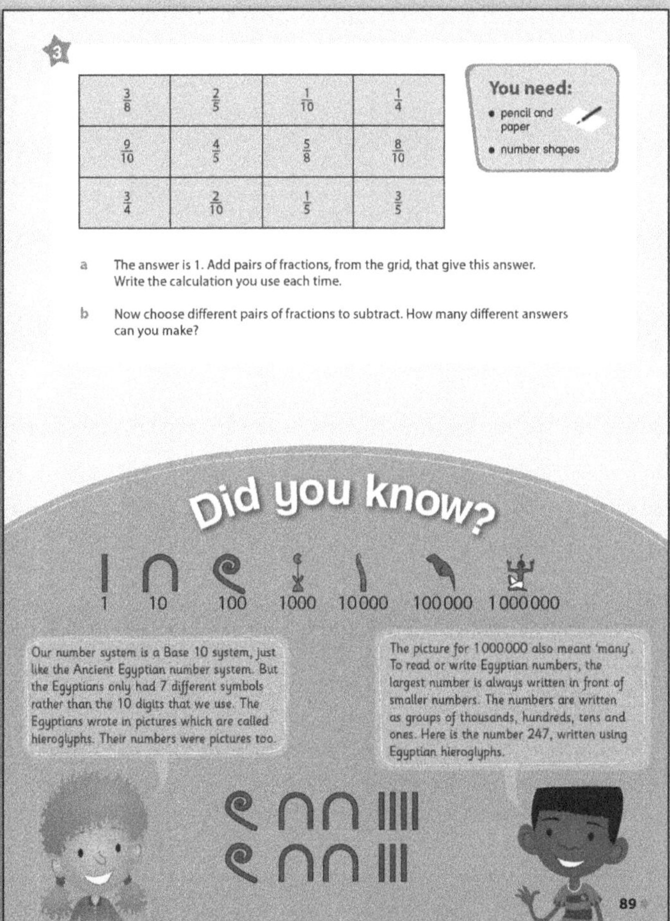

3

$\frac{3}{8}$	$\frac{2}{5}$	$\frac{1}{10}$	$\frac{1}{4}$
$\frac{9}{10}$	$\frac{4}{5}$	$\frac{5}{8}$	$\frac{8}{10}$
$\frac{3}{4}$	$\frac{2}{10}$	$\frac{1}{5}$	$\frac{3}{5}$

You need:
- pencil and paper
- number shapes

a The answer is 1. Add pairs of fractions, from the grid, that give this answer. Write the calculation you use each time.

b Now choose different pairs of fractions to subtract. How many different answers can you make?

Did you know?

1 10 100 1000 10000 100000 1000000

Our number system is a Base 10 system, just like the Ancient Egyptian number system. But the Egyptians only had 7 different symbols rather than the 10 digits that we use. The Egyptians wrote in pictures which are called hieroglyphs. Their numbers were pictures too.

The picture for 1000000 also meant 'many'. To read or write Egyptian numbers, the largest number is always written in front of smaller numbers. The numbers are written as groups of thousands, hundreds, tens and ones. Here is the number 247, written using Egyptian hieroglyphs.

89

Concepts mastered

- ☑ Children can represent numbers in different ways, applying knowledge of place value to describe the position and value of each digit in numbers up to 1000.
- ☑ Children can recognise and describe unit and non-unit fractions, referring to the value of the numerator to explain the difference between them.
- ☑ Children can draw on understanding of counting in fraction steps of a constant size to help make sense of adding and subtracting fractions with the same denominator and find pairs of fractions that total one.

Assessment task 3

Resources

Pencil and paper, number shapes.

Running the task

Ask children to describe some of the tasks they have done so far that involved adding and subtracting fractions. Perhaps they can make up a problem to go with a given addition, e.g. $\frac{3}{10} + \frac{2}{10}$ and relate it to money or length.

Children should choose pairs of fractions from the grid that give the answer one whole and write the calculation each time. You could ask them to prove their calculations using representations.

They can then work together to make a range of subtraction calculations to find as many different answers as they can. If needed, prompt them to look for pairs that share the same denominator.

Evidencing mastery

Children draw on knowledge of number bonds to help add fraction pairs that equal 1, e.g. they draw on bonds for ten for tenths, bonds for eight for eighths, etc.

Look for children who quickly spot pairs with the same denominator and add and subtract these fractions fluently.

Did you know?

The Textbook shows an example of a number written using the Ancient Egyptian number system which used hieroglyphs. Explain that, like our system, which is based on a Hindu-Arabic numeral system that uses zero as a place holder, the Egyptian system also used a notion of Base 10.

It would be useful and interesting to look at some of the similarities and differences between the Egyptian number system and the one that we use. You could point out that there are different symbols for numbers that are powers of 10 rather than being made up of digits 0–9. Also, that the numbers 1–9 are made up of multiple 'one' symbols. You could compare this with the numbers 1, 2 and 3 in Roman numerals.

Challenge children to write some 3-digit numbers using the Egyptian system and compare them to the numbers written in the symbols that we use. Discuss why the system we use is more efficient.

Unit 8

Using multiplication and division facts

Mathematical focus

- ★ Number: multiplication and division, fractions
- ★ Measurement: mass, length, money
- ★ Statistics: interpret and present data

Prior learning

Children should already be able to:

- begin to know multiplication and division facts for the two, three, four, five, eight and ten multiplication tables
- use mental calculation strategies to solve multiplication and division.

Key new learning

- Recall and use multiplication and division facts for the three, four and eight multiplication tables.
- Write and calculate mathematical statements for multiplication and division using the multiplication tables that they know, including for 2-digit numbers multiplied by single-digit numbers, using mental and progressing to formal written methods.
- Solve problems, including missing number problems, involving multiplication and division, including positive integer scaling problems and correspondence problems in which n objects are connected to m objects.

Making connections

- Recall of multiplication and division facts is essential for all areas of maths and there are many practical applications, including length, mass, volume and money, that can be exploited to give children practice in context. When working with measures, children should record their answers using the correct notation and units.
- Knowledge of multiples, and the ability to count in steps, will help children interpret information presented in scaled bar charts and pictograms and solve problems based on the information shown.
- Solving missing number problems requires good number sense and an understanding of inverse operations. Children who become adept at this will benefit later on when they come to solve equations using formal methods.
- Problems involving scaling down links to fractions, particularly finding a fraction of a given amount.

Talk about

Recap the vocabulary of multiplication and division, ensuring that children know the meaning of multiplicand, multiplier, product, dividend, divisor and quotient. It is important to talk about how the bar model shows the part-whole relationship for multiplication and its link to division. In this example, if each part represents 5, the whole would be 20 because $5 \times 4 = 20$. If the whole is 28, the parts would be 7 because $28 \div 4 = 7$. Give different values to children and ask them to tell you the parts and the whole.

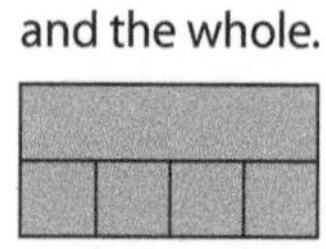

Engaging and exploring

For the picture of the spiders, ask children to estimate how many legs there are on all the spiders and write their estimate down. Then discuss how they could find out the actual number. Agree that they could count all the legs one by one, but that this is inefficient. Establish that a quicker way would be to use their multiplication table for four, doubling 4 × 9 to give 8 × 9. So the nine spiders in the photo have 72 legs in total. Ask: *How did your estimates compare to the actual answer?* Practise multiplying numbers by eight by doubling the multiplication table for four.

Looking at the picture of the toy cars, discuss how children could find out how many wheels there are on all the cars. Agree that they could use multiplication facts to find the number of cars and then double and double again to multiply by four; they could also find the products of ten and four, and of five and four and add the two products.

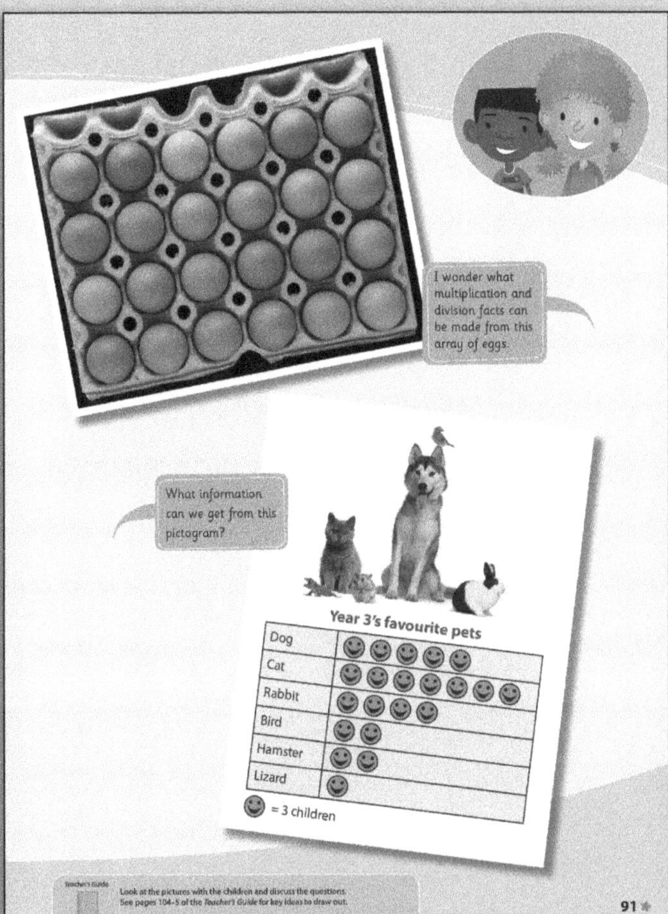

Ask other questions that involve multiplying by four by doubling twice and multiplying by 15 by multiplying by ten, halving that and adding the two products.

Look at the picture of the apples. Tell children that you would like to pack the apples in bags of four. Ask them to tell you what information they would need to know to find out how many bags are needed for the apples. Agree they will need to know how many apples there are altogether and also how many apples can fit in one bag. Tell children that there are 48 apples in the crate and that four apples can fit in a bag. Agree that to work out how many bags are needed for all the apples, they need to carry out division. Establish that they need to find out how many groups of four they can make from 48. Recap the vocabulary involved in division: dividend, divisor and quotient. Then give pairs of children counters. Ask them to count out 48 and then place them in groups of four. They should see from this that they would need 12 bags for the apples. Ask: *What other way could you have found the answer?* Agree that they could count on in fours until they get to 48.

The eggs in the picture are arranged in a six by four array. Ask children to make a matching array using counters on a piece of paper. They should describe their array to a partner, turning the paper to demonstrate commutativity. Ask them to write down the four facts that can be made (6 × 4 = 24, 4 × 6 = 24, 24 ÷ 6 = 4, 24 ÷ 4 = 6). Invite them to make other arrays using the 24 counters. Ask: *How many can you make and how many number statements can you record?*

Ask children to identify the animals in the pets photo. Do any of them have these as pets? Then ask them to tell you how they think the animals relate to the pictogram. Agree that the pictogram shows the favourite pets of a group of Year 3 children. What can children tell you about the symbols? Agree that each one represents three children. Confirm that knowing multiplication facts for three will be really helpful when it comes to identifying how many children voted for each pet. Ask children to work that out and write their answers on their whiteboards. Ask questions about the pictogram, e.g. *How many more children like cats than hamsters?*

Ask children how they come to school and make a tally to show the different modes of transport children use. Ask children to create a pictogram to show the information, using a circular symbol to represent four children. Discuss what they would need to do to the circle so that it represents one, two and three.

Checking understanding

You will know children have mastered these concepts when they can solve problems that involve using multiplication and division facts for the required tables, recalling the multiplication and corresponding division facts quickly.

Things to think about

- How will you use manipulatives and visual representations, such as the bar model, to help conceptual understanding of multiplication and division with all children?
- How will you encourage fluency, reasoning and problem solving? How can you develop the strategy another and another and another, e.g. you could ask children to give you a multiple of three and another, and another and so on.
- How could you include activities that involve the problem solving strategy sometimes, always never? This is a good one for encouraging children to reason about examples and counter examples.
- How can you ensure children experience practical opportunities to practically multiply and divide measures, such as money, length, mass and capacity?

8a Multiplication tables

- **Recall and use multiplication and division facts for the three, four and eight multiplication tables.**
- **Write and calculate mathematical statements for multiplication and division using the multiplication tables that they know, including for two-digit numbers multiplied by one-digit numbers, using mental and progressing to formal methods.**

Homework 39 and 40 | Practice Book pp 68–71

Representations and resources

Squared paper, coins, sand, plastic bags, scales, counters.

Mathematical vocabulary

Multiplication tables, double, doubling, half, halving, commutative, commutativity

Warming up

Draw a circle on the whiteboard. Around it write the numbers from one to 12 as if on a clock face. In the middle write the number of the multiplication table you wish children to practise. Point to each of the outside numbers in turn and expect children to multiply it by the number in the middle. Repeat, in a different order, revisiting numbers that they do not instantly recall. Replace the numbers around the outside with the answers to the multiplications, and ask children to tell you what number they would divide each number by to give the number in the middle.

Background knowledge

It is important that children learn their multiplication tables. Research says that children who do not know them cannot solve problems. The reason for this is that when they are working on the problem and have to stop to work out these facts, they will disengage from the problem. They then get lost and the problem becomes harder to solve. Understanding the commutative nature of multiplication is very helpful in learning multiplication facts. If we know that $8 \times 3 = 24$ we also know $3 \times 8 = 24$; we do not need to learn the second fact. Knowing that division is the inverse of multiplication is helpful for learning division facts. If we know that $24 \div 3 = 8$, we also know that $24 \div 8 = 3$. It is important to help children understand these connections.

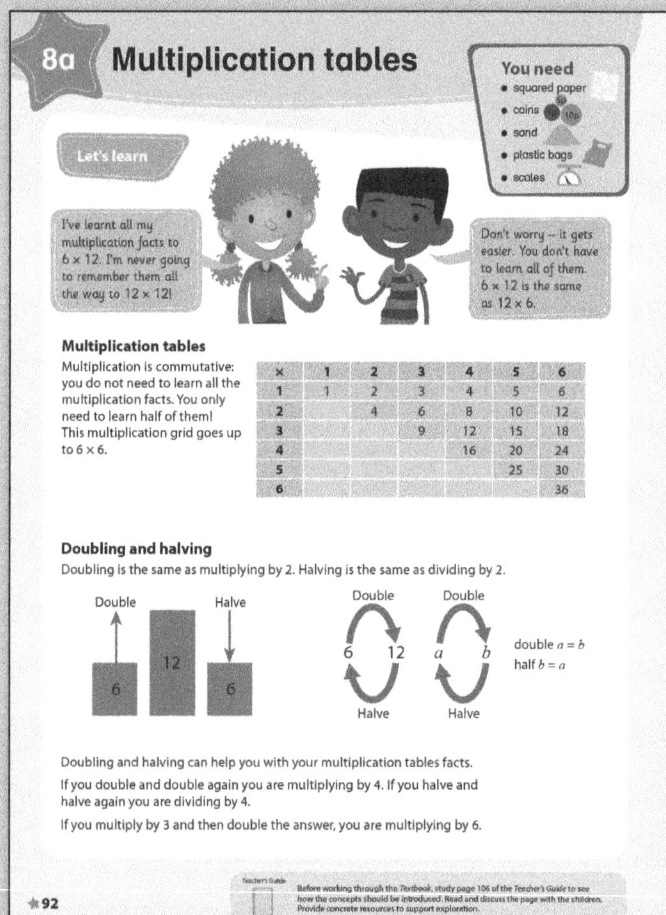

8a Multiplication tables

You need
- squared paper
- coins
- sand
- plastic bags
- scales

Let's learn

I've learnt all my multiplication facts to 6 × 12. I'm never going to remember them all the way to 12 × 12!

Don't worry – it gets easier. You don't have to learn all of them. 6 × 12 is the same as 12 × 6.

Multiplication tables

Multiplication is commutative: you do not need to learn all the multiplication facts. You only need to learn half of them! This multiplication grid goes up to 6 × 6.

×	1	2	3	4	5	6
1	1	2	3	4	5	6
2		4	6	8	10	12
3			9	12	15	18
4				16	20	24
5					25	30
6						36

Doubling and halving

Doubling is the same as multiplying by 2. Halving is the same as dividing by 2.

Doubling and halving can help you with your multiplication tables facts.

If you double and double again you are multiplying by 4. If you halve and halve again you are dividing by 4.

If you multiply by 3 and then double the answer, you are multiplying by 6.

Teacher's Guide: Before working through the Textbook, study page 106 of the Teacher's Guide to see how the concepts should be introduced. Read and discuss the page with the children. Provide concrete resources to support exploration.

92

Let's learn: Modelling and teaching

Multiplication tables

- Begin by discussing the misconception cartoon in the Textbook, in particular Oli's response. If necessary, remind children that multiplication is commutative.
- Then ask them to look at the multiplication grid and discuss, in pairs, the facts that are there and those that are missing. *Can they explain why they are missing?*
- Give them squared paper and ask them to draw their own multiplication grid to stick into their books. This should go to 12×12. Ask children to discuss with a partner how the pattern continues for the number facts to 12×6. Ask them what the first new number would be. Agree 7×7 because all the facts before 7×7 are already there.

Doubling and halving

- Call out some 2-digit numbers for children to double and halve. Include odd numbers, so that when they halve they need to think about an answer that ends with the fraction half. Then move on to simple 3-digit numbers.
- Revise doubling and halving twice for multiplying and dividing by four, as introduced in Unit 3a – 2s, 4s and 8s..
- Then look at the models in the Textbook. Establish that doubling and halving are inverse operations and that a and b can be any number. Ask children to copy the arrow model and use it to double and halve some numbers of their choice.

Let's practise: Digging deeper

Step 1

Before children begin the task, work through some examples together, encouraging children to say what they are doing in sentences, e.g. *6 × 4 = 24 is the same as 4 × 6 = 24. Multiplication is commutative – different calculation, same answer.* As they work through the task remind them to complete each number statement with its product, e.g. 4 × 9 = 9 × 4 = 36.

Step 2

Before beginning the task, call out some 2- and simple 3-digit numbers for children to double and halve. Encourage children to partition numbers in ways to make them easier to halve, e.g. 30 can be partitioned into 20 and 10. When children carry out the task, let them make jottings if they wish. They should present their answers using the model shown.

Step 3

This task is designed as a practical way of practising doubling and involves accurately weighing and reading scales. You will need to give children sand or similar, small plastic bags and a set of weighing scales. If their two answers do not match, suggest that they think about whether they have doubled incorrectly or made a mistake when weighing. Encourage them to repeat the question to find out where they went wrong.

Step 4

This task asks children to make a list of other facts that Oli could make up using his knowledge of the multiplication table for four to 12 × 4. Encourage children to write down all the commutative facts and explain that multiplication is commutative; they could draw an array as part of their explanation. In addition encourage them to make up new facts by doubling and halving, e.g. 30 × 4 = 120, 15 × 4 = 60. Expect them to be creative!

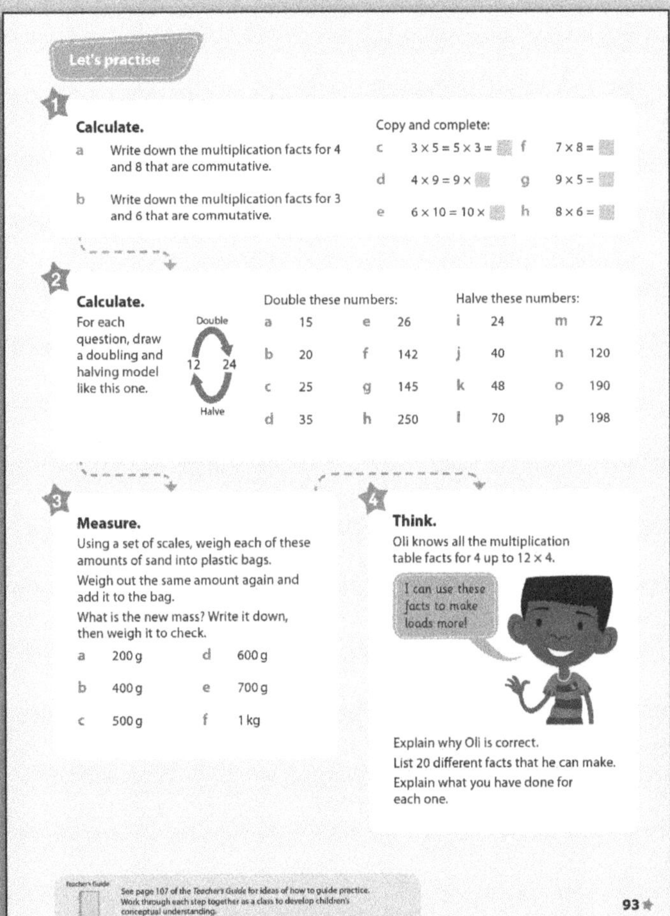

Let's practise

1 Calculate.

a Write down the multiplication facts for 4 and 8 that are commutative.

b Write down the multiplication facts for 3 and 6 that are commutative.

Copy and complete:

c 3 × 5 = 5 × 3 = ▒ f 7 × 8 = ▒

d 4 × 9 = 9 × ▒ g 9 × 5 = ▒

e 6 × 10 = 10 × ▒ h 8 × 6 = ▒

2 Calculate.

For each question, draw a doubling and halving model like this one.

Double these numbers:

a 15 e 26

b 20 f 142

c 25 g 145

d 35 h 250

Halve these numbers:

i 24 m 72

j 40 n 120

k 48 o 190

l 70 p 198

3 Measure.

Using a set of scales, weigh each of these amounts of sand into plastic bags.

Weigh out the same amount again and add it to the bag.

What is the new mass? Write it down, then weigh it to check.

a 200 g d 600 g

b 400 g e 700 g

c 500 g f 1 kg

4 Think.

Oli knows all the multiplication table facts for 4 up to 12 × 4.

Explain why Oli is correct.

List 20 different facts that he can make.

Explain what you have done for each one.

Teacher's Guide

See page 107 of the *Teacher's Guide* for ideas of how to guide practice. Work through each step together as a class to develop children's conceptual understanding.

93

Ensuring progress

Supporting understanding

Encourage children to practically create the arrays in Step 1 using counters on paper and then turn the paper so that they can see both multiplication statements. Highlight the commutativity. In Step 2, change the numbers that they work with so that they are all multiples of ten. Show them clearly how they can partition the numbers to make them easier to halve.

Broadening understanding

Adapt the numbers in Step 2 to include odd numbers and ask children to write their answers as fractions and decimals. You could also ask them to double and halve the numbers twice. In Step 3, add some masses that end with 50 grams.

Concept mastered

Children can use multiplication facts and doubling and halving to multiply numbers.

Follow-up ideas

- Children could make a doubling or halving game. They prepare cards with 2- and 3-digit numbers written on them. They place them in a pile and take it in turns to pick one at a time. They double the number and then halve it, keeping the card if both their answers are correct; the winner is the player with most cards at the end. They could then play again, this time doubling and halving twice.
- Give children bottles, water and measuring cylinders and ask them to fill the bottles with amounts in multiples of 100 ml and then show in other bottles what double and then half the volumes would look like.
- Ask children to write down pairs of commutative multiplication statements on pairs of cards. They can then use these to play a game of 'Snap' or 'Pairs'.

Answers

Step 1

a 3 × 5 = 5 × 3 = 15

b 4 × 9 = 9 × 4 = 36

c 6 × 10 = 10 × 6 = 60

d 7 × 8 = 8 × 7 = 56

e 9 × 5 = 5 × 9 = 45

f 8 × 6 = 6 × 8 = 48

Step 2

a	30	**f**	284
b	40	**g**	290
c	50	**h**	500
d	70	**i**	12
e	52	**j**	20
k	24	**n**	60
l	35	**o**	95
m	36	**p**	99

Step 3

a	400 g	**d**	1 kg 200 g
b	800 g	**e**	1 kg 400 g
c	1 kg	**f**	2 kg

Step 4

Oli knows: 4 × 1 = 4, 4 × 2 = 8, 4 × 3 = 12, 4 × 4 = 16, 4 × 5 = 20, 4 × 6 = 24, 4 × 7 = 28, 4 × 8 = 32, 4 × 9 = 36, 4 × 10 = 40, 4 × 11 = 44 and 4 × 12 = 48

Other possible facts will vary.

8b Multiplying and dividing by 5 and 20

- **Write and calculate mathematical statements for multiplication and division using the multiplication tables that they know, including for 2-digit numbers multiplied by single-digit numbers, using mental and progressing to formal written methods.**

Homework 41 and 42

Practice Book pp 72–4

Mathematical vocabulary

Multiplication tables, double, doubling, half, halving

Representations and resources

Clocks with movable hands, place-value grids, digit cards, number rods, coins, counters.

Warming up

Give each child a clock. Ask them to describe it. Ensure that they talk about the hour numbers and how many minutes pass from one to the other, making links to the multiplication table for five and the two hands. Focus on minutes past. Ask them to find different times past the same hour, e.g. five minutes past three, 40 minutes past three. Encourage them to tell you what these times would be in digital format where the hour comes first followed by the minutes, 3:05, 3:40.

Background knowledge

It is important to have a bank of mental calculation strategies. Children should all be confident with their multiplication facts for ten. They should also be able to tell you that five is half of ten and 20 is double ten. This allows you to introduce the strategy of multiplying by five by multiplying by ten and halving and multiplying by 20 by multiplying by ten and doubling. Division works in a similar way: divide by ten and double for five and divide by ten and halve for 20. Provide plenty of opportunities for children to explore this.

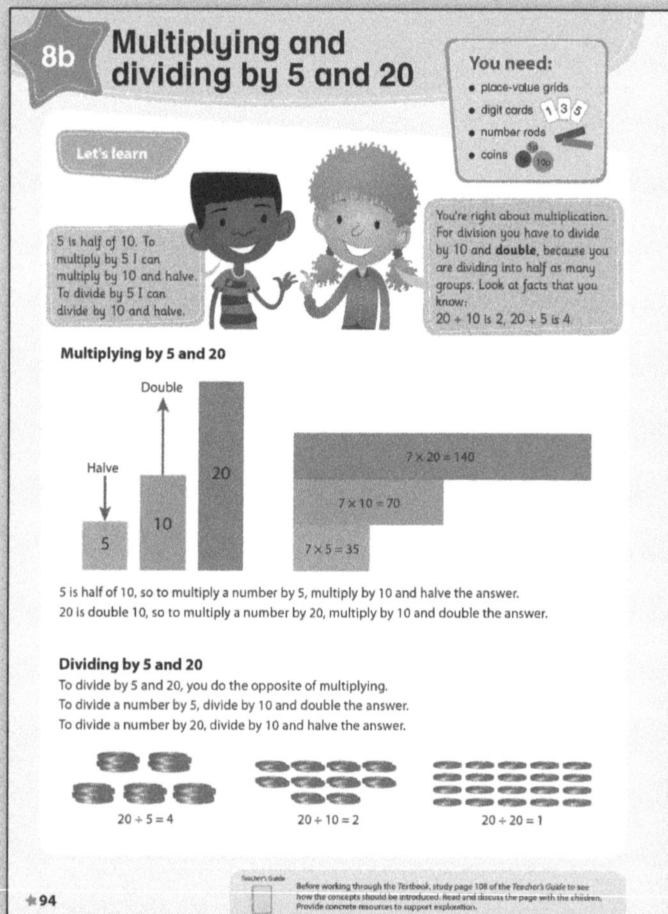

8b Multiplying and dividing by 5 and 20

You need:
- place-value grids
- digit cards
- number rods
- coins

Let's learn

5 is half of 10. To multiply by 5 I can multiply by 10 and halve. To divide by 5 I can divide by 10 and halve.

You're right about multiplication. For division you have to divide by 10 and **double**, because you are dividing into half as many groups. Look at facts that you know: 20 ÷ 10 is 2, 20 ÷ 5 is 4.

Multiplying by 5 and 20

5 is half of 10, so to multiply a number by 5, multiply by 10 and halve the answer.
20 is double 10, so to multiply a number by 20, multiply by 10 and double the answer.

Dividing by 5 and 20

To divide by 5 and 20, you do the opposite of multiplying.
To divide a number by 5, divide by 10 and double the answer.
To divide a number by 20, divide by 10 and halve the answer.

20 ÷ 5 = 4   20 ÷ 10 = 2   20 ÷ 20 = 1

94

Teacher's Guide — Before working through the *Textbook*, study page 108 of the *Teacher's Guide* to see how the concepts should be introduced. Read and discuss the page with the children. Provide concrete resources to support exploration.

Let's learn: Modelling and teaching

Multiplying by 5 and 20

- Begin by multiplying numbers by ten using place-value grids and digit cards. Expect children to be able to tell you that when multiplying the number is ten times bigger and the digits move one place to the left.
- Next refer to the halving and doubling model in the Textbook. Ask children to model this using number rods.
- Ask them to write out the facts for five up to 12 × 5 and, beside them, the facts for ten to 12 × 10. *What do they notice about the answers?* Agree that the answers for the facts for five are half those for ten because five is half of ten.
- Ask children to look at the multiplication bars and explain what happens when you multiply by 20. Finally, call out some 2-digit numbers for children to multiply by five, e.g. 24, 48, 62, and then 20, e.g. 45, 54, 63, using this strategy.

Dividing by 5 and 20

- Begin by dividing some numbers by ten using place-value grids and digit cards. Expect children to tell you that the number gets ten times smaller so the digits move one place to the right. Discuss the misconception cartoon in the Textbook. Focus on the need to double when dividing by five because they are making half as many groups as they would be if dividing by ten; agree that there would be double the number of things in each group. Model this using pennies or counters, as shown in the Textbook. Ask children to compare your model with the diagram shown in the Textbook. Call out some multiples of five for children to divide by 5 using this strategy, e.g. 30, 60, 100.
- Repeat the above for dividing by 20, first establishing that if dividing by 20 they will make twice as many groups as they would if dividing by ten. Ask children to divide some numbers by 20 using this strategy, e.g. 60, 200.

Let's practise: Digging deeper

Step 1

This task reinforces and rehearses multiplying and dividing by ten. If necessary, work through some examples before children begin using digit cards and place-value grids as in Let's learn. During the task children need to explain to a partner what is happening as a rehearsal for their written explanation. Listen for phrases such as *ten times bigger/smaller* and talk of digits moving one place to the left or right. If any children talk about adding or taking away zeros, ensure that you ask them to explain what is really happening.

Step 2

Before children begin the task, remind them that, to multiply by five, they can multiply by ten and halve. Call out some 2- and simple 3-digit numbers for practice. Similarly, remind children that, to multiply by 20, they can multiply by ten and double; again, call out a few numbers for practice.

Step 3

This task is designed as a practical way of reinforcing and practising dividing by five and 20 and also handling money. Remind children that, to divide by five, they can divide by ten and double, and, to divide by 20, they can divide by ten and halve. In both cases, ask children to explain why this works. During the task, children divide the amounts by five and 20 using these strategies; they then make the answers using the fewest coins possible.

Step 4

This task asks children to find the number that Mia was thinking of. Before they begin, give them similar problems to solve, e.g. *I multiplied my number by 20 and divided it by five. I ended up with 52. What was my number?* Encourage children to work backwards from the answer, doing the inverse operation each time; e.g. $52 \times 5 = 260$, then $260 \div 20 = 13$.

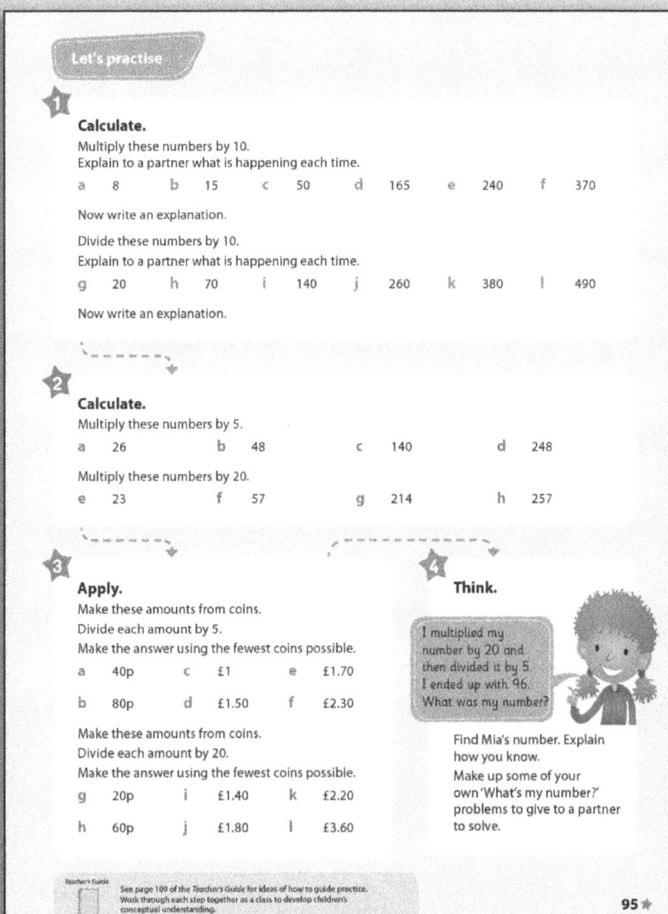

Let's practise

1 **Calculate.**

Multiply these numbers by 10.
Explain to a partner what is happening each time.

a 8 b 15 c 50 d 165 e 240 f 370

Now write an explanation.

Divide these numbers by 10.
Explain to a partner what is happening each time.

g 20 h 70 i 140 j 260 k 380 l 490

Now write an explanation.

2 **Calculate.**

Multiply these numbers by 5.

a 26 b 48 c 140 d 248

Multiply these numbers by 20.

e 23 f 57 g 214 h 257

3 **Apply.**

Make these amounts from coins.
Divide each amount by 5.
Make the answer using the fewest coins possible.

a 40p c £1 e £1.70

b 80p d £1.50 f £2.30

Make these amounts from coins.
Divide each amount by 20.
Make the answer using the fewest coins possible.

g 20p i £1.40 k £2.20

h 60p j £1.80 l £3.60

4 **Think.**

Find Mia's number. Explain how you know.
Make up some of your own 'What's my number?' problems to give to a partner to solve.

Teacher's Guide
See page 109 of the *Teacher's Guide* for ideas of how to guide practice. Work through each step together as a class to develop children's conceptual understanding.

95

Ensuring progress

Supporting understanding

Help children to grasp the fact that the number of groups halves when dividing by five (compared to dividing by ten) by giving them 30 counters (and other multiples of ten) and asking them to group them in tens and then fives. They can then group the counters in tens and then 20s to see that the number of groups doubles.

Broadening understanding

For Steps 1–3, ask children to make up a visual representation to illustrate their explanations.

Concept mastered

Children can explain the strategy for multiplying and dividing by five and 20 clearly, and show examples.

Follow-up ideas

- Children could make a card game to rehearse these strategies. They need one set of cards with 2- and simple 3-digit numbers. They need another set showing ×5, ×20, ÷5 and ÷20. They pick a number card and then an operation card and find the answer. They could make up their own rules for scoring.
- Apply the strategies, covered in this concept spread, to measures, particularly length, mass and volume. Children could measure different amounts, work out what they would be when multiplied or divided by five or 20, then measure out the answer.
- You could explore the strategy of multiplying by 15, by multiplying by ten and halving the answer, then adding the two results together.

Answers

Step 1

a 80
b 150
c 500
d 1650
e 2400
f 3700

Multiplying by ten moves every digit one place to the left (and puts 0s in the ones column).

g 2
h 7
i 14
j 26
k 38
l 49

Dividing by ten moves every digit one place to the right.

Step 2

a 130 **c** 700
b 240 **d** 1240
e 460 **g** 4280
f 1140 **h** 5140

Step 3

a 8p (5p + 2p + 1p)
b 16p (10p + 5p + 1p)
c 20p (20p)
d 30p (20p + 10p)
e 34p (20p + 10p + 2p + 2p)
f 46p (20p + 20p + 5p + 1p)
g 1p (1p)
h 3p (2p + 1p)
i 7p (5p + 2p)
j 9p (5p + 2p + 2p)
k 11p (10p + 1p)
l 18p (10p + 5p + 2p + 1p)

Step 4

Mia's number was 24.

8c Missing number problems and scaling

- **Solve problems, including missing number problems, involving multiplication and division, including positive integer scaling problems in which n objects are connected to m objects.**

Homework 43 and 44 | Practice Book pp 75–7

Representations and resources

Number rods, strips of paper, rulers, scissors, sticky tape, counters.

Mathematical vocabulary

Multiplication, division, multiplicand, multiplier, product, dividend, divisor, quotient, scaling up, scaling down, bar model, fraction

Warming up

Write a multiplication fact on the board, e.g. $3 \times 8 = 24$. Ask children to generate as many other facts as they can from this, e.g. $30 \times 8 = 240$, $240 \div 30 = 8$, $15 \times 8 = 120$, $15 \times 4 = 60$, $60 \div 4 = 15$, $15 \times 16 = 240$. Encourage them to double, halve and multiply and divide by ten and also include the inverse division facts.

Background knowledge

Scaling up and down is an effective mental calculation strategy for multiplication and division. It links well to basic ratio and will be helpful to children in later years. It also links well to fractions and provides an opportunity to rehearse this area of mathematics. Visual representations are helpful when children need to find missing numbers. The bar model is effective for solving word problems.

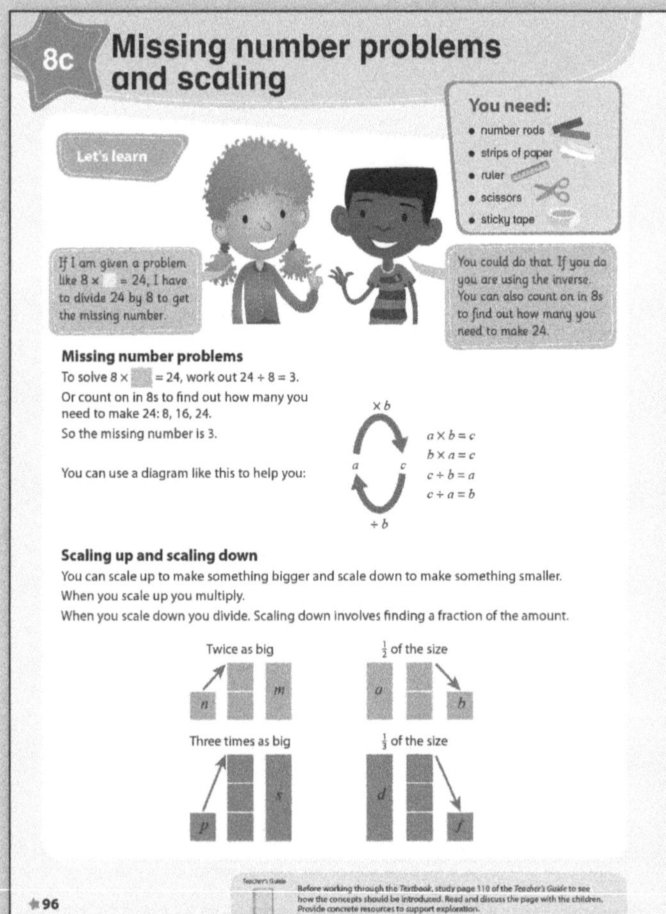

8c Missing number problems and scaling

You need:
- number rods
- strips of paper
- ruler
- scissors
- sticky tape

Let's learn

Missing number problems

To solve 8 × ▢ = 24, work out 24 ÷ 8 = 3.
Or count on in 8s to find out how many you need to make 24: 8, 16, 24.
So the missing number is 3.

You can use a diagram like this to help you:

$a \times b = c$
$b \times a = c$
$c \div b = a$
$c \div a = b$

Scaling up and scaling down

You can scale up to make something bigger and scale down to make something smaller.
When you scale up you multiply.
When you scale down you divide. Scaling down involves finding a fraction of the amount.

Teacher's Guide

Before working through the *Textbook*, study page 110 of the *Teacher's Guide* to see how the concepts should be introduced. Read and discuss the page with the children. Provide concrete resources to support exploration.

96

Let's learn: Modelling and teaching

Missing number problems

- Emphasise the fact that using multiplication facts to solve missing number statements is often simpler than using division because you can count on. Demonstrate using examples such as ▢ × 8 = 48. Agree that to find the answer children could work out 48 divided by eight to find how many groups of 8 there are in 48. However, they could use multiplication facts or count on in eights to 48. Together count back in eights from 48 and then forwards in eights to 48. Which do children think is simplest?
- Explain that using the letters a, b and c means you can use the diagram to solve other missing number problems. Work through some examples, using the diagram, with children, e.g. *If $a = 6$ and $c = 30$, what is b? If $b = 10$ and $c = 60$, what is a?* Set some more examples for children to solve themselves in the same way.

Scaling up and scaling down

- Scaling is a very useful mental calculation strategy. Look at the diagrams in the Textbook. Ask: *What do you notice?* They should be able to tell you that scaling up involves multiplying to make something bigger and that scaling down involves dividing to make something smaller. Scaling down involves finding a fraction of the amount (dividing by the denominator of the fraction). *What would you divide by to find $\frac{1}{5}$ of the size? $\frac{1}{10}$ of the size?* Ask some questions and work through them with children, using the diagram, e.g. *If $n = 12$, what is m? If $a = 50$, what is b? If $p = 6$, what is s? If $d = 12$, what is f?* Give children number rods. Ask them to take one of one colour and then place six more of the same colour in a line under the first rod to model scaling up by six. Give different values to the one and then the six for children to scale up and down. Repeat for other numbers of rods.
- Then set children some similar questions to solve. They could use strips of paper to show scaling up and down by different amounts, e.g. four and eight, and make up some questions of their own for a partner.

Let's practise: Digging deeper

Step 1

Before children begin the task, work through some examples with them, e.g., ▢ × 10 = 40, ▢ × 8 = 64, 7 × ▢ = 28, 6 × ▢ = 18. Then ask them to write down the four associated facts (e.g. 4 × 10 = 40, 10 × 4 = 40, 40 ÷ 4 = 10 and 40 ÷ 10 = 4). During the task, encourage them to use the model shown in the Textbook, substituting the known values for the letters and finding the missing number using multiplication facts. Ask children to show you the inverse operations each time.

Step 2

Prepare for the task by recapping scaling up and down. Write some numbers on the board, e.g. 6, 12, 13 and 21, for children to scale up by two, three, four, five, eight and ten. Encourage them to use their multiplication facts, partitioning the larger numbers as they did in Unit 3a – 2, 4s and 8s. Then write up some other numbers, e.g. 40, 60 and 80, for them to scale down to find $\frac{1}{2}$, $\frac{1}{3}$, $\frac{1}{4}$, $\frac{1}{5}$, $\frac{1}{8}$ and $\frac{1}{10}$. Emphasise the link to fractions, encouraging them to use their multiplication and division facts and write any amounts left as fractions, e.g. 40 scaled down by $\frac{1}{3}$, would be $13\frac{1}{3}$. Children should draw scaling models to show what they have done for all examples. Most children should then be able to work on the task independently.

Step 3

The task asks children to measure and cut strips of paper to different lengths, scale them up so they are four times the length and scale them down to find half the length. In each case, ensure they write down what they think the new length will be before they check their answers by cutting another three strips and putting them together with the first, or cutting the first length in half, and measuring. Model a similar example with children so that they know exactly what to do, then expect children to work through the task independently.

Step 4

This task asks children to investigate the possible starting numbers and how much each is scaled up by to give 64. Expect children to work systematically. Encourage them to begin with two and scale up by 32. They should use their understanding of commutativity to write the other possible number (32 scaled up by two).

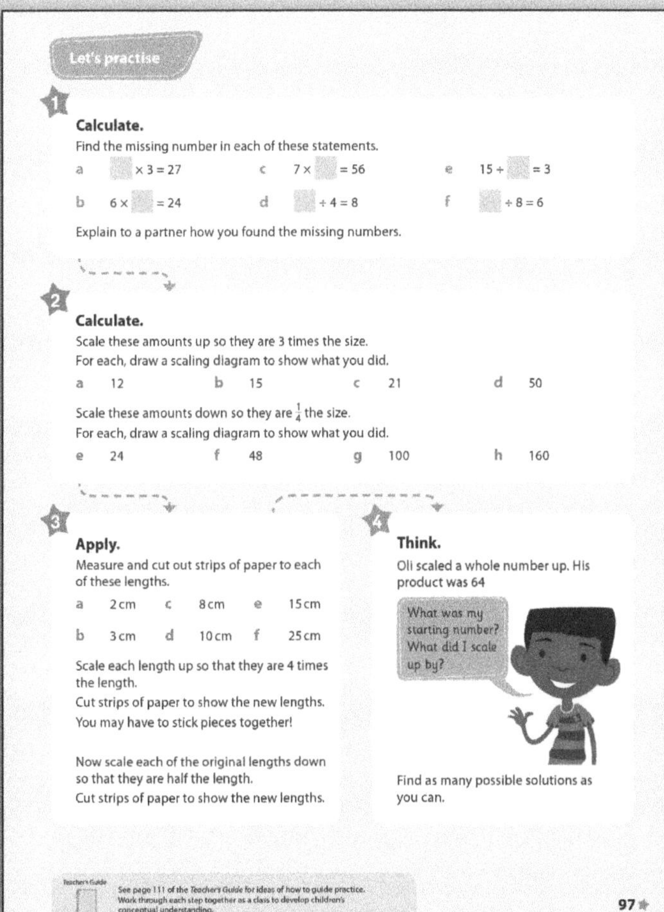

Let's practise

1 Calculate.

Find the missing number in each of these statements.

a ▢ × 3 = 27 c 7 × ▢ = 56 e 15 ÷ ▢ = 3

b 6 × ▢ = 24 d ▢ ÷ 4 = 8 f ▢ ÷ 8 = 6

Explain to a partner how you found the missing numbers.

2 Calculate.

Scale these amounts up so they are 3 times the size.
For each, draw a scaling diagram to show what you did.

a 12 b 15 c 21 d 50

Scale these amounts down so they are $\frac{1}{4}$ the size.
For each, draw a scaling diagram to show what you did.

e 24 f 48 g 100 h 160

3 Apply.

Measure and cut out strips of paper to each of these lengths.

a 2 cm c 8 cm e 15 cm

b 3 cm d 10 cm f 25 cm

Scale each length up so that they are 4 times the length.
Cut strips of paper to show the new lengths.
You may have to stick pieces together!

Now scale each of the original lengths down so that they are half the length.
Cut strips of paper to show the new lengths.

4 Think.

Oli scaled a whole number up. His product was 64

Find as many possible solutions as you can.

Teacher's Guide

See page 111 of the *Teacher's Guide* for ideas of how to guide practice. Work through each step together as a class to develop children's conceptual understanding.

97

Ensuring progress

Supporting understanding

Some children may benefit from using counters or a similar resource to help them find the missing numbers, e.g. to solve 8 × ▢ = 24 they make groups of eight counters until they reach a total of 24, and see that there are three groups.

Broadening understanding

Once children have completed the scaling up and down tasks, ask them to scale the amounts by different numbers, e.g. five and eight. They could also make up their own amounts to scale.

Concept mastered

Children can use, demonstrate and explain how to use multiplication and division to find missing numbers and also how to scale up and down.

Follow-up ideas

- Give children small plastic bags, sand and scales. They weigh, e.g. 250 g of sand and place it in a bag. They then find out how much the amount would be if scaled up by three.They check their answer by weighing out 250 g twice more and finding the mass of the three bags. They could then scale their mass down by half.
- Give children bottles, water and measuring cylinders. They measure out different volumes, scale them up or down and check by measuring, as with the sand above.
- Children could complete a similar task using money. They make, e.g. 25p using the fewest number of coins and then scale this up by three, four and five and find the new totals. They could then scale the amount down by one fifth.

Answers

Step 1

a	9	d	32
b	4	e	5
c	8	f	48

Step 2

a	36	e	6
b	45	f	12
c	63	g	25
d	150	h	40

Step 3

a	8 cm, 1 cm
b	12 cm, $1\frac{1}{2}$ cm
c	32 cm, 4 cm
d	40 cm, 5 cm,
e	60 cm, $7\frac{1}{2}$ cm
f	100 cm or 1 m, $12\frac{1}{2}$ cm

Step 4

Various answers are possible, e.g. 16 × 4 = 64.

Unit 8 High fives!

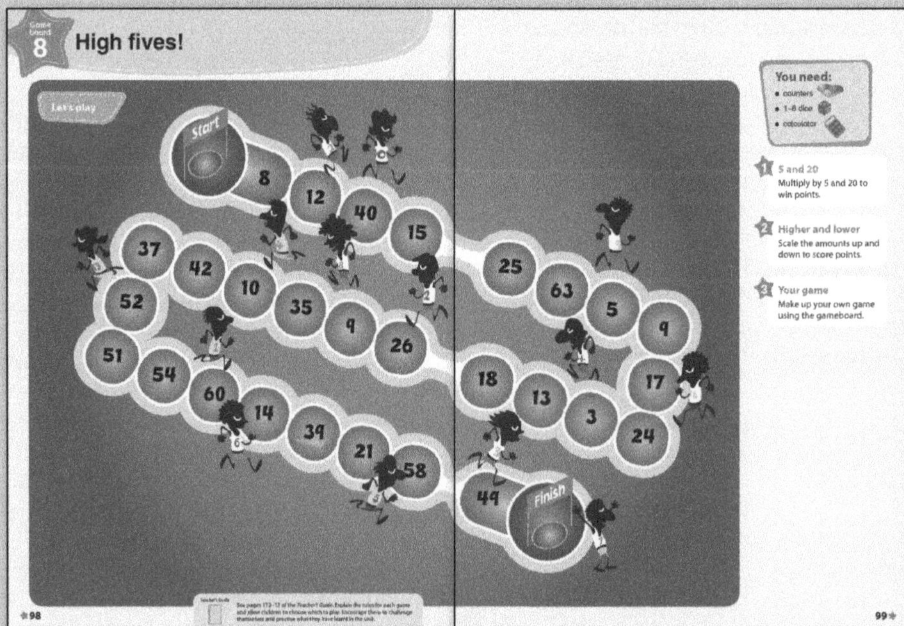

Game 1: 5 and 20

This game helps children reinforce, rehearse and consolidate multiplying by five by multiplying by ten and halving, and multiplying by 20 by multiplying by ten and doubling.

Maths focus

- Multiplying by ten and adjusting

Resources

2 counters (1 colour per player), 1–6 dice (1).

How to play

This game should be played in pairs. Children place their counters on Start. They then take it in turns to throw the dice and move their counter that number of spaces. They multiply the number they land on by five and then by 20 using the strategies they have been practising in class. They add the two answers together. If their total is higher than 100 they score one point; if it is higher than 500 they score two points. The winner is the player with the highest number of points when they have both reached Finish.

Making it easier

Children play as above, but focus on multiplying by five only, or by 20 only. Rather than scoring one or two, they keep a running total of their products; the player with the higher total at the end is the winner.

Making it harder

Encourage children to play a second game, this time dividing. They will encounter decimals this time. Some children will know about these, it will prove a useful assessment opportunity. Any children who are not familiar with decimal numbers should use the whole part of the number. Players keep a running total of their answers; this time the player with the lower total at the end is the winner.

Game 2: Higher and lower

In this game, children reinforce, rehearse and consolidate scaling up and down using doubling and halving.

Maths focus

- Scaling

Resources

2 counters (1 colour per player), 1–6 dice (1), a calculator.

How to play

This game should be played in pairs. Children place their counters on Start. They take it in turns to throw the dice and move their counter that number of spaces. They scale the number they land on up to make it twice the size and then scale it down to half the size. This will involve fractions if they land on an odd number. They find the difference between the two – this answer is the number of points they score. When both players reach Finish, they then total their points and the player with the most wins. Allow them use a calculator for this.

Making it easier

Children should scale up and down the even numbers. If they land on an odd number they stay where they are until their next go.

Making it harder

Children play as above. However, if they throw an odd number they scale the number they land on up and down by four using doubling and doubling again or halving and halving again. Some of their answers may involve the fractions of $\frac{1}{2}$ or $\frac{1}{4}$.

Game 3: Your game

Children should invent their own game designing rules that use the concepts covered in the unit. Challenge children to make their game easier or harder.

High fives!

Choose a game to play.

Game 1: 5 and 20

You need:

- 2 counters (1 colour per player)
- 1–6 dice

How to play

- Each place your counter on Start.
- Take turns to roll the dice. Move your counter that number of spaces.
- Multiply the number you land on by 5.
  Then multiply the number you land on by 20
  Add your 2 answers together.
  - If your total is higher than 100, score 1 point.
  - If your total is higher than 500, score 2 points.
- Continue to play until you both reach Finish. Then add all your points together. The winner is the player with the highest total.

Game 2: Higher and lower

You need:

- 2 counters (1 colour per player)
- 1–6 dice
- calculator

How to play

- Each place your counter on Start.
- Take turns to roll the dice. Move your counter that number of spaces.
- Scale the number you land on up by 2 to make it twice the size.
  Then scale the number you land on down to half the size.
  Find the difference between your 2 answers.
  Your answer is the number of points you score.
- Continue to play until you both reach Finish. Then use a calculator to add all your points together. The winner is the player with the highest total.

Game 3: Your game

- Make up your own game using the gameboard.
- What are the rules for your game? Explain them to someone.

Please help your child by reading the instructions and playing the game together.

Unit 8 And finally ...

Assessment task 1

Resources

Squared paper.

Running the task

Before children begin the task, recap the meaning of commutativity. Ensure that they all understand what this is. Practise saying a few facts in this way, e.g. *3 × 4 = 4 × 3. Multiplication is commutative – different calculation, same answer.* Spend some time recapping why this will not work for division. Use an example such as 12 ÷ 3 = 4; 3 ÷ 12 =. Ask children to explain why this will not work. Expect them to be able to tell you that 12 things divided into three groups would give four in each group. Three things divided into 12 groups means that there are a lot more groups to divide three into. The answer will be part of a whole number, in other words a fraction. Ask children to share their own examples.

Children need to copy the incomplete multiplication grid onto square paper. They then need to complete one half of it and explain how they can find all the facts to 12 × 12 from these facts. They also need to explain why commutativity does not work for division. Encourage them to use examples in their explanations.

Evidencing mastery

Children who can explain that multiplication is commutative and division is not, giving examples in both cases, are showing mastery.

If there are any children who have not mastered commutativity, they will need more work, with an adult, exploring arrays. They could make these using counters on paper and physically turn the paper in order to see both facts.

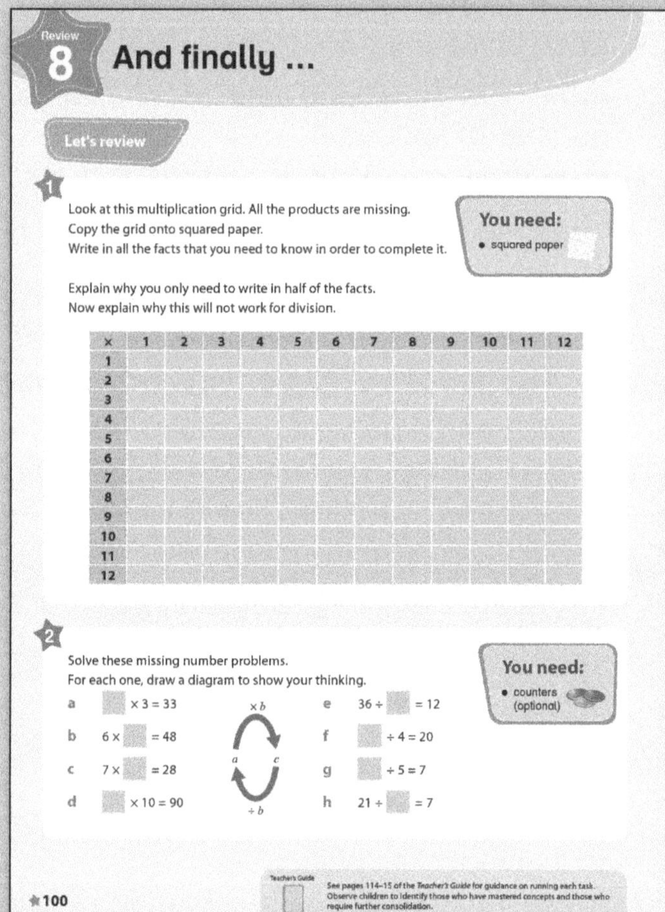

Review 8 And finally ...

Let's review

1

Look at this multiplication grid. All the products are missing.
Copy the grid onto squared paper.
Write in all the facts that you need to know in order to complete it.

You need:
- squared paper

Explain why you only need to write in half of the facts.
Now explain why this will not work for division.

×	1	2	3	4	5	6	7	8	9	10	11	12
1												
2												
3												
4												
5												
6												
7												
8												
9												
10												
11												
12												

2

Solve these missing number problems.
For each one, draw a diagram to show your thinking.

You need:
- counters (optional)

a □ × 3 = 33
b 6 × □ = 48
c 7 × □ = 28
d □ × 10 = 90

× *b*
a *c*
÷ *b*

e 36 ÷ □ = 12
f □ ÷ 4 = 20
g □ ÷ 5 = 7
h 21 ÷ □ = 7

100

Teacher's Guide

See pages 114–15 of the *Teacher's Guide* for guidance on running each task. Observe children to identify those who have mastered concepts and those who require further consolidation.

Assessment task 2

Resources

Counters (optional).

Running the task

Recap how to solve missing number problems using the arrow model from 8c – Missing number problems and scaling. Draw the model on the board and add letters to it, a as the multiplicand and c as the product with b on the top arrow as the multiplier and b on lower arrow as the divisor. Ask children to make up values for the letters and share their results with the class. Then give them values for b and c and ask them to work out what a must be, e.g.write up the missing number problem □ × 8 = 32 and draw the model on the board, substituting numbers for the letters:

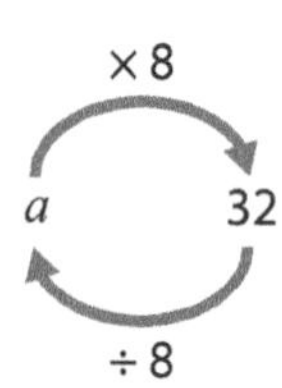

Rewrite the missing number problem as $a \times 8 = 32$ and discuss how you could solve it (by counting on in multiples of eight until you reach 32 or working out 32 ÷ 8). Encourage children to do both and then decide which is the most efficient method for them. Next give children values for a and c and ask them to use one of the ways discussed to find b.

The task asks children to solve missing number multiplication and division problems in this way. For each, they should draw the model you have been using with them. Some children may need to use counters to help them.

Evidencing mastery

Children who can solve missing number problems confidently and accurately, explaining how they worked out the answer, are showing a firm grasp of the concept. Those who need to use counters, or who can, e.g. find the missing number in a multiplication statement (e.g. □ × 3 = 33) but struggle with division statements (e.g. 36 ÷ □ = 12) require further practice.

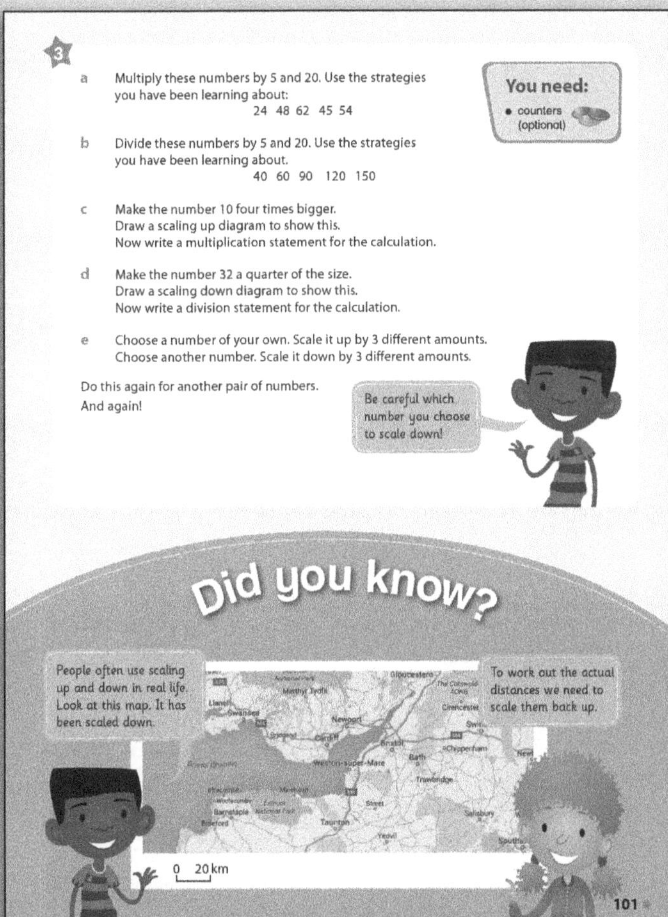

3

a Multiply these numbers by 5 and 20. Use the strategies you have been learning about:
24 48 62 45 54

b Divide these numbers by 5 and 20. Use the strategies you have been learning about.
40 60 90 120 150

c Make the number 10 four times bigger.
Draw a scaling up diagram to show this.
Now write a multiplication statement for the calculation.

d Make the number 32 a quarter of the size.
Draw a scaling down diagram to show this.
Now write a division statement for the calculation.

e Choose a number of your own. Scale it up by 3 different amounts.
Choose another number. Scale it down by 3 different amounts.

Do this again for another pair of numbers.
And again!

You need:
- counters (optional)

101

Concepts mastered

- ☑ Children can use multiplication facts and doubling and halving to multiply numbers.
- ☑ Children can explain the strategy for multiplying and dividing by five and 20 clearly, and show examples.
- ☑ Children can use, demonstrate and explain how to use multiplication and division to find missing numbers and also how to scale up and down.

Assessment task 3

Resources

Counters (optional).

Running the task

The first two questions in this task ask children to multiply and divide by five and 20 using the strategy of multiplying by ten and halving or doubling. Children need to use this strategy to be successful in this part of the task. Together, work through some examples.

Draw a scaling up diagram on the board to show that an amount has been made five times bigger. Label the small rectangle seven and ask children to tell you what the larger rectangle must be. Expect them to be able to explain what the diagram shows and how they get the answer 35. Repeat this for scaling down so that an amount is $\frac{1}{5}$ the size. Agree that to scale up you multiply, and to scale down you divide by the denominator of the fraction. Repeat this a few times with different scale factors. Ask children to draw their own scaling models as you have demonstrated. They choose how much to scale up by and then ask a partner to scale up different amounts. They repeat this for scaling down. Their partner explains how they work out their answers.

The rest of the task asks children to draw scaling models for given amounts and then to make up their own. For the scaling down part, they need to think carefully about their starting number to ensure it can be scaled down by three different amounts. Their solutions might include fractions. Provide counters if any children need extra support.

Evidencing mastery

Children who can scale up and down using a variety of scale factors, drawing diagrams and explaining what they show, have understood scaling. Children who still need to use counters, or who fail to link scaling down with fractions, have not yet mastered this concept and would benefit from further teaching.

Did you know?

People often use scaling up and down in real life. Discuss examples with children, e.g. resizing photographs, currency conversion, maps. If you have photographs of the children in the classroom you could show these and compare them with the actual children. Together look at the map in the Textbook. It has been scaled down. To work out the actual distances the measurements need to be scaled back up by the amount shown on the scale. Ask children to measure different distances using a ruler and then convert them by multiplying the number of centimetres by the number of miles represented by 1 cm to give the actual distance.

Unit 9 Exploring lines and turns

Mathematical focus

★ Geometry: properties of shapes

Prior learning

Children should already be able to:

- use confidently the terms flat, level and upright when applying to objects
- recognise right angles and compare them with quarter turns
- find right angles in shapes
- sort shapes according to shapes with/without right angles.

Key new learning

- Identify horizontal and vertical lines and pairs of perpendicular and parallel lines.
- Draw 2-D shapes and make 3-D shapes using modelling materials.
- Present data using tables.
- Recognise angles as a property of shape or a description of a turn.
- Identify right angles.
- Recognise that two right angles make a half-turn, three make three quarters of a turn and four a complete turn.
- Recognise 3-D shapes in different orientations and describe them.

Making connections

- This unit provides opportunities to connect with the art curriculum. Children should be taught to improve their mastery of art and design techniques, including drawing. They should also learn about artists such as Mondrian, whose compositions are best known for using vertical and horizontal lines, perpendicular to each other. You could show children one of his works, e.g. 'Composition with Yellow, Blue and Red'.
- Make a link to measuring time with fractions and turning at quarter turns or right angles. A quarter of an hour means a movement of the minute hand by one right angle; half an hour is equal to two quarter turns or two right angle turns.
- There is an opportunity to make a connection to the science curriculum. In this unit, as in science, children will be learning how to categorise using tables.
- In real life we all make turns and move in different directions without thinking about it, e.g. unscrewing a bottle of water, brushing teeth, turning door handles.
- Children should continue to recognise fractions in the context of shape.

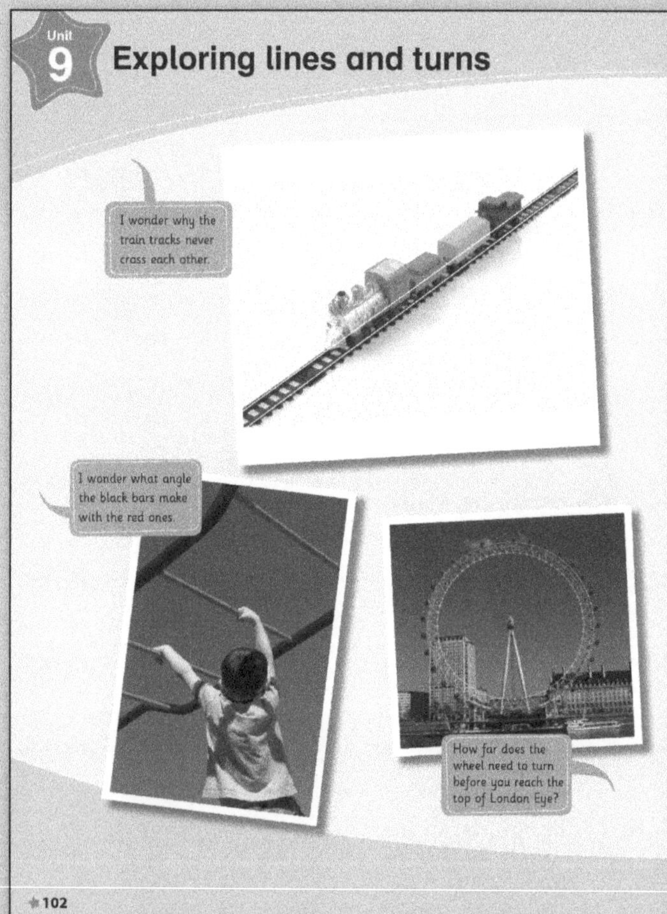

Talk about

It is important to use precise mathematical vocabulary from the beginning. Introduce children to the vocabulary they need to describe lines, including vertical, horizontal, parallel and perpendicular. Through discussion, make connections between lines and the angles that they form, e.g. perpendicular lines form right angles. Use flashcards to reinforce these ideas and secure important vocabulary.

Throughout your discussions, reinforce the concept that an angle is a measure of turn; it is not static.

Engaging and exploring

Give children some time to look at the photos in the Textbook and discuss what they notice with a partner before sharing ideas with the class. Look at the picture of the train track and ask: *What do you notice about the black tracks? What would happen to the train if the black tracks became wider or narrower?* If possible, provide a train track toy for children to see and touch. Alternatively, provide straws or interlocking cubes and ask them to build their own tracks. Ask: *Do the tracks ever meet? What would happen to the train wheels if they did?*

Ask children to describe the angles that the red bars and black ones make in the monkey bars. Encourage discussion about the reason for the right angles used. If possible, go out into the playground and look at the monkey bars. Discuss with children the angle that arms make with the body when holding onto the monkey bars. Discuss whether it would be easier or harder to balance if the angle was less than a right angle. Children could check by actually holding their arms up. Encourage them to think of other places in the playing area or school playground where objects or lines make right angles with each other.

When looking at the photo of the London Eye, ask children to imagine that they are sitting in one of the capsules. Encourage discussion about the journey that the capsule makes as the Eye turns around a full turn. Encourage comparison with the way the minute hand moves on a clock by showing a geared clock. Remind children to use appropriate mathematical language including clockwise, anticlockwise, a quarter turn, half turn and full turn.

Recap what is meant by clockwise and anticlockwise movement. Invite two children to the front of the class, facing the whiteboard and ask them to act and show slowly the movements each child needs to make so that they face each other. Encourage children to describe what they see. *Are both children turning more or less than a right angle?*

Children look at the photo of the sunset. Is the sea flat and level or wavy and stormy? Discuss the term 'horizon' as the line where the sea and sky appear to meet. Encourage children to describe other level surfaces, e.g. flat surface of a table, floor in a room. *What would happen if the table or the floor was not flat?* Ask children to look around for other flat surfaces, e.g. desk, chair.

Children discuss the tall buildings in the photo that stay upright. *Why are these buildings so tall?* Encourage discussion about buildings that stay upright and ask children to look at other objects that stay upright, e.g. door, window, wall, chair legs and notice the angles they make with the floor.

Explain to children that the tall buildings make a right angle with the sea or horizon. Establish that objects that stay upright in the classroom make a right angle with the floor. Ask children to use a book or their arms to demonstrate standing upright and at level surface. Clarify any misconceptions they may have.

Checking understanding

You will know children have mastered these concepts when they can identify horizontal and vertical lines and pairs of parallel and perpendicular lines. Children will recognise that two right angles make a half-turn, three make three quarters of a turn and four a complete turn. Children can turn a shape at right angles to make repeating patterns.

Things to think about

- What everyday objects will children use to explore parallel and perpendicular lines in different positions?
- What practical opportunities will children have to explore horizontal and vertical lines?
- What types of statistical tables can they use to record their findings?
- What shapes will children rotate to make repeating patterns?
- How will you organise groupings for discussion and activities?
- What opportunities will you give children to explain their reasoning?
- What opportunities will you provide to build fluency?
- Which problem-solving strategies are most appropriate in this unit, e.g.:
  - What do you notice?
  - What is the same? What is different?
  - Another, another, another.
  - Convince me.

9a Lines

- **Identify horizontal and vertical lines and pairs of perpendicular and parallel lines.**
- **Draw 2-D shapes and make 3-D shapes using modelling materials.**
- **Present data using tables.**

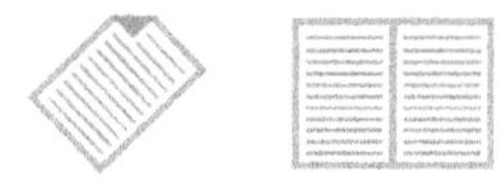

Homework 45 and 46 Practice Book pp 78–80

Representations and resources

Geostrips or straws, 2-D shapes, two large hoops, 3-D shapes, two plastic bottles, right angle tester, ruler, metre stick, cube, whiteboard and pen, modelling clay, cuboid box.

Mathematical vocabulary

Parallel, perpendicular, horizontal, vertical, extend, right angle, horizon, diagonal, grid

Warming up

Put children into two groups. Play a quick addition and subtraction game to revise adding and subtracting 100 using numbers such as 157, 278, 310. The first group adds 100, the second group subtracts 100. Discuss the different ways of asking to add or subtract 100, such as increase by 100 or find 100 more, decrease by 100 or find 100 less. Discuss the place value of each digit in the numbers. Repeat for adding or subtracting 110 by adding or subtracting ten first then 100 or vice versa.

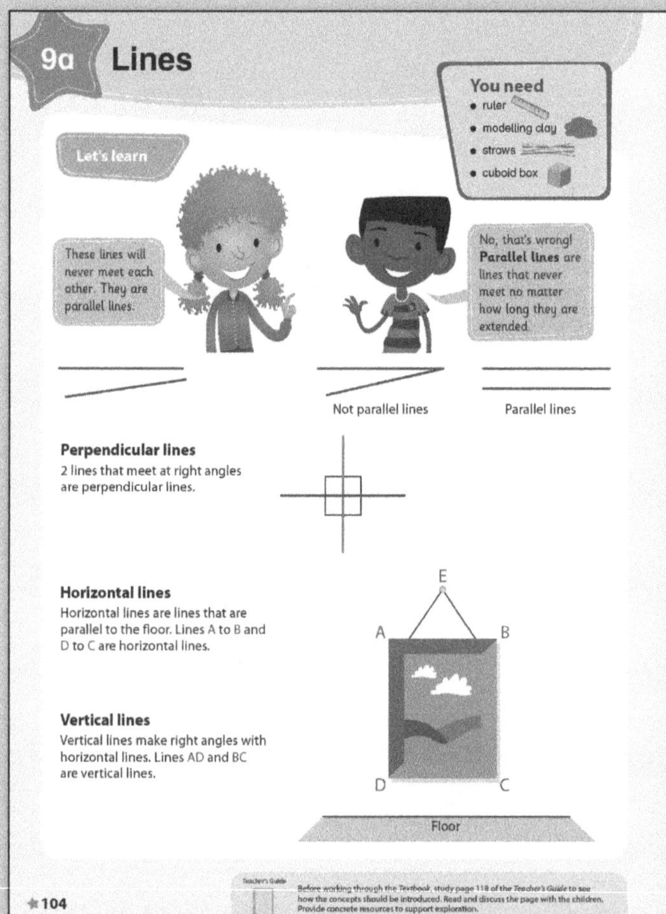

Background knowledge

Children should be familiar with terms 'flat', 'level' and 'upright' when applied to objects. In this concept you will further explore lines. A line is a set of adjacent points that has length but no width. A straight line is completely determined by two of its points, say A and B. The part of the line between any two of its points is a line segment.

A diagonal line is a slanting line that is not vertical or horizontal. Parallel lines are lines that are always an equal distance apart. Children can explore parallel lines by drawing them horizontally, vertically and diagonally. Perpendicular lines are lines that are at right angles to one another. Horizontal lines are parallel to the horizon. Vertical lines are perpendicular to the horizontal lines. It may be useful for children to relate vertical lines to height.

Let's learn: Modelling and teaching

Perpendicular lines

- Provide each table with geostrips. Explain what parallel and perpendicular lines are and draw sets of lines in different positions. Discuss the lines children see in the Textbook.
- Provide children with a variety of 2-D shapes. Make a Venn diagram on the floor using two hoops that overlap. Label them 'perpendicular' and 'parallel'. Place a shape with parallel and perpendicular sides in the middle, e.g. a rectangle. Children explain why it is there.
- Provide children with 3-D shapes such as cuboids and cubes. Explore the faces and edges that are parallel and perpendicular to each other.

Horizontal and vertical lines

- Half fill two clear plastic bottles with coloured water and place them on the table. Explain that the surface of the water is parallel to the table. Introduce horizontal, meaning parallel to the floor or table. Tilt one of the bottles and invite children to see the change in the level of the water. Draw the two bottles on the whiteboard showing their level of water and pointing to the horizontal line.
- Introduce the term vertical, meaning upright and perpendicular to a horizontal surface or line. If necessary, remind children of the definition of perpendicular. Show children vertical surfaces such as the legs of a table or chair, posters on the wall. Encourage discussion of the picture frame in the Textbook. Invite children to identify all the sets of lines that are horizontal and all the ones that are vertical.

Let's practise: Digging deeper

Step 1

Children look at the lines in different positions and identify the sets of lines that are parallel and those that are perpendicular. They have to differentiate between all the lines shown. If children are unsure, show them a pair of geostrips or straws that are parallel to each other and another pair that are perpendicular. Move each set in different positions or look at it from different angles so that children can visualise how parallel lines and perpendicular lines can look.

Step 2

This question requires children to be confident in identifying horizontal, vertical, perpendicular and parallel lines. Ask children to work with a partner. They identify the sets of lines. Ask: *Did they get the same answer? Can they identify another set of lines? And another?* Encourage children to explain their reasons for their answers.

Step 3

Prior to starting this activity, ask children to discuss the different types of lines they know and identify some lines in the classroom. If children are unsure what shapes to make, encourage them to look around them and find shapes that have no parallel lines, e.g. circle, oval, irregular shapes, sphere, shapes with parallel and perpendicular sides, e.g. rectangle, cube, cuboid, shapes made from horizontal and vertical lines, e.g. door, wall, window. Children describe the shapes they make including describing all the lines or sides/edges. Pay attention to the language they use and encourage them to use precise mathematical language. Encourage children to draw the shapes they made.

Step 4

Look out for children who guess answers; encourage them to identify all the sets of parallel and perpendicular lines first instead. Children work in pairs and discuss their answers. Children could insert the information in a table to make the comparison easier.

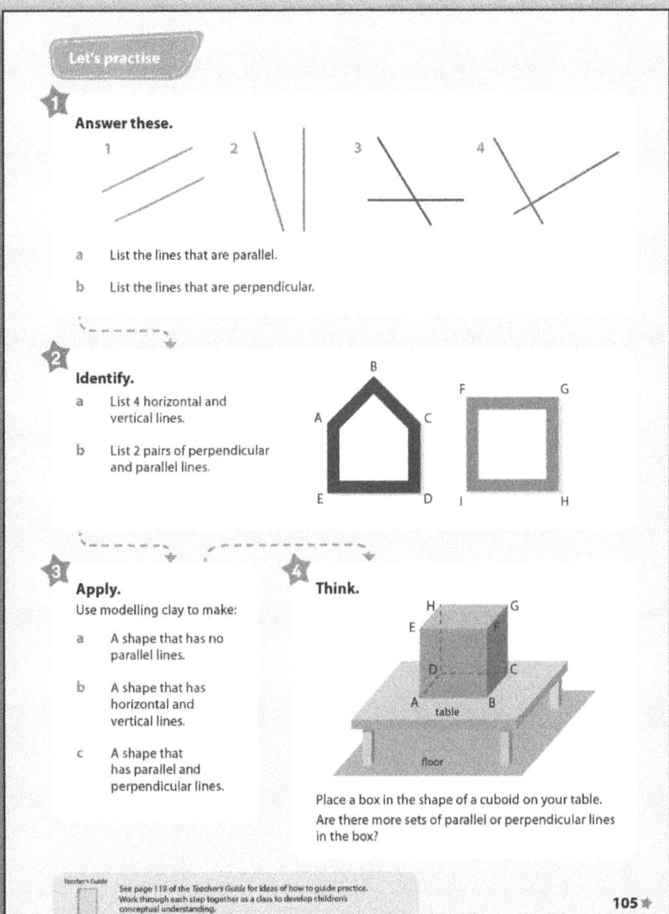

Ensuring progress

Supporting understanding

If children find Steps 1 and 2 difficult, provide them with a right angle tester to help them identify perpendicular lines. Ask them to think of parallel lines and describe them. Children could use a ruler to check the distance between the lines.

In Step 3, provide children with different shapes. Help children describe and compare the sides and edges of the shapes. Are they parallel? Are they perpendicular?

Broadening understanding

Challenge children in Step 1 to work in pairs. They make a tricky question for their partner which asks them to find a pair of parallel and perpendicular lines from four pairs of lines, including parallel and perpendicular lines in different positions. In Step 2, they could choose a line from one of the frames, e.g. A to B and insert new lines parallel to and perpendicular to it. Children work in pairs and check each other's work.

Again in pairs, in Step 3, one child could describe a 3-D shape, by describing the parallel, perpendicular, horizontal and vertical edges and faces it may have. The other child makes the shape. *Is that the correct shape?* They could take turns to make four different 3-D shapes.

Follow-up ideas

- Children work in two mixed-ability groups, the 'parallel and perpendicular' group, and the 'horizontal and vertical' group. Each group uses their group lines to make a piece of artwork to express something or describe a place or object. Children can draw the lines or use straws, string, sticks or other material to represent them.
- Ask children to research the importance of having parallel and perpendicular lines and objects. Link the maths lesson to a literacy and art one. Separate the class into 'parallel' and 'perpendicular' groups and ask each group to research and write about either 'A world without parallel lines' or 'If perpendicular lines didn't exist …'. Each group prepares a poster to illustrate their research. The best two pieces could be published in the class blog or newsletter.

Concept mastered

Children can identify horizontal and vertical lines.
Children can identify parallel and perpendicular lines.

Answers

Step 1

a 1

b 4

Step 2

ED, FG, IH are horizontal lines.

AE, CD, FI, GH are vertical lines.

There are several correct answers, e.g.: AE is parallel to CD, FI is parallel to GH

AE is perpendicular to ED, CD is perpendicular DE

Step 3

Individual answers.

Step 4

They are an equal number of sets.

9b Turning

- **Recognise angles as a property of shape or a description of a turn.**
- **Identify right angles.**
- **Recognise that two right angles make a half-turn, three make three quarters of a turn and four a complete turn.**
- **Recognise 3-D shapes in different orientations and describe them.**

Homework 47 and 48 | Practice Book pp 81–3

Representations and resources

Analogue clock, pieces of card, right angle models, straws, 3-D shapes, 2-D shapes.

Mathematical vocabulary

Right angle turn, half turn, three quarters of a turn, complete turn, clockwise, anticlockwise, rotate

Warming up

Revise fractions and discuss what they mean to children including identifying numerators and denominators in different fractions. Revise unit fractions. Children compare two different unit fractions, e.g. $\frac{1}{3}$ and $\frac{1}{5}$, $\frac{1}{10}$ and $\frac{1}{15}$, using the symbols < and >.

Encourage children to explain their reasoning. Adapt according to children's needs and ask children to show $\frac{1}{3}$ and $\frac{1}{5}$ of a shape to make it harder or help children find fractions of shapes to make it easier.

Background knowledge

An angle is a measure of a turn. It can be a fixed measure as in the size of angles of different shapes, but it can also be the amount of turn from one position to the other. Children should know that a quarter turn is called a right angle and be able to identify right angles around them.

A turn is a rotation around a fixed point. A rotation is specified by a centre and an angle. A quarter turn is rotation of 90°, a half turn is a rotation of 180°, a three quarter turn is a rotation of 270°and a full turn is a rotation of 360°. A rotation of 360° produces an identical looking shape in the same position for all 2-D shapes, including the irregular ones.

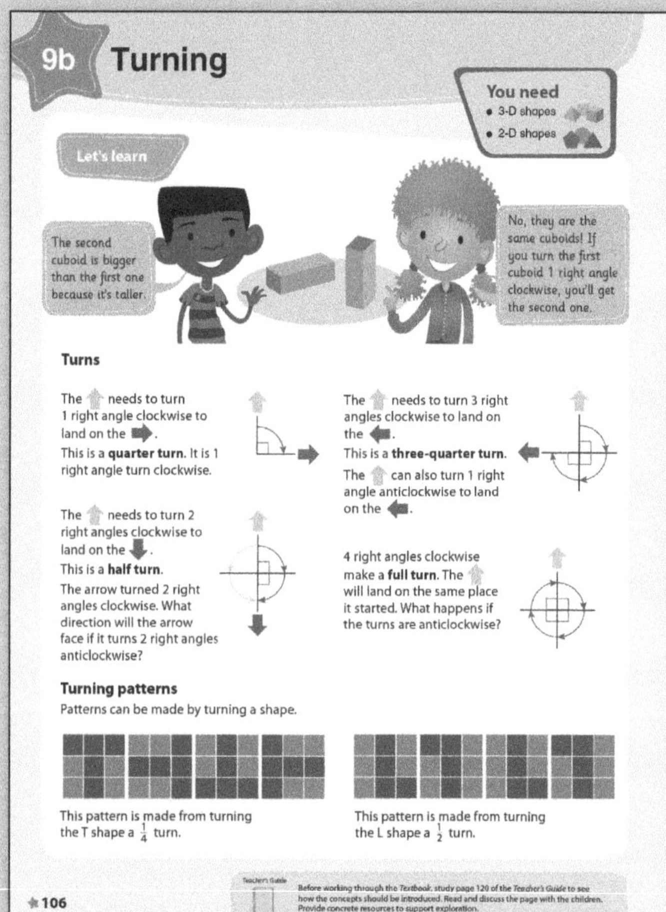
9b Turning

You need
- 3-D shapes
- 2-D shapes

Let's learn

Turns

The [arrow] needs to turn 1 right angle clockwise to land on the [arrow].
This is a **quarter turn**. It is 1 right angle turn clockwise.

The [arrow] needs to turn 2 right angles clockwise to land on the [arrow].
This is a **half turn**.
The arrow turned 2 right angles clockwise. What direction will the arrow face if it turns 2 right angles anticlockwise?

The [arrow] needs to turn 3 right angles clockwise to land on the [arrow].
This is a **three-quarter turn**.
The [arrow] can also turn 1 right angle anticlockwise to land on the [arrow].

4 right angles clockwise make a **full turn**. The [arrow] will land on the same place it started. What happens if the turns are anticlockwise?

Turning patterns

Patterns can be made by turning a shape.

This pattern is made from turning the T shape a $\frac{1}{4}$ turn.

This pattern is made from turning the L shape a $\frac{1}{2}$ turn.

106

Teacher's Guide: Before working through the *Textbook*, study page 120 of the *Teacher's Guide* to see how the concepts should be introduced. Read and discuss the page with the children. Provide concrete resources to support exploration.

Let's learn: Modelling and teaching

Turns

- Discuss the misconception cartoon. Revisit the terms 'horizontal' and 'vertical' and link the effect that turning has on the position of the shape. Remind children of how clockwise and anticlockwise turns relate to one another.
- Using an analogue clock or a paper clock, set the time at 12 o'clock. Show children a quarter turn by moving the minute hand from 12 to 3. Children recall that this is a right angle. Move the minute hand from 3 to 6. Establish that two right angles make a half turn. Move the minute hand from 6 to 9, then from 9 to 12. Establish that three right angles make three quarters of a turn and four quarter turns make one complete turn. Discuss the example in the Textbook and establish that three quarter turns clockwise is the same as moving one quarter turn anticlockwise.

Turning patterns

- Explain that patterns can be made from turning a shape or object at right angles. Draw four identical letter Ts on pieces of card and fix them to a wall. Ask a child to turn the second card by a quarter turn, the third card by a half turn and the fourth card by three quarter turns. *If there was a fifth card, what would that be? Is there a different way to turn the letter T to achieve the same results?* Help children determine the equivalent anticlockwise turn for each clockwise and generalise where possible.
- Look at the Textbook and discuss the way the shape L has turned. Model this in the same way as the letter 'T'.

Let's practise: Digging deeper

Step 1

Children identify the turns needed to move from one shape to the other, including the direction of movement and the number of right angles needed to make each turn. They could use a clock or a right-angle model to help them.

Step 2

The two questions in this step require children to first work out the result of the turn. Second, as children know where the movement starts and where it ends, they need to describe the turn required for that movement.

Step 3

Ensure that children use the correct mathematical language when they describe the turns. To extend, children can describe the number of right angles needed to make each turn.

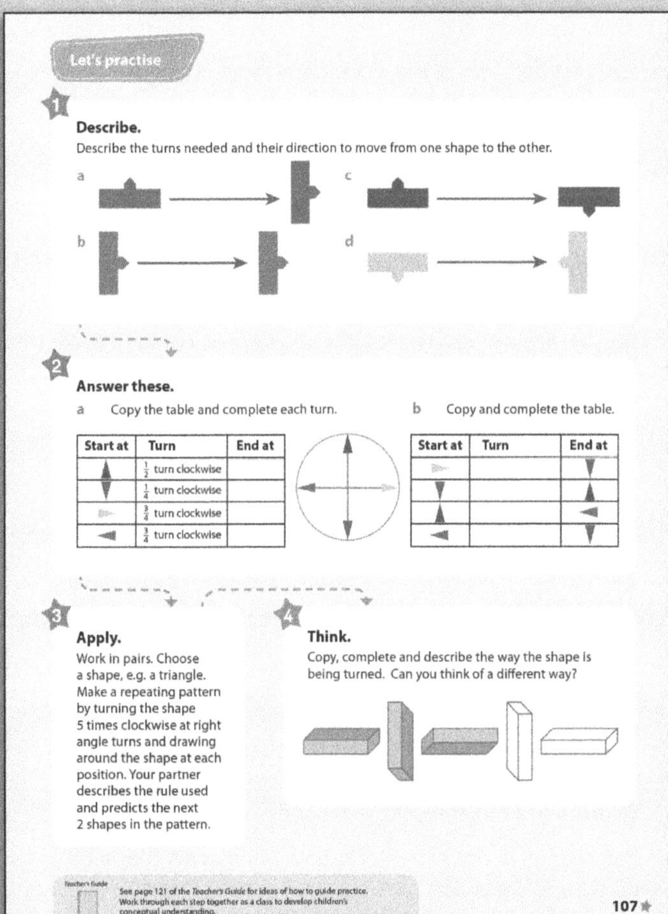

Let's practise

1 Describe.

Describe the turns needed and their direction to move from one shape to the other.

a b c d

2 Answer these.

a Copy the table and complete each turn.

Start at	Turn	End at
▲	$\frac{1}{2}$ turn clockwise	
▼	$\frac{1}{4}$ turn clockwise	
►	$\frac{3}{4}$ turn clockwise	
◄	$\frac{3}{4}$ turn clockwise	

b Copy and complete the table.

Start at	Turn	End at
►		▼
▼		▲
▲		◄
◄		▼

3 Apply.

Work in pairs. Choose a shape, e.g. a triangle. Make a repeating pattern by turning the shape 5 times clockwise at right angle turns and drawing around the shape at each position. Your partner describes the rule used and predicts the next 2 shapes in the pattern.

4 Think.

Copy, complete and describe the way the shape is being turned. Can you think of a different way?

Teacher's Guide

See page 121 of the *Teacher's Guide* for ideas of how to guide practice. Work through each step together as a class to develop children's conceptual understanding.

107

Follow-up ideas

- Children investigate the link between a complete turn followed by $\frac{1}{4}$, $\frac{1}{2}$ or $\frac{3}{4}$ turn and $\frac{1}{4}$, $\frac{1}{2}$ or $\frac{3}{4}$ turn by itself, e.g. two children stand in the middle of the playground. One turns $\frac{1}{4}$ turn, the other one a full turn first, followed by $\frac{1}{4}$ turn.
- In mixed-ability groups, show children a picture of a safe. The arrow has to point at number 8 to open. Children write down the turns needed to open the safe. The group that opens the safe first and gives clear instructions wins ten points. Repeat for a different number, e.g. 15 or 4. The group with the most points wins.

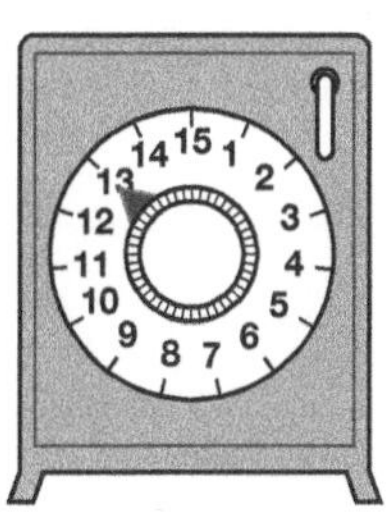

Step 4

Look out for children who colour the faces correctly because they recognise the shape of them, but cannot explain how the pattern is created. Encourage children to think of the amount of turn that is needed to move from one shape to the other.

Ensuring progress

Supporting understanding

Provide children with cut-out models of different 2-D shapes. Ask them to draw around the shape, turn it by a quarter of a turn, then draw around it again. If children are unsure, demonstrate how to place a pencil or clip at the middle of the shape and turn it by one right angle. Once children are confident with one right angle turn, repeat for two, three and four right angles. Use familiar shapes to start with, e.g. squares, rectangles and hexagons.

Broadening understanding

Challenge children to make patterns with irregular shapes. They could also use 3-D shapes such as cylinders and pyramids. Ask children to draw the shapes and describe the rule used. *Is it a clockwise or anticlockwise turn? Can you think of a different way?*

Concept mastered

Children identify that two right angles make a half turn, three make three-quarters of a turn and four a complete turn. Children make patterns by turning a shape at right angles clockwise or anticlockwise.

Answers

Step 1

a $\frac{1}{4}$ turn clockwise (or $\frac{3}{4}$ turn anticlockwise)

b complete turn clockwise (or anticlockwise)

c $\frac{1}{2}$ turn clockwise (or anticlockwise)

d $\frac{3}{4}$ turn clockwise (or $\frac{1}{4}$ turn anticlockwise)

Step 2

a

Start at	Turn	End at
▲	$\frac{1}{2}$ turn clockwise	▼
▼	$\frac{1}{4}$ turn clockwise	◄
►	$\frac{3}{4}$ turn clockwise	▲
◄	$\frac{3}{4}$ turn clockwise	▼

b

Start at	Turn	End at
►	$\frac{1}{4}$ turn clockwise or $\frac{3}{4}$ turn clockwise	▼
▼	$\frac{1}{2}$ turn clockwise or anticlockwise	▲
▲	$\frac{3}{4}$ turn clockwise or $\frac{1}{4}$ turn clockwise	◄
◄	$\frac{3}{4}$ turn clockwise or $\frac{1}{4}$ turn clockwise	▼

Step 3

Individual answers.

Step 4

The shape has been turned a quarter turn clockwise or $\frac{3}{4}$ turn anticlockwise.

Unit 9

Lines and turns

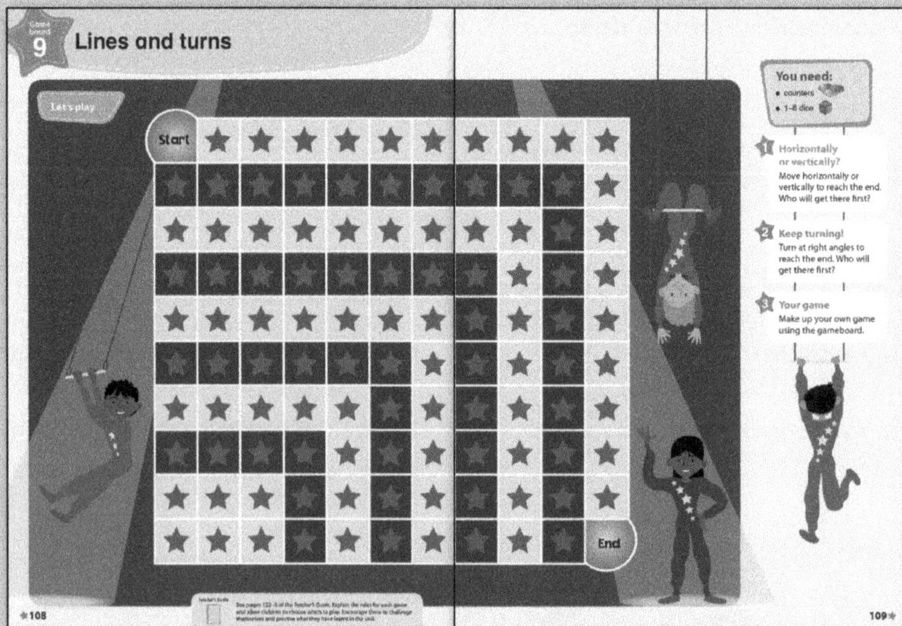

Game 1: Horizontally or vertically?

This is a simple race game. Children move horizontally or vertically only and the first player to reach the end wins.

Maths focus

- Identify horizontal and vertical lines

Resources

2 counters (1 colour per player), 1–6 dice (2).

How to play

Children place their counters on Start. One child rolls one dice. If the number is even, they will move their counter horizontally only; if the number is odd, they will move their counter vertically only. They then roll the other dice. The number rolled is the number of the squares to move their counter.

The other child then has their turn. The winner is the first to reach 'End'.

Making it easier

If stuck and unsure, children could 'call a friend' and ask for advice once during the game.

Making it harder

Children could draw a shape that has as many vertical or horizontal lines as the number that the second dice shows.

Game 3: Your game

Children should invent their own game, designing rules that use the concepts covered in the unit.

Challenge children to make their game easier or harder.

Game 2: Keep turning!

This is slightly a more complex race game. Children are required to turn at right angles, then move to reach 'End'.

Maths focus

- Recognise that 1 right angle makes a quarter turn, 2 right angles make a half turn, 3 right angles make three quarters of a turn and 4 right angles a complete turn

Resources

2 counters (1 colour per player), 1–6 dice (2).

How to play

Children place their counters on Start. One child rolls one dice. The number they throw is the number of right angles their counter will turn in the box. The direction that they end up facing is the direction that they will move. Then they roll the second dice. The number thrown is the number of steps they will move their counter.

For each go, if their counter is on a yellow box, they turn clockwise; if it is on a blue box they turn anticlockwise. If their counter is at the edge of the board, they can move in any direction. The other child then has their turn. The winner is the first to reach 'End'.

Making it easier

If stuck and unsure, children could 'call a friend' and ask for advice once during the game.

Making it harder

Children could sketch the journey they are making on squared paper, using straight lines and showing clearly the turns.

Lines and turns

Choose a game to play.

Game 1: Horizontally or vertically?

You need:

- 2 counters per player (1 colour per player)
- two 1–6 dice

How to play

- Each place your counter on Start.
- Take turns to roll both dice.
- Roll one dice to decide whether you move your counter vertically or horizontally.
- Roll the other dice to find the number of steps to move your counter.
- The winner is the first player to reach 'End'.

Game 2: Keep turning

You need:

- 2 counters per player (1 colour per player)
- two 1–6 dice

How to play

- Each place your counter on Start.
- Take turns to roll both dice.
- Roll one dice to find how many right angles your counter turns in the box.
- If your counter is on a yellow box, you turn clockwise. If it is on a blue box, you turn anti-clockwise.
- Roll the other dice to find the number of steps to move your counter.
- If your counter is at the edge of the board, you can move in any direction.
- The winner is the first player to reach 'End'.

Game 3: Your game

- Make up your own game using the gameboard.
- Can you think of a way to collect right angle turns as you move along?
- The winner could be the player who travels the longest horizontal or vertical line.
- You could continue the race back to the start or do something else.
- What are the rules for your game? Explain them to someone.

Please help your child by reading the instructions and playing the game together.

Unit 9

And finally ...

Assessment task 1

Resources

Four sheets of 4 × 4 dotted paper per group, coloured pencils, rubber, ruler.

Running the task

Children work in mixed groups to draw as many pairs of parallel and perpendicular lines as they can on the dotted paper. Every pair of lines wins a point.

Discuss the parallel and perpendicular lines in the picture of the house, including the diagonal ones. Prior to starting the task, ask children to define what parallel and perpendicular lines mean to them. Clarify any misconceptions and remind them that lines can be drawn in different positions.

Children enjoy this task, however they often start working on it, without planning ahead; lines can look messy and be on top of each other. Encourage them to think about the lines that they will draw on each piece of paper, then start working on them.

To extend the task, children count the number of lines that are the same length and record the information on a table. They may show their results on a bar chart or pictogram. *Assuming that the distance between two dots is 1 cm long, are there more pairs of lines that are 1 cm or 2 cm long? What is the longest pair of lines drawn? Are the horizontal lines the same length as the vertical ones? What about the diagonal ones?* Children measure the lines using a ruler to check their answer.

Evidencing mastery

Being able to draw parallel and perpendicular lines in different positions shows a deeper understanding of what parallel and perpendicular lines are. Describing and generalising the properties of parallel and perpendicular lines regardless of their positions shows a deep understanding of the subject.

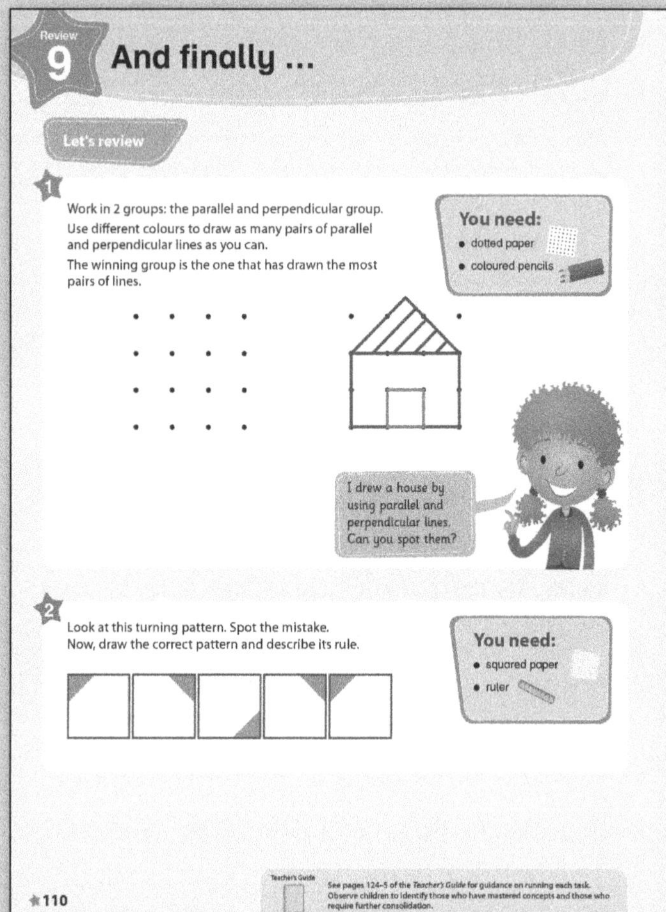

Assessment task 2

Resources

Squared paper, ruler.

Running the task

Children work in pairs. Before starting the task, revise the different ways patterns can be created. Listen for children who know that they can turn a shape at right angles to make a pattern. Encourage children to explain what a quarter turn is. Ask them to think of the other turns they know.

Some children may think that this is a 'reflecting task', hence the third square is wrong, as it needs to be the same as the first one. Though that is mathematically correct, tell children that the first square has been turned to give the second one and so on.

You may ask children to draw the next two squares. Give them time to explore what happens to the square after each turn. *How many turns did it take before your pattern looked like it did to begin with? If you turned your pattern through eight right angles clockwise, what would happen?*

To extend the task ask children to make a new pattern by turning the first square anticlockwise by a quarter turn. *What would the pattern look now? How does it differ from the pattern created when the square was moved a quarter turn clockwise?* Children predict the results and check their answers. Ask them to think of a shape that would not change whether it turned clockwise or anticlockwise. Give children time to explore the task and be confident with their results. Throughout the task encourage children to explain their thinking and encourage them to generalise where possible.

Evidencing mastery

Children who can spot the mistake in the pattern and draw the correct pattern, are showing evidence of mastery. Children who are unable to spot the mistake in the pattern need more practice in visualising what happens to a shape when turned at right angles.

Concepts mastered

- ☑ Children can identify horizontal and vertical lines. Children can identify parallel and perpendicular lines.
- ☑ Children identify that two right angles make a half turn, three make a three quarter turn and four a complete turn. Children make patterns by turning a shape at right angles clockwise or anticlockwise.

Assessment task 3

Resources

Squared paper, ruler

Running the task

Explain to children that this question has a few different answers. Ask children to recall what horizontal and vertical lines are and identify some in the classroom. Children should be able to find the first answer quickly by drawing a horizontal and vertical line perpendicular to each other.

Ask children to think of another way to split the rectangle in four equal parts. Some children may be stuck at this point and think that the question is impossible. Tell them that the answer is much easier than they think. Allow children time to think about the question and find two more answers. Remind children that only horizontal and vertical lines are used.

To extend, ask children what fraction of the whole shape each part is. *How does the quarter of a shape look different on each occasion?* Children should consider that equal fractions of a shape have the same area rather than just be parts that look the same. To check, you could ask children to cut each piece of their shapes to see if they are the same. Repeat for different shapes such as square, circle. *How many horizontal and vertical lines will you need to separate each shape in four equal parts?*

Evidencing mastery

Children who can separate each shape into four equal parts using horizontal and vertical lines only show a deep understanding of properties of horizontal and vertical lines and fractions of a shape.

Did you know?

Ask children to look at the Textbook and discuss their views on vertical cities. Why are they called vertical? *Why are architects thinking about building vertically?*

Discuss what children like about the vertical city in the photo. *What do they not like? Would they prefer to live in a vertical or horizontal city?*

Children can collect facts from the library and Internet about the increase in population in the world every day and its effects on pollution, land and life generally.

There are plans around the world for building vertical cities, e.g. the Vertical City tower in Dubai will have 400 floors and a vertical train that will move between the floors. A vertical city in the Sahara will be in the middle of the desert and include vertical gardens, schools and hospitals. There is an international vertical city competition in Asia each year which encourages young architects to design futuristic designs.

Stimulate children's curiosity in the world around us, including current and future issues and encourage them to think of what we can all do to solve these problems.

Unit 10

Using number and place value

Mathematical focus

★ Number: number and place value

★ Measurement: time, mass

★ Statistics: interpret data

Prior learning

Children should already be able to:

- recognise the place value of each digit in a 3-digit number
- represent and estimate numbers to 1000
- compare and order numbers up to 1000
- count from zero in multiples of four, eight, 50 and 100
- find ten or 100 more or less than a given number
- count on and back in fraction steps of half, one-third and one-tenth.

Key new learning

- Read and write numbers up to 1000 in numerals and words.
- Tell and read the time from an analogue clock, including using Roman numerals, and 12-hour clocks.
- Estimate and read time with increasing accuracy to the nearest minute; record and compare time in terms of seconds, minutes and hours; use vocabulary such as o'clock, a.m./p.m., morning, afternoon, noon and midnight.
- Identify, represent and compare numbers to 1000 using different representations.
- Count up and down in tenths, recognise that tenths arise from dividing an object into ten equal parts and dividing single-digit numbers or quantities by ten.
- Interpret data using bar charts.
- Know the number of seconds in a minute and thenumber of days in each month, year and leap year.
- Compare durations of events.

Making connections

- In this topic children have opportunities to solve number and practical problems, including interpreting and presenting data using bar charts, pictograms and tables.
- Children could time events in science and in PE and record and compare times in terms of minutes and seconds, using what they know about the number of seconds in a minute.
- Children can solve problems involving the number of days in each month, year and leap year, relating these to how long until their birthday and so on.

Talk about

It is important to use precise mathematical vocabulary from the beginning so that children are well equipped to talk about their mathematical learning. By the end of Year 3, children should be fluent with the language of time and be able to explain the difference between noon and midnight, which are both represented in the same way on an analogue clock. They should use the words morning and afternoon, relating them to the abbreviations a.m. and p.m. which stand for the Latin *ante meridiem* and *post meridiem*, meaning before or after midday (meridies).

Engaging and exploring

You could use the photo of the sack of rice to revise the units of mass so that children recognise and use the terms gram (g) and kilogram (kg). You could look at the language used for measurement and the relationship to place value, i.e. kilo is taken from the Greek work χίλιοι (*chilioi*) and literally means 'thousand' so a kilogram is a thousand grams.

Challenge children to think about strategies they can use to work out how much rice is needed. Agree that the counting they have been doing in steps of 50 can help them here as counting is useful for adding and subtracting. It would be useful to model this practically using measuring scales and 50 gram weights or on an interactive computer program. Explore different counts of 50 grams and the number of people that can be served each time. Begin to relate counting as repeated addition to multiplication, e.g. $50 + 50 + 50 + 50$ to 50×4. Challenge children to come up with their own counts of 50 grams, recording the steps and the number of people served each time. Make connections to 100 grams so that children are secure with the fact that there are two lots or steps of 50 in 100. Extend the count to 1000 grams or one kilogram.

For the next photo, discuss where you might see a departure board like this, e.g. bus terminal, train station. The one shown is at an airport. Talk about the types of numbers children can see and what they represent. Children should recognise that numbers are used in many different ways in our lives. Ask them to choose a gate number and show or explain what number they would need to add to it to reach the next multiple of ten. Practise bonds to 20 and 100 using these numbers.

Challenge children to find the largest number on the display board. They should prove why it is the largest, using representations and/or mathematical language to explain their thinking. These numbers represent the flight number. Ask children to either compare pairs of numbers, recording their findings using the symbols < and >, or order the set of flight numbers from smallest to largest.

Looking at the keypad, discuss the different places where we see the digits zero to nine arranged in this way. *What do you notice about this arrangement?* (Zero is at the bottom, but the digits one, two and three are at the top; the digits are arranged in threes but the zero is on its own.) Focus on the 'five' key. What do children notice about the pairs of numbers that are on either side of it in a horizontal, vertical or diagonal direction? Agree that they are all pairs of numbers that bond to ten.

Refer to the question and discuss what needs to be identified to find the fraction of the total digits that the top row represents. Agree that there are ten keys with digits so each has the value of one-tenth in the whole set of digits. You could count the keys in tenths starting from different positions up to one whole. Children should then explain why the top row represents three-tenths and perhaps find other fractions that represent other criteria, such as: *What fraction of the digits are multiples of two? What fraction of the digits show the possible values of the ones digit when we count in steps of five from zero? What fraction of the digits are odd numbers?*

Discuss some possible scenarios for the pictogram and what it may represent, e.g. the number of oranges eaten by a class at fruit time each day or the number of oranges sold in a local shop. Challenge children to identify what important information is missing from the pictogram and what we need to know. Agree that we do not yet know the value of each orange symbol and whether each represents one or more oranges. Explore the amounts shown on the pictogram when the orange symbol has the value four or eight, comparing the number of oranges eaten or sold on different days and the total number. What if the orange symbol now represents 100? What does the half orange represent? Link to the counting you have been doing in steps of four, eight and 100.

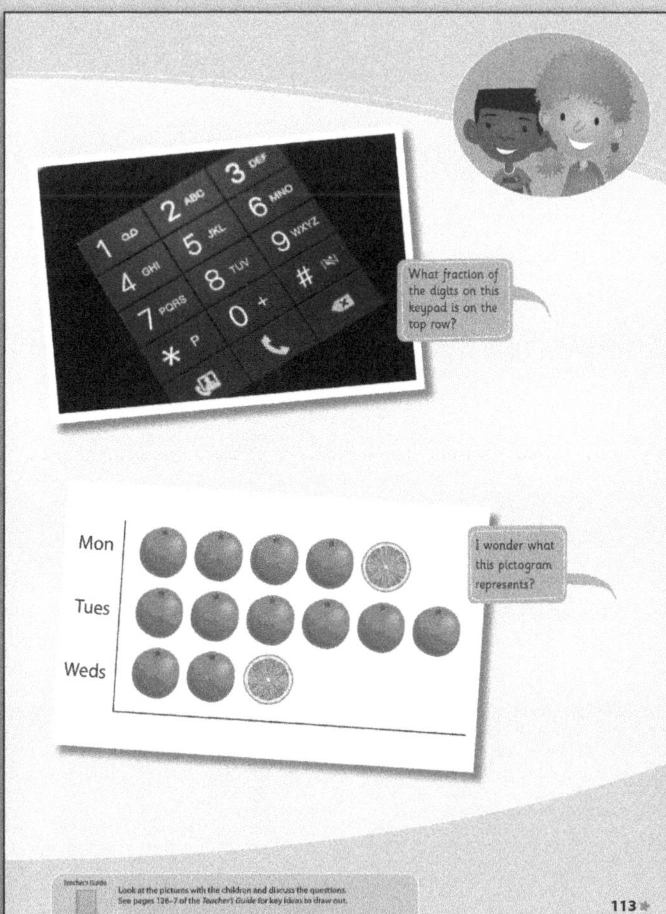

Things to think about

- How will you continue to provide opportunities to build fluency in counting in steps of a constant size, including steps related to intervals on a bar chart or steps of time, e.g. steps of five or ten minutes?
- How do you plan to organise groupings so that children who find the language of mathematics more difficult have the opportunity to work with others who use language confidently?
- Will you check conceptual understanding by encouraging children to use representations to show numbers in different ways and to show other concepts such as time intervals?
- Will you draw out reasoning through carefully planned questions that require children to think, prove and explain?

Checking understanding

You will know children have mastered these concepts when they can explain and show how and when their counting is useful for adding and subtracting. They can explain and show how to tell the time and use knowledge of different units of time to solve problems.

10a Reading and writing numbers

- Read and write numbers up to 1000 in numerals and words.
- Tell and read the time from an analogue clock, including using Roman numerals, and 12-hour clocks.
- Estimate and read time with increasing accuracy to the nearest minute; record and compare time in terms of seconds, minutes and hours; use vocabulary such as o'clock, a.m./p.m., morning, afternoon, noon and midnight.

Homework 49 and 50 | Practice Book pp 84–7 | Place Value & Abacus; Clock & Timer

Representations and resources

Base 10 apparatus, stopwatches, digit cards, clocks, place-value cards, place-value grid.

Mathematical vocabulary

Hundreds, tens, ones, place value, position, digital, analogue, minutes, seconds

Warming up

Rehearse finding 100 more or 100 less and ten more or ten less than any given number. Provide children with a table of 2- and 3-digit numbers. Include those that are close to hundreds boundaries so that children will need to count on or back over them. Invite children to randomly choose numbers from the grid, first focusing on ten more and ten less; alternatively, assign them particular rows or columns to work on. Base 10 apparatus can be used to support or confirm values each time. Quickly move on to 100 more or less as children increase their fluency.

Background knowledge

Continue to practise writing numbers in words with children, particularly focusing on the 'ty' and 'teen' words to address any misconceptions. When introducing the 12-hour digital clock, relate the five-minute intervals to counting in fives and the multiplication table for five up to 5 × 12. It is useful to show the jumps of five on a number line and then in a circular layout, perhaps around a hoop.

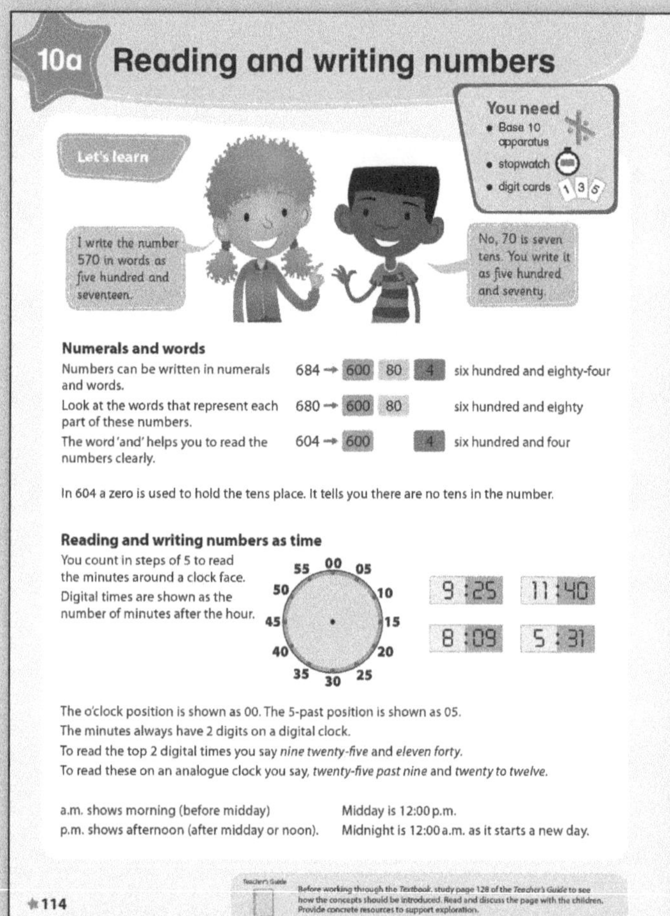

10a Reading and writing numbers

Numerals and words

Numbers can be written in numerals and words.	684 → 600 80 4	six hundred and eighty-four
Look at the words that represent each part of these numbers.	680 → 600 80	six hundred and eighty
The word 'and' helps you to read the numbers clearly.	604 → 600 4	six hundred and four

In 604 a zero is used to hold the tens place. It tells you there are no tens in the number.

Reading and writing numbers as time

You count in steps of 5 to read the minutes around a clock face.

Digital times are shown as the number of minutes after the hour.

The o'clock position is shown as 00. The 5-past position is shown as 05.

The minutes always have 2 digits on a digital clock.

To read the top 2 digital times you say *nine twenty-five* and *eleven forty.*

To read these on an analogue clock you say, *twenty-five past nine* and *twenty to twelve.*

a.m. shows morning (before midday) Midday is 12:00 p.m.

p.m. shows afternoon (after midday or noon). Midnight is 12:00 a.m. as it starts a new day.

114

Teacher's Guide

Before working through the *Textbook*, study page 128 of the *Teacher's Guide* to see how the concepts should be introduced. Read and discuss the page with the children. Provide concrete resources to support exploration.

Let's learn: Modelling and teaching

Numerals and words

- Discuss the misconception cartoon. Ask children to explain Mia's mistake and show how Base 10 apparatus could help. Talk about other numbers that may also get mixed up in this way.
- Look at how the numbers 684, 680 and 604 have been partitioned in the Textbook to show the true value of each digit and the use of zero as the place holder in the number 604. Model each number using place-value cards and invite children to match each part of the partitioned number with the word. Highlight where the word 'and' is used and where a hyphen is used to connect the words 'eighty-four'.
- Partition another number in a similar way, e.g. 576 as 500, 70 and 6 and challenge children to write the number in words. Rearrange the words as for 684 and invite children to write each one in numerals. Use Base 10 apparatus to model or confirm.

Reading and writing numbers as time

- Use the classroom clock to agree the current time, the time it will be in 30 minutes, the time it was ten minutes ago. Talk about the numbers on the clock. Discuss different styles of clock faces.
- Count in steps of five around the clock face in the Textbook and look at the examples of digital times. Explain that you read digital times as the number of minutes past the hour. Challenge children to read the two times shown on the lower two digital clocks using both the language of digital and analogue time, asking children to show the two times on an analogue clock.

Let's practise: Digging deeper

Step 1

Read the numbers that are written in words and encourage children to explain the value of each part of the number. Allow children to use Base 10 apparatus to support thinking and understanding of place value. Check that children use zero as a place holder in part b. They could write the words for each part of the number first and then think about the way to write the whole number.

Step 2

Children could use an analogue clock to display each time, carefully checking the position of each hand. Ask them to read the time using 'to' and 'past'. The clock images show faces with numbers and with Roman numerals. Children should use the clock face on the Let's learn page of the Textbook to help them decide on the value of the minutes.

Step 3

Remind children that there are 60 seconds in a minute to help them make sense of the stopwatch displays as intervals extend beyond 60 seconds. Children must estimate how many hops they can do within each given time. Alternatively, ask children to think about an activity that will take the lengths of time given, e.g. counting out 50 cubes from the tray. Children should time the activity and then compare it to their estimate. Ask: *Did the activity take longer or less time? How much more or less?*

Step 4

Discuss why Oli thinks his number will always be larger to help contextualise the problem. Children could work in pairs or groups with digit cards to investigate and reason about Oli's statement. Ask: *What is the largest or smallest number that Oli can have?* They should find examples and counter-examples to disprove the statement and show that it is sometimes true.

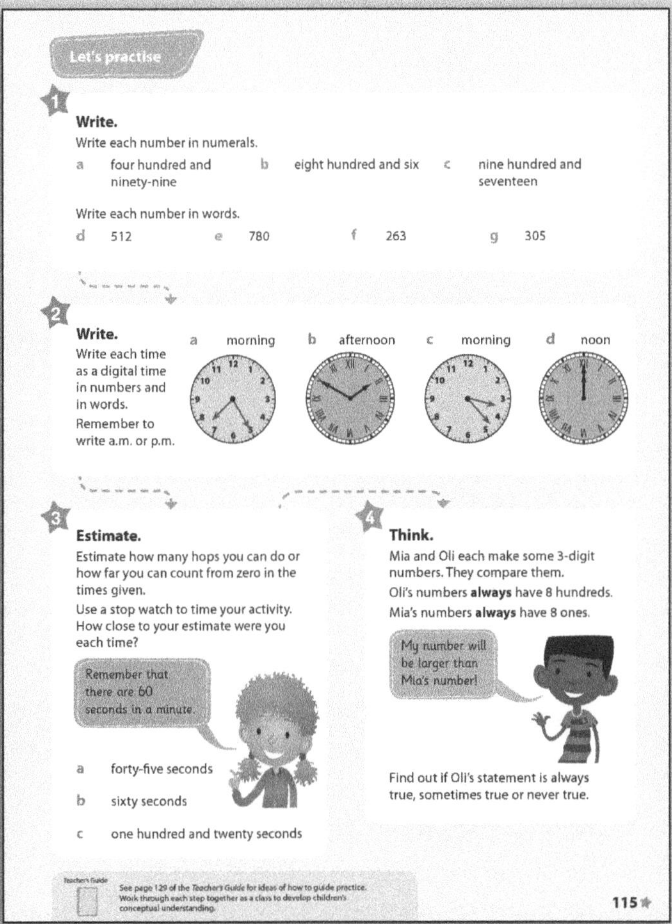

Let's practise

1 Write.

Write each number in numerals.

a four hundred and ninety-nine b eight hundred and six c nine hundred and seventeen

Write each number in words.

d 512 e 780 f 263 g 305

2 Write.

Write each time as a digital time in numbers and in words.

Remember to write a.m. or p.m.

a morning b afternoon c morning d noon

3 Estimate.

Estimate how many hops you can do or how far you can count from zero in the times given.

Use a stop watch to time your activity. How close to your estimate were you each time?

Remember that there are 60 seconds in a minute.

a forty-five seconds

b sixty seconds

c one hundred and twenty seconds

4 Think.

Mia and Oli each make some 3-digit numbers. They compare them.

Oli's numbers **always** have 8 hundreds.

Mia's numbers **always** have 8 ones.

My number will be larger than Mia's number!

Find out if Oli's statement is always true, sometimes true or never true.

Teacher's Guide

See page 129 of the *Teacher's Guide* for ideas of how to guide practice. Work through each step together as a class to develop children's conceptual understanding.

115

Ensuring progress

Supporting understanding

Children can use a place-value grid and Base 10 apparatus to help them investigate Oli's statement in Step 4. They may first find it useful to make up some different numbers for Oli that have a hundreds value of eight and some values for Mia with a ones value of eight. You could guide children to compare numbers and think about numbers that could be larger than Oli's number each time.

Broadening understanding

Extend children by asking them to consider the effect on the problem if Mia's number always had eight tens rather than eight ones. Then, encourage children to make up a problem similar to Step 4.

Concept mastered

Children can recognise the difference between a 'ty' and 'teen' number written in numerals and words. They can fluently read numbers and can write them in words and in numerals. They can fluently use the language of morning and afternoon to describe the time of day.

Follow-up ideas

- Return to the information shown on the departure board in the unit opener. Look at the different flight times, reading them using the language of digital time and challenging children to show each of the times on an analogue clock.
- Investigate different sand timers and check how accurate they are using a stopwatch. *What different timers can you get?* Ask children to think about how a one-minute timer could be used to help estimate two minutes or one and a half minutes. *What other lengths of time could it help you estimate?* Ask children to find out about sand timers that are used for longer lengths of time. *When might they be useful?*

Answers

Step 1

a 499

b 806

c 917

d five hundred and twelve

e seven hundred and eighty

f two hundred and sixty-three

g three hundred and five

Step 2

a 7:25 a.m. seven twenty-five or twenty-five past seven

b 1:50 p.m. one fifty or ten to two

c 3:23 a.m. three twenty-three or twenty-three minutes past three

d 12:00 p.m. twelve o'clock, midday

Step 4

Oli's statement is only sometimes true.

10b Using place value

- Identify, represent and compare numbers to 1000 using different representations.
- Count up and down in tenths, recognise that tenths arise from dividing an object into ten equal parts and dividing single-digit numbers or quantities by ten.
- Interpret data using bar charts.
- Know the number of seconds in a minute and the number of days in each month, year and leap year.
- Compare durations of events.

Homework 51 and 52 | Practice Book pp 88–90 | Place Value & Abacus

Representations and resources

Number rods, place-value grids, digit cards.

Mathematical vocabulary

Equal, partition, value, tenth, division, second, minute, intervals, scale

Warming up

Use the 'Zooming in' strategy to reason about months of the year. Give a criterion such as a month with an even number of days, and then 'zoom in' using the following criteria: a month where the number of days never changes; a month that is in the first half of the year; a month that is not a summer month. This will zoom in to the month of April. Look at the calendar and ask children to use the given criterion to prove that April is the correct month. Children could work in pairs to make up 'zoom in' criteria for the month of December.

Background knowledge

Use number rods to explore the relationship between numbers and place value. This will help children to develop a greater sense of multiplicative reasoning and scaling, e.g. the fact that two yellow rods (5) are equal to an orange rod (10) helps children to reason about other values for these rods, so that when the orange rod has the value 100, then the yellow rod has the value of 50.

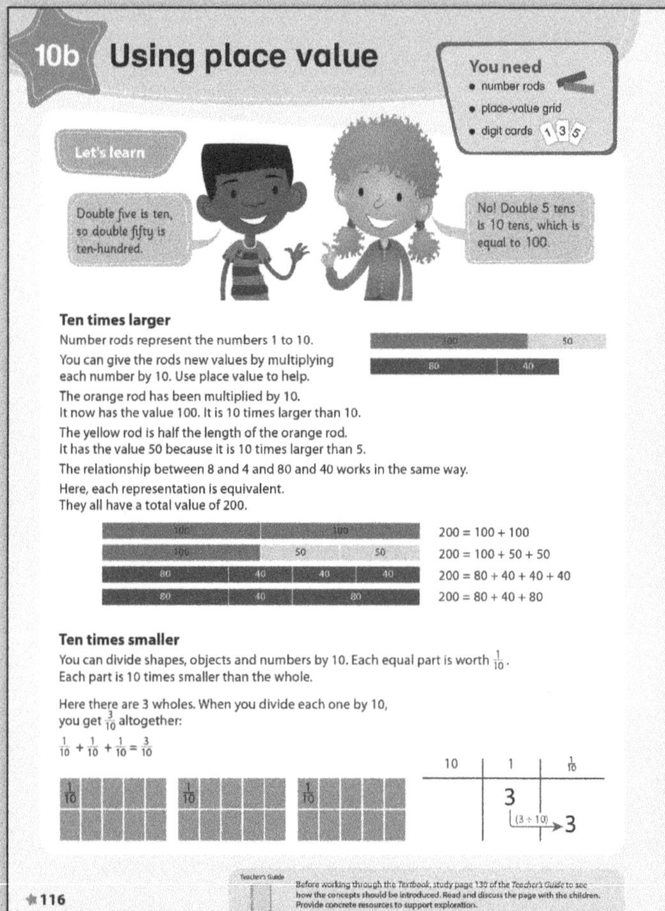

10b Using place value

You need
- number rods
- place-value grid
- digit cards

Let's learn

Double five is ten, so double fifty is ten-hundred.

No! Double 5 tens is 10 tens, which is equal to 100.

Ten times larger

Number rods represent the numbers 1 to 10.

You can give the rods new values by multiplying each number by 10. Use place value to help.

The orange rod has been multiplied by 10.
It now has the value 100. It is 10 times larger than 10.

The yellow rod is half the length of the orange rod.
It has the value 50 because it is 10 times larger than 5.

The relationship between 8 and 4 and 80 and 40 works in the same way.

Here, each representation is equivalent.
They all have a total value of 200.

200 = 100 + 100
200 = 100 + 50 + 50
200 = 80 + 40 + 40 + 40
200 = 80 + 40 + 80

Ten times smaller

You can divide shapes, objects and numbers by 10. Each equal part is worth $\frac{1}{10}$.
Each part is 10 times smaller than the whole.

Here there are 3 wholes. When you divide each one by 10, you get $\frac{3}{10}$ altogether:

$\frac{1}{10} + \frac{1}{10} + \frac{1}{10} = \frac{3}{10}$

10	1	$\frac{1}{10}$
	3	
	(3 ÷ 10) →	3

116

Teacher's Guide: Before working through the *Textbook*, study page 130 of the *Teacher's Guide* to see how the concepts should be introduced. Read and discuss the page with the children. Provide concrete resources to support exploration.

Let's learn: Modelling and teaching

Ten times larger

- Rehearse counting on and back in steps of four and eight. Look at the first representation in the Textbook. *Where can you see the digits four and eight? What do they represent?* (Four tens and eight tens.) Model the image using number rods.
- Discuss the connection between the numbers one to ten and multiples of ten to 100. Children should recognise that all numbers are ten times larger.
- Ask children to calculate the value of each set of rods, thinking about and discussing ways to bridge 100 when adding 80 and 40. Relate this to adding four and eight. The model of part-part-whole is useful here to show the calculation as 80 + 20 + 20.
- Explore the different ways that 200 is represented using number rods. Agree that each representation is equivalent as it has the same value. Write statements to describe the relationship between the parts.

Ten times smaller

- Revisit the concept that tenths arise by dividing shapes, objects and numbers by ten. Confirm that each equal part is worth one-tenth. Use the representations to practise counting in tenths up to one whole and then up to three wholes using mixed numbers to say and record the count beyond one. Ask questions, e.g. *What is $\frac{4}{10}$ more than $\frac{3}{10}$?*
- On a place-value grid you can make tenths by dividing a single-digit number by ten. Discuss the value of each column on the place-value grid and use digit cards to model three divided by ten, relating this to the image in the Textbook. Use the language, *one whole divided by ten equals one tenth so three wholes divided by ten equals three tenths – one tenth in every whole.*

Let's practise: Digging deeper

Step 1

Children should draw on the counting they have been doing to help find the total values of each representation. They should use number rods to copy each representation and use counting and calculating strategies to add the values. Encourage children to think about reordering the number rods to make calculations easier, e.g. for part b, reordering as 50, 50, 80 so 100 can be reached easily using number bonds. The numbers have been chosen carefully to emphasise the equivalence between parts a and b, and 100 more than 180 in part c.

Step 2

Children are required to use the same rods, 40, 50, 80 and 100, to represent each number in two different ways. Encourage them to use strategies, e.g. part-part-whole to cross the 100 boundary. Remind them to think carefully about the relationship between 50 and 100 and between 40 and 80 to help them find different representations. They should write two statements for each of their representations using partitioning, further securing the concept of equivalence.

Step 3

Children move digit cards one place to the right on a place-value grid to model dividing single-digit numbers by ten to result in the given fractions. They should look carefully at the fraction and identify the single digit required; this is shown by the numerator. For each example, they should write the division statement that they use, e.g. $5 \div 10 = \frac{5}{10}$. They should discuss the value of the denominator and how this relates to the divisor in the calculation. They also count in steps of two-tenths and record the steps they make.

Step 4

Encourage children to discuss the scale of the bar chart and to use language such as longer and shorter to compare the time each child has taken. All values are shown in seconds. Agree that there are 60 seconds in each minute so some children took more than a minute to find the hidden child. Children's written statements about the values shown should include, e.g. It took Mia 60 seconds to find the first person. This is exactly one minute. They should also include comparisons, e.g. It took Theo 20 seconds less than Mia.

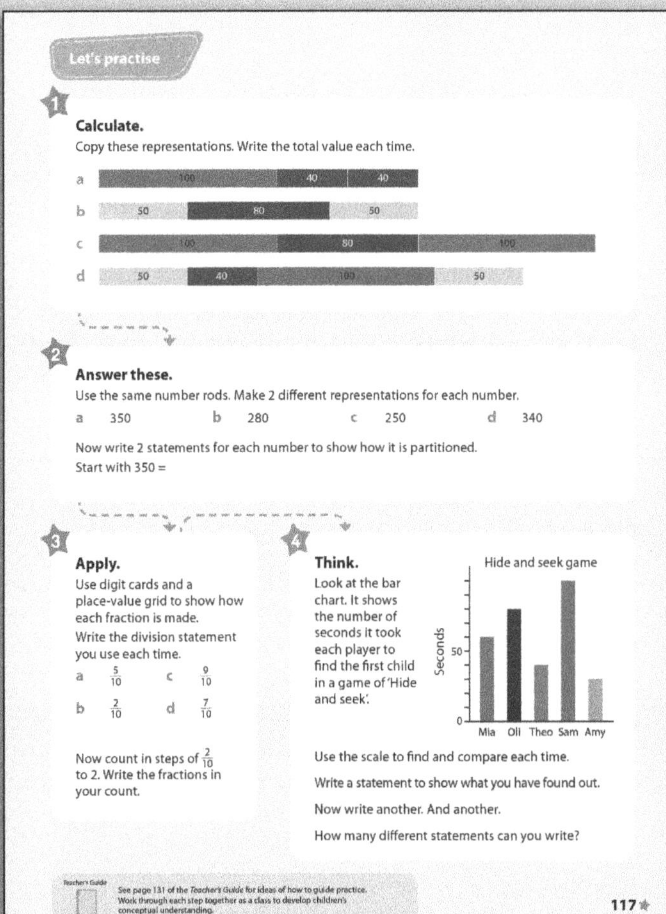
Let's practise

1 **Calculate.**
Copy these representations. Write the total value each time.

2 **Answer these.**
Use the same number rods. Make 2 different representations for each number.
a 350 b 280 c 250 d 340

Now write 2 statements for each number to show how it is partitioned.
Start with 350 =

3 **Apply.**
Use digit cards and a place-value grid to show how each fraction is made.
Write the division statement you use each time.
a $\frac{5}{10}$ c $\frac{9}{10}$
b $\frac{2}{10}$ d $\frac{7}{10}$

Now count in steps of $\frac{2}{10}$ to 2. Write the fractions in your count.

4 **Think.**
Look at the bar chart. It shows the number of seconds it took each player to find the first child in a game of 'Hide and seek'.

Use the scale to find and compare each time.
Write a statement to show what you have found out.
Now write another. And another.
How many different statements can you write?

Teacher's Guide
See page 131 of the *Teacher's Guide* for ideas of how to guide practice. Work through each step together as a class to develop children's conceptual understanding.

117

Follow-up ideas

- Return to other counts that children have done previously and in Year 2, e.g. counts of two and three, and explore them using number rods and place value to represent the numbers 20 and 30. How many different ways can they represent the number 100 or 150 this time?
- Children use stopwatches to time the length of different events in minutes or seconds. Values should be recorded to the whole second or minute, e.g. the time it takes to write their full name or to count in steps of four to 48. They should present their findings in a table and also using pictograms and bar charts. They could compare different intervals of time, describing them as longer or shorter.

Ensuring progress

Supporting understanding

In Step 1, children could initially relate the value of the rods 40, 50, 80 and 100 to the numbers four, five, eight and ten. They could explore the representations using these numbers for counting and calculating and then apply knowledge of place value, e.g. seeing part b as five, five and eight which has a total of 18 and then using the place-value grid to prove that $18 \times 10 = 180$.

Broadening understanding

In Step 4 challenge children to represent the bar chart in a different way, perhaps with a different scale or using a pictogram instead. They should explain how one representation relates to the other and that all the data shown still has the same value.

Concept mastered

Children can apply knowledge of counting in whole number and fraction steps in a variety of situations. They can relate counting to adding and subtracting, using place value and strategies such as part-part-whole to help them.

Answers

Step 1

a 180 c 280

b 180 d 240

Step 2

Answers will vary.

Step 3

a $5 \div 10 = \frac{5}{10}$ c $9 \div 10 = \frac{9}{10}$

b $2 \div 10 = \frac{2}{10}$ d $7 \div 10 = \frac{7}{10}$

Step 4

Answers will vary

Unit
10 Time travel

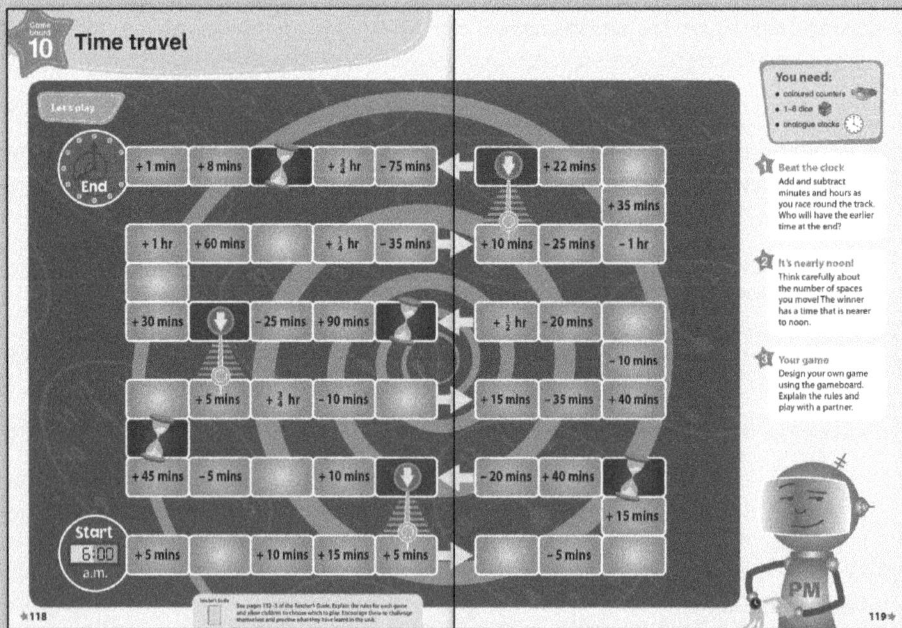

Game 1: Beat the clock

This is a simple game in which children race to the end of the track, adding and subtracting minutes and hours as they go.

Maths focus

- Tell and read the time from analogue clocks and using 12-hour clocks

Resources

1 counter per player (1 colour per player), 1–6 dice (1), analogue clocks with moving hands (2).

How to play

Both players place their counters on the 6:00 a.m. space and set their analogue clocks to 6 o'clock. They take turns to roll the dice and move their counter that number of spaces. They must add or subtract the time shown on the space from 6 o'clock, moving the hands on the clock and writing down the equivalent digital time, adding a.m. or p.m. They repeat from their new time until they reach the end of the gameboard.

If players land on a gold square they do nothing and keep the same time as before. Sand timers mean 'miss a go'. Landing on a blue square will cause them to slide down the pendulum and move back to the space below. The winner is the player who reaches the end of the track with the earlier time on their clock. The number of spaces does not need to be exact to get to the end.

Making it easier

Children can work in pairs to help when adding or subtracting times. They could also just focus on the analogue clock as they add and subtract amounts of time, carefully noting a.m. and p.m. times as they go.

Making it harder

When players land on a gold square, they must roll again and double the number of minutes they land on next, e.g. they land on '+ 10 mins' and double this time to add 20 minutes.

Game 2: It's nearly noon!

Children need to think carefully about the number of spaces to move on when playing this game. The winner is the player who ends the game with a time that is nearer to noon.

Maths focus

- Tell and read the time from digital and analogue clocks, working with durations and using the language of time

Resources

1 counter per player (1 colour per player), 1–6 dice (2), analogue clocks with moving hands (2).

How to play

Children follow the same rules as 'Beat the clock' but this time roll two dice. As each player rolls the dice, they must decide which of the numbers (and hence the time on the possible spaces) will be more useful to them. The winner is the player who reaches the end of the game with the time that is closer to noon, either before or after noon.

Making it easier

Children can work in pairs to help when adding or subtracting times. They could also just focus on the analogue clock as they add and subtract amounts of time, carefully noting a.m. and p.m. times as they go. At the end of the game they also show their time in the digital notation.

Making it harder

When players roll a double, they must double the number of minutes they land on next.

Game 3: Your game

Children should invent their own game, designing rules that use the concepts covered in the unit. Challenge children to make their game easier or harder.

Time travel

Choose a game to play.

Game 1: Beat the clock

You need:

- coloured counters (1 per player)
- 1–6 dice
- 2 analogue clocks with moving hands

How to play

- Each place your counter on 6:00 a.m. and set your clock to 6 o'clock.
- Take turns to roll the dice and move that number of spaces.
- Add or subtract the time given on the space from 6 o'clock by moving the hands on your clock.
- Write down the digital time. Use this new time for your next go.
- If you land on a gold space, do nothing and keep the same time. If you land on a sand timer miss a turn.
- Slide down pendulums to the space below!
- The winner is the player who reaches the end with the earlier time on their clock.

Game 2: It's nearly noon!

You need:

- coloured counters (1 per player)
- two 1–6 dice
- 2 analogue clocks with moving hands

How to play

- Each place your counter on 6:00 a.m. and set your clock to 6 o'clock.
- Follow the rules for Game 1 but this time roll 2 dice. Choose one of the 2 numbers to decide how many spaces to move.
- Your aim is to have a time that is closest to noon at the end of the game.
- The winner is the player who reaches the end with a time closer to noon on their clock.

Game 3: Your game

- Make up your own game using the gameboard.
- You could play 'Beat the clock' with 2 dice and choose which number to use.
- What are the rules for your game? Explain them to someone.

Please help your child by reading the instructions and playing the game together.

Unit 10 And finally ...

Assessment task 1

Resources

0–9 digit cards.

Running the task

It would be useful to start the task by asking children to use the digit cards to make a set of numbers that you read out to them, e.g. 75, 705, 463, 640.

As a group or individually, ask children to read the different number words in the Textbook. Perhaps choose one or two numbers and ask children to show you their value using digit cards.

Challenge children to use pairs or trios of words to make different 3-digit numbers. They should read each of the numbers they make and then show it in numerals. Look for children who fluently draw on numbers 11, 15 and 18 to make sense of numbers that use the box with 'ten'.

Evidencing mastery

Children who read the number words fluently and identify the value of each show mastery of this concept. They can make a range of different numbers and know where to use zero as a place holder. They can adapt the language as necessary to deal with numbers from 11 to 19.

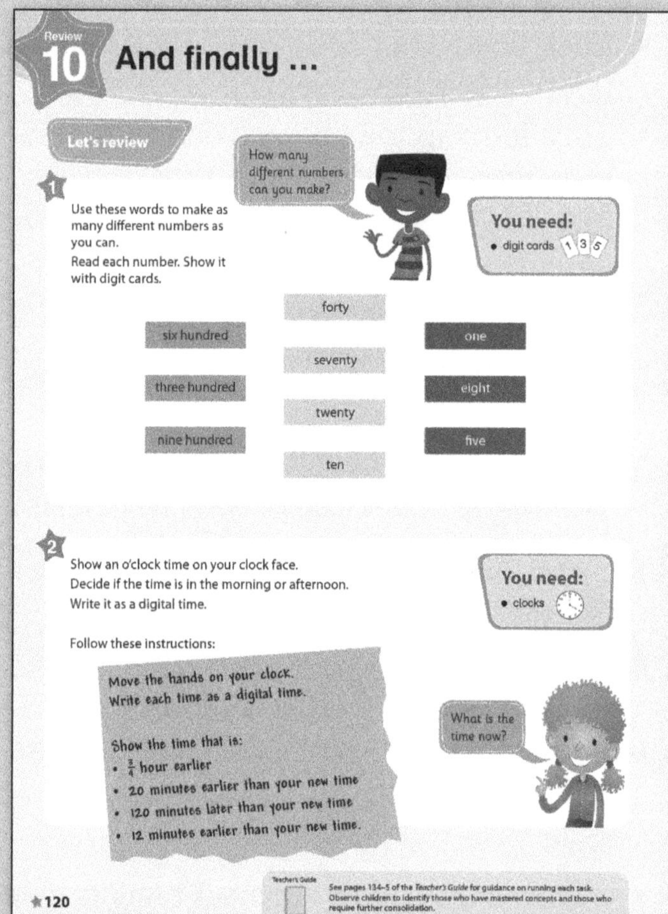
Review 10 And finally ...

Let's review

1 Use these words to make as many different numbers as you can.
Read each number. Show it with digit cards.

How many different numbers can you make?

You need:
• digit cards 1 3 5

six hundred
three hundred
nine hundred
forty
seventy
twenty
ten
one
eight
five

2 Show an o'clock time on your clock face.
Decide if the time is in the morning or afternoon.
Write it as a digital time.

You need:
• clocks

Follow these instructions:

Move the hands on your clock.
Write each time as a digital time.

Show the time that is:
• $\frac{3}{4}$ hour earlier
• 20 minutes earlier than your new time
• 120 minutes later than your new time
• 12 minutes earlier than your new time.

What is the time now?

120

Teacher's Guide
See pages 134–5 of the *Teacher's Guide* for guidance on running each task. Observe children to identify those who have mastered concepts and those who require further consolidation.

Assessment task 2

Resources

Analogue clocks.

Running the task

You may find it useful to talk about the different units of time and how they can be expressed, e.g. quarter of an hour and 15 minutes. Children should think about morning times and afternoon times and the way these can be shown.

Provide children with analogue clock faces so they can show the different times during the task and use them to help them to write the digital equivalent.

Children can start with an o'clock time of their choice, but they must decide if it is a morning or afternoon time. Read each instruction one at a time so children show the new time on the analogue clock and write it in digital notation. Prompt them to label it as a.m. or p.m. if necessary, letting them select which to use.

Children should read each time in different ways using the language associated with the analogue clock, e.g. quarter to two, and that associated with the digital clock, e.g. one forty-five.

Evidencing mastery

Children draw on the relationship between units of time, recognising 60 minutes as one hour so 120 minutes is equivalent to two hours. They are becoming more fluent with using the language associated with analogue clocks and digital clocks and can explain some of the differences.

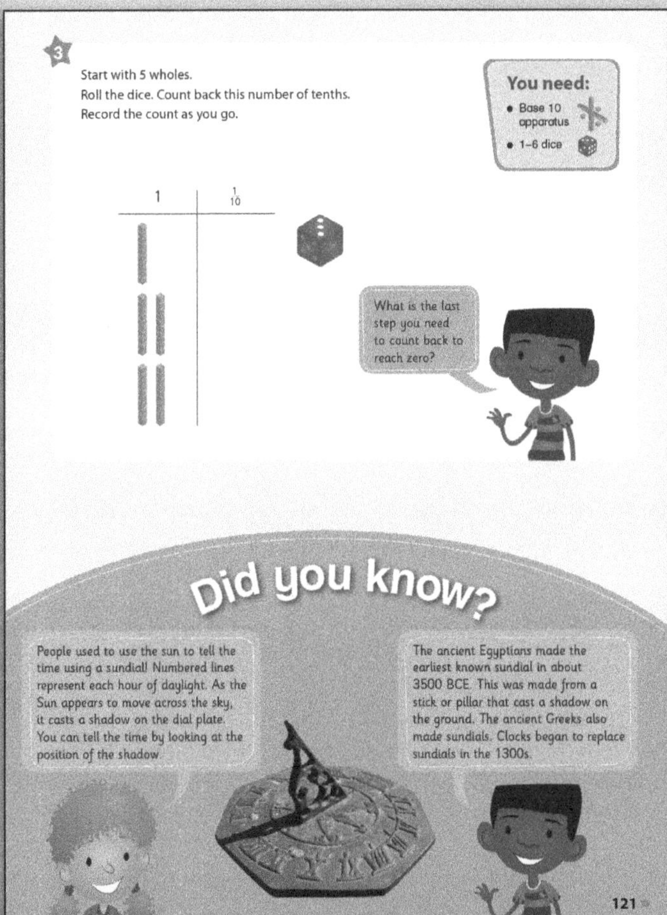

Assessment task 3

Resources

Base 10 apparatus, place-value grid, 1–6 dice.

Running the task

Remind children about some of the counting they have been doing in fraction steps. You may find it useful to rehearse counting in steps of halves and quarters to encourage them to think about mixed numbers as they cross whole boundaries.

In this task, they count back in tenths, crossing boundaries and exchanging wholes for ten-tenths as required. Children start with five wholes and represent them as five sticks in the 'ones' position on the place-value grid. Ask them to describe the value of each stick, i.e. one whole, and of each small cube, i.e. one tenth, and explain how they know.

As they roll the dice, they count back this number of tenths, e.g. they roll three and exchange one of the 'ones' sticks for ten cubes, place these in the tenths column and count back three-tenths by taking three cubes away. They then write down the number that is represented, i.e. four and seven-tenths in the Textbook example.

They continue in this way until they reach a value that is less than six-tenths and then count back the final amount required to reach zero.

Evidencing mastery

Children who count fluently back in tenths, drawing on knowledge of number bonds to help cross a ones boundary are showing evidence of mastery in this concept. They exchange one whole for ten-tenths, relating this to tens and ones.

Concepts mastered

- ☑ Children can recognise the difference between a 'ty' and 'teen' number written in numerals and words. They can fluently read numbers and can write them in words and in numerals. They can fluently use the language of morning and afternoon to describe the time of day.
- ☑ Children can apply knowledge of counting in whole number and fraction steps in a variety of situations. They can relate counting to adding and subtracting, using place value and strategies such as part-part-whole to help them.

Did you know?

Children could find out about sundials, the oldest known way that was used to tell the time. The flat surface of a sundial is called the dial plate. This plate can be made of metal, wood, stone or other materials. On the dial plate numbered lines, called hour lines, represent each hour of daylight. A gnomon sticks up at an angle from the dial plate and so casts a shadow. As the day passes, the shadow moves around the dial plate and falls on a new hour line every hour.

Children could make their own sundials, investigating where they need to mark the hour lines as the sun appears to move across the sky.

Around 1500 BCE, the Egyptians modified sundials to create shadow clocks that allowed for greater precision in determining the time of day. A more precise gnomon was also invented that divided the night time into 50 equal parts, with an additional two 'twilight' hours in the morning and evening.

You could discuss the accuracy of sundials and shadow clocks and why it was important for an instrument to be invented that would be able to tell the time with greater accuracy, i.e. to the nearest minute or second. Children could use the Internet to find examples of other early clocks, e.g. water clocks, hour glasses and candle clocks.

Unit 11

3-digit sums and differences

Mathematical focus

★ **Number: addition and subtraction**

★ **Measurement: mass, length, money, volume/capacity**

★ **Statistics: interpret and present data, solve problems**

Prior learning

Children should already be able to:

- add and subtract numbers mentally, including a 3-digit number and tens
- add and subtract numbers with up to two digits
- recognise the place value of each digit in a 3-digit number (hundreds, tens, and ones).

Key new learning

- Add and subtract numbers mentally including a 3-digit number and ones, tens and hundreds.
- Add and subtract numbers with up to three digits using the formal written methods of columnar addition and subtraction.
- Estimate the answer to a calculation and use inverse operations to check answers.
- Solve problems, including missing number problems, using number facts, place value and more complex addition.

Making connections

- Children need to be able to apply the concept of addition and subtraction to real-life situations, e.g. the total cost of two items in a shop and how much change is received. You could visit a market stall or shop to provide children with real-life practice.
- Link this unit with a science project. Children plant three sets of cress seeds and then put one in a cupboard, one on the window sill and one outside. They observe the differences in how they grow, measure the heights of the plants in centimetres or millimetres and compare the results. You could then make a connection to statistics by asking children to record their results in a table or graph.
- This unit prepares children for solving comparison, sum and difference problems using information presented in pictograms, tables and other graphs.

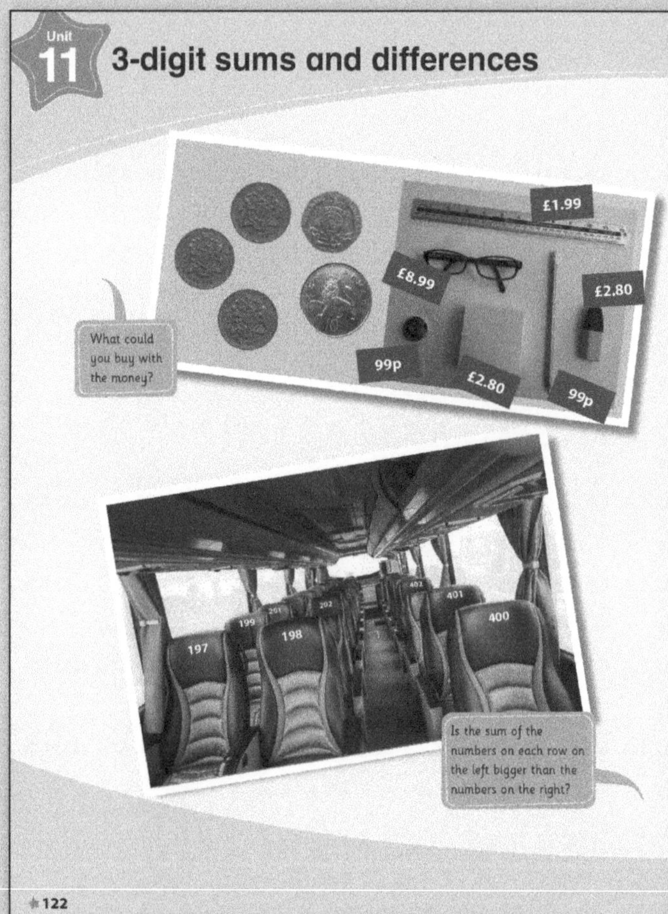

Talk about

It is important to use precise mathematical vocabulary from the beginning. Ensure children describe a digit by its place value, not just refer to it as a single-digit number, e.g. in 256, they say 50 not five. Misconceptions occur when inaccurate mathematical language is used, e.g. when calculating 345 – 123, encourage children to say 300 – 100, not refer to it as 3 – 1.

Children need to understand the concept of a 'carry' when a number totals more than ten, rather than memorise the method so they achieve an answer. Practise using Base 10 materials and talk through the calculations. Encourage use of inverse operations when calculating answers.

Engaging and exploring

Look together at the first photo. Encourage children to look at their classroom stationery. How much did their pen, pencil and rubber cost? Can they estimate how much all their stationery cost? Talk about the value of each coin. Challenge children to think about the value of different coins. *What is the least value a coin can have? What is the greatest value a coin can have? If you had five coins in your pocket what could the value be? What would the greatest value of all the coins be if they were all different? What about the least?*

Agree that in the photo there is £3.30 in total. How many pennies is that? Discuss the stationery items in the photo that could be bought with the money and the one that cannot be bought. *What coins would you need to have to buy the items?* Help children who are unsure by providing them with real or plastic coins so that they can picture each sum of money. Challenge children to estimate how much more money they would need if they wanted to buy the glasses. *What coins could they be?* Adapt the items and prices according to children's needs and help children estimate 3-digit numbers.

For the second photo, talk about the numbers on seats in trains and planes. *Why are the numbers needed? Why do the train companies need to know how many people are travelling in total or how many more tickets they need to sell?* Ask children to use estimation to predict whether for each row the sum of the numbers on the left is greater or less than the number on the right. Ask children to add the numbers on the left to confirm. When adding, children should use an appropriate mental calculation strategy and not a written method. Discuss whether their predictions were correct. Ask: *Which strategies did you use to add the two numbers in each row on the left? Why was your strategy the most efficient?* Challenge children to write number statements that use the symbols $<$, $>$, $=$ to show their findings.

Discuss the question related to the basketball photo and decide how many minutes until the end of the match. Explain that when using time children need to learn that bridging through ten or 100 is not appropriate. When working with minutes and hours, it is necessary to bridge through 60 as there are 60 minutes in one hour, e.g. a digital clock displaying 9:59 will, in two minutes time, read 10:01 not 10:61. Provide children with digital or geared clocks or they could make paper ones with Roman numerals. They should use these to answer questions, e.g. *What is 20 minutes after 8:50? 8:50 + 10 minutes takes us to 9:00, then add another 10 minutes. Can you show 20 minutes before 11:00? 5 minutes after 7:59?*

Look at the pictogram of snowy days. *Why is it important to record such information? What does sum mean? And difference?* Establish that sum is the result of one or more additions and difference is found by comparing the quantity of one set of objects with another. Provide interlocking cubes to make towers of 100 and demonstrate that one full snowflake can be represented by a tower of 100 cubes.

Children work in groups and each table constructs the pictogram shown in the Textbook using interlocking cubes. *What does half of a snowflake mean? What about a quarter?* Link number and fractions and explain that if one snowflake or tower = 100, then half of it will be 50 and $\frac{1}{4}$ of it will be 25. Encourage children to find the difference by using estimation, then use a mental strategy to work out the actual sums.

This work could be linked to a geography lesson. Children could revisit information they have collected about temperature or rainfall in different countries. Recording and comparing data helps children develop ideas about weather conditions around the world.

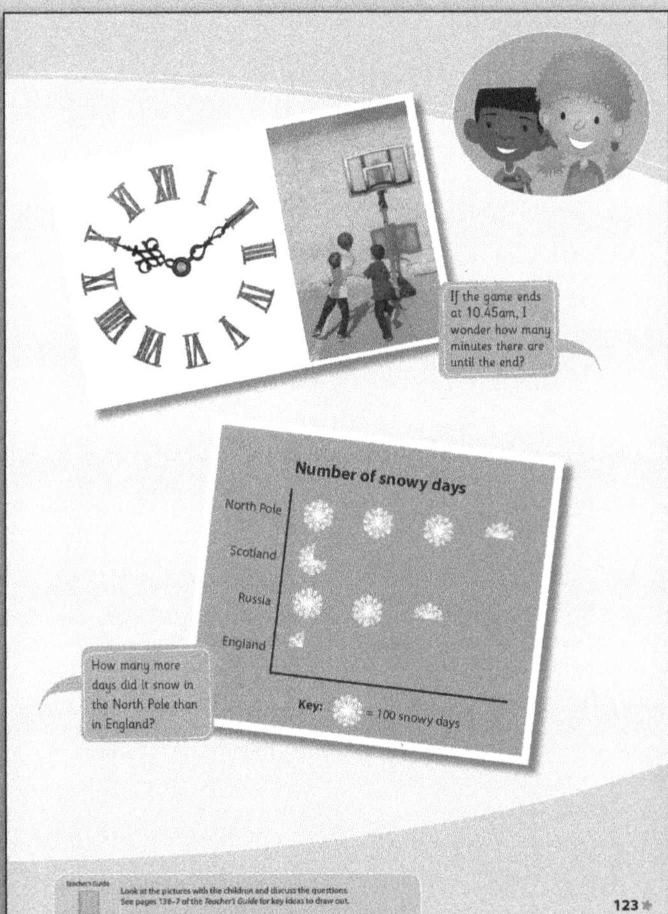

Things to think about

- What type of manipulatives and visual representations will you use?
- How will you create opportunities for children to practise addition and subtraction in real-life situations, including opportunities for meaningful role play?
- How will you build time and opportunities for children to explain their reasoning?
- How will you organise your groupings?
- What opportunities will you provide to build fluency?
- Which problem-solving strategies are most appropriate in this unit, e.g. What do you notice? What's the same? What's different? Convince me.

Checking understanding

You will know children have mastered these concepts when they can solve addition and subtraction problems with 3-digit numbers in different contexts, appropriately choosing and using number facts, showing understanding of place value, counting, mental and written methods. They will be able to find missing calculations and use estimating and inverse operations to check their answers. They can explain their decision-making and justify their solutions.

11a Adding 3-digit numbers

- Add numbers mentally including a 3-digit number and ones, tens and hundreds.
- Add numbers with up to three digits using the formal written methods of columnar addition.
- Estimate the answer to a calculation and use inverse operations to check answers.
- Solve problems, including missing number problems, using number facts, place value and more complex addition.

Homework 53 and 54 | Practice Book pp 91–3 | Place Value & Abacus

Representations and resources

Whiteboards and pens, building blocks, counters, small classroom items, balance scales, 500 g weights, interlocking cubes, number lines, place-value counters, Base 10 apparatus.

Mathematical vocabulary

Addition, adding, total, sum, altogether, equal, estimate, multiple

Warming up

Ask quick addition questions which require children to revisit their number facts to ten and 20, doubles and near doubles and bridging a multiple of ten, e.g.: What is 23 + 7? 24 + 8? 32 + 33? To extend write on the board five numbers, e.g. 14, 28, 36, 5, 12 and ask them to group them so that they can add them quickly. Children should add 36 + 14 = 50, 28 + 12 = 40, 50 + 40 + 5 = 95. Adapt the numbers to make the task easier/harder.

Background knowledge

Addition has a commutative property, 100 + 200 = 200 + 100. Numbers can be added in any order and it is easier to add the smallest number to the biggest one. This property is useful in problem solving, hence it is important for children to understand and it. Addition has an associative property. When three or more numbers are added together, they can be added in any order, e.g. 87 + 3 + 110 = (87 + 3) + 110 = 90 + 110 = 200. Addition has an inverse relationship with subtraction. Every addition calculation can be replaced by a subtraction one and vice versa, e.g. if 80 + 200 = 280, 280 – 80 = 200 and 280 – 200 = 80.

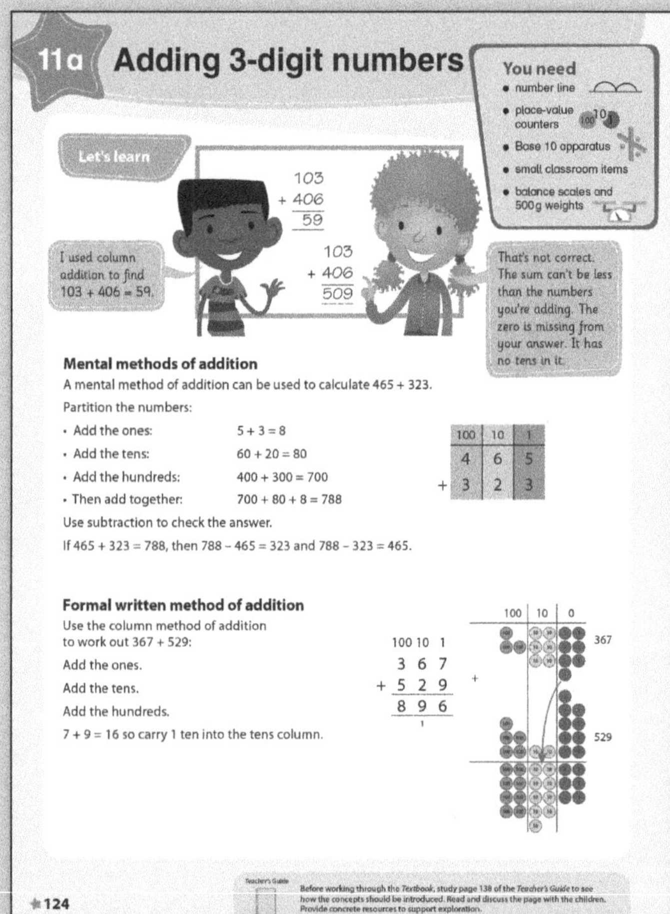
11a Adding 3-digit numbers

You need
- number line
- place-value counters
- Base 10 apparatus
- small classroom items
- balance scales and 500g weights

Let's learn

Mental methods of addition

A mental method of addition can be used to calculate 465 + 323.

Partition the numbers:

- Add the ones: 5 + 3 = 8
- Add the tens: 60 + 20 = 80
- Add the hundreds: 400 + 300 = 700
- Then add together: 700 + 80 + 8 = 788

	100	10	1
	4	6	5
+	3	2	3

Use subtraction to check the answer.

If 465 + 323 = 788, then 788 – 465 = 323 and 788 – 323 = 465.

Formal written method of addition

Use the column method of addition to work out 367 + 529:

Add the ones.

Add the tens.

Add the hundreds.

7 + 9 = 16 so carry 1 ten into the tens column.

	100	10	1
	3	6	7
+	5	2	9
	8	9	6
		1	

124

Teacher's Guide
Before working through the *Textbook*, study page 138 of the *Teacher's Guide* to see how the concepts should be introduced. Read and discuss the page with the children. Provide concrete resources to support exploration.

Let's learn: Modelling and teaching

Mental methods of addition

- Discuss the misconception cartoon. Can children explain the error that Oli has made? Provide further examples of addition calculations where there is an error in the tens or units column. Can children to identify and correct the errors?
- Discuss the use of addition to solve Mia's problem. *Why do you have to add? How can you check that the answer is correct? Can you think of an example where you added two numbers (calculating sum of points in a game, pocket money, sweet in a jar)?* Establish that addition is required to calculate a sum or total of two quantities.

Formal written method of addition

- Ask children to discuss what the question requires before attempting it. Explain that they always start with ones. Demonstrate by showing Base 10 apparatus. Say: *7 + 9 = 16. What are the ones in 16? We can rearrange 16 as one ten + six ones. One ten must go in the ten column. I cannot write it in the answer line as I know there are more tens to add. Finally, add all the ones, tens and hundreds.*
- Repeat for other questions, e.g. find 235 more than 712, increase 127 by 136. Explain what the words 'increase, sum, total, more' mean and establish when addition is used to solve problems. *Can you estimate the answer?* Allow children time to understand and explore the concept of carrying one ten to the tens column.
- Provide further practice of column addition.

Let's practise: Digging deeper

Step 1

Encourage children to explain the mental method they choose. Revisit the number facts to 100 prior to the task and allow children time to talk through each calculation and work out the answer. After discussing the method used in part a, ask: *Which other sum can you find in the same way?* Establish that in parts a and b children can treat the numbers as 2-digit numbers while remembering the place value. Establish that partitioning can be used in parts c, d and e and encourage children to work in pairs and explain their method to their partner. *How can you calculate the sum in part f? Can you think of a different way?* Encourage children to explain their answers.

Step 2

Children should make an estimate first and then use column addition or a mental calculation strategy to calculate each sum. They could use place-value counters as a support. Share the strategies that children used. Observe whether all children used the same strategies and ask them to justify their approach.

Step 3

Children must find pairs of items that weigh less than 500 g, weigh them, estimate their total mass and then calculate their total mass. Children should record their answers in number statements. Encourage discussion about the method used to calculate the sum. To challenge children, ask them to give you a silly estimate, e.g. the total weight being 200 grams when each weight is over 200 grams. Encourage children to explain the reasons for their answers.

Step 4

Children should be able to notice and understand that to make the largest sum, they need to add the two largest numbers and to make the smallest sum, they need to add the two smallest numbers. For parts c and d, revisit odd and even numbers and encourage children to generalise.

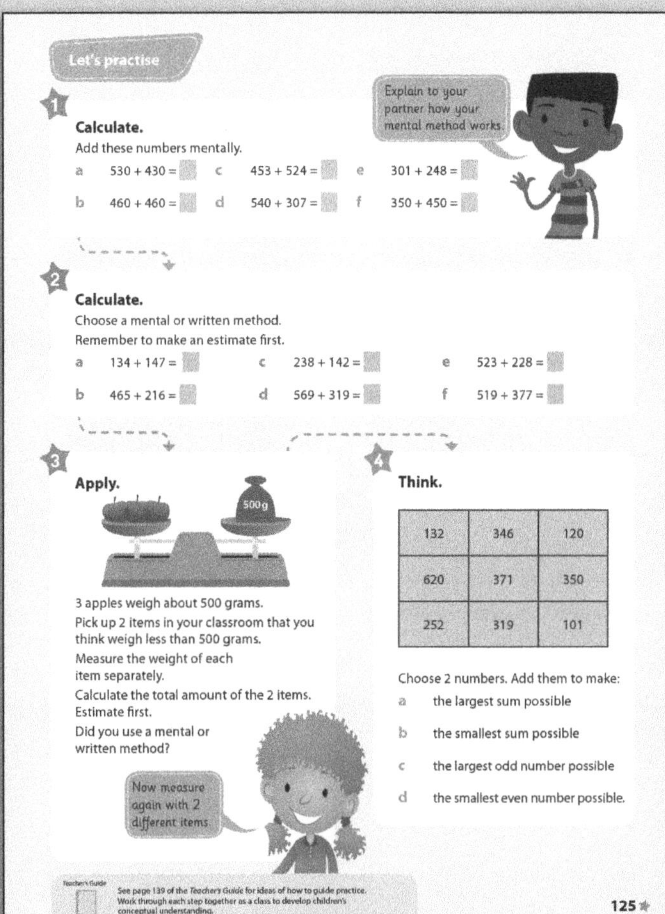
Let's practise

1 Calculate.

Add these numbers mentally.

a 530 + 430 =
c 453 + 524 =
e 301 + 248 =

b 460 + 460 =
d 540 + 307 =
f 350 + 450 =

2 Calculate.

Choose a mental or written method.

Remember to make an estimate first.

a 134 + 147 =
c 238 + 142 =
e 523 + 228 =

b 465 + 216 =
d 569 + 319 =
f 519 + 377 =

3 Apply.

3 apples weigh about 500 grams.

Pick up 2 items in your classroom that you think weigh less than 500 grams.

Measure the weight of each item separately.

Calculate the total amount of the 2 items. Estimate first.

Did you use a mental or written method?

4 Think.

132	346	120
620	371	350
252	319	101

Choose 2 numbers. Add them to make:

a the largest sum possible

b the smallest sum possible

c the largest odd number possible

d the smallest even number possible.

Teacher's Guide: See page 139 of the *Teacher's Guide* for ideas of how to guide practice. Work through each step together as a class to develop children's conceptual understanding.

125

Ensuring progress

Supporting understanding

Allow plenty of time for children to explore and understand addition of 3-digit numbers. Use real-life examples so that children can understand why addition is needed. As children become more confident with mentally adding 2-digit numbers, introduce prices that are 3-digit numbers (in pennies).

Broadening understanding

Encourage children to generalise where possible, e.g. encourage them to explore whether it is always, sometimes or never true that when you add a hundreds number (e.g. 200) to a 3-digit number only the value of the hundreds column changes. *Why do the tens and units columns not change?*

Concept mastered

✓ Children can explain when a mental method is more appropriate than a written method and fluently apply knowledge of number facts and place value to support mental work. They can explain the additive property of numbers and refer to it when using a formal written method.

Follow-up ideas

- Work in 2 groups. Throw the dice three times and make a 3-digit target number with the numbers shown. Write this on the whiteboard and ask each group to write as many addition number facts as possible in two minutes, e.g. if the target is 335, the number facts could be 100 + 235, 200 + 135. The group with the most facts wins one point. The winning group is the first to reach five points.
- Investigate what happens when children create an addition pyramid with three rows when the values on the bottom of the pyramid are given, e.g. children need to add the values on the third row to find the values in the second row, then add the values in the second row to find the value on the top row. Children work in two mixed-ability groups.

Answers

Step 1

a 960 **d** 847
b 920 **e** 549
c 977 **f** 800

Step 2

a 281 **d** 888
b 681 **e** 751
c 380 **f** 896

Step 4

a 620 + 371 = 991
b 101 + 120 = 221
c 620 + 371 = 991
d 132 + 120 = 252

11b Subtracting 3-digit numbers

- **Subtract numbers mentally including a 3-digit number and ones, tens and hundreds.**
- **Subtract numbers with up to three digits using formal written methods of columnar subtraction.**
- **Estimate the answer to a calculation and use inverse operations to check answers.**
- **Solve problems, including missing number problems, using number facts, place value and more complex subtraction.**

Homework 55 and 56 Practice Book pp 94–6

Representations and resources

Whiteboards and pens, string, Base 10 apparatus, number lines, tape measures, beanbags.

Mathematical vocabulary

Subtract, difference, take away, less than, more than, equal, estimate, inverse, addition

Warming up

Ask children missing number questions, e.g ▢ + 70 = 100, 35 + ▢ = 45. Choose easy sums to ensure that the focus of the task is revisiting and exploring the link between addition and subtraction. Establish that addition is the inverse operation to subtraction. Use bar models if children find the concept difficult. *How can you check the answer?* Put the number back in the question. *Does it work?* e.g. ▢ + 23 = 30. ▢ = 7 because 23 + 7 = 30.

Background knowledge

Subtraction does not have a commutative property. The order of subtraction does matter, e.g. 800 – 250 ≠ 250 – 800. A series of consecutive subtractions can be made in any order, e.g. 800 – 40 – 200 = 800 – 200 – 40. Every subtraction calculation has an inverse relationship with an addition calculation, e.g. if 900 – 250 = 650, then 650 + 250 = 900. Subtraction can be used when: a) a quantity is reduced, b) to complete a set or a certain quantity, how many more do you need, or c) when finding a difference.

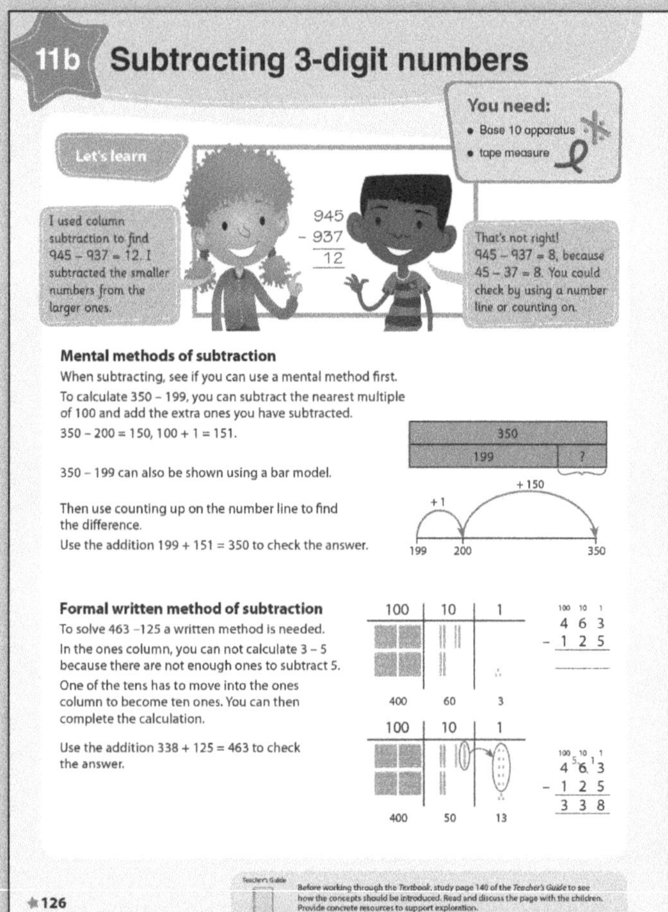
11b Subtracting 3-digit numbers

You need:
- Base 10 apparatus
- tape measure

Let's learn

I used column subtraction to find 945 – 937 = 12. I subtracted the smaller numbers from the larger ones.

That's not right! 945 – 937 = 8, because 45 – 37 = 8. You could check by using a number line or counting on.

Mental methods of subtraction

When subtracting, see if you can use a mental method first.

To calculate 350 – 199, you can subtract the nearest multiple of 100 and add the extra ones you have subtracted.

350 – 200 = 150, 100 + 1 = 151.

350 – 199 can also be shown using a bar model.

Then use counting up on the number line to find the difference.

Use the addition 199 + 151 = 350 to check the answer.

Formal written method of subtraction

To solve 463 –125 a written method is needed.

In the ones column, you can not calculate 3 – 5 because there are not enough ones to subtract 5.

One of the tens has to move into the ones column to become ten ones. You can then complete the calculation.

Use the addition 338 + 125 = 463 to check the answer.

126

Before working through the *Textbook*, study page 140 of the *Teacher's Guide* to see how the concepts should be introduced. Read and discuss the page with the children. Provide concrete resources to support exploration.

Let's learn: Modelling and teaching

Mental methods of subtraction

- Use the misconception cartoon to explain that, when subtracting one number from the other, moving some of the digits around will give the wrong answer. Give children examples using lower values, e.g. Is 21 – 18 = 3 or = 7? Ask them to explain their answers by referring to commutativity.
- Discuss the use of subtraction to solve Oli's problem. *Why do we have to subtract? When do we subtract and when do we add?* Give examples of subtractions and additions and ask children to discuss whether they will subtract or add, e.g. *15 points less, take 100 away, spent £1.20 from £4, temperature decreased by 5 degrees. What method will you use?*
- Discuss how mental methods can be used to subtract numbers that are close together or numbers that can be adjusted. Demonstrate subtracting 199 by subtracting 200 and adding one back, or by counting up on a number line (as shown in the Textbook).

Formal written method of subtraction

- Prior to starting the task revisit the ideas from Warming up that addition and subtraction are reverse operations to each other. Compare 463 – 125 with other subtractions children have made. The numbers are not multiples of ten, are not close together on the number line and cannot be adjusted easily. Explain that a formal written method would, therefore, be appropriate. Use Base 10 apparatus to show how when removing 125 cubes from 463, 338 are left. Ask a child to put 338 and 125 cubes together to show that the total is 463 again.
- Model the calculation using Base 10 apparatus, as shown in the Textbook.

Let's practise: Digging deeper

Step 1

Children should make an estimate before completing each calculation. The calculations should be solved mentally.
Ask children to explain why a mental calculation strategy is appropriate in each case, and to explain their strategy, e.g. finding the difference because the numbers are close together; using related number facts for two 2-digit numbers or round numbers to the nearest ten or 100 then adjust the answer. *Were the actual answers close, less than or more than the estimated answers?*

Step 2

Children need to identify that they should use the column written method. They could use Base 10 apparatus to support the written method. Look out for those who are using the method correctly in particular when they 'borrow one ten' from the tens column. In parts e to h, children subtract different measurements that involve 3-digit numbers. *Will the measurement affect the answer?* Encourage the use of the correct mathematical vocabulary when writing word problems.

Step 3

During this practical task, children should choose to use mental or written methods as appropriate. Encourage them to explain their choices. To extend, children could find the difference in prices between the items. *How much cheaper was one item than the other? If you had £9 to start with and your change is £1.30, what items did you buy? How can you check your answer?*

Step 4

As only one of the digits in each mystery number has been specified, some children may find it difficult to make decisions as to what the other two digits might be. Ask children to draw a grid where each digit can be placed. Read the question slowly and place each digit in the right box.

	100	10	1
Number 1			
Number 2			

You may read the question for them, changing the intonation on the key areas to highlight what is required.

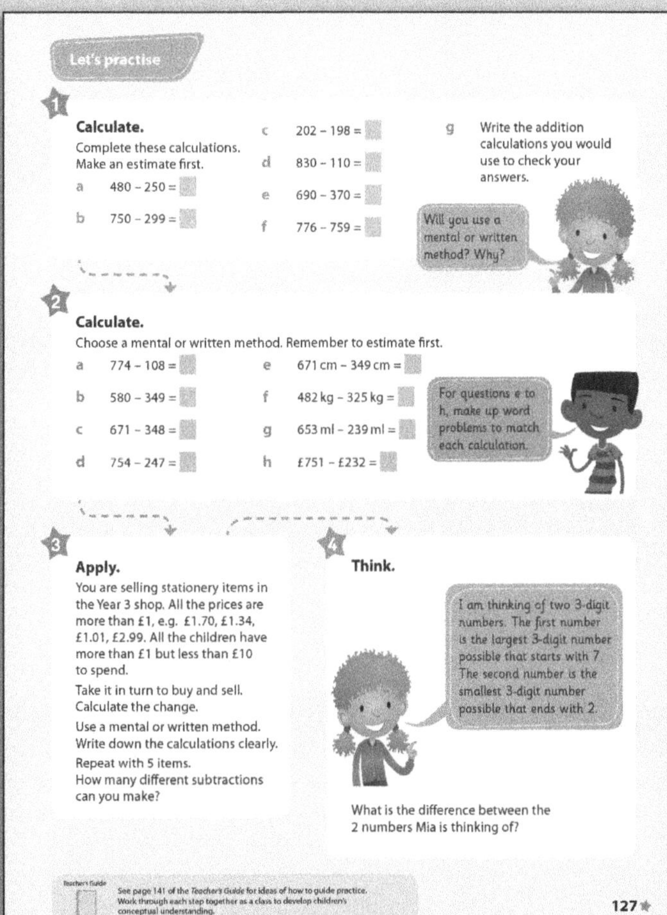

Let's practise

1 **Calculate.**
Complete these calculations. Make an estimate first.

a 480 – 250 =
b 750 – 299 =
c 202 – 198 =
d 830 – 110 =
e 690 – 370 =
f 776 – 759 =
g Write the addition calculations you would use to check your answers.

2 **Calculate.**
Choose a mental or written method. Remember to estimate first.

a 774 – 108 =
b 580 – 349 =
c 671 – 348 =
d 754 – 247 =
e 671 cm – 349 cm =
f 482 kg – 325 kg =
g 653 ml – 239 ml =
h £751 – £232 =

3 **Apply.**
You are selling stationery items in the Year 3 shop. All the prices are more than £1, e.g. £1.70, £1.34, £1.01, £2.99. All the children have more than £1 but less than £10 to spend.
Take it in turn to buy and sell. Calculate the change.
Use a mental or written method. Write down the calculations clearly.
Repeat with 5 items.
How many different subtractions can you make?

4 **Think.**

What is the difference between the 2 numbers Mia is thinking of?

Teacher's Guide
See page 141 of the *Teacher's Guide* for ideas of how to guide practice. Work through each step together as a class to develop children's conceptual understanding.

127

Ensuring progress

Supporting understanding

Work with children in a focus group. Revisit number bonds to 20, number facts to 100 and subtracting single-digit and 2-digit numbers from a given 3-digit number. Allow time for children to practise and ask questions. Clarify any misconceptions they may have. Discuss the importance of the place value of each digit in a 3-digit number and using estimates to check the answer is correct.

Broadening understanding

Challenge children to create problems similar to the one in Step 4 and swap with a partner. Encourage the use of correct mathematical vocabulary.

Concept mastered

Children can use a written method and their knowledge of partitioning to subtract 3-digit numbers.

Follow-up ideas

- Split the class into two teams. Throw a dice three times and make a 3-digit number using the numbers shown. Children write five subtraction number facts for that number as quickly as possible. The group that writes the number facts first wins the challenge. Repeat for different values.
- Children work in small groups. Tell them that they have £150 spending money to buy toys for 60 children in Years 1 and 2; so far they have spent £9.99. Children work out how much money they have left. They could research which toys they could buy for the younger children to use at break time. What if the budget was £300 or £800?

Answers

Step 1

a	230	c	4	e	320
b	451	d	720	f	17

g 250 + 230 = 480
451 + 299 = 750
4 + 198 = 202
720 + 110 = 830
320 + 370 = 690
17 + 759 = 776

Step 2

a	666	e	322 cm
b	231	f	157 kg
c	323	g	414 ml
d	507	h	£519

Step 4

799 – 102 = 697

Unit 11

Add-venture take-away pizza

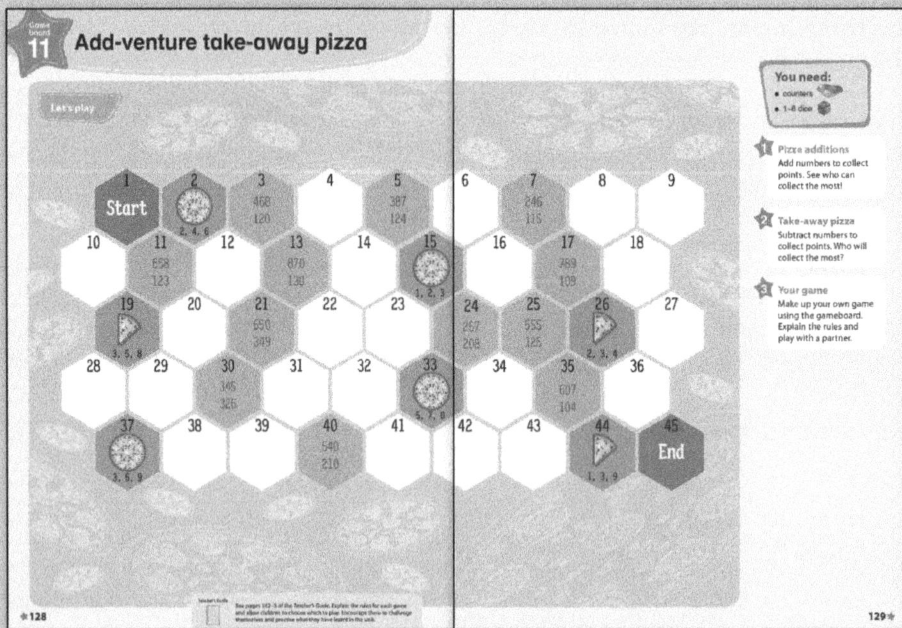

Game 1: Pizza additions

In this game, children race around the track, collecting points for correct addition.

Maths focus

Add 3-digit numbers mentally or using a written method

Resources

1–6 dice (1), 1 counter per player (1 colour per player).

How to play

Children place their counters on Start. They take turns to roll the dice and move that number of spaces. If children land on a white space, they roll the dice three times and make a 3-digit number using the numbers rolled. Children collect four points if they find two numbers that add up to the 3-digit number, e.g. if they make number 150, they say 80 + 70 = 150. If children land on an orange space with two 3-digit numbers, they collect four points if they add up the numbers correctly. If they land on a full pizza, they collect 20 points if they use the three single-digit numbers, make the two biggest possible 3-digit numbers and add them together correctly. If the two numbers are not the biggest but are added correctly, eight points are added to their score. If children land on a slice of a pizza, they collect ten points if they use the three single-digits, make the two smallest possible 3-digit numbers and add them correctly. If the two numbers are not the smallest but are added correctly, four points are added to their score. The winner is the player who collects the most points by the End.

Making it easier

Players could 'call a friend' and ask for advice twice during the game. If the numbers are difficult to add, children can use estimation rather than exact values.

Making it harder

Children get an extra ten points for correctly explaining the reasons for using a mental or a written method.

Game 2: Take-away pizza

Children add and subtract values using mental arithmetic or written methods.

Maths focus

Subtract 3-digit numbers mentally or using a written method

Resources

1–6 dice (1), 1 counter per player (1 colour per player).

How to play

Children start as in Game 1. This time, if they land on a white space, they collect four points if they find two numbers that have a difference equal to the 3-digit number they made, e.g. if they make number 150, they say 200 – 50 = 150. If children land on an orange space with two 3-digit numbers, they collect four points if they subtract the numbers correctly, choosing a mental or written method. If children land on a full pizza, they collect 20 points if they use the numbers to make the two biggest possible 3-digit numbers and subtract them correctly. If children land on a slice of a pizza, they collect ten points if they use the numbers to make the two smallest possible 3-digit numbers and subtract them correctly. The winner is the player who collects the most points by the End.

Making it easier

Children can use estimation rather than exact values.

Making it harder

Children collect an extra ten points for finding another set of numbers that have a difference equal to the 3-digit number they made. They write all the number facts related to this subtraction.

Game 3: Your game

Children should invent their own game, designing rules that use the concepts covered in the unit. Challenge children to make their game easier or harder.

Add-venture take-away pizza

Choose a game to play.

Game 1: Pizza additions

You need:
- 1–6 dice
- 1 counter per player (1 colour per player)

How to play
- Each place your counter on Start.
- Take turns to roll the dice. Move that number of spaces.
- If you land on a white shape, roll the dice 3 times to make a 3-digit number. Find 2 numbers that add up to make this 3-digit number. Collect 4 points.
- If you land on orange space with two 3-digit numbers, add up the numbers correctly. Collect 4 points.
- If you land on a full pizza, use the numbers to make the two biggest 3-digit numbers you can. Add them correctly. Collect 20 points.
- If you land on a slice of a pizza, use the numbers to make the two smallest 3-digit numbers you can. Add them correctly. Collect 10 points.
- The winner is the player who collects the most points by the End.

Game 2: Take-away pizza

You need:
- 1–6 dice
- 1 counter per player (1 colour per player)

How to play
- Each place your counter on Start.
- Take turns to roll the dice. Move that number of spaces.
- If you land on a white shape, roll the dice 3 times to make a 3-digit number. Find 2 numbers that have a difference equal to this 3-digit number. Collect 4 points.
- If you land on a space with two 3-digit numbers, subtract the numbers correctly. Collect 4 points.
- If you land on a full pizza, use the 3 numbers to make the 2 biggest 3-digit numbers possible. Subtract them correctly. Collect 20 points.
- If you land on a slice of a pizza, use the 3 numbers to make the 2 smallest 3-digit numbers you can. Subtract them correctly. Collect 10 points.
- The winner is the player who collects the most points by the End.

Game 3: Your game

- Make up your own game using the gameboard.
- Explain the rules and play with a partner.

Please help your child by reading the instructions and playing the game together.

Unit 11 And finally ...

Assessment task 1

Running the task

In this task children should use a mental method of addition or subtraction as the numbers are easy to partition and add or subtract. Begin by providing a simpler example to illustrate the question. This provides an opportunity for children to focus reasoning, without worrying about the calculations involved, e.g. There are 7 lizards and 50 snakes. *How many more lizards are there?* Remind them to use estimation to check that the answers make sense. Do not tell them the answer; instead ask them to use the inverse operation to check their calculations.

Children can then work on the first part of the task independently. In the second part of the task, children complete the pictogram. Before they start, discuss different scales that can be used, e.g. If one box represents 40, half of the box represents 20, and a quarter represents ten. Repeat for different values.

Encourage discussion on how children would represent 375 in the table using this scale. Challenge children to think of other ways to represent the data, e.g. using bar graphs or ICT. Encourage discussion about what is the same and what is different between the different methods they suggest. Provide time for children to work in mixed-ability groups, supporting each group as needed and developing reasoning.

Evidencing mastery

Children who recognise that they need to subtract to find how many more lizards than snakes show a clear understanding of the concepts of addition and subtraction, and the mathematical language used. They can distinguish between correct and false statements to explore the concept of mathematical proof, making generalisations and developing their mathematical thinking, demonstrating a deeper fluency and mastery.

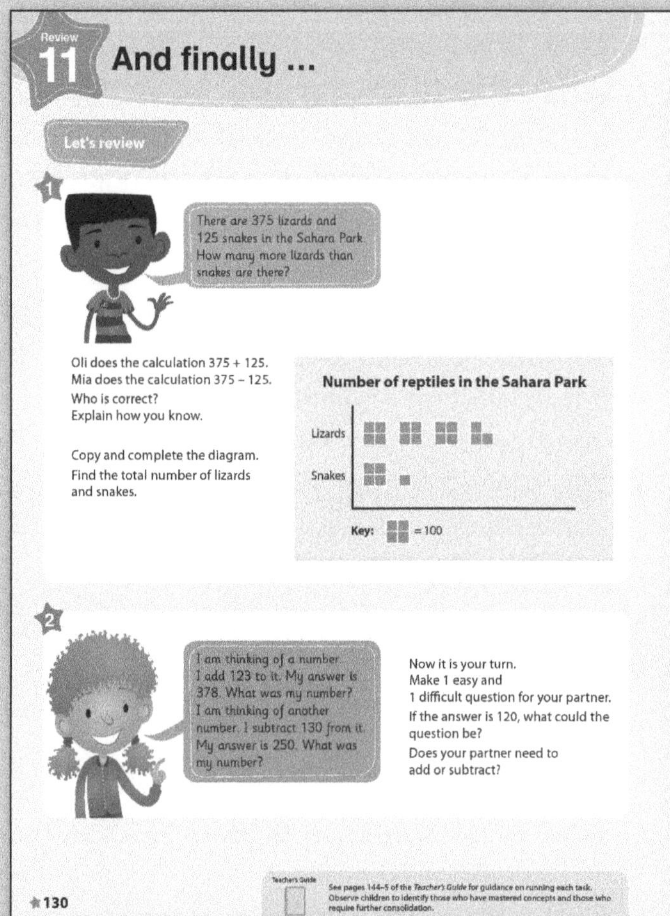
Review 11 And finally ...

Let's review

1

There are 375 lizards and 125 snakes in the Sahara Park. How many more lizards than snakes are there?

Oli does the calculation 375 + 125.
Mia does the calculation 375 − 125.
Who is correct?
Explain how you know.

Copy and complete the diagram.
Find the total number of lizards and snakes.

Number of reptiles in the Sahara Park

Lizards
Snakes
Key: = 100

2

I am thinking of a number. I add 123 to it. My answer is 378. What was my number? I am thinking of another number. I subtract 130 from it. My answer is 250. What was my number?

Now it is your turn.
Make 1 easy and 1 difficult question for your partner.
If the answer is 120, what could the question be?
Does your partner need to add or subtract?

130

Teacher's Guide
See pages 144–5 of the *Teacher's Guide* for guidance on running each task. Observe children to identify those who have mastered concepts and those who require further consolidation.

Assessment task 2

Running the task

Children need to decide whether to add or subtract to find the missing numbers. Encourage them to write number statements to show their workings and check the answer by substituting the number they found back in the question.

Before starting the task, you may introduce children to simpler examples, so that they can focus on the development of reasoning skills without worrying about the subject knowledge, e.g. *I am thinking of a number. I add 20 to it. My answer is 100. What is my number?*

In the second part of the task, children are encouraged to think creatively to make questions when the answer is given. Some children may prefer to stick to one type of question, e.g. addition. Encourage them to make their next question different. To help them, ask them to use some of the vocabulary they have been using in the lesson, e.g. total, difference, how many more, how many less. You could also ask children to include different values, such as two 3-digit numbers; money (e.g. £5.20, £3.10); hours and minutes (e.g. 3 hours, 29 minutes) or measurements (e.g. 250 ml or 750 g).

Evidencing mastery

Look for children who are able to apply reverse operations to find the missing number questions. They fluently round the numbers and estimate to check answers. Children show reasoning skills when making addition or subtraction questions with 3-digit numbers. They are able to explain why a question is easy or difficult and add or subtract fluently using a mental or a written method.

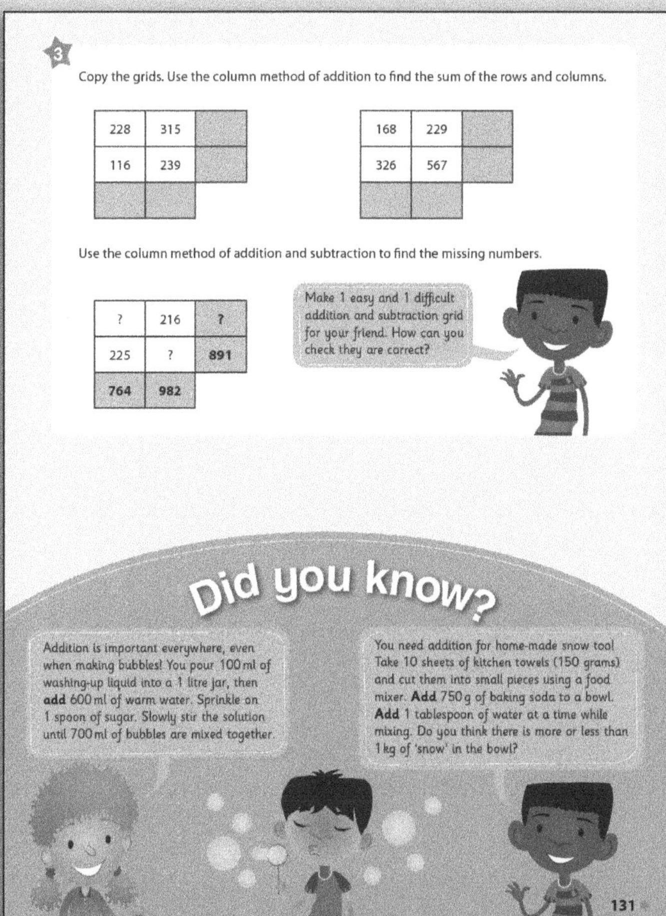

3

Copy the grids. Use the column method of addition to find the sum of the rows and columns.

228	315	
116	239	

168	229	
326	567	

Use the column method of addition and subtraction to find the missing numbers.

?	216	**?**
225	?	**891**
764	**982**	

Did you know?

Addition is important everywhere, even when making bubbles! You pour 100 ml of washing-up liquid into a 1 litre jar, then **add** 600 ml of warm water. Sprinkle on 1 spoon of sugar. Slowly stir the solution until 700 ml of bubbles are mixed together.

You need addition for home-made snow too! Take 10 sheets of kitchen towels (150 grams) and cut them into small pieces using a food mixer. **Add** 750 g of baking soda to a bowl. **Add** 1 tablespoon of water at a time while mixing. Do you think there is more or less than 1 kg of 'snow' in the bowl?

131

Concepts mastered

- ✓ Children can explain when a mental method is more appropriate than a written method and fluently apply knowledge of number facts and place value to support mental work. They can explain the additive property of numbers and refer to it when using a formal written method.
- ✓ Children use a written method and their knowledge of partitioning to subtract 3-digit numbers.

Assessment task 3

Running the task

This task encourages children to see the links between addition and subtraction and use the column written methods. Before starting it write a number bond on the whiteboard, e.g. $40 + 60 = 100$. Ask children to think of what else they know based on this statement. To add an element of competition, ask them to write down in 30 seconds three more facts based on the statement. Once children are confident in deriving new number statements from a number bond, ask them to attempt the task.

Ensure children understand how the grid works. Remind them not to write the numbers too close to each other, and emphasise the importance of placing the digit they carry in the calculations in the right column.

Ask children to estimate and use addition and subtraction to check their answers. You could ask children to check a partner's answers. Finding a mistake and correcting it is a good way of learning. Look out for any misconceptions and help children clarify them.

Evidencing mastery

You will know that children have mastered these concepts when they are able to create their own grids and apply their knowledge that addition and subtraction are reverse operations to each other. Children understand that addition is commutative, but subtraction is not, and are able to use their knowledge of column addition and subtraction to find out all the answers.

Did you know?

Ask questions about the information given, using the mathematical language children have learnt in the unit. *Do you use more water or washing-up liquid? How much more? How much less?* Encourage children to think of places where they use addition and subtraction, e.g. making squash, making paint, playdough.

You could link this unit with a 'make and raise money' project for a school fund or charity. Children make cupcakes and sell them. *How much of each ingredient do you need to buy and how much will each cost? How much money will each cupcake sell for? How much money will you raise? Do you add or subtract? Do you calculate the sums mentally or use a written method?* Being able to add and subtract with 3-digit numbers is needed to calculate all of these figures.

Unit 12 Representing whole numbers and fractions

Mathematical focus

★ Number: number and place value, fractions

★ Measurement: length, money, mass

Prior learning

Children should already be able to:

- count from zero in multiples of four, eight, 50 and 100
- find ten or 100 more or less than a given number
- recognise the place value of each digit in a 3-digit number (hundreds, tens, ones)
- compare and order numbers up to 1000; read numbers in numerals and words.

Key new learning

- Identify, represent and compare numbers up to 1000 using different representations.
- Count up and down in tenths, recognise that tenths arise from dividing an object into ten equal parts and dividing single-digit numbers or quantities by ten.
- Solve number and practical problems involving measure and compare lengths (m/cm/mm).
- Recognise and use fractions as numbers; unit and non-unit fractions with small denominators.
- Compare and order unit fractions and fractions with the same denominator.
- Add and subtract amounts of money to give change, using both £ and p in practical contexts.
- Recognise and show, using diagrams, equivalent fractions with small denominators.
- Add and subtract fractions with the same denominator within one whole.
- Solve number and practical problems involving measure; compare, add and subtract: mass (kg/g).

Making connections

- This unit offers several opportunities to solve number problems and to link number to measure. Children should solve practical problems that require them to add and subtract lengths, masses and capacities using a range of units. They should recognise and explain how they have applied knowledge of number and place value.
- Children should understand that mathematics has a wide variety of real-life applications, such as adding and subtracting amounts of money to give change. Children should use both £ and p in a range of practical contexts, e.g. buying cakes at a school cake sale.

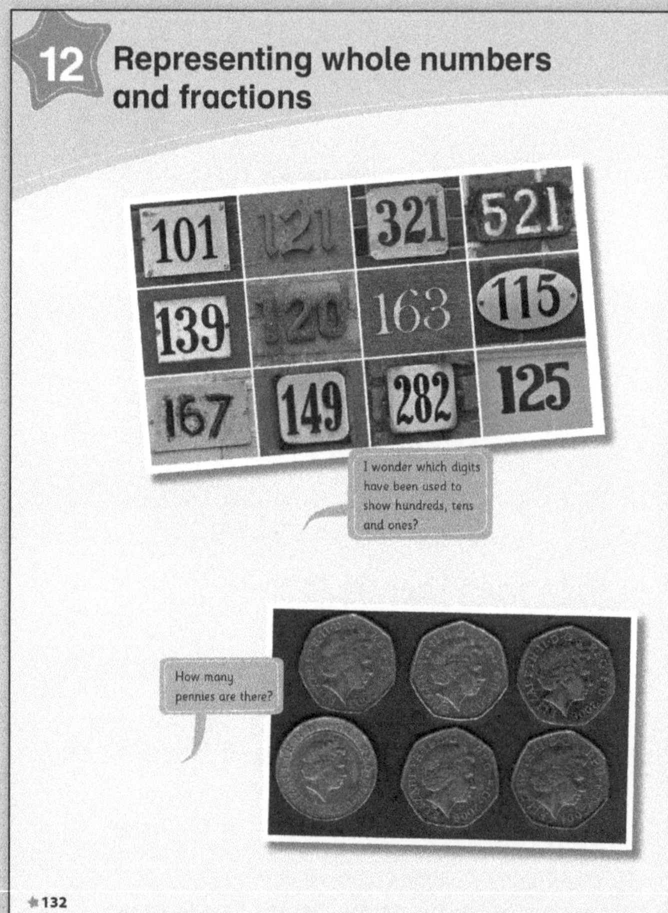

Talk about

It is important to use precise mathematical vocabulary from the beginning, so that children become fluent with the mathematical language they need to explain their reasoning and convince others of their ideas and solutions. The language of fractions introduces new terminology, as children recognise and identify unit and non-unit fractions and how the terms relate to the numerator and denominator of a fraction. In this unit, they recognise equivalent fractions and explain when a fraction is larger or equivalent to another. Develop language such as *it has the same value but may not look the same*, to support the concept of equivalence.

Engaging and exploring

Explore the positional and multiplicative aspect of the digits in a given house number. You could ask children to find other house numbers in the photo where a digit has the same value. Investigate the question posed to find digits that have been used in all positions. Use place-value grids to support the discussion. Only digits seven, eight and nine are not used in all positions. Children could suggest some other numbers where the same digits have been used in different positions.

Represent one of the numbers using Base 10 apparatus or place-value counters and invite children to find the matching house number. You could ask them to give 'silly answers', explaining why this would be the case, e.g. show 116 in Base 10 and a child suggests that 136 is a 'silly answer' because it has three tens and the representation only has one ten.

Children could select a row or column and order the numbers from smallest to largest or pick pairs of numbers to compare using the symbols < and >. Challenge children to find sets of three or four numbers where one number in each set is the odd one out, e.g. 120, 160, 282 and 305, with 282 as the odd one out because it is not a multiple of five.

Children can use coins to recreate the image, counting the number of 50p coins and identifying the odd one out as a £2 coin. Discuss the ways that the question can be answered, linking it to counting in steps of 50. Children should count in fifties up to 250 and be able to say how many steps of 50 have been counted, e.g. 50, 100, 150 (that is three steps of 50), 200, 250 (that is five steps of 50). Children should recognise that there are two steps of 100 in a £2 coin as they draw on knowledge of 100 pence in a pound. Link finding the total of 250 and 200 to finding 100 more than any given number, using manipulatives to represent the concept that the tens and ones value remain unchanged.

Ask children to look at the photo of the orange juice and discuss the meaning of sharing 'equally' and how this will influence the question posed, i.e. there must be the same amount in each part. First suggest that the juice is shared equally between two glasses. *What fraction of the whole bottle will each part represent?* Challenge children to explain their ideas, i.e. there is one whole divided into two equal parts so each part has the value of a half.

Children should continue to suggest sharing equally between other numbers of glasses, explaining the fraction each time. They should reason about the sizes of different fractions as they explore and explain why $\frac{1}{5}$, for example, is smaller than $\frac{1}{4}$ but larger than $\frac{1}{6}$. Revisit the term 'unit fraction' and 'non-unit fraction', relating these to the number of equal parts.

Discuss how the windows are formed and challenge children to investigate the total number of rectangles. They should recognise that there are rectangles of different sizes, including two larger ones that make up the main window frames.

Suggest that you can see four halves. Children should explain where the four halves can be seen, recognising that, as long as each window is divided into two equal parts, the halves do not necessarily have to look the same as long as they are equivalent in value.

Ask children to explore other fractions they can see, e.g. quarters (quarters in a main frame and quarters in each quarter pane), counting them as they go up to two wholes. They should recognise that two quarters have the same value as one half, and four quarters have the same value as one whole. You could model the counts on a number line to further secure the concept that fractions are numbers.

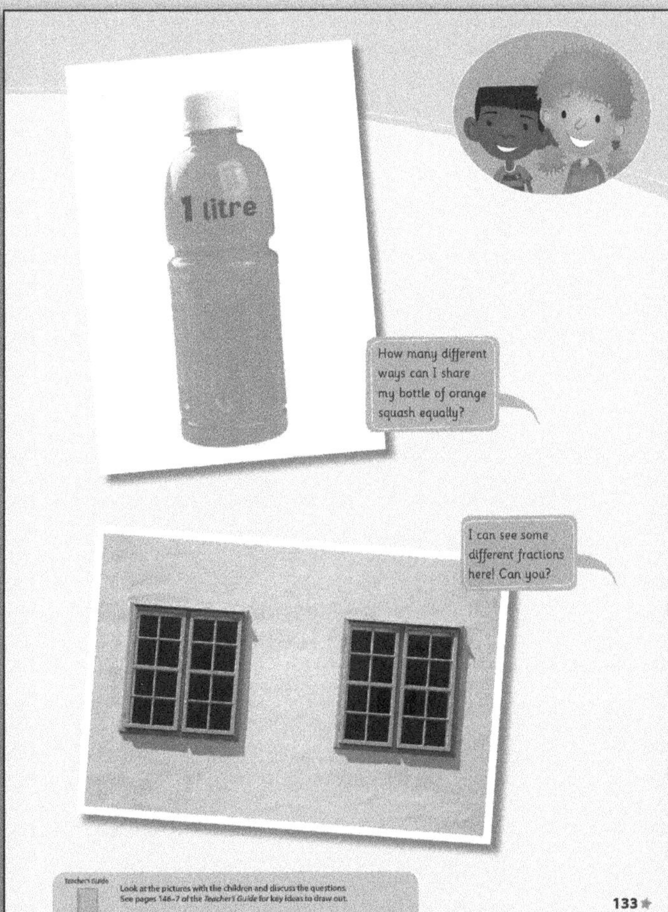

Things to think about

- How will you model and encourage the use of precise mathematical vocabulary when talking and reasoning about fractions and whole numbers?
- How will you use manipulatives and visual representations to help all children with their conceptual understanding of fractions and their equivalents? What have children used before? How can these be developed?
- How will you make effective use of additional adults? Could they support children to practise explanations and model their own thinking?
- How will you build in problem solving so that children apply what they have learnt, including in the context of money, length, capacity and mass?

Checking understanding

You will know children have mastered these concepts when they can represent fractions as numbers, explaining and showing how they know one fraction is bigger than or equivalent to another.

12a Representing whole numbers and tenths

- **Identify, represent and compare numbers to 1000 using different representations.**
- **Count up and down in tenths, recognise that tenths arise from dividing an object into ten equal parts and dividing single-digit numbers or quantities by ten.**
- **Solve number and practical problems involving measure and compare lengths (m/cm/mm).**

Homework 57 and 58 | Practice Book pp 97–100 | Numerals & Symbols; Place Value & Abacus

Representations and resources

Ten frames or squared paper, counters, cubes, counting stick, number lines, rulers, pencils, bead strings, Base 10 apparatus, place-value counters, place-value grid, 10p coins.

Mathematical vocabulary

Hundreds, tens, ones, whole, tenths, partition, equivalent

Warming up

Practise the multiplication facts for ten using a counting stick to represent each step of ten. Use the language *10 one time, 10 twice or two times, 10 three times* as children recall 10, 20, 30 and so on. Ask questions such as *If 110 is the answer, how many tens is that?* to relate division to multiplication. Use a place-value grid to model how we can use our multiplication facts for ten to multiply single-digit numbers by ten, e.g. $10 \times 3 = 30$ so $3 \times 10 = 30$. Ask questions such as: *If* $10 \times 6 = 60$, $6 \times 10 = ?$

Background knowledge

This concept provides opportunities to explore numbers using ten frames and partitioning. Partitioning in different ways prepares children for the formal methods of subtraction that involves decomposition, e.g. for 543 – 127, we can partition 543 into 500, 30 and 13, making it easier to subtract seven. You can see this partitioning within the column method as a ten is exchanged for ten ones, giving 13 altogether and leaving three tens.

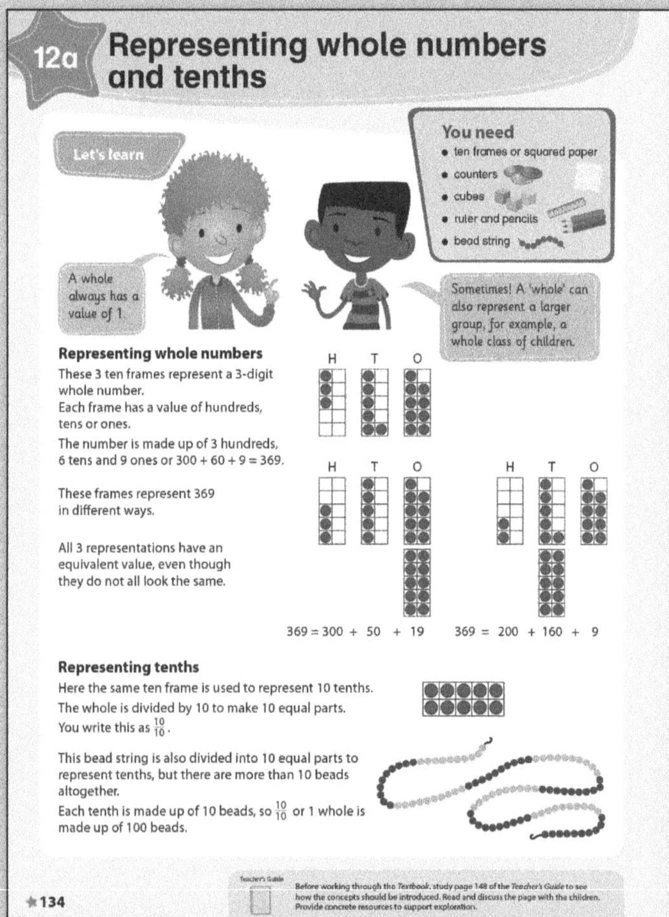
12a Representing whole numbers and tenths

Let's learn

You need
- ten frames or squared paper
- counters
- cubes
- ruler and pencils
- bead string

Representing whole numbers

These 3 ten frames represent a 3-digit whole number.
Each frame has a value of hundreds, tens or ones.
The number is made up of 3 hundreds, 6 tens and 9 ones or 300 + 60 + 9 = 369.

These frames represent 369 in different ways.

All 3 representations have an equivalent value, even though they do not all look the same.

Representing tenths

Here the same ten frame is used to represent 10 tenths.
The whole is divided by 10 to make 10 equal parts.
You write this as $\frac{10}{10}$.

This bead string is also divided into 10 equal parts to represent tenths, but there are more than 10 beads altogether.
Each tenth is made up of 10 beads, so $\frac{10}{10}$ or 1 whole is made up of 100 beads.

134

Teacher's Guide

Before working through the *Textbook*, study page 148 of the *Teacher's Guide* to see how the concepts should be introduced. Read and discuss the page with the children. Provide concrete resources to support exploration.

Let's learn: Modelling and teaching

Representing whole numbers

- Discuss the way that the ten frames have been used to represent 369 in the Textbook. Encourage children to count in hundreds: 100, 200, 300 and in tens: 10, 20, 30, 40, 50, 60 and then in ones to confirm that the frames represent the number 369.
- Look at the two other representations that show 369 partitioned in different ways. Model the images using ten frames and counters. Ask: *What is the same and what is different about the representations? How do you know they both represent 369?* Encourage children to use counting and knowledge of place value in their explanations. Confirm that ten tens are equivalent to 100 and ten ones are equivalent to ten. Match the partitioned statements with the parts of the image they represent. Use counters and a ten frame to explore further ways that 369 can be partitioned.

Representing tenths

- Fill three ten frames with counters of one colour. Explain that each ten frame has the value of one whole. Ask them to explain the fraction that each part represents using fractional language, i.e. *each whole is divided into ten equal parts, so each part is worth* $\frac{1}{10}$. *There are* $\frac{10}{10}$ *in a whole.*
- Count in tenths up to the first whole, and then continue up to three wholes, expressing the count in mixed numbers. Confirm that 30 tenths have been counted, ten in each whole.
- Discuss the similarities and differences between the bead string and a ten frame representation. Agree that although each representation is divided into ten equal parts and represents tenths, they do not look the same. A tenth of the ten frame is one counter, while a tenth on the bead string is made up of ten beads. This is because the 'whole' has a different value.

Engaging and exploring

Step 1

Children should explain that the number 742 is represented and show this as the partitioned statement $700 + 40 + 2 = 742$. They should then use ten frames or counters to explore partitioning 742 in different ways, recording the matching statement each time.

Step 2

Children should explain which fractions each frame represents using fractional language, explaining that each frame shows tenths and saying how many tenths they can see. Encourage them to look for number bonds to complete wholes, as well as counting. A number line can also be used to confirm counts and the value of each row.

Step 3

Children measure the pencil to find its length is made up of seven whole centimetres and $\frac{3}{10}$ of a whole centimetre. They should explain that the fraction is shown in tenths because each whole centimetre is divided into ten equal parts. Look at representing 7 cm and $\frac{3}{10}$ cm in different ways, e.g. with bead strings or number rods. Develop the task so that each length is then shown in centimetres and millimetres, e.g. 7 cm 3 mm.

Step 4

Children should use cubes or counters to make a row of ten and add subsequent rows as the investigation develops. Encourage them to identify how many cubes or counters are represented by the whole and the value of $\frac{1}{10}$. Discuss any patterns that children notice and ask why this may be the case.

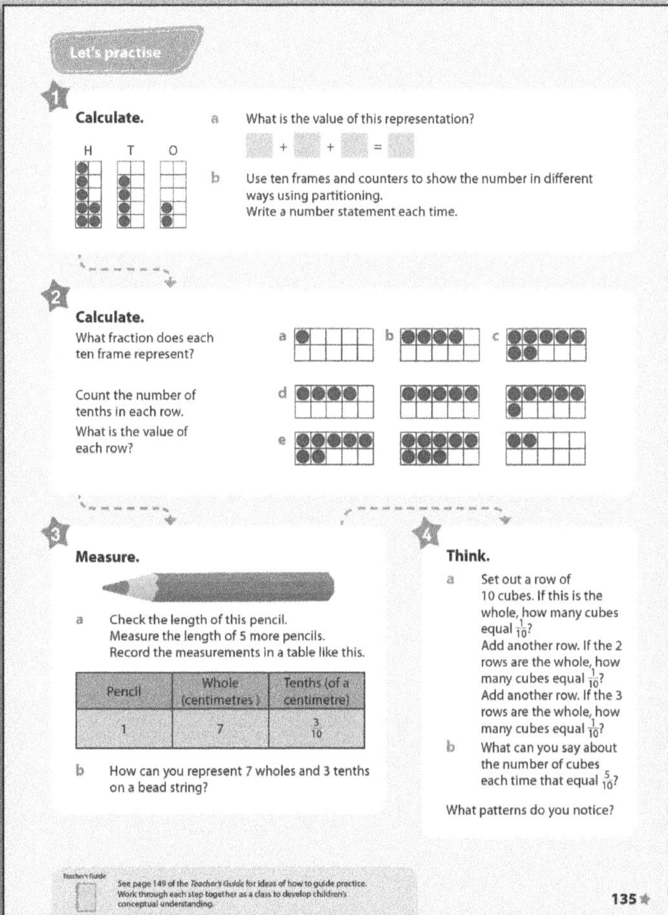
Let's practise

1 **Calculate.**

H T O

a What is the value of this representation?

□ + □ + □ = □

b Use ten frames and counters to show the number in different ways using partitioning.
Write a number statement each time.

2 **Calculate.**

What fraction does each ten frame represent?

Count the number of tenths in each row.

What is the value of each row?

a b c d e

3 **Measure.**

a Check the length of this pencil.
Measure the length of 5 more pencils.
Record the measurements in a table like this.

Pencil	Whole (centimetres)	Tenths (of a centimetre)
1	7	$\frac{3}{10}$

b How can you represent 7 wholes and 3 tenths on a bead string?

4 **Think.**

a Set out a row of 10 cubes. If this is the whole, how many cubes equal $\frac{1}{10}$?
Add another row. If the 2 rows are the whole, how many cubes equal $\frac{1}{10}$?
Add another row. If the 3 rows are the whole, how many cubes equal $\frac{1}{10}$?

b What can you say about the number of cubes each time that equal $\frac{5}{10}$?

What patterns do you notice?

Teacher's Guide

See page 149 of the *Teacher's Guide* for ideas of how to guide practice. Work through each step together as a class to develop children's conceptual understanding.

135

Follow-up ideas

- Use the pencil measurements to create pictograms to compare the lengths. Children could use the ten frames to represents wholes and parts e.g. for $7\frac{3}{10}$ cm, they could show this as:

Pencil 1 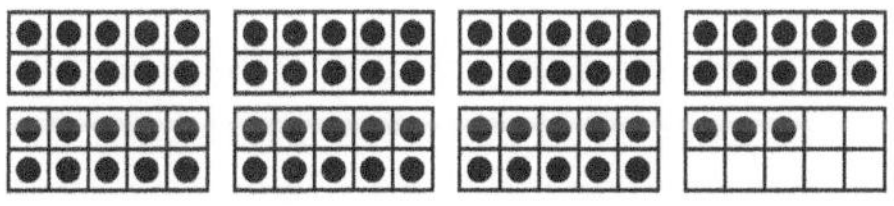

- Children could further develop the relationship between millimetres and centimetres by counting measurements in steps of $\frac{1}{10}$ cm and then in millimetres along a ruler or number line.

Ensuring progress

Supporting understanding

Encourage children to use Base 10 apparatus alongside the ten frames, so that they can see the relationship between the two representations. Discuss the positional and multiplicative aspect of each digit in the numbers 369 and 742, relating this to the column headings and the Base 10 apparatus.

Broadening understanding

You could further develop Step 4 into the context of money, building up the rows using 10 pence coins. Encourage children to identify the whole each time and the value of $\frac{1}{10}$ as rows are added. They should discuss the similarities and differences between this representation and the one used with cubes, e.g. each row is also in tenths, but the whole has a different value.

Concept mastered

Children can explain the value of each digit in a 3-digit number and use representations to show how the number can be partitioned in different ways. They can count on and back in tenths, recognising that tenths arise when an object or a quantity is divided into ten equal parts.

Answers

Step 1

a $700 + 40 + 2 = 742$

b Answers will vary.

Step 2

a $\frac{1}{10}$

b $\frac{4}{10}$

c $\frac{7}{10}$

d $1\frac{5}{10}$ or $1\frac{1}{2}$

e $1\frac{7}{10}$

Step 3

a Children's own measuring displayed in a table using whole centimetres and tenths of a centimetre.

b e.g. 7 sets of 10 beads to represent 7 wholes and 3 beads to represent $\frac{3}{10}$ of the next whole.

Step 4

a Children's recording will vary, but should show that:

1 whole equals 10, so $\frac{1}{10}$ is 1
2 wholes equal 20, so $\frac{1}{10}$ is 2
3 wholes equal 30, so $\frac{1}{10}$ is 3
4 wholes equal 40, so $\frac{1}{10}$ is 4

Children should notice that the value of the whole is ten times larger than the value of the tenth and/or the value of $\frac{1}{10}$ is ten times smaller than the value of the whole.

b Explanations will vary, but could include:

1 whole equals 10, so $\frac{5}{10}$ is 5
2 wholes equal 20, so $\frac{5}{10}$ is 10
$\frac{5}{10}$ is the same as $\frac{1}{2}$ because half of ten is five and half of 20 is ten.

12b Finding and using unit and non-unit fractions

- **Recognise and use fractions as numbers; unit and non-unit fractions with small denominators.**
- **Compare and order unit fractions and fractions with the same denominator.**
- **Add and subtract amounts of money to give change, using both £ and p in practical contexts.**

Homework 59 and 60 | Practice Book pp 101–4 | Fraction Wall

Representations and resources

Fraction bars, number line, rulers, 50p coins, counters.

Mathematical vocabulary

Unit fraction, non-unit fraction, numerator, denominator, operator, divide, division

Warming up

Challenge children to complete the diagram in as many ways as they can to show part-part-whole. This will allow for children to draw on their multiplication facts and place value, perhaps extending beyond 12 × 4 and 4 × 12. Reinforce the inverse relationship between multiplication and division.

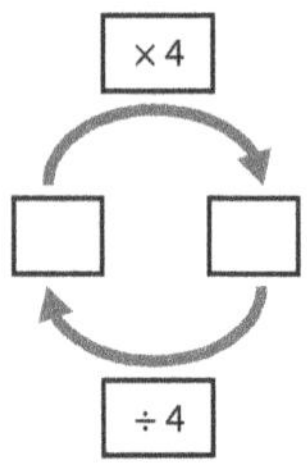

Background knowledge

Fractions are numbers on the number line. A unit fraction is a fraction with a numerator of one, e.g. $\frac{1}{3}$ or $\frac{1}{2}$. A non-unit fraction has a numerator with a value that is not one, e.g. $\frac{3}{4}$ or $\frac{2}{5}$.

Finding a unit fraction of an amount, e.g. $\frac{1}{5}$, is the same as dividing an amount by five. By dividing by five, an amount is split into five equal parts which are called fifths. For non-unit fractions, e.g. $\frac{3}{5}$, we must still find the value of $\frac{1}{5}$ by dividing by five, but then scaling this up to show $\frac{1}{5}$ three times or three lots of $\frac{1}{5}$.

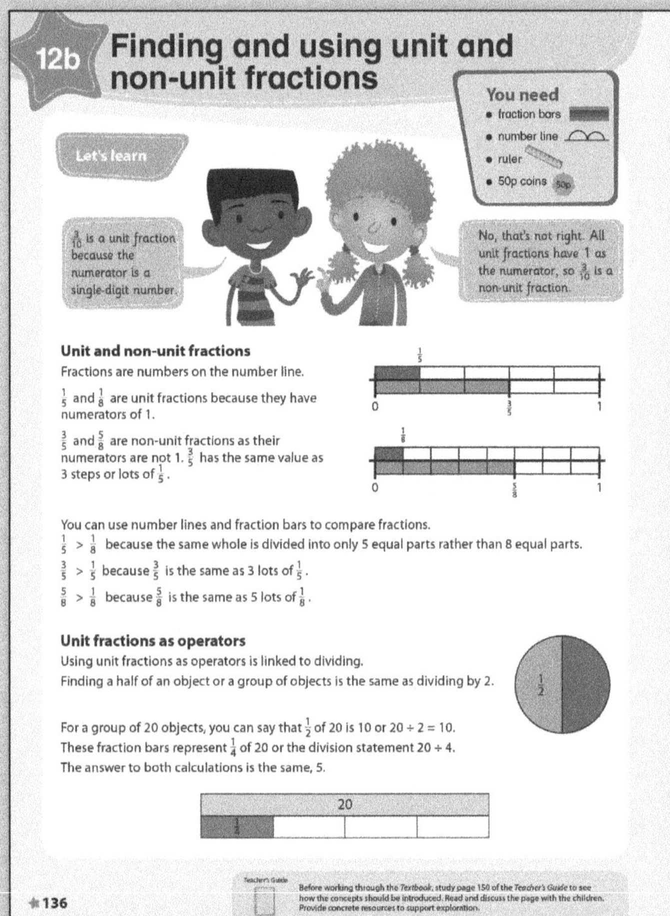

12b Finding and using unit and non-unit fractions

You need
- fraction bars
- number line
- ruler
- 50p coins

Let's learn

$\frac{3}{10}$ is a unit fraction because the numerator is a single-digit number.

No, that's not right. All unit fractions have 1 as the numerator, so $\frac{3}{10}$ is a non-unit fraction.

Unit and non-unit fractions

Fractions are numbers on the number line.

$\frac{1}{5}$ and $\frac{1}{8}$ are unit fractions because they have numerators of 1.

$\frac{3}{5}$ and $\frac{5}{8}$ are non-unit fractions as their numerators are not 1. $\frac{3}{5}$ has the same value as 3 steps or lots of $\frac{1}{5}$.

You can use number lines and fraction bars to compare fractions.

$\frac{1}{5} > \frac{1}{8}$ because the same whole is divided into only 5 equal parts rather than 8 equal parts.

$\frac{3}{5} > \frac{1}{5}$ because $\frac{3}{5}$ is the same as 3 lots of $\frac{1}{5}$.

$\frac{5}{8} > \frac{1}{8}$ because $\frac{5}{8}$ is the same as 5 lots of $\frac{1}{8}$.

Unit fractions as operators

Using unit fractions as operators is linked to dividing.

Finding a half of an object or a group of objects is the same as dividing by 2.

For a group of 20 objects, you can say that $\frac{1}{2}$ of 20 is 10 or 20 ÷ 2 = 10.

These fraction bars represent $\frac{1}{4}$ of 20 or the division statement 20 ÷ 4.

The answer to both calculations is the same, 5.

136

Teacher's Guide

Before working through the *Textbook*, study page 150 of the *Teacher's Guide* to see how the concepts should be introduced. Read and discuss the page with the children. Provide concrete resources to support exploration.

Let's learn: Modelling and teaching

Unit and non-unit fractions

- Discuss Oli's misconception about unit fractions. Ask children to suggest some of the unit fractions they know and to represent them in different ways by drawing shapes or other images to match the written fraction.
- Use a number line to count on and back in fraction steps to one, e.g. in quarters or eighths. Pause to note which fractions are unit fractions and which are non-unit fractions.
- Use the fraction bars in the Textbook to discuss the position of fifths and eighths on the number line.
- Invite children to compare fifths and eighths using > and <.
- Ask children to draw their own number line and fraction bars to represent quarters and sixths. Call out pairs of fractions, e.g. $\frac{1}{4}$ and $\frac{1}{6}$, $\frac{3}{4}$ and $\frac{2}{6}$. Ask them to write comparison statements.

Unit fractions as operators

- Discuss the relationship between the terms 'half' or 'half of' and 'divide by two' or 'shared between two'.
- Establish that all terms have the same meaning and would result in the same image, e.g. the circle in the Textbook, or the same value, e.g. half of 20 is 10 and 20 ÷ 2 = 10.
- Use the fraction bars to compare the whole (20) and the fraction ($\frac{1}{4}$). Remind children that a whole does not always have a value of one. The fraction bars clearly show that a whole has been divided into four equal parts and that each part is one quarter. Record the statements $\frac{1}{4}$ of 20 = 5 and 20 ÷ 4 = 5. Explain to children that both answers are the same because they have used the same operation of division.
- Establish that the denominator is the same number as the divisor in the division calculation.

Let's practise: Digging deeper

Step 1

Children use fraction bars and a number line to compare pairs of unit fractions and pairs of non-unit fractions that share the same denominator. Encourage children to describe non-unit fractions as 'so many steps or lots of the unit fraction'. This helps them make comparisons, e.g. $\frac{3}{10}$ can be described as three steps or lots of $\frac{1}{10}$, which is smaller than seven steps or lots of $\frac{1}{10}$.

Step 2

Not all unit fractions are labelled in the representations, so children will need to identify these first before they write the matching fraction and division statements. Look for those who fluently draw on multiplication and division facts. For the final part of the task, children should relate the divisor five to fifths to help them write the matching fraction statement.

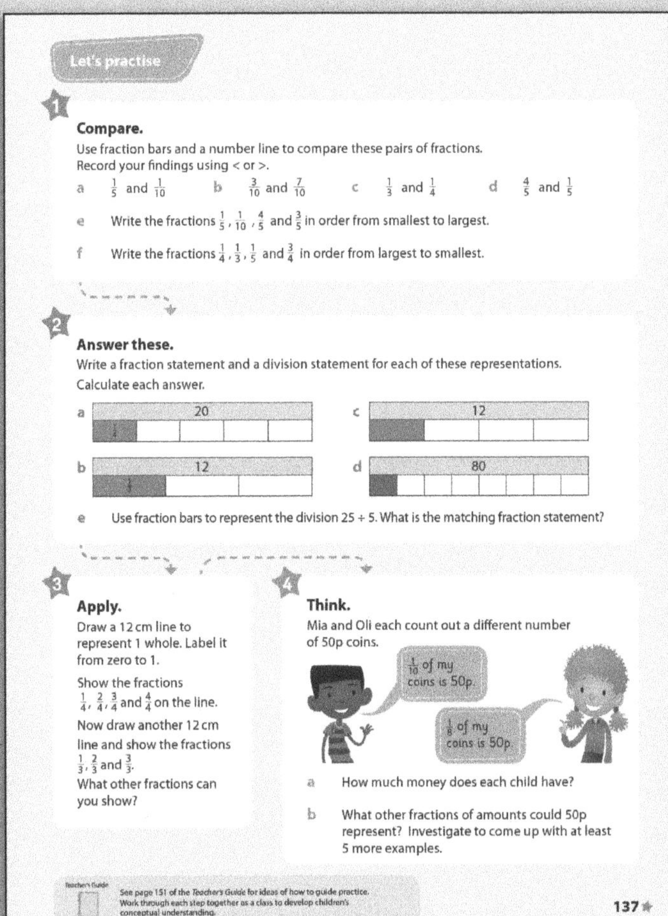
Let's practise

1 Compare.
Use fraction bars and a number line to compare these pairs of fractions.
Record your findings using < or >.
a $\frac{1}{5}$ and $\frac{1}{10}$ b $\frac{3}{10}$ and $\frac{7}{10}$ c $\frac{1}{3}$ and $\frac{1}{4}$ d $\frac{4}{5}$ and $\frac{1}{5}$
e Write the fractions $\frac{1}{5}$, $\frac{1}{10}$, $\frac{4}{5}$ and $\frac{3}{5}$ in order from smallest to largest.
f Write the fractions $\frac{1}{4}$, $\frac{1}{3}$, $\frac{1}{5}$ and $\frac{3}{4}$ in order from largest to smallest.

2 Answer these.
Write a fraction statement and a division statement for each of these representations.
Calculate each answer.
a 20 c 12
b 12 d 80
e Use fraction bars to represent the division 25 ÷ 5. What is the matching fraction statement?

3 Apply.
Draw a 12 cm line to represent 1 whole. Label it from zero to 1.
Show the fractions $\frac{1}{4}$, $\frac{2}{4}$, $\frac{3}{4}$ and $\frac{4}{4}$ on the line.
Now draw another 12 cm line and show the fractions $\frac{1}{3}$, $\frac{2}{3}$ and $\frac{3}{3}$.
What other fractions can you show?

4 Think.
Mia and Oli each count out a different number of 50p coins.

a How much money does each child have?
b What other fractions of amounts could 50p represent? Investigate to come up with at least 5 more examples.

Teacher's Guide
See page 151 of the *Teacher's Guide* for ideas of how to guide practice. Work through each step together as a class to develop children's conceptual understanding.

137

Follow-up ideas

- Compare the same unit fraction of different amounts, e.g. $\frac{1}{5}$ of 20p or 20 kg, relating these to multiplication and division facts. Compare different unit fractions of different amounts, so that children recognise the importance of the value of the whole. *Would you rather have $\frac{1}{10}$ of £100 or $\frac{1}{2}$ of £10?*
- Investigate the different unit fractions of different numbers of children you can make in the classroom. Children record their finding in different ways, relating each to the matching division statement. You could have calculation cards, e.g. $\frac{1}{3}$ of 18, and invite children to arrange themselves to represent the fraction and also record it as 18 ÷ 3.

Step 3

Children should be encouraged to describe non-unit fractions as 'so many steps or lots of the unit fraction' to help them make sense of their positions on the number line. Encourage children to show other sets of fractions, e.g. halves and sixths, on other 12 cm lines.

Step 4

Children should explore the statements and explain what they notice about the fraction each time and the amount of money, i.e. eight 50p coins and $\frac{1}{8}$. It would be useful to use fraction bars to represent the solutions each time, comparing the whole and the parts so that the relationship is clear.

Ensuring progress

Supporting understanding

Children could do Step 2 practically, using counters to model the whole for representations a, b and c. The counters could then be shared equally between the number of equal parts, so that children relate equal sharing to division. Children then count the number of counters in one part and recognise this as the answer to the division.

Broadening understanding

Develop Step 4 so that children begin to think about non-unit fractions as well as unit fractions. If the fraction of the amount is two 50p coins (£1) each time, what could the fractions and the amounts be? e.g. $\frac{2}{5}$ of £2.50 or $\frac{1}{2}$ of £1 or $\frac{2}{10}$ of £5 which is equivalent to $\frac{1}{5}$ of £5 or $\frac{2}{6}$ of £3 which is equivalent to $\frac{1}{3}$ of £3.

Concept mastered

Children can compare pairs of unit fractions and explain which is larger. They can relate unit fractions as operators to dividing by integers, using representations and manipulatives to support their thinking

Answers

Step 1

a $\frac{1}{5} > \frac{1}{10}$ or $\frac{1}{10} < \frac{1}{5}$

b $\frac{7}{10} > \frac{3}{10}$ or $\frac{3}{10} < \frac{7}{10}$

c $\frac{1}{3} > \frac{1}{4}$ or $\frac{1}{4} < \frac{1}{3}$

d $\frac{4}{5} > \frac{1}{5}$ or $\frac{1}{5} < \frac{4}{5}$

e $\frac{1}{10}, \frac{1}{5}, \frac{3}{5}, \frac{4}{5}$ **f** $\frac{3}{4}, \frac{1}{3}, \frac{1}{4}, \frac{1}{5}$

Step 2

a $\frac{1}{5}$ of 20 = 4 and 20 ÷ 5 = 4

b $\frac{1}{3}$ of 12 = 4 and 12 ÷ 3 = 4

c $\frac{1}{4}$ of 12 = 3 and 12 ÷ 4 = 3

d $\frac{1}{8}$ of 80 = 10 and 80 ÷ 8 = 10

e $\frac{1}{5}$ of 25 = 5

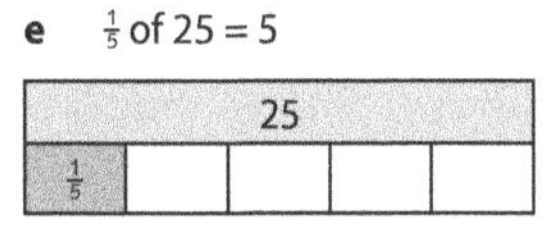

Step 3

Children's own 12 cm lines with fractions drawn.
e.g.

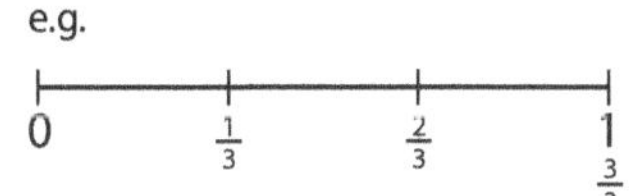

Step 4

a Oli has £5 and Mia has £4.

b e.g. $\frac{1}{2}$ of £1 = 50p or $\frac{1}{3}$ of £1.50 or $\frac{1}{12}$ of £6.

12c Equivalent fractions

- **Recognise and show, using diagrams, equivalent fractions with small denominators.**
- **Add and subtract fractions with the same denominator within one whole.**
- **Solve number and practical problems involving measure; compare, add and subtract: mass (kg/g).**

Homework 61 and 62 Practice Book pp 105–7 Fraction Wall

Representations and resources

Fraction bars, counters, number lines, folded or cut shapes.

Mathematical vocabulary

Whole, fraction, numerator, denominator, equivalent, multiply, divide, add, subtract

Warming up

Oli and Mia are comparing lengths of ribbon. The difference between two lengths of ribbon is 12 cm. What could the two lengths be? Work in pairs to find as many differences of 12 cm as you can. Share some of the possible solutions, but then give a further criteria that the total length of the two ribbons is a multiple of ten. Children should use their findings and draw on bonds for ten to find solutions that fit both criteria, e.g. 16 cm and 4 cm, 36 cm and 24 cm or 126 cm and 114 cm.

Background knowledge

Equivalent fractions are important in comparing and calculating with fractions.

Equivalent fractions share the same position on a number line because the values are the same. It is important to link finding equivalent fractions with multiplication – to keep the fraction equivalent, both the numerator and denominator are multiplied by the same number.

In Year 3, children add and subtract fractions with the same denominator. Relate this to counting on and back in fraction steps of the same size. Use fraction bars to support this and make links to the number line.

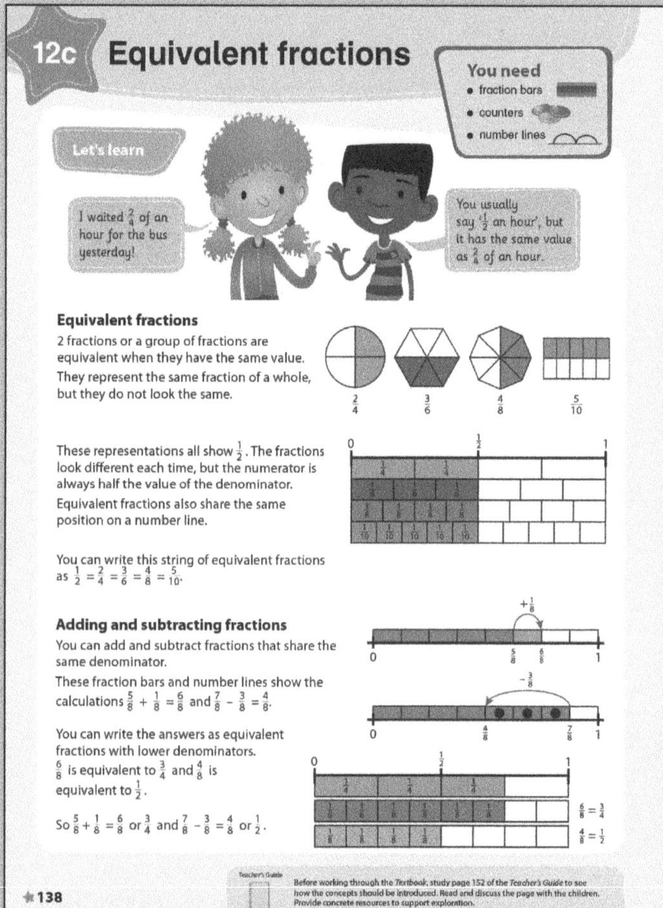

12c Equivalent fractions

You need
- fraction bars
- counters
- number lines

Let's learn

Equivalent fractions

2 fractions or a group of fractions are equivalent when they have the same value. They represent the same fraction of a whole, but they do not look the same.

$\frac{2}{4}$ $\frac{3}{6}$ $\frac{4}{8}$ $\frac{5}{10}$

These representations all show $\frac{1}{2}$. The fractions look different each time, but the numerator is always half the value of the denominator.

Equivalent fractions also share the same position on a number line.

You can write this string of equivalent fractions as $\frac{1}{2} = \frac{2}{4} = \frac{3}{6} = \frac{4}{8} = \frac{5}{10}$.

Adding and subtracting fractions

You can add and subtract fractions that share the same denominator.

These fraction bars and number lines show the calculations $\frac{5}{8} + \frac{1}{8} = \frac{6}{8}$ and $\frac{7}{8} - \frac{3}{8} = \frac{4}{8}$.

You can write the answers as equivalent fractions with lower denominators. $\frac{6}{8}$ is equivalent to $\frac{3}{4}$ and $\frac{4}{8}$ is equivalent to $\frac{1}{2}$.

So $\frac{5}{8} + \frac{1}{8} = \frac{6}{8}$ or $\frac{3}{4}$ and $\frac{7}{8} - \frac{3}{8} = \frac{4}{8}$ or $\frac{1}{2}$.

$\frac{6}{8} = \frac{3}{4}$ $\frac{4}{8} = \frac{1}{2}$

138

Teacher's Guide Before working through the *Textbook*, study page 152 of the *Teacher's Guide* to see how the concepts should be introduced. Read and discuss the page with the children. Provide concrete resources to support exploration.

Let's learn: Modelling and teaching

Equivalent fractions

- Refer to the misconception cartoon and relate this to the corresponding circle shape. Explore the other shapes in the Textbook, the numerator each time and the fractions they represent. Encourage children to use fractional language to describe them, e.g. *There are four equal parts, so each part is a quarter. The fraction is $\frac{2}{4}$ because two of these four parts are shaded.*
- Ask children what they notice about the shapes: *what is the same and what is different?* Remind children that they have met the word 'equivalence' when partitioning numbers in different ways. *Something is equivalent when it has the same value, even if it does not look the same.*
- Use the fraction wall and paper fraction bars to confirm that all the shaded shapes represent $\frac{1}{2}$, as the relationship between the numerator and denominator stays the same.

Adding and subtracting fractions

- Model the calculations $\frac{5}{8} + \frac{1}{8}$ and $\frac{7}{8} - \frac{3}{8}$ using fraction bars and the number line. Agree that the answers are $\frac{6}{8}$ and $\frac{4}{8}$. Refer children back to the equivalent fractions they were exploring earlier and to the fraction wall image in the Textbook.
- Write the answers using both the original fractions and the equivalent fractions with lower denominators.

Let's practise: Digging deeper

Step 1

Children must first identify the fraction bars they need to use by referring to the denominator. Encourage them to explain their decisions using language such as: *The denominator tells me there are five equal parts, so I need to look for the fraction bar showing fifths.* They will find that some pairs of fractions are equivalent and some are not.

Step 2

Children can use fraction bars and the number line to help with the addition and subtraction of fraction pairs. For part g, children should draw upon counting back in quarters from one whole or expressing the whole as $\frac{4}{4}$. Look for children who also express the answer $\frac{5}{5}$ as one.

Step 3

Children work together to represent the equivalent positions of Mia and Oli in races using fraction bars and counters. Encourage them to begin by revisiting the fraction pairs they have already worked with. Ask questions such as: *How do you know that the fractions are equivalent?* Encourage children to record the equivalent pairs using the equals sign. Once they have found all equivalent fractions for the tracks, ask them to create their own track and repeat the task.

Step 4

In this finding all possibilities problem, children only have certain weights they can use. They should apply what they have found out about equivalent fractions to help them find a range of solutions. Support them in doing this by asking questions, e.g. *What do you know about the number of quarters that have the same value $\frac{1}{2}$? How can this help you?* Remind them that they have more than one of each weight, so a solution of $\frac{1}{4}$ kg + $\frac{1}{4}$ kg is possible.

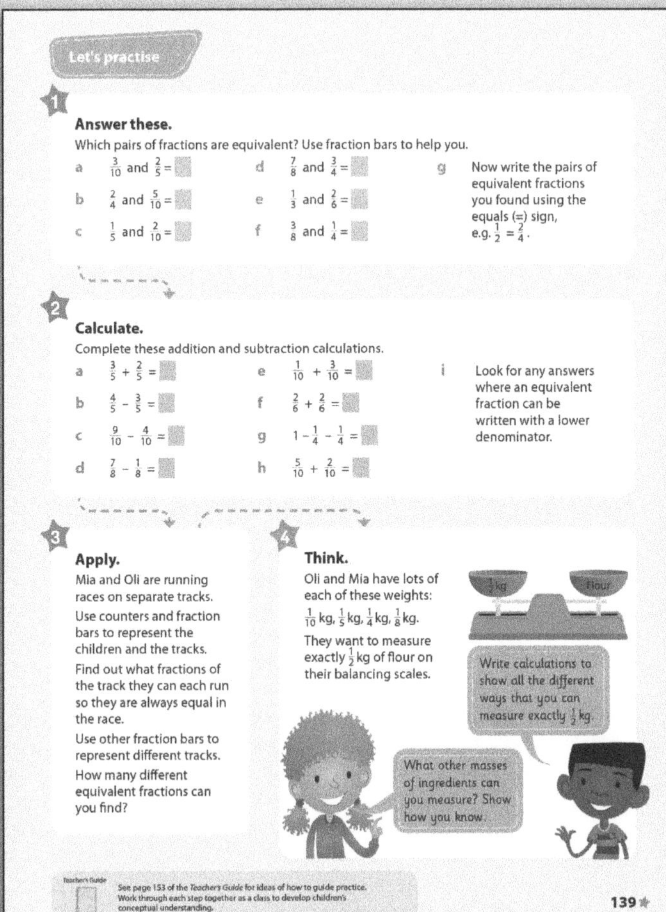
Let's practise

1 Answer these.

Which pairs of fractions are equivalent? Use fraction bars to help you.

a $\frac{3}{10}$ and $\frac{2}{5}$ =

b $\frac{2}{4}$ and $\frac{5}{10}$ =

c $\frac{1}{5}$ and $\frac{2}{10}$ =

d $\frac{7}{8}$ and $\frac{3}{4}$ =

e $\frac{1}{3}$ and $\frac{2}{6}$ =

f $\frac{3}{8}$ and $\frac{1}{4}$ =

g Now write the pairs of equivalent fractions you found using the equals (=) sign, e.g. $\frac{1}{2} = \frac{2}{4}$.

2 Calculate.

Complete these addition and subtraction calculations.

a $\frac{3}{5} + \frac{2}{5}$ =

b $\frac{4}{5} - \frac{3}{5}$ =

c $\frac{9}{10} - \frac{4}{10}$ =

d $\frac{7}{8} - \frac{1}{8}$ =

e $\frac{1}{10} + \frac{3}{10}$ =

f $\frac{2}{6} + \frac{2}{6}$ =

g $1 - \frac{1}{4} - \frac{1}{4}$ =

h $\frac{5}{10} + \frac{2}{10}$ =

i Look for any answers where an equivalent fraction can be written with a lower denominator.

3 Apply.

Mia and Oli are running races on separate tracks.

Use counters and fraction bars to represent the children and the tracks.

Find out what fractions of the track they can each run so they are always equal in the race.

Use other fraction bars to represent different tracks.

How many different equivalent fractions can you find?

4 Think.

Oli and Mia have lots of each of these weights:

$\frac{1}{10}$ kg, $\frac{1}{5}$ kg, $\frac{1}{4}$ kg, $\frac{1}{8}$ kg.

They want to measure exactly $\frac{1}{2}$ kg of flour on their balancing scales.

Teacher's Guide

See page 153 of the *Teacher's Guide* for ideas of how to guide practice. Work through each step together as a class to develop children's conceptual understanding.

139

Ensuring progress

Supporting understanding

Folded or cut shapes can be used to support the concept of equivalence and calculating with fractions. They also provide a strong visual for children.

Broadening understanding

Provide opportunities for children to practise adding non-unit fractions, as well as strings of unit fractions, e.g. $\frac{1}{8}$ kg + $\frac{1}{8}$ kg + $\frac{1}{8}$ kg + $\frac{1}{8}$ kg can also be recorded as $\frac{2}{8}$ kg + $\frac{2}{8}$ kg and $\frac{3}{8}$ kg + $\frac{1}{8}$ kg. Children should also recognise that $\frac{2}{8}$ kg + $\frac{2}{8}$ kg can be written using fractions with lower denominators as $\frac{1}{4}$ kg + $\frac{1}{4}$ kg.

Concept mastered

Children can explain and show when a pair of fractions are equivalent and write answers to addition and subtraction calculations as fractions with lower denominators.

Follow-up ideas

- Return to the window image in the unit opener and ask children to look for examples of equivalent fractions. You could also encourage them to make up addition and subtraction calculations using the fractions shown by different parts of the windows.
- Children can create fraction art and make up statements about the fractions in their picture, e.g. $\frac{2}{4} + \frac{2}{4} = \frac{4}{4}$, $\frac{4}{4} = 1$, $\frac{5}{8} + \frac{3}{8} = 1$, $\frac{2}{8} = \frac{1}{4}$ and so on.

Answers

Step 1

a Not equivalent

b Equivalent

c Equivalent

d Not equivalent

e Equivalent

f Not equivalent

g $\frac{2}{4} = \frac{5}{10}$; $\frac{1}{5} = \frac{2}{10}$ and $\frac{1}{3} = \frac{2}{6}$

Step 2

a $\frac{3}{5} + \frac{2}{5} = \frac{5}{5}$ or 1

b $\frac{4}{5} - \frac{3}{5} = \frac{1}{5}$

c $\frac{9}{10} - \frac{4}{10} = \frac{5}{10}$

d $\frac{7}{8} - \frac{1}{8} = \frac{6}{8}$

e $\frac{1}{10} + \frac{3}{10} = \frac{4}{10}$

f $\frac{2}{6} + \frac{2}{6} = \frac{4}{6}$

g $1 - \frac{1}{4} - \frac{1}{4} = \frac{2}{4}$

h $\frac{5}{10} + \frac{2}{10} = \frac{7}{10}$

i $\frac{5}{5} = 1$, $\frac{5}{10} = \frac{1}{2}$, $\frac{6}{8} = \frac{3}{4}$, $\frac{4}{10} = \frac{2}{5}$, $\frac{4}{6} = \frac{2}{3}$, $\frac{2}{4} = \frac{1}{2}$.

Step 3

Children's own investigations using fraction bars and counters to show pairs of equivalent fractions, e.g.

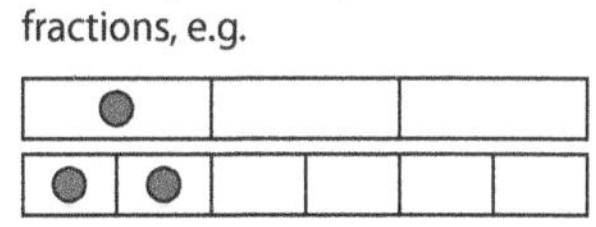

To show that $\frac{1}{3} = \frac{2}{6}$.

Step 4

Answers will vary.

e.g. $\frac{1}{4}$ kg + $\frac{1}{4}$ kg = $\frac{1}{2}$ kg

$\frac{1}{10}$ kg + $\frac{1}{10}$ kg + $\frac{1}{10}$ kg + $\frac{1}{10}$ kg + $\frac{1}{10}$ kg = $\frac{1}{2}$ kg

They could also weigh $\frac{3}{4}$ kg:

$\frac{1}{4}$ kg + $\frac{1}{4}$ kg + $\frac{1}{4}$ kg = $\frac{3}{4}$ kg

Unit 12 Fraction action!

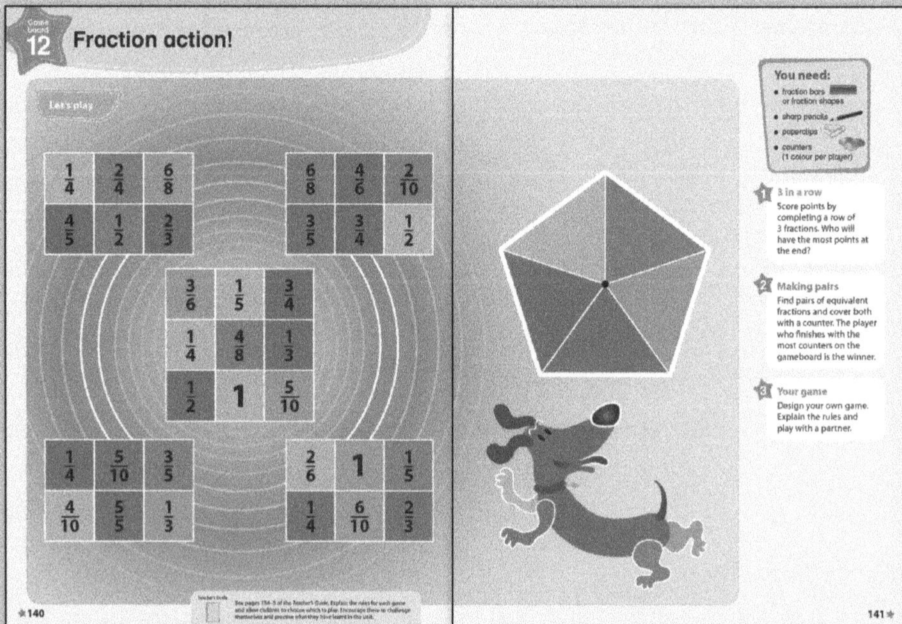

Game 1: 3 in a row

Children use equivalent fractions to score points and complete rows on the gameboard.

Maths focus

- Recognise equivalent fractions

Resources

Fraction bars or fraction shapes, counters (1 colour per player), sharp pencils, paperclips.

How to play

Players take turns to spin for a colour. They choose a fraction from any gameboard that has the same colour. To win that square, they must find an equivalent fraction on their fraction bars and prove to their partner how they know it is equivalent. If they are correct, they place a counter on that square. Players score one point for a row of three fractions so they need to think carefully about the fractions they choose each time, not only to fill their own rows but also to block their partner. The player with the most points at the end is the winner.

Making it easier

Children could use the square board only (which does not include non-unit fractions) or pick a fraction of their choice and show an equivalent on a fraction bar.

Making it harder

The rules could be adapted so that for the square board, a row, column or diagonal scores a point.

Game 3: Your game

Children should invent their own game designing rules that use the concepts covered in the unit. Challenge children to make their game easier or harder.

Game 2: Making pairs

Children find matching pairs of equivalent fractions and cover both with a counter.

Maths focus

- Recognise equivalent fractions

Resources

Fraction bars or fraction shapes, counters (1 colour per player), sharp pencils, paperclips.

How to play

Players take turns to spin for a colour. They choose a fraction on that coloured square from any gameboard. The player must find an equivalent fraction from any other gameboard to win both squares. Players use fraction bars to prove to their partner that the fractions are equivalent. If they are correct, they cover both equivalent fractions on the gameboards with counters.

If no matching pair is available, the player can make up their own equivalent fraction but they only win the original square. The aim is to have the most counters on the gameboards at the end.

Making it easier

Players could work with a partner to make equivalent pairs and discuss their thinking. The game could also be adapted so that the spinner is not used. Players could pick fraction pairs of their choice and show an equivalent.

Making it harder

Children could use the same rules, but when an equivalent fraction pair is not available, players could miss a turn or suggest another equivalent fraction that is not given on any of the gameboards, e.g. for a $\frac{1}{3}$, they could suggest the fraction $\frac{3}{9}$ to win the square.

Fraction action!

Choose a game to play.

Game 1: 3 in a row

You need:

- fraction bars or fraction shapes
- counters (1 colour per player)
- sharp pencils
- paperclips

How to play

- The aim is to cover rows of 3 fractions with your counters.
- Take turns to spin for a colour.
- Choose a fraction on that colour from any gameboard.
- Win the square by showing your partner an equivalent fraction on your fraction bars.
- Score a point for a row of 3 fractions.
- The winner is the player with the most points at the end of the game.

Game 2: Making pairs

You need:

- fraction bars or fraction shapes
- counters (1 colour per player)
- sharp pencils
- paperclips

How to play

- The aim is to find pairs of equivalent fractions.
- Take turns to spin for a colour.
- Choose a fraction on that colour from any gameboard.
- Find an equivalent fraction from any other gameboard.
- Win both squares by showing your partner the equivalent fractions on your fraction bars. Cover each square with a counter.
- If there is no equivalent fraction on the gameboards, make up your own but you only win 1 square.
- The winner is the player with the most counters on the gameboards at the end of the game.

Game 3: Your game

- Make up your own game using the gameboards.
- You could score 2 points for a row of 3 fractions and 1 point for a column of 2 fractions on a gameboard.
- For Game 1, players could choose 2 gameboards each, but share the square gameboard.
- Explain the rules and play with a partner.

Please help your child by reading the instructions and playing the game together.

Unit 12 And finally …

Assessment task 1

Resources

Digit cards 0-9, Base 10 apparatus, place-value counters and/or ten frames.

Running the task

Children can work on their own or in pairs to make up 3-digit numbers using digit cards.

Encourage them to describe the positional and multiplicative aspect of each digit, drawing on their knowledge of place value, e.g. for the number 469, the digit 4 is positioned in the hundreds column. We know its true value when we multiply it by 100.

Children should choose how to represent the number. Encourage them to use a mixture of manipulatives and pictorial representations. Ask them to rearrange the digits to make two more numbers, representing them in the same way. Challenge them to compare the digits in each number and the value they have when positioned in different places. Children should apply this knowledge to help them order the numbers.

Another set of three digits can then be picked.

Evidencing mastery

Children represent 3-digit numbers in a variety of ways and can describe the value of each digit using positional and multiplicative language. They can order a set of 3-digit numbers, looking first at the value of the hundreds digit and explaining why this digit is the most significant for numbers of this size.

Review 12 And finally …

Let's review

1

4 6 9

You need:
- digit cards 0-9
- Base 10 apparatus
- place-value counters and/or ten frames

Use 3 digit cards each time to make a 3-digit number.
Show the number using manipulatives or a drawing.
Rearrange the digits to make another number and then another.

Order the 3 numbers, starting with the smallest.

2

You need:
- fraction bars
- counters
- number lines

Oli and I made equivalent fraction pairs.
Here is what we found out.

$\frac{4}{8} = \frac{2}{4}$ $\frac{3}{4} = \frac{7}{8}$

$\frac{1}{2} = \frac{5}{10}$ $\frac{1}{5} = \frac{3}{10}$

$\frac{1}{3} = \frac{3}{6}$ $\frac{2}{8} = \frac{1}{4}$

Mark the children's work using fraction bars or a method of your choice.

142

Teacher's Guide

See pages 156–7 of the Teacher's Guide for guidance on running each task. Observe children to identify those who have mastered concepts and those who require further consolidation.

Assessment task 2

Resources

Fraction bars, counters, number lines.

Running the task

You could start by asking children to make as many equivalent fraction pairs as they can using fraction bars or other representations. They should explain how they know that the fractions are equivalent. Encourage reasoning such as, *they cover or represent the same part of the whole.*

They should then mark the work completed by Mia and Oli, showing and explaining carefully when they are correct and when they have made a mistake. Again, encourage children to refer back to the fraction bars in order to explore whether they agree or disagree with Mia and Oli's work. For fractions that are not equivalent, you could ask children to compare the fractions and discuss which is larger and how they know. Encourage reasoning using precise mathematical language, e.g. *It covers or represents a larger part of the whole.* Or, *there is a smaller part needed to make or complete the whole'*

Encourage children to suggest some possible fractions that Mia and Oli could have used to correct any mistakes.

Evidencing mastery

Children showing mastery use representations to prove when two fractions are equivalent. They can explain that they have the same value even though they do not look the same, by describing the number of parts in each whole, based on the size of the denominator, and the number of parts represented by the numerator.

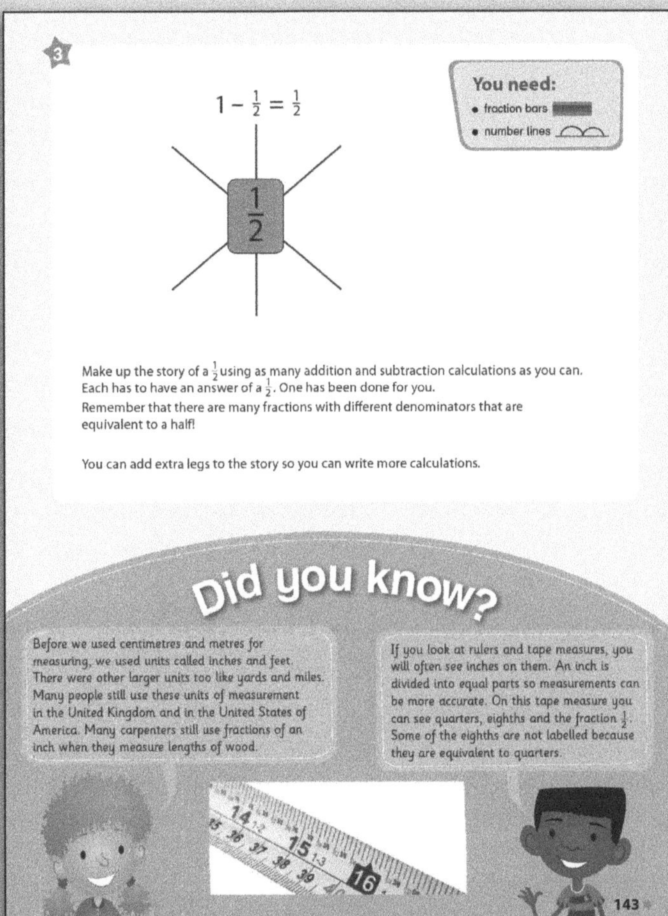
3

$1 - \frac{1}{2} = \frac{1}{2}$

$\frac{1}{2}$

You need:
• fraction bars
• number lines

Make up the story of a $\frac{1}{2}$ using as many addition and subtraction calculations as you can. Each has to have an answer of a $\frac{1}{2}$. One has been done for you.
Remember that there are many fractions with different denominators that are equivalent to a half!

You can add extra legs to the story so you can write more calculations.

Did you know?

Before we used centimetres and metres for measuring, we used units called inches and feet. There were other larger units too like yards and miles. Many people still use these units of measurement in the United Kingdom and in the United States of America. Many carpenters still use fractions of an inch when they measure lengths of wood.

If you look at rulers and tape measures, you will often see inches on them. An inch is divided into equal parts so measurements can be more accurate. On this tape measure you can see quarters, eighths and the fraction $\frac{1}{2}$. Some of the eighths are not labelled because they are equivalent to quarters.

143

Assessment task 3

Resources

Fraction bars, number lines.

Running the task

You could run this task in pairs or small groups, so that children can work together to find a greater range of calculations. They use the approach of 'Maths stories' to tell the story of a half. In this case, $\frac{1}{2}$ is the answer to different addition and subtraction calculations.

Children should use number lines, fraction bars and other representations to make up additions and subtractions. You may wish to start by finding equivalent fractions that have the value $\frac{1}{2}$, so that children are guided to think about other denominators, such as eighths, tenths and sixths.

Evidencing mastery

Children showing mastery fluently apply their knowledge of counting on and back in fraction steps, and can explain how their counting is useful for adding and subtracting. They draw on a range of representations to support their calculations and recognise that it is easier to add and subtract fractions that share the same denominator.

Did you know?

Although the UK changed to the metric system in 1971, the changeover from inches, feet, yards and miles has taken far longer. Many people still use these measurements; they are agreed as international measures and used daily in countries like the USA. Although children do not meet imperial measurement until Year 5, many of them will have heard them being used.

Look at some of the rulers and tape measures in the classroom and compare the number of equal parts that a centimetre is divided into (ten) and the number of equal divisions in an inch. This is often eight, but may be 16 or even 32, depending on the accuracy. Count in fraction steps of $\frac{1}{8}$ along the inch and look at how equivalent fractions with lower denominators have replaced some of the fractions in the eighths count.

Concepts mastered

- ☑ Children can explain the value of each digit in a 3-digit number and use representations to show how the number can be partitioned in different ways. They can count on and back in tenths, recognising that tenths arise when an object or a quantity is divided into ten equal parts.
- ☑ Children can compare pairs of unit fractions and explain which is larger. They can relate unit fractions as operators to dividing by integers, using representations and manipulatives to support their thinking.
- ☑ Children can explain and show when a pair of fractions are equivalent and write answers to addition and subtraction calculations as fractions with lower denominators.

Unit 13

Written methods for multiplication and division

Mathematical focus

★ **Number: number and place value, multiplication and division**

★ **Measurement: money**

Prior learning

Children should already be able to:

- recall and use multiplication and division facts for the two, three, four, five, eight and ten multiplication tables
- use mental calculation strategies to solve multiplication and division problems
- use arrays to show multiplication and division.

Key new learning

- Write and calculate mathematical statements for multiplication and division using known multiplication tables, including for 2-digit numbers multiplied by single-digit numbers, using mental and progressing to formal written methods.

Making connections

- The ability to multiply and divide larger numbers relies on knowledge of multiplication table facts, and on an understanding of place value. Children need to see connections, both between the different known facts (e.g. the multiplication facts for four are double the multiplication facts for two) and between known facts and larger numbers (e.g. they know $3 \times 2 = 6$, and 60 is ten times larger than six, so they can work out that $3 \times 20 = 60$, or $60 \div 3 = 20$).
- Mastery of the formal written methods for multiplication and division enables children to work with increasingly large numbers. They will apply these skills in other areas of maths, including area, volume and correspondence problems, as well as in other school subjects (e.g. science) and everyday life (e.g. cooking).
- Children need to multiply and divide in the context of measures, including money (e.g. finding the cost of multiple items) and time (e.g. finding how many five-minute appointments can be accommodated in a given time period), as well as length, mass and capacity/volume.

Talk about

It is important to use precise mathematical vocabulary from the beginning. Discuss what an array is and how it can be used to show multiplication and division. You can also use arrays to revise the idea that division is the inverse of multiplication, and that multiplication is commutative (different calculation, same answer) but division is not. For multiplication, children need to know that the multiplicand is multiplied by the multiplier to give the product. For division, the dividend is divided by the divisor to give the quotient.

Engaging and exploring

Look at the photos of the plants in the Textbook. Discuss that a seedling is a young plant and ask children to think about what plants are shown. Then ask children how the seedlings are arranged. They should recognise that they are set out in arrays. Discuss what arrays show and establish that an array is a way of representing multiplication and division. In the aerial view example, there are five rows of eight seeds. *What multiplication statements can you write from this?* Agree $8 \times 5 = 40$ and $5 \times 8 = 40$. Recap commutativity, agreeing that it does not matter which order you multiply numbers, the answer will be the same: different calculation, same answer. Then focus on division. We know there are 40 seeds altogether, so the division statements are $40 \div 5 = 8$ (if we take away groups of five, there will be eight groups) and $40 \div 8 = 5$ (if we take away groups of eight, there will be five groups). Recap that division is not commutative and that division and multiplication are inverse operations. Ask children to model the arrays for the other seedlings using counters and to write the corresponding multiplication and division statements.

Looking at the picture of the juice carton, find out whether children remember the mental calculation strategy for multiplying by five. If not, remind them that because five is half of ten, they could multiply 68p by ten and halve the answer. Give other prices for the juice and ask children to find the cost of five cartons in each case. Ensure they write their answers using monetary notation. You could also ask children to find the cost of 20 cartons, using the fact that 20 is twice ten, they can multiply by ten and double.

Look at the picture of the chessboard. *Have you ever played chess?* Discuss different ways of working out the total number of squares on the board. Agree that they could count the squares individually, but this could take a while. A quicker way could be to count one row and then add that number repeatedly. Establish that the chessboard is an array, so they could find how many squares in a row and how many rows and multiply the two numbers together. Ask children what division they could make from the array. Agree that there are 64 squares altogether and eight rows, so the division would be $64 \div 8 = 8$. Give children counters and ask them to make an array. *What multiplication and division facts do they show?*

Looking at the courgettes, discuss with children how they would divide by four using a mental calculation strategy. Agree that they could halve and halve again, because this is the opposite of doubling and doubling again for multiplying by four. Give children numbers to divide by four using this strategy. You could include some calculations that result in a whole number and the fraction $\frac{1}{2}$ or $\frac{1}{4}$. Then ask children to work out how much one courgette would cost. You could refer to the seedling picture, and ask questions relating to multiplying and dividing by four using the doubling and halving strategies.

Ask children to look at the picture of the coins and discuss how multiplication could help them to work out how much money there is altogether. Establish that they could multiply the value of each coin by the number there are of that coin. Ask them to do this for the 2p coin. Ask them to make the result (14p) using 2p coins and then to exchange these for other coins, so that they use the fewest possible coins (10p + 2p + 2p). Repeat for the other coins. Finally, ask children to find how much money there is altogether by adding the results for each coin (14p + 60p + 30p + 80p + £2.50 + £3 + £4 = £11.34). Ask them to exchange the coins they have collected to make the total using the fewest possible coins and notes (£10 + £1 + 30p + 10p + 2p + 2p).

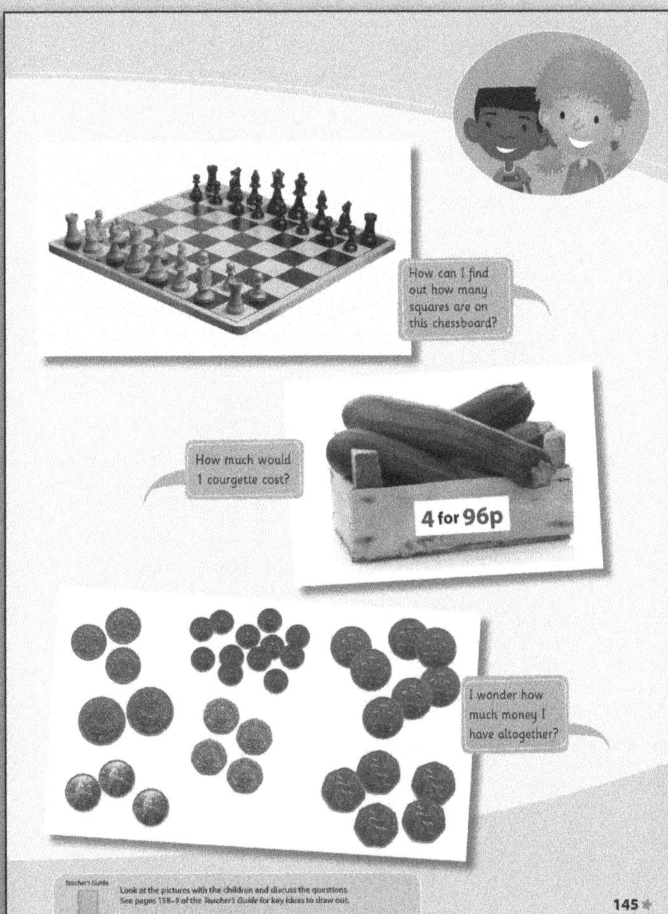

Things to think about

- How will you use manipulatives to help all children develop a conceptual understanding of the written methods for multiplication and division?
- How will you help children understand the link between the array, the grid method and the written method?
- How will you ensure children experience practical opportunities to multiply and divide measures, such as money, length, mass and capacity?

Checking understanding

You will know that children have mastered these concepts when they can explain how arrays relate to multiplication and division. They will be able to multiply and divide 2-digit and single-digit numbers using known facts and formal written methods.

13a Towards the written method for multiplication

- **Write and calculate mathematical statements for multiplication and division using known multiplication tables, including for 2-digit numbers multiplied by single-digit numbers, using mental and progressing to formal methods.**

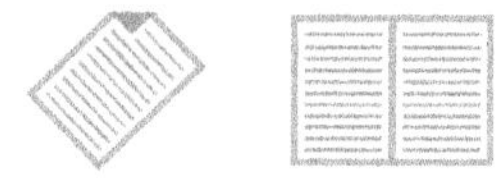

Homework 63 and 64 | Practice Book pp 108–13

Representations and resources

Clocks with movable hands, Base 10 apparatus, coins (1p, 10p, £1).

Mathematical vocabulary

Multiplication, multiplicand, multiplier, product, commutative, commutativity

Warming up

Give each child a clock with movable hands. Call out different analogue times for children to show on the clocks (e.g. 20 minutes past seven, 40 minutes past three, 55 minutes past nine); ensure that they have positioned the hour hand in the correct position. Ask children to write down what each time is in digital time (e.g. 7:20, 3:40, 9:55).

Background knowledge

It is important that children gain conceptual understanding as well as procedural fluency in the written method for multiplication. Children need the opportunity to explore the progression through the different stages from arrays to the formal written method. Work through this slowly to ensure that children gain an understanding that will enable them to, for example, explain in their own words the similarities and differences in the models explored. It is also important that the calculations you give them cannot easily be answered using mental calculation strategies covered in this unit. Therefore multipliers of two, four and five should be avoided.

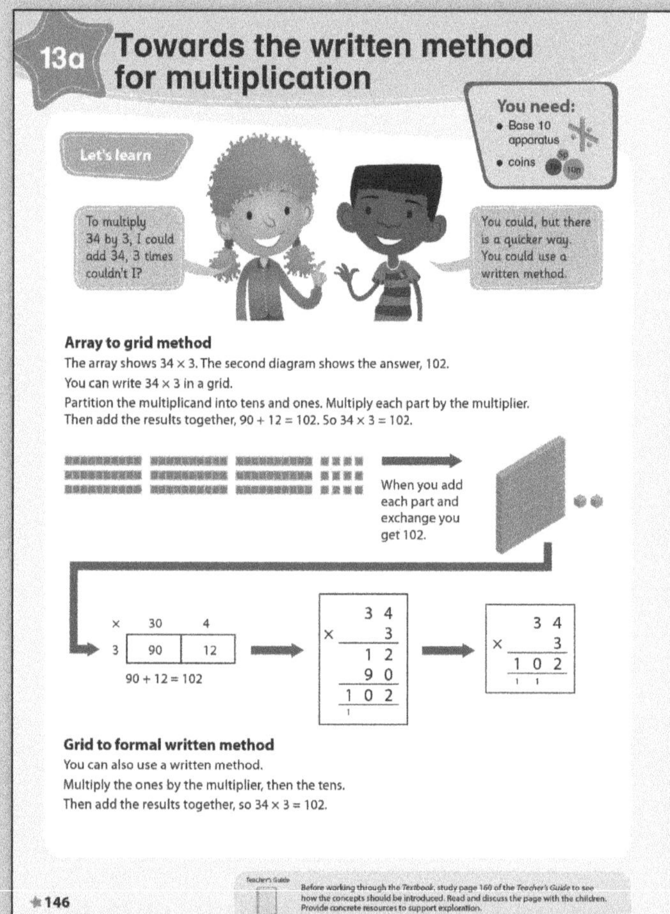

13a Towards the written method for multiplication

You need:
- Base 10 apparatus
- coins

Let's learn

To multiply 34 by 3, I could add 34, 3 times couldn't I?

You could, but there is a quicker way. You could use a written method.

Array to grid method

The array shows 34 × 3. The second diagram shows the answer, 102.

You can write 34 × 3 in a grid.

Partition the multiplicand into tens and ones. Multiply each part by the multiplier. Then add the results together, 90 + 12 = 102. So 34 × 3 = 102.

When you add each part and exchange you get 102.

×	30	4
3	90	12

90 + 12 = 102

Grid to formal written method

You can also use a written method.

Multiply the ones by the multiplier, then the tens.

Then add the results together, so 34 × 3 = 102.

146

Teacher's Guide

Before working through the Textbook, study page 160 of the Teacher's Guide to see how the concepts should be introduced. Read and discuss the page with the children. Provide concrete resources to support exploration.

Let's learn: Modelling and teaching

Array to grid method

- Begin by discussing the misconception cartoon in the Textbook. Agree that adding 34 three times is not particularly efficient. Tell children they will be learning about the more efficient written method, looking at each step in the progression from array to written method.
- Ask children to make the array shown in the Textbook using Base 10 apparatus. Then ask them to combine the ones and exchange them for tens. They should then combine and exchange the tens. *Do your results match the second diagram shown?* Next ask them to make the initial array again. Demonstrate how this translates to the grid method as shown. Ask children what is similar about the two models and what is different.
- Repeat this process for different calculations, e.g. 46 × 3. Children could also practise multiplying money (using £1, 10p and 1p coins) and length (using Base 10 apparatus to represent the metres and the tens and ones the centimetres).

Grid to formal written method

- Look at the grid and demonstrate how it translates to the expanded written method. Ask children what is similar and what is different about the two methods. Agree that in both cases you multiply the ones and tens by the multiplier separately, then add the results. Check that children understand how to carry 10 tens into the hundreds column.
- Next look at the final way to set out a multiplication. *How is this the same as the expanded written method? How is it different?* Agree that it is the same, but this time you do not write the products for the ones, tens and hundreds separately. Pay close attention to the carried digits.
- Repeat using 57 × 6, then give children other calculations to solve using first the grid and then the two written methods.

Let's practise: Digging deeper

Step 1

This task reinforces the links between the array and grid method. Before they begin, work through some examples using Base 10 apparatus. Ask children to make the array and use it to form the grid showing the tens and ones, and the multiplier. Return to the array and ask children to combine and exchange the ones, then the tens, and find the total. Finally, ask them to total the amounts in the grid. Do they get the same product? For each example, ask children to tell you what is the same and what is different about the two methods. Children can then work on the task independently.

Step 2

This task reinforces the links between the grid method and the expanded and formal written methods. As for Step 1, work through some examples before beginning. Ensure all three models are covered and that children are able to translate from one to the other with understanding. Some children may not be ready to do this independently, so work with them as a group, setting out the array first.

Step 3

This task is designed as a practical way of practising moving from the array to the grid method. Children need to set out the array using 10p and 1p coins. Ensure that children can make the appropriate amounts of money and that they exchange ten 10p coins for £1 coins. Emphasise the place value of the different coins so that they can link pound coins with hundreds, 10p coins with tens and 1p coins with ones. Encourage children to look at their products for the threes and sixes and discuss what they notice. They should be able to tell you that the products for multiplying by six are double those by three. Ask them to explain their reasoning and to convince you that what they say is correct.

Step 4

This task expects children to use their ability to reason about numbers. They need to work out the missing numbers, using what has been presented and known facts to reason about the missing numbers. Once they have completed the first part, they explain how they found the missing numbers to a partner and then make up their own missing number calculations.

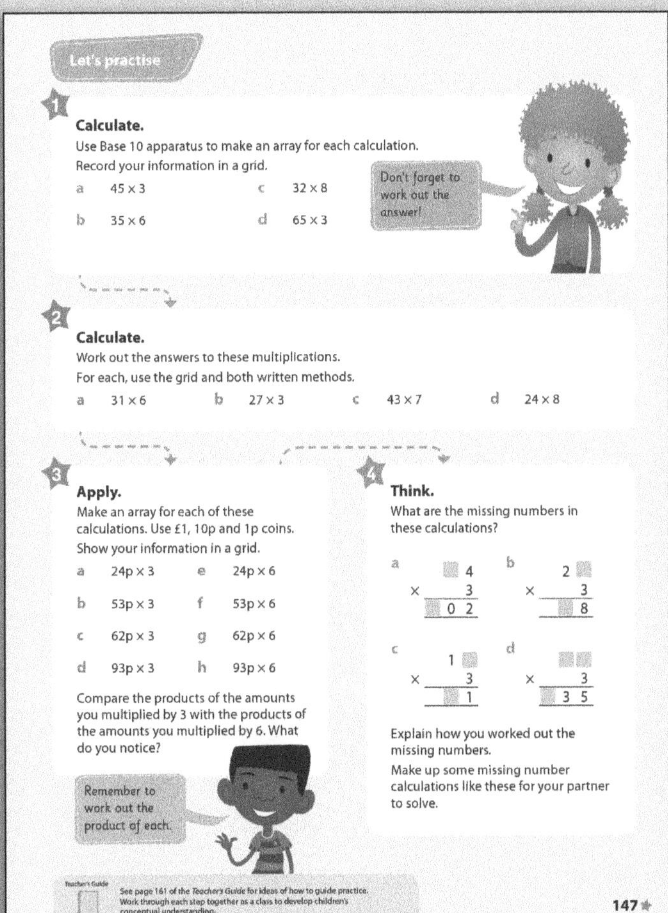
Let's practise

1 Calculate.
Use Base 10 apparatus to make an array for each calculation.
Record your information in a grid.
a 45 × 3 c 32 × 8
b 35 × 6 d 65 × 3

2 Calculate.
Work out the answers to these multiplications.
For each, use the grid and both written methods.
a 31 × 6 b 27 × 3 c 43 × 7 d 24 × 8

3 Apply.
Make an array for each of these calculations. Use £1, 10p and 1p coins.
Show your information in a grid.
a 24p × 3 e 24p × 6
b 53p × 3 f 53p × 6
c 62p × 3 g 62p × 6
d 93p × 3 h 93p × 6
Compare the products of the amounts you multiplied by 3 with the products of the amounts you multiplied by 6. What do you notice?

4 Think.
What are the missing numbers in these calculations?
a ☐4 × 3 = ☐02
b 2☐ × 3 = ☐☐8
c 1☐ × 3 = ☐1
d ☐☐ × 3 = 135
Explain how you worked out the missing numbers.
Make up some missing number calculations like these for your partner to solve.

See page 161 of the Teacher's Guide for ideas of how to guide practice. Work through each step together as a class to develop children's conceptual understanding.

147

Ensuring progress

Supporting understanding

If any children are struggling to move to the written method, they may not be ready for it at this stage. Work with them in a group, demonstrating the array for each calculation and modelling how the array transfers to the grid method. When they are confident with these models introduce the written model alongside these.

Broadening understanding

Give children calculations with more missing numbers to find. These could involve finding different possibilities.

Concept mastered

Children can explain and demonstrate the progression from the array to the formal written method for multiplication.

Follow-up ideas

- Make up some word problems for children to solve, e.g. *Samir had 36 marbles. Sam had three times as many. How many marbles did Sam have? Alexir had 84 books and wanted to put them in boxes, six in a box. How many boxes did she need?*
- Give children a selection of multiplication calculations with a variety of multipliers including two, three, four, five and six. Children need to decide which is the most appropriate strategy to answer them. They should consider the mental calculation strategies studied in previous units, so could look back in their Textbooks to help.
- Give children a toy catalogue and ask them to choose toys to buy and work out the cost of three or six.

Answers

Step 1

a 135 **c** 256

b 210 **d** 195

Step 2

a 186 **c** 301

b 81 **d** 192

Step 3

a 72p **d** £2.79

b £1.59 **e** £1.44

c £1.86 **f** £3.18

g £3.72 **h** £5.58

Children should notice that the product of an amount multiplied by six is twice the product of the same amount multiplied by three.

Step 4

a 34 × 3 = 102

b 26 × 3 = 78

c 17 × 3 = 51

d 45 × 3 = 135

Answers will vary.

13b Towards the written method for division

- **Write and calculate mathematical statements for multiplication and division using known multiplication tables, including for 2-digit numbers multiplied by single-digit numbers, using mental and progressing to formal methods.**

Homework 65 and 66 | Practice Book pp 114–16

Representations and resources

Counting stick, Base 10 apparatus, counters, squared paper, coins (10p, 1p).

Mathematical vocabulary

Division, dividend, divisor, quotient, commutative, inverse.

Warming up

Show children the counting stick. Tell them that one end is zero and the other is 80. *What multiples should we count in to get from one end to the other?* Agree eights. Place your finger on each division in turn. Children count in eights to 80 and back. *What two numbers would be added if there were 12 divisions?* Agree 88 and 96. Repeat, but jump your finger around the stick. Pause on different divisions and ask children to give the multiplication statement and its commutative equivalent (e.g. $4 \times 8 = 32$ and $8 \times 4 = 32$). Also ask them to give you the two division statements. Take the opportunity to recap the vocabulary of multiplication and division.

Background knowledge

It is important that children gain conceptual understanding as well as procedural fluency in the written method for division. Children need the opportunity to develop this practically. Arrays are a good way to visually demonstrate links between multiplication and division and to reinforce the fact that multiplication is commutative but division is not. Base 10 apparatus allows children to see the effects of partitioning numbers into multiples of the divisor. It can also be used to model the formal written method, making concrete phrases such as *three tens go into seven tens twice with one ten left over*, as well as the meaning of any carried digits. It is important that the calculations you give children cannot easily be answered using mental calculation strategies covered in previous units.

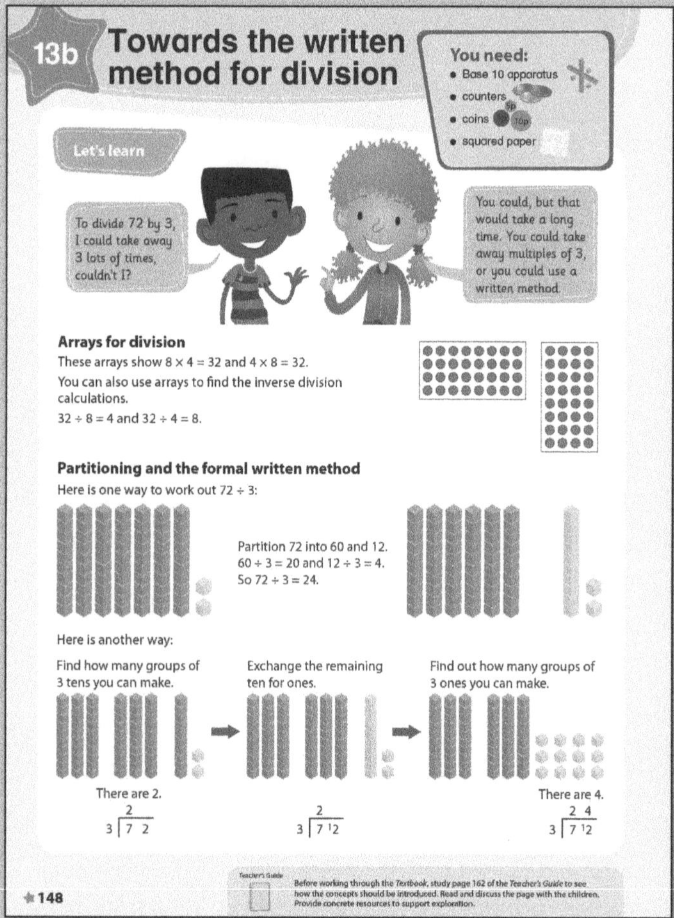
13b Towards the written method for division

You need:
- Base 10 apparatus
- counters
- coins
- squared paper

Let's learn

To divide 72 by 3, I could take away 3 lots of times, couldn't I?

You could, but that would take a long time. You could take away multiples of 3, or you could use a written method.

Arrays for division

These arrays show $8 \times 4 = 32$ and $4 \times 8 = 32$.

You can also use arrays to find the inverse division calculations.

$32 \div 8 = 4$ and $32 \div 4 = 8$.

Partitioning and the formal written method

Here is one way to work out $72 \div 3$:

Partition 72 into 60 and 12.
$60 \div 3 = 20$ and $12 \div 3 = 4$.
So $72 \div 3 = 24$.

Here is another way:

Find how many groups of 3 tens you can make. There are 2.

Exchange the remaining ten for ones.

Find out how many groups of 3 ones you can make. There are 4.

148

Teacher's Guide: Before working through the *Textbook*, study page 162 of the *Teacher's Guide* to see how the concepts should be introduced. Read and discuss the page with the children. Provide concrete resources to support exploration.

Let's learn: Modelling and teaching

Arrays for division

- Look at the arrays in the Textbook. Agree that they show 8 four times and 4 eight times respectively. Discuss how this relates to repeated addition. Establish that $8 \times 4 = 32$ and $4 \times 8 = 32$. Remind children that division is the inverse of multiplication and agree that you can use the arrays to deduce that $32 \div 8 = 4$ and $32 \div 4 = 8$. Use the four facts to review the idea that multiplication is commutative (different calculation, same answer), but division is not.
- Give children counters and ask them to make different arrays (e.g. to show five multiplied by six). For each array, ask them to write the multiplication and division statement they can make from it, then turn it around and write the other two statements.

Partitioning and the formal written method

- Give children Base 10 apparatus and ask them to make 72. Establish that they know six is a multiple of three, and 60 must be ten times that multiple, so they can partition 72 into 60 and 12. Ask them to model this, exchanging one of the tens for ones and grouping to work out $60 \div 3 = 20$ and $12 \div 3 = 4$, so $72 \div 3 = 24$. Agree that splitting the dividend into multiples of the divisor is quicker than Oli's method in the cartoon. Give them other examples to explore in the same way.
- Work through the example of the formal written method in the Textbook step by step, using Base 10 apparatus. Discuss similarities and differences between this and what they did for partitioning. Give them other calculations to answer using the written method in this way.

Let's practise: Digging deeper

Step 1

This task asks children to make arrays for the multiplication calculations, then write down the inverse division calculation. Encourage children to use counters to set out their arrays. Alternatively, they could cut out their arrays from squared or dotted paper. You could encourage those that are confident to find the commutative multiplication calculation and its inverse division as well.

Step 2

This task asks children to use a partitioning strategy and known facts to answer division calculations. Before they begin, work through some examples, e.g. for 48 ÷ 3, agree that they know 10 × 3 = 30, so they can partition 48 into 30 and 18; 30 ÷ 3 = 10, 18 ÷ 3 = 6, so the answer is 16. You could practise the three, six and eight multiplication facts and then ask them to work independently on the task. Encourage children to check their answers using the written method.

Step 3

This task is designed as a practical way of using the formal written method for division. Children first need to make the amounts using 10p and 1p coins. They then group the 10p coins according to the divisor and exchange any 10p coins left over for 1p coins (each child will need at least 16 1p coins). Finally, they group the 1p coins according to the divisor. They record their work using the formal written method, as shown in the Textbook. You may need to work with less confident children in a focus group to ensure understanding.

Step 4

This task expects children to work out all the possible arrays using 48 counters. You could give each pair a sheet of paper so that they can make their arrays on it and, when they have made each one, they can turn the paper to show the commutative array. Make sure they write down the multiplication and division statement related to each array as they go along.

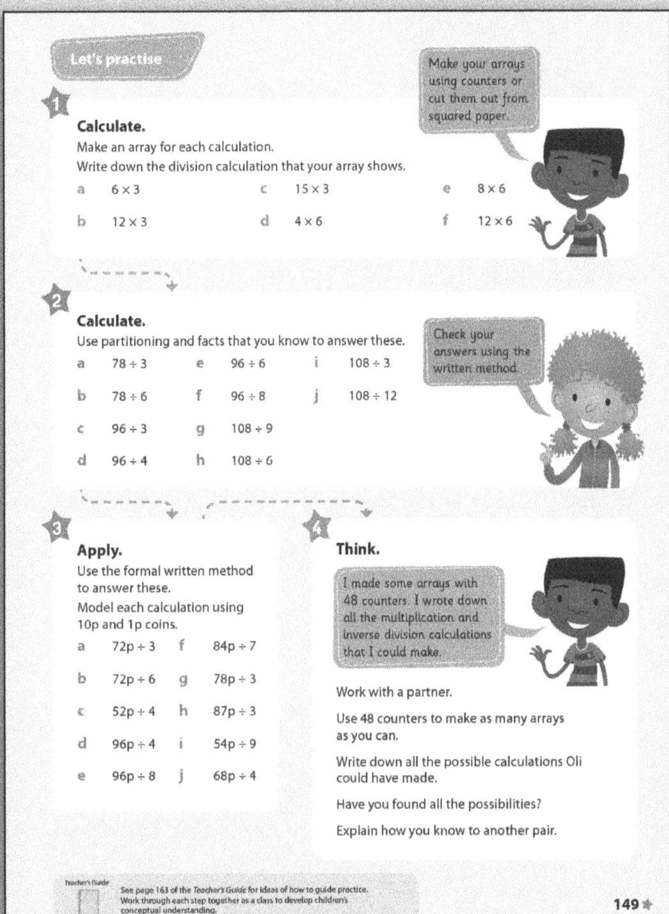
Let's practise

1 Calculate.
Make an array for each calculation.
Write down the division calculation that your array shows.

a 6 × 3	c 15 × 3	e 8 × 6
b 12 × 3	d 4 × 6	f 12 × 6

Make your arrays using counters or cut them out from squared paper.

2 Calculate.
Use partitioning and facts that you know to answer these.

a 78 ÷ 3	e 96 ÷ 6	i 108 ÷ 3
b 78 ÷ 6	f 96 ÷ 8	j 108 ÷ 12
c 96 ÷ 3	g 108 ÷ 9	
d 96 ÷ 4	h 108 ÷ 6	

Check your answers using the written method.

3 Apply.
Use the formal written method to answer these.
Model each calculation using 10p and 1p coins.

a 72p ÷ 3	f 84p ÷ 7
b 72p ÷ 6	g 78p ÷ 3
c 52p ÷ 4	h 87p ÷ 3
d 96p ÷ 4	i 54p ÷ 9
e 96p ÷ 8	j 68p ÷ 4

4 Think.
I made some arrays with 48 counters. I wrote down all the multiplication and inverse division calculations that I could make.
Work with a partner.
Use 48 counters to make as many arrays as you can.
Write down all the possible calculations Oli could have made.
Have you found all the possibilities?
Explain how you know to another pair.

Teacher's Guide
See page 163 of the Teacher's Guide for ideas of how to guide practice. Work through each step together as a class to develop children's conceptual understanding.

149

Follow-up ideas

- Give children missing number questions that involve multiplication and division, e.g. 24 × ▢ = 144, ▢ ÷ 3 = 24. Encourage them to use the array models included in this unit to understand what the question is asking and to help solve it.
- Ask children to investigate other numbers to see how many arrays they can make, as in Step 4. Ask them to write the multiplication and corresponding division statements for each one.
- Ask children to work in pairs. One child multiplies a number between 12 and 20 by a single digit. They give their number to their partner who works out, through a division method, what possible pair of numbers were multiplied.

Ensuring progress

Supporting understanding

For any children who might be struggling use variation, particularly for the division calculations, e.g. for Step 2 a, ask them to use partitioning to divide 39, 42, 48, 51 and 66 by three before they answer 78 ÷ 3. Model this carefully with children using Base 10 apparatus.

Broadening understanding

You could give children extra calculations to solve with divisors of seven and nine. You could also ask children to make up their own examples and then incorporate them into word problems that involve grouping.

✓ Concept mastered

Children can explain and demonstrate how arrays relate to division. They can divide 2-digit numbers by single-digit numbers using known facts.

Answers

Step 1

a	18 ÷ 3 = 6	**d**	24 ÷ 6 = 4
b	36 ÷ 3 = 12	**e**	48 ÷ 6 = 8
c	45 ÷ 3 = 15	**f**	72 ÷ 6 = 12

Step 2

a	26	**f**	12
b	13	**g**	12
c	32	**h**	18
d	24	**i**	36
e	16	**j**	9

Step 3

a	24p	**d**	24p
b	12p	**e**	12p
c	13p	**f**	12p
g	26p	**i**	6p
h	29p	**j**	17p

Step 4

1 × 48 = 48, 48 ÷ 48 = 1

48 × 1 = 48, 48 ÷ 1 = 48

2 × 24 = 48, 48 ÷ 24 = 2

24 × 2 = 48, 48 ÷ 2 = 24

3 × 16 = 48, 48 ÷ 16 = 3

16 × 3 = 48, 48 ÷ 3 = 16

4 × 12 = 48, 48 ÷ 12 = 4

12 × 4 = 48, 48 ÷ 4 = 12

6 × 8 = 48, 48 ÷ 8 = 6

8 × 6 = 48, 48 ÷ 6 = 8

Unit

13 Seeing stars

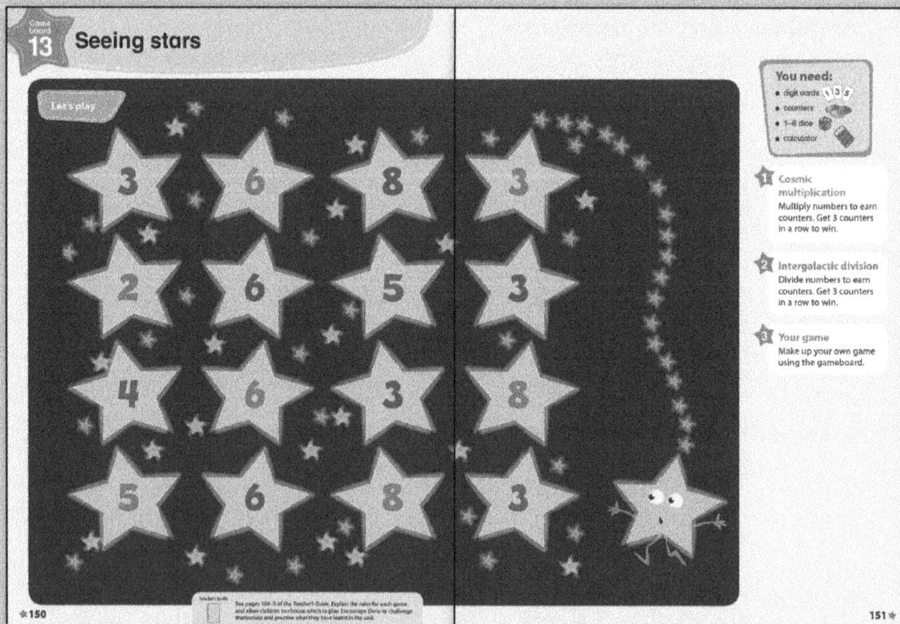

Game 1: Cosmic multiplication

This game gives children practice multiplying a 2-digit number by a single-digit number. It also encourages them to consider which strategy to use: a mental calculation strategy, the grid method or the formal written method.

Maths focus

- Write and calculate mathematical statements for multiplication

Resources

Counters (1 colour per player), 0–9 digit cards (2 sets), 1–6 dice (1), calculator.

How to play

This game should be played in pairs. Children shuffle the digit cards and place them in a pile face down on the table. They choose which colour counters each will use and roll the dice to establish who will go first. They take it in turns to pick two digit cards and use them to make a 2-digit number. On each turn, they pick a star. They multiply their 2-digit number by the number in the star. They can choose whichever method, mental or written, they think is appropriate. If they choose a star with a two or four, encourage them to use a doubling strategy. If they choose a star with five in it, encourage them to multiply by ten and halve (or vice versa), using jottings to help. Their partner checks their answer using a calculator. If they are correct, they place a counter on that star. The winner is the first player to have three counters in a row, either horizontally, vertically or diagonally.

Making it easier

Encourage children to make the lowest 2-digit number possible with the two digit cards they have picked.

Making it harder

Encourage children to make the highest 2-digit number they can with their digit cards, or challenge them to pick three digit cards and make a 3-digit number to multiply.

Game 2: Intergalactic division

This game gives children practice dividing a 2-digit number by a single-digit number. They have the option to use partitioning or the formal written method.

Maths focus

- Write and calculate mathematical statements for division

Resources

Counters (1 colour per player), 0–9 digit cards (2 sets), 1–6 dice (1), calculator.

How to play

This game should be played in pairs. Children shuffle the digit cards together and place them in a pile face down on the table. They choose which colour counters each will use and roll the dice to establish who will go first. They then take it in turns to pick two digit cards and make a 2-digit number. On each turn, they pick a star. They divide their 2-digit number by the number in the star. They can choose the method that they are most confident with. Their partner checks their answer using a calculator. If they are correct, they place a counter on that star. The winner is the first player to have three counters in a row, either horizontally, vertically or diagonally.

Making it easier

Encourage children to use partitioning, using known facts, to work out their answers.

Making it harder

Encourage children to consider a sensible mental calculation strategy or the formal written method for their calculations.

Game 3: Your game

Children should invent their own game designing rules that use the concepts covered in the unit. Challenge children to make their game easier or harder.

Seeing stars

Choose a game to play.

Game 1: Cosmic multiplication

You need:

- counters (1 colour per player)
- two sets of 0–9 digit cards
- 1–6 dice
- calculator

How to play

- Shuffle the digit cards and place them in a pile face down on the table. Choose which colour counter each player will use. Roll the dice to decide who goes first.
- Take turns to pick 2 digit cards. Use them to make a 2-digit number.
- Choose a star and multiply your 2-digit number by the star number. Use whichever method you think best. It can be a mental method or a written method.
- Ask your partner to check your answer. If you are correct, put a counter on the star.
- The winner is the first player to have 3 counters in a row. The row can be horizontal, vertical or diagonal.

Game 2: Intergalactic division

You need:

- counters (1 colour per player)
- two sets of 0–9 digit cards
- 1–6 dice
- calculator

How to play

- Shuffle the digit cards and place them in a pile face down on the table. Choose which colour counter each player will use. Roll the dice to decide who goes first.
- Take turns to pick 2 digit cards. Use them to make a 2-digit number.
- Choose a star and divide your 2-digit number by the star number. Use whichever method you think best.
- Ask your partner to check your answer. If you are correct, put a counter on the star.
- The winner is the first player to have 3 counters in a row. The row can be horizontal, vertical or diagonal.

Game 3: Your game

- Make up your own game using the gameboard.
- Perhaps you could use the dice to decide whether to multiply or divide.
- What are the rules for your game? Explain them to someone.

Please help your child by reading the instructions and playing the game together.

Unit 13 And finally ...

Assessment task 1

Resources

Base 10 apparatus.

Running the task

Before children begin, recap the vocabulary related to multiplication: multiplicand, multiplier, product, commutative, inverse, dividend, divisor and quotient. Ensure understanding and encourage them to give their definitions to a partner in a full sentence. Then discuss the importance of knowing multiplication facts and practise the facts for the three and six and then the four and eight multiplication tables. Emphasise that knowing these will help when answering both multiplication and division problems.

The task asks children to work through the progression from array to the formal written method using the calculation 45 × 3. Before children tackle the task independently, you might like to work through a similar example with the class: ask them to describe each stage to a partner and comment on what is the same and what is different. When they have completed the task, you could ask them to repeat it for different calculations (e.g. 36 × 3, 42 × 6).

The final part of the task asks children to explain which of the four methods they prefer and why. Use their answers, and your observations of their work during the task, to assess their progress. Some children may need further practice in order to fully master one stage, moving on to the next when they are ready. Initially children are likely to prefer the array method, as this allows them to visualise what is happening. However, in time they are likely to prefer the later methods, as these are progressively more efficient.

Evidencing mastery

If children can explain and demonstrate the stages from the array to the formal written method, they are showing mastery.

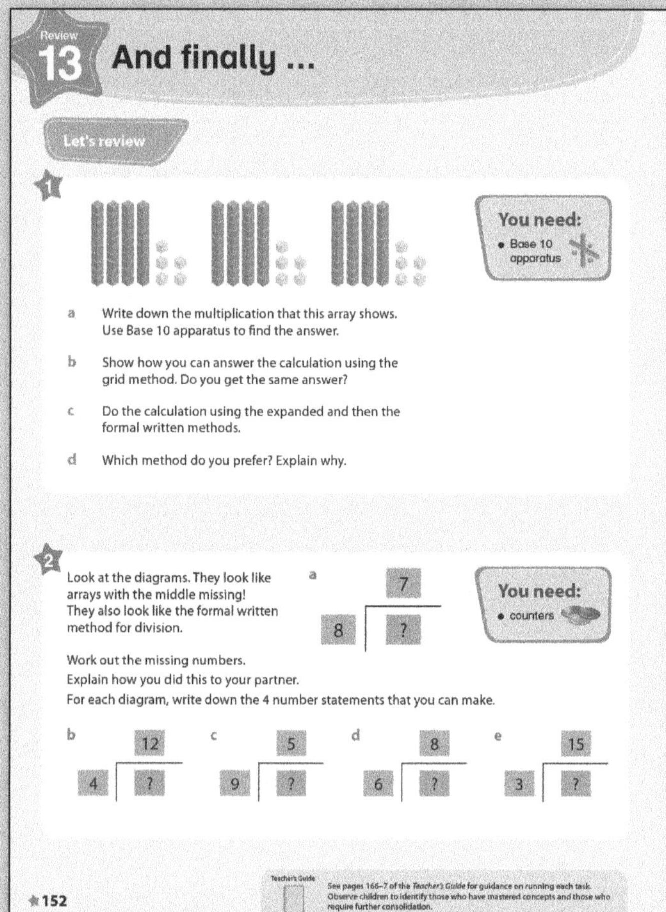
Review 13 And finally ...

Let's review

1

You need:
• Base 10 apparatus

a Write down the multiplication that this array shows. Use Base 10 apparatus to find the answer.

b Show how you can answer the calculation using the grid method. Do you get the same answer?

c Do the calculation using the expanded and then the formal written methods.

d Which method do you prefer? Explain why.

2

Look at the diagrams. They look like arrays with the middle missing! They also look like the formal written method for division.

a 7 / 8 ?

You need:
• counters

Work out the missing numbers.
Explain how you did this to your partner.
For each diagram, write down the 4 number statements that you can make.

b 12 / 4 ?　c 5 / 9 ?　d 8 / 6 ?　e 15 / 3 ?

152

Teacher's Guide
See pages 166–7 of the *Teacher's Guide* for guidance on running each task. Observe children to identify those who have mastered concepts and those who require further consolidation.

Assessment task 2

Resources

Counters.

Running the task

This task assesses children's understanding of the inverse nature of multiplication and division. Look at the first diagram. They will be familiar with the layout from the formal written method for division. The diagram also looks like an array, with the counters missing. Help children make this connection by asking them to set out the array (eight counters, seven times) and then to work out the total number of counters by multiplying eight by seven. Then ask them to explain what they did to their partner. Encourage them to use precise mathematical vocabulary. Relate their results to the diagram in the Textbook; they should see that the missing number is the product of the two given numbers. Children should then be able to write down the four number statements that the diagram shows (8 × 7 = 56, 7 × 8 = 56, 56 ÷ 7 = 8, 56 ÷ 8 = 7).

Children should then be able to tackle the remaining four diagrams independently. Allow them to set out the arrays using counters but, if appropriate, challenge some children to answer at least one part without this support.

Evidencing mastery

If children can explain and demonstrate the relationship between multiplication and division, they are evidencing mastery.

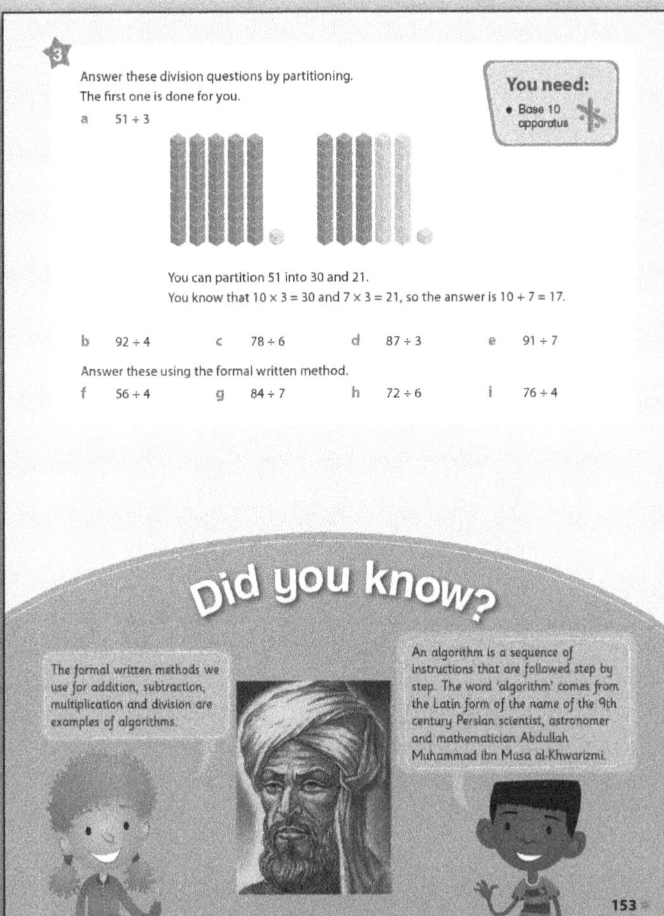

3

Answer these division questions by partitioning.
The first one is done for you.

a 51 ÷ 3

You can partition 51 into 30 and 21.
You know that 10 × 3 = 30 and 7 × 3 = 21, so the answer is 10 + 7 = 17.

b 92 ÷ 4 c 78 ÷ 6 d 87 ÷ 3 e 91 ÷ 7

Answer these using the formal written method.

f 56 ÷ 4 g 84 ÷ 7 h 72 ÷ 6 i 76 ÷ 4

You need:
- Base 10 apparatus

Did you know?

The formal written methods we use for addition, subtraction, multiplication and division are examples of algorithms.

An algorithm is a sequence of instructions that are followed step by step. The word 'algorithm' comes from the Latin form of the name of the 9th century Persian scientist, astronomer and mathematician Abdullah Muhammad ibn Musa al-Khwarizmi.

153

Concepts mastered

- ☑ Children can explain and demonstrate the progression from the array to the formal written method for multiplication.
- ☑ Children can explain and demonstrate how arrays relate to division. They can divide 2-digit numbers by single-digit numbers using known facts.

Assessment task 3

Resources

Base 10 apparatus.

Running the task

Remind children that division is essentially finding the number of groups of the divisor that can be made from the dividend. Discuss the partitioning method using the example in the Textbook (51 ÷ 3). If necessary, make up some more examples to give children more practice before asking them to work independently on parts b–e. Give them Base 10 apparatus but, as in Task 2, you could challenge some children to answer at least one part without this support.

Before children move on to the second part of the task, ask them to consider how they solved the calculations in 13b – Towards the written method for division using the formal written method. Give pairs Base 10 apparatus and ask them to use it to solve a division such as 78 ÷ 3, describing what they are doing to their partner and recording their work using the formal written method. They could practise a few examples in this way before answering parts f–j independently. Again, can some children carry out the formal written method without using Base 10 apparatus?

Evidencing mastery

If children can explain and demonstrate division by partitioning and the formal written method, they are evidencing mastery.

Did you know?

An algorithm is a sequence of instructions that are followed step by step. The formal written methods for addition, subtraction, multiplication and division are examples of algorithms – each comprises a set of steps which need to be followed to attain a correct answer. These steps are always the same. It has been said that these straightforward steps can usually be followed by any human of average intelligence!

Algorithms can be found everywhere. They have been developed to ease our daily life. They are used in computing and data processing, as well as in areas such as artificial intelligence and molecular biology. Google is one of the products of the development of the algorithm.

The word 'algorithm' can be traced back to the ninth century, when the Persian scientist, astronomer and mathematician Abdullah Muhammad ibn Musa al-Khwarizmi introduced Arabic numerals to the Western world. He developed algorism, a method of arithmetic using these numerals. Both 'algorism' and 'algorithm' stem from the Latin form of his name.

Unit 14 2-D shapes and perimeter

Mathematical focus

- ★ Geometry: properties and shapes
- ★ Measurement: length
- ★ Statistics: interpret and present data

Prior learning

Children should already be able to:

- identify and describe the properties of 2-D shapes, including the number of sides and line symmetry in a vertical line
- use a right angle tester to check whether or not an angle in a 2-D shape is a right angle
- identify horizontal, vertical, parallel and perpendicular lines in shapes.

Key new learning

- Draw 2-D shapes and describe them.
- Interpret and present data using bar charts, pictograms and tables.
- Measure, compare, add and subtract lengths (m/cm/mm).
- Measure the perimeter of simple 2-D shapes.

Making connections

- For an art and design topic, children could draw 2-D images of 3-D shapes. Discuss the work of Picasso and investigate how he turns 3-D objects into 2-D shapes. Children could create their own piece of artwork, e.g. draw a cylindrical bottle as a pair of rectangles.
- Encourage children to recognise fractions in the context of shape. Give them a selection of regular and irregular shapes and ask them to investigate whether they could be halved.
- When finding a perimeter, make the connection to calculating efficiently, using mental calculation strategies and known facts, e.g. to find the perimeter of a regular hexagon with sides of eight centimetres children can draw on their multiplication facts ($6 \times 8 = 48$ cm).
- Enlarging shapes can be linked to simple scaling by integers. Children could draw small shapes, measure their sides to the nearest centimetres and calculate their perimeter. They then scale them up, e.g. double each size, draw the new shape, calculate the new perimeter and compare it to the original.

Talk about

It is important to use precise mathematical vocabulary from the beginning. Throughout your discussions, ensure that children are able to name the 2-D shapes correctly, including irregular shapes and use more complex vocabulary such as 'composite' with confidence. Use visual aids to support and reinforce key definitions.

From the outset, establish a clear definition of perimeter as the distance measured around a 2-D shape.

Engaging and exploring

For the first photo, ask children to work in pairs and consider the shapes that gardens and hedges around them can be. Discuss the answers as a class and write the names of the 2-D shapes on the whiteboard. Show corresponding plastic 2-D shapes and confirm their properties. Then identify the shape of the hedge in the picture. You could discuss how long any garden hedges they know might be. You could go outside and measure the length of the hedges or another area in the playground. Revisit measuring lengths in metres (m), centimetres (cm) and millimetres (mm). Discuss different examples where each unit could be used.

Next look at the photo of the parachute. Ask children to identify how many triangles the parachute is made up of. Confirm 12 by counting. Encourage children to discuss the reason the parachute is made of triangles in different colours. Ask children to think of other places in which they can see shapes 'stuck together' or a shape being split into different parts, e.g. windows, doors, sports pitches. Children work in small groups. Give each group 12 paper triangles. Ask: *Can you glue them on a piece of paper to make a small parachute? Is there a gap between the triangles? Why is that?*

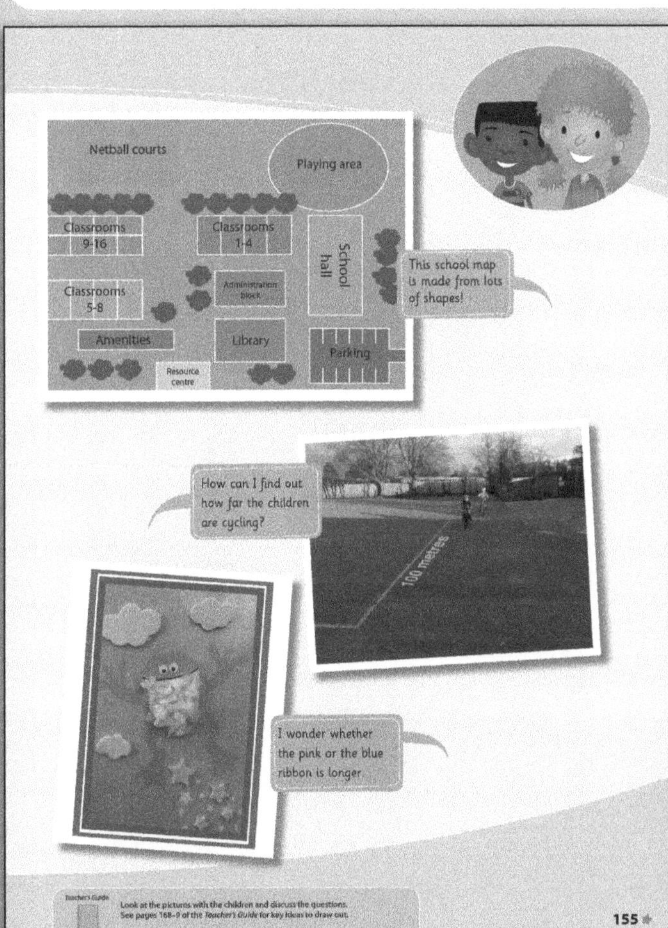

Ask children to discuss the shapes they see on the school map and what they represent in real life. Recap parallel, perpendicular, horizontal and vertical lines and ask children to identify them in the shapes on the map. Talk together about the use of maps and the use of 2-D shapes in them. Link shapes and measurement and explain how scaling is used in constructing maps. Ask children to think about constructing a map or a plan of their classroom or school and what they need to do. Consider measuring the length and width, the tools they will use and the shapes that each area will be. Emphasise the importance of drawing 2-D shapes accurately and their use in real life. Look at a map or plan of the school. Ask: *What is the shape of your classroom? How many times smaller is the width in the plan compared to the real life?*

Now refer to the photo of children cycling. Ask: *How can we find out how far they will cycle?* Focus children's attention on the fact that the playground has four sides of equal length and that the length of each has to be added together. Ask: *If each side of the playground was 100 metres long, how far would the children have cycled?* Ask children to discuss in pairs and collect feedback on the whiteboard. Which children add 100 four times and which children use multiplication? Ask: Which method is the hardest and which is the easiest? Why? Which method is the most efficient? Why? Guide children to understand that it is more efficient to calculate the answer mentally using multiplication facts. Highlight that they must include the units in the answer.

For the photo of the card, ask children which ribbon is the longest. Listen for those who notice that one rectangle is bigger than the other so it will need more ribbon to go around it. Ask children to think how they can prove why the blue ribbon is longer. *What would they do if they could not remove the ribbon and measure it?* Encourage children to sketch the rectangles formed by the ribbons and use mathematical statements and/or mathematical language to explain their reasoning.

Checking understanding

You will know children have mastered these concepts when they can name and draw different 2-D shapes. Children can measure, compare, add and subtract the lengths of the shapes and can measure the perimeter of simple 2-D shapes.

Things to think about

- What everyday objects will children use to measure perimeter?
- What practical opportunities will children have to make 2-D shapes?
- What types of statistical tables can they use to record their findings?
- How will you organise groupings for discussion and activities?
- What opportunities will you give children to explain their reasoning?
- What opportunities will you provide for children to build fluency?
- Which problem-solving strategies are most appropriate in this unit, e.g.:
  - Explain why
  - What do you notice?
  - What is the same? What is different?
  - Another, another, another
  - Convince me.

14a All about 2-D shapes

- **Draw 2-D shapes and describe them.**
- **Interpret and present data using bar charts, pictograms and tables.**

Homework 67 and 68 Practice Book pp 117–19

Mathematical vocabulary

2-D shapes, polygon, semicircle, regular, irregular, shapes, quadrilateral, pentagon, hexagon, heptagon, octagon

Representations and resources

Whiteboards and pens, 2-D shapes, two large hoops, right angle models, rulers, mirrors, coloured pencils, squared paper, scissors.

Warming up

Revise finding doubles of numbers up to and including double 20. You say a number, e.g. 13, children write its double on their whiteboard and show the result (26). Discuss how children doubled the number. Look out for children who find it difficult to double the numbers, in particular those between 15 and 20. Revise finding doubles of five, six, seven, eight and nine and the multiplication table for two. Once children are confident with these, encourage them to partition the numbers into tens and units and double them. Adapt the task according to children's needs. To extend, revise halving even numbers up to and including half of 40.

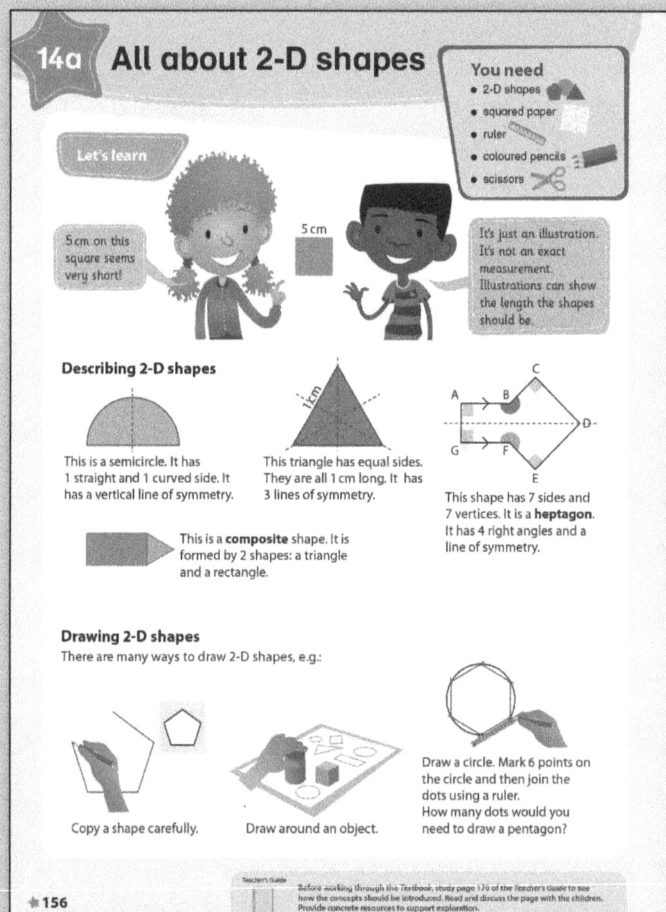

Background knowledge

Children should be familiar with most 2-D shapes. Watch out for children who only recognise regular pentagons, hexagons and octagons. Provide a range of irregular shapes to clarify and describe what makes a shape a pentagon, hexagon or octagon. It is important to understand that plastic 2-D shapes are technically 3-D shapes. Some children may raise this point; clarify that 2-D shapes are the face of the 3-D shapes they are using.

Regular 2-D shapes such as squares, rectangles and regular pentagons have the same number of lines of symmetry as their number of sides.

Let's learn: Modelling and teaching

Describing 2-D shapes

- Provide groups of children with a variety of cut-out regular and irregular 2-D shapes. Include circles and semicircles. Children name the shapes they recognise. Write down on the whiteboard the names of the shapes they are unsure of. Explain that all sides of a regular shape are equal in length. Ask children to separate the shapes in two groups using two large hoops – regular and irregular.
- Discuss the composite shape in the Textbook. Explain that by composing or combining different shapes, new shapes can be created. Invite children to make two new shapes by using three of the 2-D shapes.
- Choose a selection of 2-D shapes and identify the parallel, perpendicular, horizontal and vertical lines and clarify any misconceptions. Ask children to identify shapes with and without parallel and perpendicular lines. Repeat for horizontal and vertical lines. Discuss the angles of one of the shapes. *Are they bigger or smaller than a right angle?* Emphasise that an angle is formed by straight lines meeting at a point.
- Discuss lines of symmetry the shapes have including horizontal, vertical and diagonal. Demonstrate them in a square by folding it or using a mirror.

Drawing 2-D shapes

- Ask children to draw a triangle, quadrilateral and pentagon. Look out for those who are confident and invite them to share their tips. Explain the different ways of drawing shapes in the Textbook. Allow them time to experience each one of them. Which method is the easiest? Hardest?

Let's practise: Digging deeper

Step 1

Children work in pairs. If they are unsure where to start, remind them to count the sides or vertices of each shape and name them accordingly. Before they start drawing, ask them to describe the 2-D shapes, paying attention to whether they have horizontal, vertical, perpendicular or parallel sides. When drawing the triangle and hexagon, children may find it easier to place the vertices first, then join them together. Ask children to reason about how they know what each shape is, using the vocabulary of lines, angles and sides.

Step 2

Children work in pairs or small groups. This question requires children to visualise the shapes and then draw them accordingly. Can they describe each shape? Ask: *Is it a regular or irregular shape? How do you know?* Encourage children to describe the properties of each shape they draw including horizontal lines, vertical lines and right angles. Challenge them to check whether the shape has any lines of symmetry. Encourage discussion about the method used to draw each shape. Ask them to share their best methods and tips.

Step 3

Children could make the face of a cat, dog or rabbit by using hexagons, triangles and circles. They could make a train by using rectangles, squares and circles. Taking turns, the first child draws the shape, then the second child describes the properties of the shapes used and guesses the object. Encourage the use of precise mathematical language.

Step 4

Children compare the properties of the rectangle and square they draw. They work individually and then discuss their answers with a partner. Children can insert the information in a table to make the comparison easier. Encourage them to compare sides, including the lengths, angles and lines of symmetry in each shape.

Square	Rectangle

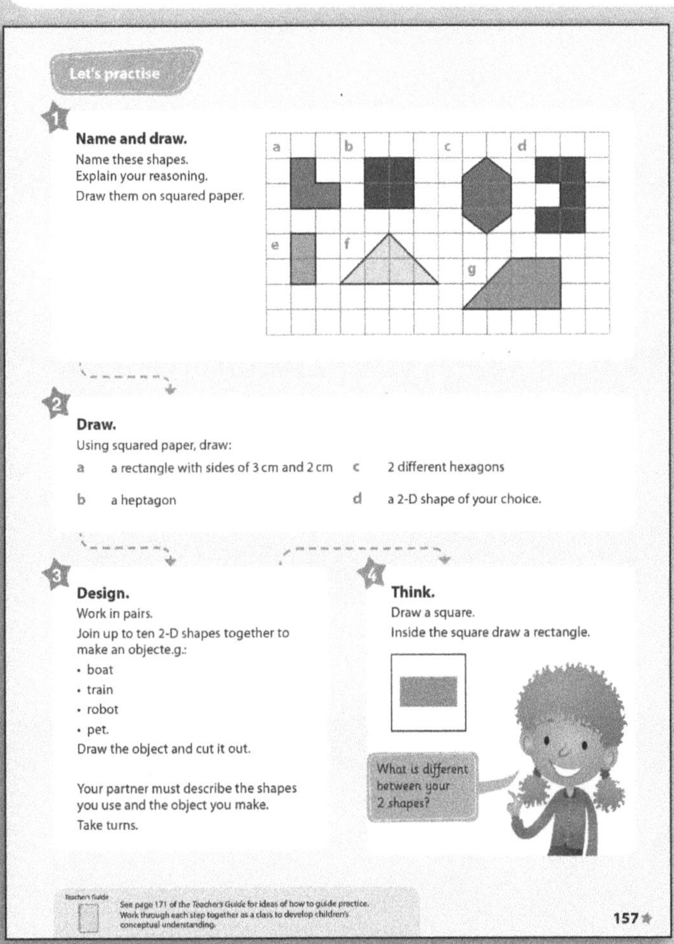
Let's practise

1 **Name and draw.**
Name these shapes.
Explain your reasoning.
Draw them on squared paper.

2 **Draw.**
Using squared paper, draw:
a a rectangle with sides of 3 cm and 2 cm
b a heptagon
c 2 different hexagons
d a 2-D shape of your choice.

3 **Design.**
Work in pairs.
Join up to ten 2-D shapes together to make an objecte.g.:
- boat
- train
- robot
- pet.

Draw the object and cut it out.

Your partner must describe the shapes you use and the object you make.
Take turns.

4 **Think.**
Draw a square.
Inside the square draw a rectangle.

Teacher's Guide
See page 171 of the *Teacher's Guide* for ideas of how to guide practice. Work through each step together as a class to develop children's conceptual understanding.

157

Ensuring progress

Supporting understanding

If the shapes children need to draw have a line of symmetry, help by drawing half of the shape and the line of symmetry. Ask children to draw the reflection of the shape. Use this opportunity to discuss the different types of symmetry shapes may have and remind children of the 'mirror method' they learnt in Year 2.

Work with children in a focus group to make compound shapes. Provide them with different 2-D shapes that have some equal lengths so that they can match the sides that are equal together. Prior to working on the tasks, revisit the concepts learnt in Years 2 and 3.

Broadening understanding

Challenge children to draw a group of quadrilaterals, pentagons, hexagons, heptagons and octagons, each shape within each group looking as different as possible from the others. Ask them to make compound shapes by using different-size triangles. *Can you make hexagons and pentagons by using triangles only? What if you use squares only?*

Follow-up ideas

- In small groups, children research how to make simple origami shapes and make three different ones. The 2-D shapes used in each origami shape should be clear to see. Photograph the best ones and display them or publish them in the class blog or newsletter.
- Swap roles. Children are the 'teacher' and give you instructions to draw a shape. For each instruction, draw anything but the shape, e.g. children say, 'Draw a pentagon with five sides'; you draw a shape with five sides but one of them is curved. Continue until they have given you all the information that is needed to define the properties of a pentagon.

Concept mastered

Children can draw 2-D shapes and describe their properties.

Answers

Step 1

a irregular hexagon

b square

c irregular hexagon

d irregular octagon

e rectangle

f isoceles triangle

g irregular quadrilateral

Step 4

Both are quadrilaterals with 4 right angles. The rectangle has opposite sides equal.

The square has all 4 sides equal.

14b Measuring perimeter

- **Measure, compare, add and subtract lengths (m/cm/mm).**
- **Measure the perimeter of simple 2-D shapes.**
- **Interpret and present data using bar charts, pictograms and tables.**

Homework 69 and 70 | Practice Book pp 120–3

Mathematical vocabulary

Perimeter, centimetre (cm), metre (m), millimetres (mm)

Representations and resources

Whiteboards and pens, 2-D shapes (regular and irregular), string, squared paper, rulers, coloured pencils, metre stick, chalk or washable paint, paintbrushes.

Warming up

Revise multiples of five that total to 100, e.g. you say 15, children write on their whiteboards 85. Ask children to think about the numbers in the multiplication table for five and what they have in common. To make it easier, children could find multiples of ten that add to 100. To make it more challenging, they could find multiples of two that total 100. Adapt the task according to children's needs and help children revise the two, five, and ten multiplication tables.

Background knowledge

Perimeter is the length of the boundary or sides of a 2-D shape. It is measured in units of lengths such as millimetres (mm), centimetres (cm) or metres (m). The perimeter of a circle is called the circumference.

Later in Key Stage 2, children will learn about area, which is a measure of surface and measured in square units, e.g. mm^2, cm^2 or m^2. While children will not have learnt about area of shapes, one of the most common mistakes is confusing area and perimeter of 2-D shapes. Provide lots of opportunities to help children understand that perimeter is the length around the shape, using practical equipment.

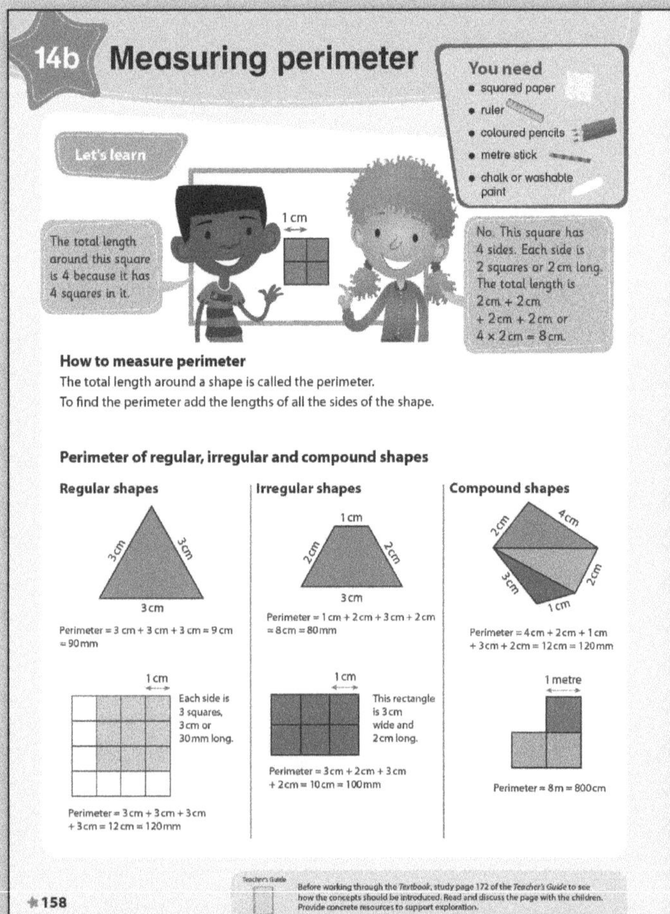
14b Measuring perimeter

You need
- squared paper
- ruler
- coloured pencils
- metre stick
- chalk or washable paint

Let's learn

The total length around this square is 4 because it has 4 squares in it.

1 cm

No. This square has 4 sides. Each side is 2 squares or 2 cm long. The total length is 2 cm + 2 cm + 2 cm + 2 cm or 4 × 2 cm = 8 cm.

How to measure perimeter

The total length around a shape is called the perimeter.
To find the perimeter add the lengths of all the sides of the shape.

Perimeter of regular, irregular and compound shapes

Regular shapes

3 cm, 3 cm, 3 cm

Perimeter = 3 cm + 3 cm + 3 cm = 9 cm = 90 mm

1 cm

Each side is 3 squares, 3 cm or 30 mm long.

Perimeter = 3 cm + 3 cm + 3 cm + 3 cm = 12 cm = 120 mm

Irregular shapes

1 cm, 2 cm, 2 cm, 3 cm

Perimeter = 1 cm + 2 cm + 3 cm + 2 cm = 8 cm = 80 mm

1 cm

This rectangle is 3 cm wide and 2 cm long.

Perimeter = 3 cm + 2 cm + 3 cm + 2 cm = 10 cm = 100 mm

Compound shapes

2 cm, 4 cm, 2 cm, 3 cm, 1 cm

Perimeter = 4 cm + 2 cm + 1 cm + 3 cm + 2 cm = 12 cm = 120 mm

1 metre

Perimeter = 8 m = 800 cm

158

Teacher's Guide

Before working through the *Textbook*, study page 172 of the *Teacher's Guide* to see how the concepts should be introduced. Read and discuss the page with the children. Provide concrete resources to support exploration.

Let's learn: Modelling and teaching

How to measure perimeter

- Refer to the Textbook to define perimeter. Explain in terms of the boundaries or the outside length/sides of a shape. Tell children to go outside and measure the perimeter of a part of the garden or playing area using a metre stick. Measure the perimeter of one face of your book and pencil case using a ruler. Discuss the different measurements used in each case (m, cm, mm).

Perimeter of regular, irregular and compound shapes

- Provide each table with a mixture of regular and irregular 2-D shapes. Children work in two groups. The first group measures the lengths of the sides of the triangles to the nearest centimetre and finds the perimeter by adding the values. The second group measures the perimeter of the same shapes by placing a piece of string all around the sides of the shapes, then measuring the length. Check the two groups have found the same perimeter and record as modelled in the Textbook. Discuss which method is easier. Repeat for other shapes.
- Ask children to pick up two shapes, e.g. two identical squares, make a compound shape and draw around the sides of it. *What 2-D shape have you created?* They estimate the perimeter of the new shape and measure it. Explain that when measuring the perimeter of a compound shape we only measure and add the lengths of the outside sides/boundaries. Ask children to halve the compound shape into the original two squares used to make it. *Will the perimeter of each square be half of the perimeter of the compound shape?* Children measure the new perimeter and establish that though the shape is halved the perimeter is not.
- Repeat for different shapes, linking fractions of shapes and finding the perimeter of compound shapes.

Let's practise: Digging deeper

Step 1

Children measure the shapes. Ensure they show their calculations clearly and add all the sides of the shape. Encourage children to think of different ways to find the perimeter and to say the answer in centimetres and millimetres.

Step 2

This step requires children to understand how to measure the perimeter of different 2-D shapes and also group polygons according to their perimeter and number of sides. Ask children to describe the properties of each shape using precise mathematical vocabulary.

Step 3

Children work in small groups, using a metre stick. Some may find it easier to change the perimeter to centimetres only. Advise children to sketch the shapes they will make so that they know the length of the sides they will draw. Support children to identify what is different: *How many sides does each shape have? What is it called? Are any of the sides equal size?*

Step 4

Revisit what a regular shape is. Discuss children's strategies to find the perimeter of each shape. Start with the triangle. If children have not thought about using multiplying instead of adding, help them by sketching each shape and write the calculation next to it, e.g. for the triangle write 2 + 2 + 2 or 3 × 2. Encourage children to generalise that to find the perimeter of a regular shape, they multiply the length of one side by the number of sides the shape has.

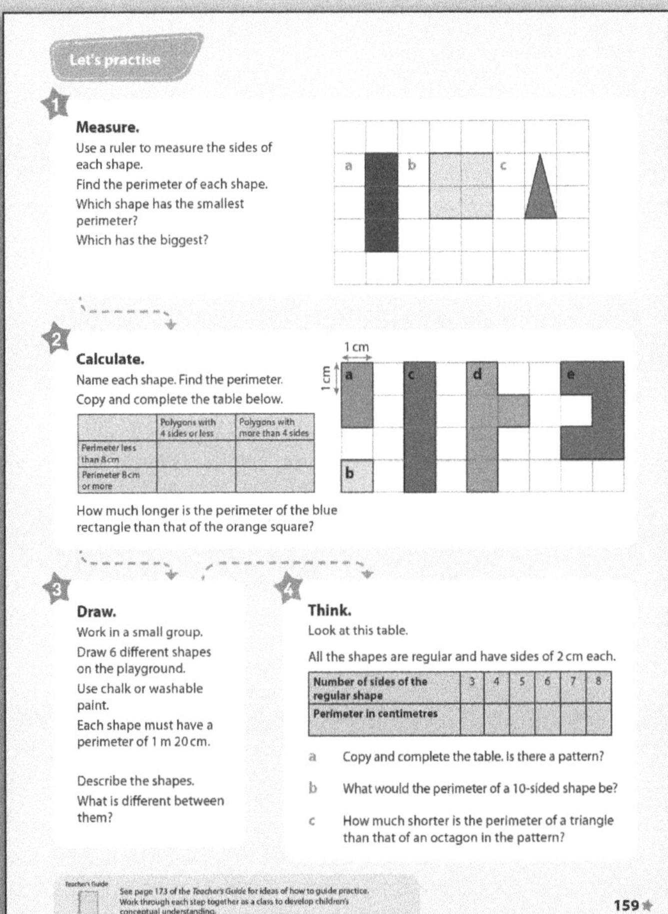

Follow-up ideas

- Working in four small groups, children use interlocking squares or triangles to build quadrilaterals, pentagons, hexagons and octagons. They draw around each shape and measure its perimeter. They then separate the shape in half. *Will the perimeter be halved? Can you halve the shape in a different way? Has the perimeter of each half changed?* Encourage children to investigate for different shapes from each group, generalise and share their results.
- Children work in two groups. Each group throws a 1–6 dice and adds ten to the number shown. The answer is the perimeter of the 2-D shapes children need to make. *How many different 2-D shapes can you make in three minutes?* The group that makes the most wins.

Ensuring progress

Supporting understanding

Work with children in a focus group to revisit the concept of perimeter prior to completing the tasks. Look out for children who only add the values of two of the sides of a rectangle or a regular shape. It might be helpful to mark the sides they have added.

Broadening understanding

Challenge children to recognise that opposite sides in a rectangle are equal, so to find the perimeter they can just add the lengths of the shorter and longer side together, then double the answer. Encourage generalising and share their views. Challenge children to find the perimeter of regular shapes of three centimetres and five centimetres, notice the pattern the values of the perimeter follow, and generalise.

Concept mastered

Children can measure, compare, add and subtract lengths in metres, centimetres and millimetres. They can measure the perimeter of simple 2-D shapes.

Answers

Step 1

Perimeters:

a rectangle: 8 cm

b square: 8 cm

c triangle: 5 cm

Rectangle and square have the largest perimeter and triangle has the smallest.

Step 2

Perimeters:

a rectangle 6 cm

b square 4 cm

c rectangle 10 cm

d octagon 12 cm

e octagon 12 cm

Perimeter less than 8 cm	Polygons with 4 sides or less	Polygons with more than 4 sides
	a, b	
Perimeter 8 cm or more	c	d, e

Step 4

a Multiply the number of sides by 2.

Number of sides of the regular shape	3	4	5	6	7	8
Perimeter in centimetres	6	8	10	12	14	16

b 20 cm

c 10 cm

Unit 14 Black or white?

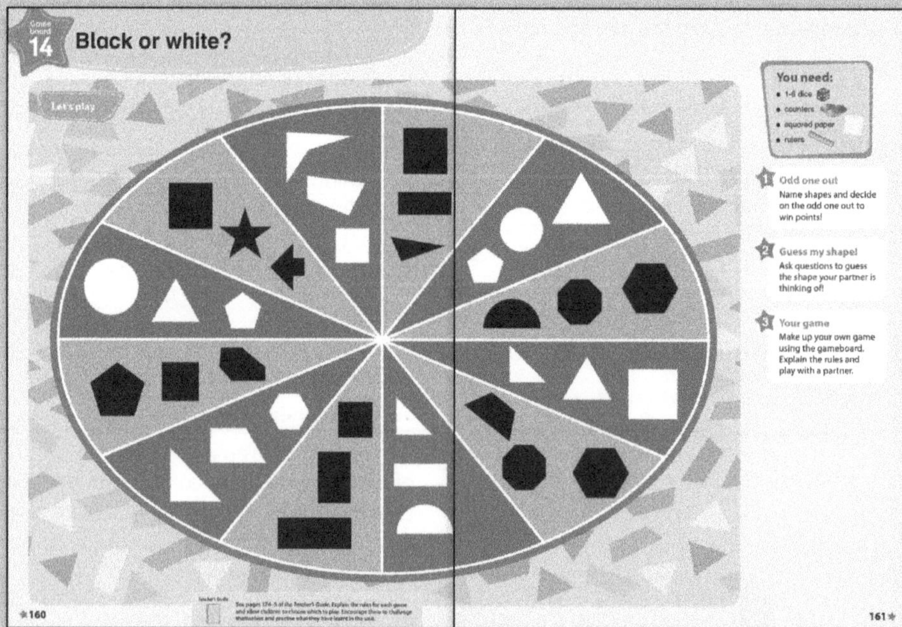

Game 1: Odd one out

In this simple game, children choose the shape that is the odd one out and draw it to collect points.

Maths focus

- Name, describe and draw 2-D shapes

Resources

Squared paper, 1–6 dice (2), rulers, 12 counters.

How to play

Play in pairs. Each child rolls a dice and the child with the higher score chooses a section on the gameboard. If the same child has the higher score on their third consecutive turn, they choose a section for the other child. If both children have the same score, they both roll the dice again.

On their turn, children name and describe all three shapes in their chosen section to win three points. They then draw the shape that they think is the odd one out in the group and justify their answer to win two points. Children place a counter on each section once it has been chosen.

The winner is the child with the most points when all 12 sections have been selected.

Making it easier

If unsure, children could 'call a friend' and ask for advice once during the game.

Making it harder

Children could be asked to show the lines of symmetry in the shapes that they draw.

Game 3: Your game

Children should invent their own game, designing rules that use the concepts covered in the unit.

Challenge children to make their game easier or harder.

Game 2: Guess my shape!

This is a more difficult game where children have to guess a shape and draw it to win points.

Maths focus

- Name, describe and draw 2-D shapes including regular and irregular shapes, with and without lines of symmetry

Resources

Squared paper, 1–6 dice (2), rulers.

How to play

Play in pairs. Each child rolls a dice and the child with the higher score starts the game. The child chooses a black or white shape and secretly draws it on a piece of paper. They then put the piece of paper away.

The other child asks up to eight questions about the shape that has been drawn, to which the first child can only answer 'yes' or 'no'. The second child guesses the shape, draws it and names it. Children then compare their drawn shapes. The second child then chooses a shape for their partner to guess. For each turn, if the correct shape is named within three guesses, the child gets three points; if named within six guesses the child gets two points; for eight guesses, one point. The winner is the first player to collect 22 points.

Making it easier

If stuck and unsure, children can ask their partner for a clue about the shape.

Making it harder

Children could ask questions about the lines of symmetry that shapes may have and whether they are regular or irregular shapes.

Black or white?

Choose a game to play.

Game 1: Odd one out

You need:
- two 1–6 dice
- squared paper and pencils
- ruler
- 12 counters

How to play
- Play with a partner.
- Each roll a dice. The player with the higher number chooses a section of shapes on the gameboard.
- Name and describe all 3 shapes in your section to win 3 points.
- Draw the shape you think is the odd one out. Justify your answer to win 2 points.
- Place a counter on that section.
- The winner is the player who collects the most points when all 12 sections have been selected.

Game 2: Guess my shape!

You need:
- two 1–6 dice
- squared paper and pencils
- ruler

How to play
- Play with a partner. Each roll a dice.
- If your number is higher, choose a shape on the board. Draw the shape secretly and put to one side.
- Your partner asks you up to 8 questions about the shape. You can only answer 'yes' or 'no'.
- When your partner has guessed the shape, they draw and name it. If it is correct:
  - ▶ within 3 guesses – 3 points
  - ▶ within 6 guesses – 2 points
  - ▶ for 8 guesses – 1 point.
- Your partner then chooses a shape for you to guess.
- The winner is the first player to collect 22 points.

Game 3: Your game

- Make up your own game using the gameboard.
- Can you think of a way to collect regular or irregular shapes as you move along?
- What are the rules for your game? Explain them to someone.

Please help your child by reading the instructions and playing the game together.

Unit 14 And finally ...

Assessment task 1

Resources

Dotted paper (4 × 4), colouring pencils, rulers.

Running the task

Encourage children to visualise the quadrilateral prior to drawing it. *Will it be a rectangle, a square or an irregular quadrilateral?* It is important that children are confident in the properties of quadrilaterals and understand that they can exist in any orientations. Children should identify all squares, rectangles and other quadrilaterals and draw the one with the largest perimeter. Children measure the sides of each shape including the ones with diagonal sides. They should notice that the diagonal lines are longer than the horizontal or vertical ones. Children measure the perimeter to the nearest centimetre and compare the results. Discuss the different units used to measure the shapes. Challenge children to use the actual values in centimetres and millimetres when measuring the shapes. Recap that 1 cm = 10 mm.

Emphasise the importance of working together as a pair and of working systematically. You could extend the task by asking children to identify all the right angles in the shapes with the longest perimeter. Children could also explore the horizontal and vertical sides the shape may have. You could challenge them to find the rectangle, square or equilateral triangle with the longest perimeter.

Evidencing mastery

When children are convinced that they have not only drawn a 2-D shape, but also the one with the longest possible perimeter, they show that they are confident in the properties of the shapes and how to measure perimeter. Children showing mastery can visualise the shapes in the dotted grid and identify the one that has the longest perimeter.

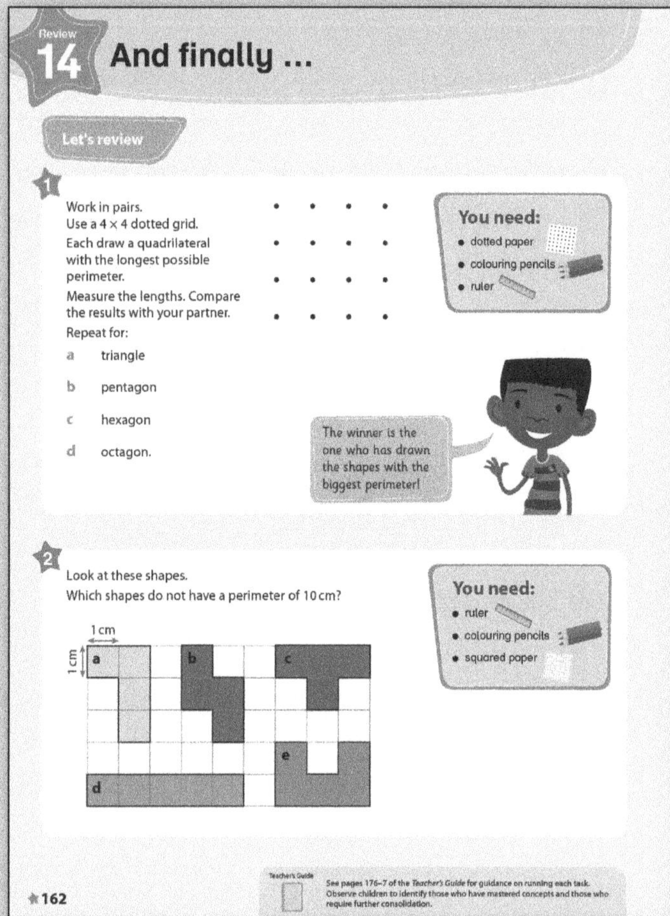
Review 14 And finally ...

Let's review

1 Work in pairs.
Use a 4 × 4 dotted grid.
Each draw a quadrilateral with the longest possible perimeter.
Measure the lengths. Compare the results with your partner.
Repeat for:

a triangle

b pentagon

c hexagon

d octagon.

You need:
- dotted paper
- colouring pencils
- ruler

The winner is the one who has drawn the shapes with the biggest perimeter!

2 Look at these shapes.
Which shapes do not have a perimeter of 10 cm?

You need:
- ruler
- colouring pencils
- squared paper

162

Teacher's Guide
See pages 176–7 of the *Teacher's Guide* for guidance on running each task. Observe children to identify those who have mastered concepts and those who require further consolidation.

Assessment task 2

Resources

Squared paper, ruler, colouring pencils.

Running the task

Children work in pairs. Prior to starting the task, revisit what compound shapes are and how they are formed. Children look at the shapes and firstly find the length of each side by counting the number of squares. Remind them to include all the sides of the shapes. They add all the sides to find the perimeter and identify the shapes which do not have a perimeter of ten centimetres.

Give children time to copy the shapes on to squared paper. Revisit some of the learning from previous work, e.g. ask them to mark a pair of parallel sides with an arrow head (>) and to explain how they know they are parallel. Listen for children who say that the squared paper shows that parallel sides stay the same distance apart, which is what parallel sides are. *What do all the shapes have in common?* Listen for children who notice that all the angles are right angles. Discuss regular shapes children may draw. Ask them to think of what a regular triangle is called (equilateral triangle), regular quadrilateral (square), regular pentagon and so on.

To extend the task, you could ask children to draw other shapes that have a perimeter of ten centimetres. *If you draw regular shapes, how long will each side be to give a perimeter of ten centimetres? Why is it difficult to draw a triangle and heptagon?* Listen for children who know that ten is not in the three or seven multiplication tables. Give children time to explore the task and be confident with their results. Throughout the task encourage them to explain their thinking and to generalise where possible.

Evidencing mastery

Children who can calculate the perimeter of each shape and use their calculations to identify which shapes do not have a perimeter of 10 cm, are showing clear evidence of mastery.

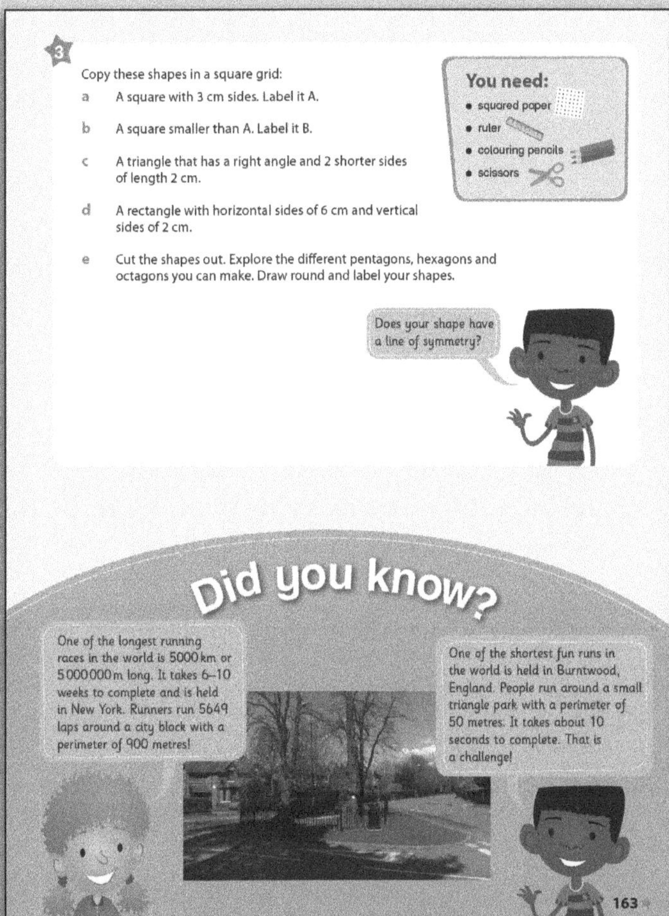

3

Copy these shapes in a square grid:

a A square with 3 cm sides. Label it A.

b A square smaller than A. Label it B.

c A triangle that has a right angle and 2 shorter sides of length 2 cm.

d A rectangle with horizontal sides of 6 cm and vertical sides of 2 cm.

e Cut the shapes out. Explore the different pentagons, hexagons and octagons you can make. Draw round and label your shapes.

You need:
- squared paper
- ruler
- colouring pencils
- scissors

Does your shape have a line of symmetry?

Did you know?

One of the longest running races in the world is 5000 km or 5 000 000 m long. It takes 6–10 weeks to complete and is held in New York. Runners run 5649 laps around a city block with a perimeter of 900 metres!

One of the shortest fun runs in the world is held in Burntwood, England. People run around a small triangle park with a perimeter of 50 metres. It takes about 10 seconds to complete. That is a challenge!

163

Assessment task 3

Resources

Squared paper, rulers, colouring pencils, scissors.

Running the task

Provide children with squared paper. Ask: *If one square is 1 cm long, how many squares will your shape be?* Children explore the different shapes they can draw. Ask them to place the ruler firmly on the paper before drawing the lines. Help children cut out the shapes and place them next to each other.

Extend the task by asking them to fold each shape. What do they notice? *Does one half overlap the other one? How many right angles does each shape have?*

Ask children to put some or all pieces together to make a new shape. *What is the largest number of right angles your shape can have? What is the smallest number of sides your shape can have?* To extend, children can describe their shape to their partner in four sentences. *Can you draw or name the shape without seeing it? Take turns and compare the shapes. Describe their properties. What do you notice? How do they differ?*

Evidence of mastery

Children who draw the shapes correctly and explore the different ways of making new shapes show a deep understanding of properties of 2-D shapes. Children who do not notice all the sides of the shapes or do not count them properly show that they need more practice in recognising irregular shapes in different positions.

Concepts mastered

- ☑ Children can draw 2-D shapes and describe their properties.
- ☑ Children can measure, compare, add and subtract lengths in metres, centimetres and millimetres. They can measure the perimeter of simple 2-D shapes.

Did you know?

Encourage discussion about the importance of knowing the perimeter of a park or running area. *Do you know anyone who has run a race? How long was it? How do you think they measured that distance?* Discuss the reasons so many people nowadays complete marathons, from raising money for charities, schools and hospitals to setting challenges for themselves.

Share interesting facts about the perimeter of different parks, e.g. Phoenix Park in Dublin is one of the largest walled city parks in Europe. Its perimeter wall is about 11 kilometres or 11 000 metres long. It was built 350 years ago as a royal deer park. You may link perimeter and distance to speed and time and discuss how different animals run the perimeter of the park at different times according to how fast or slow they run, e.g. a cheetah can run 11 kilometres in ten minutes, a deer in 15 minutes and a sloth in two days. Can children estimate how long the perimeter of their local park is and how long it would take them to run or walk around it?

1a Measuring in centimetres and converting to millimetres

You need:

- 30 cm ruler marked in cm and mm
- small items from the house
- paper and pencil

- Find 5 items from around the house which each measure less than 30 cm.
- Write a list of their measurements to the nearest centimetre.
- Convert your measurements to millimetres by counting in tens. If your toy measures 13 cm, count up 10 mm for every cm: 10, 20, 30 ... 120, 130 mm.

- Write your lengths in order of size from shortest to longest.
- Compare the cm measurements with the mm equivalents.
- What do you notice?

Please help your child by reading the instructions and doing the activity together.

1a Finding possibilities using £1, 10p and 1p coins

You need:

- 3 coins – £1, 10p and 1p
- pencil and paper
- a partner

- You and your partner must share these 3 coins between you.
- Who has which coins?
- Make a list or draw round the coins to show the different possibilities.
- Which of the arrangements of coins would you like to have?
- Explain why.

Please help your child by reading the instructions and doing the activity together.

1b Hundreds, tens and ones

Year 3 Unit 1 Homework 3

You need:
- digit cards 1–9
- paper and pencil
- a partner

- Each player draws a place-value grid like this:

100	10	1

- Spread out the digit cards face down on the table.
- Take turns to pick a card. Decide what value your number will have. It can be ones, tens or hundreds, e.g. if you pick a 3 it could be 3 hundreds, 3 tens or 3 ones.
- Once you have decided, write the number in your place-value grid. Put the digit card back on the table.
- Pick 2 more cards each. Write them in your place-value grid.
- The winner is the person who has created the largest number.
- Play a few times.

Talk about how to be a winner. Think about strategies to use and good positions for particular numbers.

Please help your child by reading the instructions and doing the activity together.

1b Combining hundreds, tens and ones

Year 3 Unit 1 Homework 4

You need:
- bag of coins (at least 5 × £1, 5 × 10p, 5 × 1p)
- paper and pencil

- Choose a small handful of coins from the bag without looking.
- Sort them into groups of coins with the same value.
- Write the value of each group.
- Add the amounts together to find the total in pence.
- Set your calculation out as a place-value addition.

300 + 20 + 3 = 323p

- Do this 3 times.
- Now try to make a large total without looking in the bag. Think which coins you will need more of. Think about how you can recognise these coins by touch.

Please help your child by reading the instructions and doing the activity together.

1c

Comparing volumes

Year 3 Unit 1
Homework 5

You need:

- measuring jug
- squash in another jug
- 4 glasses
- a grownup

- Together make up about a litre of squash in a jug or bottle.
- Use the measuring jug to measure out 225 ml of squash. Pour this into a glass.
- Measure and pour 150 ml, 250 ml and 175 ml of squash into the other 3 glasses. Make labels for each glass showing the volume of squash in it.
- Does each glass contain the same volume of squash? Order the glasses by volume from greatest to smallest.
- Now make each glass contain the same volume of squash. You will need to pour squash from the fuller glasses into the less full glasses. Write down how much squash you are moving between the glasses.
- How much does every glass contain at the end?

225 ml 150 ml 250 ml 175 ml

Please help your child by reading the instructions and doing the activity together.

1c

Inequality signs

Year 3 Unit 1
Homework 6

You need:

- Internet access or animal books
- pencil and paper

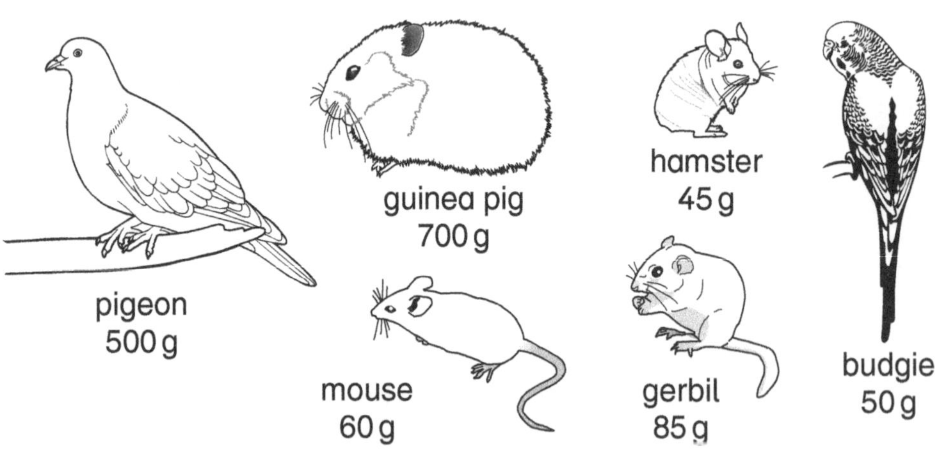

- Here are the masses of 6 small animals.
- Write their masses in order from greatest to smallest.
- Now use inequality signs to compare the masses, e.g. 500 g > 60 g.
- Use the Internet or books to find the masses of 6 other animals.
- Write some inequality statements about them.

Please help your child by reading the instructions and doing the activity together.

1d

Numbers used when measuring

Year 3 Unit 1
Homework 7

You need:

- ruler
- pencil and paper

Numbers are used for many different things. They are on measuring equipment too.

- Divide a large piece of paper into 4 sections. Give each section a different heading: 'length', 'capacity', 'mass' and 'time'.
- Look around your house to find numbers that are being used for these measures.
- Draw pictures of any equipment or labels or instructions you find. Make sure you put them in the correct section.
- Add drawings of other equipment you know or have used at school, even if you do not have them in your own house.

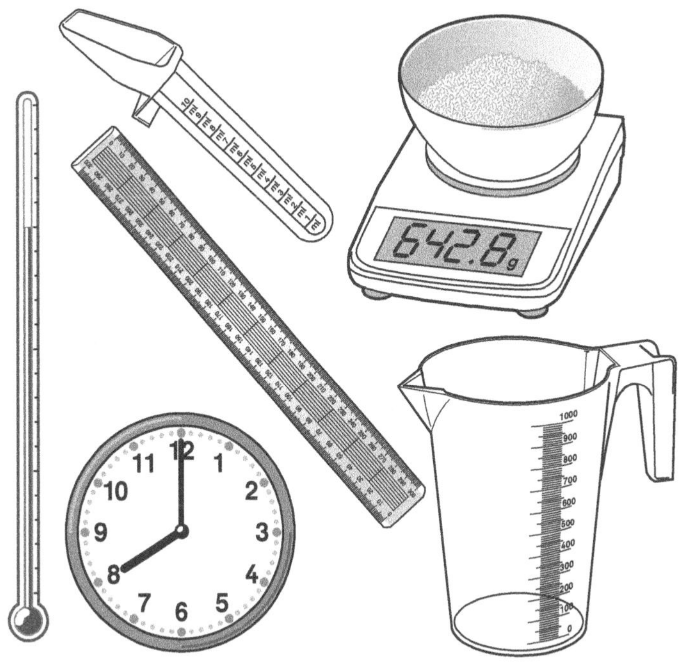

Please help your child by reading the instructions and doing the activity together.

1d

Ways to represent numbers

Year 3 Unit 1
Homework 8

You need:

- coloured pencils
- pencil and paper
- a grownup

- Choose a 2-digit number which is not a multiple of 10. Write it in the centre of a large piece of paper.
- Draw different ways of showing that number. Here is an example:

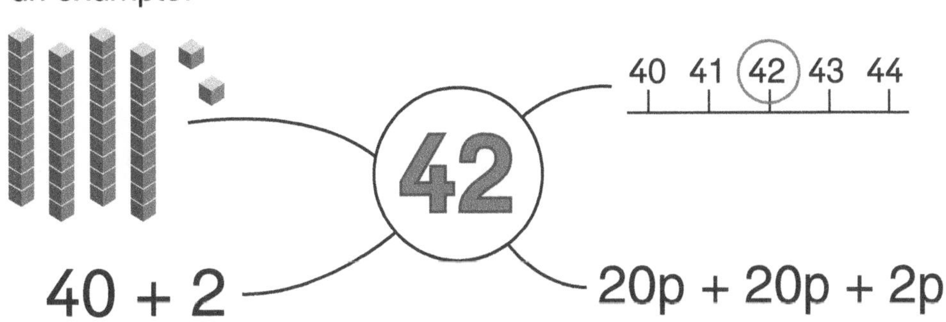

- Explain to the grownup what each drawing means. Can they add any other drawings?
- Look out for numbers around you when you are out and about. Make a list. Write where you saw them and what they were used for, e.g. bus numbers linked to a timetable.

Please help your child by reading the instructions and doing the activity together.

2a Adding near multiples of 10

Year 3 Unit 2
Homework 9

You need:

- 18 paper circles
- pencil and paper
- a partner

- Write these numbers on the paper circles: 8, 9, 18, 19, 28, 29. Make 3 sets.
- The aim is to race to 100 by adding these numbers.
- Shuffle the numbered paper circles. Arrange them face down in 2 rows, 1 row for each player.
- Start with a score of 20. Each player takes turns to turn over the next circle in their row. Add that number to your running score. Jot it down on paper.
- The player to reach 100 first is the winner.

Start at 20
Turn over 19 → 39
Turn over 8 → 47
Turn over 28 → 75 …

To add these numbers, you need to practise a **rounding and adjustment** strategy. To add 28 to another number, first add 30 and then subtract 2.

Please help your child by reading the instructions and doing the activity together.

2a Reducing prices by 39p using adjustment

Year 3 Unit 2
Homework 10

You need:

- pencil and paper

- All the items in this shop will be reduced in price by 39p. Find the new prices.

- Which items are now for sale at less than half the original price?
- Theo bought 2 items at the new reduced prices. He paid with £1 and received 23p change. Which items did he buy?
- Is there more than 1 possible answer?

Please help your child by reading the instructions and doing the activity together.

Adding using written methods

You need:

- pencil and paper

The post office has sorted letters into 8 bags for delivery.

Each post person takes 2 bags. Each person must deliver a certain number of letters.

Must deliver 557 | Must deliver 537 | Must deliver 555 | Must deliver 556

- Work out which post person took which bags.
- Use a written addition strategy to try out different combinations of bags until each post person has the total number of letters they need.

Please help your child by reading the instructions and doing the activity together.

Subtracting 3-digit numbers

You need:

- drink containers
- pencil and paper

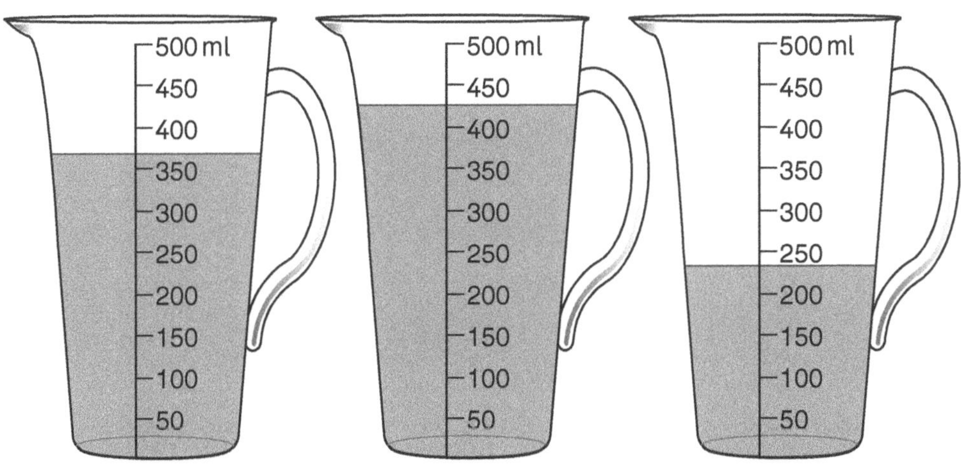

362 ml | 425 ml | 239 ml

- Look at the volume of juice in each jug.
- During a party, 153 ml is drunk from each jug.
- Work out how much juice is left in each jug. Draw Base 10 pictures to help you carry out the subtractions.
- Mark the new levels on the measuring jugs.
- Look at drink containers in your kitchen. How many millilitres of drink does each hold?
- Subtract 153 ml from those volumes too!

Please help your child by reading the instructions and doing the activity together.

3a

Adding 2p, 4p and 8p to create totals

You need:
- pencil and paper

- The local post office only has stamps valued 2p, 4p and 8p.
- Work out if you can combine the stamps to pay for these letters. Use the fewest stamps possible for each letter.
- Is it possible to pay for all the letters?
- If not, which amounts cannot be made? Can you explain why?
- How many different ways can you find to pay for a letter costing 16p?

15p

16p

17p

18p

19p

20p

Please help your child by reading the instructions and doing the activity together.

3a

Showing information on a pictogram

You need:
- squared paper and pencil
- a grownup

- With your grownup, find a safe place to stand where you can see cars driving along a road.
- Count the number of cars of different colours including silver, red, green and black.
- Keep a tally to show how many of each colour drove past.
- At home, show your findings on a pictogram. Think of a symbol you can use to represent 2 cars.
- How can you show 3 cars on your pictogram, if 1 symbol stands for 2 cars?
- Which colour car did you see most of?
- How many more silver cars did you see than green cars?
- Write 2 facts about your findings.

silver	
red	
green	
black	

Please help your child by reading the instructions and doing the activity together.

3b

Finding arrays at home

Year 3 Unit 3
Homework 15

You need:

- food packaging
- pencil and paper

- With a grownup's permission, have a look at home for packaging which stores food in arrays.

$2 \times 3 = 6$
$3 \times 2 = 6$

- Draw a picture of each array.
- Write 2 multiplication facts to describe each array.
- Next time you are at the supermarket, look out for more arrays.
- Draw them when you get home. Write the matching multiplications alongside them.

Please help your child by reading the instructions and doing the activity together.

3b

Drawing arrays for multiplication facts

Year 3 Unit 3
Homework 16

You need:

- ruler
- squared paper and pencil

- List as many multiplication facts as you can which have a product of 30.
- Draw a rectangle made of small squares to represent each multiplication fact.
- How many rectangles have you drawn for 30?
- Try to work out which numbers create lots of rectangles.
- Try 24, 27 and 32. Explain your findings.

3

10 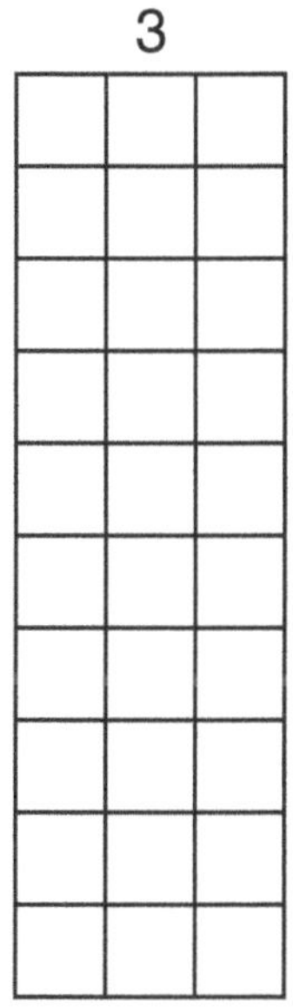 $3 \times 10 = 30$

Please help your child by reading the instructions and doing the activity together.

3c

School pudding combinations

You need:

- pencil and paper

There are 4 available choices for pudding at school today:

- shortbread biscuit
- milkshake
- ice-cream
- fruit

- You are allowed to choose 2 different items. Which 2 would you choose?
- How many different possible combinations of 2 items are there?
- List them.
- If you were allowed to choose 3 items, would there be more or fewer possible combinations?

Please help your child by reading the instructions and doing the activity together.

3c

Sharing items fairly

You need:

- small items, e.g. dried pasta pieces, grapes or raisins
- pencil and paper

- Count out 12 items.
- Imagine you are sharing these between 2 people. How many would they get each?
- Record this as a division: 12 ÷ 2 = _______ each.
- Explore which numbers of people you could share 12 items between so that each person has the same amount.
- Now try this with 15 items. Do you think there will be more ways to share these because 15 is a bigger number?
- Explore different numbers. Try to come up with a rule.
- How do you know if a number can be shared equally between lots of different numbers of people?

Please help your child by reading the instructions and doing the activity together.

4a

Investigating cuboids

Year 3 Unit 4
Homework 19

You need:

- empty boxes of all sizes (from cereals, biscuits, toothpaste ...)

- Carefully open up each box along the glued seams so that the cardboard lies flat on the table.
- Look at each of these opened cuboids. These are called 'nets'. What do you notice?
- How many faces does each box have? What shape are these faces?
- Are the faces always joined up in the same arrangement?
- Find different ways of arranging the faces on the opened net so that they still create a cuboid when they are folded up again.
- How would the nets of a cube be different from a cuboid?

Please help your child by reading the instructions and doing the activity together.

4a

Searching for 3-D shapes

Year 3 Unit 4
Homework 20

You need:

- pencil and paper
- a grownup

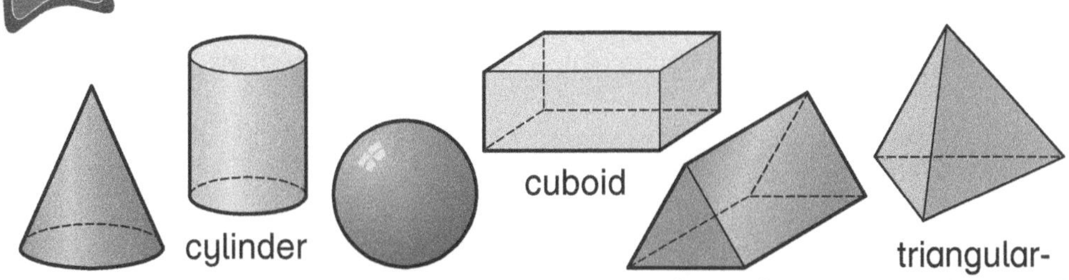

- You are going to look for these 6 shapes.
- Make yourself a reminder sheet of these 3-D shapes.
- Look around the house for objects that are these shapes.
  - ▶ Look in food cupboards at boxes, tins and packaging.
  - ▶ Look in bedrooms at bottles, creams and containers.
  - ▶ Look in play areas at toys.
- Which shapes are easy to find? Which are harder? Why?
- Think how products are moved from a warehouse to the shop. Would it be sensible to package cereals and baked beans in spherical shaped containers?

Please help your child by reading the instructions and doing the activity together.

4b Identifying angles

Year 3 Unit 4
Homework 21

You need:

- ruler
- 3 coloured pencils
- Internet access or reference books
- pencil and paper

- Design your own flag. Here is an example:

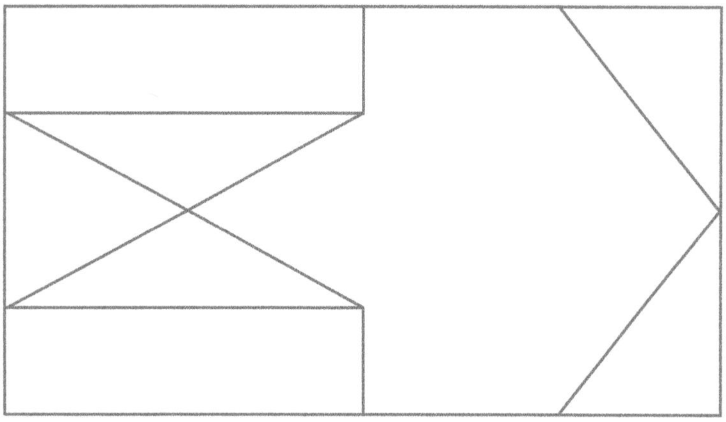

- Make a right angle tester from the corner of a piece of A4 paper.
- Use your right angle tester to find the right angles in your flag design. Colour them in the first colour.
- Then colour all the angles **less** than a right angle in a second colour.
- Colour all the angles **more** than a right angle in a third colour.
- Which type of angle are there most of? Is there a reason for this?
- Have a look at flags from different countries on the Internet or in books.
- Search for right angles.

Please help your child by reading the instructions and doing the activity together.

4b Making 2-D shapes

Year 3 Unit 4
Homework 22

You need:

- 5 drinking straws (or pencils all of the same length)
- ruler
- 3 coloured pencils
- pencil and paper

- Arrange the straws into a house shape like this.
- Draw a diagram of your shape.
- Use 3 different colours. Mark the right angles, angles greater than a right angle and angles smaller than a right angle.

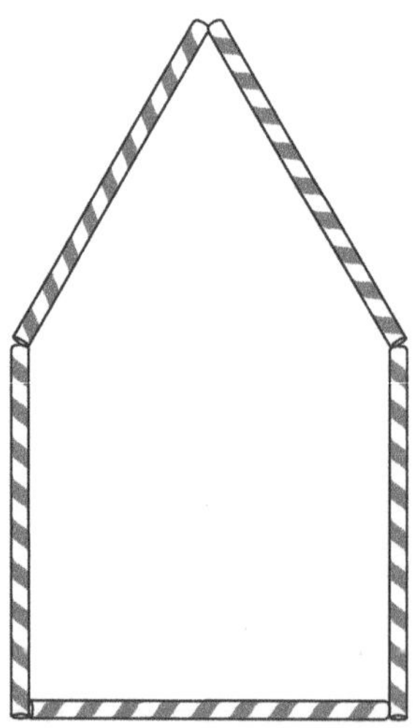

- Now rearrange your 5 straws into a different shape.
- Again, draw a diagram and colour the different angles.
- Make 4 different shapes in total.
- Is it possible to make a shape with no right angles, 2 angles smaller than a right angle and 2 angles greater than a right angle?

Please help your child by reading the instructions and doing the activity together.

5a

Counting in fours and eights

You need:

- pencil and paper

Amy is inviting the whole class to her party. There will be 32 children in total.

The party room has some tables that seat 4 children and some tables that seat 8 children.

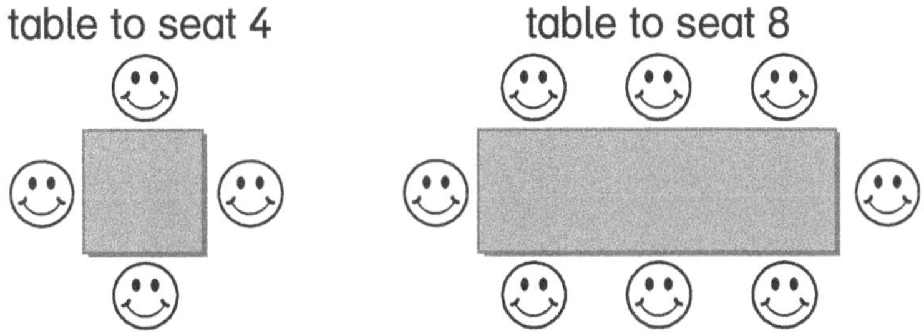

- Which tables should Amy use? Find different ways to set out the room so that each child has a seat at a table.
- Amy has decided to join the tables together in a long line. Find out whether it is better to join 4 large tables of 8 or 8 small tables of 4. Which arrangement will seat the most children?
- Remember, some seats will be lost where the tables join together. Draw diagrams to help with your thinking.

Please help your child by reading the instructions and doing the activity together.

5a

Counting in steps of 50

You need:

- 12 pieces of card or paper
- pencil and paper
- a partner

- Make a set of 12 number cards with these numbers on: 200, 250, 300, 350, 400, 450, 500, 550, 600, 650, 700, 750.
- Shuffle the number cards. Place them face down on the table in a pile.
- Take turns to turn over the top number of the pile.
- Count how many steps of 50 from zero are needed to reach that number. Score 1 point for each step.

= 7 steps, so score 7 points

- Keep a record of the points scored.
- When all the cards have been revealed, the winner is the person with the most points.

Please help your child by reading the instructions and doing the activity together.

5b Making 3-digit numbers with hundreds, tens and ones

You need:
- green, yellow and red coloured pencils
- paper
- scissors
- bag or box
- a partner

- Make a set of 27 small circles (like counters).
- Colour 9 of them green – these will represent hundreds.
- Colour 9 of them yellow – these will represent tens.
- Colour 9 of them red – these will represent ones.
- Put these place-value circles into a small bag or box and shake them.
- Pick out a small handful of circles.
- What number do they represent?
- Sort out the hundreds, tens and ones. Count the number of each.
- Do you always make a 3-digit number? When would you not?
- Have a few practice goes. Then play this as a game with a partner. The winner makes the smallest number!

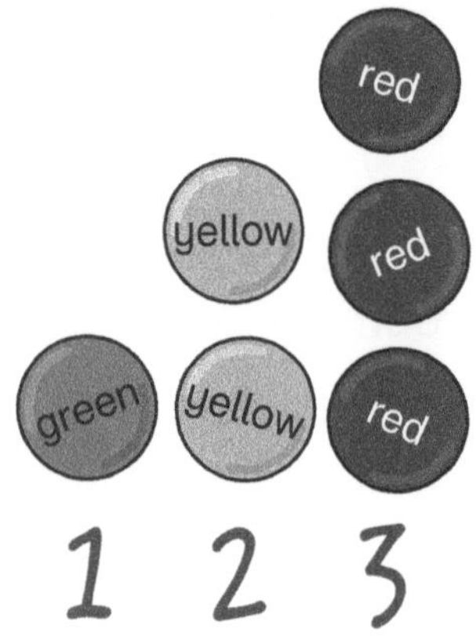

Please help your child by reading the instructions and doing the activity together.

5b Comparing and ordering numbers

You need:
- 1– 6 dice (3)
- pencil and paper
- a grownup

- Roll 3 dice. Record the digits rolled, e.g. 3, 5 and 2.
- How many different 3-digit numbers can you make with these digits? Make a list.
- Roll a different set of 3 digits. Again list the numbers you can make.
- Try this 3 more times so you have 5 lists in total.
- Put the numbers in each list into order with the smallest first.

Do you always get the same amount of numbers in each list? When might you get fewer? Look at your results. Talk about any patterns you notice with your grownup.

Please help your child by reading the instructions and doing the activity together.

5c Counting forwards and backwards in tenths

You need:
- 1–6 dice
- 1 counter or coin
- pencil and paper
- a partner

- Draw a big number line from zero to 4 marked in tenths. Remember there are 10 tenths in each whole 1.

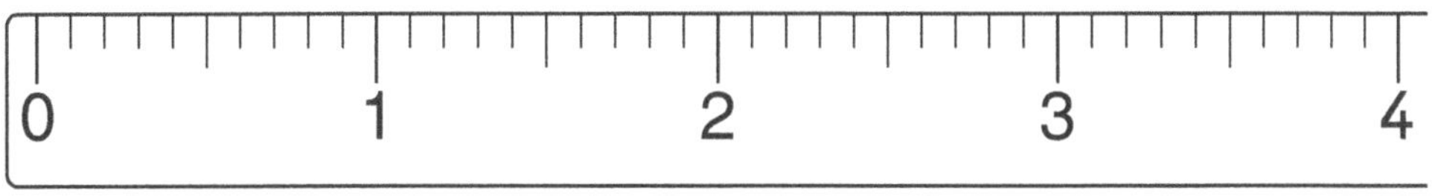

- The game starts with a counter on the number 2. Both players are moving the same counter.
- One player is subtracting tenths with every dice number rolled, aiming to get the counter to zero.
- The other player is adding tenths with every dice number rolled, aiming to get the counter to 4.
- Take turns to roll the dice. Add or subtract that number of tenths and move the counter. Keep a note of the new number reached each time, e.g. $2\frac{3}{10}$.
- Keep playing until 1 person reaches their target or until an agreed number of turns have been taken. Who is closest to their target?

Please help your child by reading the instructions and doing the activity together.

5c Adding tenths to make 1 whole

You need:
- fruit
- bowl
- spoon
- pencil and paper

To make 1 whole fruit drink
Orange: $\frac{3}{10}$ squash, the rest water
Blackcurrant: $\frac{2}{10}$ squash, the rest water
Apple: $\frac{5}{10}$ squash, the rest water
Lime: $\frac{1}{10}$ squash, the rest water

- How many tenths of water are needed for each drink? Remember you need $\frac{10}{10}$ in total to make 1 whole fruit drink.

Making 1 whole fruit salad
$\frac{4}{10}$ orange
$\frac{1}{10}$ banana
$\frac{2}{10}$ pear
The rest is apple.

- How many tenths of apple are needed?
- Try making a fruit salad with your own quantities of fruit.
- Count 1 spoonful as $\frac{1}{10}$. Write down how much of each fruit you use.
- Remember you need $\frac{10}{10}$ in total to make 1 whole fruit salad.

Please help your child by reading the instructions and doing the activity together.

6a

Adding multiples of 100

Year 3 Unit 6
Homework 29

You need:
- 1–6 dice
- pencil and paper
- a partner

- Each player chooses a start number. It must be a 3-digit number between 123 and 456. Write it down.
- Take turns to roll the dice. Whatever number the dice lands on tells you the number of hundreds to add to your start number, e.g. roll 3 and so add 300.
- Complete the addition mentally by counting on. Write the number you have reached.
- Which player is closest to 1000?
- Keep going until 1 player's score crosses 1000.
- Try with different starting numbers.
- Does the starting number matter?

Which dice numbers do you hope to roll? Explain why.

Please help your child by reading the instructions and doing the activity together.

6a

Adding 3-digit numbers

Year 3 Unit 6
Homework 30

You need:
- pencil and paper

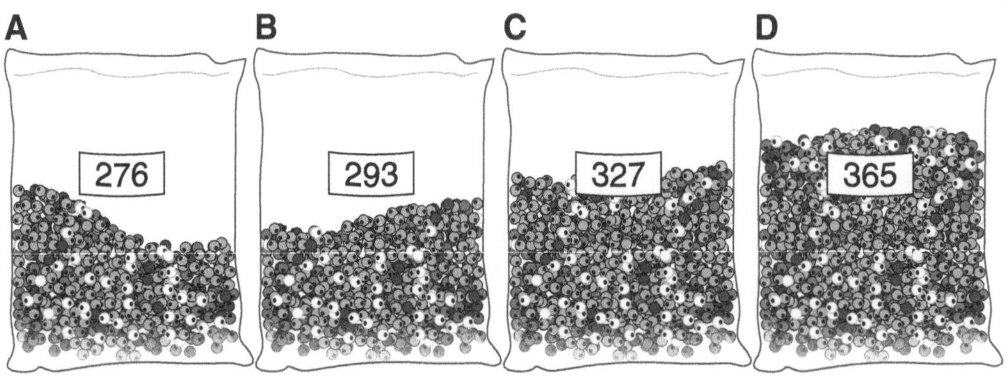

- Euan has these 4 large bags of beads. He has agreed to give 2 bags to his friend Mohinder.
- Work out all the possible combinations of 2 bags. Also work out the totals when the beads in each pair of bags are added together.
- Euan would like them both to have roughly the same number of beads.
- Which 2 bags should Euan give Mohinder for this to happen?

Please help your child by reading the instructions and doing the activity together.

6b

Investigating differences

Year 3 Unit 6
Homework 31

You need:

- pencil and paper

- Choose 2 numbers in the range 368 and 373. Write them in the circles.
- Find the difference between the 2 numbers. Write it into the box above.
- Repeat this for other pairs of numbers in the range given.
- Can you find differences from 1 to 5?
- Is there more than 1 way to make some of the differences?

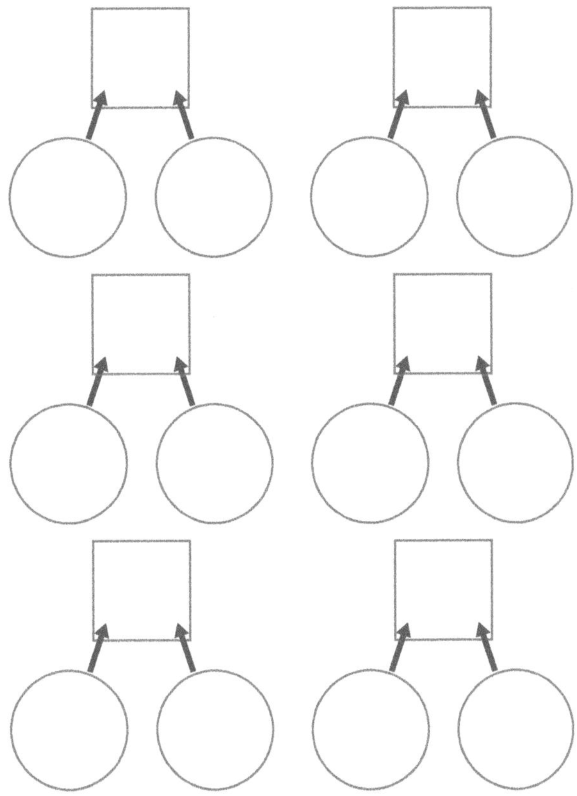

Please help your child by reading the instructions and doing the activity together.

6b

Compare mass by finding differences

Year 3 Unit 6
Homework 32

You need:

- Internet access or animal books
- pencil and paper

- Find the difference in mass between the lion and the polar bear.
- Which 2 animals have a difference in mass of 106 kg?
- How much heavier is the dolphin compared with the lion?

Animal mass in kilograms	
Giraffe	800
Polar bear	475
Dolphin	425
Zebra	384
Brown bear	278
Lion	175

- Which 2 animals have the smallest difference in mass? What is the difference?
- Find 3 other differences. Write a sentence explaining each one.
- Use the Internet or animal books to find the mass of farm animals.
- Compare these and order them from heaviest to lightest.

Please help your child by reading the instructions and doing the activity together.

7a

Adding multiples of 10

Year 3 Unit 7
Homework 33

You need:
- pencil and paper

- Start at 216 and add 30.
- Keep adding 30 and recording the numbers you arrive at.
- Can you see any patterns? Describe them.
- Does the pattern in the tens and ones column repeat? How long does it take before 1 section is repeated?
- Now start on 216 and add 40 each time. What do you notice?
- Compare the two patterns.
- Does the pattern in the tens and ones column repeat? How long does it take before 1 section is repeated?
- Add other multiples of 10 (e.g. 20, 50, 60) to 216 and compare results.

Please help your child by reading the instructions and doing the activity together.

7a

Add and subtract hundreds, tens and ones

Year 3 Unit 7
Homework 34

You need:
- pencil and paper

- Start with 537. Draw a representation of it on the paper using Base 10 pictures.
- You must reach the target number of 142 by adding or subtracting hundreds or tens or ones. How many steps does it take you to reach 142?

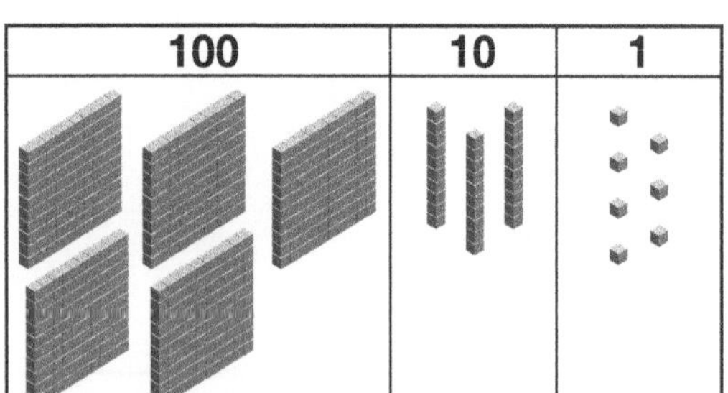

537, subtract 400, add 10, subtract 5 and reach the target in 3 steps.

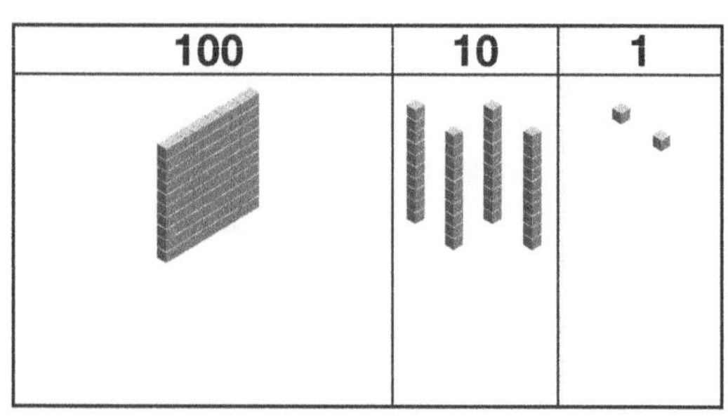

142

- Does it always take the same number of steps?
- Try different 3-digit start numbers that are larger than 500. Count the number of steps needed to reach 142.
- What do you discover?
- If the 3-digit start number was less than 500, would it take fewer steps?

Please help your child by reading the instructions and doing the activity together.

7b

Comparing unit and non-unit fractions

Year 3 Unit 7
Homework 35

You need:

- ruler
- scissors
- pencil and paper

- Cut some paper strips each measuring 24 cm in length and 2 cm wide.
- Take 1 strip and draw lines on it to divide it into 3 equal parts.

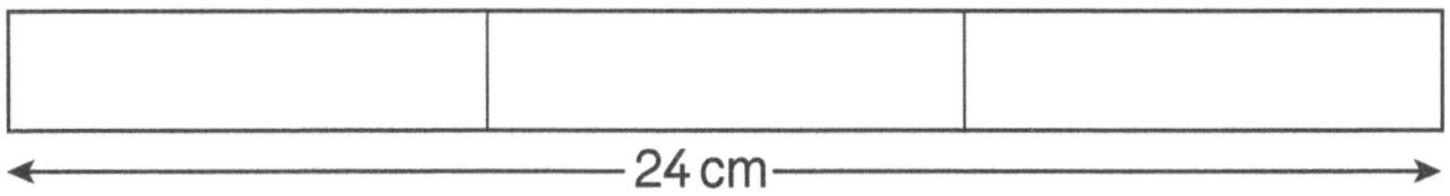

- How long is $\frac{1}{3}$ of the strip? How long is $\frac{2}{3}$ of the strip?
- Take a second strip. This time divide it into 4 equal parts.
- Calculate the length of $\frac{1}{4}$, $\frac{2}{4}$ and $\frac{3}{4}$ of the strip.
- Repeat for a strip divided into 6 equal parts. Find the length of $\frac{1}{6}$, $\frac{2}{6}$, $\frac{3}{6}$, $\frac{4}{6}$ and $\frac{5}{6}$ of the strip.
- Repeat for a strip divided into 8 equal parts. Find the length of $\frac{1}{8}$, $\frac{2}{8}$, $\frac{3}{8}$, $\frac{4}{8}$, $\frac{5}{8}$, $\frac{6}{8}$ and $\frac{7}{8}$ of the strip.
- Look at your results. Can you see any number patterns? Explain them.

Please help your child by reading the instructions and doing the activity together.

7b

Shading fractions of a rectangle

Year 3 Unit 7
Homework 36

You need:

- squared paper
- coloured pencils
- ruler
- pencil and paper

- Draw a rectangle on the squared paper. It should be made up of 8 small squares in a 4 × 2 arrangement.

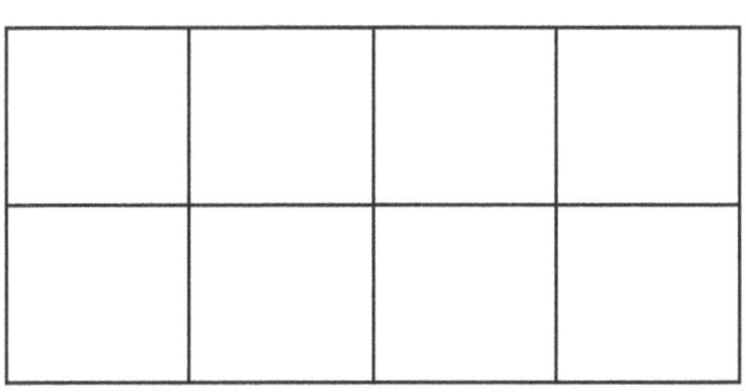

- Shade $\frac{1}{8}$ of the rectangle in 1 colour.
- Draw more rectangles. Find different ways to shade $\frac{1}{8}$ of the rectangle. You may only colour whole squares. How many different ways are there?
- Now find different ways to shade $\frac{2}{8}$ of the same rectangle shape.
- Will there be a greater number of ways? Is it possible to find them all?

Please help your child by reading the instructions and doing the activity together.

7c Fraction puzzle

Year 3 Unit 7
Homework 37

You need:

- pencil and paper

Jack has a chocolate bar made of 12 pieces.

He shares it with his friends.

He gives $\frac{1}{4}$ to Annabelle.

He gives $\frac{1}{6}$ to Freddie.

He gives $\frac{1}{3}$ to Kapil.

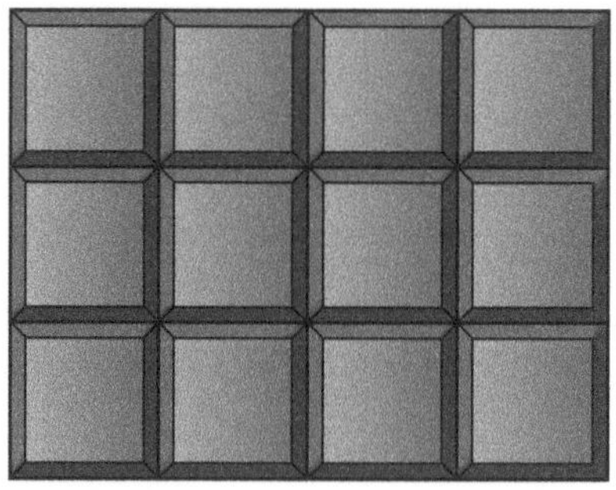

- How many pieces does he give to each person?
- What fraction of the whole bar does he have left? How many pieces is that?
- When Jack gets home he gives 1 of the remaining pieces to Mum. He eats the rest himself. What fraction of the original bar does he actually eat?

Please help your child by reading the instructions and doing the activity together.

7c Adding tenths to make 1 whole

Year 3 Unit 7
Homework 38

You need:

- digit cards 1–9 (2 sets)
- pencil and paper
- a partner

- The aim of the game is to create pairs of 'tenth' fractions which add to a total of 1, e.g. $\frac{3}{10} + \frac{7}{10} = 1$.
- Take turns to pick a digit card. The number picked is the numerator in a tenth fraction.

- Write the fraction.
- Keep picking cards and writing tenth fractions.
- Look out for pairs of fractions that add to a total of 1, e.g. $\frac{3}{10}$ and $\frac{7}{10}$.
- When you find a pair like this, join them on your paper. Each fraction can only be used once in a pair.
- The winner is the first to make all the possible pairs which total 1.

Please help your child by reading the instructions and doing the activity together.

8a

Halving prices

You need:

- pencil and paper

- The clothing shop has a half-price sale. Work out how much each item will cost in the sale.
- Mum wants to go shopping! She has £60 to spend.
- Which 3 sale items could she choose? List different possibilities.
- How much would it cost to buy every item in the sale?
- How much more money would Mum need?

Please help your child by reading the instructions and doing the activity together.

8a

Making cookies

You need:

- pencil and paper

Chocolate chip cookies

Makes 20

100 g butter (melted)
125 g caster sugar
200 g self-raising flour
100 g chocolate (chopped)
1 egg

- Adjust the recipe to make only 10 cookies.
- Write the new ingredients list.
- What did you have to do to each measurement?
- Now adjust the original recipe to make 40 cookies.
- Write the new ingredients list.
- What did you have to do to each measurement?

To enjoy eating the cookies!

- Get a grownup to help.
- Choose how many cookies to make.
- Measure out the ingredients. Mix them all together.
- Make small flattened balls of mixture.
- Place them on a baking tray lined with greaseproof paper.
- Cook them in an oven at a temperature of 170°C for 10 minutes.

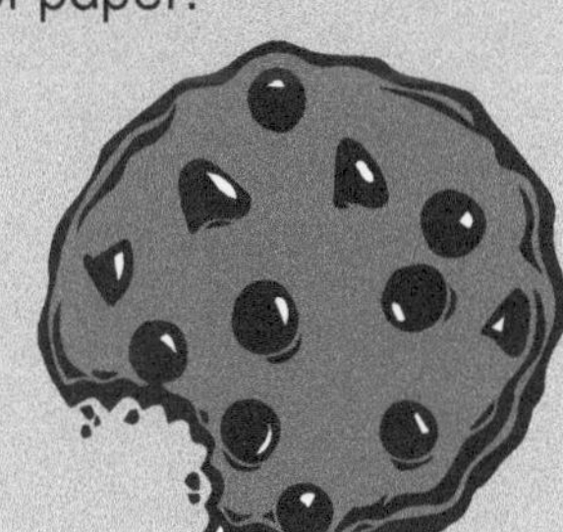

Please help your child by reading the instructions and doing the activity together.

Year 3 Unit 8
Homework 41

8b Ways to multiply by 5 and 20

You need:
- pencil and paper

A set of numbers enter the function machine.

Each number is first multiplied by 10 and then halved.

Numbers in

2
4
5
10
12
20

Numbers out

- Find the numbers that come out of the function machine.
- Another machine with only 1 action creates the same 'in' and 'out' numbers. What is the action on the front?
- Make your own function machine for '×10 and then double'.
- Test it with different 'in' numbers. Write the numbers that come out.
- Which single function could replace '×10 and then double'?

Please help your child by reading the instructions and doing the activity together.

Year 3 Unit 8
Homework 42

8b Multiplying by 10 and 100

You need:
- pencil and paper

A special tree grows in the school grounds.

Thick branches grow from a central trunk.

10 small twigs grow from every thick branch.

There are 10 green leaves on every small twig.

- Draw sketches to help you answer these questions:
  - If the tree has 4 thick branches, how many small twigs are there?
  - If the tree has 7 thick branches, how many green leaves are there?
  - If there are 600 green leaves, how many thick branches must there be?
  - If the tree has 80 small twigs, how many thick branches and how many green leaves are there?
- Describe the relationship between thick branches, small twigs and green leaves.

Please help your child by reading the instructions and doing the activity together.

8c Scaling up and down

Year 3 Unit 8
Homework 43

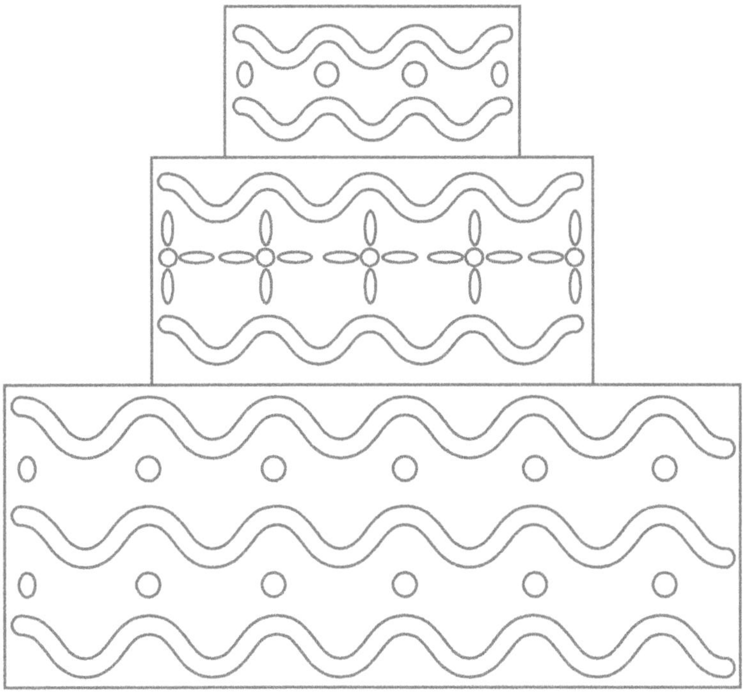

You need:
- ruler
- pencil and paper
- book

- This party cake has 3 tiers. Measure the size of each tier.
- Use scaling up to draw a party cake twice as big.
- Now draw a party cake half the size of the original cake.
- Find a book in your house. Measure its front cover.
- Draw a diagram of the front cover which is half the size of the actual book.

Please help your child by reading the instructions and doing the activity together.

8c Missing numbers

Year 3 Unit 8
Homework 44

You need:
- pencil and paper
- a partner

- One number is missing from each of these calculations.
- Can you work out what the number is?
- Check that it works for each calculation.

$\square \times 3 = 24$ $\quad$ $4 \times 12 = 4\square$

$1\square = 2 \times 9$ $\quad$ $\square \div 2 = 4$

$10 \times \square = \square 0$

- Now write another set of 5 mystery calculations which each have the same missing number.
- Challenge your partner to work out the missing number.

Please help your child by reading the instructions and doing the activity together.

Straight lines around us

You need:

- ruler
- pencil and paper

- Look around the house for different straight lines and edges. Look on objects and furniture.
- Decide if the lines you see are:

▶ parallel	▶ horizontal
▶ perpendicular	▶ vertical

- Divide a sheet of paper into 4 quarters. Draw examples of each type of straight line that you find.
- Try to find at least 4 examples of each, e.g. parallel lines could be the top and bottom edges of a picture frame.

Please help your child by reading the instructions and doing the activity together.

Types of straight lines

You need:

- ruler
- coloured pencils
- pencil and paper

- Study the picture. Colour the different types of lines that you can see.

▶ parallel = red	▶ horizontal = green
▶ perpendicular = blue	▶ vertical = yellow

- Do you need to colour the same line in more than 1 colour? Can you explain why?
- Are any of the lines coloured in just 1 colour?
- Is it possible to add a detail to the picture to include a straight line that is only coloured once. Can you add a horizontal line which is not parallel or perpendicular?
- Make other drawings of your own using straight lines.

Please help your child by reading the instructions and doing the activity together.

9b

Turning an image

You need:

- card
- scissors
- ruler
- pencil and paper

- Draw the initial letter of your name on card in block writing. Use a ruler and straight lines only.
- Cut the letter out to use as a template.
- Now draw a line of these letters on your paper. First draw around the template. Then turn it $\frac{1}{4}$, $\frac{1}{2}$ or $\frac{3}{4}$ of a turn either anticlockwise or clockwise and draw around it again.
- Make and explore different patterns. Here are some examples for the letter J:

Draw | $\frac{1}{4}$ turn clockwise | draw | $\frac{1}{4}$ turn clockwise | draw | $\frac{1}{4}$ turn clockwise ...

Draw | $\frac{3}{4}$ turn anticlockwise | draw | $\frac{1}{2}$ turn clockwise | draw | $\frac{3}{4}$ turn anticlockwise | draw | $\frac{1}{2}$ turn clockwise ...

Please help your child by reading the instructions and doing the activity together.

9b

Using turning vocabulary

You need:

- blindfold
- a partner

- Ask your partner to put on a blindfold so they cannot see.
- Now you must direct them!
- Use this vocabulary:
  - forward (any number) of steps
  - backwards (any number) of steps
  - $\frac{1}{4}$ turn
  - $\frac{1}{2}$ turn
  - $\frac{3}{4}$ turn
  - full turn
  - clockwise
  - anticlockwise
- For example, forward 2 steps, $\frac{1}{4}$ turn anticlockwise, forward 5 steps, $\frac{1}{4}$ turn clockwise, stop.
- Give 1 instruction at a time. Direct your partner around the room or to a particular place such as the fridge.
- Which turns do you use a lot? Which are less useful?

Please help your child by reading the instructions and doing the activity together.

10a

Writing 3-digit numbers in words

Year 3 Unit 10
Homework 49

You need:
- pencil

Gita is counting the number of fans in some of the stands at Wembley Stadium.

She uses an automatic clicker machine which counts in hundreds, tens and ones.

Stand 1	Stand 2	Stand 3	Stand 4	Stand 5	Stand 6
			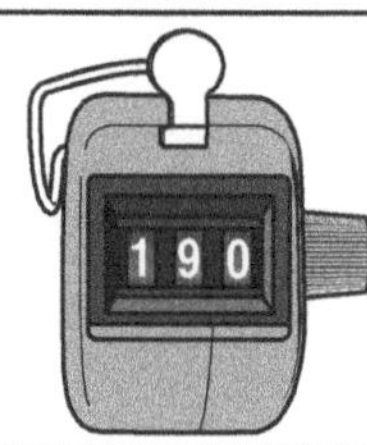		

- Write the number of fans in each stand in words rather than numerals.
- Which stand has the greatest number of fans?
- Which number is made of only hundreds and tens?
- Does stand 5 or stand 1 have more fans?
- How many fewer fans are in stand 6 compared with stand 2?

Please help your child by reading the instructions and doing the activity together.

10a

Digital and analogue times

Year 3 Unit 10
Homework 50

You need:
- digital clock or watch
- pencil and paper
- a grownup

- Choose 5 events that usually happen on 1 of your weekend days. Or choose something that you know is going to happen, e.g. get up, play in the park, go out for lunch, watch TV, go to bed.
- Write them in a list.
- As these 5 events happen, ask an adult to help you look at the time on a digital watch. Write it beside the event on your list, e.g. get up 8:09 a.m.
- Now show these 5 digital times on these analogue clock faces.

			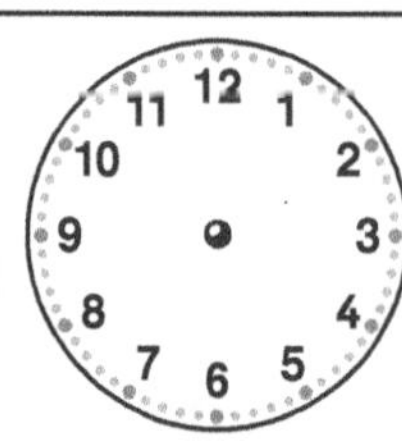		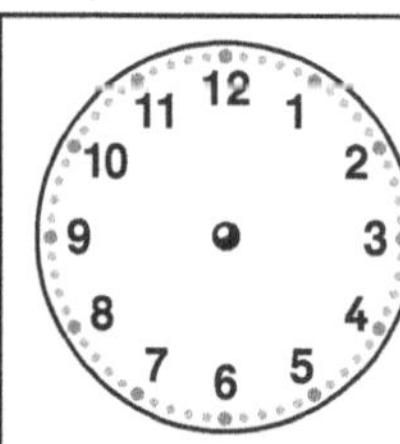
Event: Get up	Event:	Event:	Event:	Event:	Event:
Time: 8:09 a.m.	Time:	Time:	Time:	Time:	Time:

Please help your child by reading the instructions and doing the activity together.

10b

Partitioning 3-digit numbers into multiples of 10

You need:
- pencil and paper

- Choose a 3-digit multiple of 10. 420
- Partition your chosen number into hundreds and tens. 400 + 20
- Now partition further into individual hundreds and tens. 100 + 100 + 100 + 100 + 20
- Can you partition the same number into different chunks, making sure each chunk is a multiple of 10? 200 + 220 or 50 + 50 + 300 + 20
- Find at least 10 different ways to partition your chosen number.
- Repeat with another 3-digit multiple of 10.
- Estimate how many different ways you might be able to partition your number into multiple of 10 chunks.

Please help your child by reading the instructions and doing the activity together.

10b

Collecting tenths

You need:
- 1–6 dice
- squared paper
- pencil
- a partner

- Draw 5 rectangles on your squared paper. Each one must enclose 10 small squares as shown here.

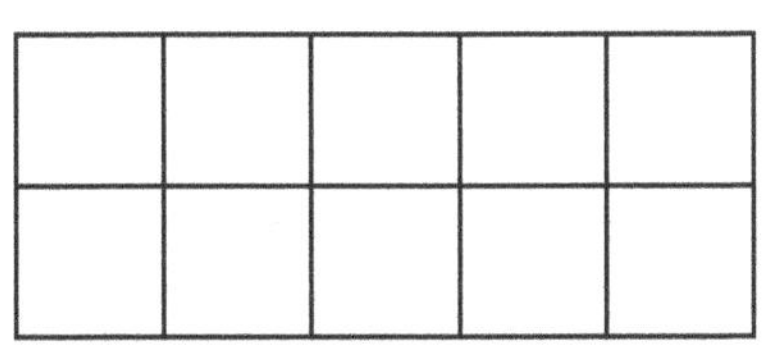

- Each rectangle is made up of 10 tenths. You have drawn 5 rectangles so there are 50 tenths altogether.
- Roll the dice and colour that many tenths of the first rectangle.
- See how many rolls of the dice are needed before all 10 tenths have been coloured.
- Estimate how many rolls of the dice will be needed to colour the remaining 4 rectangles (40 tenths in total).
- Carry on rolling the dice to find out. How close was your estimate?
- You could play this against a partner. The winner colours the agreed number of tenths first.

Please help your child by reading the instructions and doing the activity together.

11a

Adding 3-digit numbers using mental methods

Year 3 Unit 11 Homework 53

You need:

- pencil and paper for jottings

- The motor mechanics have ordered some new equipment for their workshop.
- How many of each item do they now have?

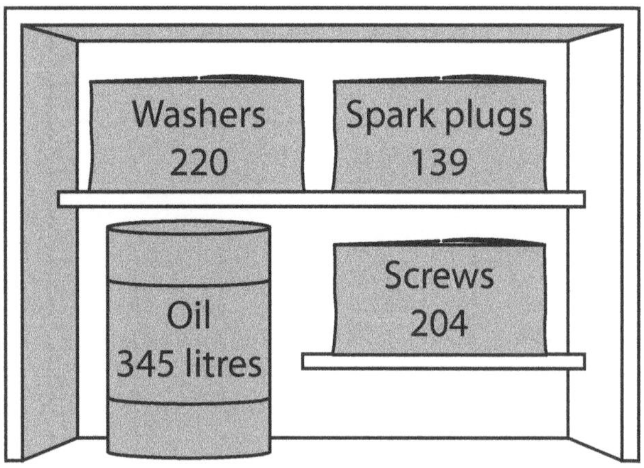

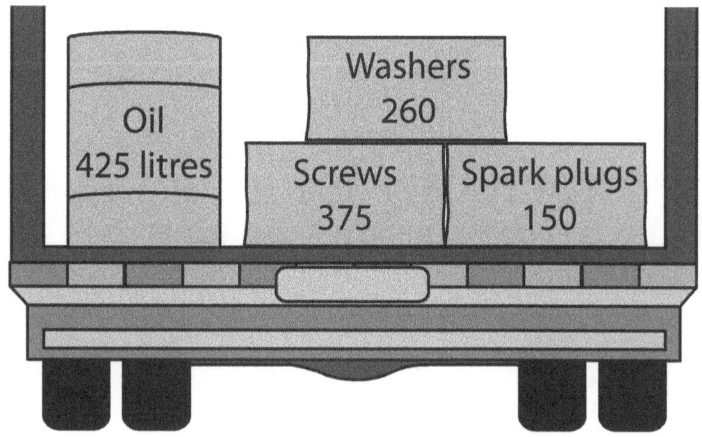

- The screws and washers need to be paired – 1 screw with 1 washer.
- Do they have the same number of each to do the pairing?
- If not, what should they do?

Please help your child by reading the instructions and doing the activity together.

11a

Adding 3-digit numbers using written methods

Year 3 Unit 11 Homework 54

You need:

- Internet access
- pencil and paper
- a grownup

Some big cats have arrived at the safari park in safe containers. There is a lion, a tiger, a lynx, a leopard, a hyena and a puma.

Their masses are written on the containers, but the animal names have rubbed off.

- Find out which big cat is in each container.
- Write the names beside the correct container.
- Can you convert the pounds to kilograms using an Internet conversion tool? Ask a grownup to help

The lynx is the lightest of the cats.

The lynx and leopard have a combined mass of 145 pounds.

The lion and puma together have a mass of 525 pounds.

The hyena is around half the mass of the puma.

The tiger is the heaviest of the big cats.

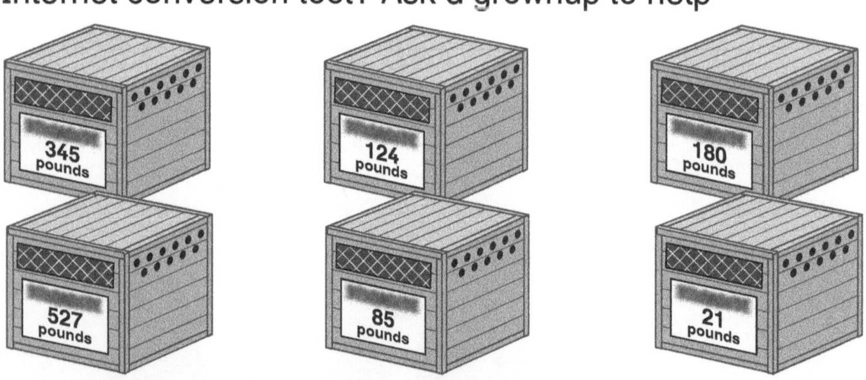

Please help your child by reading the instructions and doing the activity together.

11b

Counting up to find a difference

Year 3 Unit 11
Homework 55

You need:
- Internet access or shop
- pencil and paper for jottings

Amelia is checking stock at the local supermarket.

She counts the number of items left on each shelf.

Then she calculates how many more need to be ordered from the warehouse.

Item	Number left on shelf	Total number required	Number to be ordered?
Cans of baked beans	467	500	
Packets of dried pasta	623	840	
Bottles of lemonade	382	525	
Cartons of orange juice	502	780	

- Count up to calculate how many more of each item is needed.
- Which item on the shelf has the largest reorder number?
- Use the Internet or look in a shop to find out the approximate price of a carton of orange juice and a bottle of lemonade. Will it cost more to restock the bottles of lemonade or the cartons of juice?

Please help your child by reading the instructions and doing the activity together.

11b

Subtracting 3-digit numbers using written methods

Year 3 Unit 11
Homework 56

You need:
- 1–6 dice
- pencil and paper
- a partner

- Decide which person will collect odd differences and who will collect even differences.
- Each player rolls a dice 3 times to create a 3-digit number.
- Compare the numbers. Whose is larger?
- Subtract the smaller number from the larger number using a written subtraction method.
- Is the difference odd or even?
- The player collecting odd differences scores 1 point for each odd difference made.
- The player collecting even differences scores 1 point for each even difference made.
- Repeat the game a number of times.
- Is 1 player more likely to win than the other, or is it a fair game?

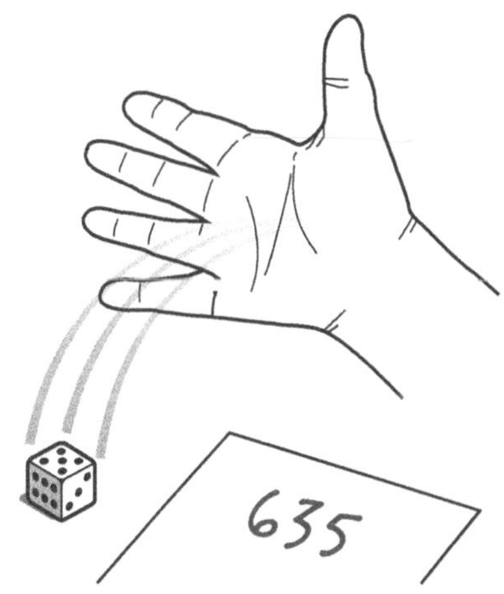

Please help your child by reading the instructions and doing the activity together.

12a Making 999 with hundreds, tens and ones

You need:

- £1 coins × 9, 10p coins × 9, 1p coins × 9
- small bag (or pot)
- pencil and paper
- a partner

- Each player copies out this blank set of 10 frames.

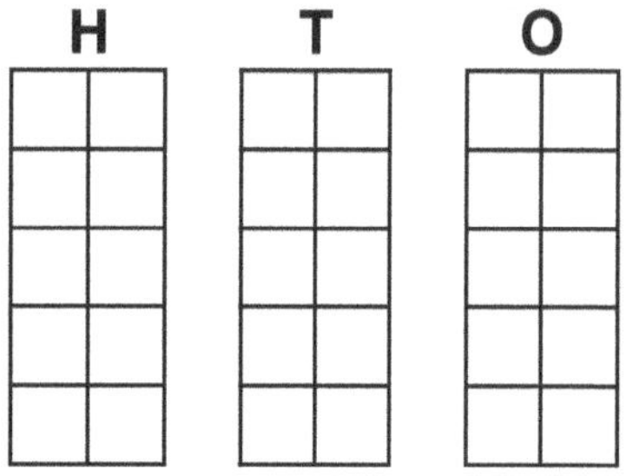

- Take it in turns to pick 3 coins from the bag without looking.
- Depending on the coins, shade the corresponding cells on the 10 frames.

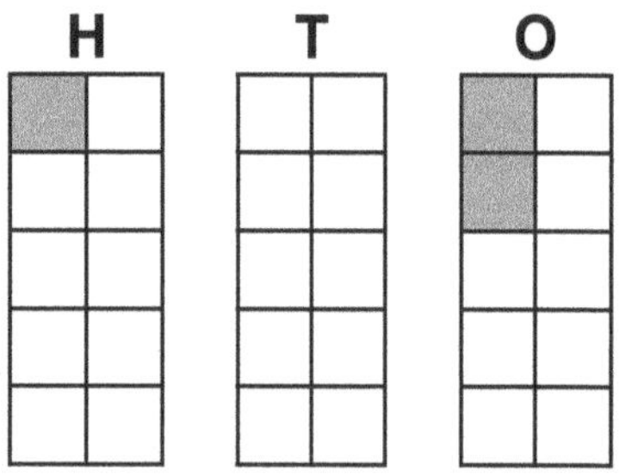

- Return the coins to the bag for the next player's turn.
- Keep picking sets of 3 coins from the bag and shading cells on the frames.
- The first player to shade the number 999 is the winner.

Please help your child by reading the instructions and doing the activity together.

12a Measuring length in cm and mm

You need:

- 0–30 cm ruler, showing mm divisions
- small items from your bedroom
- pencil and paper

- Look closely at your ruler.
- You can see that 1 centimetre (cm) is made up of 10 millimetres (mm). Each mm is $\frac{1}{10}$ of a cm.
- Measure the length of 5 small items (less than 30 cm in length) from your bedroom.
- Write the measurements in different ways. Show them in a diagram like the one here.
- How many more tenths of a cm need adding to each length to make the next whole cm?

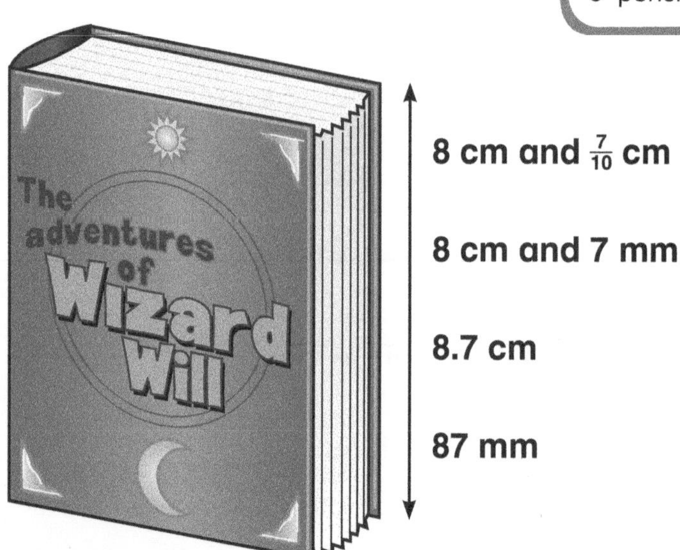

Add another $\frac{3}{10}$ cm to make 9 cm

Please help your child by reading the instructions and doing the activity together.

12b Making, comparing and ordering thirds and sixths

You need:

- small pieces of paper
- card and pencil
- scissors
- sharp pencil and paperclip
- pencil and paper
- a partner

- Each player draws a set of 6 fractions, each on a separate small piece of paper. They must all have 3 or 6 as the denominator (the number on the bottom) and a space for the numerator.

- Make the spinner out of card by placing a sharp pencil on the dot at the centre through the end of the paperclip. Flick the paperclip to select a number.
- Take turns to spin for numerators (the number on the top) for the fractions you have written. Each fraction must have a smaller number on top and a larger number on the bottom. If you roll a number you cannot use, miss that go.
- When each player has a set of 6 fractions, compare them.
- Who has the largest fraction? Who has the smallest?
- Put your set of fractions in order from smallest to largest.
- Now talk to your partner about how to merge all your fractions together into a single ordered list.

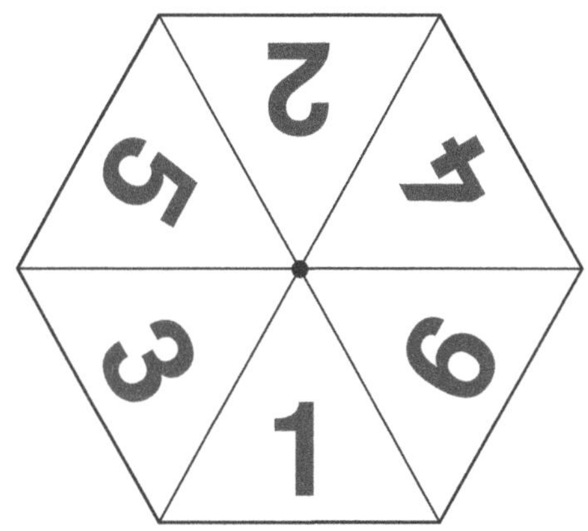

Please help your child by reading the instructions and doing the activity together.

12b Halves, quarters and eighths

You need:

- scissors
- ruler
- pencil and paper

- Cut out 6 strips of paper like this:

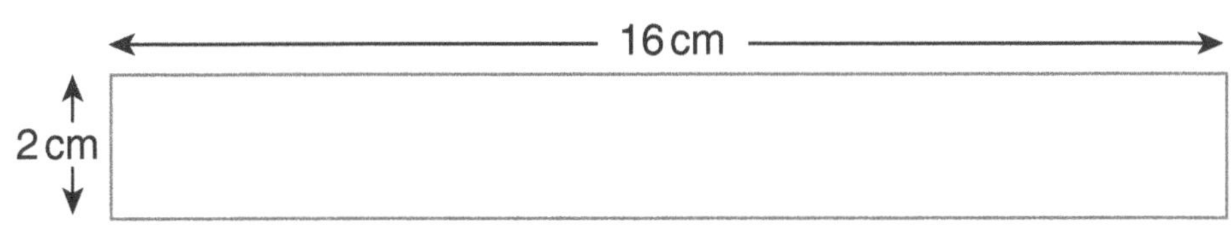

- Keep 1 strip whole. Using division to help you, mark and then cut each strip to show the fractions in the box.
- Make sure each strip is labelled with the fraction it shows and its length, e.g. '$\frac{1}{2}$ of 16 cm = 8 cm'.
- Now look at the pieces of each strip that are left over.
- Measure them. Then try to work out what fraction of 16 cm each shows.
- You can use your whole 16 cm strip to help with your thinking.

$\frac{1}{2}$ of 16 cm
$\frac{1}{4}$ of 16 cm
$\frac{1}{8}$ of 16 cm
$\frac{3}{4}$ of 16 cm
$\frac{5}{8}$ of 16 cm

Please help your child by reading the instructions and doing the activity together.

12c Fractions equivalent to $\frac{1}{4}$

Year 3 Unit 12
Homework 61

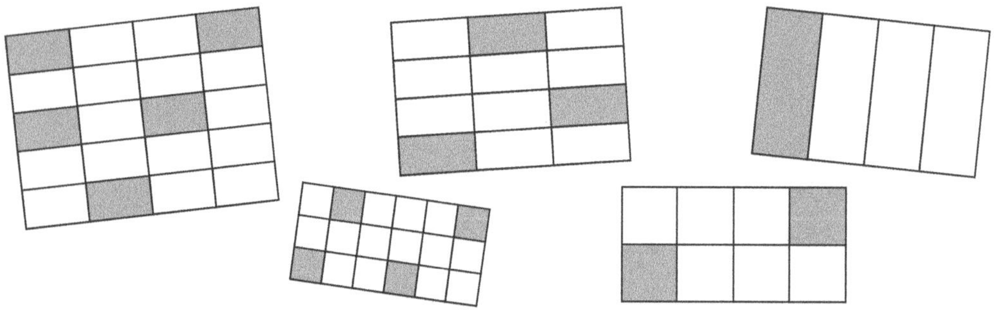

You need:

- pencil and paper
- a grownup

- What fraction of each rectangle has been shaded?
- Count the shaded parts to provide the numerator (number on top) and count the total number of parts to provide the denominator (number on the bottom).
- Write the fraction next to each shape.
- Now write the fractions in a list.
- Can you put them into an order? Discuss the order you have chosen with a grownup.
- Can you see any patterns? Describe them.
- If the next rectangle is split into 24 parts, how many parts do you think will be shaded?
- Each of these fractions is equal to $\frac{1}{4}$ because the numerator (the number of parts shaded) is $\frac{1}{4}$ of the denominator (the total number of parts). Discuss this with a grownup.

Please help your child by reading the instructions and doing the activity together.

12c Adding and subtracting eighths

Year 3 Unit 12
Homework 62

You need:

- 32 counters (or 5p coins)
- sharp pencil and paperclip
- ruler
- scissors
- pencil and paper
- a partner

- Each player draws 2 grids of 8 equal squares to fit their counters.

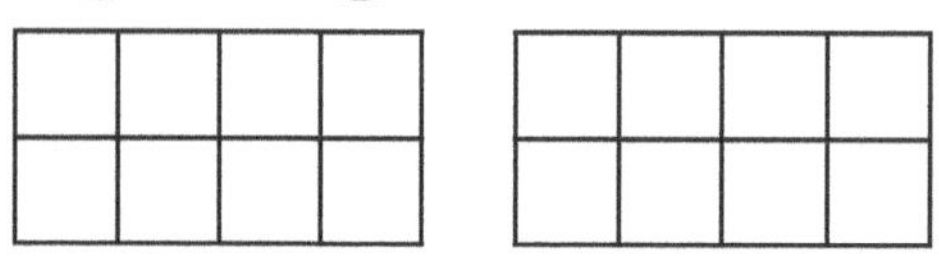

- Make the spinner by placing the sharp pencil on the centre through the end of the paperclip.
- Place 8 counters on 1 grid, 1 counter per small square. Each counter represents $\frac{1}{8}$.
- Look at your grids. You have 1 grid full showing $\frac{8}{8}$ or 1 whole. The other grid is empty showing zero.
- Take turns to spin the spinner. Either add or subtract that number of eighths from your grids, e.g. spin $-\frac{3}{8}$ and remove 3 counters, spin $+\frac{1}{8}$ and add 1 counter.
- Agree how many spins each player will have.
- When the game is over, work out the fraction shown by your counters. You might have 1 whole and some eighths.
- Can you write this fraction in a different way? Is there a fraction equivalent to this?

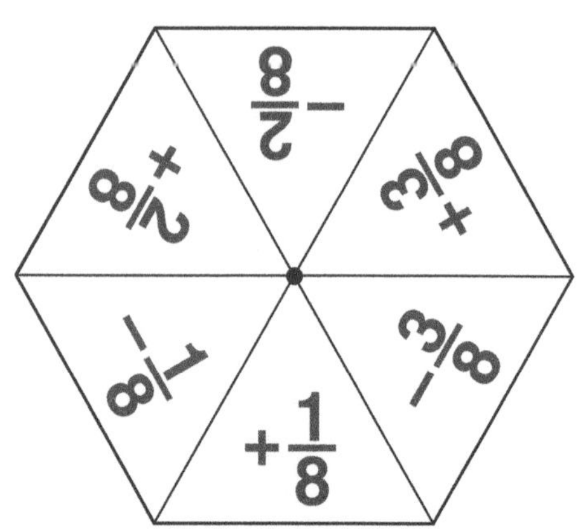

Please help your child by reading the instructions and doing the activity together.

13a Grid method of multiplication

Year 3 Unit 13
Homework 63

You need:

- pencil and paper
- a grownup

Sammy's family is going on a trip to MagicLand.

They need to choose 1 of these meal packages.

There are 2 adults and 3 children in the family. They need food for 6 days.

	Adult	Child
Package 1: breakfast, lunch and dinner	£35.00 per day	£20.00 per day
Package 2: breakfast and dinner	£20.00 per day	£12.00 per day

- Use the grid method to calculate the total cost of each package.
- How much more expensive is Package 1 compared to Package 2?
- Buying lunch separately at the theme park would cost £15 per person per day.
- Is it cheaper to buy Package 1 or to buy Package 2 and get lunch separately at the theme park each day?
- Explain your thinking and working out to a grownup.

Please help your child by reading the instructions and doing the activity together.

13a Written multiplication methods

Year 3 Unit 13
Homework 64

You need:

- pencil and paper

- Choose a 2-digit number between 35 and 65, e.g. 42. It must not include any zeros.
- Use a written multiplication method to multiply your number by 2, 3, 4, 5 and 6.
- Look at your answers and compare them.
- Can you see any patterns? Explain why they have resulted.
- Put your answers in order from smallest to largest.
- What is the difference between each of the answers?

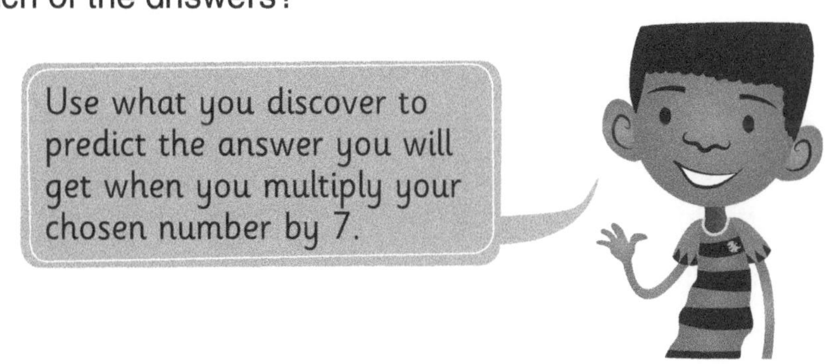

Please help your child by reading the instructions and doing the activity together.

13b

Using arrays to show divisions

Year 3 Unit 13
Homework 65

You need:

- squared paper
- ruler
- pencil and paper

- On your squared paper, draw rectangles which enclose 36 small squares.
- Each array you have created could be used to represent a division where the dividend is 36.
- Write all the divisions possible for the rectangles you have drawn.
- Are there 2 divisions for each rectangle?
- Jack says '37 is a bigger number than 36, so there will be more rectangles and more divisions for 37'. Is he right? Explain your answer.

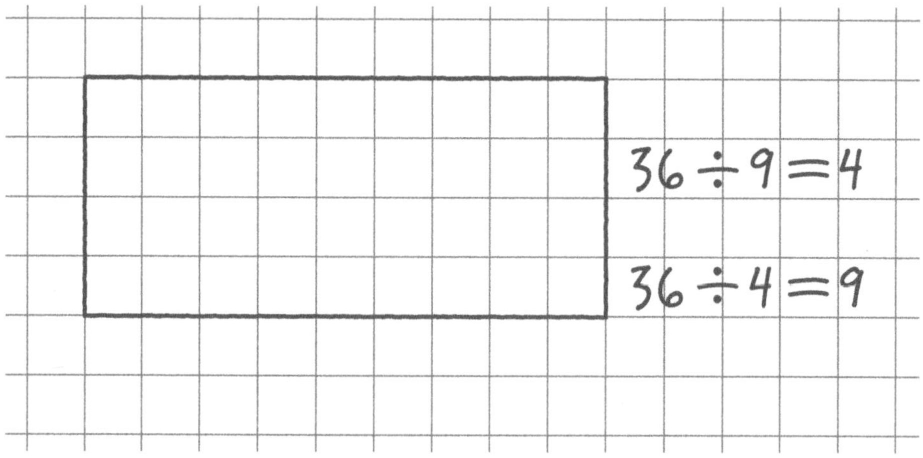

Please help your child by reading the instructions and doing the activity together.

13b

Compact division

Year 3 Unit 13
Homework 66

You need:

- pencil and paper

- There are 4 lengths of string measuring 96 cm, 84 cm, 90 cm and 76 cm.

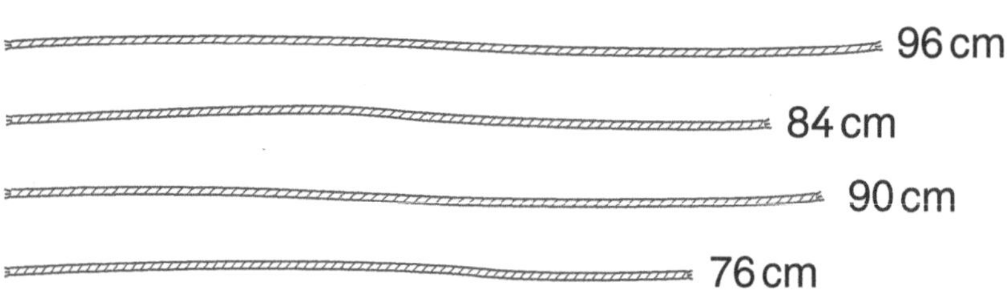

- You can choose to have $\frac{1}{3}$ of one of the lengths, $\frac{1}{4}$ of another, $\frac{1}{5}$ of another and $\frac{1}{6}$ of another.
- You are trying to end up with the longest possible length of string when you add the 4 sections together at the end.
- Choose which fraction of each length to have. Use a written division method to calculate the lengths you would be given. Round any answers to the nearest whole centimetre.
- Which divisions give you the longest possible length?
- What about the shortest possible length?

Please help your child by reading the instructions and doing the activity together.

14a

Making and drawing 2-D shapes

Year 3 Unit 14
Homework 67

You need:

- string
- scissors
- felt tip pen
- ruler
- pencil and paper

- Cut a piece of string exactly 36 cm long.
- Use a felt tip pen to put marks along the string. Work from one end and put a mark every 3 cm to the other end. This should create 12 equal sized sections.
- Arrange the string on the table to make a triangle. Sketch the triangle you create on paper, showing the markers.
- Make different triangles. For each triangle you make, there must be a marker at each corner. Look at the diagram.

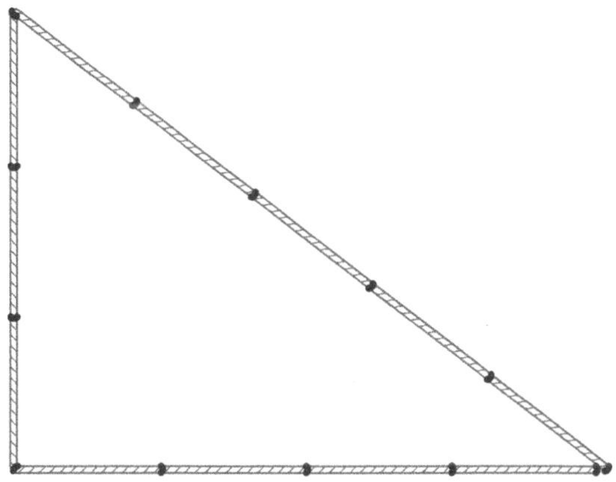

- Now try to make other shapes with the string. Then draw them. You can make regular and irregular shapes.
- Label each drawing with its 2-D shape name.

Please help your child by reading the instructions and doing the activity together.

14a

Drawing quadrilaterals

Year 3 Unit 14
Homework 68

You need:

- ruler
- coloured pencils
- pencil and paper

- This circle has 8 equally spaced dots around its curved side.
- Join any 4 dots using a ruler. How many different quadrilaterals (shapes with 4 straight sides) can you draw in this way?
- You can use this circle and choose a different colour for each shape or you can copy out lots of these blank circles first and draw each shape in its own circle.

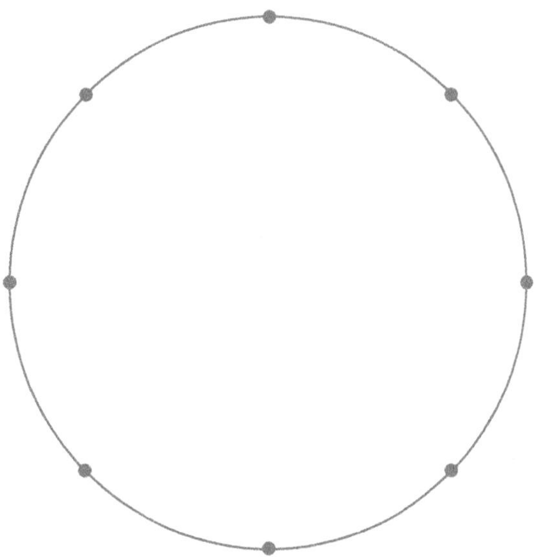

- Explore other 2-D shapes you can make by joining 3 or more dots. Can you draw a hexagon? A heptagon? An octagon?

Please help your child by reading the instructions and doing the activity together.

14b Shapes with the same area but different perimeters

You need:
- cm squared paper
- ruler
- pencil and paper

- Draw shapes which enclose 12 small centimetre squares on your squared paper.
- Start with rectangles, but then draw other shapes too.
- Each of the 12 small squares must have at least 1 side in contact with the side of another small square – they cannot just meet at the corner.
- Work out the perimeter of each shape you have drawn by counting around the outside of the enclosed centimetre squares.

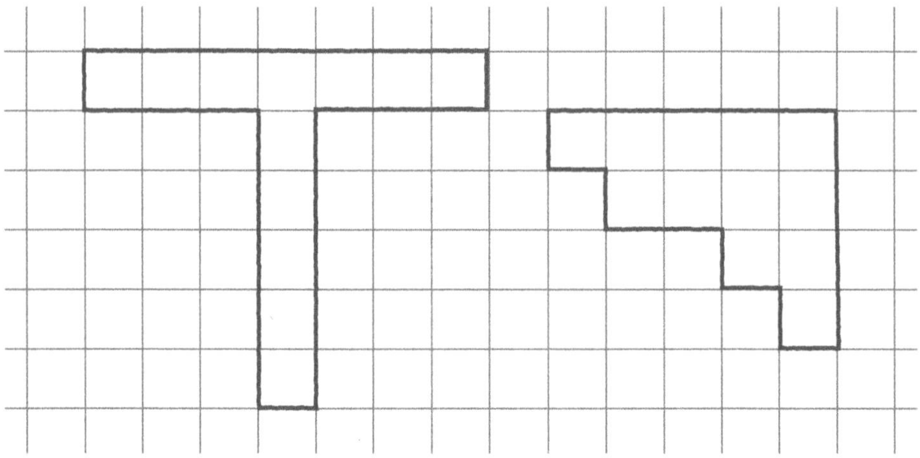

- Try to arrange the 12 small squares to create the shape with the longest perimeter and the shape with the shortest perimeter.

Please help your child by reading the instructions and doing the activity together.

14b Finding perimeters of objects

You need:
- pillow or cushion
- ruler
- pencil and paper

- Here is some beading – it is lots of beads strung together to decorate things.
- It costs £1.50 per 10 cm. You can only buy it in lengths which are multiples of 10 cm.

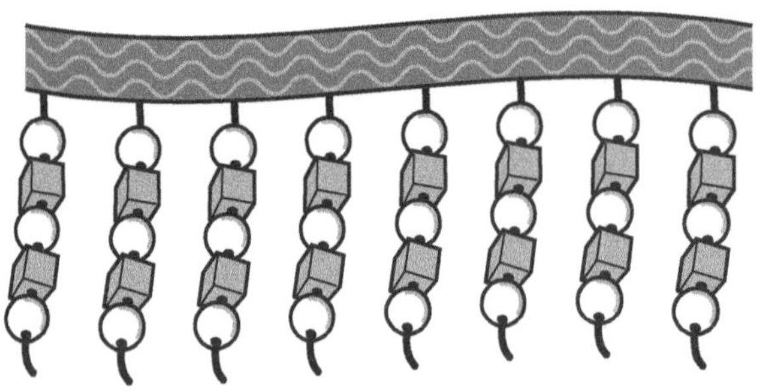

- Imagine you would like some of this beading to go all the way around the edge of your pillow.
- Work out the length of beading you need for your pillow. Work out the amount you would need to buy. How much would it cost?
- Repeat this for cushions of other sizes in your house.
- You can also use this beading to go around the edge of sofas and chairs.
- Choose 3 other items in your house which could have beading around their edge (perimeter).
- Work out the length of beading required for each, the amount you would need to buy and the cost.

Please help your child by reading the instructions and doing the activity together.

Homework sheets answers

Homework 1 1a

Measuring in centimetres and converting to millimetres

Notice that the digits have moved to the left and a zero has appeared, e.g. 24 cm → 240 mm.

Homework 2 1a

Finding possibilities using £1, 10p and 1p coins

Possible arrangements of the 3 coins are: £1, 10p / 1p; £1, 1p / 10p; 10p, 1p / £1; £1 / 10p, 1p; 10p / £1, 1p; 1p / £1, 10p

Homework 3 1b

Hundreds, tens and ones

To win, put the largest digits into the highest value columns.

Homework 4 1b

Combining hundreds, tens and ones

To make a large total, try to pick lots of £1 coins. They are thicker than the 10p and 1p coins.

Homework 5 1c

Comparing volumes

Pour 25 ml from the 225 ml glass into the 175 ml glass.

Pour 50 ml from the 250 ml glass into the 150 ml glass.

Now each glass contains 200 ml of squash.

Homework 6 1c

Inequality signs

700 g, 500 g, 85 g, 60 g, 50 g, 45 g

Various comparisons possible.

Homework 10 2a

Reducing prices by 39p using adjustment

84p → 45p, 58p → 19p, 97p → 58p, 64p → 25p, 71p → 32p, 87p → 48p

The items now priced at 19p (bricks), 25p (rings), 32p (robot).

Theo bought the items now priced at 45p (teddy) and 32p (robot) or at 58p (train) and 19p (bricks) as they both total 77p.

Homework 11 2b

Adding using written methods

557 = 134 + 423

537 = 123 + 414

555 = 213 + 342

556 = 244 + 312

Homework 12 2b

Subtracting 3-digit numbers

209 ml, 272 ml, 86 ml juice left in each jug.

Homework 13 3a

Adding 2p, 4p and 8p to create totals

15p not possible

16p = 8p + 8p

17p not possible

18p = 8p + 8p + 2p

19p not possible

20p = 8p + 8p + 4p

You can only make even number totals when combining even numbers (2, 4 and 8 are all even).

16p = 8p + 8p, 8p + 4p + 4p, 8p + 4p + 2p + 2p, 8p + 2p + 2p + 2p + 2p, 4p + 4p + 4p + 4p, 4p + 4p + 4p + 2p + 2p, 4p + 4p + 2p + 2p + 2p + 2p, 4p + 2p + 2p + 2p + 2p + 2p + 2p, 2p + 2p + 2p + 2p + 2p + 2p + 2p + 2p

Homework 16 3b

Drawing arrays for multiplication facts

Product of 30: 1 × 30, 30 × 1, 2 × 15, 15 × 2, 3 × 10, 10 × 3, 5 × 6, 6 × 5; 4 rectangles

24 also has 4 rectangles and 8 facts; 27 has only 1 rectangle of 1 × 27; 32 has 3 rectangles and 6 facts.

Numbers with lots of factors (or which are in lots of multiplication tables) have more rectangles.

Homework 17 3c

School pudding combinations

There are 6 combinations if you can choose 2 items: S + M, S + IC, S + F, M + IC, M +F, IC + F.

There are only 4 combinations if you can choose 3 items: S + M + IC, S + M + F, S + IC + F, M + IC + F.

Homework 18 3c

Sharing items fairly

12 can be shared equally between 2, 3, 4, 6 or 12 people.

15 can only be shared between 3, 5 and 15 people.

If the number has lots of factors it can be divided by lots of different numbers.

Homework 19 4a

Investigating cuboids

Nets of cuboids can have different arrangements but they always have 6 faces, which can be rectangles and perhaps some squares. Nets of cubes also have 6 faces but they are all squares. Examples of nets:

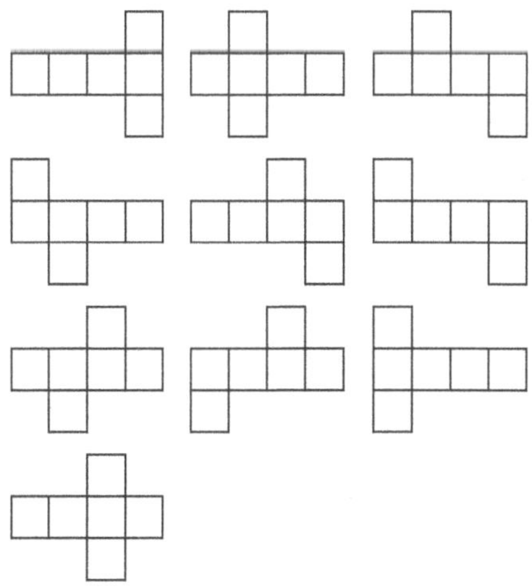

Homework 20 4a

Searching for 3-D shapes

Cylinders and cuboids are usually easier to find than cones and pyramids.

More things fit packaging that is this shape and these shapes are easier to stack.

Homework 22 4b

Making 2-D shapes

One example is a trapezium – it has no right angles, 2 angles smaller than a right angle and 2 angles greater than a right angle.

Homework 23 5a

Counting in fours and eights

Amy could set out the room in any of these ways to seat 32 children:

4 4 4 4 4 4 4 4
8 4 4 4 4 4 4
8 8 4 4 4 4
8 8 8 4 4
8 8 8 8

Joining 4 large tables loses 6 seats, so will now only seat 26 children.

Joining 8 small tables loses14 seats, so will now only seat 18 children.

It is better to have fewer larger tables.

Homework 25 5b

Making 3-digit numbers with hundreds, tens and ones

You will not make a 3-digit number if you don't pick out any green hundreds counters.

Homework 26 5b

Comparing and ordering numbers

You can make 6 different numbers, assuming the 3 digits rolled are different, e.g. 352, 325, 532, 523, 235, 253.

If a number is repeated, e.g. you roll 1, 3 and 3, you will only be able to make 3 numbers: 133, 313, 331. If you roll 3 numbers the same, e.g. 4, 4 and 4, you will only be able to make 1 number (444)!

Homework 28 5c

Adding tenths to make 1 whole

Orange: $\frac{7}{10}$ water

Blackcurrant: $\frac{8}{10}$ water

Apple: $\frac{5}{10}$ water

Lime: $\frac{9}{10}$ water

Apple: $\frac{3}{10}$ water

$\frac{3}{10}$ apple

Homework 29 6a

Adding multiples of 100

You are more likely to reach 1000 first if you start with a higher number, e.g. 456 is better than 256, but there would be no difference between 412 and 499 as you are only adding hundreds.

You hope to roll big numbers like 5 or 6 because the more hundreds you add, the quicker you will reach 1000.

Homework 30 6a

Adding 3-digit numbers

(A + B) 276 + 293 = 569, (A + C) 276 + 327 = 603, (A + D) 276 + 365 = 641, (B + C) 293 + 327 = 620, (B + D) 293 + 365 = 658, (C + D) 327 + 365 = 692

One child should have bags A and D (641). The other should have bags B and C (620) as these combinations have the smallest difference of only 21 beads.

Homework 31 6a

Investigating differences

Look for systematic working. There will be 15 different pairs leading to five differences of 1, four differences of 2, three differences of 3, two differences of 4 and one difference of 5:

368/369 = 1, 368/370 = 2, 368/371 = 3, 368/372 = 4, 368/373 = 5

369/370 = 1, 369/371 = 2, 369/372 = 3, 369/373 = 4

370/371 = 1, 370/372 = 2, 370/373 = 3

371/372 = 1, 371/373 = 2

372/373 = 1

Homework 32 6b

Compare mass by finding differences

Difference between lion and polar bear = 300 kg

Zebra and brown bear difference = 106 kg

Dolphin 250 kg heavier than lion

Dolphin and zebra have smallest difference = 41 kg

Homework 33 7a

Adding multiples of 10

Add 30: 216, 246, 276, 306, 336, 366, 396, 426, 456, 486, 516 …

The pattern in the tens and ones column repeats every 10 jumps.

Add 40: 216, 256, 296, 336, 376, 416 ...

The pattern in the tens and ones column repeats every 5 jumps.

Homework 34 7a

Add and subtract hundreds, tens and ones

It will not always take the same number of steps if one of the HTO digits in the start number is the same as that of the target number.

The only thing that will reduce the number of steps is if the HT or O digit in the start number is the same as in target number.

Homework 35 7b

Comparing unit and non-unit fractions

$\frac{1}{3} = 8$ cm, $\frac{2}{3} = 16$ cm; $\frac{1}{4} = 6$ cm, $\frac{2}{4} = 12$ cm, $\frac{3}{4} = 18$ cm; $\frac{1}{6} = 4$ cm, $\frac{2}{6} = 8$ cm, $\frac{3}{6} = 12$ cm, $\frac{4}{6} = 16$ cm, $\frac{5}{6} = 20$ cm; $\frac{1}{8} = 3$ cm, $\frac{2}{8} = 6$ cm, $\frac{3}{8} = 9$ cm, $\frac{4}{8} = 12$ cm, $\frac{5}{8} = 15$ cm, $\frac{6}{8} = 18$ cm, $\frac{7}{8} = 21$ cm

Counting up in multiple strings/ links to multiplication tables, e.g. 3, 6, 9, 12, 15, 18, 21, 24 for eighths.

Equivalent fractions: $\frac{1}{3} = \frac{2}{6}$, $\frac{1}{4} = \frac{2}{8}$, $\frac{2}{4} = \frac{3}{6} = \frac{4}{8}$, $\frac{2}{3} = \frac{4}{6}$, $\frac{3}{4} = \frac{6}{8}$

Homework 36 7b

Shading fractions of a rectangle

Only colouring 1 square each time means there are 8 different ways to shade $\frac{1}{8}$.

There are 28 ways to shade 2 squares.

Shading $\frac{6}{8}$ would give the same answers and arrangements as for $\frac{2}{6}$, but those left unshaded for $\frac{2}{8}$ would be shaded for $\frac{6}{8}$.

Homework 37 7b

Fraction puzzle

Annabelle $\frac{1}{4}$ of 12 = 3 pieces

Freddie $\frac{1}{6}$ of 12 = 2 pieces

Kapil $\frac{1}{3}$ of 12 = 4 pieces

Left 3 pieces = $\frac{1}{4}$

Freddie 2 pieces = $\frac{1}{6}$

Homework 38 7c

Adding tenths to make a whole

$\frac{1}{10} + \frac{9}{10}$, $\frac{2}{10} + \frac{8}{10}$, $\frac{3}{10} + \frac{7}{10}$, $\frac{4}{10} + \frac{6}{10}$, $\frac{5}{10} + \frac{5}{10}$

Homework 39 8a

Halving prices

Dress £24, long-sleeved top £13, trousers £17, t-shirt £8, shoes £32, bag £27

Mum could choose various combinations:

Shoes, trousers, t-shirt: £57; Shoes, long-sleeved top, t-shirt: £53; Bag, dress, t-shirt: £59; Bag, trousers, long-sleeved top: £57; Bag, trousers, t-shirt: £48; Bag, long-sleeved top, t-shirt: £48; Dress, trousers, long-sleeved top: £54; Dress, trousers, t-shirt: £49; Dress, long-sleeved top, t-shirt: £45; Trousers, long-sleeved top, t-shirt: £38

Buy everything in sale for £121.

Mum needs another £61.

Homework 41 8b

Ways to multiply by 5 and 20

Numbers out: 10, 20, 25, 50, 60, 100

Single function is '×5'

'×20' could replace '×10 and then double'

Homework 42 8b

Multiplying by 10 and 100

4 thick branches: 40 small twigs

7 thick branches: 700 green leaves

600 green leaves: 6 thick branches

80 small twigs: 8 thick branches and 800 green leaves

There are 10 times as many small twigs as thick branches and 10 times as many green leaves as small twigs. So there are 100 times as many green leaves as thick branches.

Homework 43 8c

Scaling up and down

Twice as big:
rectangles 4 × 8 cm, 6 × 12 cm, 8 × 20 cm

Half the size:
rectangles 1 × 2 cm, 1.5 × 3 cm, 2 × 5 cm

Homework 44 8c

Missing numbers

8

Homework 46 9a

Types of straight lines

All the lines will be in more than 1 colour as the parallel lines are also either horizontal or vertical and some are also perpendicular to another line.

Homework 48 9b

Using turning vocabulary

There is a tendency to do $\frac{1}{4}$ turns anticlockwise or clockwise rather than using $\frac{3}{4}$ turns. $\frac{1}{2}$ turns just take you back in the opposite direction so are less useful when directing a path (as are whole turns).

Homework 49 10a

Writing 3-digit numbers in words

three hundred and twenty-five, four hundred and forty-seven, two hundred and twenty-one, one hundred and ninety, three hundred and fifty-two, one hundred and forty-seven

Stand 2 has the most. Stand 4 is made of only hundreds and tens. Stand 5 has more fans than stand 1. There are 300 fewer in stand 6 than stand 2.

Homework 51 10b

Partitioning 3-digit numbers into multiples of 10

Estimates should be high as there will be lots of combinations.

Homework 53 11a

Adding 3-digit numbers using mental methods

Washers 480, spark plugs 289, oil 770 litres, screws 579. As the numbers of screws and washers is different, they need to order another 99 washers.

Homework 54 11a

Adding 3-digit numbers using written methods

Tiger 527 pounds (239 kg), lion 345 pounds (156 kg), puma 180 pounds (82 kg), leopard 124 pounds (56 kg), hyena 95 pounds (43 kg), lynx 21 pounds (10 kg)

Homework 55 11a

Counting up to find a difference

Order: 33 baked beans, 217 pasta, 143 lemonade, 278 juice. Largest reorder: juice.

Homework 56 11b

Subtracting 3-digit numbers using written methods

Odd and even is a fair game as there is a 50/50 chance of it being either.

Homework 60 12b

Halves, quarters and eighths

$\frac{1}{2}$ of 16 cm = 8 cm; leftover 8 cm = $\frac{1}{2}$ of 16 cm

$\frac{1}{4}$ of 16 cm = 4 cm; leftover 12 cm = $\frac{3}{4}$ of 16 cm

$\frac{1}{8}$ of 16 cm = 2 cm; leftover 14 cm = $\frac{7}{8}$ of 16 cm

$\frac{3}{4}$ of 16 cm = 12 cm; leftover 4 cm = $\frac{1}{4}$ of 16 cm

$\frac{5}{8}$ of 16 cm = 10 cm; leftover 6 cm = $\frac{3}{8}$ of 16 cm

Homework 61 12c

Fractions equivalent to $\frac{1}{4}$

Might choose $\frac{1}{4}, \frac{2}{8}, \frac{3}{12}, \frac{4}{16}, \frac{5}{20}$. The numerators increase by 1 and the denominators increase by 4/counting in fours. The pattern is 1, 2, 3, 4, 5 for the numerators and 4, 8, 12, 16, 20 for the denominators.

A rectangle split into 24 parts will have 6 parts shaded.

Homework 62 12c

Adding and subtracting eighths

16; $\frac{16}{8}$ or 2 wholes

Homework 63 13a

Grid method of multiplication

Total cost of Package 1 = £780, Package 2 = £456. So Package 1 is £324 more.

Package 2 plus lunch = £456 + £450 = £906, so it is cheaper to buy Package 1 with all meals included.

Homework 64 13a

Written multiplication methods

The answers get bigger because the chosen number is multiplied by a bigger number each time so the product is also larger.

The difference between the answers is equal to the chosen number, e.g. with 42 each answer is 42 more than the previous answer.

Multiplying by 7 will add one more of the chosen number, e.g. 42, to the answer found when multiplying the chosen number by 6.

Homework 65 13b

Using arrays to show divisions

36 ÷ 36 = 1, 36 ÷ 1 = 36, 36 ÷ 18 = 2, 36 ÷ 2 = 18, 36 ÷ 12 = 3, 36 ÷ 3 = 12, 36 ÷ 9 = 4, 36 ÷ 4 = 9, 36 ÷ 6 = 6

There are 2 divisions for each rectangle, except for the 6 × 6 special rectangle which is a square and only has 1 division.

37 only has 1 rectangle (1 × 37), so it will only have 2 divisions: 37 ÷ 1 = 37 and 37 ÷ 37 = 1.

37 is a prime number with only 2 factors, 1 and itself. Although the children have not yet learnt this vocabulary it may be useful for the parents.

Homework 66 13b

Compact division

To get the longest length, find the largest fraction of the largest amount, so $\frac{96}{3} = 23$, $\frac{90}{4} = 23$, $\frac{84}{5} = 17$, $\frac{76}{6} = 13$ (rounded to nearest whole number):
32 + 23 + 17 + 13 = 85

To get the shortest length, find the smallest fraction of the largest amount, so $\frac{96}{6} = 16$, $\frac{90}{5} = 18$, $\frac{84}{4} = 21$, $\frac{76}{3} = 25$ (rounded):
16 + 18 + 21 + 25 = 80

Homework 69 14b

Shapes with the same area but different perimeters

A 3×4 rectangle has a perimeter of 14 cm,
a 2×6 rectangle has a perimeter of 16 cm,
a 1×12 rectangle has a perimeter of 26 cm.
The children will have drawn plenty of other composite shapes.

Appendix

A Glossary of mathematical terms

1, 2, 3

2-dimensional (2-D)
Points in 2-dimensional space lie on a flat surface.

3-dimensional (3-D)
Points in 3-dimensional space occupy a space or a volume.

5, 10, 15… minutes past
Ways of counting minutes on an analogue clock. The minute hand takes five minutes to move between each hour mark on the clock face. See also *analogue clock*.

12-hour time
Counting hours of the day in two blocks of twelve. 12.01-12 noon as a.m. and 12.01-12 midnight as p.m. Often told on a 12-hour clock and known as analogue time.

24-hour time
Counting hours of the day from 0-24. Used on digital clocks. 2 p.m. is written as 14:00.

A

a.m.
From Latin ante-meridian, meaning before midday. See also *12-hour time*.

above/below zero
Temperatures are measured relative to 0°C – the freezing point of water, e.g. 4° below zero is –4°C.

acute angle
An angle between 0° and 90°. See also *obtuse, reflex angle*.

add
A mathematical operation to increase one number (the augend) by another to give the sum.

addend
The number being added in an addition calculation. See also *augend*.

addition
A mathematical operation combining two or more numbers to find a total. Augend + addend = sum (or total).

addition fact
An addition statement likely to be frequently used, so worth memorising.

algebra
Generalised calculation using symbols (variables) instead of numbers. It can be used to prove statements and show general relationships.

analogue clock
A dial with hands used to show time. The dial shows 12 hours in a full circle. The minute hand moves one complete turn every hour. Times on these clocks are read, e.g. 20 past five or five to four.

angle
The amount of turn between two straight lines that meet at a point. Usually measured in degrees. Symbol: °. See also *acute, obtuse, reflex angle*.

anticlockwise
A rotation or turn in the opposite direction to the movement of the hands on a clock. See also *clockwise*.

approximate, approximately
A number that is not exact, e.g. 2028 is approximately 2000. Symbol: ≈.

arc
Part of the circumference of a circle.

area
The 2-D measure of the size of a surface. Measured in 'square' units: mm^2, cm^2, m^2, km^2.

array
An arrangement of numbers, shapes or objects in rows of equal size and columns of equal size, used to find out how many altogether.

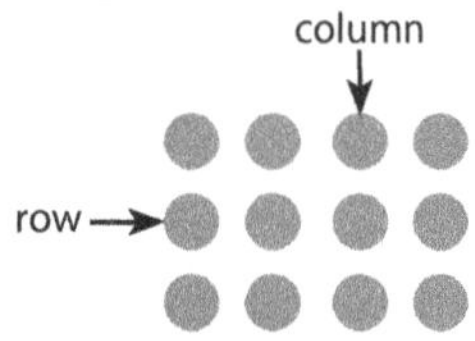

$4 \times 3 = 12$

ascending/descending order
Ascending order: rank values from smallest to largest.
Descending order: rank values from largest to smallest.

associative law
A mathematical law or rule where numbers can be grouped in different ways when adding or multiplying, without changing the total, e.g. $(a + b) + c = a + (b + c)$ and $(a \times b) \times c = a \times (b \times c)$.

augend
The number being added to in an addition calculation. See also *addend*.

average
The middle value of a set of numbers. It is found by adding all the numbers together and dividing by how many numbers there are. See also *mean*.

axis, axes
Scale lines, usually vertical and horizontal, used to define positions of points on a grid or graph.

axis of symmetry
An axis of symmetry divides the shape into two identical parts. Also called a mirror line.

B

balance
Things are balanced when both sides have equal value, e.g. 1000 g = 1 kg, 3 + 6 = 10 – 1.

bar chart
A statistical diagram using bars to show the frequency of outcomes.

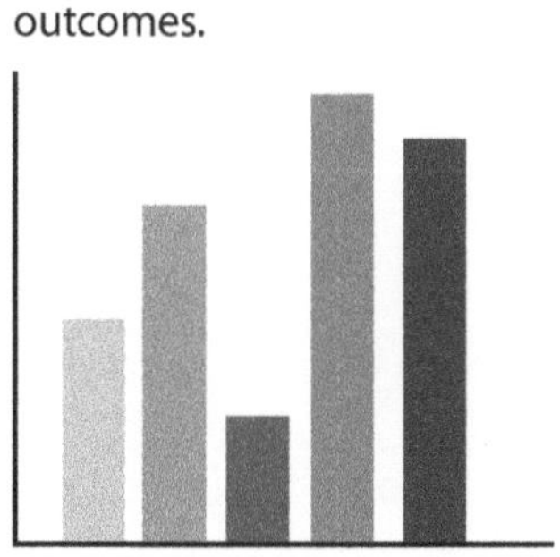

bar line chart
A statistical diagram using lines to show the frequency of discrete outcomes.

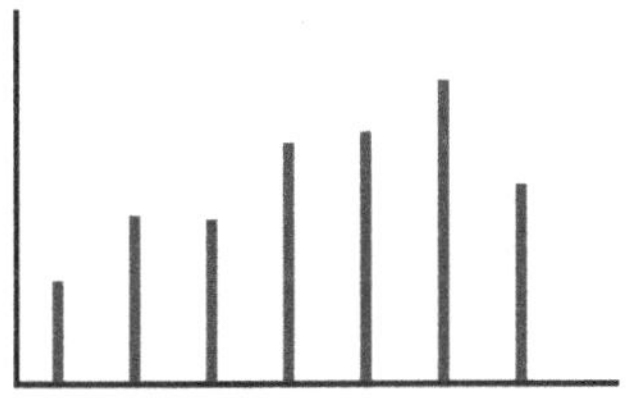

base, square-based
The flat surface underneath a 3-D shape. A square-based pyramid has one square base and four triangular faces.

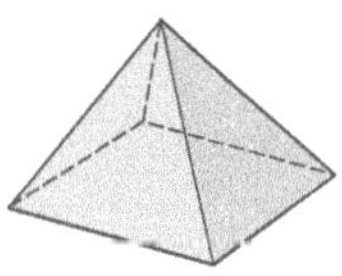

Base 10 system
This is another name for the decimal number system. It increases and decreases by powers of 10. When we multiply a number by, e.g. 10, the digits move one place to the left because the number is made ten times bigger. When we divide by, e.g. 100, the number is 100 times smaller and the digits move two places to the right.

block diagram
A diagram showing statistical information. Each block stands for one object or event.

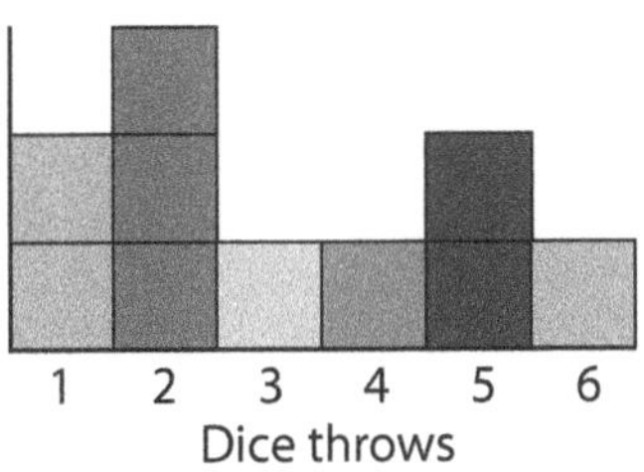

breadth
The same as width.

C

calendar
A list of the days of the year, arranged by month, week and day.

capacity
The amount a container can hold, e.g. the capacity of a 2 l bottle is 2 litres, the capacity of a football stadium is the amount of people it will hold. See also *volume*.

Carroll diagram
A Carroll diagram sorts objects according to a criteria and not that criteria. Can be several criteria but always the criteria and not the criteria, e.g. odd numbers/not odd numbers, multiples of 5/not multiples of 5, dogs/not dogs.

category
A group of elements or numbers all with the same property, e.g. dogs, cats, rats are all in the category 'animals'.

Celsius
A scale used to measure temperature. Sometimes called Centigrade. Units are °C.

centilitre
One hundredth of a litre. Symbol: cl. 100 cl = 1 l.

centimetre
A unit of length, $\frac{1}{100}$ of 1 metre. Symbol: cm.

centre
A point at the exact middle of a shape. The centre of a circle is the same distance from all points on its circumference.

century
100 years.

change
The money left over when buying something with a note or coin bigger than the amount needed. The change is given back to the buyer.

chart
A statistical diagram.

circle, circular
A set of points that are all a fixed distance (the radius) from a point (the centre). Like a circle.

circumference
The perimeter of a circle. The set of points a fixed distance from the centre of a circle. See also *arc*.

clock, clock face, hands
A clock is used to show and record time. It can have a circular face with revolving hands to mark hours and minutes, or it can have a digital display.

clockwise
A rotation or turn in the same direction as the movement of the hands on a clock. See also *anticlockwise*.

column
A vertical list of elements or numbers, usually in a table or an array.

combinations
Different combinations made from a selection, e.g. the various different outfits which can be made by choosing one hat and one coat to wear from three hats and four coats.

commutative
Addition and multiplication are commutative. It doesn't matter which way you add or mulitply in, the answer is always the same. Same answer, different calculation, e.g. $3 + 4 = 4 + 3$. But subtraction and division are not commutative, e.g. $7 - 2 \neq 2 - 7$.

compound number
A number that is not a prime number.

compound shape
A compound shape consists of two or more simple shapes such as a triangle placed on a square or oblong on top of a square. Also known as a composite shape.

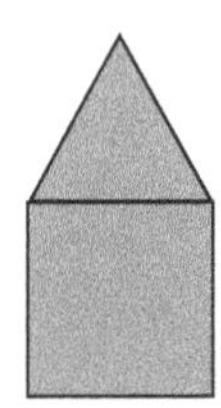

concentric
Circles which share the same centre.

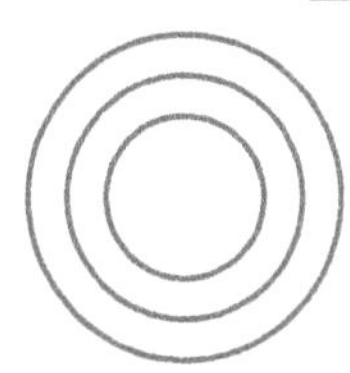

cone
A 3-D shape with a flat, circular face and a curved face. It has one apex directly above the circular base.

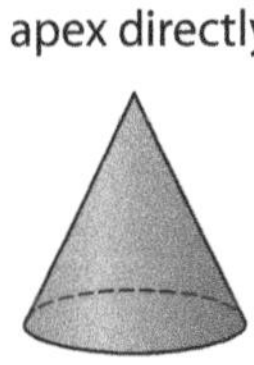

congruent
Shapes are congruent if they are exactly the same shape and size.

consecutive
Numbers that follow each other in a linear pattern, e.g. 3, 4, 5; 60, 70, 80; 17, 19, 21.

Glossary

construct
To draw a shape accurately using a ruler, compasses and a protractor.

coordinate
An ordered pair of (x, y) values that define the position of a point on a Cartesian plane. In 3-D (x, y, z).

corner
A point on a 2-D shape where sides meet. Properly called a vertex (plural, vertices).

cube
A 3-D shape made from six identical squares which all meet at right angles, e.g. a cube of sugar.

cube number, cubed
Formed when a number is multiplied by itself and then by itself again. 2 cubed = $2 \times 2 \times 2 = 8$. The cube numbers are a sequence $1^3, 2^3, 3^3$ and so on, which gives the numbers 1, 8, 27, 64, 125 and so on. See also *square number*.

cubic millimetres (mm^3), cubic centimetres (cm^3), cubic metres (m^3), cubic kilometres (km^3)
Metric measurements of liquid and solid volume. 1 mm^3 is the volume enclosed in a cube of length 1 mm, etc.

cuboid
A 3-D shape made from six rectangles. Two or four of the rectangles could be squares, e.g. a cereal box. A cube is a special sort of cuboid.

currency
A money system. In the UK, the currency is pounds sterling (£). In the EU, the currency is the euro (€).

curved
A line that is not straight, e.g. a circle, or a surface that is not flat, e.g. an egg.

curved surface
A surface of a 3-D shape which is not flat, e.g. the surface of a sphere or cylinder.

cylinder, cylindrical
A 3-D object with circular ends and a uniform cross-section. The top is vertically above the base. Like a cylinder.

D

data
Numbers collected from a questionnaire or survey. Pieces of information usually represented in a special way, e.g. on bar charts and pie charts.

database
A method of storing data, often in large tables on a computer.

date
How we record the passing of time. Usually given as day of the month, month and then year, e.g. 3rd April 2015.

decimal, decimal fraction, decimal point, decimal place, decimal equivalent
Fractions as tenths, hundredths and so on represented as digits after a decimal point, e.g. 0.253 is equivalent to $\frac{2}{10} + \frac{5}{100} + \frac{3}{1000}$ or $\frac{253}{1000}$.

degree
Symbol: °. A unit used to measure the size of an angle. There are 360° in one complete turn. Also a unit of temperature.

denominator
The number underneath the vinculum in a fraction. Also called the divisor.

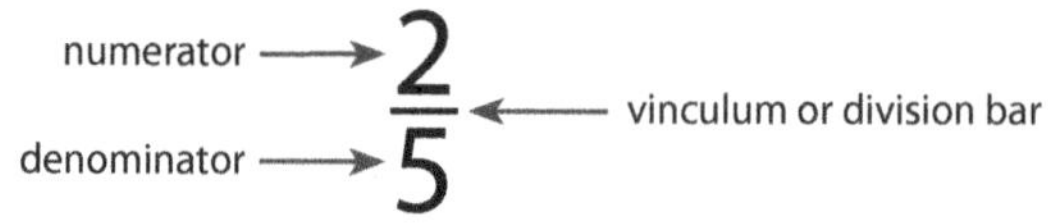

diagonal
A straight line inside a shape that goes from one corner to another (but not an edge).

diagram
A sketch or accurate drawing of a mathematical shape or problem.

diameter
A line passing across a circle, or a sphere, which passes through the centre. See also *radius*.

difference
The result of a subtraction. The difference between 12 and 5 is 7. See also *minuend, subtrahend*.

digit
A symbol from 0–9 in the decimal system. Used to show value. The value of each digit depends on its position, e.g. in 200, the digit 2 represents two hundreds.

digit total/sum
The sum of all the digits in a number, e.g. the digit sum of 435 is $4 + 3 + 5 = 12$. This carries on to $1 + 2 = 3$, so the digit total of 435 is 3.

digital clock, digital time
A system that shows the time as numbers. It can use the 12-hour or the 24-hour clock. 6 o'clock in the evening would show as 06.00 p.m. or 18:00.

discount
A reduction offered on the price of an item for sale.

distance apart ... between ... to ... from
The length of the shortest line joining two points.

distribution
In statistics. The distribution of a set of values.

distributive law
When adding or multiplying, the numbers can be rearranged to support calculating, e.g. $2 \times 13 \times 5 = (2 \times 5) \times 13 = 10 \times 13 = 130$ and $a(b + c) = ab + ac$.

dividend
The number that is divided in a division calculation, e.g. in $12 \div 6 = 2$, 12 is the dividend. See also *denominator, division bracket, divisor, quotient*.

dividing
The process of division.

divisibility
Whether a number can be divided without remainder. All even numbers are divisible by 2.

division
A mathematical operation which groups a number into a given number of parts, e.g. $12 \div 4$ is 12 divided into four parts each of value 3. It is the inverse operation to multiplication.

division bracket
The half box around the dividend in a division. See also *dividend*.

division fact
A division statement likely to be frequently used, so worth memorising.

division (on a scale)
The intervals on a scale, on a ruler or a graph axis.

divisor
The number that is used to divide in a division sum, e.g. in $12 \div 6 = 2$, 6 is the divisor. See also *denominator, dividend, quotient*.

dodecahedron
A 3-D polyhedron with 12 faces. A regular dodecahedron has pentagonal faces.

double
To multiply by 2.

E

edge
The line made where two faces of a 3-D shape meet.
See also *face, vertex*.

eighths
The fraction of a whole obtained when it is shared into eight equal pieces.

equal sharing
To divide a number or set of items into equal parts.

equals
Symbol: =. Is the same as and equivalent to, e.g. $5 + 3 = 7 + 1$.

equation
A mathematical statement showing an equality,
e.g. $10 \times 2 = 4 \times 5$ or $2x + 6 = 16$.

equilateral triangle
A triangle with three equal sides and three equal angles of 60°.

equivalent, equivalent to
Symbol: ≡. Two numbers or expressions that are equal, but which can be in a different form, e.g. £1 ≡ 100p.

equivalent fractions
Fractions with the same value, e.g. $\frac{1}{4} = \frac{2}{8} = \frac{3}{12}$. These are equivalent fractions.

estimate
An approximate answer, often used to check a complex calculation.

even
A whole number which is divisible by 2. It is a multiple of 2. See also *odd*.

F

face
A flat surface of a 3-D shape. See also *edge* and *vertex*.

factor
Numbers that divide exactly into a number are its factors, e.g. the factors of 12 are 1, 2, 3, 4, 6, 12.

factor pair
Two factors that multiply together to give the number. The factor pairs of 12 are 1×12, 2×6, 3×4.

factorise
To write a number or algebraic expression as a product of two or more factors.

flat
In 2-D and faces of 3-D shapes, not curved.

foot, feet
An imperial unit of length, approximately 30 cm.
12 inches = 1 foot and 3 feet = 1 yard.

formula, formulae
A mathematical sentence using letters or symbols (variables), e.g. area of a rectangle = length × width or $a = l \times w$.

fraction
Part of a whole, written as one number divided by another. In the fraction $\frac{3}{5}$, the numerator 3 is above the vinculum and the denominator 5 is below.

frequency table
A statistical table listing various outcomes and the frequency that they occur.

G

gallon
An imperial measure of capacity. 1 gallon is approximately 4.5 litres. See also *pint*.

gram
Symbol: g. A unit of mass. There are 1000 grams in a kilogram. See also *kilogram*.

graph
A diagram showing the relationship between two sets of numbers.

greater than
Also called more than. Symbol: >. Used when comparing the size of two quantities or measures. 10 is greater than 7, or $10 > 7$. See also *less than*.

greater than or equal to
Symbol: ≥. An inequality showing the lowest value a number can take. $n \geq 7$ means n can have any value from 7 upwards. See also *less than or equal to*.

greatest value, least value
The highest or lowest value that can occur.

grouping
To divide, objects and numbers can be shared or grouped. Grouping is putting objects or numbers into groups of a particular size.

H

half
When a whole is divided into two equal parts.

half past
A measure of time. Half (an hour) past, so half past 5 is the same as 5:30 and 30 minutes past 5. See also *o'clock*.

halfway between
The midpoint between two values, e.g. 15 is halfway between 10 and 20.

heavier than, lighter than
Comparing two masses or weights, e.g. 4 kg is heavier than 3 kg, 3 kg is lighter than 4 kg.

heaviest, lightest
Comparing two or more masses or weights, e.g. of 5 kg, 6 kg and 10 kg, 5 kg is the lightest, 10 kg is the heaviest.

heavy, light
Words used to compare mass or weight.

Glossary

hemisphere
Half of a sphere.

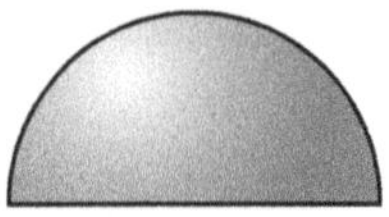

heptagon, heptagonal
A 2-D shape with seven straight sides.

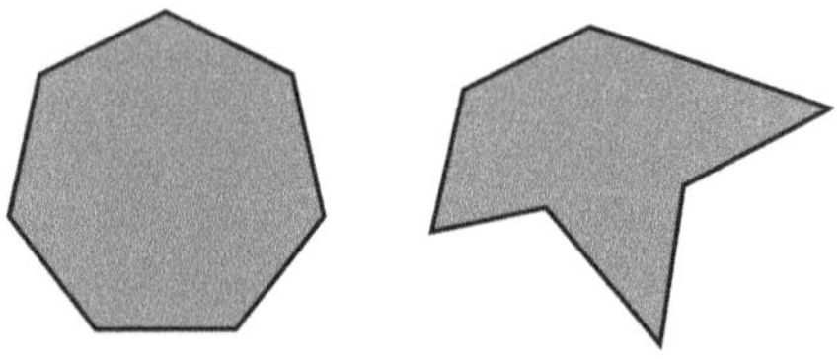

hexagon, hexagonal
A 2-D shape with six straight sides.

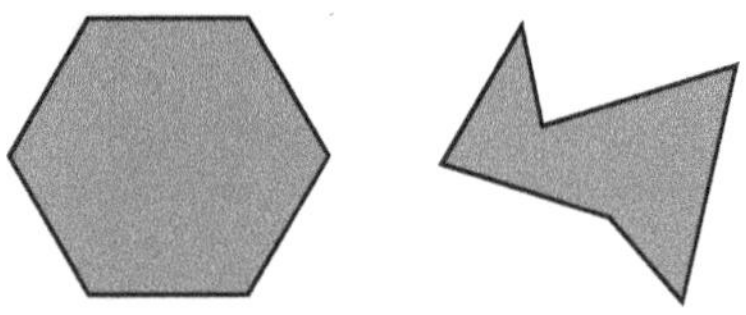

hollow
Having an outline or surface that curves inwards, e.g. the inside of a hemisphere.

horizontal
Parallel to the horizon. See also *vertical*.

hour
Symbol: h. A measure of time. There are 24 hours in a day and 60 minutes in one hour. See also *minute, second*.

hour hand
The hand on a clock that measures the hours. One complete revolution takes 12 hours. See also *minute hand*.

hundred
One hundred, 100, is ten tens or one more than 99.

hundred thousand
100 000.

hundreds
The position in a number where the digit represents hundreds, e.g. in 278 there is a digit 2 in the hundreds place, so there are 2 hundreds.

hundreds boundary
When counting from tens to hundreds, the hundreds boundary is crossed.

hundredths
A fraction $\frac{1}{100}$ or 0.01.

I

imperial unit
A non-metric unit of measure, e.g. inches, yards, miles, pints. Many are still in common use.

in every, for every
A way of expressing proportion (in every) and ratio (for every), e.g. One in every ten pupils has a dog; For every teacher there are 15 students. See also *ratio*.

inch, inches
An imperial unit of length, approximately 2.5 cm.
12 inches = 1 foot.

integer, positive, negative
An integer is a whole number which can be positive or negative, e.g. –4, –2, 4, 100.

intersecting, intersection
Where two lines or curves cross.

inverse
Inverse operations leave the original value unchanged. The inverse of + 4 is – 4. The inverse of $\times$ 4 is $\div$ 4 or $\times \frac{1}{4}$. The inverse 'undoes' the action.

irregular
Not regular. A shape with sides and angles that are not equal.

isosceles triangle
A triangle with two equal sides and two equal base angles.
A right-angled isosceles triangle has one right angle.

K

kilogram
Symbol: kg. A unit of mass. There are 1000 grams in a kilogram. See also *gram*.

kilometre
A metric measure of distance. 1 km = 1000 m.

kite
A quadrilateral with two pairs of equal adjacent sides.

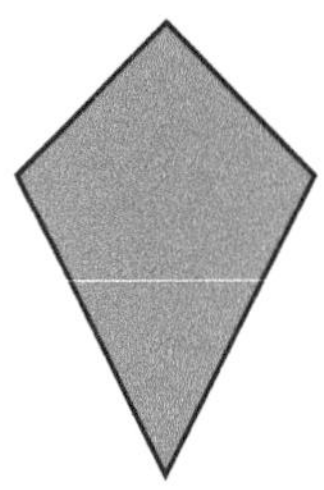

L

least popular, least common
In statistics. The value or outcome that happens least often. See also *most common*.

length, height, width, depth
Words used to describe lengths of lines and shapes, e.g. a cuboid has length 5 cm, width 3 cm and height 6 cm.

less than
Used when comparing the size of two quantities or measures, e.g. 7 is less than 10. See also *more than*.

less than or equal to
Symbol: ≤. An inequality showing the highest value a number can take. $n \leq 7$ means n can have any value up to and including 7. See also *greater than or equal to*.

line
A line is straight. It has no thickness and extends in both directions without ending.

line graph
A statistical graph with a continuous line showing the trend or variation in a value.

line segment
Part of a line that has a starting and ending point.

line symmetry
A 2-D object has line symmetry if it can be folded into two identical halves along a mirror line. Each half is a mirror image of the other.

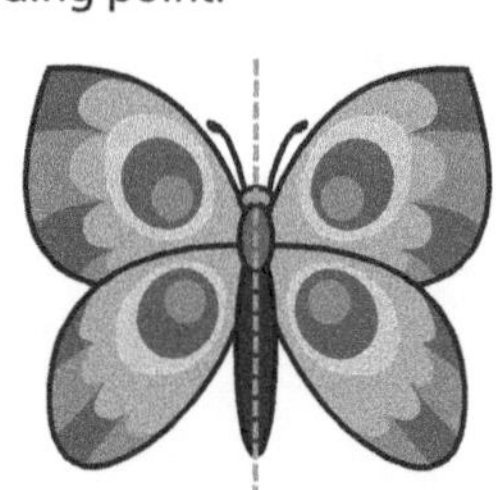
line of symmetry

linear number sequence
A sequence of numbers that increases by a constant difference, e.g. 9, 13, 17, 21, 25, and so on.

litre
Symbol: l. A measure of capacity. 1000 millilitres = 1 litre.

long, longer, longest
A comparison of lengths, e.g. a line is 3 cm, 3 cm is longer than 2 cm. Three lines are 4 cm, 6 cm and 8 cm. The longest length is 8 cm.

M

mass
A metric measure of the amount of matter in an object. Measured in grams (g), kilograms (kg) or tonnes (t). The mass of an object does not change, but its weight alters with any changes in the force of gravity.

maximum/minimum value
The largest/smallest value a number or variable can take.

mean
A measure of average. Mean = total of all data values ÷ number of data points. See also *median, range.*

measure, measurement
The size of a unit, e.g. we can measure area in square metres. Also means the act of measuring something.

measuring cylinder
A graduated cylinder for measuring volume and capacity accurately.

measuring scale
A way of measuring using a line or a dial with equal divisions, like on a ruler.

median
A measure of average. The middle number or value when all the elements of the data set are in ascending (or descending) order. If there is no middle value, then the mean of the two middle values. See also *mean, mode, range.*

mental calculation
Doing a calculation in your head, but perhaps with jottings.

metre
Symbol: m. A unit of length equal to 100 centimetres. 100 centimetres = 1 metre.

metric unit
Any unit used to measure on a metric scale, e.g. kilograms, centimetres, litres. All based on the decimal system.

mile
An imperial measure of distance. Used in the UK and US to measure distances between places. 5 miles is approximately equivalent to 8 kilometres.

millennium
A thousand years (10 centuries).

millilitre
Symbol: ml. A measure of capacity. 1000 millilitres = 1 litre.

millimetre
One thousandth of a metre. 1000 mm = 1 m.

million
1 000 000.

minuend
The starting number in a subtraction calculation, e.g. 10 (the minuend) – 3 (the subtrahend) = 7 (the difference). See also *subtrahend, difference.*

minus
Symbol. Another word for subtract.

minute
Symbol: min. A measure of time. See also *second, hour.*

minute hand
The hand on a clock face that measures the minutes. One complete revolution takes 60 minutes (one hour). See also *hour hand.*

mixed number
A number with both a whole number part and a fractional part, e.g. $3\frac{1}{2}$.

money
Coins and notes used to buy goods and services.

more than
Also called greater than. Symbol: >. Used when comparing the size of two quantities or measures. 10 is more than 7 or 10 > 7. See also *less than.*

more than or equal to
Symbol: ≥. An inequality showing the lowest value a number can take. $n \geq 7$ means n can have any value from 7 upwards. See also *less than or equal to.*

most common
In statistics. The most frequently occurring outcome. See also *least common.*

multiple, multiple of
A multiple is the product of two numbers, e.g. the multiples of 7 are 7, 14, 21, 28 and so on.

multiplicand
A number to be multiplied, e.g. in 6 × 3 = 18, 6 is the multiplicand. See also *multiplier.*

multiplication
A mathematical operation.

multiplication fact
A multiplication statement likely to be frequently used, so worth memorising, e.g. the multiplication table.

multiplication table
A list of multiplication facts for a given multiple, often learned by heart.

multiplier
The multiplying number, e.g. in 6 × 3 = 18, 3 is the multiplier. See also *multiplicand.*

multiply
Symbol: ×. A mathematical process equivalent to repeated addition, e.g. 2 × 4 = 2 + 2 + 2 + 2 = 8 or repeated grouping.

N

negative numbers
Numbers below zero on the number line. Read as negative 1, negative 2 and so on. See also *integer.*

net (open, closed)
The compound shape resulting from opening out a 3-D shape to show its 2-D faces and how they are connected. A one-piece set of connected 2-D shapes which can be folded to make a 3-D shape.

nth term
An algebraic expression that gives the value of any term in a sequence from its position in the sequence. An unknown value.

number
A label given to a quantity, using numerals. There are many different types of number, including counting numbers 0, 1, 2, 3 and so on; fractions; negative numbers; ordinal numbers.

Glossary

number bonds/pairs
Pairs of numbers with a particular total, e.g. the number bonds for 10 are all pairs of whole numbers, like 2 and 8, which add up to 10.

number statement
A mathematical statement using numbers, also called a number sentence, e.g. $4 + 5 - 1 = 8$.

numeral
A symbol used to represent a number. We use arabic numerals 0-9, but there are also Roman numerals and other systems.

numerator
The number above the vinculum in a fraction.

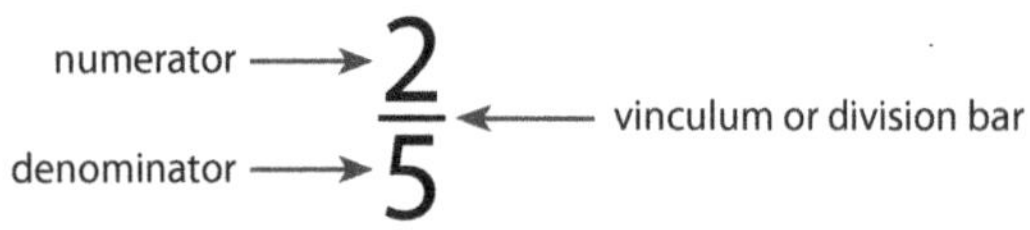

O

oblong
An irregular rectangle. A 2-D shape with two pairs of opposite sides that are equal and the angles are 90°. See also *square*.

obtuse angle
An angle between 90° and 180°. See also *acute, reflex angle*.

octagon, octagonal
A 2-D shape with eight straight sides.

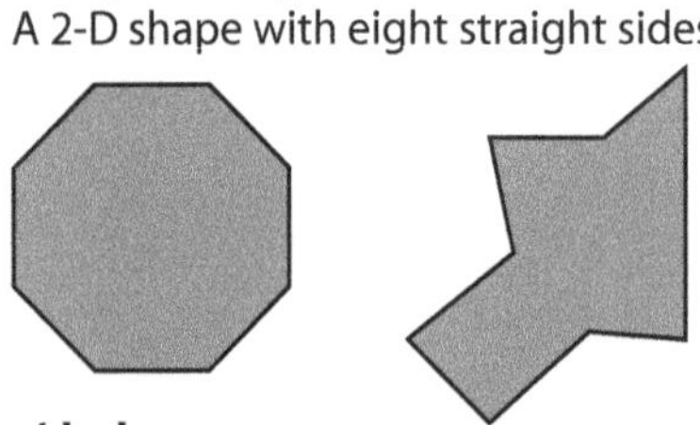

o'clock
A way of describing an exact hour time, e.g. 5 o'clock means the time is 5:00. See also *half past*.

octahedron, octahedral
A 3-D shape with eight triangular faces.

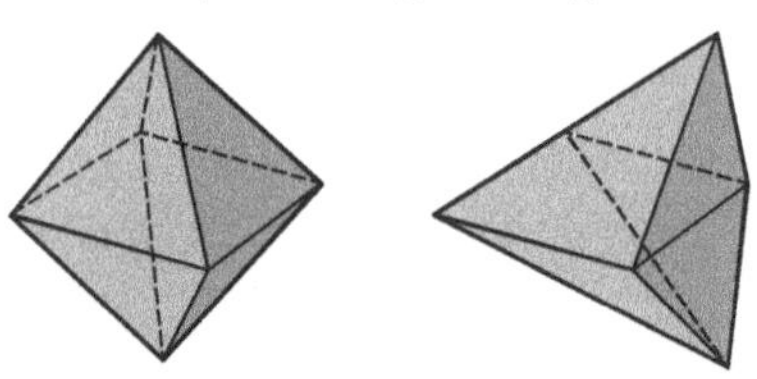

odd
A whole number which has a remainder of 1 when divided by 2. It is not a multiple of 2. See also *even*.

one hundred less/more
A number one hundred whole units more or less than another number. 900 is a hundred less than 1000 and 100 more than 800.

one less
The number one whole before that number on an number line, e.g. 9 is one less than 10.

one more
The number one whole after that number on a number line, e.g. 9 is one more than 8.

one third
A fraction obtained when a whole is divided into three equal parts.

ones
When counting individual items, the next counting number is allocated to the set each time one more is counted. 9 is the largest number of ones. See also *single-digit*.

ones boundary
When counting from a decimal to a whole number, the ones boundary is crossed. See also *tenths boundary*.

ordinal number
A number that tells the order of something, e.g. in a list 1st, 2nd, 3rd, and so on.

ounce
An imperial measure of mass. Symbol: oz. 1 ounce is approximately 28 g. 16 oz = 1 pound.

outcome
One of the possible results from a statistical experiment or trial, e.g. when tossing a coin there are two equally-likely outcomes: heads or tails.

P

p.m.
From Latin post-meridian, meaning after midday. 14:00 on the 24-hour clock is 2:00 p.m. See also *12-hour time*.

parallel
Lines that are the same distance apart and never meet.

parallelogram
A 2-D shape with two pairs of opposite sides that are equal and parallel. A rectangle is a special parallelogram, with all the angles 90°.

parts of a whole
A fraction of a whole number or object. If there are five equal parts of a whole then each part is $\frac{1}{5}$.

pattern
A regular arrangement of shapes or numbers that follows a rule.

pentagon, pentagonal
A 2-D shape with five straight sides.

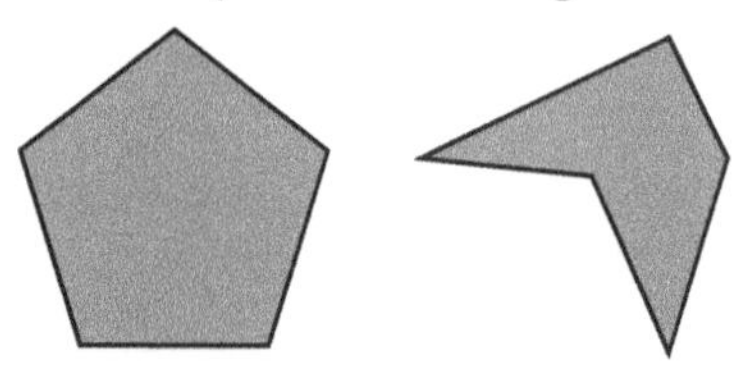

percentage, per cent, %
A fraction or mixed number expressed as hundredth parts, e.g. $\frac{1}{2} = \frac{50}{100} = 50\%$.

perimeter
The total distance measured around the outside of a 2-D shape or area. Calculated by adding the lengths of all the sides.

perpendicular
At right-angles to. Horizontal lines are always perpendicular to vertical lines.

pictogram
A picture to show statistical information. A picture is used to represent one or a number of elements.

pie chart
A statistical diagram that shows proportions of quantities as slices of a circle (a pie).

pint
An imperial measure of capacity. There are 8 pints in 1 gallon. 1 litre is approximately 1.75 pints.

place, place value
Place value has several aspects to it. One is positional, which is where the digit of a number is placed, e.g. in 345, the digit 3 is positioned in the hundreds. Another is multiplicative, which is when we multiply the digit by its position to get its true value. So the 3 in 345 is multiplied by 100 to give 300. A third is additive. This is when all the individual values of the digits are added together to give the whole number, e.g. $300 + 40 + 5 = 345$.

plane
A flat surface.

polygon
The general name for 2-D shapes with three or more straight sides. Includes triangle (three sides), quadrilateral (four sides), pentagon (five sides), and so on.

polyhedron
The general name for 3-D shapes with straight sides. Plural polyhedra. Includes tetrahedron, prisms, pyramids.

pound
An imperial measure of mass. Symbol: lb. 2.2 lb is approximately 1 kg. See also *ounce*.

prime factor
A factor of a number that is also a prime number, e.g. the prime factors of 12 are 2 and 3, since $12 = 2 \times 2 \times 3 = 2^2 \times 3$.

prime number
A number with only two factors, itself and 1. 1 is not a prime number.

prism
A 3-D shape with two identical and parallel ends, joined by rectangular faces. The cross-section of a prism is always the same shape and size as the ends.

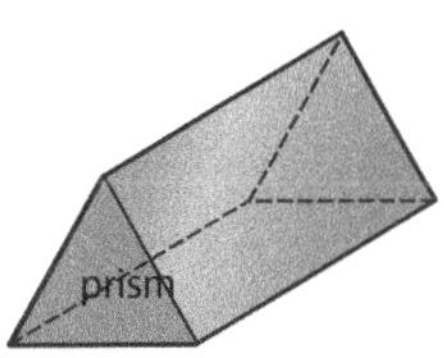

product
The result of multiplying two numbers, e.g. the product of 4 and 3 is $4 \times 3 = 12$.

profit, loss
The money made or lost in a financial transaction. Can be expressed as a money value or as a percentage.

proper/improper fraction
A proper fraction is a fraction that is less that 1, with the numerator less than the denominator, e.g. $\frac{2}{5}$. In an improper fraction, the numerator is larger than the denominator, e.g. $\frac{5}{2}$.

pyramid, square-based
A 3-D shape with a square base and four triangular faces.

Q

quadrant
One of the four regions formed by the x- and y-axes on a Cartesian graph.

quadrilateral
A 2-D shape with four straight sides.

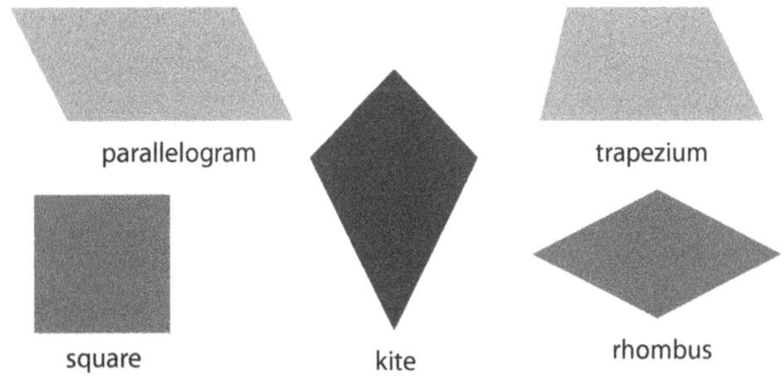

quarter
When a whole is divided into four equal parts.

quarter past, quarter to
15 minutes past the hour or 15 minutes before the hour, e.g. quarter to 12 is 11:45, quarter past 12 is 12:15.

questionnaire
A set of questions given to people to fill in, in order to collect data for analysis. See also *survey, data*.

quotient
The answer to a division calculation, e.g. in $12 \div 6 = 2$, 2 is the quotient. See also *denominator, dividend, divisor*.

R

radius
Any straight line segment from the centre of a circle to the edge (circumference). The radius is half of the diameter. See also *diameter*.

range
A measure of statistical spread. The difference between the highest and lowest values in a set of data. See also *mean, median*.

ratio
A comparison of parts, usually expressed in its simplest form, using a colon, e.g. 12 boys and 15 girls expressed as a ratio is 12:15 or 4:5.

rectangle, rectangular
A four-sided 2-D shape with four right angles and equal opposite sides. A square is a regular rectangle with all four sides equal. An oblong is an irregular rectangle.

rectilinear
A rectangular shape.

reduced to, simplify
To reduce or simplify a fraction or ratio, divide both numbers by the highest common factor, e.g. $\frac{6}{9} = \frac{2}{3}$.

reflect, reflection
To transform an object by reflecting it in a mirror line. The image is the same shape and size as the object.

reflective symmetry
A figure or object has reflective symmetry if there is a line (2-D) or a plane (3-D) which divides the shape into two identical parts.

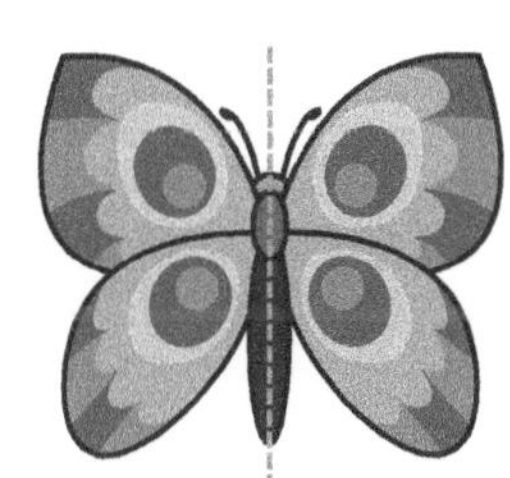
line of symmetry

Glossary

reflex angle
An angle greater than 180°. See also *acute, obtuse angle.*

regular
A 2-D shape with all the sides equal length and equal angles.

remainder
The number left over after a division sum, e.g. 13 ÷ 3 = 4 remainder 1.

rhombus
A 2-D shape with four equal sides and equal opposite angles.

right angle
A quarter of a full turn. 90°.

right-angled triangle
A triangle with one right angle. Can be isosceles or scalene.

Roman numerals
Numbers used by the Romans. Digits have no place value, e.g. II = 2 , VI = 6, LX = 60.

rotate, rotation
To transform an object by turning it a given direction and angle round a fixed point. The image is the same shape and size as the object.

round up, round down
A method of approximation. 37 rounds up to the nearest 10 so gives an approximation of 40, but 34 rounds down to the nearest 10 so gives an approximation of 30. Digits 4 or less round down and digits 5 or more round up, so 750 to the nearest 100 is 800.

row
A horizontal arrangement of, e.g. objects, shapes or numbers. See also *array.*

rule
An instruction for carrying out a mathematical operation or continuing a pattern. It can be written using symbols or words. See also *sequence.*

S

scalene triangle
A triangle with no equal sides or angles.

scales
A way of measuring using a line with equal divisions, like on a ruler. Also a device for measuring weight.

second
Symbol: s. A measure of time. There are 60 seconds in one minute. See also *minute, hour.*

semi-circle
Half of a circle, made from half of the curved circumference and a diameter.

sequence
A set of numbers made by following a given rule, e.g. the multiples of 3 are 3, 6, 9 and so on.

sevenths
The fraction of a whole obtained when it is cut into seven equal pieces.

shape
A 2-D or 3-D object.

sharing
A model for division, e.g. 10 ÷ 2 = 5 is 10 shared between 2, giving 5 each. Links closely with fractions, e.g. 10 shared between 2 is 5, so 5 is half of 10.

short, shorter, shortest
Words used when comparing lengths or height, e.g. a line is 3 cm, 2 cm is shorter than 3 cm, three lines are 4 cm, 6 cm and 8 cm. The shortest length is 4 cm.

side
A 2-D shape or figure has sides which are line segments. These line segments form the boundary of the shape. See also *corner.*

single-, 2-, 3-digit numbers
The number of digits in a number, e.g. 3 is a single-digit number, 13 is a 2-digit number and 213 is a 3-digit number.

sixths
The fraction of a whole obtained when it is cut into six equal pieces.

sorting
Classifying objects, shapes or numbers into groups according to their properties.

sphere, spherical
A 3-D shape where every point on the surface is the same distance from the centre, like a ball.

square
A regular quadrilateral where all the sides are equal.

square millimetre (mm^2), square centimetre (cm^2), square metre (m^2)
Metric units of measure of area equivalent to a square 1 mm by 1 mm, a square 1 cm by 1 cm or a square 1 m by 1 m. Symbols: mm^2, cm^2 and m^2.

square number, squared
The square numbers are a sequence 1^2, 2^2, 3^2, formed by multiplying each number by itself. This gives the numbers 1, 4, 9, 16, 25 and so on. See also *cube number.*

statement
A number sentence, e.g. 2 + 4 = 6.

statistics
The branch of mathematics which studies the collection, representation and interpretation of data.

subtract
To do a subtraction calculation.

subtraction
A subtraction finds the difference between two numbers. Also called taking away, e.g. 10 (the minuend) – 3 (the subtrahend) = 7 (the difference). See also *minuend.*

subtraction fact
A subtraction statement likely to be frequently used, so worth memorising.

subtrahend
The number that is subtracted from the minuend.

sum
The answer to an addition calculation. The sum of 4 and 5 is 9. See also *total.*

surface
The face or faces of a 3-D shape. They can be flat like the face of a cube or curved like a sphere.

survey
A survey collects data for analysis. See also *questionnaire, data.*

symmetry, symmetrical
A figure has line symmetry if it can be folded along a mirror line into two halves which are mirror images of each other. It has rotational symmetry if it can be rotated to give an identical shape.

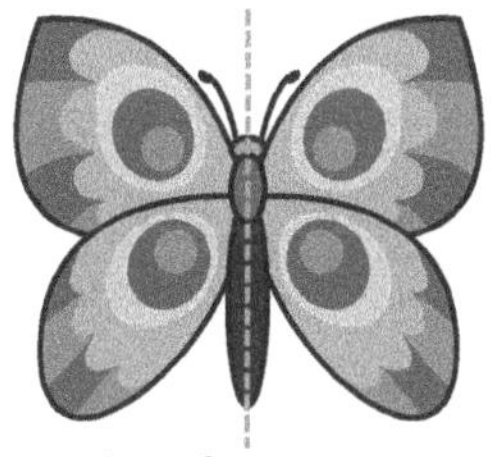
line of symmetry

T

table
An arrangement of numbers or objects in rows and columns. See also *array*.

take away
Another name for subtraction. See also *subtraction*.

tall, taller, tallest
A comparison of two or more heights, e.g. Janet is 130 cm tall and John is 128 cm tall. Janet is taller than John, but Sam is the tallest.

tally
A set of marks used for quick and accurate counting. Usually counting in sets of 5 with four downward strokes and the 5th stroke is a diagonal line across the four downward strokes.

tally chart
A table used to collect information using tally counting.

temperature
A measure of hotness. Usually in degrees Celsius or degrees Fahrenheit. Symbol: °C or °F.

ten less
The number ten before that number on a number line, e.g. 40 is ten less than 50.

ten more
The number ten after that number on a number line, e.g. 50 is ten more than 40.

ten thousand
10 000.

tens boundary
When counting from ones to tens, the tens boundary is crossed.

tenths
The fraction of a whole obtained when it is cut into ten equal pieces. The basis for the decimal system of counting.

tenths boundary
When counting from a hundredth to a tenth, the tenths boundary is crossed. See also *ones boundary*.

tetrahedron
A 3-D shape with four triangular faces.

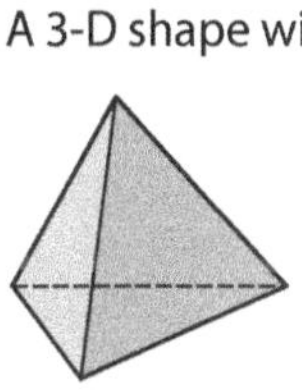

thousand less/more
The number one thousand whole units more or less than another number. 9000 is a thousand less than 10 000 and 11 000 is a thousand more than 10 000.

thousandths
$\frac{1}{1000} = 0.001$.

three-quarters
A fraction of a whole. Three parts of a whole that has been divided into four equal parts.

$\frac{3}{4}$

timetable
A table listing start and finish or arrival and departure times of activities or events, e.g. a school timetable or a public transport timetable.

title
A sentence to describe or explain a chart, graph or diagram.

tonne
A metric measure of mass. 100 kilograms = 1 tonne.

total
The answer to an addition calculation. The total of 4, 3 and 5 is 12. See also *sum*.

translate, translation
To transform an object by moving it a given distance and direction. The image is the same shape and size as the object and in the same orientation.

trapezium
A quadrilateral with one pair of parallel sides. It can also be isosceles.

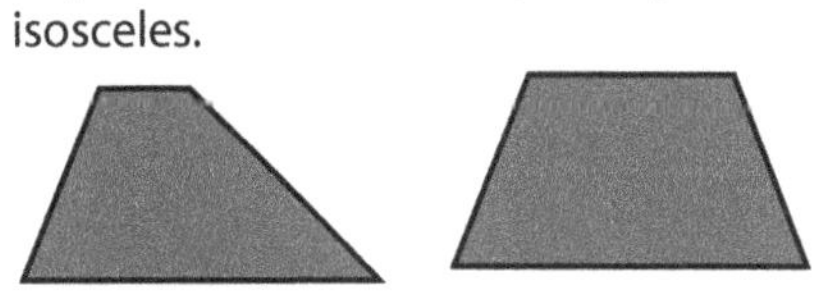

triangle, triangular
A 2-D shape with three straight sides.

triangular prism
A 3-D shape with two identical and parallel triangular ends, joined by three rectangular faces.

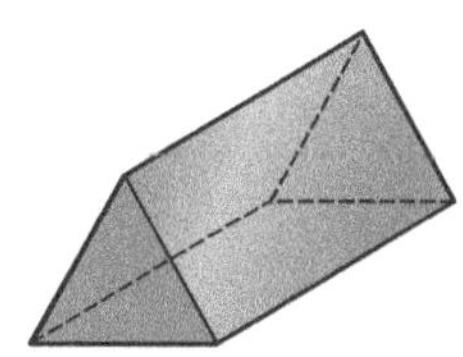

turn (whole turn, half turn, quarter turn, three-quarter turn)
A rotation about a point or line, like a hand around the clock face or a door about the join to the door frame. A whole turn is one complete revolution.

U

units
The standard measures, e.g. the units of length are metres, centimetres.

unknowns
Numbers to be found by solving equations and formulae. Represented by letters or shapes.

V

variable
A quantity that can take a range of different values. Represented by letters.

Venn diagram
A diagram of interlocking circles, used to sort numbers or objects by category.

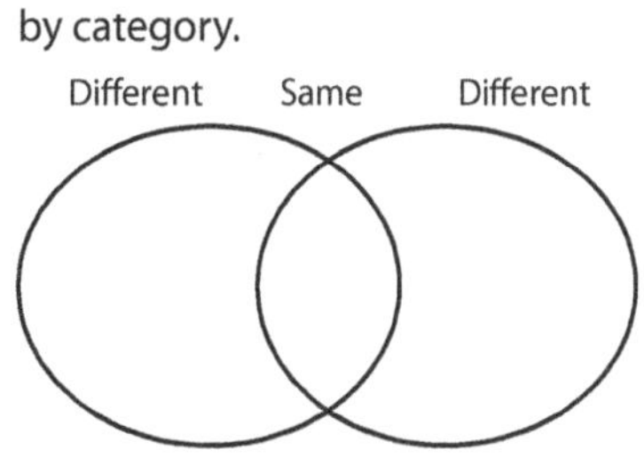

vertex, vertices
The point where two sides meet on a 2-D shape and where three or more faces meet on a 3-D shape. See also *face, edge*.

vertical
At right-angles (90°) to the horizontal plane.
See also *perpendicular.*

vinculum
The line that separates the numerator from the denominator.

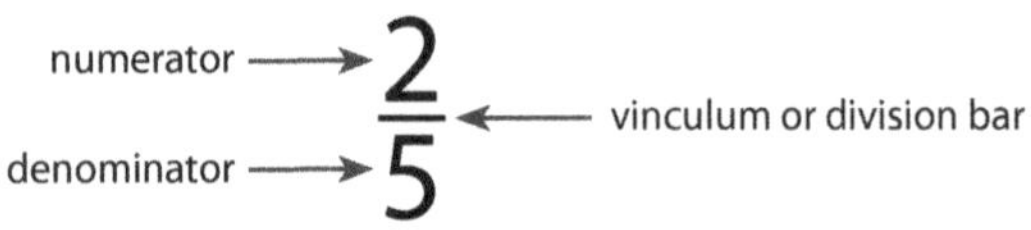

volume
Liquid volume is the amount of liquid in a container, e.g. 250 ml of water in a 2 l bottle. Measured in cubic ml, litres and so on.

Solid volume is the space a 3-D object takes up, e.g. a fridge in the kitchen. Measured in cubic mm, cm, metres and so on.

See also *capacity*.

W

weight
The force exerted on a mass by gravity. The units are units of force (Newtons). Often confused with mass.

whole-part relationship
How the parts are related to the whole, often illustrated with bars. This can be used when describing relationships between, e.g. addition and subtraction, fractions, percentages and ratio.

written calculation
A mathematical operation using a particular method.

X

x-axis
The horizontal line on a graph or coordinate grid that runs through zero.

Y

y-axis
The vertical line on a graph or coordinate grid that runs through zero.

yard
An imperial unit of length, approximately 90 cm. Symbol: yd. 36 inches = 3 feet = 1 yard. See also *foot, feet, inch, inches*.

Bibliography and further reading

Alexander, R. (2008). *Essays on pedagogy.* Abingdon: Routledge.

Alexander, R. (2012). *Neither national nor a curriculum?* York: Cambridge Primary Review.

Askew, M., Brown, M., Rhodes, V., Johnson, D., and Wiliam, D. (1997). *Effective teachers of numeracy.* London: King's College.

Askew, M., Hodgen, J., Hossain, S. and Bretscher, N. (2010). Theme 10 Textbooks. *Values and variables: mathematics education in high-performing countries.* London: Nuffield Foundation. 34-35.

Barber, M. and Mourshed, M. (2007). *How the world's best-performing school systems come out on top.* McKinsey Education.

Barmby, P., Bilsborough, L., Harries, T. and Higgins, S. (2009). *Primary mathematics: teaching for understanding.* Maidenhead: Open University Press.

Barmby, P., Harries, A.V. and Higgins, S.E. (2010). Teaching for understanding/ understanding for teaching. Thompson, I. (Ed.) *Issues in teaching numeracy in primary schools.* Buckingham: Open University Press. 45-57. http://dro.dur.ac.uk/7939/1/7939.pdf

Benton, T. (2014). *A re-evaluation of the link between autonomy, accountability and achievement in PISA 2009.* Cambridge: Cambridge Assessment.

Carpenter, T.P. et al. (1999). *Children's mathematics: cognitively guided instruction.* Portsmouth NH: Heinemann.

DfE. (2011). *The National Strategies 1997-2011: A brief summary of the impact and effectiveness of the National Strategies.* https://www.gov.uk/government/uploads/system/uploads/attachment_data/file/175408/DFE-00032-2011.pdf

DfE. (2014). *National Curriculum in England: mathematics programmes of study.* https://www.gov.uk/government/publications/national-curriculum-in-england-mathematics-programmes-of-study

Drury, H. (2014). *Mastering mathematics: teaching to transform achievement.* Oxford: Oxford University Press.

Fan, L., Zhu, Y., and Miao, Z. (2013). Textbook research in mathematics education: development status and directions. *ZDM: The International Journal on Mathematics Education*, 45: 633-646.

Goldin, G.A. (1998). Representational systems, learning and problem solving in mathematics. *Journal of Mathematical Behavior*, 17(2): 137-65.

Gu, L., Huang, R., and Marton, F. (2004). Teaching with variation: a Chinese way of promoting effective mathematics learning. Lianghuo, F., Ngai-Ying, W., Jinfa, C., and Shiqi, L. (Eds.) *How Chinese learn mathematics: perspectives from insiders.* Singapore: World Scientific Publishing Co. Pte. Ltd. 309-347.

Haggerty, L., and Pepin, B. (2002). An investigation of mathematics textbooks and their use in English, French and German classrooms: who gets an opportunity to learn what? *British Educational Research Journal,* 28(4): 567-590.

Harries, T., and Sutherland, R. (1999). Primary school mathematics textbooks: an international comparison. Thompson, I. (Ed.) *Issues in teaching numeracy in primary schools.* Buckingham: Open University Press. 1-66.

Hiebert, J. and Carpenter, T.P. (1992). Learning and teaching with understanding. Grouws, D.A. (Ed.) *Handbook of Research on Mathematics Teaching and Learning.* New York: Macmillan. 66-97.

Hodgen, J., Brown, M., Coe, R. and Kuchemann, D. (2012). Why have educational standards changed so little over time: the case of school mathematics in England. Paper presented at the *British Educational Research Association* (BERA) annual conference. Institute of Education, University of London.

Howson, G. (2013). The development of mathematics textbooks: historical reflections from a personal perspective. *ZDM: The International Journal on Mathematics Education*, 45(5): 647-658.

Hoyles, C., Morgan, C. and Woodhouse, G. (1999). *Rethinking the maths curriculum.* London: Falmer Press.

Jianhua, L. (2004). Thorough understanding of the textbook: a significant feature of Chinese teacher manuals. Lianghuo, F., Ngai-Ying, W., Jinfa, C., and Shiqi, L. (Eds.) *How Chinese learn mathematics: perspectives from insiders.* Singapore: World Scientific Publishing Co. Pte. Ltd. 262-280.

Lai, M.Y. and Murray, S. (2012). Teaching with procedural variation: a Chinese way of promoting deep understanding of mathematics. *International Journal for Mathematics Teaching and Learning.* Retrieved on 12th May 2015 from http://www.cimt.plymouth.ac.uk/journal/default.htm

Lo, M.L., and Marton, F. (2012). Towards a science of the art of teaching: using variation theory as a guiding principle of pedagogical design. *International Journal of Lesson and Learning Studies*, 1(1): 7-22.

Macintyre, T. and Hamilton, S. (2010). Mathematics learners and mathematics textbooks: a question of identity? Whose curriculum? Whose mathematics? *Curriculum Journal*, 21(1): 3-23.

Maclellan, E. (1997). The role of concrete materials in constructing mathematical meaning. *Education 3-13*, 25(3): 31-35.

Mason, J. and Johnston-Wilder, S. (Eds.) (2004). Learners powers. *Fundamental constructs in Mathematics Education.* London: Routledge Falmer. 115-142.

McCulloch, J. (2011). *Subject to change: should primary schools structure learning around subjects or themes?* London: Pearson Centre for Policy and Learning.

Merttens, R. (2012). The "concrete-pictorial-abstract" heuristic. *Mathematics Teaching*, 228: 33-38.

Morris, P. and Adamson, B. (2010). *Curriculum, schooling and society in Hong Kong.* Hong Kong: Hong Kong University Press.

Morris, P. and Auld, E. (2013). Comparative education, the 'new paradigm' and policy borrowing: constructing knowledge for educational reform. *Comparative Education,* 13th August 2013.

National Centre for Excellence in the Teaching of Mathematics. (2010). Developing mathematics in primary schools. Headteachers talk about creating and sustaining excellence in the teaching of mathematics. *National Centre for Excellence in the Teaching of Mathematics*, 24.

National Centre for Excellence in the Teaching of Mathematics. (2014). *Mastery approaches to mathematics and the new National Curriculum.* https://www.ncetm.org.uk/public/files/19990433/Developing_mastery_in_mathematics_october_2014.pdf

National Centre for Excellence in the Teaching of Mathematics. (2015). *NCETM Mathematics Textbook Guidance.* https://www.ncetm.org.uk/files/21383193/NCETM+Textbook+Guidance.pdf

Nisbet, I. (2013). Is there a place for China's wise laoshi? *TES*, 14th June 2013.

Nuñes, T., Bryant, P. and Watson, A. (2009). *Key understandings in mathematics learning.* London: The Nuffield Foundation.

Oates, T. (2010). *Could do better: using international comparisons to refine the National Curriculum in England.* Cambridge: Cambridge Assessment.

Oates, T. (2014). *Why textbooks count: a policy paper.* Cambridge: Cambridge Assessment.

OECD. (2010). *Strong performers and successful reformers in education: lessons from PISA for the United States.* Paris: Organisation for Economic Co-operation and Development.

Ofsted (Office for Standards in Education). (2011). *Good practice in primary mathematics: evidence from successful schools.* London: Ofsted. https://www.gov.uk/government/publications/good-practice-in-primary-mathematics-evidence-from-successful-schools

Ofsted (Office for Standards in Education). (2008). *Mathematics: understanding the score.* London: Ofsted. https://www.gov.uk/government/publications/mathematics-made-to-measure

Ofsted (Office for Standards in Education). (2012). *Mathematics: made to measure.* London: Ofsted. https://www.gov.uk/government/publications/mathematics-made-to-measure

Rabel, S. and Wooldridge, I. (2013). Exploratory talk in mathematics: what are the benefits? *Education 3-13*, 41(1): 15-22.

Raiker, A. (2002). Spoken language and mathematics. *Cambridge Journal of Education*, 32(1): 45-60.

Reynolds, D. and Farrell, S. (1996). *Worlds apart? A review of international studies of educational achievement involving England.* London: HMSO for OFSTED.

Rowland, T., Huckstep, P. and Thwaites, A. (2003). The knowledge quartet. *Proceedings of the British Society for Research into Learning Mathematics*, 23(3): 97-103.

Shulman, L.S. (1986). Those who understand: knowledge growth in teaching. *Educational Researcher*, 15(2): 4-14.

Sierpinska, A. (1994). *Understanding in mathematics.* London: Falmer Press.

Sowell, E.J. (1989). Effects of manipulative materials in mathematics education. *Journal for Research in Mathematics Education*, 20(5): 498-505.

Sun, X. (2011). "Variation problems" and their roles in the topic of fraction division in Chinese mathematics textbook examples. *Educational Studies in Mathematics*, 76: 65-85.

White, R. and Gunston, R. (1992). *Probing understanding.* London: Falmer Press.

Williams, P. (2008). Independent review of mathematics teaching in Early Years settings and primary schools. *Department for Children, Schools and Families,* 90.

Xu, B. (2013). The development of school mathematics textbooks in China since 1950. *ZDM: The International Journal on Mathematics Education*, 45(5): 725-736.

Yan, Z. and Lianghuo, F. (2006). Focus on the representation of problem types in intended curriculum: a comparison of selected mathematics textbooks from mainland China and the United States. *International Journal of Science and Mathematics Education*, 4(4): 609-626.

Yang, D.C. and Huang, F.Y. (2004). Relationships among computational performance, pictorial representation, symbolic representation and number sense of sixth-grade students in Taiwan. *Educational Studies*, 30(4): 373-389.